CW00518354

William H. Prescott

History of the Conquest of Peru

with a preliminary view of the civilization of the Incas - Vol. 1

William H. Prescott

History of the Conquest of Peru
with a preliminary view of the civilization of the Incas - Vol. 1

ISBN/EAN: 9783337840266

Printed in Europe, USA, Canada, Australia, Japan

Cover: Foto ©ninafisch / pixelio.de

More available books at **www.hansebooks.com**

MEXICO

AND THE LIFE OF THE CONQUEROR
FERNANDO CORTES

BY
WILLIAM H. PRESCOTT

IN TWO VOLUMES

ILLUSTRATED

VOL. I

NEW YORK
PETER FENELON COLLIER
MDCCCXCVIII

PREFACE.

As the Conquest of Mexico has occupied the pens of Solís and of Robertson, two of the ablest historians of their respective nations, it might seem that little could remain at the present day to be gleaned by the historical inquirer. But Robertson's narrative is necessarily brief, forming only part of a more extended work ; and neither the British, nor the Castilian author, was provided with the important materials for relating this event, which have been since assembled by the industry of Spanish scholars. The scholar who led the way in these researches was Don Juan Baptista Muñoz, the celebrated historiographer of the Indies, who, by a royal edict, was allowed free access to the national archives, and to all libraries, public, private, and monastic, in the kingdom and its colonies. The result of his long labors was a vast body of materials, of which unhappily he did not live to reap the benefit himself. His manuscripts were deposited, after his death, in the archives of the Royal Academy of History at Madrid ; and that collection was subsequently augmented by the manuscripts of Don Vargas Ponçe, President of the Academy, obtained, like those of Muñoz, from different quarters, but especially from the archives of the Indies at Seville.

On my application to the Academy, in 1838, for permission to copy that part of this inestimable collection relating to Mexico and Peru, it was freely acceded to, and an eminent German scholar, one of their own number, was appointed to superintend the collation and transcription of the manuscripts ; and this, it may be added, before I had any claim on the courtesy of that respectable body, as one of its associates. This conduct shows the advance of a liberal spirit in the Peninsula since the time of Dr. Robertson, who complains that he was denied admission to the most important public repositories. The favor with which my own application was regarded, however, must chiefly be attributed to the kind offices of the venerable President of the Academy, Don Martin Fernandez de Navarrete ; a scholar whose

persona! character has secured to him the same high considera-
ion at home, which his literary labors have obtained abroad.
To this eminent person I am under still further obligations, for
the free use which he has allowed me to make of his own manuscripts,—the fruits of a life of accumulation, and the basis of
those valuable publications, with which he has at different times
illustrated the Spanish colonial history.

From these three magnificent collections, the result of half a
century's careful researches, I have obtained a mass of unpublished documents, relating to the Conquest and Settlement of
Mexico and of Peru, comprising altogether about eight thousand
folio pages. They consist of instructions of the Court, military
and private journals, correspondence of the great actors in the
scenes, legal instruments, contemporary chronicles, and the like,
drawn from all the principal places in the extensive colonial
empire of Spain, as well as from the public archives in the
Peninsula.

I have still further fortified the collection, by gleaning such
materials from Mexico itself as had been overlooked by my
illustrious predecessors in these researches. For these I am indebted to the courtesy of Count Cortina, and, yet more, to that
of Don Lucas Alaman, Minister of Foreign Affairs in Mexico;
but, above all, to my excellent friend, Don Angel Calderon de
la Barca, late Minister Plenipotentiary to that country from the
Court of Madrid,—a gentleman whose high and estimable
qualities, even more than his station, secured him the public
confidence, and gained him free access to every place of interest
and importance in Mexico.

I have also to acknowledge the very kind offices rendered to
me by the Count Camaldoli at Naples; by the Duke of Ser-
radifalco in Sicily, a nobleman, whose science gives additional
lustre to his rank; and by the Duke of Monteleone, the present
representative of Cortés, who has courteously opened the archives of his family to my inspection. To these names must also
be added that of Sir Thomas Phillips, Bart., whose precious collection of manuscripts probably surpasses in extent that of any
private gentleman in Great P.itain, if not in Europe; that of
Mons. Ternaux-Compans, the proprietor of the valuable literary
collection of Don Antonio Uguina, including the papers of
Muñoz, the fruits of which he is giving to the world in his excellent translations; and, lastly, that of my friend and countryman,
Arthur Middleton, Esq., late Chargé d'Affaires from the United
States, at the Court of Madrid, for the efficient aid he has afforded
me in prosecuting my inquiries in that capital.

In addition to this stock of original documents obtained

through these various sources, I have diligently provided myself with such printed works as have reference to the subject, including the magnificent publications, which have appeared both in France and England, on the Antiquities of Mexico, which, from their cost and colossal dimensions, would seem better suited to a public than to a private library.

Having thus stated the nature of my materials, and the sources whence they are derived, it remains for me to add a few observations on the general plan and composition of the work.—Among the remarkable achievements of the Spaniards in the sixteenth century, there is no one more striking to the imagination than the conquest of Mexico. The subversion of a great empire by a handful of adventurers, taken with all its strange and picturesque accompaniments, has the air of romance rather than of sober history ; and it is not easy to treat such a theme according to the severe rules prescribed by historical criticism. But, notwithstanding the seductions of the subject, I have conscientiously endeavored to distinguish fact from fiction, and to establish the narrative on as broad a basis as possible of contemporary evidence ; and I have taken occasion to corroborate the text by ample citations from authorities, usually in the original, since few of them can be very accessible to the reader. In these extracts I have scrupulously conformed to the ancient orthography, however obsolete and even barbarous, rather than impair in any degree the integrity of the original document.

Although the subject of the work is, properly, only the Conquest of Mexico, I have prepared the way for it by such a view of the Civilization of the ancient Mexicans, as might acquaint the reader with the character of this extraordinary race, and enable him to understand the difficulties which the Spaniards had to encounter in their subjugation. This introductory part of the work, with the essay in the Appendix which properly belongs to the Introduction, although both together making only half a volume, has cost me as much labor, and nearly as much time, as the remainder of the history. If I shall have succeeded in giving the reader a just idea of the true nature and extent of the civilization to which the Mexicans had attained, it will not be labor lost.

The story of the Conquest terminates with the fall of the capital. Yet I have preferred to continue the narrative to the death of Cortés, relying on the interest which the development of his character in his military career may have excited in the reader. I am not insensible to the hazard I incur by such a course. The mind, previously occupied with one great idea, that of the subversion of the capital, may feel the prolongation of the story beyond that point superfluous, if not tedious ; **and**

may find it difficult after the excitement caused by witnessing a great national catastrophe, to take an interest in the adventures of a private individual. Solís took the more politic course
of concluding his narrative with the fall of Mexico, and thus
leaves his readers with the full impression of that memorable
event, undisturbed, on their minds. To prolong the narrative is
to expose the historian to the error so much censured by the
French critics in some of their most celebrated dramas, where
the author by a premature *énouement* has impaired the interest
of his piece. It is the defect that necessarily attaches, though
in a greater degree, to the history of Columbus, in which petty
adventures among a group of islands make up the sequel of a
life that opened with the magnificent discovery of a World ; a
defect, in short, which has required all the genius of Irving and
the magical charm of his style perfectly to overcome.

Notwithstanding these objections, I have been induced to
continue the narrative, partly from deference to the opinion of
several Spanish scholars, who considered that the biography of
Cortés had not been fully exhibited, and partly from the circumstance of my having such a body of original materials for
this biography at my command. And I cannot regret that I
have adopted this course ; since, whatever lustre the Conquest
may reflect on Cortés as a military achievement, it gives but an
imperfect idea of his enlightened spirit, and of his comprehensive
and versatile genius.

To the eye of the critic there may seem some incongruity in
a plan which combines objects so dissimilar as those embraced
by the present history ; where the Introduction, occupied with
the antiquities and origin of a nation, has somewhat the character of a *philosophic* theme, while the conclusion is strictly
biographical, and the two may be supposed to match indifferently
with the main body, or *historical* portion of the work. But I
may hope that such objections will be found to have less weight
in practice than in theory ; and, if properly managed, that the
general views of the Introduction will prepare the reader for the
particulars of the Conquest, and that the great public events
narrated in this will, without violence, open the way to the remaining personal history of the hero who is the soul of it. Whatever incongruity may exist in other respects, I may hope that
the *unity* of *interest*, the only unity held of much importance
by modern critics, will be found still to be preserved.

The distance of the present age from the period of the narrative might be presumed to secure the historian from undue
prejudice or partiality. Yet to American and English readers,
acknowledging so different a moral standard from that of the

sixteenth century, ⅄ may possibly be thought too indulgent to the errors of the Conquerors ; while to a Spaniard, accustomed to the undiluted panegyric of Solís, I may be deemed to have dealt too hardly with them. To such I can only say, that, while, on the one hand, I have not hesitated to expose in their strongest colors the excesses of the Conquerors ; on the other, I have given them the benefit of such mitigating reflections as might be suggested by the circumstances and the period in which they lived. I have endeavored not only to present a picture true in itself, but to place it in its proper light, and to put the spectator in a proper point of view for seeing it to the best advantage. I have endeavored, at the expense of some repetition, to surround him with the spirit of the times, and, in a word, to make him, if I may so express myself, a contemporary of the sixteenth century. Whether, and how far, I have succeeded in this, he must determine.

For one thing, before I conclude, I may reasonably ask the reader's indulgence. Owing to the state of my eyes, I have been obliged to use a writing-case made for the blind, which does not permit the writer to see his own manuscript. Nor have I ever corrected, or even read, my own original draft. As the chirography, under these disadvantages, has been too often careless and obscure, occasional errors, even with the utmost care of my secretary, must have necessarily occurred in the transcription, somewhat increased by the barbarous phraseology imported from my Mexican authorities. I cannot expect that these errors have always been detected even by the vigilant eye of the perspicacious critic to whom the proof-sheets have been subjected.

In the Preface to the "History of Ferdinand and Isabella," I lamented, that, while occupied with that subject, two of its most attractive parts had engaged the attention of the most popular of American authors, Washington Irving. By a singular chance, something like the reverse of this has taken place in the composition of the present history, and I have found myself unconsciously taking up ground which he was preparing to occupy. It was not till I had become master of my rich collection of materials, that I was acquainted with this circumstance ; and, had he persevered in his design, I should unhesitatingly have abandoned my own, if not from courtesy, at least from policy ; for, though armed with the weapons of Achilles, this could give me no hope of success in a competition with Achilles himself. But no sooner was that distinguished writer informed of the preparations I had made, than, with the gentlemanly spirit which will surprise no one who has the pleasure of his acquaintance, he instantly announced to me his intention of leaving the subject open to me. While I do but justice to Mr. Irving by this statement, I feel the prejudice it does to myself in the unavailing regret I am exciting in the bosom of the reader.

I must not conclude this Preface, too long protracted as it is already, without a word of acknowledgment to my friend George Ticknor, Esq.,—the friend of many years,—for his patient revision of my manuscript; a labor of love, the worth of which those only can estimate, who are acquainted with his extraordinary erudition and his nice critical taste. If I have reserved his name for the last in the list of those to whose good offices I am indebted, it is most assuredly not because I value his services least.

WILLIAM H. PRESCOTT.

BOSTON, October 1, 1843.

CONTENTS.

OF

VOLUME FIRST.

BOOK I.

INTRODUCTION.—VIEW OF THE AZTEC CIVILIZATION

CHAPTER I.

CHAPTER II.

CHAPTER III.

CHAPTER IV.

BOOK II.

DISCOVERY OF MEXICO.

CHAPTER I.

CHAPTER II.

CHAPTER III.

JEALOUSLY OF VELASQUEZ.—CORTES EMBARKS.—EQUIPMENT OF HIS FLEET.—HIS
PERSON AND CHARACTER.— RENDEZVOUS AT HAVANA.—STRENGTH OF HIS
ARMAMENT... 182

CHAPTER IV.

VOYAGE TO COZUMEL.—CONVERSION OF THE NATIVES.—JERONIMO DE AGUILAR.—
ARMY ARRIVES AT TABASCO.— GREAT BATTLE WITH THE INDIANS.—CHRIS-
TIANITY INTRODUCED... 191

CHAPTER VIII.

BOOK III.

MARCH TO MEXICO.

CHAPTER I.

CHAPTER II.

REPUBLIC OF TLASCALA.—ITS INSTITUTIONS.—EARLY HISTORY.—DISCUSSIONS IN THE SENATE.—DESPERATE BATTLES... 279

CHAPTER III.

DECISIVE VICTORY.—INDIAN COUNCIL.—NIGHT ATTACK.—NEGOTIATIONS WITH THE ENEMY.—TLASCALAN HERO... 293

CHAPTER IV.

DISCONTENTS IN THE ARMY.—TLASCALAN SPIES.—PEACE WITH THE REPUBLIC.—EMBASSY FROM MONTEZUMA... 306

CHAPTER V.

CHAPTER VI.

CHAPTER VII.

CHAPTER VIII.

CHAPTER IX.

BOOK IV.

RESIDENCE IN MEXICO.

CHAPTER I.

CHAPTER II.

CHAPTER III.

CHAPTER IV.

CHAPTER V.

CHAPTER VI.

LIST OF ILLUSTRATIONS

MEXICO

VOL. I

CONQUEST OF MEXICO.

BOOK I.

INTRODUCTION.

VIEW OF THE AZTEC CIVILIZATION.

CHAPTER I.

ANCIENT MEXICO.—CLIMATE AND PRODUCTS.—PRIMITIVE RACES
—AZTEC EMPIRE.

Of all that extensive empire which once acknowledged the
authority of Spain in the New World, no portion, for interest
and importance, can be compared with Mexico ; — and this
equally, whether we consider the variety of its soil and climate ;
the inexhaustible stores of its mineral wealth ; its scenery, grand
and picturesque beyond example ; the character of its ancient
inhabitants, not only far surpassing in intelligence that of the
other North American races, but reminding us, by their monuments, of the primitive civilization of Egypt and Hindostan ; or
lastly, the peculiar circumstances of its Conquest, adventurous
and romantic as any legend devised by Norman or Italian bard
of chivalry.   It is the purpose of the present narrative to exhibit
the history of this Conquest, and that of the remarkable man by
whom it was achieved.

But, in order that the reader may have a better understanding
of the subject, it will be well, before entering on it, to take a
general survey of the political and social institutions of the races
who occupied the land at the time of its discovery.

The country of the ancient Mexicans, or Aztecs as they were
called, formed but a very small part of the extensive territories

comprehended in the modern republic of Mexico.[1] Its bound·
aries cannot be defined with certainty. They were much enlarged
in the latter days of the empire, when they may be considered
as reaching from about the eighteenth degree north, to the
twenty-first, on the Atlantic ; and from the fourteenth to the nineteenth, including a very narrow strip, on the Pacific.[2] In its
greatest breadth, it could not exceed five degrees and a half,
dwindling, as it approached its south-eastern limits, to less than
two. It covered, probably, less than sixteen thousand square
leagues.[3] Yet such is the remarkable formation of this country,
that, though not more than twice as large as New England, it
presented every variety of climate, and was capable of yield·
ing nearly every fruit, found between the equator and the Arctic
circle.

All along the Atlantic, the country is bordered by a broad
track, called the *tierra caliente,* or hot region, which has the usual

---

[1] Extensive indeed, if we may trust Archbishop Lorenzana, who tells us,
" It is doubtful if the country of New Spain does not border on *Tartary* and
Greenland ; — by the way of California, on the former, and by New Mexico,
on the latter " ! Historia de Nueva España, (México, 1770,) p, 38, nota.

[2] I have conformed to the limits fixed by Clavigero. He has probably,
examined the subject with more thoroughness and fidelity than most of his
countrymen, who differ from him, and who assign a more liberal extent to
the monarchy. (See his Storia Antica del Messico, (Cesena, 1780,) dissert.
7.) The Abbé, however, has not informed his readers on what frail founda·
tions his conclusions rest. The extent of the Aztec empire is to be gathered
from the writings of historians since the arrival of the Spaniards, and from
the picture-rolls of tribute paid by the conquered cities ; both sources ex·
tremely vague and defective. See the MSS. of the Mendoza collection, in
Lord Kingsborough's magnificent publication (Antiquities of Mexico, comprising Facsimiles of Ancient Paintings and Hieroglyphics, together with the
Monuments of New Spain. London, 1830). The difficulty of the inquiry is
much increased by the fact of the conquests having been made, as will be
seen hereafter, by the united arms of three powers, so that it is not always
easy to tell to which party they eventually belonged. The affair is involved
in so much uncertainty, that Clavigero, notwithstanding the positive assertions in his text, has not ventured, in his map, to define the precise limits of
the empire, either towards the north, where it mingles with the Tezcucan
empire, or towards the south, where, indeed, he has fallen into the egregious
blunder of asserting, that, while the Mexican territory reached to the four·
teenth degree, it did not include any portion of Guatemala. (See tom. I. p.
29, and tom. IV. dissert. 7.) The Tezcucan chronicler, Ixtlilxochitl, puts in
a sturdy claim for the paramount empire of his own nation. Historia
Chichemeca, MS., cap. 39, 53, et alibi.

[3] Eighteen to twenty thousand, according to Humboldt, who considers the
Mexican territory to have been the same with that occupied by the modern
intendancies of Mexico, Puebla, Vera Cruz, Oaxaca, and Valladolid. (Essai
Politique sur le Royaume de Nouvelle Espagne, (Paris, 1825,) tom. I. p.
196.) This last, however, was all, or nearly all, included in the rival kingdom of Mechoacan, as he himself **more correctly** states in another part of his
work. Comp. tom. II. p. 164.

high temperature of equinoctial lands. Parched and sandy plains are intermingled with others, of exuberant fertility, almost impervious from thickets of aromatic shrubs and wild flowers, in the midst of which tower up trees of that magnificent growth which is found only within the tropics. In this wilderness of sweets lurks the fatal *malaria*, engendered, probably, by the decomposition of rank vegetable substances in a hot and humid soil. The season of the bilious fever,—*vómito*, as it is called,—which scourges these coasts, continues from the spring to the autumnal equinox, when it is checked by the cold winds that descend from Hudson's Bay. These winds in the winter season frequently freshen into tempests, and, sweeping down the Atlantic coast, and the winding Gulf of Mexico, burst with the fury of a hurricane on its unprotected shores, and on the neighboring West India islands. Such are the mighty spells with which Nature has surrounded this land of enchantment, as if to guard the golden treasures locked up within its bosom. The genius and enterprise of man have proved more potent than her spells.

After passing some twenty leagues across this burning region, the traveller finds himself rising into a purer atmosphere. His limbs recover their elasticity. He breathes more freely, for his senses are not now oppressed by the sultry heats and intoxicating perfumes of the valley. The aspect of nature, too, has changed, and his eye no longer revels among the gay variety of colors with which the landscape was painted there. The vanilla, the indigo, and the flowering cacao-groves disappear as he advances. The sugar-cane and the glossy-leaved banana still accompany him ; and, when he has ascended about four thousand feet, he sees in the unchanging verdure, and the rich foliage of the liquid-amber tree, that he has reached the height where clouds and mists settle, in their passage from the Mexican Gulf. This is the region of perpetual humidity ; but he welcomes it with pleasure, as announcing his escape from the influence of the deadly *vómito*.[4] He has entered the *tierra templada*, or temperate region, whose character resembles that of the temperate zone of the globe. The features of the scenery become grand, and even

---

[4] The traveller, who enters the country across the dreary sand-hills of Vera Cruz, will hardly recognize the truth of the above description. He must look for it in other parts of the *tierra caliente*. Of recent tourists, no one has given a more gorgeous picture of the impressions made on his senses by these sunny regions than Latrobe, who came on shore at Tampico; (Rambler in Mexico, (New York, 1836.) chap. 1;) a traveller, it may be added, whose descriptions of man and nature, in our own country, where we can judge, are distinguished by a sobriety and fairness that entitle him to confidence in his delineation of other countries.

terrible. His ̩ad sweeps along the base of mighty mountains, once gleami̩ with volcanic fires, and still resplendent in their mantles of snow, which serve as beacons to the mariner, for many a league at sea. All around he beholds traces of their ancient combustion, as his road passes along vast tracts of lava, bristling in the innumerable fantastic forms into which the fiery torrent has been thrown by the obstacles in its career. Perhaps, at the same moment, as he casts his eye down some steep slope, or almost unfathomable ravine, on the margin of the road, he sees their depths glowing with the rich blooms and enamelled vegetation of the tropics. Such are the singular contrasts presented, at the same time, to the senses, in this picturesque region !

Still pressing upwards, the traveller mounts into other climates, favorable to other kinds of cultivation. The yellow maize, or Indian corn, as we usually call it, has continued to follow him up from the lowest level ; but he now first sees fields of wheat, and the other European grains brought into the country by the Conquerors. Mingled with them, he views the plantations of the aloe or maguey (*agave Americana*), applied to such various and important uses by the Aztecs. The oaks now acquire a sturdier growth, and the dark forests of pine announce that he has entered the *tierra fria*, or cold region,—the third and last of the great natural terraces into which the country is divided. When he has climbed to the height of between seven and eight thousand feet, the weary traveller sets his foot on the summit of the Cordillera of the Andes,—the colossal range, that, after traversing South America and the Isthmus of Darien, spreads out, as it enters Mexico, into that vast sheet of table-land, which maintains an elevation of more than six thousand feet, for the distance of nearly two hundred leagues, until it gradually declines in the higher latitudes of the north.[5]

Across the mountain rampart a chain of volcanic hills stretches, in a westerly direction, of still more stupendous dimensions, forming, indeed, some of the highest land on the globe. Their peaks, entering the limits of perpetual snow, diffuse a grateful coolness over the elevated *plateaus* below ; for these last, though termed ' cold,' enjoy a climate, the mean temperature of which is not lower than that of the central parts of Italy.[6] The air is exceedingly dry ; the soil, though naturally

---

[5] This long extent of country varies in elevation from 5570 to 8856 feet,—equal to the height of the passes of Mount Cenis, or the Great St. Bernard. The table-land stretches still three hundred leagues further, before it declines to a level of 2624 feet. Humboldt, Essai Politique, tom. I. pp. 157, 255.

[6] About 62o Fahrenheit, or 17o Réaumur. (Humboldt, Essai Politique,

good, is rarely clothed with the luxuriant vegetation of the lower regions. It frequently, indeed, has a parched and barren aspect, owing partly to the greater evaporation which takes place on these lofty plains, through the diminished pressure of the atmosphere ; and partly, no doubt, to the want of trees to shelter the soil from the fierce influence of the summer sun. In the time of the Aztecs, the table-land was thickly covered with larch, oak, cypress, and other forest trees, the extraordinary dimensions of some of which, remaining to the present day, show that the curse of barrenness in later times is chargeable more on man than on nature. Indeed, the early Spaniards made as indiscriminate war on the forest as did our Puritan ancestors, though with much less reason. After once conquering the country, they had no lurking ambush to fear from the submissive, semicivilized Indian, and were not, like our forefathers, obliged to keep watch and ward for a century. This spoliation of the ground, however, is said to have been pleasing to their imaginations, as it reminded them of the plains of their own Castile,—the table-land of Europe ;[7] where the nakedness of the landscape forms the burden of every traveller's lament, who visits that country.

Midway across the continent, somewhat nearer the Pacific than the Atlantic ocean, at an elevation of nearly seven thousand five hundred feet, is the celebrated Valley of Mexico. It is of an oval form, about sixty-seven leagues in circumference,[8] and is encompassed by a towering rampart of porphyritic rock, which nature seems to have provided, though ineffectually, to protect it from invasion.

The soil, once carpeted with a beautiful verdure, and thickly sprinkled with stately trees, is often bare, and, in many places, white with the incrustation of salts, caused by the draining of

tom. I. p 273.) The more elevated plateaus of the table-land, as the Valley of Toluca, about 8500 feet above the sea, have a stern climate, in which the thermometer, during a great part of the day, rarely rises beyond 45° F. Idem, (loc. cit.,) and Malte-Brun, (Universal Geography, Eng. Trans., book 83,) who is, indeed, in this part of his work, but an echo of the former writer.

[7] The elevation of the Castiles, according to the authority repeatedly cited, is about 350 toises or 2100 feet above the ocean. (Humboldt's Dissertation, apud Laborde, Itinéraire Descriptif de l'Espagne, (Paris, 1827,) tom I. p. 5) It is rare to find plains in Europe of so great a height.

[8] Archbishop Lorenzana estimates the circuit of the Valley at ninety leagues, correcting at the same time the statement of Cortés, which puts it at seventy, very near the truth, as appears from the result of M. de Humboldt's measurement, cited in the text. Its length is about eighteen leagues, by twelve and a half in breadth. (Humboldt, Essai Politique, tom. II. p. 29.—Lorenzana, His. de Nueva España, p. 101.) Humboldt's map of the Valley of Mexico forms the third in his " Atlas Géographique et Physique," and, like all the others in the collection, will be found of inestimable value to the traveller, the geologist, and the historian.

the waters. Five lakes are spread over the Valley, occupying one tenth of its surface.[9] On the opposite borders of the largest of these basins, much shrunk in its dimensions [10] since the days of the Aztecs, stood the cities of Mexico and Tezcuco, the capitals of the two most potent and flourishing states of Anahuac, whose history, with that of the mysterious races that preceded them in the country, exhibits some of the nearest approaches to civilization to be met with anciently on the North American continent.

Of these races the most conspicuous were the Toltecs. Advancing from a northerly direction, but from what region is uncertain, they entered the territory of Anahuac,[11] probably before the close of the seventh century. Of course, little can be gleaned, with certainty, respecting a people, whose written records have perished, and who are known to us only through the extraditionary legends of the nations that succeeded them,[12]

[9] Humboldt, Essai Politique, tom. II. pp. 29 44–49—Malte Brun, book 85. This latter geographer assigns only 6700 feet for the level of the Valley, contradicting himself, (comp. book 83,) or rather, Humboldt, to whose pages he helps himself, *plenis manibus*, somewhat too liberally, indeed, for the scanty references at the bottom of his page.

[10] Torquemada accounts, in part, for this diminution, by supposing, that as God permitted the waters, which once covered the whole earth, to subside, after mankind had been nearly exterminated for their iniquities, so he allowed the waters of the Mexican lake to subside, in token of good-will and reconciliation, after the idolatrous races of the land had been destroyed by the Spaniards! (Monarchia Indiana, (Madrid, 1723,) tom. I. p. 309.) Quite as probable, if not as orthodox an explanation, may be found in the active evaporation of these upper regions, and in the fact of an immense drain having been constructed, during the lifetime of the good father, to reduce the waters of the principal lake, and protect the capital from inundation,

[11] Anahuac, according to Humboldt, comprehended only the country between the 14th and 21st degrees of N. latitude. (Essai Politique, tom. I. p. 197.) According to Clavigero, it included nearly all since known as New Spain. (Stor. del Messico, tom. I. p. 27.) Veytia uses it, also, as synonymous with New Spain. (Historia Antigua de Méjico, (Méjico, 1836,) tom. I. cap. 12.) The first of these writers probably allows too little, as the latter do too much, for, its boundaries. Ixtlilxochitl says it extended four hundred leagues south of the Otomie country. (Hist. Chichemeca. MS., cap. 73.) The word Anahuac signifies *near the water*. It was, probably, first applied to the country around the lakes in the Mexican Valley, and gradually extended to the remoter regions occupied by the Aztecs, and the other semicivilized races. Or, possibly, the name may have been intended, as Veytia suggests, (Hist. Antig., lib. 1, cap. 1,) to denote the land between the waters of the Atlantic and Pacific.

[12] Clavigero talks of Boturini's having written " on the faith of the Toltec historians." (Stor. del Messico, tom. I. p. 128.) But that scholar does not pretend to have ever met with a Toltec manuscript, himself, and had heard of only one in the possession of Ixtlilxochitl. (See his Idea de una Kueva Historia General de la América Septentrional, (Madrid, 1746,) p. 110.) The latter writer tells us, that his account of the Toltec and Chichemec races was

By the general agreement of these, however, the Toltecs were well
instructed in agriculture, and many of the most useful mechanic
arts; were nice workers of metals; invected the complex arrangement of time adopted by the Aztecs; and, in short, were
the true fountains of the civilization which distinguished this
part of the continent in latter times.[13] They established their
capital at Tula, north of the Mexican Valley, and the remains of
extensive buildings were to be discerned there at the time of
the Conquest.[14] The noble ruins of religious and other edifices,
still to be seen in various parts of New Spain, are referred to
this people, whose name, *Toltec*, has passed into a synonyme for
architect.[15] Their shadowy history reminds us of those primitive
races, who preceded the ancient Egyptians in the march of civilization; fragments of whose monuments, as they are seen at
this day, incorporated with the buildings of the Egyptians themselves, give to these latter the appearance of almost modern
constructions.[16]

After a period of four centuries, the Toltecs, who had extended their sway over the remotest borders of Anahuac,[17] having been greatly reduced, it is said, by famine, pestilence, and
unsuccessful wars, disappeared from the land as silently and
mysteriously as they had entered it. A few of them still lingered behind, but much the greater number, probably, spread
over the region of Central America and the neighboring isles;
and the traveller now speculates on the majestic ruins of Mitla
and Palenque, as possibly the work of this extraordinary people.[18]

"derived from interpretation," (probably, of the Tezcucan paintings,) " and
from the traditions of old men " ; poor authority for events which had passed,
centuries before. Indeed, he acknowledges that their narratives were so full
of absurdity and falsehood, that he was obliged to reject nine-tenths of them.
(See his Relaciones, MS., no. 5.) The cause of truth would not have suffered
much, probably, if he had rejected nine-tenths of the remainder.

[13] Ixtlilxochitl, Hist. Chich., MS., cap. 2.—Idem, Relaciones, MS., no. 2.—
Sahagun, Historia General de las Cosas de Nueva España, (México, 1829,)
lib. 10, cap. 29.—Veytia, Hist. Antig., lib. 1, cap. 27.

[14] Sahagun, Hist. de Nueva España, lib. 10, cap. 29.

[15] Idem, ubi supra.—Torquemada, Monarch. Ind lib. 1, cap. 14.

[16] Description de l'Egypte, (Paris, 1809,) Antiquités, tom. I. cap. 1. Veytia
has traced the migrations of the Toltecs with sufficient industry, scarcely re-
warded by the necessarily doubtful credit of the results. Hist. Antig., lib. 2,
cap. 21–33.

Ixtlilxochitl, Hist. Chich., MS., cap. 73.

- Veytia, Hist. Antig., lib. 1, cap. 33.—Ixtlilxochitl, Hist Chich, MS,
cap. 3.—Idem, Relaciones, MS., no. 4, 5.—Father Torquemada—perhaps
misinterpreting the Tezcucan hieroglyphics—has accounted for the mysterious disappearance of the Toltecs, by such *tetfastum* stories of giants and
demons, as show his appetite for the marvellous was fully equal to that of
any of his calling. See his Monarch. Ind., lib. 1, cap. 14.

After the lapse of another hundred years, a numerous and rude tribe, called the Chichemecs, entered the deserted country from the regions of the far Northwest. They were speedily followed by other races, of higher civilization, perhaps of the same family with the Toltecs, whose language they appear to have spoken. The most noted of these were the Aztecs or Mexicans, and the Acolhuans. The latter, better known in later times by the name of Tezcucans, from their capital, Tezcuco,[19] on the eastern border of the Mexican lake, were peculiarly fitted, by their comparatively mild religion and manners, for receiving the tincture of civilization which could be derived from the few Toltecs that still remained in the country. This, in their turn, they communicated to the barbarous Chichemecs, a large portion of whom became amalgamated with the new settlers as one nation.[20]

Availing themselves of the strength derived, not only from this increase of numbers, but from their own superior refinement, the Acolhuans gradually stretched their empire over the ruder tribes in the north ; while their capital was filled with a numerous population, busily employed in many of the more useful and even elegant arts of a civilized community. In this palmy state, they were suddenly assaulted by a warlike neighbor, the Tepanecs, their own kindred, and inhabitants of the same valley as themselves. Their provinces were overrun, their armies beaten, their king assassinated, and the flourishing city of Tezcuco became the prize of the victor. From this abject condition the uncommon abilities of the young prince, Nezahualcoyotl, the rightful heir of the crown, backed by the efficient aid of his Mexican allies, at length, redeemed the state, and opened to it a new career of prosperity, even more brilliant than the former.[21]

The Mexicans, with whom our history is principally concerned, came, also, as we have seen, from the remote regions of the North,—the populous hive of nations in the New World, as it has been in the Old. They arrived on the borders of Anahuac, towards the beginning of the thirteenth century, some time after the occupation of the land by the kindred races. For a

---

[19] *Tezcuco* signifies " place of detention " ; as several of the tribes who successively occupied Anahuac were said to have halted some time at the spot. Ixtlilxochitl, Hist, Chich., MS., cap. 10.

[20] The historian speaks, in one page, of the Chichemecs' burrowing in caves, or, at best, in cabins of straw ;—and, in the next, talks gravely of their *señoras, infantas,* and *caballeros !* Ibid., cap. 9, et seq.· ·Veytia, Hist. Antig., lib. 2, cap. 1–10.—Camargo, Historia de Tlascala, MS.

[21] Ixtlilxochitl, Hist. Chich., MS., cap. 9–20.—Veytia, Hist. Antig., lib. 2, cap. 29–54.

long time they did not establish themselves in any permanent residence; but continued shifting their quarters to different parts of the Mexican Valley, enduring all the casualties and hardships of a migratory life. On one occasion, they were enslaved by a more powerful tribe; but their ferocity soon made them formidable to their masters.[22] After a series of wanderings and adventures, which need not shrink from comparison with the most extravagant legends of the heroic ages of antiquity, they at length halted on the southwestern borders of the principal lake, in the year 1325. They there beheld, perched on the stem of a prickly pear, which shot out from the crevice of a rock that was washed by the waves, a royal eagle of extraordinary size and beauty, with a serpent in his talons, and his broad wings opened to the rising sun. They hailed the auspicious omen, announced by the oracle, as indicating the site of their future city, and laid its foundations by sinking piles into the shallows; for the low marshes were half buried under water. On these they erected their light fabrics of reeds and rushes; they sought a precarious subsistence from fishing, and from the wild fowl which frequented the waters, as well as from the cultivation of such simple vegetables as they could raise on their floating gardens. The place was called Tenochtitlan, in token of its miraculous origin, though only known to Europeans by its other name of Mexico, derived from their war-god, Mexitli.[23] The legend of its foundation is still further commemorated by the device of the eagle and the cactus, which form the arms of the modern Mexican republic. Such were the humble beginnings of the Venice of the Western World.[24]

[22] These were the Colhuans, not Acolhuans, with whom Humboldt, and most writers since, have confounded them. See his Essai Politique, tom. I. p. 414; II. p. 37.

[23] Clavigero gives good reasons for preferring the etymology of Mexico above noticed, to various others. (See his Stor. del Messico, tom. I. p. 168, nota.) The name *Tenochtitlan* signifies *tunal* (a cactus) *on a stone.* Esplicacion de la Col. de Mendoza, apud Antiq. of Mexico, vol. IV.

[24] "Datur hæc venia antiquitati," says Livy, "ut, miscendo humana divinis, primordia urbium augustiora faciat." Hist. Præf.—See for the above paragraph, Col. de Mendoza, plate 1, apud Antiq. of Mexico. vol. I.,—Ixtlilxochitl, Hist. Chich., MS., cap. 10,—Toribio, Historia de los Indios, MS., Parte 3, cap. 8,—Veytia, Hist. Antig., lib. 2, cap. 15.—Clavigero, after a laborious examination, assigns the following dates to some of the prominent events noticed in the text. No two authorities agree on them; and this is not strange considering that Clavigero—the most inquisitive of all—does not always agree with himself. (Compare his dates for the coming of the Acolhuans; tom. I. p. 147, and tom. IV. dissert. 2.)—

	A. D.
The Toltecs arrived in Anahuac	648
They abandoned the country .	1051

The forlorn condition of the new settlers was made still worse by domestic feuds. A part of the citizens seceded from the main body, and formed a separate community on the neighboring marshes. Thus divided, it was long before they could aspire to the acquisition of territory on the main land. They gradually increased, however, in numbers, and strengthened themselves yet more by various improvements in their polity and military discipline, while they established a reputation for courage as well as cruelty in war, which made their name terrible throughout the Valley. In the early part of the fifteenth century, nearly a hundred years from the foundation of the city, an event took place which created an entire revolution in the circumstances, and, to some extent, in the character of the Aztecs. This was the subversion of the Tezcucan monarchy by the Tepanecs, already noticed. When the oppressive conduct of the victors had at length aroused a spirit of resistance, its prince, Nezahualcoyotl, succeeded, after incredible perils and escapes, in mustering such a force, as, with the aid of the Mexicans, placed him on a level with his enemies. In two successive battles, these were defeated with great slaughter, their chief slain, and their territory, by one of those sudden reverses which characterize the wars of petty states, passed into the hands of the conquerors. It was awarded to Mexico, in return for its important services.

Then was formed that remarkable league, which, indeed, has no parallel in history. It was agreed between the states of Mexico, Tezcuco, and the neighboring little kingdom of Tlacopan, that they should mutually support each other in their wars, offensive and defensive, and that, in the distribution of the spoil, one fifth should be assigned to Tlacopan, and the remainder be divided, in what proportions is uncertain, between the other powers. The Tezcucan writers claim an equal share for their nation with the Aztecs. But this does not seem to be warranted by the immense increase of territory subsequently appropriated by the latter. And we may account for any advantage conceded to them by the treaty, on the supposition, that, however inferior they may have been originally, they were

The Chichemecs arrived	.	.	.	.	.	1170
The Acolhuans arrived about	.	.	.	.	1200
The Mexicans reached Tula		.	.	.	.	1196
They founded Mexico	.		.	.	.	1325

See his dissert. 2, sec. 12. In the last date, the one of most importance, he is confirmed by the learned Veytia, who differs from him in all the others. Hist. Antig., lib. 2, cap. 15.

at the time of making it, in a more prosperous condition than their allies, broken and dispirited by long oppression. What is more extraordinary than the treaty itself, however, is the fidelity with which it was maintained. During a century of uninterrupted warfare that ensued, no instance occurred where the parties quarrelled over the division of the spoil, which so often makes shipwreck of similar confederaces among civilized states.[26]

The allies for some time found sufficient occupation for their arms in their own valley ; but they soon overleaped its rocky ramparts, and by the middle of the fifteenth century, under the first Montezuma, had spread down the sides of the table-land to the borders of the Gulf of Mexico. Tenochtitlan, the Aztec capital, gave evidence of the public prosperity. Its frail tenements were supplanted by solid structures of stone and lime. Its population rapidly increased. Its old feuds were healed. The citizens who had seceded were again brought under a common government with the main body, and the quarter they occupied was permanently connected with the parent city ; the dimensions of which, covering the same ground, were much larger than those of the modern capital of Mexico.[27]

Fortunately, the throne was filled by a succession of able princes, who knew how to profit by their enlarged resources and by the martial enthusiasm of the nation. Year after year saw them return, loaded with the spoils of conquered cities, and with throngs of devoted captives, to their capital. No state

---

[26] The loyal Tezcucan chronicler claims the supreme dignity for his own sovereign, if not the greatest share of the spoil, by this imperial compact. (Hist. Chich., cap. 32.) Torquemada, on the other hand, claims one half of all the conquered lands for Mexico. (Monarch. Ind., lib. 2, cap. 40.) All agree in assigning only one fifth to Tlacopan; and Veytia (Hist. Antig., lib. 3, cap. 3) and Zurita (Rapport sur les Differentes Classes de chefs de la Nouvelle Espagne, trad. de Ternaux, (Paris, 1840,) p. 11), both very competent critics acquiesce in an equal division between the two principal states in the confederacy. An ode, still extant, of Nezahualcovotl, in its Castilian version, bears testimony to the singular union of the three powers.

> " solo se acordaran en las Naciones
> lo bien que gobernaron
> las *tres Cabezas* que el Imperio honraron."
> CANTARES DEL EMPERADOR
> NEZAHUALCOYTL, MS.

[27] See the plans of the ancient and modern capital, in Bullock's "Mexico," first edition. The original of the ancient map was obtained by that traveller from the collection of the unfortunate Boturini; if, as seems probable, it is the one indicated on page 13 of his Catalogue, I find no warrant for Mr. Bullock's statement, that it was the same prepared for Cortés by the order of Montezuma.

was able long to re‹‹ ‚ the accumulated strength of the confed‹ erates.   At the beginning of the sixteenth century, just before the arrival of the Spaniards, the Aztec dominion reached across the continent, from the Atlantic to the Pacific ; and, under the bold and bloody Ahuitzotl, its arms had been carried far over the limits already noticed as defining its permanent territory, into the farthest corners of Guatemala and Nicaragua.   This extent of empire, however limited in comparison with that of many other states, is truly wonderful, considering it as the acquisition of a people whose whole population and resources had so recently been comprised within the walls of their own petty city ; and considering, moreover, that the conquered territory was thickly settled by various races, bred to arms like the Mexicans, and little inferior to them in social organization.   The history of the Aztecs suggests some strong points of resemblance to that of the ancient Romans, not only in their military successes, but in the policy which led to them.[27]

[27] Clavigero, Stor. del Messico, tom. I. lib. 2.—Torquemada, Monarch. Ind., tom. I. lib. 2,—Boturini, Idea, p. 146.—Col. of Mendoza, Part 1, and Codex Telleriano-Remensis, apud antiq. of Mexico, vols. I., VI.

Machiavelli has noticed it as one great cause of the military successes of the Romans, "that they associated themselves, in their wars, with other states, as the principal"; and expresses his astonishment that a similar policy should not have been adopted by ambitious republics in later times. (See his Discorsi sopra T. Livio, lib. 2, cap. 4, apud Opere (Geneva, 1798).) This, as we have seen above, was the very course pursued by the Mexicans.

———

The most important contribution, of late years, to the early history of Mexico is the *Historia Antigua* of the Lic. Don Mariano Veytia, published in the city of Mexico, in 1836. This scholar was born of an ancient and highly respectable family at Puebla, 1718. After finishing his academic education, he went to Spain, where he was kindly received at court. He afterwards visited several other countries of Europe, made himself acquainted with their languages, and returned home well stored with the fruits of a discriminating observation and diligent study. The rest of his life he devoted to letters; especially to the illustration of the national history and antiquities. As the executor of the unfortunate Boturini, with whom he had contracted an intimacy in Madrid, he obtained access to his valuable collection of manuscripts in Mexico, and from them, and every other source which his position in society and his eminent character opened to him, he composed various works, none of which, however, except the one before us, has been admitted to the honors of the press. The time of his death is not given by his editor, but it was probably not later than 1780.

Veytia's history covers the whole period, from the first occupation of Anahuac to the middle of the fifteenth century, at which point his labors were unfortunately terminated by his death. In the early portion he has endeavored to trace the migratory movements and historical annals of the principal races who entered the country. Every page bears testimony to the extent and fidelity of his researches; and, if we feel but moderate confidence in the results, the fault is not imputable to him, so much as to the dark and doubtful nature of the subject. As he descends to later ages, he is more occupied with the fortunes of the Tezcucan than with those of the Aztec dynasty, which have been amply discussed by others of his countrymen. The premature close of his labors prevented him, probably, from giving that attention to the domestic institutions of the people he describes, to which they are entitled as the most important subject of inquiry to the historian. The deficiency has been supplied by his judicious editor, Orteaga, from other sources. In the early part of his work, Veytia has explained the chronological system of the Aztecs, but, like most writers preceding the accurate Gama, with indifferent success. As a critic, he certainly ranks much higher than the annalists who preceded him; and, when his own religion is not involved, shows a discriminating judgment. When it is, he betrays a full measure of the credulity which still maintains its hold on too many even of the well informed of his countrymen. The editor of the work has given a very interesting letter from the Abbé Clavigero to Veytia, written when the former was a poor and humble exile, and in the tone of one addressing a person of high standing and literary eminence. Both were employed on the same subject. The writings of the poor Abbé, published again and again, and translated into various languages, have spread his fame throughout Europe; while the name of Veytia, whose works have been locked up in their primitive manuscript, is scarcely known beyond the boundaries of Mexico.

CHAPTER II.

SUCCESSION TO THE CROWN.—AZTEC NOBILITY.—JUDICIAL SYS-
TEM.—LAWS AND REVENUES.—MILITARY INSTITUTIONS.

THE form of government differed in the different states of
Anahuac. With the Aztecs and Tezcucans it was monarchical
and nearly absolute. The two nations resembled each other so
much, in their political institutions, that one of their historians
has remarked, in too unqualified a manner indeed, that what is
told of one may be always understood as applying to the other.[1]
I shall direct my inquiries to the Mexican polity, borrowing an
illustration occasionally from that of the rival kingdom.

The government was an elective monarchy. Four of the
principal nobles, who had been chosen by their own body in the
preceding reign, filled the office of electors, to whom were added,
with merely an honorary rank however, the two royal allies of
Tezcuco and Tlacopan. The sovereign was selected from the
brothers of the deceased prince, or, in default of them, from his
nephews. Thus the election was always restricted to the same
family. The candidate preferred must have distinguished himself in war, though, as in the case of the last Montezuma, he
were a member of the priesthood.[2] This singular mode of
supplying the throne had some advantages. The candidates
received an education which fitted them for the royal dignity,
while the age, at which they were chosen, not only secured the
nation against the evils of minority, but afforded ample means
for estimating their qualifications for the office. The result, at
all events, was favorable ; since the throne, as already noticed,
was filled by a succession of able princes, well qualified to rule
over a warlike and ambitious people. The scheme of election,
however defective, argues a more refined and calculating policy
than was to have been expected from a barbarous nation.[3]

---

[1] Ixtlilxochitl, Hist. Chich., MS., cap. 36.

[2] This was an exception.—In Egypt, also, the king was frequently taken
from the warrior caste, though obliged afterwaʳ ˒ to be instructed in the
mystries of the priesthood: ὁ δὲ ἐκ μαχίμων ατ ˴εδειγμένος ευϑὺς ἐγίνετο τῶν
ἱέρων. Plutarch,, de Isid. et Osir., sec. 9.

[3] Torquemada, Monarch. Ind., lib. 2, cap. 18; lib. 11, cap. 27.—Clavigero,

The new monarch was installed in his regal dignity with much parade of religious ceremony ; but not until, by a victorious campaign, he had obtained a sufficient number of captives to grace his triumphal entry into the capital, and to furnish victims for the dark and bloody rites which stained the Aztec superstition. Amidst this pomp of human sacrifice, he was crowned. The crown, resembling a mitre in its form, and curiously ornamented with gold, gems, and feathers, was placed on his head by the lord of Tezcuco, the most powerful of his royal allies. The title of *King*, by which the earlier Aztec princes are distinguished by Spanish writers, is supplanted by that of *Emperor* in the later reigns, intimating, perhaps, his superiority over the confederated monarchies of Tlacopan and Tezcuco.[4]

The Aztec princes, especially towards the close of the dynasty, lived in a barbaric pomp, truly Oriental. Their spacious palaces were provided with halls for the different councils, who aided the monarch in the transaction of business. The chief of these was a sort of privy council, composed in part, probably, of the four electors chosen by the nobles after the accession, whose places, when made vacant by death, were immediately supplied as before. It was the business of this body, so far as can be gathered from the very loose accounts given of it, to advise the king, in respect to the government of the provinces, the administration of the revenues, and, indeed, on all great matters of public interest.[5]

In the royal buildings were accommodations, also, for a numerous body-guard of the sovereign, made up of the chief nobility. It is not easy to determine with precision, in these barbarian governments, the limits of the several orders. It is certain, there was a distinct class of nobles, with large landed possessions, who held the most important offices near the person

Stor. del Messico, tom, II. p. 112.—Acosta, Naturall and Moral Historie of the East and West Indies, Eng. trans. (London, 1604.)

According to Zurita, an election by the nobles took place only in default of heirs of the deceased monarch. (Rapport, p. 15.) The minute historical investigation of Clavigero may be permitted to outweigh this general assertion.

[4] Sahagun, Hist, de Nueva España, lib. 6, cap. 9, 10, 14 ; lib. 8, cap. 31, 34.—See also, Zurita, Rapport, pp. 20–23.

Ixtlilxochitl stoutly claims this supremacy for his own nation. (Hist. Chich., MS., cap. 34.) His assertions are at variance with facts stated by himself elsewhere, and are not countenanced by any other writer whom I have consulted.

[5] Sahagun, who places the elective power in a much larger body, speaks of four senators, who formed a stated council. (Hist. de Nueva España, lib. 8, cap. 30.) Acosta enlarges the council beyond the number of the electors. (Lib. 6, ch. 26.) No two writers agree.

an appeal lay *t* his tr*i*.unal. Besides these courts, there was a body of infei*i*or magistrates, distributed through the country, chosen by the people themselves in their several districts. Their authority was limited to smaller causes, while the more important were carried up to the higher courts. There was still another class of subordinate officers, appointed also by the people, each of whom was to watch over the conduct of a certain number of families, and report any disorder or breach of the laws to the higher authorities.[12]

In Tezcuco the judicial arrangements were of a more refined character; [13] and a gradation of tribunals finally terminated in a general meeting or parliament, consisting of all the judges, great and petty, throughout the kingdom, held every eighty days in the capital, over which the king presided in person. This body determined all suits, which, from their importance, or difficulty, had been reserved for its consideration by the lower tribunals. It served, moreover, as a council of state, to assist the monarch in the transaction of public business.[14]

Such are the vague and imperfect notices that can be gleaned, respecting the Aztec tribunals, from the hieroglyphical paintings still preserved, and from the most accredited Spanish writers. These, being usually ecclesiastics, have taken much less interest in this subject, than in matters connected with religion. They find some apology, certainly, in the early destruction of most of the Indian paintings, from which their information was, in part, to be gathered.

On the whole, however, it must be inferred, that the Aztecs were sufficiently civilized to evince a solicitude for the rights both of

[12] Clavigero, Stor. del Messico, tom. II. pp. 127, 128.—Torquemada, Monarch. Ind., ubi supra.

In this arrangement of the more humble magistrates we are reminded of the Anglo-Saxon hundreds and tithings, especially the latter, the members of which were to watch over the conduct of the families in their districts, and bring the offenders to justice. The hard penalty of mutual responsibility was not known to the Mexicans.

[13] Zurita, so temperate, usually, in his language, remarks, that, in the capital, "Tribunals were instituted which might compare in their organization with the royal audiences of Castile." (Rapport, p. 93.) His observations are chiefly drawn from the Tezcucan courts, which, in their forms of pro cedure, he says, were like the Aztec. (Loc. cit.)

[14] Boturini, Idea, page. 87. Torquemada, Monarch. Ind., lib. 11, cap. 26.

Zurita compares this body to the Castilian córtes. It would seem, however, according to him, to have consisted only of twelve principal judges, besides the king. His meaning is somewhat doubtful. (Rapport, pp. 94, 101, 106.) M. de Humboldt, in his account of the Aztec courts, has confounded them with the Tezcucan Comp. Vues des Cordillères et Monumens des peuples Indigénes del' Amérique, (Paris, 1810,) p. 55, and Clavigero, Stor del Messico, tom. II. pp. 128, 129.

property and of persons. The law, authorizing an appeal to the highest judicature in criminal matters only, shows an attention to personal security, rendered the more obligatory by the extreme severity of their penal code, which would naturally have made them more cautious of a wrong conviction. The existence of a number of co-ordinate tribunals, without a central one of supreme authority to control the whole, must have given rise to very discordant interpretations of the law in different districts. But this is an evil which they shared in common with most of the nations of Europe.

The provision for making the superior judges wholly independent of the crown was worthy of an enlightened people. It presented the strongest barrier, that a mere constitution, could afford, against tyranny. It is not, indeed, to be supposed, that, in a government otherwise so despotic, means could not be found for influencing the magistrate. But it was a great step to fence round his authority with the sanction of the law ; and no one of the Aztec monarchs, as far as I know, is accused of an attempt to violate it.

To receive presents or a bribe, to be guilty of collusion in any way with a suitor, was punished, in a judge, with death. Who, or what tribunal, decided as to his guilt, does not appear. In Tezcuco this was done by the rest of the court. But the king presided over that body. The Tezcucan prince, Nezahualpilli, who rarely tempered justice with mercy, put one judge to death for taking a bribe, and another for determining suits in his own house,—a capital offence, also, by law.[15]

The judges of the higher tribunals were maintained from the produce of a part of the crown lands, reserved for this purpose. They, as well as the supreme judge, held their offices for life. The proceedings in the courts were conducted with decency and order. The judges wore an appropriate dress, and attended to business both parts of the day, dining, always, for the sake of despatch in an apartment of the same building where they held their session ; a method of proceeding much commended by the Spanish chroniclers, to whom despatch was not very familiar in their own tribunals. Officers attend to preserve order, and others summoned the parties, and produced them in court. No counsel was employed ; the parties stated their own case, and supported it by their witnesses. The oath of the accused was also admitted in evidence. The statement of

---

[15] " Ah ! si esta se repitiera hoy, que bueno seria !" exclaims Sahagun's Mexican editor. Hist. de Nueva España, tom. II. p. 304, nota —Zurita. Rapport, p. 102.—Torquemada, Monarch. Ind., ubi supra.—Ixtlilxochitl, Hist. Chich., MS., cap. 67.

the case, the tes' .ony, and the proceedings of the trial, were all set forth by a clerk, in hieroglyphical paintings, and handed over to the court. The paintings were executed with so much accuracy, that, in all suits respecting real property, they were allowed to be produced as good authority in the Spanish tribunals, very long after the Conquest; and a chair for their study and interpretation was established at Mexico in 1553, which has long since shared the fate of most other provisions for learn. ing in that unfortunate country.[16]

A capital sentence was indicated by a line traced with an arrow across the portrait of the accused. In Tezcuco, where the king presided in the court, this, according to the national chronicler, was done with extraordinary parade. His description ¬hich is of rather a poetical cast, I give in his own words. ·' In the royal palace of Tezcuco was a courtyard, on the opposite sides of which were two halls of justice. In the principal one, called the 'tribunal of God,' was a throne of pure gold, inlaid with turquoises and other precious stones. On a stool, in front, was placed a human skull, crowned with an immense emerald, of a pyramidal form, and surmounted by an aigrette of brilliant plumes and precious stones. The skull was laid on a heap of military weapons, shields, quivers, bows, and arrows. The walls were hung with tapestry, made of the hair of different wild animals, of rich and various colors, festooned by gold rings, and embroidered with figures of birds and flowers. Above the throne was a canopy of variegated plumage, from the centre of which shot forth re. splendent rays of gold and jewels. The other tribunal, called ' the King's,' was also surmounted by a gorgeous canopy of feathers, on which were emblazoned the royal arms. Here the sovereign gave public audience, and communicated his despatches. But, when he decided important causes, or confirmed a capital sentence, he passed to the ' tribunal of God,' attended by the fourteen great lords of the realm, marshalled according to their rank. Then, putting on his mitred crown, incrusted with pre. cious stones, and holding a golden arrow, by way of sceptre, in his left hand, he laid his right upon the skull, and pronounced judgment." [17] All this looks rather fine for a court of justice, it

[16] Zurita, Rapport, pp. 95, 100, 103.—Sahagun, Hist. de Nueva España, loc. cit.—Humboldt, Vues des Cordillères, pp. 55, 56.—Torquemada, Monarch. Ind., lib. 11, cap. 25.
Clavigero says, the accused might free himself by oath; " Il reo poteva gurgarsi col giuramento." (Stor. del Messico, tom. II. p. 129.) What rogue, then, could ever have been convicted?
[17] Ixtlilxochitl, Hist. Chich., MS., cap. 36.
These various objects had a symbolical meaning, according to Boturin, Idea, p. 84.

must be owned. But it is certain, that the Tezcucans, as we shall see hereafter, possessed both the materials, and the skill requisite to work them up in this manner. Had they been a little further advanced in refinement, one might well doubt their having the bad taste to do so.

The laws of the Aztecs were registered, and exhibited to the people, in their hieroglyphical paintings. Much the larger part of them, as in every nation imperfectly civilized, relates rather to the security of persons, than of property. The great crimes against society were all made capital. Even the murder of a slave was punished with death. Adulterers, as among the Jews, were stoned to death. Thieving, according to the degree of the offence, was punished by slavery or death. Yet the Mexicans could have been under no great apprehension of this crime, since the entrances to their dwellings were not secured by bolts, or fastenings of any kind. It was a capital offence to remove the boundaries of another's lands ; to alter the established measures ; and for a guardian not to be able to give a good account of his ward's property. These regulations evince a regard for equity in dealings, and for private rights, which argues a considerable progress in civilization. Prodigals, who squandered their patrimony, were punished in like manner ; a severe sentence since the crime brought its adequate punishment along with it. Intemperance, which was the burden, moreover, of their religious homilies, was visited with the severest penalties ; as if they had foreseen in it the consuming canker of their own, as well as of the other Indian races in later times. It was punished in the young with death, and in older persons with loss of rank and confiscation of property. Yet a decent conviviality was not meant to be proscribed at their festivals, and they possessed the means of indulging it, in a mild fermented liquor, called *pulque*, which is still popular, not only with the Indian, but the European population of the country.[18]

The rites of marriage were celebrated with as much formality

---

[18] Paintings of the Mendoza Collection, Pl. 72, and Interpretation ap. Antiqu. of Mexico, vol. VI. p. 87.—Torquemada, Monarch. Ind., lib. 12, cap. 7.— Clavigero, Stor. del Messico, tom. II. pp. 130–134.— Camargo, Hist. de Tlascala, MS.

They could scarcely have been an intemperate people, with these heavy penalties hanging over them. Indeed, Zurita bears testimony that those Spaniards, who thought they were, greatly erred. (Rapport, p. 112.) Mons, Ternaux's translation of a passage of the Anonymous Conqueror, " aucun peuple n'est aussi sobre," (Recueil de Pièces Relatives à la Conquête de Mexique, ap. Voyage, &c., (Paris, 1838,) p. 54,) may give a more favorable impression, however, than that intended by his original, whose remark is confined to abstemiousness in eating. See the Relatione, ap. Ramusio, Raccolta delle Navigationi et Viaggi. (Venetia, 1554-1565.)

as in any Christian country ; and the institution was held in such reverence, that a tribunal was instituted for the sole pur-pose of determining questions relating to it. Divorces could not be obtained, until authorized by a sentence of this court, after a patient hearing of the parties.

But the most remarkable part of the Aztec code was that relating to slavery. . There were several descriptions of slaves : prisoners taken in war, who were almost always reserved for the dreadful doom of sacrifice ; criminals, public debtors, persons who, from extreme poverty, voluntarily resigned their freedom, and children who were sold by their own parents. In the last instance, usually occasioned also by poverty, it was common for the parents, with the master's consent, to substitute others of their children successively, as they grew up ; thus distributing the burden, as equally as possible, among the different members of the family. The willingness of freemen to incur the penal-ties of this condition is explained by the mild form in which it existed. The contract of sale was executed in the presence of at least four witnesses. The services to be exacted were limited with great precision. The slave was allowed to have his own family, to hold property, and even other slaves. His children were free. No one could be born to slavery in Mexico ; [19] an honorable distinction, not known, I believe, in any civilized community where slavery has been sanctioned.[20] Slaves were not sold by their masters, unless when these were driven to it by poverty. They were often liberated by them at their death, and sometimes, as there was no natural repugnance founded on difference of blood and race, were married to them. Yet a refractory or vicious slave might be led into the market, with a collar round his neck, which intimated his bad character, and there be publicly sold, and, on a second sale, reserved for sac-rifice.[21]

Such are some of the most striking features of the Aztec

[19] In Ancient Egypt the child of a slave was born free, if the father were free. (Diodorus, Bibl. Hist., lib. 1, sec. 80.) This, though more liberal than the code of most countries, fell short of the Mexican.

[20] In Egypt the same penalty was attached to the murder of a slave, as to that of a freeman. (Ibid., lib. 1, sec. 77.) Robertson speaks of a class of slaves held so cheap in the eye of the Mexican law, that one might kill them with impunity. (History of America, (ed. London, 1776,) vol. III. p. 164.) This, however, was not in Mexico, but in Nicaragua, (see his own authority, Herrera, Hist. General, dec. 3, lib. 4, cap. 2,) a distant country, not incorpo-rated in the Mexican empire, and with laws and institutions very different from those of the latter.

[21] Torquemada, Monarch. Ind., lib. 12, cap. 15; lib. 14, cap. 16, 17.— Sahagun, Hist. de Nueva España, lib. 8, cap. 14.—Clavigero, Stor. del Messico, tom. II. pp. 134-136.

code, to which the Tezcucan bore great resemblance.[22] With some exceptions, it is stamped with the severity, the ferocity indeed, of a rude people; hardened by familiarity with scenes of blood, and relying on physical, instead of moral means, for the correction of evil.[23] Still, it evinces a profound respect for the great principles of morality, and as clear a perception of these principles as is to be found in the most cultivated nations.

The royal revenues were derived from various sources. The crown lands, which appear to have been extensive, made their returns in kind. The places in the neighborhood of the capital were bound to supply workmen and materials for building the king's palaces, and keeping them in repair. They were also to furnish fuel, provisions, and whatever was necessary for his ordinary domestic expenditure, which was certainly on no stinted scale.[24] The principal cities, which had numerous villages and a large territory dependent on them, were distributed into districts, with each a share of the lands allotted to it, for its support. The inhabitants paid a stipulated part of the produce to the crown. The vassals of the great chiefs, also, paid a portion of their earnings into the public treasury; an arrangement not at all in the spirit of the feudal institutions.[25]

[22] Ixtlilxochitl, Hist. Chich., MS., cap. 38, and Relaciones, MS.
The Tezcucan code, indeed, as digested under the great Nezahualcoyotl, formed the basis of the Mexican, in the latter days of the empire. Zurita, Rapport, p. 95.
[23] In this, at least, they did not resemble the Romans; of whom their countryman could boast, "Gloriari licet, nulli gentium mitiores placuisse pœnas." Livy, Hist., lib. 1, cap. 28.
[24] The Tezcucan revenues were, in like manner, paid in the produce of the country. The various branches of the royal expenditure were defrayed by specified towns and districts; and the whole arrangements here, and in Mexico, bore a remarkable resemblance to the financial regulations of the Persian empire, as reported by the Greek writers; (see Herodotus, Clio, sec. 192;) with this difference, however, that the towns of Persia proper were not burdened with tributes, like the conquered cities. Idem, Thalia, sec. 97.
[25] Lorenzana, Hist. de Nueva España, p. 172.—Torquemada, Monarch. Ind., lib. 2, cap. 89; lib. 14, cap, 7.—Boturini, Idea, p. 166.—Camargo, Hist. de Tlascala, MS.—Herrera, Hist. General, dec. 2, lib. 7, cap 13.
The people of the provinces were distributed into *calpulli* or tribes, who held the lands of the neighborhood in common. Officers of their own appointment parcelled out these lands among the several families of the *calpulli*; and, on the extinction or removal of a family, its lands reverted to the common stock, to be again distributed. The individual proprietor had no power to alienate them. The laws regulating these matters were very precise, and had existed ever since the occupation of the country by the Aztecs. Zurita, Rapport, pp. 51-62.

In addition to this tax on all the agricultural produce of the kingdom, there was another on its manufactures. The nature and variety of the tributes will be best shown by an enumeration of some of the principal articles. These were cotton dresses, and mantles of featherwork exquisitely made ; ornamented armor ; vases and plates of gold ; gold dust, bands and bracelets ; crystal, gilt, and varnished jars and goblets ; bells, arms, and utensils of copper ; reams of paper ; grain, fruits, copal, amber, cochineal, cacao, wild animals and birds, timber, lime, mats, &c.[26] In this curious medley of the most homely commodities, and the elegant superfluities of luxury, it is singular that no mention should be made of silver, the great staple of the country in later times, and the use of which was certainly known to the Aztecs.[27]

Garrisons were established in the larger cities,—probably those at a distance, and recently conquered,—to keep down revolt, and to enforce the payment of the tribute.[28] Tax-gatherers

[26] The following items of the tribute furnished by different cities will give a more precise idea of its nature :—20 chests of ground chocolate ; 40 pieces; of armor, of a particular device; 2400 loads of large mantles, of twisted cloth; 800 loads of small mantles, of rich wearing apparel; 5 pieces of armor of rich feathers; 60 pieces of armor, of common feathers; a chest of beans; a chest of *chian;* a chest of maize; 8000 reams of paper; likewise 2000 loaves of very white salt, refined in the shape of a mould, for the consumption only of the lords of Mexico; 8000 lumps of unrefined copal; 400 small baskets of white refined copal; 100 copper axes; 80 loads of red chocolate; 800 *xicaras*, out of which they drank chocolate ; a little vessel of small turquoise stones; 4 chests of timber, full of maize; 4000 loads of lime ; tiles of gold, of the size of an oyster, and as thick as the finger; 40 bags of cochineal; 20 bags of gold dust, of the finest quality; a diadem of gold, of a specified pattern; 20 lip-jewels of clear amber, ornamented with gold; 200 loads of chocolate: 100 pots or jars of liquid-amber; 8000 *handfuls* of rich scarlet feathers; 40 tiger-skins; 1600 bundles of cotton, &c., &c. Col. de Mendoza, part 2, ap. Antiqu. of Mexico, vols. I., VI.

[27] Mapa de Tributos, ap. Lorenzana, Hist. de Nueva España.—Tribute-roll, ap. Antiq. of Mexico, vol. I., and Interpretation, vol. VI., pp. 17–44.

The Mendoza Collection, in the Bodleian Library at Oxford, contains a roll of the cities of the Mexican empire, with the specific tributes exacted from them. It is a copy made after the Conquest with a pen on European paper (See Foreign Quarterly Review, No. XVII. Art. 4.) An original painting of the same roll was in Boturini's museum. Lorenzana has given us engravings of it, in which the outlines of the Oxford copy are filled up, though somewhat rudely. Clavigero considers the explanations in Lorenzana's edition very inaccurate, (Stor. del Messico, tom. I. p. 25,) a judgment confirmed by Aglio, who has transcribed the entire collection of the Mendoza papers, in the first volume of the Antiquities of Mexico. It would have much facilitated reference to his plates, if they had been numbered;—a strange omission !

[28] The caciques, who submitted to the allied arms, were usually confirmed in their authority, and the conquered places allowed t' :tain their laws and usages. (Zurita, Rapport, p. 67.) The conquests were ..ot always partitioned, but sometimes, singularly enough, were held in common by the three powers. Ibid., p. 11.

were also distributed throughout the kingdom, who were recognized by their official badges, and dreaded from the merciless rigor of their exactions. By a stern law, every defaulter was liable to be taken and sold as a slave. In the capital were spacious granaries and warehouses for the reception of the tributes. A receiver-general was quartered in the palace, who rendered in an exact account of the various contributions, and watched over the conduct of the inferior agents, in whom the least malversation was summarily punished. This functionary was furnished with a map of the whole empire, with a minute specification of the imposts assessed on every part of it. These imposts, moderate under the reigns of the early princes, became so burdensome under those at the close of the dynasty, being rendered still more oppressive by the manner of collection, that they bred disaffection throughout the land, and prepared the way for its conquest by the Spaniards.[29]

Communication was maintained with the remotest parts of the country by means of couriers. Post-houses were established on the great roads, about two leagues distant from each other. The couriers, bearing his despatches in the form of a hieroglyphical painting, ran with them to the first station, where they were taken by another messenger and carried forward to the next, and so on till they reached the capital. These couriers, trained from childhood, travelled with incredible swiftness; not four or five leagues an hour, as an old chronicler would make us believe, but with such speed that despatches were carried from one to two hundred miles a day.[30] Fresh fish was frequently served at Montezuma's table in twenty-four hours from the time it had been taken in the Gulf of Mexico, two hundred miles from the capital. In this way intelligence of the movements of the royal armies was rapidly brought to court; and the dress of the

---

[29] Collec. of Mendoza, ap. Antiq. of Mexico, vol. VI, p. 17.—Carta de Cortés, ap. Lorenzana, Hist. de Nueva España, p. 110.—Torquemada, Monarch. Ind., lib. 14, cap. 6. 8.—Herrera, Hist. General, dec. 2, lib 7, cap. 13.—Sahagun, Hist. de Nueva España, ib. 8, cap. 18, 19.

[30] The Hon. C. A. Murray, whose imperturbable good humor under real troubles forms a contrast, rather striking, to the sensitiveness of some of his predecessors to imaginary ones, tells us, among other marvels, that an Indian of his party travelled a hundred miles in four and twenty hours. (Travels in N. America, (New York, 1839,) vol. I. p. 193.) The Greek, who, according to Plutarch, brought the news of victory to Platæa, a hundred and twenty-five miles, in a day, was a better traveler still. Some interesting facts on the pedestrian capabilities of man in the savage state are collected by Buffon, who concludes, truly enough, "L'homme civilisé ne connait pas ses forces." (Histoire Naturelle; De la Jeunesse.)

courier, denoting by its color that of his tidings, spread joy or consternation in the towns through which he passed.

But the great aim of the Aztec institutions, to which private discipline and public honors were alike directed, was the profession of arms. In Mexico, as in Egypt, the soldier shared with the priest the highest consideration. The king, as we have seen, must be an experienced warrior. The tutelary deity of the Aztecs was the god of war. A great object of their military expeditions was, to gather hecatombs of captives for his altars. The soldier, who fell in battle, was transported at once to the region of ineffable bliss in the bright mansions of the Sun.[33] Every war therefore, became a crusade ; and the warrior, animated by a religious enthusiasm, like that of the early Saracen, or the Christian crusader, was not only raised to a contempt of danger, but courted it, for the imperishable crown of martyrdom. Thus we find the same impulse acting in the most opposite quarters of the globe, and the Asiatic, the European, and the American, each earnestly invoking the holy name of religion in the perpetration of human butchery.

The question of war was discussed in a council of the king and his chief nobles. Ambassadors were sent, previously to its declaration, to require the hostile state to receive the Mexican gods, and to pay the customary tribute. The persons of ambassadors were held sacred throughout Anahuac. They were lodged and entertained in the great towns at the public charge, and were everywhere received with courtesy, so long as they did not deviate from the highroads on their route. When they did, they forfeited their privileges. If the embassy proved unsuccessful, a defiance, or open declaration of war, was sent ; quotas were drawn from the conquered provinces, which were always subjected to military service, as well as the payment of taxes ;

---

[31] Torquemada, Monarch. Ind., lib. 14, cap. 1.

The same wants led to the same expedients in ancient Rome, and still more ancient Persia. " Nothing in the world is borne so swiftly," says Herodotus, " as messages by the Persian couriers " ; which his commentator, Valckenaer, prudently qualifies by the exception of the carrier pigeon. (Herodotus, Hist., Urania, sec. 98, nec non Adnot. ed. Schweighäuser.) Couriers are noticed, in the thirteenth century, in China, by Marco Polo. Their stations were only three miles apart, and they accomplished five days' journey in one. (Viaggi di Marco Polo, lib. 2, cap. 20, ap. Ramusio, tom. II.) A similar arrangement for posts subsists there at the present day, and excites the admiration of a modern traveller. (Anderson, British Embassy to China, (London, 1796,) p. 282.) In all these cases, the posts were for the use of government only.

[32] Sahagun, Hist. de Nueva España, lib. 3, Apend.,cap. 3.

and the royal army, usually with the monarch at its head, began its march.[33]

The Aztec princes made use of the incentives employed by European monarchs to excite the ambition of their followers. They established various military orders, each having its privileges and peculiar insignia. There seems, also, to have existed a sort of knighthood, of inferior degree. It was the cheapest reward of martial prowess, and whoever had not reached it was excluded from using ornaments on his arms or his person, and obliged to wear a coarse white stuff, made from the threads of the aloe, called *nequen*. Even the members of the royal family were not excepted from this law, which reminds one of the occasional practice of Christian knights, to wear plain armor, or shields without device, till they had achieved some doughty feat of chivalry. Although the military orders were thrown open to all, it is probable that they were chiefly filled with persons of rank, who, by their previous training and connexions, were able to come into the field under peculiar advantages.[34]

The dress of the higher warriors was picturesque and often magnificent. Their bodies were covered with a close vest of quilted cotton, so thick as to be impenetrable to the light missiles of Indian warfare. This garment was so light and serviceable, that it was adopted by the Spaniards. The wealthier chiefs sometimes wore, instead of this cotton mail, a cuirass made of thin plates of gold, or silver. Over it was thrown a surcoat of the gorgeous featherwork in which they excelled.[35] Their helmets were sometimes of wood, fashioned like the heads of wild animals, and sometimes of silver, on the top of which waved a *panache* of variegated plumes, sprinkled with precious stones

[33] Zurita; Rapport, pp. 68, 120.—Col. of Mendoza, ap. Antiq. of Mexico,vol. 1 Pl. 67; vol. VI. p. 74.—Torquemada, Monarch. Ind., lib. 14, cap. 1.
The reader will find a remarkable resemblance to these military usages, in those of the early Romans. Comp. Liv., Hist., lib. 1, caps. 32; lib. 4, cap. 30, et alibi.

[34] Ibid., lib. 14, cap. 4, 5.—Acosta, lib. 6, ch. 26.—Collec. of Mendoza, ap. Antiq. of Mexico, vol. 1. Pl. 65; vol. VI. p. 72.—Camargo, Hist. de Tlascala, MS

[35] " Their mail if mail, it may be called, was woven
    Of vegetable down, like finest flax,
    Bleached to the whiteness of newfallen snow.
    *   *   *   *   *   *   *
    Others, of higher office, were arrayed
    In feathery breastplates, of more gorgeous hue
    Than the gay plumage of the mountain-cock,
    Than the pheasant's glittering pride. But what were those,
    Or what the thin gold hauberk, when opposed
    To arms like ours in battle ? "
                                        MADOC, P. 1, canto 7.

Beautiful painting ! One may doubt, however, the propriety of the Welshman's vaunt, before the use of fire-arms.

and ornaments of gol¹ They wore also collars, bracelets, and ear-rings, of the sar.., rich materials.[36]

Their armies were divided into bodies of eight thousand men; and these again, into companies of three or four hundred, each with its own commander. The national standard, which has been compared to the ancient Roman, displayed, in its embroidery of gold and feather-work, the armorial ensigns of the state. These were significant of its name, which, as the names of both persons and places were borrowed from some material object, was easily expressed by hieroglyphical symbols. The companies and the great chiefs had also their appropriate banners and devices, and the gaudy hues of their many-colored plumes gave a dazzling splendor to the spectacle.

Their tactics were such as belong to a nation, with whom war, though a trade, is not elevated to the rank of a science. They advanced singing, and shouting their war-cries, briskly charging the enemy, as rapidly retreating, and making use of ambuscades, sudden surprises, and the light skirmish of guerilla warfare. Yet their discipline was such as to draw forth the encomiums of the Spanish conquerors. "A beautiful sight it was," says one of them, "to see them set out on their march, all moving forward so gayly, and in so admirable order!"[37] In battle, they did not seek to kill their enemies, so much as to take them prisoners; and they never scalped, like other North American tribes. The valor of a warrior was estimated by the number of his prisoners; and no ransom was large enough to save the devoted captive.[38]

Their military code bore the same stern features as their other laws. Disobedience of orders was punished with death. It was death, also, for a soldier to leave his colors, to attack the enemy before the signal was given, or to plunder another's booty or prisoners. One of the last Tezcucan princes, in the spirit of an

---

[36] Sahagun, Hist. de Nueva España, lib. 2, cap. 27 ; lib. 8, cap. 12.. Relatione d'un gentil' huomo, ap. Ramusio, tom. III. p. 305.—Torquemada, Monarch. Ind., ubi supra.

[37] Relatione d'un gentil' huomo, ubi supra.

[38] Col. of Mendoza, ap. Antiq. of Mexico, vol. I. Pl. 65, 66; vol. VI. p. 73. —Sahagun, Hist. de Nueva España, lib. 8, cap. 12.—Toribio, Hist. de los Indios, MS., Parte I. cap. 7.—Torquemada, Monarch Ind., lib. 14, cap. 3.— Relatione d'un gentil' huomo, ap. Ramusio, loc. cit.

Scalping may claim high authority, or, at least, antiquity. The Father of History gives an account of it among the Scythians, showing that they performed the operation, and wore the hideous trophy, in the same manner as our North American Indians. (Herodot., Hist. Melpomene, sec. 64.) Traces of the same savage custom are also found in the laws of the Visigoths, among the Franks, and even the Anglo-Saxons. See Guizot, Cours d'Histoire Moderne, (Paris, 1829,) tom. I. p. 283.

ancient Roman, put two sons to death,—after having cured their
wounds,—for violating the last-mentioned law.[39]

I must not omit to notice here an institution, the introduction of which, in the Old World, is ranked among the beneficent
fruits of Christianity. Hospitals were established in the principal cities, for the cure of the sick, and the permanent refuge
of the disabled soldiers; and surgeons were placed over them,
"who were so far better than those in Europe," says an old
chronicler, "that they did not protract the cure, in order to increase the pay."[40]

Such is the brief outline of the civil and military polity of the
ancient Mexicans; less perfect than could be desired, in regard to the former, from the imperfection of the sources whence
it is drawn. Whoever has had occasion to explore the early
history of modern Europe has found how vague and unsatisfac-
tory is the political information which can be gleaned from the
gossip of monkish annalists. How much is the difficulty increased in the present instance, where this information, first
recorded in the dubious language of hieroglyphics, was interpreted in another language, with which the Spanish chroniclers
were imperfectly acquainted, while it related to institutions of
which their past experience enabled them to form no adequate
conception! Amidst such uncertain lights, it is in vain to expect nice accuracy of detail. All that can be done is, to attempt an outline of the more prominent features, that a correct
impression, so far as it goes, may be produced on the mind of
the reader.

Enough has been said, however, to show that the Aztec and
Tezcucan races were advanced in civilization very far beyond
the wandering tribes of North America.[41] The degree of civili-

[39] Ixtlilxochitl, Hist. Chich., MS., cap. 67.
[40] Torquemada, Monarch. Ind., lib. 12, cap. 6; lib. 14, cap. 3.—Ixtlilxochitl, Hist Chich., MS., cap. 36.
[41] Zurita is indignant at the epithet of *barbarians* bestowed on the Aztecs;
an epithet, he says, "which could come from no one who had personal knowledge of the capacity of the people, or their institutions, and which, in some
respects, is quite as well merited by the European nations." (Rapport, p.
200, et seq.) This is strong language. Yet no one had better means of
knowing than this eminent jurist, who, for nineteen years, held a post in the
royal *audiences* of New Spain, During his long residence in the country he
had ample opportunity of acquainting himself with its usages, both through
his own personal observation and intercourse with the natives, and through
the first missionaries who came over after the Conquest. On his return to
Spain, probably about 1560, he occupied himself with an answer to queries
which have been propounded by the government, on the character of the
Aztec laws and institutions and on that of the modifications introduced by
the Spaniards. Much of his treatise is taken up with the latter subject. In
what relates to the former he is more brief than could be wished, from the

zation which they had reached, as inferred by their political institutions, may be considered, perhaps, not much short of that
enjoyed by our Saxon ancestors, under Alfred.   In respect to
the nature of it, they may be better compared with the Egyptians ; and the examination of their social relations and culture
may suggest still stronger points of resemblance to that ancient
people.

Those familiar with the modern Mexicans will find it difficult
to conceive that the nation should ever have been capable of
devising the enlightened polity which we have been considering.
But they should remember that in the Mexicans of our day they
see only a conquered race ; as different from their ancestors as
are the modern Egyptians from those who built,—I will not say,
the tasteless pyramids,—but the temples and palaces, whose
magnificent wrecks strew the borders of the Nile, at Luxor and
Karnac.   The difference is not so great as between the ancient
Greek, and his degenerate descendant, lounging among the
master-pieces of art which he has scarcely taste enough to admire,—speaking the language of those still more imperishable
monuments of literature which he has hardly capacity to comprehend.   Yet he breathes the same atmosphere, is warmed by the
same sun, nourished by the same scenes, as those who fell at
Marathon, and won the trophies of Olympic Pisa.   The same
blood flows in his veins that flowed in theirs.   But ages of tyranny
have passed over him ; he belongs to a conquered race.

The American Indian has something peculiarly sensitive in
his nature.   He shrinks instinctively from the rude touch of a
foreign hand.   Even when this foreign influence comes in the
form of civilization, he seems to sink and pine away beneath it.
It has been so with the Mexicans.   Under the Spanish domina-
tion, their numbers have silently melted away.   Their energies
are broken.   They no longer tread their mountain plains with
the conscious independence of their ancestors.   In their faltering step, and meek and melancholy aspect, we read the sad
characters of the conquered race.   The cause of humanity, indeed, has gained.   They live under a better system of laws, a
more assured tranquillity, a purer faith.   But all does not avail.

difficulty, perhaps, of obtaining full and satisfactory information as to the
details.   As far as he goes, however, he manifests a sound and discriminating
judgment.   He is very rarely betrayed into the extravagance of expression
so visible in the writers of the time; and this temperance, combined with his
uncommon sources of information, makes his work one of highest authority
on the limited topics within its range.—The original manuscript was consulted by Clavigero, and, indeed, has been used by other writers.   The work
is now accessible to all, as one of the series of translations from the pen of
the indefatigable Ternaux.

Their civilization was of the hardy character which belongs to the wilderness. The fierce virtues of the Aztec were all his own. They refused to submit to European culture,—to be engrafted on a foreign stock. His outward form, his complexion, his lineament, are substantially the same. But the moral characteristics of the nation, all that constituted its individuality as a race, are effaced forever.

Two of the principal authorities for this chapter are Torquemada and Clavigero. The former, a Provincial of the Franciscan order, came to the New World about the middle of the sixteenth century. As the generation of the Conquerors had not then passed away, he had ample opportunities of gathering the particulars of their enterprise from their own lips. Fifty years, during which he continued in the country, put him in possession of the traditions and usages of the natives, and enabled him to collect their history from the earliest missionaries, as well as from such monuments as the fanaticism of his own countrymen had not then destroyed. From these ample sources he compiled his bulky tomes, beginning, after the approved fashion of the ancient Castilian chroniclers, with the creation of the world, and embracing the whole circle of the Mexican institutions, political, religious, and social, from the earliest period to his own time. In handling these fruitful themes, the worthy father has shown a full measure of the bigotry which belonged to his order at that period. Every page, too, is loaded with illustrations from Scripture or profane history, which form a whimsical contrast to the barbaric staple of his story ; and he has sometimes fallen into serious errors, from his misconception of the chronological system of the Aztecs. But, notwithstanding these glaring defects in the composition of the work, the student, aware of his author's infirmities, will find few better guides than Torquemada in tracing the stream of historic truth up to the fountain head ; such is his manifest integrity, and so great were his facilities for information on the most curious points of Mexican antiquity. No work, accordingly, has been more largely consulted and copied, even by some, who, like Herrera, have affected to set little value on the sources whence its information was drawn. —(Hist. General, dec. 6, lib. 6, cap, 19.) The *Monarchia Indiana* was first published at Seville, 1615, (Nic Antonio, Bibliotheca Nova, (Matriti, 1783,) tom. II. p. 787,) and since, in a better style, in three volumes folio, at Madrid, in 1723.

The other authority, frequently cited in the preceding pages, is the Abbé Clavigero's *Storia Antica del Messico.* It was originally printed towards the close of the last century, in the Italian language, and in Italy, whither the author, a native of Vera Cruz, and a member of the order of the Jesuits, had retired, on the expulsion of that body from America, in 1767. During a residence of thirty-five years in his own country, Clavigero had made himself intimately acquainted with its antiquities, by the careful examination of paintings, manuscripts, and such other remains as were to be found in his day. The plan of his work is nearly as comprehensive as that of his predecessor, Torquemada ; but the later and more cultivated period, in which he wrote, is visible in the superior address with which he has managed his complicated subject. In the elaborate disquisitions in his concluding volume, he has done much to rectify the chronology, and the various inaccuracies of preceding writers. Indeed, an avowed object of his work was, to vindicate his countrymen from what he conceived to be the misrepresentations of Robertson

Raynal, and De Pau. In regard to the last two, he was perfectly successful. Such an ostensible design might naturally suggest unfavorable ideas of his impartiality. But, on the whole, he seems to have conducted the discussion with good faith ; and, if he has been led by national zeal to overcharge the picture with brilliant colors, he will be found much more temperate, on this score, than those who preceded him, while he has applied sound principles of criticism, of which they were incapable. In a word, the diligence of his researches has gathered into one focus the scattered lights of tradition and antiquarian lore, purified in a great measure from the mists of superstition which obscure the best productions of an earlier period. From these causes, the work, notwithstanding its occasional prolixity, and the disagreeable aspect given to it by the profusion of uncouth names in the Mexican orthography, which bristle over every page, has found merited favor with the public, and created something like a popular interest in the subject. Soon after its publication at Cesena, in 1780, it was translated into English, and more lately, into Spanish and German.

CHAPTER III.

MEXICAN MYTHOLOGY.—THE SACERDOTAL ORDER.—THE
TEMPLES.—HUMAN SACRIFICES.

THE civil polity of the Aztecs is so closely blended with their religion, that, without understanding the latter, it is impossible to form correct ideas of their government or their social institutions. I shall pass over, for the present, some remarkable traditions, bearing a singular resemblance to those found in the Scriptures, and endeavor to give a brief sketch of their mythology, and their careful provisions for maintaining a national worship.

Mythology may be regarded as the poetry of religion,—or rather as the poetic development of the religious principles in a primitive age. It is the effort of untutored man to explain the mysteries of existence, and the secret agencies by which the operations of nature are conducted. Although the growth of similar conditions of society, its character must vary with that of the rude tribes in which it originates ; and the ferocious Goth, quaffing mead from the skulls of his slaughtered enemies, must have a very different mythology from that of the effeminate native of Hispaniola, loitering away his hours in idle pastimes, under the shadow of his bananas.

At a later and more refined period, we sometimes find these primitive legends combined into a regular system under the hands of the poet, and the rude outline moulded into forms of ideal beauty, which are the objects of adoration in a credulous age, and the delight of all succeeding ones. Such were the beautiful inventions of Hesiod and Homer, " who," says the Father of History, " created the theogony of the Greeks "; an assertion not to be taken too literally, since it is hardly possible that any man should create a religious system for his nation.[1] They only filled up the shadowy outlines of tradition with the bright touches of their own imaginations, until they had clothed them

---

[1] ποιήσαντες θεογονίην "Ελλησι Herodotus, Euterpe, sec. 53 – Heeren hazards a remark equally strong, respecting the epic poets of India, " who," says he, " have supplied the numerous gods that fill her Pantheon." Historical Researches, Eng. trans., (Oxford, 1833,) vol. III. p. 139.

in beauty which kindled the imaginations of others. The power of the poet, indeed, may be felt in a similar way in a much riper period of society. To say nothing of the "Divina Commedia," who is there that rises from the perusal of "Paradise Lost," without feeling his own conceptions of the angelic hierarchy quickened by those of the inspired artist, and a new and sensible form, as it were, given to images which had before floated dim and undefined before him ?

The last-mentioned period is succeeded by that of philosophy ; which, disclaiming alike the legends of the primitive age, and the poetical embellishments of the succeeding one, seeks to shelter itself from the charge of impiety by giving an allegorical interpretation to the popular mythology, and thus to reconcile the latter with the genuine deductions of science.

The Mexican religion had emerged from the first of the periods we have been considering, and, although little affected by poetical influences, had received a peculiar complexion from the priests, who had digested as thorough and burdensome a ceremonial, as ever existed in any nation. They had, moreover, thrown the veil of allegory over early tradition, and invested their deities with attributes, savoring much more of the grotesque conceptions of the eastern nations in the Old World, than of the lighter fictions of Greek mythology, in which the features of humanity, however exaggerated, were never wholly abandoned.[2]

In contemplating the religious system of the Aztecs, one is struck with its apparent incongruity, as if some portion of it had emanated from a comparatively refined people, open to gentle influences, while the rest breathes a spirit of unmitigated ferocity. It naturally suggests the idea of two distinct sources, and authorizes the belief that the Aztecs had inherited from their predecessors a milder faith, on which was afterwards engrafted their own mythology. The latter soon became dominant, and gave its dark coloring to the creeds of the conquered nations, —which the Mexicans, like the ancient Romans, seem willingly to have incorporated into their own,—until the same funereal superstitions settled over the farthest borders of Anahuac.

The Aztecs recognized the existence of a supreme Creator and Lord of the universe. They addressed him in their prayers as " the God by whom we live," " omnipresent, that knoweth

---

[2] The Hon. Mountstuart Elphinstone has fallen into a similar train of thought, in a comparison of the Hindoo and Greek Mythology, in his " History of India," published since the remarks in the text were written. (See Book I. ch. 4.) The same chapter of this truly philosophic work suggests some curious points of resemblance to the Aztec religious institutions, that may furnish pertinent illustrations to the ·mind bent on tracing the affinities of the Asiatic and American races

all thoughts, and giveth all gifts," " without whom man is as nothing," " invisible, incorporeal, one God, of *perfect perfection and purity*," " under whose wings we find repose and a sure defence." These sublime attributes infer no inadequate conception of the true God. But the idea of unity—of a being, with whom volition is action, who has no need of inferior ministers to execute his purposes—was too simple or too vast, for their understandings ; and they sought relief, as usual, in a plurality of deities, who presided over the elements, the changes of the seasons, and the various occupations of man.[3] Of these, there were thirteen principal deities, and more than two hundred inferior ; to each of whom some special day, or appropriate festival, was consecrated.[4]

At the head of all stood the terrible Huitzilopotchli, the Mexican Mars ; although it is doing injustice to the heroic wargod of antiquity to identify him with this sanguinary monster. This was the patron deity of the nation. His fantastic image was loaded with costly ornaments. His temples were the most stately and august of the public edifices ; and his altars reeked with the blood of human hecatombs in every city of the empire. Disastrous, indeed, must have been the influence of such a superstition on the character of the people.[5]

[3] Ritter has well shown, by the example of the Hindoo system, how the idea of unity suggests, of itself, that of plurality. History of Ancient philosophy, Eng. trans., (Oxford, 1838,) book 2, ch. 1.

[4] Sahagun, Hist. de Nueva España, lib. 6, passim.—Acosta, lib. 5, ch. 9.—Boturini, Idea, p. 8. et seq.—Ixtlilxochitl, Hist. Chich., MS., cap. 1—Camargo, Hist. de Tlascala, MS.

The Mexicans, according to Clavigero, believed in an evil Spirit, the enemy of the human race, whose barbarous name signified "Rational Owl." (Stor. del. Messico, tom. II. p. 2) The curate Bernaldez speaks of the Devil being embroidered on the dresses of Columbus's Indians, in the likeness of an owl. (Historia de los Reyes Católicos, MS., cap. 131.) This must not be confounded, however, with the evil Spirit in the mythology of the North American Indians, (See Heckewelder's account, ap. Transactions of the American Philosophical Society, Philadelphia, vol. I, p 205,) still less with the evil Principle of the Oriental nations of the Old World. It was only one among many deities, for evil was found too literally mingled in the natures of most of the Aztec gods,—in the same manner as with the Greek, to admit of its personification by any one.

[5] Sagahun, Hist. de Nueva España, lib. 3, cap. 1, et seq.—Acosta, lib. 5, ch. 9.—Torquemada, Monarch. Ind., lib. 6, cap. 21.—Boturini, Idea, pp. 27, 28.

Huitzilopotchli is compounded of two words, signifying " hummingbird," and " left," from his image having the feathers of this bird on its left foot; (Clavigero, Stor. del Messico, tom. II. p. 17.) an amiable etymology for so ruffian a deity.—The fantastic forms of the Mexican idols were in the highest degree symbolical. See Gama's learned exposition of the devices on the statue of the goddess found in the great square of Mexico (Description de

A far more int̤r̤ es̤ ̤ ̤g personage in their mythology was Quetzalcoatl, gou ̤f ̤.̤e air, a divinity who, during his residence on earth, instructed the natives in the use of metals, in agriculture, and in the arts of government. He was one of those benefactors of their species, doubtless, who have been deified by the gratitude of posterity. Under him, the earth teemed with fruits and flowers, without the pains of culture. An ear of Indian corn was as much as a single man could carry. The cotton, as it grew, took, of its own accord, the rich dyes of human art. The air was filled with intoxicating perfumes and the sweet melody of birds. In short, these were the halcyon days, which find a place in the mythic systems of so many nations in the Old World. It was the *golden age* of Anahuac,

From some cause, not explained, Quetzalcoatl incurred the wrath of one of the principal gods, and was compelled to abandon the country. On his way, he stopped at the city of Cholula, where a temple was dedicated to his worship, the massy ruins of which still form one of the most interesting relics of antiquity in Mexico. When he reached the shores of the Mexican Gulf, he took leave of his followers, promising that he and his descendants would revisit them hereafter, and then, entering his wizard skiff, made of serpents' skins embarked on the great ocean for the fabled land of Tlapallan. He was said to have been tall in stature, with a white skin, long, dark hair, and a flowing beard. The Mexicans looked confidently to the return of the benevolent diety; and this remarkable tradition, deeply cherished in their hearts, prepared the way, as we shall see hereafter, for the future success of the Spaniards.[6]

las Dos Piedras, (México, 1832,) Parte 1, pp. 34-44) The tradition respecting the origin of this god, or, at least, his appearance on earth, is curious. He was born of a woman. His mother, a devout person, one day, in her attendance on the temple, saw a ball of bright-colored feathers floating in the air. She took it, and deposited it in her bosom. She soon after found herself pregnant, and the dread deity was born, coming into the world, like Minerva, all armed,—with a spear in the right hand, a shield in the left, and his head surmounted by a crest of green plumes. (See Clavigero, Stor. del Messico, tom. II. p. 19, et seq.) A similar notion in respect to the incarnation of their principal deity existed among the people of India beyond the Ganges, of China, and of Thibet. " Budh," says Milman, in his learned and luminous work on the History of Christianity, " according to a tradition known in the West, was born of a virgin. So were the Fohi of China, and the Schakaof of Thibet, no doubt the same, whether a mythic or a real personage. The Jesuits in China, says Barrow, were appalled at finding in the mythology of that country the counterpart of the Virgo Deipara." (Vol. I. p. 99, note. The existence of similar religious ideas in remote regions, inhabited by different races, is an interesting subject of study; furnishing, as it does, one of the most important links in the great chain of communication which binds together the distant families of nations.

[6] Codex Vaticanus, Pl. 15, and Codex Telleriano-Remensis, Part 2. Pl

We have not space for further details respecting the Mexican divinities, the attributes of many of whom were carefully defined, as they descended, in regular gradation, to the *penates* or household gods, whose little images were to be found in the humblest dwelling.

The Aztecs felt the curiosity, common to man in almost every stage of civilization, to lift the veil which covers the mysterious past, and the more awful future. They sought relief, like the nations of the Old Continent, from the oppressive idea of eternity, by breaking it up into distinct cycles, or periods of time, each of several thousand years' duration, There were four of these cycles, and at the end of each, by the agency of one of the elements, the human family was swept from the earth, and the sun blotted out from the heavens, to be again rekindled.[2]

They imagined three separate states of existence in the future life. The wicked, comprehending the greater part of mankind,

2. ap. Antiq of Mexico, vols. I., VI.—Sahagun, Hist. de Nueva España, lib. 3, cap. 3, 4, 13, 14.—Torquemada, Monarch. Ind., lib. 6, cap. 24.—Ixtlilxochitl, Hist. Chich., MS., cap. 1.—Gomara, Cronica de la Nueva España, cap. 222, ap. Barcia, Historiadores Primitivos de las Indias Occidentales, (Madrid, 1749,) tom II.

Quetzalcoatl signifies "feathered serpent." The last syllable means, likewise, a "twin"; which furnished an argument for Dr. Siguenza to identify this god with the apostle Thomas, (Didymus signifying also a twin,) who, he supposes, came over to America to preach the Gospel. In this rather startling conjecture he is supported by several of his devout countrymen, who appear to have as little doubt of the fact as of the advent of St. James, for a similar purpose, in the mother country. See the various authorities and arguments set forth with becoming gravity in Dr. Mier's dissertation in Bustamante's edition of Sahagun, (lib. 3, Suplem.,) and Veytia, (tom. I. pp. 16-200.) Our ingenious countryman, McCulloh, carries the Aztec god up to a still more respectable antiquity, by identifying him with the patriarch Noah. Researches, Philosophical and Antiquarian, concerning the Aboriginal History of America, (Baltimore, 1829,) p. 233.

[7] Cod. Vat., Pl. 7-10, ap. Antiq. of Mexico, vols. I., VI.—Ixtlilxochitl, Hist. Chich., MS., cap. 1.

M de Humboldt has been at some pains to trace the analogy between the Aztec cosmogony and that of Eastern Asia. He has tried, though in vain, to find a multiple which might serve as the key to the calculations of the former. (Vues des Cordillères, pp. 202-212.) In truth, there seems to be a material discordance in the Mexican statements, both in regard to the number of revolutions and their duration. A manuscript before me, of Ixtlilxochitl, reduces them to three, before the present state of the world, and allows only 4394 years for them; (Sumaria Relacion, MS., No. 1;) Gama, on the faith of an ancient Indian MS., in Boturini's Catalogue, (VIII. 13,) reduces the duration still lower; (Descripcion de las Dos Piedras, Parte I, p. 40, et seq.;) while the cycles of the Vatican paintings take up near 18,000 years. It is interesting to observe how the wild conjectures of an ignorant age have been confirmed by the more recent discoveries in geology, making it probable that the earth has experienced a number of convulsions, possibly thousands of years distant from each other, which have swept away the races then existing, and given a new aspect to the globe.

were to expiate their sins in a place of everlasting darkness. Another class, with no other merit than that of having died of certain diseases, capriciously selected, were to enjoy a negative existence of indolent contentment.   The highest place was re-served, as in most warlike nations, for the heroes who fell in battle, or in sacrifice.   They passed, at once, into the presence of the Sun, whom they accompanied with songs and choral dances, in his bright progress through the heavens ; and, after some years, their spirits went to animate the clouds and singing birds of beautiful plumage, and to revel amidst the rich blossoms and odors of the gardens of paradise.[8]   Such was the heaven of the Aztecs ; more refined in its character than that of the more polished pagan, whose elysium reflected only the martial sports, or sensual gratifications, of this life.[9]   In the destiny they assigned to the wicked, we discern similar traces of refinement ; since the absence of all physical torture forms a striking con-trast to the schemes of suffering so ingeniously devised by the fancies of the most enlightened nations.[10]   In all this, so con-trary to the natural suggestions of the ferocious Aztec, we see the evidences of a higher civilization, inherited from their pre-decessors in the land.

Our limits will allow only a brief allusion to one or two of their most interesting ceremonies.   On the death of a person, his corpse was dressed in the peculiar habiliments of his tutelar

---

[8] Sahagun, Hist. de Nueva España , lib. 3, Apend.—Cod. Vat., ap. Antiq. of Mexico, Pl. 1–5.—Torquemada, Monarch. Ind., lib. 13, cap 48.

The last writer assures us, " that as to what the Aztecs said of their going to hell, they were right; for as they died in ignorance of the true faith, they have, without question, all gone there to suffer everlasting punishment "! Ubi supra.

[9] It conveys but a poor idea of these pleasures, that the shade of Achilles can say, " he had rather be the slave of the meanest man on earth, than sov-ereign among the dead." (Odyss. A. 488–490.)   The Mahometans believe that the souls of martyrs pass, after death, into the bodies of birds, that haunt the sweet waters and bowers of Paradise.   (Sale's Koran, (London, 1825,) vol. I. p. 106.)—The Mexican heaven may remind one of Dante's, in its *ma-terial* enjoyments; which, in both, are made up of light, music, and motion. The sun, it must also be remembered, was a spiritual conception with the Aztec:

> " He sees with other eyes than theirs ; where they
> Behold a sun, he spies a deity."

[10] It is singular that the Tuscan bard, while exhausting his invention in devising modes of bodily torture, in his " Inferno." should have made so little use of the *moral* sources of misery.   That he has not done so might be reckoned a strong proof of the rudeness of the time, did ᵕ ᵕ not meet with examples of it in our own day ; in which a serious and sublime writer, like Dr. Watts, does not disdain to employ the same coarse machinery for mov-ing the conscience of the reader.

deity. It was strewed with pieces of paper, which operated as charms against the dangers of the dark road he was to travel. A throng of slaves, if he were rich, was sacrificed at his obsequies. His body was burned, and the ashes, collected in a vase, were preserved in one of the apartments of his house. Here we have successively the usages of the Roman Catholic, the Mussulman, the Tartar, and the Ancient Greek and Roman; curious coincidences, which may show how cautious we should be in adopting conclusions founded on analogy.[11]

A more extraordinary coincidence may be traced with Christian rites, in the ceremony of naming their children. The lips and bosom of the infant were sprinkled with water, and "the Lord was implored to permit the holy drops to wash away the sin that was given to it before the foundation of the world; so that the child might be born anew."[12] We are reminded of Christian morals, in more than one of their prayers, in which they used regular forms. "Wilt thou blot us out, O Lord, for ever? Is this punishment intended, not for our reformation, but for our destruction?" Again, "Impart to us, out of thy great mercy, thy gifts, which we are not worthy to receive through our own merits." "Keep peace with all," says another petition; "bear injuries with humility; God, who sees, will avenge you." But the most striking parallel with Scripture is in the remarkable declaration, that "he, who looks too curiously on a woman, commits adultery with his eyes." These pure and elevated maxims, it is true, are mixed up with others of a puerile, and even brutal character, arguing that confusion of the moral perceptions, which is natural in the twilight of civilization. One would not expect, however, to meet, in such a state of society, with doctrines as sublime as any inculcated by the enlightened codes of ancient philosophy.[13]

---

[11] Carta del Lic. Zuazo, (Nov., 1521,) MS.—Acosta, lib. 5, cap 8.—Torquemada, Monarch. Ind., lib. 13, cap. 45—Sahagun, Hist. de Nueva España. lib. 3, Apend.

Sometimes the body was buried entire, with valuable treasures, if the deceased was rich. The "Anonymous Conqueror," as he is called, saw gold to the value of 3000 castellanos drawn from one of these tombs. Relatione d' un gentil' huomo, ap. Ramusio, tom. III. p. 310.

[12] This interesting rite, usually solemnized with great formality, in the presence of the assembled friends and relatives, is detailed with minuteness by Sahagun, (Hist. de Nueva España, lib. 6, cap. 37,) and by Zuazo, (Carta, MS.,) both of them eyewitnesses. For a version of part of Sahagun's account, see *Appendix, Part 1, note* 26.

[13] "¿Es possible, que esteazote y este castigo no se nos da para nuestra correccion y enmienda, sino para total destruccion y asolamiento?" (Sahagun, Hist. de Nueva España lib. 6, cap. 1.) "Y esto por sola vuestra liberalidad y magnificencia lo habeis de hacer, que ninguno es digno ni merecedor

But, although the Aztec mythology gathered nothing from the beautiful inventions of the poet, nor from the refinements of philosophy, it was much indebted, as I have noticed, to the priests, who endeavored to dazzle the imagination of the people by the most formal and pompous ceremonial. The influence of the priesthood must be greatest in an imperfect state of civilization, where it engrosses all the scanty science of the time in its own body. This is particularly the case, when the science is of that spurious kind which is less occupied with the real phenomena of nature, than with the fanciful chimeras of human superstition. Such are the sciences of astrology and divination, in which the Aztec priests were well initiated ; and, while they seemed to hold the keys of the future in their own hands, they impressed the ignorant people with sentiments of superstitious awe, beyond that which has probably existed in any other country,—even in ancient Egypt.

The sacerdotal order was very numerous ; as may be inferred from the statement, that five thousand priests were, in some way or other, attached to the principal temple in the capital. The various ranks and functions of this multitudinous body were discriminated with great exactness. Those best instructed in music took the management of the choirs. Others arranged the festivals conformably to the calendar. Some superintended the education of youth, and others had charge of the hieroglyphical paintings and oral traditions ; while the dismal rites of sacrifice were reserved for the chief dignitaries of the order. At the head of the whole establishment were two high-priests, elected from the order, as it would seem, by the king and principal nobles, without reference to birth, but solely for their qualifications, as shown by their previous conduct in a subordinate station. They were equal in dignity, and inferior only to the sovereign, who rarely acted without their advice in weighty matters of public concern.[14]

de recibir vuestras larguezas por su dignidad y merecimiento, sino que por vuestra benignidad." (Ibid., lib. 6, cap. 2.) "Sed sufridos y reportados, que Dios bien os vé y responderá por vosotros, y él os vengará (á) sed humildes con todos y con esto dos hará Dios merced y tambien honra." (Ibid., lib. 6, cap. 17.) "Tampoco mires con curiosidad el gesto y disposicion de la gente principal, mayormente de las mugeres, y sobre todo de las casadas, porque dice el refran que él que curiosamente mira à la muger adultera con la vista." (Ibid., lib. 6, cap. 22.)

[14] Sahagun, Hist. de Nueva Espana, lib. 2, Apend ; lib. 3. cap. 9.—Torquemada, Monarch. Ind., lib, 8, cap. 20; lib 9, cap. 3, 56.—Gomara, Cron., cap. 215, ap. Barcia, tom. II.—Toribio, Hist. de los Indios, MS., Parte 1, cap. 4.

Clavigero says that the highpriest was necessarily a person of rank. (Stor. del Messico, tom. II. p. 37.) I find no authority for this, not even in his

The priests were each devoted to the service of some particular deity, and had quarters provided within the spacious precincts of their temple ; at least, while engaged in immediate attendance there,—for they were allowed to marry, and have families of their own. In this monastic residence they lived in all the stern severity of conventual discipline. Thrice during the day, and once at night, they were called to prayers. They were frequent in their ablutions and vigils, and mortified the flesh by fasting and cruel penance,—drawing blood from their bodies by flagellation, or by piercing them with the thorns of the aloe ; in short, by practising all those austerities to which fanaticism (to borrow the strong language of the poet) has resorted, in every age of the world,

> " In hopes to merit heaven by making earth a hell." [15]

The great cities were divided into districts placed under the charge of a sort of parochial clergy, who regulated every act of religion within their precincts. It is remarkable that they administered the rites of confession and absolution. The secrets of the confessional were held inviolable, and penances were imposed of much the same kind as those enjoined in the Roman Catholic Church. There were two remarkable peculiarities in the Aztec ceremony. The first was, that, as the repetition of an offence, once atoned for, was deemed inexpiable, confession was made but once in a man's life, and was usually deferred to a late period of it, when the penitent unburdened his conscience, and settled, at once, the long arrears of iniquity. Another peculiarity was, that priestly absolution was received in place of the legal punishment of offences, and authorized an acquittal in case of arrest. Long after the Conquest, the simple natives, when they came under the arm of the law, sought to escape by producing the certificate of their confession. [16]

oracle, Torquemada, who expressly says, " There is no warrant for the assertion, however probable the fact may be." (Monarch. Ind., lib. 9, cap. 5.) it is contradicted by Sahagun, whom I have followed as the highest authority in these matters. Clavigero had no other knowledge of Sahagun's work than what was filtered through the writings of Torquemada, and later authors.

[15] Sahagun, Hist de Nueva Espana, ubi supra.—Torquemada, Monarch. Ind., lib. 9, cap 25.—Gomara. Cron., ap. Barcia, ubi supra.—Acosta, lib 5 cap. 14, 17.

[16] Sahagun, Hist. de Nueva Espana, lib 1, cap. 12 ; lib 6, cap. 7.

The address of the confessor, on these occasions, contains some things too remarkable to be omitted " O merciful Lord," he says, in his prayer. " thou who knowest the secrets of all hearts, let thy forgiveness and favor descend, like the pure waters of heaven, to wash away the stains from the

One of the ' most important duties of the priesthood was that of education, to which certain buildings were appropriated within the inclosure of the principal temple. Here the youth of both sexes, of the higher and middling orders, were placed at a very tender age. The girls were intrusted to the care of priestesses; for women were allowed to exercise sacerdotal functions, except those of sacrifice.[17]. In these institutions the boys were drilled in the routine of monastic disipline; they decorated the shrines of the gods with flowers, fed the sacred fires, and took part in the religious chants and festivals. Those in the higher schools—the *Calmecac*, as it was called—were initiated in their traditionary lore, toe mysteries of hieroglyphics, the principles of government, and such branches of astronomical and natural science as were within the compass of the priesthood. The girls learned various feminine employments, especially to weave and embroider rich coverings for the altars of the gods. Great attention was paid to the moral discipline of both sexes. The most perfect decorum prevailed; and offences were punished with extreme rigor, in some instances with death itself. Terror, not love, was the spring of education with the Aztecs.[18]

At a suitable age for marrying, or for entering into the world,

soul　Thou knowest that this poor man *has sinned, not from his own free will*, but from the influence of the sign in under which he was born." After a copious exhortation to the penitent, enjoying a variety of mortifications and minute ceremonies by way of penance, and particularly urging the necessity of instantly procuring *a slave for sacrifice* to the Deity, the priest concludes with inculcating charity to the poor. "Clothe the naked and feed the hungry, whatever privations it may cost thee; for remember, *their flesh is like thine, and they are men like thee*" Such is the strange medley of truly Christian benevolence and heathenish abominations which pervade the Aztec litany,—intimating sources widely different.

[17] The Egyptian gods were also served by priestesses. (See Herodotus, Euterpe, sec. 54.) Tales of scandal similar to those which the Greeks circulated respecting them, have been told of the Aztec virgins (See Le Noir's dissertation, ap. Antiquités Mexicaines, (Paris, 1834,) tom. II. p. 7. note) The early missionaries, credulous enough certainly, give no countenance to such reports; and father Acosta, on the contrary, exclaims, "In truth, it is very strange to see that this false opinion of religion hath so great force among these young men and maidens of Mexico, that they will serve the Divell with so great rigor and austerity, which many of us doe not in the service of the most high God; the which is a great shame and confusion." Eng. Trans., lib. 5, cap. 16.

[18] Toribio, Hist. de los Indios, MS., Parte 1, cap. 9.—Sahagun, Hist. de Nueva España, lib. 2,, Apend.; lib. 3, cap. 4–8.—Zurita, Rapport, pp. 123-126.—Acosta, lib. 5, cap. 15, 16.—Torquemada, Monarch. Ind., lib. 9, cap. 11–14, 30, 31.

"They were taught," says the good father last cited, "to eschew vice, and cleave to virtue,—*according to their notions of them*; namely, to abstain from wrath, to offer violence and do wrong to no man,—in short to perform the duties plainly pointed out by natural religion."

the pupils were dismissed, with much ceremony, from the con‑ vent, and the recommendation of the principal often introduced those most competent to responsible situations in public life Such was the crafty policy of the Mexican priests, who, by reserving to themselves the business of instruction, were enabled to mould the young and plastic mind according to their own wills, and to train it early to implicit reverence for religion and its ministers ; a reverence which still maintained its hold on the iron nature of the warrior, long after every other vestige of education had been effaced by the rough trade to which he was devoted.

To each of the principal temples, lands were annexed for the maintenance of the priests. These estates were augmented by the policy or devotion of successive princes, until, under the last Montezuma, they had swollen to an enormous extent, and covered every district of the empire. The priests took the management of their property into their own hands ; and they seem to have treated their tenants with the liberality and indulg‑ ence characteristic of monastic corporations. Besides the large supplies drawn from this source, the religious order was enriched with the first-fruits, and such other offerings as piety or supersti‑ tion dictated. The surplus beyond what was required for the support of the national worship was distributed in alms among the poor ; a duty strenuously prescribed by their moral code. Thus we find the same religion inculcating lessons of pure philanthropy, on the one hand, and of merciless extermination, as we shall soon see, on the other. The inconsistency will not appear incredible to those who are familiar with the history of the Roman Catholic Church, in the early ages of the Inquisition.[10]

The Mexican temples—*teocallis,* "houses of God," as they were very numerous. There were several hundreds in each of the principal cities, many of them, doubtless, very humble edi‑ fices. They were solid masses of each, cased with brick, or stone, and in their form somewhat resembled the pyramida' structures of ancient Egypt. The bases of many of them were more than a hundred feet square, and they towered to a still

---

[10] Torquemada, Monarch. Ind , lib. 8, cap. 20, 21.—Camargo, Hist. de Tlascala, MS.

It is impossible not to be struck with the great resemblance, not merely in a few empty forms, but in the whole way of life, of the Mexican and Egyptian priesthood. Compare Herodotus (Euterpe, passim) and Diodorus (lib. 1, sec. 73, 81). The English reader may consult, for the same purpose, Heeren, (Hist. Res., vol. V. chap 2,) Wilkinson, (Manners and Customs of the Ancient Egyptians, (London, 1837,) vol. I. pp. 257-279,) the last writer especially,—who has contributed, more than all others, towards opening to us the interior of the social life of this interesting people.

greater height.   They were distributed into four or five stories, each of smaller dimensions than that below.   The ascent wa by a flight of steps, at an angle of the pyramid, on the out side.   This led to a sort of terrace, or gallery, at the base of the second story, which passed quite round the building to another flight of stairs, commencing also at the same angle as the preced· ing and directly over it, and leading to a similar terrace ; so that one had to make the circuit of the temple several times, before reaching the summit.   In some instances the stairway led directly up the centre of the western face of the building.   The top was a broad area, on which were erected one or two towers, forty or fifty feet high, the sanctuaries in which stood the sacred images of the presiding deities.   Before these towers stood the dreadful stone of sacrifice, and two lofty altars, on which fires were kept, as inextinguishable as those in the temple of Vesta.   There were said to be six hundred of these altars, on smaller buildings within the inclosure of the great temple of Mexico, which, with those on the sacred edifices in other parts of the city, shed a brilliant illumination over its streets, through the darkest night.[20]

From the construction of their temples, all religious services were public.   The long processions of priests, winding round their massive sides, as they rose higher and higher towards the summit, and the dismal rites of sacrifice performed there, were all visible from the remotest corners of the capital, impressing on the spectator's mind a superstitious veneration for the mys· teries of his religion, and for the dread ministers by whom they were interpreted.

This impression was kept in full force by their numerous festivals.   Every month was consecrated to some protecting deity ; and every week, nay, almost every day, was set down in their calendar for some appropriate celebration ; so that it is difficult to understand how the ordinary business of life could have been compatible with the exactions of religion.   Many of their ceremonies were of a light and cheerful complexion, con· sisting of the national songs and dances, in which both sexes joined.   Processions were made of women and children crowned

---

[20] Rel. d'un gent., ap. Ramusio, tom. III. fol. 307.—Camargo, Hist. de Tlascala, MS —Acosta, lib. 5, cap. 13.—Gomara, Cron., cap. 80, ap. Barcia, tom. II.—Toribio, Hist. de los Indios, MS., Parte 1, cap. 4.—Carta del Lic. Zuazo, MS.
This last writer, who visited Mexico immediately after the Conquest, in 1521, assures us that some of the smaller temples, or pyramids, were filled with earth impregnated with odoriferous gums and gold dust ; the latter. sometimes in such quantities as probably to be worth a million of *castellanos!* (Ubi supra.) These were the temples of Mammon, indeed ! But I find no confirmation of such golden reports.

with garlands and bearing offerings of fruits, and ripened maize, or the sweet incense of copal and other odoriferous gums, while the altars of the deity were stained with no blood save that of animals.[21] These were the peaceful rites derived from their Toltec predecessors, on which the fierce Aztecs engrafted a superstition too loathsome to be exhibited in all its nakedness, and one over which I would gladly draw a veil altogether, but that it would leave the reader in ignorance of their most striking institution, and one that had the greatest influence in forming the national character.

Human sacrifices were adopted by the Aztecs early in the fourteenth century, about two hundred years before the Conquest.[22] Rare at first, they became more frequent with the wider extent of their empire : till, at length, almost every festival was closed with this cruel abomination. These religious ceremonials were generally arranged in such a manner as to afford a type of the most prominent circumstances in the character or history of the deity who was the object of them. A single example will suffice.

One of their most important festivals was that in honor of the god Tezcatlipoca, whose rank was inferior only to that of the Supreme Being. He was called "the soul of the world," and supposed to have been its creator. He was depicted as a handsome man, endowed with perpetual youth. A year before the intended sacrifice, a captive, distinguished for his personal beauty, and without a blemish on his body, was selected to represent this deity. Certain tutors took charge of him, and instructed him how to perform his new part with becoming grace and dignity. He was arrayed in a splendid dress, regaled with incense and with a profusion of sweet-scented flowers, of which the ancient Mexicans were as fond as their descendants at the present day. When he went abroad, he was attended by a train of the royal pages, and, as he halted in the streets to play some favorite melody, the crowd prostrated themselves before him, and did him homage as the representative of their good deity. In this way he led an easy, luxurious life, till within a month

---

[21] Cod. Tel. Rem.,Pl. 1, and Cod. Vat. passim, ap. Antiq. of Mexico, vols. I., VI.—Torquemada, Monarch. Ind., lib. 10, cap. 10, et seq.—Sahagun, Hist. de Nueva Espana, lib. 2, passim.

Among the offerings, quails may be particularly noticed, for the incredible quantities of them sacrificed and consumed at many of the festivals.

[22] The traditions of their origin have somewhat of a fabulous tinge. But, whether true or false, they are equally indicative of unparalleled ferocity in the people who could be the subject of them. Clavigero, Stor. del Messico, tom. I. p. 167, et seq.; also Humboldt, (who does not appear to doubt them,) Vues des Cordilleres, p. 95.

of his sacrifice. Four beautiful girls, bearing the names of the principal goddesses, were then selected to share the honors of his bed; and with them he continued to live in idle dalliance, feasted at the banquets of the principal nobles, who paid him all the honors of a divinity.

At length the fatal day of sacrifice arrived. The term of his short-lived glories was at an end. He was stripped of his gaudy apparel, and bade adieu to the fair partners of his revelries. One of the royal barges transported him across the lake to a temple which rose on its margin, about a league from the city. Hither the inhabitants of the capital flocked, to witness the consummation of the ceremony. As the sad procession wound up the sides of the pyramid, the unhappy victim threw away his gay chaplets of flowers, and broke in pieces the musical instruments with which he had solaced the hours of captivity. On the summit he was received by six priests, whose long and matted locks flowed disorderly over their sable robes, covered with hieroglyphic scrolls of mystic import. They led him to the sacrificial stone, a huge block of jasper, with its upper surface somewhat convex. On this the prisoner was stretched. Five priests secured his head and his limbs; while the sixth clad in a scarlet mantle, emblematic of his bloody office, dexterously opened the breast of the wretched victim with a sharp razor of *itztli*,—a volcanic substance, hard as flint,—and, inserting his hand in the wound, tore out the palpitating heart. The minister of death, first holding this up towards the sun, an object of worship throughout Anahuac, cast it at the feet of the deity to whom the temple was devoted, while the multitudes below prostrated themselves in humble adoration. The tragic story of this prisoner was expounded by the priests as the type of human destiny, which, brilliant in its commencement, too often closes in sorrow and disaster.[23]

Such was the form of human sacrifice usually practiced by the Aztecs. It was the same that often met the indignant eyes of the Europeans, in their progress through the country, and from the dreadful doom of which they themselves were not exempted. There were, indeed, some occasions when preliminary tortures, of the most exquisite kind,—with which it is unneces-

[23] Sahagun, Hist. de Nueva Espana, lib. 2, cap. 2, 5, 24, et alibi.—Herrera, Hist. General, dec. 3, lib. 2, cap. 16.—Torquemada, Monarch. Ind., lib. 7, cap. 19; lib. 10, cap. 14—Rel. d'un gent., ap. Ramusio, tom III. fol. 307.— Acosta, lib. 5, cap. 9–21.—Carta del Lic. Zuazo, M⌐—Relacion por el Regimiento de Vera Cruz, (Julio, 1519,) MS.
Few readers probably, will sympathize with the sentence of Torquemada, who concludes his tale of woe by coolly dismissing "the soul of the victim, to sleep with those of his false gods, in hell!" Lib. 10, cap. 23.

sary to shock the reader,—were inflicted, but they always terminated with the bloody ceremony above described. It should be remarked, however, that such tortures were not the spontaneous suggestions of cruelty, as with the North American Indians; but were all rigorously prescribed in the Aztec ritual, and doubtless were often inflicted with the same compunctious visitings which a devout familiar of the Holy Office might at times experience in executing its stern decrees.[24] Women, as well as the other sex, were sometimes reserved for sacrifice. On some occasions, particularly in seasons of drought, at the festival of the insatiable Tlaloc, the god of rain, children, for the most part infants, were offered up. As they were borne along in open litters, dressed in their festal robes, and decked with the fresh blossoms of spring, they moved the hardest heart to pity, though their cries were drowned in the wild chant of the priests, who read in their tears a favorable augury for their petition. These innocent victims were generally bought by the priests of parents who were poor, but who stifled the voice of nature, probably less at the suggestions of poverty, than of a wretched superstition.[25]

The most loathsome part of the story—the manner in which the body of the sacrificed captive was disposed of—remains yet to be told. It was delivered to the warrior who had taken him in battle, and by him, after being dressed, was served up in an entertainment to his friends. This was not the coarse repast of famished cannibals, but a banquet teeming with delicious beverages and delicate viands, prepared with art, and attended by both sexes, who, as we shall see hereafter, conducted themselves with all the decorum of civilized life. Surely, never were re-

[24] Sahagun, Hist de Nueva España, lib. 2, cap. 10, 29.—Comara, Cron., cap. 219, ap. Barcia, tom. II.—Toribio, Hist. de los Indios, MS., Parte I, cap. 6-11.
The reader will find a tolerably exact picture of the nature of these tortures in the twenty-first canto of the " Inferno." The fantastic creations of the Florentine poet were nearly realized, at the very time he was writing, by the barbarians of an unknown world. One sacrifice, of a less revolting character, deserves to be mentioned. The Spaniards called it the "gladiatorial sacrifice," and it may remind one of the bloody games of antiquity. A captive of distinction was sometimes furnished with arms, and brought against a number of Mexicans in succession. If he defeated them all, as did occasionally happen, he was allowed to escape If vanquished, he was dragged to the block and sacrificed in the usual manner. The combat was fought on a huge circular stone, before the assembled capital. Sahagun, Hist. de Nueva España, lib. 1, cap. 21.—Rel. d'un gent., ap. Ramusio, tom. III fol. 305.
[25] Sahagun, Hist. de Nueva España, lib. 2, cap. 1, 4, 21, et alibi.—Torquemada., Monarch. Ind., lib. 10, cap 10.—Clavigero, Stor. del Messico. tom. II. pp. 76, 82.

finement and the extreme of barbarism brought so closely in contact with each other![26]

Human sacrifices have been practiced by many nations, not excepting the most polished nations of antiquity,[27] but never by any, on a scale to be compared with those in Anahuac. The amount of victims immolated on its accursed altars would stagger the faith of the least scrupulous believer. Scarcely any author pretends to estimate the yearly sacrifices throughout the empire at less than twenty thousand, and some carry the number as high as fifty![28]

On great occasions, as the coronation of a king, or the consecration of a temple, the number becomes still more appalling. At the dedication of the great temple of Huitzilopotchli, 1486, the prisoners, who for some years had been reserved for the purpose, were drawn from all quarters to the capital. They were ranged in files, forming a procession nearly two miles long. The ceremony consumed several days, and seventy thousand captives are said to have perished at the shrine of this terrible deity! But who can believe that so numerous a body would have suffered themselves to be led unresistingly like sheep to the slaughter? Or how could their remains, too great for consumption in the ordi-

---

[26] Carta del Lic. Zuazo, MS.—Torquemada, Monarch. Ind., lib. 7, cap. 19.—Herrera, Hist. General, dec. 3, lib. 2, cap. 17.—Sahagun, Hist. de Nueva España, lib. 2, cap. 21, et alibi.—Toribio Hist. de los Indios, MS., Parte 1, cap. 2.

[27] To say nothing of Egypt where, notwithstanding the indications on the monuments, there is strong reason for doubting it. (Comp. Herodotus, Euterpe, sec. 45.) It was of frequent occurrence among the Greeks, as every schoolboy knows. In Rome, it was so common as to require to be interdicted by an express law, less than a hundred years before the Christian era,—a law recorded in a very honest strain of exultation by Pliny; (Hist, Nat., lib. 30, sec. 3, 4;) notwithstanding which traces of the existence of the practice may be discerned to a much later period. See, among others, Horace, Epod., In Canidiam.

[28] See Clavigero, Stor. del Messico, tom. II. p. 49.

Bishop Zumarraga, in a letter written a few years after the Conquest, states that 20,000 victims were yearly slaughtered in the capital. Torquemada turns this into 20,000 *infants* (Monarch. Ind., lib. 7, cap. 21., Herrera, following Acosta, says 20.000 victims on a specified day of the year, throughout the kingdom. (Hist, General, dec. 2, lib. 2, cap. 16.) Clavigero, more cautious, infers that this number may have been sacrificed annually throughout Anahuac. (Ubi supra.) Las Casas. however, in his reply to Sepulveda's assertion. that no one who had visited the New World put the number of yearly sacrifices at less than 20.000, declares that " this is the estimate of brigands, who wish to find an apology for their own atrocities, and that the real number was not above 50 "! (Œuvres. ed. Llorente, (Paris 1822,) tom. I. pp. 365, 386.) Probably the good ' .nop's arithmetic, here, as in most other instances, came more from his heart than his head. With such loose and contradictory *data*, it is clear that any specific number is mere conjecture, undeserving the name of calculation.

nary way, be disposed of, without breeding a pestilence in the capital ? Yet the event was of recent date, and is unequivocally attested by the best informed historians.[29] One fact may be considered certain. It was customary to preserve the skulls of the sacrificed, in buildings appropriated to the purpose. The companions of Cortés counted one hundred and thirty-six thousand in one of these edifices![30] Without attempting a precise calculation, therefore, it is safe to conclude that thousands were yearly offered up, in the different cities of Anahuac, on the bloody altars of the Mexican divinities.[31]

Indeed, the great object of war, with the Aztecs, was quite as much to gather victims for their sacrifices, as to extend their empire. Hence it was, that an enemy was never slain in battle, if there were a chance of taking him alive. To this circumstance the Spaniards repeatedly owed their preservation. When Montezuma was asked, "why he had suffered the republic of Tlascala to maintain her independence on his borders," he replied, "that she might furnish him with victims for his gods"! As the supply began to fail, the priests, the Dominicans of the New World, bellowed aloud for more, and urged on their superstitious sovereign by the denunciations of celestial wrath. Like the militant churchmen of Christendom in the Middle Ages, they mingled themselves in the ranks, and were conspicuous in the thickest of the fight, by their hideous aspect and frantic gestures. Strange, that, in every country, the most

[29] I am within bounds. Torquemada states the number most precisely, at 72,344. (Monarch. Ind., lib. 2. cap. 63.) Ixtilxochitl, with equal precision, at 80,400. (Hist. Chich., MS.) *Quien sabe !* The latter adds, that the captives massscred in the capital, in the course of that memorable year, exceeded 100,000 ! (Loc. cit.) One, however, has to read but a little way, to find out that the science of numbers—at least, where the party was not an eyewitness—is anything but an exact science with these ancient chroniclers. The Codex Tel-Remensis, written some fifty years after the Conquest, reduces the amount to 20,000 (Antiq. of Mexico, vol I. Pl 19; vol. VI p. 141, Eng. note) Even this hardly warrants the Spanish interpreter in calling king Ahuitzotl a man " of a mild and a moderate disposition," *templada y benigna condicion !* Ibid., vol. V. p. 49.

[30] Gomara states the number on the authority of two soldiers, whose names he gives, who took the trouble to count the grinning horrors in one of these Golgothas, where they were so arranged as to produce the most hideous effect. The existence of these conservatories is attested by every writer of the time.

[31] The "Anonymous Conqueror" assures us, as a fact beyond dispute, that the Devil introduced himself into the bodies of the idols, and persuaded the silly priests that his only diet was human hearts! It furnishes a very satisfactory solution, to his mind, of the frequency of sacrifices in Mexico. Rel. d'un gent., ap. Ramusio, tom. III. fol. 307.

fiendish passions of the human heart have been those kindled in the name of religion ! [32]

The influence of these practices on the Aztec character was as disastrous as might have been expected. Familiarity with the bloody rites of sacrifice steeled the heart against human sympathy, and begat a thirst for carnage, like that excited in the Romans by the exhibitions of the circus. The perpetual recurrence of ceremonies, in which the people took part, associated religion with their most intimate concerns, and spread the gloom of superstition over the domestic hearth, until the character of the nation wore a grave and even melancholy aspect, which belongs to their descendants at the present day. The influence of the priesthood, of course, became unbounded. The sovereign thought himself honored by being permitted to assist in the services of the temple. Far from limiting the authority of the priests to spiritual matters, he often surrendered his opinion to theirs, where they were least competent to give it. It was their opposition that prevented the final capitulation which would have saved the capital. The whole nation, from the peasant to the prince, bowed their necks to the worst kind of tyranny, that of a blind fanaticism.

In reflecting on the revolting usages recorded in the preceding pages, one finds it difficult to reconcile their existence with anything like a regular form of government, or an advance in civilization. Yet the Mexicans had many claims to the character of a civilized community. One may, perhaps, better understand the anomaly, by reflecting on the condition of some of the most polished countries in Europe, in the sixteenth century, after the establishment of the modern Inquisition; an institution, which yearly destroyed its thousands, by a death more painful than the Aztec sacrifices ; which armed the hand of brother against brother, and, setting its burning seal upon the

---

[32] The Tezcucan priests would fain have persuaded the good king Neza-aualcoyotl, on occasion of a pestilence, to appease the gods by the sacrifice of some of his own subjects, instead of his enemies ; on the ground, that, not only they would be obtained more easily, but would be fresher victims, and more acceptable. (Ixtlilxochitl, Hist. Chich., MS., cap. 41.) This writer mentions a cool arrangement entered into by the allied monarchs with the republic of Tlascala and her confederates. A battlefield was marked out, on which the troops of the hostile nations were to engage at stated seasons, and thus supply themselves with subjects for sacrifice. The victorious party was not to pursue his advantage by invading the other's territory, and they were to continue, in all other respects, on the most amicable footing. (Ubi supra.) The historian, who follows in the track of the Tezcucan Chronicler, may often find occasion to shelter himself, like Ariosto, with

" Mettendolo Turpin, lo metto anch' io."

lip, did more to stay the march of improvement than any other scheme ever devised by a human cunning.

Human sacrifice, however cruel, has nothing in it degrading to its victim. It may be rather said to ennoble him by devoting him to the gods. Although so terrible with the Aztecs, it was sometimes voluntarily embraced by them, as the most glorious death, and one that opened a sure passage into paradise.[33] The Inquisition, on the other hand, branded its victims with infamy in this world, and consigned them to everlasting perdition in the next.

One detestable feature of the Aztec superstition, however, sunk it far below the Christian. This was its cannibalism; though, in truth, the Mexicans were not cannibals, in the coarsest acceptation of the term. They did not feed on human flesh merely to gratify a brutish appetite, but in obedience to their religion. Their repasts were made of the victims whose blood had been poured out on the altar of sacrifice. This is a distinction worthy of notice.[34] Still, cannibalism, under any form, or whatever sanction, cannot but have a fatal influence on the nation addicted to it. It suggests ideas so loathsome, so degrading to man, to his spiritual and immortal nature, that it is impossible the people who practice it should make any great progress in moral or intellectual culture. The Mexicans furnish no exception to this remark. The civilization, which they possessed, descended from the Toltecs, a race who never stained their altars, still less their banquets, with the blood of man. All that deserved the name of science in Mexico came from this source; and the crumbling ruins of edifices, attributed to them, still extant in various parts of New Spain, show a decided superiority in their architecture over that of the later races of Anahuac. It is true, the Mexicans made great proficiency in many of the social and mechanic arts, in that material culture,—if I may so call it,—the natural growth of increasing opulence, which ministers to the gratification of the senses. In purely intellectual progress, they were behind the Tezcucans, whose wise sovereigns came into the abominable rites of their neighbors with reluctance, and practised them on a much more moderate scale.[35]

[33] Rel. d'un gent. ap. Ramusio, tom. III. fol. 307.

Among other instances, is that of Chimalpopoca, third king of Mexico, who doomed himself, with a number of his lords, to this death, to wipe off an indignity offered him by a brother monarch. (Torquemada, Monarch. Ind., lib. 2, cap. 28.) This was the law of honor with the Aztecs.

[34] Voltaire, doubtless, intends this, when he says, "Ils n'étaient point anthropophages, comme un très-petit nombre de peuplades Américaines." (Essai sur les Mœurs, chap. 147.)

[35] Ixtlilxochitl, Hist. Chich., MS., cap. 45, et alibi.

In this state of things, it was beneficently ordered by Providence that the land should be delivered over to another race, who would rescue it from the brutish superstitions that daily extended wider and wider, with extent of empire.[36] The debasing institutions of the Aztecs furnish the best apology for their conquest. It is true, the conquerors brought along with them the Inquisition. But they also brought Christianity, whose benign radiance would still survive, when the fierce flames of fanaticism should be extinguished ; dispelling those dark forms of horror which had so long brooded over the fair regions of Anahuac.

[36] No doubt the ferocity of character engendered by their sanguinary rites greatly facilitated their conquests. Machiavelli attributes to a similar cause, in part, the military successes of the Romans. (Discorsi sopra T. Livio, lib. 2, cap. 2.) The same chapter contains some ingenious reflections— much more ingenious than candid—on the opposite tendencies of Christianity.

The most important authority in the preceding chapter, and, indeed, wherever the Aztec religion is concerned, is Bernardino de Sahagun, a Franciscan friar, contemporary with the conquest. His great work, *Historia Universal de Nueva España,* has been recently printed for the first time. The circumstances attending its compilation and subsequent fate form one of the most remarkable passages in literary history.

Sahagun was born in a place of the same name, in old Spain. He was educated at Salamanca, and, having taken the vows of St. Francis, came over as a missionary to Mexico in the year 1529. Here he distinguished himself by his zeal, the purity of his life, and his unwearied exertions to spread the great truths of religion among the natives. He was the guardian of several conventual houses, successively, until he relinquished these cares, that he might devote himself more unreservedly to the business of preaching, and of compiling various works designed to illustrate the antiquities of the Aztecs. For these literary labors he found some facilities in the situation which he continued to occupy, of reader, or lecturer, in the College of Santa Cruz, in the capital.

The "Universal History" was concocted in a singular manner. In order to secure to it the greatest possible authority, he passed some years in a Tezcucan town, where he conferred daily with a number of respectable natives unacquainted with Castilian. He propounded to them queries, which they, after deliberation, answered in their usual method of writing, by hieroglyphical paintings. These he submitted to other natives, who had been educated under his own eye in the college of Santa Cruz, and the latter, after a consultation among themselves, gave a written version, in the Mexican tongue, of the hieroglyphics. This process he repeated in another place in some part of Mexico, and subjected the whole to a still further revision by a third body in another quarter. He finally arranged the combined results into a regular history, in the form it now bears; composing it in the Mexican language, which he could both write and speak with great accuracy and elegance,—greater, indeed, than any Spaniard of the time.

The work presented a mass of curious information, that attracted much attention among his brethren. But they feared its influence in keeping alive in the natives a too vivid reminiscence of the very superstitions which it was the great object of the Christian clergy to eradicate. Sahagun had views more liberal than those of his order, whose blind zeal would willingly have annihilated every monument of art and human ingenuity, which had not been produced under the influence of Christianity. They refused to allow him the necessary aid to transcribe his papers, which he had been so many years in preparing, under the pretext that the expense was too great for their order to incur. This occasioned a further delay of several years. What was worse, his provincial got possession of his manuscripts, which were soon scattered among the different religious houses in the country,

In this forlorn state of his affairs, Sahagun drew up a brief statement of the nature and contents of his work, and forwarded it to Madrid. It fell into the hands of Don Juan de Ovando, president of the Council for the Indies, who was so much interested in it, that he ordered the manuscripts to be re-stored to their author, with the request that he would at once set about translating them into Castilian. This was accordingly done. His papers were recovered, though not without the menace of ecclesiastical censures; and the octogenarian author began the work of translation from the Mexican, in which they had been originally written by him thirty years before. He had the satisfaction to complete the task, arranging the Spanish version in a parallel column with the original, and adding a vocabulary, explaining the difficult Aztec terms and phrases; while the text was supported by the numerous paintings on which it was founded, In this form, making two bulky volumes in folio, it was sent to Madrid. There seemed now to be no further reason for postponing its publication. the importance of which could not be doubted. But from this moment it disappears; and we hear nothing further of it, for more than two centuries, except only as a valuable work, which had once existed, and was probably buried in some one of the numerous ceme-teries of learning in which Spain abounds.

At length, towards the close of the last century, the indefatigable Muñoz succeeded in disinterring the long lost manuscript from the place tradition had assigned to it,—the library of a convent at Tolosa, in Navarre, the north-ern extremity of Spain. With his usual ardor, he transcribed the whole work with his own hands, and added it to the inestimable collection. of which, alas! he was destined not to reap the full benefit himself. From this transcript Lord Kingsborough was enabled to procure the copy which was published in 1830, in the sixth volume of his magnificent compilation. In it he expresses an honest satisfaction at being the first to give Sahagun's work to the world. But in this supposition he was mistaken The very year pre-ceding, an edition of it, with annotations, appeared in Mexico, in three vol-umes 8vo. It was prepared by Bustamante,—a scholar to whose editorial activity his country is largely indebted,—from a copy of the Muñoz manu-script which came into his possession. Thus this remarkable work, which was denied the honors of the press during the author's lifetime, after passing into oblivion, reappeared, at the distance of nearly three centuries, not in his own country, but in foreign lands widely remote from each other, and that almost simultaneously. The story is extraordinary though unhappily not so extraordinary in Spain as it would be elsewhere.

Sahagun divided his history into twelve books. The first eleven are occupied with the social institutions of Mexico, and the last with the Conquest. On the religion of the country he is particularly full. His great object evidently was, to give a clear view of its mythology, and of the burdensome ritual which belonged to it. Religion entered so intimately into the most private concerns and usages of the Aztecs, that Sahagun's work must be a text-book for every student of their antiquities. Torquemada availed himself of a man-uscript copy, which fell into his hands before it was sent to Spain, to enrich his own pages,— a circumstance more fortunate for his readers than for Sahagun's reputation, whose work, now that it is published, loses much of the originality and interest which would otherwise attach to it. In one respect it is invaluable; as presenting a complete collection of the various forms of prayer, accommodated to every possible emergency, in use by the Mexicans. They are often clothed in dignified and beautiful language, showing, that sublime speculative tenets are quite compatible with the most degrading practices of superstition. It is much to be regretted that we have not the eighteen hymns, inserted by the author in his book, which would have particular interest, as the only specimen of devotional poetry preserved of the Aztecs. The hieroglyphical paintings, which accompanied the text, are also missing. If they have escaped the hands of fanaticism, both may reappear at some future day.

Sahagun produced several other works, of a religious or philological character. Some of these were voluminous, but none have been printed. He lived to a very advanced age, closing a life of activity and usefulness, in 1590, in the capital of Mexico. His remains were followed to the tomb by a numerous concourse of his own countrymen, and of the natives, who lamented in him the loss of unaffected piety, benevolence, and learning.

CHAPTER IV.

Mexican Hieroglyphics.—Manuscripts.—Arithmetic.—Chronology.—Astronomy.

It is a relief to turn from the gloomy pages of the preceding chapter, to a brighter side of the picture, and to contemplate the same nation in its generous struggle to raise itself from a state of barbarism, and to take a positive rank in the scale of civilization. It is not the less interesting, that these efforts were made on an entirely new theatre of action, apart from those influences that operate in the Old World ; the inhabitants of which, forming one great brotherhood of nations, are knit together by sympathies, that make the faintest spark of knowledge, struck out in one quarter, spread gradually wider and wider, until it has diffused a cheering light over the remotest. It is curious to observe the human mind, in this new position, conforming to the same laws as on the ancient continent, and taking a similar direction in its first inquiries after truth,—so similar, indeed, as, although not warranting, perhaps, the idea of imitation, to suggest, at least, that of a common origin.

In the eastern hemisphere, we find some nations, as the Greeks, for instance, early smitten with such a love of the beautiful as to be unwilling to dispense with it, even in the graver productions of science ; and other nations, again, proposing a severer end to themselves, to which even imagination and elegant art were made subservient. The productions of such a people must be criticised, not by the ordinary rules of taste, but by their adaptation to the peculiar end for which they were designed. Such were the Egyptians in the Old World,[1] and the Mexicans in the New. We have already had occasion to notice the resemblance borne by the latter nation to the former in their religious economy. We shall be more struck with it in their scientific culture, especially their hieroglyphical writing and their astronomy.

---

[1] "An Egyptian temple," says Denon, strikingly, " is an open volume, in which the teachings of science, morality, and the arts are recorded. Every thing seems to speak one and the same language, and breathes one and the same spirit." The passage is cited by Heeren, Hist. Res., vol. V. p. 178.

To describ⌐ ⌐ction⌐ ⌐d events by delineating visible objects seems to be a natural suggestion, and is practised, after a certain fashion, by the rudest savages. The North American Indian carves an arrow on the bark of trees to show his followers the direction of his march, and some other sign to show the success of his expeditions. But to paint intelligibly a consecutive series of these actions—forming what Warburton has happily called *picture-writing* [2]— requires a combination of ideas, that amounts to a positively intellectual effort. Yet further, when the object of the painter, instead of being limited to the present, is, to pen· etrate the past, and to gather from its dark recesses lessons of instruction for coming generations, we see the dawnings of a literary culture,—and recognize the proof of a decided civiliza- tion in the attempt itself, however imperfectly it may be executed.

The literal imitation of objects will not answer for this more complex and extended plan. It would occupy too much space, as well as time, in the execution. It then becomes necessary to abridge the pictures, to confine the drawing to outlines, or to such prominent parts of the bodies delineated, as may readily suggest the whole. This is the *representative* or *figurative* writing, which forms the lowest stage of hieroglyphics.

But there are things which have no type in the material world ; abstract ideas, which can only be represented by visible objects supposed to have some quality analogous to the idea intended. This constitutes *symbolical* writing, the most difficult of all to the interpreter since the analogy between the material and immaterial object is often purely fanciful, or local in its application. Wo, for instance, could suspect the association which made a beetle represent the universe, as with the Egyptians, or a serpent typify time, as with the Aztecs?

The third and last division is the *phonetic,* in which signs are made to represent sounds, either entire words, or parts of them. This is the nearest approach of the hieroglyphical series to that beautiful invention, the alphabet, by which language is resolved into its elementary sounds, and an apparatus supplied for easily and accurately expressing the most delicate shades of thought.

The Egyptians were well skilled in all three kinds of hierogly- phics. But, although their public monuments display the first class, in their ordinary intercourse and written records, it is now certain, they almost wholly relied on the phonetic character. Strange, that, having thus broken down the thin partition which divided them from an alphabet, their latest monuments should

---

[2] Divine Legation, ap. Works, (London, 1811,) vol. IV. b. 4, sec. 4. The bishop of Gloucester, in his comparison of the various hieroglyphical systems of the world, shows his characteristic sagacity and boldness by an.

exhibit no nearer approach to it than their earliest.[1] The Aztecs, also, were acquainted with the several varieties of hieroglyphics. But they relied on the figurative infinitely more than on the others. The Egyptians were at the top of the scale, the Aztecs at the bottom.

In casting the eye over a Mexican manuscript, or map, as it is called, one is struck with the grotesque caricatures it exhibits of the human figure ; monstrous, overgrown heads, on puny, misshapen bodies, which are themselves hard and angular in their outlines, and without the least skill in composition. On closer inspection, however, it is obvious that it is not so much a rude attempt to delineate nature, as a conventional symbol, to express the idea in the most clear and forcible manner ; in the same way as the pieces of similar value on a chess-board, while they correspond with one another in form, bear little resemblance, usually, to the objects they represent. Those parts of the figure are most distinctly traced, which are the most important. So, also, the coloring, instead of the delicate gradations of nature, exhibits only gaudy and violent contrasts, such as may produce the most vivid impression. " For even colors," as Gama observes, "speak in the Aztec hieroglyphics."[4]

But in the execution of all this the Mexicans were much inferior to the Egyptians. The drawing of the latter, indeed, are exceedingly defective, when criticised by the rules of art ; for they were as ignorant of perspective as the Chinese, and only exhibited the head in profile, with the eye in the centre, and with total absence of expression. But they handled the pencil more gracefully than the Aztecs, were more true to the natural forms of objects, and, above all, showed great superiority in abridging the original figure by giving only the outline, or some characteristic or essential feature. This simplified the process, and facilitated the communication of thought. An Egyptian

nouncing opinions little credited then, though since established. He affirmed the existence of an Egyptian alphabet, but was not aware of the phonetic property of hieroglyphics,—the great literary discovery of our age.

[3] It appears that the hieroglyphics on the most recent monuments of Egypt contain no larger infusion of phonetic characters than those which existed eighteen centuries before Christ ; showing no advance, in this respect, for twenty-two hundred years ! (See Champollion, Précis du Système Hiéroglyphique des Anciens Egyptiens, (Paris, 1824,) pp. 242, 281.) It may seem more strange that the enchorial alphabet, so much more commodious, should not have been substituted. But the Egyptians were familiar with their hieroglyphics from infancy, which, moreover, took the fancies of the most illiterate, probably in the same manner as our children are attracted and taught by the picture-alphabets in an ordinary spelling-book.

[4] Descripcion Histórica y Cronologica de las Dos Piedras, (México, 1832,) Parte 2, p. 39.

text has almost the appearance of alphabetical writing in its re‑ gular lines of minute figures. A Mexican text book looks usually like a collection of pictures, each one forming the subject of a separate study. This is particularly the case with the delinea‑ tions of mythology; in which the story is told by a conglomera‑ tion of symbols, that may remind one more of the mysterious anaglyphs sculptured on the temples of the Egyptians, than of their written records.

The Aztecs had various emblems for expressing such things as, from their nature, could not be directly represented by the painter; as, for example, the years, months, days, the seasons, the elements, the heavens, and the like. A "tongue" denoted speaking; a "foot-print," travelling; a "man sitting on the ground," an earthquake. These symbols were often very arbitrary, varying with the caprice of the writer; and it requires a nice discrimination to interpret them, as a slight change in the form or position of the figure intimated a very different mean‑ ing.[5] An ingenious writer asserts that the priests devised secret symbolic characters for the record of their religious mysteries. It is possible. But the researches of Champollion lead to the conclusion, that the similar opinion, formerly en‑ tertained respecting the Egyptian hieroglyphics, is without foundation.[6]

Lastly, they employed, as above stated, phonetic signs, though these were chiefly confined to the names of persons and places; which, being derived from some circumstance, or characteristic quality, were accommodated to the hieroglyphical system. Thus the town *Cimatlan* was compounded of *cimatl,* a "root," which grew near it, and *tlan,* signifying "near"; *Tlaxcallan* meant "the place of bread," from its rich fields of corn : *Huexotzinco,* "a place surrounded by willows." The names of persons were often significant of their adventures and achieve‑ ments. That of the great Tezcucan prince, Nezahualcoyotl, signified "hungry fox," intimating his sagacity, and his dis‑

---

[5] Ibid., pp. 32, 44.—Acosta, lib. 6. cap. 7.

The continuation of Gama's work, recently edited by Bustamante, in Mexico, contains, among other things, some interesting remarks on the Aztec hieroglyphics, The editor has rendered a good service by this further publi‑ cation of the writings of this estimable scholar, who has done more than any of his countrymen to explain the mysteries of Aztec science.

[6] Gama, Descripcion, Parte 2, p. 32.

Warburton, with his usual penetration, rejects the idea of mystery in the figurative hieroglyphics. (Divine Legation, b. 4. sec. 4.) If there was any mystery reserved for the initiated, Champollion thinks it may have been the system of the anaglyphs. (Précis, p. 360.) May not this be true, likewise, of the monstrous symbolical combinations which represented the Mexican deities ?

tresses in early life.[7] The emblems of such names were no sooner seen, than they suggested to every Mexican the person and place intended; and, when painted on their shields, or embroidered on their banners, became the armorial bearings, by which city and chieftain were distinguished, as in Europe, in the age of chivalry.[8]

But, although the Aztecs were instructed in all the varieties of hieroglyphical painting, they chiefly resorted to the clumsy method of direct representation. Had their empire lasted, like the Egyptian, several thousand instead of the brief space of two hundred years, they would, doubtless, like them, have advanced to the more frequent use of the phonetic writing. But, before they could be made acquainted with the capabilities of their own system, the Spanish Conquest, by introducing the European alphabet, supplied their scholars with a more perfect contrivance for expressing thought, which soon supplanted the ancient pictorial character.[9]

Clumsy as it was, however, the Aztec picture-writing seems to have been adequate to the demands of the nation, in their imperfect state of civilization. By means of it were recorded all their laws, and even their regulations for domestic economy; their tribute-rolls, specifying the imposts of the various towns; their mythology, calendars, and rituals; their political annals, carried back to a period long before the foundation of the city. They digested a complete system of chronology, and could specify with accuracy the dates of the most important events in their history; the year being inscribed on the margin, against the particular circumstance recorded. It is true, history, thus executed, must necessarily be vague and fragmentary. Only a few leading incidents could be presented. But in this it did not differ much from the monkish chronicles of the dark ages,

---

[7] Boturini, Idea, pp. 77–83.—Gama, Descripcion, Parte 2, pp. 34–43.

Heeren is not aware, or does not allow, that the Mexicans used phonetic characters of any kind. (Hist. Res., vol. V. p. 45.—) They, indeed, reversed the usual order of proceeding, and, instead of adapting the hieroglyphic to the name of the object, accommodated the name of the object to the hieroglyphic. This of course, could not admit of great extension. We find phonetic characters, however, applied, in some instances, to common, as well as proper names.

[8] Boturini, Idea, ubi supra.

[9] Clavigero has given a catalogue of the Mexican historians of the sixteenth century,—some of whom are often cited in this history,—which bears honorable testimony to the literary ardor and intelligence of the native races. Stor. del Messico, tom. I., Pref.—Also, Gama, Descripcion, Parte 1, passim.

which often dispose of years in a few brief sentences ;—quite
long enough for the annals of barbarians.[10]

In order to estimate aright the picture-writing of the Aztecs
one must regard it in connexion with oral tradition, to which it
was auxiliary.   In the colleges of the priests the youth were
instructed in astronomy, history, mythology, &c. ; and those
who were to follow the profession of hieroglyphical painting
were taught the application of the characters appropriated to
each of these branches.   In an historical work, one had charge
of the chronology, another of the events.   Every part of the
labor was thus mechanically distributed.[11]   The pupils, instructed
in all that was before known in their several departments, were
prepared to extend still further the boundaries of their imperfect science.   The hieroglyphics served as a sort of stenography,
a collection of notes, suggesting to the initiated much more
than could be conveyed by a literal interpretation.   This combination of the written and the oral comprehended what may be
called the literature of the Aztecs.[12]

[10] M. de Humboldt's remark, that the Aztec annals, from the close of the
eleventh century, " exhibit the greatest method, and astonishing minuteness,"
(Vues des Cordillères, p. 137,) must be received with some qualification.
The reader would scarcely understand from it, that there are rarely more
than one or two facts recorded in any year, and sometimes not one in a dozen
or more.   The necessary looseness and uncertainty of these historical
records are made apparent by the remarks of the Spanish interpreter of the
Mendoza codex, who tells us that the natives to whom it was submitted
were very long in coming to an agreement about the proper signification of
the paintings.   Antiq. of Mexico, vol. VI. p. 87,

[11] Gama, Descripcion, Parte 2, p. 30.—Acosta, lib. 6, cap. 7.
"Tenian para cada género," says Ixtlilxochitl, "sus Escritores, unos que
trataban de los Anales, poniendo por su órden las cosas que acaecian en cada
un año, con dia, mes, y hora ; otros tenian á su cargo las Genealogías, y
descendencia del los Reyes, Senores, y Personas de linaje, asentando por
cuenta y razon los que nacian, y borraban los que morian con la misma
cuenta.   Unos tenian cuidado de las pinturas, de los términos, límites, y
mojoneras de las Ciudades, Provincias, Pueblos, y Lugares, y de las suertes,
y repartimiento de las tierras, cuyas eran, y á quien pertenecian; otros de
los libros de Leyes, ritos, y seremonias que usaban." Hist. Chich., MS.,
Prólogo.

[12] According to Boturini, the ancient Mexicans were acquainted with the
Peruvian method of recording events, by means of the *quippus*,—knotted
strings of various colors,—which were afterwards superseded by hieroglyphical painting. (Idea, p. 86.)   He could discover, however, but a single
specimen, which he met with in Tlascala, and that had nearly fallen to pieces
with age.   McCulloh suggests that it may have been only a wampum belt,
such as is common among our North America Indians. (Researches, p.
201.)   The conjecture is plausible enough.   Strings of wampum, of various
colors, were used by the latter people for the similar purpose of registering
events.   The insulated fact, recorded by Boturini, is hardly sufficient—un-
supported, as far as I know, by any other testimony—to establish the

Their manuscripts were made of different materials,— of cotton cloth, or skin, closely prepared ; of a composition of silk and gum ; but, for the most part, of a fine fabric from the leaves of the aloe, *agava Americana,* called by the natives, *maguey,* which grows luxuriantly over the table-lands of Mexico. A sort of paper was made from it, resembling somewhat the Egyptian *papyrus,*[13] which, when properly dressed and polished, is said to have been more soft and beautiful than parchment. Some of the specimens, still existing, exhibit their original fresh-ness, and the paintings on them retain their brilliancy of colors. They were sometimes done up into rolls, but more frequently into volumes, of moderate size, in which the paper was shut up, like a folding-screen, with a leaf or tablet of wood at each ex-tremity, that gave the whole, when closed, the appearance of a book. The length of the strips was determined only by con-venience. As the pages might be read and referred to sepa-rately, this form had obvious advantages over the rolls of the ancients.[14]

At the time of the arrival of the Spaniards, great quantities of these manuscripts were treasured up in the country. Numerous persons were employed in painting, and the dexterity of their operations excited the astonishment of the Conquerors. Un-fortunately, this was mingled with other, and unworthy feelings. The strange, unknown characters inscribed on them excited sus-picion. They were looked on as magic scrolls; and were re-garded in the same light with the idols and temples, as the symbols of a pestilent superstition, that must be extirpated. The first archbishop of Mexico, Don Juan de Zumarraga,—a name that should be as immortal as that of Omar,—collected these paintings from every quarter, especially from Tezcuco, the

existence of *quippus* among the Aztecs, who had but little in common with the Peruvians.

[13] Pliny, who gives a minute account of the *papyrus* reed of Egypt, notices the various manufactures obtained from it, as ropes, cloth, paper, &c. It also served as a thatch for the roofs of houses, and as food and drink for the natives. (Hist. Nat. lib. 11, cap. 20-22.) It is singular that the American *agave,* a plant so totally different, should also have been applied to all these various uses.

[14] Lorenzana, Hist. de Nueva España, p. 8.—Boturini, Idea, p. 96.—Humboldt, Vues des Cordillères, p. 52.—Peter Martyr Anglerius, De Orbe Novo, (Compluti, 1530,) dec. 3, cap. 8; dec. 5, cap. 10.

Martyr has given a minute description of the Indian maps, sent home soon after the invasion of New Spain. His inquisitive mind was struck with the evidence they afforded of a positive civilization. Ribera, the friend of Cortés, brought back a story, that the paintings were designed as patterns for embroiderers and jewellers. But Martyr had been in Egypt, and he felt little hesitation in placing the Indian drawings in the same class with those he had seen on the obelisks and temples of that country.

most cultivated capital in Anahuac, and the great depository of the national archives. He then caused them to be piled up in a "mountain-heap,"—as it is called by the Spanish writers themselves,—in the market-place of Tlatelolco, and reduced them all to ashes![15] His greater countryman, Archbishop Ximenes, had celebrated a similar *auto-da-fe* of Arabic manuscripts, in Granada, some twenty years before. Never did fanaticism achieve two more signal triumphs, than by the annihilation of so many curious monuments of human ingenuity and learning.[16]

The unlettered soldiers were not slow in imitating the example of their prelate. Every chart and volume which fell into their hands was wantonly destroyed; so that, when the scholars of a later and more enlightened age anxiously sought to recover some of these memorials of civilization, nearly all had perished, and the few surviving were jealously hidden by the natives.[17] Through the indefatigable labors of a private individual, however, a considerable collection was eventually deposited in the archives of Mexico; but was so little heeded there, that some were plundered, others decayed piecemeal from the damps and mildews, and others, again, were used up as waste-paper.[18] We contemplate with indignation the cruelties inflicted by the early conquerors. But indignation is qualified with contempt, when we see them thus ruthlessly trampling out the spark of knowledge, the common boon and property of all mankind. We may well doubt, which has the strongest claims to civilization, the victor, or the vanquished.

A few of the Mexican manuscripts have found their way, from time to time, to Europe, and are carefully preserved in the public libraries of its capitals. They are brought together in the magnificent work of Lord Kingsborough; but not one is there from Spain. The most important of them, for the light it throws on the Aztec institutions, is the Mendoza Codex; which, after its mysterious disappearance for more than a century, has

---

[15] Ixtlilxochitl, Hist. Chich., MS., Prologo.—Idem, Sum. Relac., MS.
Writers are not agreed whether the conflagration took place in the square of Tlatelolco or Tezcuco. Comp. Clavigero, Stor. del Messico, tom. II. p. 188, and Bustamante's Pref. to Ixtlilxochitl, Cruautés des Conquérans, trad. de Ternaux, p. xvii.

[16] It has been my lot to record both these displays of human infirmity, so humbling to the pride of intellect. See the History of Ferdinand and Isabella, Part 2, chap. 6.

[17] Sahagun, Hist. de Nueva-España, lib. 10, cap. 27.—Bustamante, Mañanas de Alameda, (México, 1836,) tom. II. Prologo.

[18] The enlightened governor, Don Lorenzo Zavala sold the documents in the archives of the Audience of Mexico, according to Bustamante, as wrapping paper, to apothecaries, shopkeepers, and rocket-makers! Boturini's noble collection has not fared much better.

at length reappeared in the Bodleian library at Oxford. It has been several times engraved.[19] The most brilliant in coloring, probably, is the Borgian collection, in Rome.[20] The most curious, however, is the Dresden Codex, which has excited less attention than it deserves. Although usually classed among Mexican manuscripts, it bears little resemblance to them in its execution ; the figures of objects are more delicately drawn, and the characters, unlike the Mexican, appear to be purely arbitrary, and are possibly phonetic.[21] Their regular arrangement

[19] The history of this famous collection is familiar to scholars. It was sent to the Emperor Charles the Fifth, not long after the Conquest, by the viceroy Mendoza, Marques de Mondejar. The vessel fell into the hands of a French cruiser, and the manuscript was taken to Paris. It was afterwards bought by the chaplain of the English embassy, and, coming into the possession of the antiquary Purchas, was engraved, *in extenso*, by him, in the third volume of his "Pilgrimage." After its publication, in 1625, the Aztec original lost its importance, and fell into oblivion so completely, that, when at length the public curiosity was excited in regard to its fate, no trace of it could be discovered. Many were the speculations of scholars, at home and abroad, respecting it, and Dr. Robertson settled the question as to its existence in England, by declaring that there was no Mexican relic in that country, except a golden goblet of Montezuma. (History of America, (London, 1796,) vol. III. p. 370.) Nevertheless, the identical Codex, and several other Mexican paintings, have been since discovered in the Bodleian library. The circumstance has brought some obloquy on the historian, who, while prying into the collections of Vienna and the Escurial, could be so blind to those under his own eyes. The over-sight will not appear so extraordinary to a thorough-bred collector, whether of manuscripts, or medals, or any other rarity. The Mendoza Codex is, after all, but a copy, coarsely done with a pen on European paper. Another copy, from which Archbishop Lorenzana engraved his tribute-rolls, in Mexico, existed in Boturini's collection. A third is in the Escurial, according to the Marquess of Spineto. (Lectures on the Elements of Hieroglyphics, (London,) lect. 7.) This may possibly be the original painting. The entire Codex, copied from the Bodleian maps, with its Spanish and English interpretations is included in the noble compilation of Lord Kingsborough. (Vols. I., V., VI.) It is distributed into three parts; embracing the civil history of the nation, the tributes paid by the cities, and the domestic economy and discipline of the Mexicans; and, from the fulness of the interpretation, is of much importance in regard to these several topics.

[20] It formerly belonged to the Giustiniani family; but was so little cared for, that it was suffered to fall into the mischievous hands of the domestics' children, who made sundry attempts to burn it. Fortunately it was painted on deerskin, and, though somewhat singed, was not destroyed. (Humboldt, Vues Cordillères, p. 89, et seq.) It is impossible to cast the eye over this brilliant assemblage of forms and colors without feeling how hopeless must be the attempt to recover a key to the Aztec mythological symbols; which are here distributed with the symmetry, indeed, but in all the endless combinations, of the kaleidoscope. It is in the third volume of Lord Kingsborough's work.

[21] Humboldt, who has copied some pages of it in his "Atlas Pittoresque," intimates no doubt of its Aztec origin. (Vues des Cordillères, pp. 266 267.) M. Le Noir even reads in it an exposition of Mexican Mythology, with occa-

is quite equal to th´ Egyptian. The whole infers a much higher civilization than the Aztec, and offers abundant food for curious speculation.[22]

Some few of these maps have interpretations annexed to them, which were obtained from the natives after the Conquest.[23] The greater part are without any, and cannot now be unriddled. Had the Mexicans made free use of a phonetic alphabet, it might have been originally easy, by mastering the comparatively few signs employed in this kind of communication, to have got a permanent key to the whole.[24] A brief inscription has furnished a clue to the vast labyrinth of Egyptian hieroglyphics. But the Aztec characters, representing individuals, or, at most, species, require to be made out separately; a hopeless task, for which little aid is to be expected from the vague and general

sional analogies to that of Egypt and of Hindostan. (Antiquites Mexicaines, tom. II., Introd.) The fantastic forms of hieroglyphic symbols may afford analogies for almost anything.

[22] The history of this Codex, engraved entire in the third volume of the "Antiquities of Mexico," goes no further back than 1739, when it was pur-chased at Vienna for the Dresden library. It is made of the American *agave*. The figures painted on it bear little resemblance, either in feature or form, to the Mexican. They are surmounted by a sort of head-gear, which looks something like a modern peruke. On the chin of one we may notice a beard, a sign often used after the conquest to denote a European. Many of the persons are sitting cross-legged. The profiles of the faces and the whole contour of the limbs, are sketched with a spirit and freedom, very unlike the hard, angular outlines of the Aztecs. The characters, also are delicately traced, generally in an irregular, but circular form, and are very minute. They are arranged, like the Egyptian, both horizontally and perpendicularly, mostly in the former manner, and, from the prevalent direction of the profiles would seem to have been read from right to left. Whether phonetic or ideographic, they are of that compact and purely conventional sort which belongs to a well-digested system for the communication of thought. One cannot but regret, that no trace should exist of the quarter whence this MS. was obtained; perhaps, some part of Central America; from the region of the mysterious races who built the monuments of Mitla and Palenque. Though, in truth, there seems scarcely more resemblance in the symbols to the Palenque *bas-reliefs*, than to the Aztec paintings.

[23] There are three of these; the Mendoza Codex: the Telleriano Rem-ensis,—formerly the property of Archbishop Tellier,—in the Royal library of Paris; and the Vatican MS., No. 3738. The interpretation of the last bears evident marks of its recent origin; probably as late as the close of the sixteenth, or the beginning of the seventeenth century, when the ancient hieroglyphics were read with the eye of faith, rather than of reason. Who-ever was the commentator. (comp. Vues des Cordillères, pp. 203, 204: and Antiq. of Mexico, vol. VI. pp. 155, 222,) he has given such an exposition, as shows the old Aztecs to have been as orthodox Christians, as any subjects of the Pope.

[24] The total number of Egyptian hieroglyphics discovered by Champollion amounts to 864; and of these 130 only are phonetic, notwithstanding that this kind of character is used far more frequently than both the others. Précis, p. 263,—also Spineto, Lectures, lec. 3.

tenor of the few interpretations now existing. There was, as already mentioned, until late in the last century, a professor in the University of Mexico, especially devoted to the study of the national picture-writing. But, as this was with a view to legal proceedings, his information, probably, was limited to deciphering titles. In less than a hundred years after the Conquest, the knowledge of the hieroglyphics had so far declined, that a diligent Tezcucan writer complains he could find in the country only two persons, both very aged, at all competent to interpret them.[26]

It is not probable, therefore, that the art of reading these picture-writings will ever be recovered ; a circumstance certainly to be regretted. Not that the records of a semi-civilized people would be likely to contain any new truth or discovery important to human comfort or progress ; but they could scarcely fail to throw some additional light on the previous history of the nation, and that of the more polished people who before occupied the country. This would be still more probable, if any literary relics of their Toltec predecessors were preserved ; and if report be true, an important compilation from this source was extant at the time of the invasion, and may have perhaps contributed to swell the holocaust of Zumarraga.[27] It is no great stretch of fancy, to suppose that such records might reveal the successive links in the mighty chain of migration of the primitive races, and, by carrying us back to the seat of their possessions in the Old World, would have solved the mystery which has so long

---

[26] Ixtlilxochitl., Hist. Chich., MS., Dedic.
Boturini, who travelled through ever part of the country, in the middle of the last century, could not meet with an individual who could afford him the least clue to the Aztec hieroglyphics. So completely had every vestige of their ancient language been swept away for the memory of the natives. (Idea, p. 116.) If we are to believe Bustamante, however, a complete key to the whole system is, at this moment, *somewhere* in Spain. It was carried home, at the time of the process against father Mier, in 1795. The name of the Mexican Champollion who discovered it is Borunda. Gama, Descripcion, tom. II. p. 33, nota.

[27] *Teoamoxtli,* "the divine book," as it was called. According to Ixtlilxochitl, it was composed by a Tezcucan doctor, named Huematzin, towards the close of the seventh century. (Relaciones, MS.) It gave an account of the migrations of his nation from Asia, of the various stations on their journey, of their social and religious institutions, their science, arts, &c., &c., a good deal too much for one book. *Ignotum pro ma nifico.* It has never been seen by a European. A copy is said to have been in possession of the Texcucan chroniclers, on the taking of their capital. (Bustamante, Cronica Mexicana, (Mexico, 1822,) carta 3.) Lord Kingsborough, who can scent out a Hebrew root, be it buried never so deep, has discovered that the *Teoamoxtli* was the Pentateuch. Thus,—*teo* means "divine," *amotl,* "paper" or "book," and *moxtli* "*appears* to be Moses,"—"Divine Book of Moses,"! Antiq. of Mexico, vol. VI. p. 204, nota.

perplexed the learned, in regard to the settlement and civilization of the New.

Besides the hieroglyphical maps, the traditions of the country
were embodied in the songs and hymns, which, as already mentioned, were carefully taught in the public schools.   These were
various, embracing the mythic legends of a heroic age, the warlike achievements of their own, or the softer tales of love and
pleasure.[27]   Many of them were composed by scholars and persons of rank, and are cited as affording the most authentic record of events.[28]   The Mexican dialect was rich and expressive,
though inferior to the Tezcucan, the most polished of the idioms
of Anahuac.   None of the Aztec compositions have survived,
but we can form some estimate of the general state of poetic
culture from the odes which have come down to us from the
royal house of Tezcuco.[29]   Sahagun has furnished us with translations of their more elaborate prose, consisting of prayers and
public discourses, which give a favorable idea of their eloquence, and show that they paid much attention to rhetorical
effect.   They are said to have had, also, something like theatri-
cal exhibitions, of a pantomimic sort, in which the faces of the
performers were covered with masks, and the figures of birds or
animals were frequently represented ; an imitation to which they
may have been led by the familiar delineation of such objects in
their hieroglyphics.[30]   In all this we see the dawning of a literary culture, surpassed, however, by their attainments in the severer walks of mathematical science.

They devised a system of notation in their arithmetic, sufficiently simple.   The first twenty numbers were expressed by a
corresponding number of dots.   The first five had specific
names ; after which they were represented by combining the
fifth with one of the four preceding; as five and one for six,
five and two for seven, and so on.   Ten and fifteen had each a
separate name, which was also combined with the first four, to
express a higher quantity.   These four, therefore, were the rad-

---

[27] Boturini, Idea, pp. 90–97.—Clavigero, Stor. del Messico, tom. II. pp.
174–178.
[28] " Los cantos con que las observaban Autores muy graves en su modo
de ciencia y facultad, pues fuéron los mismos Reyes, y de la gente mas ilustre
y entendida, que siempre observáron y adquiriéron la verdad, y esta con
tanta, y razon, quanta pudiéron tener los mas graves y fidedignos Autores."
Ixtlilxochitl, Hist. Chich., MS., Prólogo.
[29] See Chap. 6, of this Introduction.
[30] See some account of these mummeries in A _osta, (lib. 5, cap. 30,)—
also Clavigero (Stor. del Messico, ubi supra).   Stone models of masks are
sometimes found among the Indian ruins, and engravings of them are both
in Lord Kingsborough's work, and in the Antiquités Mexicaines.

ical characters of their oral arithmetic, in the same manner as they were of the written with the ancient Romans: a more simple arrangement, probably, than any existing among Europeans.[81] Twenty was expressed by a separate hieroglyphic,—a flag. Larger sums were reckoned by twenties, and, in writing, by repeating the number of flags. The square of twenty, four hundred, had a separate sign, that of a plume, and so had the cube of twenty, or eight thousand, which was denoted by a purse, or sack. This was the whole arithmetical apparatus of the Mexicans, by the combination of which they were enabled to indicate any quantity. For greater expedition, they used to denote fractions of the larger sums by drawing only a part of the object. Thus, half or three fourths of a plume, or of a purse, represented that proportion of their respective sums, and so on.[82] With all this, the machinery will appear very awkward to us, who perform our operations with so much ease, by means of the Arabic, or, rather, Indian ciphers. It is not much more awkward, however, than the system pursued by the great mathematicians of antiquity, unacquainted with the brilliant invention, which has given a new aspect to mathematical science, of determining the value, in a great measure, by the relative position of the figures.

In the measurement of time, the Aztecs adjusted their civil year by the solar. They divided it into eighteen months of twenty days each. Both months and days were expressed by peculiar hieroglyphics,—those of the former often intimating the season of the year, like the French months, at the period of the Revolution. Five complementary days, as in Egypt,[83] were added, to make up the full number of three hundred and sixty-five. They belonged to no month, and were regarded as peculiarly unlucky. A month was divided into four weeks, of five days each, on the last of which was the public fair, or market day.[84] This arrangement, differing from that of the nations of the Old Continent, whether of Europe or Asia,[85] has the advantage of giving an

---

[81] Gama, Descripcion, Parte 2, Apend 28.

Gama, in comparing the language of Mexican notation with the decimal system of the Europeans, and the ingenious binary system of Leibnitz, confounds oral with written arithmetic.

[82] Ibid., ubi supra.

This learned Mexican has given a very satisfactory treatise on the arithmetic of the Aztecs, in his second part.

[83] Herodotus, Euterpe, sec. 4.

[84] Sahagun, Hist. de Nueva España, lib. 4, Apend.

According to Clavigero, the fairs were held on the days bearing the sign of the year. Stor. del Messico, tom. II. p. 62.

[85] The people of Java, according to Sir Stamford Raffles, regulated their markets, also, by a week of five days. They had, besides, our week of

equal number of days to each month, and of comprehending entire weeks, without a fraction, both in the month and in the year.[86]

As the year is composed of nearly six hours more than three hundred and sixty-five days, there still remained an excess, which, like other nations who have framed a calendar, they provided for by intercalation ; not, indeed, every fourth year, as the Europeans,[37] but at longer intervals, like some of the Asiatics.[38] They waited till the expiration of fifty-two vague years, when they interposed thirteen days, or rather twelve and a half, this being the number which had fallen in arrear. Had they inserted thirteen, it would have been too much, since the annual excess over three hundred and sixty-five is about eleven minutes less than six hours. But, as their calendar, at the time of the Conquest, was found to correspond with the European, (making allowance for the subsequent Gregorian reform,) they would seem to have adopted the shorter period of twelve days and a half,[39] which brought them, within an almost inappreci-

seven. (History of Java. (London, 1830,) vol. I., pp. 531, 532.) The latter division of time, of general use throughout the East, is the oldest monument existing of astronomical science. See La Place, Exposition du Système du Monde, (Paris, 1808,) lib. 5, chap. 1.

[36] Veytia, Historia Antigua de Méjico, (Méjico, 1806,) tom. I. cap. 6, 7. —Gama, Descripcion, Parte 1, pp. 33, 34, et alibi.—Boturini, Idea, pp. 4, 44, et seq.—Cod. Tel. Rem., ap. Antiq. of Mexico, vol. VI. p. 104.— Camargo, Hist. de Tlascala, MS.—Toribio, Hist. de los Indios, MS., Parte I. cap. 5.

[37] Sahagun intimates doubts of this. " Otra fiesta hacian de cuatro en cuatro años á honra del fuego, y en esta fiesta *es verosimil, y hay congeturas* que hacian su visiesto contando seis dias de *nemontemi* " ; the five unlucky complementary days were so called. (Hist. de Nueva España, lib. 4, Apend.) But this author, however good an authority for the superstitions, is an indifferent one for the science of the Mexicans.

[38] The Persians had a cycle of one hundred and twenty years, of three hundred and sixty-five days each at the end of which they intercalated thirty days. (Humboldt, Vues des Cordillères, p. 177.) This was the same as thirteen after the cycle of fifty-two years of the Mexicans ; but it was less accurate than their probable intercalation of twelve days and a half. It is obviously indifferent, as far as accuracy is concerned, which multiple of four is selected to form the cycle ; though the shorter the interval of intercalation, the less of course, will be the temporary departure from the true time.

[39] This is the conclusion to which Gama arrives, after a very careful investigation of the subject. He supposes that the " bundles," or cycles, of fifty-two years,—by which, as we shall see, the Mexicans computed time, —ended, alternately, at midnight and midday. (Descripcion, Parte 1, p. 52, et seq.) He finds some warrant for this in Acosta's account, (lib. 6, cap. 2,) though contradicted by Torquemada, (Monarch. Ind., lib. , cap. 33,) and, as it appears, by Sahagun,—whose work, however, Gama never saw,— (Hist. de Nueva España, lib. 7, cap. 9,) both of whom place the close of the year at midnight. Gama's hypothesis derives confirmation from a circumstance I have not seen noticed. Besides the " bundle " of fifty-two years, the

able fraction, to the exact length of the tropical year, as established by the most accurate observations.[40]   Indeed, the intercalation of twenty-five days, in every hundred and four year shows a nicer adjustment of civil to solar time than is presenteo by any European calendar ; since more than five centuries must elapse, before the loss of an entire day.[41]   Such was the astonishing precision displayed by the Aztecs, or, perhaps, by their more polished Toltec predecessors, in these computations, so difficult as to have baffled, till a comparatively recent period, the most enlightened nations of ·Christendom ! [42]

The chronological system of the Mexicans, by which they determined the date of any particular event, was, also, very re-

Mexicans had a larger cycle of one hundred and four years, called " an old age."   As this was not used in their reckonings, which were carried on by their " bundles," it seems highly probable that it was designed to express the period which would bring round the commencement of the smaller cycles to the same hour, and in which the intercalary days, amounting to twenty-five, might be comprehended without a fraction.

[40] This length, as computed by Zach, at 365d. 5h. 48m. 48sec., is only 2m. 9sec. longer than the Mexican ; which corresponds with the celebrated calculation of the astronomers of the Caliph Almamon, that fell short about two minutes of the true time. See La Place, Exposition, p. 350.

[41] "El corto exceso de 4hor. 38min. 40seg., que hay de mas de las 25 dias en el período de 104 años, no puede componer un dia entero, hasta que pasen mas de cinco de estos periodos maximos ó 538 años." Gama, Descripcion, Parte I, p. 23.) Gama estimates the solar year at 365d. 5h. 48m. 50sec.

[42] The ancient Etruscans arranged their calendar in cycles of 110 solar years, and reckoned the year at 365d. 5h. 40m.; at least. this seems probable, says Niebuhr. (History of Rome, Eng. trans., (Cambridge 1828.) vol, I. p. 113, 238.) The early Romans had not wit enough to avail themselves of this accurate measurement, which came within nine minutes of the true time. The Julian reform, which assumed 365d. 5¼h. as the length of the year, erred as much, or rather more, on the other side. And when the Europeans, who adopted this calendar, landed in Mexico, their reckoning was nearly eleven days in advance of the exact time,—or, in other words, of the reckoning of the barbarous Aztecs ; a remarkable fact.

Gama's researches lead to the conclusion, that the year of the new cycle began with the Aztecs on the ninth of January ; a date considerably earliei than that usually assigned by the Mexican writers. (Descripcion, Parte I, pp. 49-52.) By postponing the intercalation to the end of fifty-two years, the annual loss of six hours made every fourth year begin a day earlier. Thus, the cycle commencing on the ninth year of January, the fifth year of it began on the eighth, the ninth year on the seventh, and so on ; so that the last day of the series of fifty-two years fell on the twenty-sixth of December. when tho intercalation of thirteen days rectified the chronology, and carried the commencement of the new year to the ninth of January again. Torquemada, puzzled by the irregularity of the new-year's day, asserts that the Mexicans were unacquainted with the annual excess of six hours, and therefore never intercalated ! (Monarch. Ind., lib. 10, cap. 36.) The interpreter of the Vatican Codex has fallen into a series of blunders on the same subject, still more ludicrous. (Antiq. of Mexico, vol. VI. Pl. 16.) So soon had Aztec science fallen into oblivion, after the Conquest !

markaðle. T'.e epo⁓., from which they reckoned, corresponded
with the yea. 1091, ⌣f the Christian era. It was the period of
the reform of their calendar, soon after their migration from
Aztlan. They threw the years, as already noticed, into great
cycles, of fifty-two each, which they called "sheafs," or "bun·
dles," and represented by a quantity of reeds bound together
by a string. As often as this hieroglyphic occurs in their maps,
it shows the number of half centuries. To enable them to
specify any particular year, they divided the great cycle into four
smaller cycles, or indictions, of·thirteen years each. They then
adopted two periodical series of signs, one consisting of their
numerical dots, up to thirteen, the other, of four hieroglyphics
of the years.[43] These latter they repeated in regular succession,
setting against each one a number of the corresponding series
of dots, continued also in regular succession up to thirteen.
The same system was pursued through the four indictions, which
thus, it will be observed, began always with a different hieroglyphic of the year from the preceding; and in this way, each of
the hieroglyphics was made to combine successively with each
of the numerical signs, but never twice with the same; since
four, and thirteen, the factors of fifty-two,—the number of years
in the cycle,—must admit of just as many combinations as are
equal to their product. Thus every year had its appropriate
symbol, by which it was, at once, recognized. And this symbol,
preceded by the proper number of "bundles," indicating the
half centuries, showed the precise time which had elapsed since
the national epoch of 1091.[44] The ingenious contrivance of a
periodical series, in place of the cumbrous system of hieroglyphical notation, is not peculiar to the Aztecs, and is to be found
among various people, on the Asiatic continent,—the same in
principle, though varying materially in arrangement.[45]

[43] These hieroglyphics were a "rabbit," a "reed," a "flint," a "house."
They were taken as symbolical of the four elements, air, water, fire, earth,
according to Veytia. (Hist. Antig., tom. I. cap. 5.) It is not easy to see
the connexion between the terms "rabbit" and "air," which lead the respective series.
[44] The following table of two of the four indictions of thirteen years each
will make the text more clear. The first column shows the actual year of the
great cycle, or "bundle." The second, the numerical dots used in their

[45] Among the Chinese, Japanese, Moghols, Mantchous, and other families
of the Tartar race. Their series are composed of symbols of their five ele·
ments, and the twelve zodiacal signs making a cycle of sixty years' duration.
Their several systems are exhibited, in connection with the Mexican, in the
luminous pages of Humboldt, (Vues des Cordillères, p. 149,) who draws important consequences from the comparison, to which we shall have occasion
to return hereafter.

The solar calendar, above described, might have answered all the purposes of the nation ; but the priests chose to con-

arithmetic. The third is composed of their hieroglyphics for rabbit, reed, flint, house, in their regular order.

FIRST INDICTION.		SECOND INDICTION.	
Year of the Cycle.		Year of the Cycle.	
1.	.	14.	.
2.	. .	15.	. .
3.	. . .	16.	. . .
4.	. . . .	17.	. . . .
5.	. . . . .	18.	. . . . .
6.	:	19.	. . . . . .
7.	: : . . .	20.	: . . .
8.	: : : . .	21.	: : . .
9.	: : : . .	22.	: : : . .
10.	: : : . :	23.	: : : .
11.	: : : : :	24.	: : : . .
12.	: : : : :	25.	: : : : :
13.	: : : : . :	26.	: : : : :

By pursuing the combinations through the two remaining Indictions, it will be found that the same number of dots will never coincide with the same hieroglyphic.

These tables are generally thrown into the form of wheels, as are those, also, of their months and days, having a very pretty effect. Several have been published, at different times, from the collections of Siguenza and Boturini. The wheel of the great cycle of fifty-two years is encompassed by

struct another for themselves.   This was called a " lunar reckon.
ing," though nowise accommodated to the revolutions of the
moon.[46]   It was formed, also, of two periodical series, one of
them consisting of thirteen numerical signs, or dots, the other.
of the twenty hieroglyphics of the days.   But, as the product of
these combinations would only be 260, and, as some confusion
might arise from the repetition of the same terms for the remaining 105 days of the year, they invented a third series, consisting
of nine additional hieroglyphics, which, alternating with the two
preceding series, rendered it impossible that the three should
coincide twice in the same year, or indeed in less than 2340
days; since $20 \times 13 \times 9 = 2340$.[47]   Thirteen was a mystic number
of frequent use in their tables.[48]   Why they resorted to that of
nine, on this occasion, is not so clear.[49]

a serpent, which was also the symbol of "an age," both with the Persians
and Egyptians.   Father Toribio seems to misapprehend the nature of these
chronological wheels ; "Tenian rodelas y escudos, y en ellas pintadas las
figuras y armas de sus Demonios con su blason."   Hist. de los Indios, MS.,
Parte 1, cap. 4.

[46] In this calendar, the months of the tropical year were distributed into
cycles of thirteen days, which, being repeated twenty times,—the number of
days in a solar month,—completed the lunar, or astrological, year of 260 days;
when the reckoning began again.   "By the contrivance of these *trecenas*
(terms of thirteen days) and the cycle of fifty-two years," says Gama, "they
formed a luni-solar period, most exact for astronomical purposes." (Descripcion, Parte 1, p. 27.)   He adds, that these *trecenas* were suggested by the
periods in which the moon is visible before and after, conjunction.   (Loc.
cit.)   It seems hardly possible that a people, capable of constructing a calendar so accurately on the true principles of solar time, should so grossly err
as to suppose, that, in this reckoning, they really "represented the daily
revolutions of the moon."   "The whole Eastern world," says the learned
Niebuhr, "has followed the moon in its calendar ; the free scientific division
of a vast portion of time is peculiar to the West.   Connected with the
West is that primeval extinct world which we call the New."   History of
Rome, vol. I. p. 239.

[47] They were named "companions," and "lords of the night," and were
supposed to preside over the night, as the other signs did over the day.
Boturini, Idea, p. 57.

[48] Thus, their astrological year was divided into months of thirteen days,
there were thirteen years in their indictions, which contained each three
hundred and sixty-five periods of thirteen days, &c.   It is a curious fact, that
the number of lunar months of thirteen days, contained in a cycle of fifty-two
years, with the intercalation, should correspond precisely with the number of
years in the great Sothic period of the Egyptians, namely, 1491 ; a period, in
which the seasons and festivals came round to the same place in the year
again.   The coincidence may be accidental.   But a people employing periodical series, and astrological calculations, have generally some meaning in the
numbers they select and the combinations to which they lead.

[49] According to Gama, (Descripcion, Parte 1 pp. 75, 76,) because 360.
can be divided by nine without a fraction ; the nine "companions" not being
attached to the five complementary days.   But 4, a mystic number much used
in their arithmetical combinations, would have answered the same purpose,

This second calendar rouses a holy indignation in the early Spanish missionaries, and father Sahagun loudly condems it, as "most unhallowed, since it is founded neither on natural reason, nor on the influence of the planets, nor on the true course of the year ; but it is plainly the work of necromancy, and the fruit ot a compact with the Devil!"[50] One may doubt, whether the superstition of those who invented the scheme was greater than that of those who thus impugned it. At all events, we may, without having recourse to supernatural agency, find in the human heart a sufficient explanation of its origin ; in that love of power, that has led the priesthood of many a faith to affect a mystery, the key to which was in their own keeping.

By means of this calendar, the Aztec priests kept their own records, regulated the festivals and seasons of sacriftce, and made all their astrological calculations.[61] The false science of astrology is natural to a state of society partially civilized, where the mind, impatient of the slow and cautious examination by which alone it can arrive at truth, launches, at once, into the regions of speculation, and rashly attempts to lift the veil, —the impenetrable veil, which is drawn around the mysteries of nature. It is the characteristic of true science, to discern the impassable, but not very obvious, limits which divide the province of reason from that of speculation. Such knowledge

equally well. In regard to this, McCulloh observes, with much shrewdness, "It seems impossible that the Mexicans so careful in constructing their cycle. should abruptly terminate it with 360 revolutions, whose natural period of termination is 2340." And he supposes the nine "companions" were used in connexion with the cycles of 260 days, in order to throw them into the larger ones, of 2340; eight of which, with a ninth of 260 days, he ascertains to be equal to the great solar period of 52 years. (Researches, pp. 207, 208.) This is very plausible. But in fact the combinations of the two first series, forming the cycle of 260 days, were always interrupted at the end of the year, since each new year began with the same hieroglyphic of the days. The third series of the "companions" was intermitted, as above stated, on the five unlucky days which closed the year, in order, if we may believe Boturini, that the first day of the solar year might have annexed to it the first of the nine "companions," which signified "lord of the year" ; (Idea, p. 57 :) a result which might have been equally well secured, without any intermission at all, by taking 5, another favorite number, instead of 9, as the divisor. As it was, however, the cycle, as far as the third series was concerned, did terminate with 360 revolutions. The subject is a perplexing one; and I can hardly hope to have presented it in such a manner as to make it perfectly clear to the reader.

[50] Hist. de Nueva España, lib. 4, Introd.
[61] "Dans les pays les plus differents," says Benjamin Constant, concluding some sensible reflections on the sources of the sacerdotal power, "chez les peuples de mœurs les plus opposées, le sacerdoce a dû au culte des elements et des astres un pouvoir dont aujourd'hui nous concevons a peine l'idee." De la Religion. (Paris, 1825,) lib. 3, ch. 5.

comes tardily. How many ages have rolled away, in which powers, that, rightly directed, might have revealed the great laws of nature, have been wasted in brilliant, but barren, reveries on alchemy and astrology !

The latter is more particularly the study of a primitive age; when the mind, incapable of arriving at the stupendous fact, that the myriads of minute lights, glowing in the firmament, are the centres of systems as glorious as our own, is naturally led to speculate on their probable uses, and to connect them in some way or other with man, for whose convenience every other object in the universe seems to have been created. As the eye of the simple child of nature watches, through the long nights, the stately march of the heavenly bodies, and sees the bright hosts coming up, one after another, and changing with the changing seasons of the year, he naturally associates them with those seasons, as the periods over which they hold a mysterious influence. In the same manner, he connects their appearance with any interesting event of the time, and explores, in their flaming characters, the destinies of the newborn infant.[52] Such is the origin of astrology, the false lights of which have continued from the earliest ages to dazzle and bewilder mankind, till they have faded away in the superior illumination of a comparatively recent period.

The astrological scheme of the Aztecs was founded less on the planetary influences, than on those of the arbitrary signs they had adopted for the months and days. The character of the leading sign, in each lunar cycle of thirteen days, gave a complexion to the whole ; though this was qualified, in some degree, by the signs of the succeeding days, as well as by those of the hours. It was in adjusting these conflicting forces that the great art of the diviner was shown. In no country, not even in ancient Egypt, were the dreams of the astrologer more implicity deferred to. On the birth of a child, he was instantly summoned. The time of the event was accurately ascertained ; and the family hung in trembling suspense, as the minister of Heaven cast the horoscope of the infant, and unrolled the dark

---

[52] " It is a gentle and affectionate thought,
    That, in immeasurable heights above us,
    At our first birth the wreath of love was woven
    With sparkling stars for flowers."

COLERIDGE, Translation of Wallenstein, Act 2, sc. 4.

Schiller is more true to poetry than history, when he tells us, in the beautiful passage of which this is part, that the worship of the stars took the place of classic mythology. It existed long before it.

volume of destiny. The influence of the priest was confessed by the Mexican, in the very first breath which he inhaled.[53]

We know little further of the astronomical attainments of the Aztecs. That they were acquainted with the cause of eclipses is evident from the representation, on their maps, of the disk of the moon projected on that of the sun.[54] Whether they had arranged a system of constellations is uncertain ; though, that they recognized some of the most obvious, as the Pleiades, for example, is evident from the fact that they regulated their festivals by them. We know of no astronomical instruments used by them, except the dial.[55] An immense circular block of carved stone, disinterred in 1790, in the great square in Mexico, has supplied an acute and learned scholar with the means of establishing some interesting facts in regard to Mexican science.[56] This colossal fragment, on which the calendar is engraved, shows that they had the means of settling the hours of the day with precision, the periods of the solstices and of the equinoxes, and that of the transit of the sun across the zenith of Mexico.[57]

---

[53] Gama has given us a complete almanac of the astrological year, with the appropriate signs and divisions, showing with what scientific skill it was adapted to its various uses. (Descripcion, Parte 1, pp. 25-31 ; 62-76.) Sahagun has devoted a whole book to explaining the mystic import and value of these signs, with a minuteness that may enable one to cast up a scheme of nativity for himself. (Hist. de Nueva España, lib. 4.) It is evident he fully believed the magic wonders which he told. "It was a deceitful art," he says, "pernicious and idolatrous ; and was never contrived by human reason." The good father was certainly no philosopher.

[54] See, among others, the Cod. Tel.-Rem., Part 4, Pl. 22, ap. Antiq. of Mexico, vol. I.

[55] "It can hardly be doubted," says Lord Kingsborough, "that the Mexicans were acquainted with many scientifical instruments of strange invention, as compared with our own ; whether the *telescope* may not have been of the number is uncertain; but the thirteenth plate of M. Dupaix's *Monuments*, Part Second, which represents a man holding something of a similar nature to his eye, affords reason to suppose that they knew how to improve the powers of vision." (Antiq. of Mexico, vol. VI. p. 15, note.) The instrument alluded to is rudely carved on a conical rock. It is raised no higher than the neck of the person who holds it, and looks—to my thinking—as much like a musket as a telescope; though I shall not infer the use of firearms among the Aztecs from this circumstance. (See vol. IV. Pl. 15.) Captain Dupaix, however, in his commentary on the drawing, sees quite as much in it as his Lordship. Ibid., vol. V. p. 241.

[56] Gama, Descripcion, Parte 1, sec. 4 ; Parte 2, Apend.

Besides this colossal fragment, Gama met with some others, designed, probably, for similar scientific uses, at Chapoltepec. Before he had leisure to examine them, however, they were broken up for materials to build a furnace ! A fate not unlike that which has too often befallen the monuments of ancient art in the Old World.

[57] In his second treatise on the cylindrical stone, Gama dwells more at large on its scientific construction, as a vertical sun-dial, in order to dispel

We cannot contemplate the astronomical science of the Mexicans, so disproportioned to their progress in other walks of civilization, without astonishment.   An acquaintance with some of
the more obvious principles of astronomy is within the reach of
the rudest people.   With a little care, they may learn to connect
the regular changes of the seasons with those of the place of the
sun at his rising and setting.   They may follow the march of the
great luminary through the heavens, by watching the stars that
first brighten on his evening track, or fade in his morning beams.
They may measure a revolution of the moon, by marking her
phases, and may even form a general idea of the number of such
revolutions in a solar year.   But that they should be capable of
accurately adjusting their festivals by the movements of the
heavenly bodies, and should fix the true length of the tropical
year, with a precision unknown to the great philosophers of an·
tiquity, could be the result only of a long series of nice and patient observations, evincing no slight progress in civilization.[58]
But whence could the rude inhabitants of these mountain regions
have derived this curious erudition?   Not from the barbarous
hordes who roamed over the higher latitudes of the North ; nor
from the more polished races on the Southern continent, with
whom, it is apparent, they had no intercourse.   If we are driven,
in our embarrassment, like the greatest astronomer of our age
to seek the solution among the civilized communities of Asia,
we shall still be perplexed by finding, amidst general resemblance
of outline, sufficient discrepancy in the details, to vindicate, in
the judgments of many, the Aztec claim to originality.[59]

I shall conclude the account of Mexican science, with that of
a remarkable festival, celebrated by the natives at the termination of the great cycle of fifty-two years.   We have seen, in the
preceding chapter, their tradition of the destruction of the
world at four successive epochs.   They looked forward confi-

the doubts of some sturdy sceptics on this point. (Descripcion, Parte 2.
Apend. I.)   The civil day was distributed by the Mexicans into sixteen parts;
and began, like that of most of the Asiatic nations, with sunrise.   M. de
Humboldt, who probably never saw Gama's second treatise, allows only
eight intervals.   Vues des Cordilères, p. 128.

[58] Un calendrier,'' exclaims the enthusiastic Carli, " qui est réglé sur la
révolution annuelle du soleil, non seulement par l'addition de cinq jours tous
les ans, mais encore par la correction du bissextile, doit sans doute être re-
gardé comme une opération déduite d'une étude réfléchie, et d'une grande
combinaison.   Il faut donc supposer chez ces peuples une suite d'observations astronomiques, une idée distincte de la sphère, de la déclinaison de
l'écliptique, et l'usage d'un calcul concernant les jours et les heures des apparitions solaires,'' Lettres Américaines, tom. I. let. 23.

[59] La Place, who suggests the analogy, frankly admits the difficulty.
Système du Monde, lib. 5, ch 3.

dently to another such catastrophe, to take place, like the preceding, at the close of a cycle, when the sun was to be effaced from the heavens, the human race, from the earth, and when the darkness of chaos was to settle on the habitable globe. The cycle would end in the latter part of December, and, as the dreary season of the winter solstice approached, and the diminished light of day gave melancholy presage of its speedy extinction, their apprehensions increased; and, on the arrival of the five "unlucky" days which closed the year, they abandoned themselves to despair.[60] They broke in pieces the little images of their household gods, in whom they no longer trusted. The holy fires were suffered to go out in the temples, and none were lighted in their own dwellings. Their furniture and domestic utensils were destroyed; their garments torn in pieces; and everything was thrown into disorder, for the coming of the evil genii who were to descend on the desolate earth

On the evening of the last day, a procession of priests, assuming the dress and ornaments of their gods, moved from the capital towards a lofty mountain, about two leagues distant. They carried with them a noble victim, the flower of their captives, and an apparatus for kindling the *new fire*, the success of which was an augury of the renewal of the cycle. On reaching the summit of the mountain, the procession paused till midnight; when, as the constellation of the Pleiades approached the zenith,[61] the *new fire* was kindled by the friction of the sticks placed on the wounded breast of the victim.[62] The flame was soon communicated to a funeral pile, on which the body of the slaughtered captive was thrown. As the light streamed up towards heaven, shouts of joy and triumph burst forth from the countless multitudes who covered the hills, the terraces of the temples and the

[60] M. Jomard errs in placing the *new fire*, with which ceremony the old cycle properly concluded, at the winter solstice. It was not till the 26th day of December, if Gama is right. The cause of M. Jomard's error is his fixing it before, instead of after, the complementary days. See his sensible letter on the Aztec calendar, in the Vues des Cordillères p. 309.

[61] At the actual moment of their culmination, according to both Sahagun (Hist. de Nueva España, lib. 4, Apend.) and Torquemada (Monarch. Ind., lib. 10, cap. 33, 36). But this could not be, as that took place at midnight, in November; so late as the last secular festival, which was early in Montezuma's reign, in 1507. (Gama, Descripcion, Parte 1, p. 50, nota —Humboldt, Vues des Cordillères, pp. 181, 182.) The longer we postpone the beginning of the new cycle, the greater still must be the discrepancy.

[62] "On his bare breast the cedar boughs are laid;
On his bare breast, dry sedge and odorous gums
Lay ready to receive the sacred spark
And blaze, to herald the ascending Sun,
Upon his living altar."
SOUTHEY's Madoc, part 2, canto 16.

house-tops, with yet anxiously bent on the mount of sacrifice. Couriers, with torches lighted at the blazing beacon, rapidly bore them over every part of the country; and the cheering element was seen brightening on altar and hearthstone, for the circuit of many a league, long before the sun, rising on his accustomed track, gave assurance that a new cycle had commenced its march, and that the laws of nature were not to be reversed for the Aztecs.

The following thirteen days were given up to festivity. The houses were cleansed and whitened. The broken vessels were replaced by new ones. The people, dressed in their gayest apparel, and crowned with garlands and chaplets of flowers, thronged in joyous procession, to offer up their oblations and thanksgivings in the temples. Dances and games were instituted, emblematical of the regeneration of the world. It was the carnival of the Aztecs; or rather the national jubilee, the great secular festival, like that of the Romans, or ancient Etruscans, which few alive had witnessed before,—or could expect to see again.[63]

[63] I borrow the words of the summons by which the people were called to the *ludi seculares*, the secular games of ancient Rome, "*quos nec spectâsset quisquam, nec spectaturus esset.*" (Suetonius, Vita Tib. Claudii, lib. 5.) The old Mexican chroniclers warm into something like eloquence in their descriptions of the Aztec festival, (Torquemada, Monarch. Ind., lib. 10, cap. 33.—Toribio, Hist de los Indios, MS., Parte 1, cap. 5.—Sahagun, Hist. de Nueva España, lib. 7, cap. 9-12. See also, Gama Descripcion, Parte 1, pp. 52-54,—Clavigero, Stor. del Messico, tom. II. pp. 84-86.) The English reader will find a more brilliant coloring of the same scene in the canto of Madoc, above cited,—" On the Close of the Century."

M. de Humboldt remarked, many years ago, It were to be wished that some government would publish at its own expense the remains of the ancient American civilization; for it is only by the comparison of several monuments, that we can succeed in discovering the meaning of these allegories, which are partly astronomical, and partly mystic." This enlightened wish has now been realized, not by any government, but by a private individual Lord Kingsborough. The great work, published under his auspices, and so often cited in this Introduction, appeared in London in 1830. When completed, it will reach to nine volumes, seven of which are now before the public. Some idea of its magnificence may be formed by those who have not seen it, from the fact, that copies of it, with colored plates, sold originally at £175, and, with uncolored, at £120. The price has been since much reduced. It is designed to exhibit a complete view of the ancient Aztec MSS., with such few interpretations as exist; the beautiful drawings of Castañeda relating to Central America, with the commentary of Dupaix; the unpublished history of father Sahagun; and, last, not least, the copious annotations of his Lordship.

Too much cannot be said of the mechanical execution of the book,—its splendid typography, the apparent accuracy and the delicacy of the drawings, and the sumptuous quality of the materials. Yet the purchaser would have been saved some superfluous expense, and the reader much inconvenience, if the letter-press had been in volumes of an ordinary size. But it is not uncommon, in works on this magnificent plan, to find utility in some measure sacrificed to show.

The collection of Aztec MSS., if not perfectly complete, is very extensive and reflects great credit on the diligence and research of the compiler. It strikes one as strange, however, that not a single document should have been drawn from Spain. Peter Martyr speaks of a number having been brought thither in his time. (De Insulis nuper Inventis, p. 368.) The Marquis Spineto examined one in the Escurial, being the same with the Mendoza Codex, and perhaps the original, since that at Oxford is but a copy. (Lectures, lec. 7.) Mr. Waddilove, chaplain of the British embassy to Spain, gave a particular account of one to Dr. Robertson, which he saw in the same library, and considered an Aztec calendar. Indeed, it is scarcely possible that the frequent voyagers to the New World should not have furnished the mother-country with abundant specimens of this most interesting feature of Aztec civilization. Nor should we fear that the present liberal government would seclude these treasures from the inspection of the scholar.

Much cannot be said in favor of the arrangement of these codices. In some of them, as the Mendoza Codex, for example, the plates are not even numbered; and one who would study them by the corresponding interpretations, must often bewilder himself in the maze of hieroglyphics, without a clue to guide him. Neither is there any attempt to enlighten us as to the positive value and authenticity of the respective documents, or even their previous history beyond a barren reference to the particular library from which they have been borrowed. Little light, indeed can be expected on these matters; but we have not that little.—The defect of arrangement is chargeable on other parts of the work. Thus, for instance, the sixth book of Sahagun is transferred from the body of the history to which it belongs, to a preceding volume; while the grand hypothesis of his lordship, for which the work was concocted, is huddled into notes, hitched on random passages of the text, with a good deal less connection than the stories of queen Scheherazade, in the " Arabian Nights," and not quite so entertaining.

The drift of Lord Kingsborough's speculations is, to establish the colonization of Mexico by the Israelites. To this the whole battery of his logic and learning is directed. For this hieroglyphics are unriddled, manuscripts compared, monuments delineated. His theory, however, whatever be its merits, will scarcely become popular; since, instead of being exhibited in a clear and comprehensive form, readily embraced by the mind, it is spread over an infinite number of notes, thickly sprinkled with quotations, from languages ancient and modern, till the weary reader, floundering about in the ocean of fragments, with no light to guide him, feels like Milton's Devil, working his way through chaos,—

> " neither sea
> Nor good dry land ; nigh foundered, on he fares."

It would be unjust, however, not to admit that the noble author, if his logic is not always convincing, shows much acuteness in detecting analogies; that he displays familiarity with his subject, and a fund of erudition, though it often runs to waste ; that whatever be the defects of arrangement, he has brought together a most rich collection of unpublished materials to illustrate the Aztec, and in a wider sense, American antiquities ; and that, by this munificent undertaking, which no government, probably, would have and few individuals coul⌐ .⌐ , executed, he has entitled himself to the lasting gratitude of every friend oʻ .ence.

Another writer, whose works must be diligently consulted by every student of Mexican antiquities, is Antonio Gama. His life contains as few incidents as those of most scholars. He was born at Mexico, in 1735, of a respectable family, and was bred to the law. He early showed a preference for mathematical studies, conscious that in this career lay his strength. In 1771, he communicated his observations on the eclipse of that year to the French astronomer M. de Lalande, who published them in Paris, with high commendations, of the author. Gama's increasing reputation attracted the attention of government; and he was employed by it, in various scientific labors of importance. His great passion, however, was the study of Indian antiquities. He made himself acquainted with the history of the native races, their traditions. their languages, and, as far as possible, their hieroglyphics. He had an oportunity of showing the fruits of this preparatory training, and his skill as an antiquary, on the discovery of the great calendar-stone, in 1790. He produced a masterly treatise on this, and another Aztec monument, explaining the objects to which they were devoted, and pouring a flood of light on the astronomical science of the Aborigines, their mythology, and their astrological system. He afterwards continued his investigations in the same path and wrote treatises on the dial, hieroglyphics, and arithmetic of the Indians. These, however, were not given to the world till a few years since, when they were published, together with a reprint of the former work, under the auspices of the industrious Bustamante. Gama died in 1802; leaving behind him a reputation for great worth in private life; one, in which the bigotry, that seems to enter too frequently into the character of the Spanish-Mexican, was tempered by the liberal feelings of a man of science. His reputation as a writer stands high for patient acquisition, accuracy and acuteness. His conclusions are neither warped by the love of theory so common in the philosopher, nor by the easy credulity so natural to the antiquary. He feels his way with the caution of a mathematician, whose steps are demonstrations. M. de Humboldt was largely indebted to his first work, as he has emphatically acknowledged. But not withstanding the eulogiums of this popular writer, and his own merits, Gama's treatises are rarely met with out of New Spain, and his name can hardly be said to have a transatlantic reputation.

CHAPTER V.

AZTEC AGRICULTURE.—MECHANICAL ARTS.—MERCHANTS.—
DOMESTIC MANNERS.

IT is hardly possible that a nation, so far advanced as the
Aztecs in mathematical science, should not have made considerable progress in the mechanical arts, which are so nearly connected with it. Indeed, intellectual progress of any kind implies
a degree of refinement, that requires a certain cultivation of
both useful and elegant art. The savage, wandering through
the wide forest, without shelter for his head, or raiment for his
back, knows no other wants than those of animal appetites ; and,
when they are satisfied, seems to himself to have answered the
only ends of existence. But man, in society, feels numerous
desires, and artificial tastes spring up, accommodated to the
various relations in which he is placed, and perpetually
stimulating his invention to devise new expedients to gratify
them.

There is a wide difference in the mechanical skill of different
nations ; but the difference is still greater in the inventive
power which directs this skill, and makes it available. Some
nations seem to have no power beyond that of imitation ; or, if
they possess invention, have it in so low a degree, that they are
constantly repeating the same idea, without a shadow of alteration or improvement ; as the bird builds precisely the same
kind of nest which those of its own species built at the beginning
of the world. Such, for example, are the Chinese, who have,
probably, been familiar for ages with the germs of some discoveries, of little practical benefit to themselves, but which,
under the influence of European genius, have reached a degree
of excellence, that has wrought an important change in the constitution of society.

Far from looking back, and forming itself slavishly on the
past, it is characteristic of the European intellect to be ever on
the advance. Old discoveries become the basis of new ones.
It passes onward from truth to truth, connecting the whole by a
succession of links, as it were, into the great chain of science
which is to encircle and bind together the universe. The light
of learning is shed over the labors of art. New avenues are

opened for the communication both of person and of thought. New facilities are devised for subsistence. Personal comforts, of every kind, are inconceivably multiplied, and brought within the reach of the poorest. Secure of these, the thoughts travel into a nobler region than that of the senses ; and the appliances of art are made to minister to the demands of an elegant taste, and a higher moral culture.

The same enlightened spirit, applied to agriculture, raises it from a mere mechanical drudgery, or the barren formula of traditional precepts, to the dignity of a science. As the composition of the earth is analyzed, man learns the capacity of the soil that he cultivates ; and, as his empire is gradually extended over the elements of nature, he gains the power to stimulate her to her most bountiful and various production. It is with satis-faction that we can turn to the land of our fathers, as the one in which the experiment has been conducted on the broadest scale, and attended with results that the world has never before wit-nessed. With equal truth, we may point to the Anglo-Saxon race in both hemispheres, as that whose enterprising genius has contributed most essentially to the great interests of humanity, by the application of science to the useful arts.

Husbandry, to a very limited extent, indeed, was practised by most of the rude tribes of North America. Wherever a natural opening in the forest, or a rich strip of *interval*, met their eyes, or a green slope was found along the rivers, they planted it with beans and Indian corn.[1] The cultivation was slovenly in the extreme, and could not secure the improvident natives from the frequent recurrence of desolating famines. Still, that they tilled the soil at all was a peculiarity which hon-orably distinguished them from other tribes of hunters, and raised them one degree higher in the scale of civilization.

Agriculture in Mexico was in the same advanced state as the other arts of social life. In few countries, indeed, has it been more respected. It was closely interwoven with the civil and religious institutions of the nation. There were peculiar deities to preside over it ; the names of the months and of the religious festivals had more or less reference to it. The public taxes, as we have seen, were often paid in agricultural produce. All, except the soldiers and great nobles, even the inhabitants

---

[1] This latter grain, according to Humboldt, was found by the **Europeans in** the New World, from the South of Chili to Pennsylvania ; (Essai Politique, tom. II. p. 408 ;) he might have added, to the St. Lawrence. Our Puritan fathers found it in abundance on the New England coast, wherever they landed. See Morton, New England's Memorial, (Boston. 1826,) p. 68. –Gookin, Massa-chusetts Historical Collections, chap. 3.

of the cities, cultivated the soil. The work was chiefly done by the men ; the women scattering the seed, husking the corn, and taking part only in the lighter labors of the field.[2] In this they presented an honorable contrast to the other tribes of the continent, who imposed the burden of agriculture, severe as it is in the North, on their women.[8] Indeed, the sex was as tenderly regarded by the Aztecs in this matter, as it is, in most parts of Europe, at the present day.

There was no want of judgment in the management of their ground. When somewhat exhausted, it was permitted to recover by lying fallow. Its extreme dryness was relieved by canals, with which the land was partially irrigated ; and the same end was promoted by severe penalties against the destruction of the woods, with which the country, as already noticed, was well covered before the Conquest. Lastly, they provided for their harvests ample granaries, which were admitted by the Conquerors to be of admirable construction. In this provision we see the forecast of civilized man.[4]

Among the most important arcticles of husbandry, we may notice the banana, whose facility of cultivation and exuberant returns are so fatal to habits of systematic and hardy industry.[t] Another celebrated plant was the cacao, the fruit of which

---

[2] Torquemada, Monarch. Ind., lib. 13, cap. 31.

"Admirable example for our times," exclaims the good father, "when women are not only unfit for the labors of the field, but have too much levity to attend to their own household ! "

[8] A striking contrast also to the Egyptians, with whom some antiquaries are disposed to 'dentify the ancient Mexicans. Sophocles notices the effeminacy of the men in Egypt, who stayed at home tending the loom, while their wives were employed in severe labors out of doors.

> "Ὦ πάντ'ἐκείνω τοῖς ἐν Αἰγύπτῳ νόμοις
> Φύσιν κατεικασθέντε καὶ βίου τροφάς.
> Ἐκεῖ γὰρ οἱ μὲν ἄρσενες κατὰ στέγας
> Θακοῦσιν ἰστουργοῦντες · αἱ δὲ σύννομοι
> Τἄξω βίου τροφεῖα πορσύνουσ' ἀεί."
>
> SOPHOCL., Œdip Col., v. 337-341.

[4] Torquemada, Monarch. Ind., lib. 13. cap 32.—Clavigero, Stor. del Messico, tom II. pp. 153-155.

"Jamas pedeciéron hambre," says the former writer, sino en pocas ocasiones." If these famines were rare, they were very distressing, however, and lasted very long. Comp. Ixtlilxochitl, Hist. Chich., MS., cap 41, 71, et alibi.

[t] Oviedo considers the *musa* an important plant ; and Hernandez, in his copious catalogue, makes no mention of it at all. But Humboldt, who has given much attention to it, concludes, that if some species were brought into the country, others were indigenous. (Essai Politique, tom. II. pp. 382-388) If we may credit Clavigero, the bananas was the forbidden fruit that tempted our poor mother Eve ! Stor. del Messico, tom. 1. p. 49. nota.

furnished the chocolate,—from the Mexican *chocolatl*,—now so common a beverage throughout Europe.[6] The vanilla, confined to a small district of the seacoast, was used for the same purposes, of flavoring their food and drink, as with us.[7] The great staple of the country, as, indeed, of the American continent, was maize, or Indian corn, which grew freely along the valleys, and up the steep sides of the Cordilleras to the high level of the table-land. The Aztecs were as curious in its preparation, and as well intructed in its manifold uses, as the most expert New England housewife. Its gigantic stalks, in these equinoctial regions, afford a saccharine matter, not found to the same extent in northern latitudes, and supplied the natives with sugar little inferior to that of the cane itself, which was not introduced among them till after the Conquest.[8] But the miracle of nature was the great Mexican aloe, or *maguey*, whose clustering pyramids of flowers, towering above their dark coronals of leaves, were seen sprinkled over many a broad acre of the table-land. As we have already noticed, its bruised leaves afforded a paste from which paper was manufactured;[9] its juice was fermented into an intoxicating beverage, *palque*, of which the natives, to this day, are excessively fond;[10] its leaves further supplied an impenetrable thatch for the more humble dwellings; thread, of which coarse stuffs were made, and strong cords, were drawn from its tough and twisted fibres; pins and needles were made of the thorns at the extremity of its leaves; and the root, when properly cooked, was converted into a palatable and nutritious food. The *agave*, in short, was meat, drink, clothing, and writing materials, for the Aztec! Surely, never

---

[6] Rel. d'un gent., ap. Ramusio, tom III. fol. 306.—Hernandez, De Historiâ Plantarum Novæ Hispanæ, (Matriti, 1790,) lib. 6, cap. 87.

[7] Sahagun, Hist. de Nueva España, lib. 8. cap. 13, et alibi.

[8] Carta del. Lic. Zuazo, MS.
He extols the honey of the maize, as equal to that of bees.
(Also Oviedo, Hist. Naturel de las Indias, cap. 4, ap. Barcia, tom. I.) Hernandez, who celebrates the manifold ways in which the maize was prepared, derives it from the Haytian word, *mahiz*. Hist. Plantarum, lib. 6, cap. 44, 45.

[9] And is still, in one spot at least, San Angel,—three leagues from the capital. Another mill was to have been established, a few years since, in Puebla. Whether this has actually been done I am ignorant. See the Report of the Committee on Agriculture to the Senate of the United States, March 12, 1838.

[10] Before the Revolution, the duties on the *pulque* formed so important a branch of revenue, that the cities of Mexico, Puebla, and Toluca alone, paid $817,739 to government. (Humboldt, Essai Politique, tom. II. p. 47.) It requires time to reconcile Europeans to the peculiar flav- of this liquor, on the merits of which they are consequently much divided. There is but one opinion among the natives. The English reader will find a good account of its manufacture in Ward's Mexico, vol. II. pp. 55-60.

did Nature enclose in so compact a form so many of the ele‑ ments of human comfort and civilization![11]

It would be obviously out of place to enumerate in these pages all the varieties of plants, many of them of medicinal virtue, which have been introduced from Mexico into Europe. Still less can I attempt a catalogue of its flowers, which, with their variegated and gaudy colors, form the greatest attraction of our greenhouses. The opposite climates embraced within the narrow latitudes of New Spain have given to it properly, the richest and most diversified Flora to be found in any country on the globe. These different products were systematically arranged by the Aztecs, who understood their properties, and collected them into nurseries, more extensive than any then existing in the Old World. It is not improbable that they suggested the idea of those " gardens of plants " which were introduced into Europe not many years after the Conquest.[12]

The Mexicans were as well acquainted with the mineral, as with the vegetable treasures of their kingdom. Silver, lead, and tin they drew from the mines of Tasco ; copper from the mountains of Zacotollan. These were taken not only from the crude masses on the surface, but from veins wrought in the solid rock, into which they opened extensive galleries. In fact, the traces of their labors furnished the best indications for the early Spanish miners. Gold, found on the surface, or gleaned from the beds of rivers, was cast into bars, or, in the form of dust, made part of the regular tribute of the southern provinces

[11] Hernandez enumerates the several species of the maguey, which are turned to these manifold uses, in his learned work, De Hist. Plantarum. Lib. 7, cap. 71 et seq.) M. de Humboldt considers them all varieties of the *agave Americana,* familiar in the southern parts, both of the United States and Europe. (Essai Politique, tom. II p. 487. et seq.) This opinion has brought on him a rather sour rebuke from our countryman, the late Dr. Perrine, who pronounces them a distinct species from the American *agave ;* and regards one of the kinds, the *pita,* from which the fine thread is obtained, as a totally distinct genus. (See the Report of the Committee on Agriculture). Yet the Baron may find authority for all the properties ascribed by him to the maguey, in the most accredited writers, who have resided more or less time in Mexico. See, among others, Hernandez, ubi supra.—Sahagun, Hist. de Nueva España, lib. 9, cap. 2 ; lib. 11, cap. 7.—Toribio, Hist. de los Indios, MS., Parte 3, cap. 19 —Carta del Lic. Zuazo, MS The last, speaking of the maguey, which produces the fermented drink, says expressly, " De lo que queda de las dichas hojas se aprovechan, como de lino mui delgado, ó de Olanda, de que hacen lienzos mui primos para vestir, é bien delgados." It cannot be denied, however, that Dr. Perrine shows himself intimately acquainted with the structure and habits of the tropical plants, which, with such patriotic spirit, he proposed to introduce into Florida.

[12] The first regular establishment of this kind, according to Carli, was at Padua, in 1545. Lettres Améric., tom. 1. chap. 21.

of the empire. The use of iron, with which the soil was impregnated, was unknown to them. Notwithstanding its abundance, it demands so many processes to prepare it for use, that
it has commonly been one of the last metals pressed into the
service of man. The age of iron has followed that of brass, in
fact as well as in fiction.[13]

They found a substitute in an alloy of tin and copper; and,
with tools made of this bronze, could cut not only metals, but,
with the aid of a silicious dust, the hardest substances, as basalt,
porphyry, amethysts, and emeralds.[14] They fashioned these
last, which were found very large, into many curious and fantastic forms. They cast, also, vessels of gold and silver, carv-
ing them with their metallic chisels in a very delicate manner.
Some of the silver vases were so large that a man could not
encircle them with his arms. They imitated very nicely the
figures of animals, and, what was extraordinary, could mix the
metals in such a manner, that the feathers of a bird, or the
scales of a fish, should be alternately of gold and silver. The
Spanish goldsmiths admitted their superiority over themselves
in these ingenious works.[15]

---

[13] P. Martyr, De Orbe Novo, Decades, (Compluti, 1530,) dec. 5, p. 191.—
Acosta lib. 4, cap. 3.—Humboldt, Essai Politique, tom. III. pp. 114—125.—
Torquemada, Monarch. Ind., lib. 13, cap. 34.
  "Men wrought in brass," says Hesiod, "when iron did not exist."

Χαλκῷ δ᾽ ἐργάζοντο μέλας δ᾽ οὐκ ἔσκε σίδηρος.

HESIOD.

The Abbé Raynal contends that the ignorance of iron must necessarily have
kept the Mexicans in a low state of civilization, since without it "they could
have produced no work in metal, worth looking at, no masonry nor architecture, engraving, nor sculpture." (History of the Indies, Eng. trans., vol. III.
b. 6.) Iron, however, if known, was little used by the Ancient Egyptians,
whose mighty monuments were hewn with bronze tools, while their weapons
and domestic utensils were of the same material, as appears from the green
color given to them in their paintings.
[14] Gama, Descripcion, Parte 2, pp. 25-29.—Torquemada, Monarch, Ind.,
ubi supra.
[15] Sahagun, Hist. de Nueva España, lib. 9, cap. 15-17.—Boturini, Idea, p.
77.—Torquemada, monarch. Ind., loc. cit.
  Herrera, who says they could also enamel, commends the skill of the Mexican goldsmiths in making birds and animals with movable wings and limbs,
in a most curious fashion. (Hist. General, dec. 2, lib. 7, cap. 15.) Sir John
Maundeville, as usual,

                               " with his hair on end
          At his own wonders,"

notices the "gret marvayle" of similar pieces of mechanism, at the court of
the grand Chane of Cathay. See his Voiage and Travaile, chap. 20.

They employed another tool, made of *itztli*, or obsidian, a dark transparent mineral, exceedingly hard, found in abundance in their hills. They made it into knives, razors, and their serrated swords. It took a keen edge, though soon blunted. With this they wrought the various stones and alabasters employed in the construction of their public works and principal dwellings. I shall defer a more particular account of these to the body of the narrative, and will only add here, that the entrances and angles of the buildings were profusely ornamented with images, sometimes of their fantastic deities, and frequently of animals.[16] The latter were executed with great accuracy. "The former," according to Torquemada, "were the hideous reflection of their own souls. And it was not till after they had been converted to Christianity, that they could model the true figure of a man."[17] The old chronicler's facts are well founded. whatever we may think of his reasons. The allegorical phantasms of his religion, no doubt, gave a direction to the Aztec artist, in his delineation of the human figure ; supplying him with an imaginary beauty in the personification of divinity itself. As these superstitions lost their hold on his mind, it opened to the influences of a purer taste ; and, after the Conquest, the Mexicans furnished many examples of correct, and some of beautiful portraiture.

Sculptured images were so numerous, that the foundations of the cathedral in the *plaza mayor*, the great square of Mexico, are said to be entirely composed of them.[18] This spot may, indeed, be regarded as the Aztec forum,—the great depository of the treasures of ancient sculpture, which now lie hid in its bosom. Such monuments are spread all over the capital, however, and a new cellar can hardly be dug, or foundation laid, without turning up some of the mouldering relics of barbaric art. But they are little heeded, and, if not wantonly broken in pieces at once, are usually worked into the rising wall, or supports of the new edifice.[19] Two celebrated bas-reliefs, of the last Montezuma and his father, cut in the solid rock, in the beautiful groves of Chapoltepec, was deliberately destroyed, as late as the last cen-

[16] Herrera, Hist. General, dec. 2, lib. 7, cap. 11. Torquemada, Monarch. Ind., lib. 13, cap. 34.—Gama, Description, Parte 2, pp. 27, 28.

[17] " Parece, que permitia Dios, que la figure de sus cuerpos se asimilase á la que tenian sus almas, por el pecado, en que siempre permanecian." Monarch. Ind., lib. 13, cap. 34.

[18] Clavigero, Stor. del Messico, tom. II. p. 195.

[19] Gama, Descripcion, Parte I. p. 1. Besides the *plaza mayor*, Gama points out the Square of Tlatelolco, as a great cemetery of ancient relics. It was the quarter to which the Mexicans retreated, on the siege of the capital

tury, by order of *t'.-* government![20]   The monuments of the
barbarian meet with as little respect from civilized man, as those
of the civilized man from the barbarian.[21]

The most remarkable piece of sculpture yet disinterred is the
great calendar-stone, noticed in the preceding chapter. It con-
sists of dark porphyry, and, in its original dimensions, as taken
from the quarry, is computed to have weighed nearly fifty tons.
It was transported from the mountains beyond Lake Chalco, a
distance of many leagues, over a broken country intersected by
water-courses and canals.   In crossing a bridge which traversed
one of these latter, in the capital, the supports gave way, and
the huge mass was precipitated into the water, whence it was
with difficulty recovered.   The fact that so enormous a fragment
of porphyry could be thus safely carried for leagues, in the face
of such obstacles, and without the aid of cattle,—for the Aztecs,
as already mentioned, had no animals of draught,—suggests to
us no mean ideas of their mechanical skill, and of their ma
chinery ; and implies a degree of cultivation, little inferior to
that demanded for the geometrical and astronomical science displayed in the inscriptions on this very stone.[22]

The ancient Mexicans made utensils of earthern ware for the
ordinary purposes of domestic life, numerous specimens of which
still exist.[23]   They made cups and vases of a lackered or painted

[20] Torquemada, Monarch. Ind., lib. 13, cap. 34.—Gama, Descripcion,
Parte 2, pp. 81–83.

These statues are repeatedly noticed by the old writers. The last was
destroyed in 1754, when it was seen by Gama, who highly commends the
execution of it. Ibid.

[21] This wantonness of destruction provokes the bitter animadversion of
Martyr, whose enlightened mind respected the vestiges of civilization wherever found. "The conquerors," he says, "seldom repaired the buildings
that were defaced. They would rather sack twenty stately cities, than
erect one good edifice." De Orbe Novo, dec. 5, cap. 10.

[22] Gama, Descripcion, Parte I. pp. 110–114.—Humboldt, Essai Politique,
tom. II, p. 40.

Ten thousand men were employed in the transportation of this enormous
mass, according to Tezozomoc, whose narrative, with all the accompanying
prodigies, is minutely transcribed by Bustamante. The Licentiate shows an
appetite for the marvellous, which might excite the envy of a monk of the
Middle Ages. (See Descripcion, nota, loc. cit.) The English traveller,
Latrobe, accommodates the wonders of nature and art very well to each other
by suggesting that these great masses of stone were transported by means of
the mastodon, whose remains are occasionally disinterred in the Mexican
Valley. Rambler in Mexico, p. 145.

[23] A great collection of ancient pottery, with various other specimens of
Aztec art, the gift of Messrs Poinsett and Keating, is deposited in the
Cabinet of the American Philosophical Society, at Philadelphia. See the
Catalogue, ap. Transactions, vol. III. p. 510.

wood, impervious to wet and gaudily colored. Their **dyes were** obtained from both mineral and vegetable substances. Among them was the rich crimson of the cochineal, the modern rival of the famed Tyrian purple. It was introduced into Europe from Mexico, where the curious little insect was nourished with great care on plantations of cactus, since fallen into neglect.[24] The natives were thus enabled to give a brilliant coloring to the webs, which were manufactured of every degree of fineness, from the cotton raised in abundance throughout the warmer regions of the country. They had the art, also, of interweaving with these the delicate hair of rabbits and other animals, which made a cloth of great warmth as well as beauty, of a kind altogether original ; and on this they often laid a rich embroidery, of birds, flowers or some other fanciful device.[25]

But the art in which they most delighted was their *plumaje,* or feather-work. With this they could produce all the effect of a beautiful mosaic. The gorgeous plumage of the tropical birds, especially of the parrot tribe, afforded every variety of color ; and the fine down of the humming bird, which revelled in swarms among the honeysuckle bowers of Mexico, supplied them with soft aërial tints that gave an exquisite finish to the picture. The feathers, pasted on a fine cotton web, were wrought into dresses for the wealthy, hangings for apartments, and ornaments for the temples. No one of the American fabrics excited such admiration in Europe, whither numerous specimens were sent by the Conquerors. It is to be regretted, that so graceful an art should have been suffered to fall into decay.[26]

There were no shops in Mexico, but the various manufactures

---

[24] Hernandez, Hist. Plantarum, lib. 6, cap. 116.

[25] Carta del Lic. Zuazo, MS.—Herrera, Hist. General, dec. 2, lib. 7 cap. 15. —Boturini, Idea, p. 77.

It is doubtful how far they were acquainted with the manufacture of silk. Carli supposes that what Cortés calls silk was only the fine texture of hair, or down, mentioned in the text. (Lettres Améric., tom. I. let. 21.) But it is certain they had a species of caterpillar, unlike our silkworm, indeed, which spun a thread that was sold in the markets of ancient Mexico. See the Essai Politique, (tom. III. pp. 66–69,) where M. de Humboldt has collected some interesting facts in regard to the culture of silk by the Aztecs. Still, that the fabric should be matter of uncertainty at all shows that it could not have reached any great excellence or extent.

[26] Carta del Lic. Zuazo, MS.—Acosta, lib. 4. cap. 37.—Sahagun, Hist. de Nueva España, lib. 9, cap. 18–21.—Toribio, Hist de los Indios, MS., Parte I, cap. 15,—Rel. d'un gent., ap. Ramusio, tom. III. fol. 306.

Count Carli is in raptures with a specimen of feather-painting which he saw in Strasbourg. "Never did I behold anything so exquisite," he says, "for brillancy and nice gradation of color, and for beauty of design. No European artist could have made such a thing " (Lettres Améric., let. 21,

and agricultural products were brought together for sale in the
great market-places of the principal cities. Fairs were held
there every fifth day, and were thronged by a numerous concourse of persons, who came to buy or sell from all the neighboring country. A particular quarter was allotted to each kind
of article. The numerous transactions were conducted without
confusion, and with entire regard to justice, under the inspection of magistrates appointed for the purpose. The traffic was
carried on partly by barter, and partly by means of a regulated
currency, of different values. This consisted of transparent
quills of gold dust ; of bits of tin, cut in the form of a T ; and of
bags of cacao, containing a specified number of grains. " Blessed
money," exclaims Peter Martyr, " which exempts its possessors
from avarice, since it cannot be long hoarded, nor hidden under
ground ! " [27]

There did not exist in Mexico that distinction of castes found
among the Egyptian and Asiatic nations. It was usual, however, for the son to follow the occupation of his father. The
different trades were arranged into something like guilds ; having, each, a particular district of the city appropriated to it, with
its own chief, its own tutelar deity, its peculiar festivals, and the
like. Trade was held in avowed estimation by the Aztecs.
" Apply thyself, my son," was the advice of an aged chief, " to
agriculture, or to feather-work, or some other honorable calling.
Thus did your ancestors before you. Else, how would they have
provided for themselves and their families? Never was it heard
that nobility alone was able to maintain its possessor." [28] Shrewd
maxims, that must have sounded somewhat strange in the ear of
a Spanish *hidalgo!* " [29]

note.) There is still one place, Patzquaro, where, according to Bustamante,
they preserve some knowledge of this interesting art, though it is practised
on a very limited scale, and at great cost. Sahagun, ubi supra, nota.

[27] " O felicem monetam, quæ suavem utilemque præbet humano generi
potum, et a tartareu peste avaritiæ sous immunes servat possessores; quod
suffodi aut diu servari nequeat ! " De Orbe Novo, dec. 5, cap. 4.—(See, also.
Carta de Cortés, ap. Lorenzana, p, 100 et seq.—Sahagun, Hist. de Nueva
España, lib. 8, cap. 36.—Toribio, Hist. de los Indios, MS., Parte 3, cap. 8,
—Carta del Lic. Zuazo, MS.) The substitute for money throughout the
Chinese empire was equally simple in Marco Polo's time, consisting of bits
of stamped paper, made from the inner bark of the mulberry-tree. See
Viaggi di Messer Marco Polo, gentil'huomo Venetiano, lib. 2, cap. 18, ap.
Ramusio, tom. II.

[28] " Procurad de saber algun *oficio honroso* como es el hacer obras de pluma
à otros oficios mecenicos. . . . . . Mirad que tengais cuidado de lo tocante
á la agricultura. . . . . En ninguna parte he visto que alguno se mantenga
por su nobleza." Sahagun, Hist. de Nueva España, lib. 6, cap. 17.

[29] Col. de Mendoza, ap Antiq. of Mexico, vol. I. Pl. 71; vol. VI. p. 86.—
Torquemada, Monarch. Ind., lib. 2. cap. 41.

But the occupation peculiarly respected was that of the merchant. It formed so important and singular a feature of their social economy, as to merit a much more particular notice than it has received from historians. The Aztec merchant was a sort of itinerant trader, who made his journeys to the remotest borders of Anahuac, and to the countries beyond, carrying with him merchandise of rich stuffs, jewelry, slaves, and other valuable commodities. The slaves were obtained at the great market of Azcapozalco, not many leagues from the capital, where, fairs were regularly held for the sale of these unfortunate beings. They were brought thither by their masters, dressed in their gayest apparel, and instructed to sing, dance, and display their little stock of personal accomplishments, so as to recommend themselves to the purchaser. Slave-dealing was an honorable calling among the Aztecs.[30]

With this rich freight, the merchant visited the different provinces, always bearing some present of value from his own sovereign to their chiefs, and usually receiving others in return, with a permission to trade. Should this be denied him, or should he meet with indignity or violence, he had the means of resistance in his power. He performed his journeys with a number of companions of his own rank, and a large body of inferior attendants who were employed to transport the goods. Fifty or sixty pounds were the usual load for a man. The whole caravan went armed, and so well provided against sudden hostilities, that they could make good their defence, if necessary, till reinforced from home. In one instance, a body of these militant traders stood a siege of four years in the town of Ayotlan, which they finally took from the enemy.[31] Their own government, however, was always prompt to embark in a war on this ground, finding it a very convenient pretext for extending the Mexican empire. It was not unusual to allow the merchants to raise levies themselves, which were placed under their command. It was, moreover, very common for the prince to employ the merchants as a sort of spies, to furnish him information of the state of the countries through which they passed, and the dispositions of the inhabitants towards himself.[32]

Thus their sphere of action was much enlarged beyond that of a humble trader, and they acquired a high consideration in the body politic. They were allowed to assume insignia and devices

---

[30] Sahagun, Hist. de Nueva España, lib. 9. cap. 4, 10-14.

[31] Ibid., lib. 9, cap. 2.

[32] Ibid., lib. 9, cap. 2, 4.

In the Mendoza Codex is a painting, representing the execution of a cacique and his family, with the destruction of his city, for maltreating the persons of some Aztec merchants. Antiq. of Mexico, vol. I. Pl. 67

of their own. Some of their number composed what is called
by the Spanish writers a council of finance ; at least, this was
the case in Tezcuco.[33] They were much consulted by the monarch, who had some of them constantly near his person ; addressing them by the title of "uncle," which may remind one of that
of *primo*, or " cousin " by which a grandee of Spain is saluted by
his sovereign. They were allowed to have their own courts, in
which civil and criminal cases, not excepting capital, were determined ; so that they formed an independent community, as it
were, of themselves. And, as their various traffic supplied them
with abundant stores of wealth, they enjoyed many of the most
essential advantages of an hereditary aristocracy.[34]

That trade should prove the path to eminent political preferment in a nation but partially civilized, where the names of
soldier and priest are usually the only titles to respect, is certainly an anomaly in history. It forms some contrast to the
standard of the more polished monarchies of the Old World, in
which rank is supposed to be less dishonored by a life of idle
ease or frivolous pleasure, than by those active pursuits which
promote equally the prosperity of the state and of the individual.
If civilization corrects many prejudices, it must be allowed that
it creates others.

We shall be able to form a better idea of the actual refinement of the natives, by penetrating into their domestic life and
observing the intercourse between the sexes. We have fortunately the means of doing this. We shall there find the ferocious
Aztec frequently displaying all the sensibility of a cultivated
nature ; consoling his friends under affliction, or congratulating
them on their good fortune, as on occasion of a marriage, or of
the birth or the baptism of a child, when he was punctilious in
his visits, bringing presents of costly dresses and ornaments, or
the more simple offering of flowers, equally indicative of his
sympathy. The visits, at these times, though regulated with all

---

[33] Torquemada, Monarch. Ind., lib. 2, cap. 41.

Ixtlilxochitl gives a curious story of one of the royal family of Tezcuco, who
offered, with two *other* merchants *otros mercaderes,* to visit the court of a hostile cacique, and bring him dead or alive to the capital. They availed themselves of a drunken revel, at which they were to have been sacrificed, to effect
their object. Hist. Chich., MS., cap. 62.

[34] Sahagun, Hist. de Nueva España, lib. 9, cap. 2, 5.

The ninth book is taken up with an account of the merchants, their pilgrimages, the religious rites on their departure, and the sumptuous way of living
on their return. The whole presents a very remarkable picture, showing they
enjoyed a consideration, among the half-civilized nations of Anahuac, to which
there is no parallel, unless it be that possessed by the merchant-princes of an
Italian republic, or the princely merchants of our own.

the precision of Oriental courtesy, were accompanied by expressions of the most cordial and affectionate regard.[35]

The discipline of children, especially at the public schools, as stated in a previous chapter, was exceedingly severe.[36] But after she had come to a mature age, the Aztec maiden was treated by her parents with a tenderness, from which all reserve seemed banished. In the counsels to a daughter about to enter into life, they conjured her to preserve simplicity in her manners and conversation, uniform neatness in her attire, with strict attention to personal cleanliness. They inculcated modesty, as the great ornament of a woman, and implicit reverence for her husband ; softening their admonitions by such endearing epithets as showed the fullness of a parent's love.[37]

Polygamy was permitted among the Mexicans, though chiefly confined, probably, to the wealthiest classes.[38] And the obligations of the marriage vow, which was made with all the formality of a religious ceremony, were fully recognized, and impressed on both parties. The women are described by the Spaniards as pretty, unlike their unfortunate descendants, of the

[36] Sahagun, Hist. de Nueva España, lib. 6, cap. 23-37.—Camargo, Hist. de Tlascala, MS.

These complimentary attentions were paid at stated seasons, even during pregnancy. The details are given with abundant gravity and minuteness by Sahagun, who descends to particulars which his Mexican editor, Bustamante, has excluded, as somewhat too unreserved for the public eye. If they were more so than some of the editor's own notes, they must have been very communicative indeed.

[36] Zurita, Rapport, pp, 112-134.

The Third Part of the Col. de Mendoza (Antiq. of Mexico, vol. I.) exhibits the various ingenious punishments devised for the refractory child. The flowery path of knowledge was well strewed with thorns for the Mexican tyro.

[37] Zurita, Rapport, pp. 151-160.

Sahagun has given us the admonitions of both father and mother to the Aztec maiden, on her coming to years of discretion. What can be more tender than the beginning of the mother's exhortation? "Hija mia muy amada, muy querida palomita: ya has oido y notado las palabras que tu señor padre te ha dicho; ellas son palabras preciosas, y que raramente se dicen ni se oyen, las quales han procedido de las entrañas y corazon en que estaban atesoradas ; y tu muy amado padre bien sabe que eres su hija, engendra de él, eres su sangre y su carne, y sabe Dios nuestro señor que es asi ; aunque eres muger, é imagen de tu padre? que mas, te puedo decir, hija mia, de lo que ya esta dicho?" (Hist. de Nueva España lib. 6, cap. 19.) The reader will find this interesting document, which enjoins so much of what is deemed most essential among civilized nations, translated entire in the *Appendix, Part 2, No 1.*

[38] Yet we find the remarkable declaration, in the counsels of a father to nis son, that, for the multiplication of the species, God ordained one man only for one woman. "Nota, hijo mio, lo que te digo, mira que el mundo ya tiene este estilo de engendrar y multiplicar, y para esta generacion y mul tiplicacion, ordeno Dios que una muger ••• • de un varon, y un varon de una muger." Ibid. lib. 6, cap. 21.

present day, though ·.ith .he same serious and rather melancholy
cast of countenan.... .'heir long black hair, covered in some
parts of the country, by a veil made of the fine web of the *pita*,
might generally be seen wreathed with flowers, or, among the
richer people, with strings of precious stones, and pearls from
the Gulf of California. They appear to have been treated with
much consideration by their husbands; and passed their time in
indolent tranquillity, or in such feminine occupations as spinning,
embroidery, and the like ; while their maidens beguiled the hours
by the rehearsal of traditionary tales and ballads.[39]

The women partook equally with the men of social festivities
and entertainments. These were often conducted on a large
scale, both as regards the number of guests and the costliness of
the preparations. Numerous attendants, of both sexes, waited
at the banquet. The halls were scented with perfumes, and
the courts strewed with odoriferous herbs and flowers, which
were distributed in profusion among the guests, as they arrived.
Cotton napkins and ewers of water were placed before them, as
they took their seats at the board; for the venerable ceremony
of ablution,[40] before and after eating, was punctiliously observed
by the Aztecs.[41] Tobacco was then offered to the company, in
pipes, mixed up with aromatic substances, or in the form of
cigars, inserted in tubes of tortoise-shell or silver. They com-
pressed the nostrils with the fingers, while they inhaled the

---

[39] Ibid., lib. 6, cap. 21-23; lib 8, cap. 23.—Rel. d'un gent., ap Ramusio,
tom. III. fol. 305.—Carta del Lic. Zuazo, MS.

[40] As old as the heroic age of Greece, at least. We may fancy ourselves at
the table of Penelope, where water in golden ewers was poured into silver
basins for the accommodation of her guests, before beginning the repast.

"Χέρνιβα δ' ἀμφίπολος προχόῳ ἐπέχευε φέρουσα
Καλῇ, χρυσείῃ, ὑπὲρ ἀργυρέοιο λέβητος,
Νίψασθαι · παρὰ δὲ ξεστὴν ἐτάνυσσε τράπεζαν.

The feast affords many other points of analogy to the Aztec, inferring a similar
stage of civilization in the two nations. One may be surprised, however,
to find a greater profusion of the precious metals in the barren isle of Ithaca,
than in Mexico. But the poet's fancy was a richer mine than either.

[41] Sahagun, Hist. de Nueva España, lib. 6, cap. 22.
Amidst some excellent advice of a parent to his son, on his general deportment, we find the latter punctilously enjoined not to take his seat at the board
till he has washed his face and hands, and not to leave it till he has repeated
the same thing, and *cleansed his teeth*. The directions are given with a precision worthy of an Asiatic. " Al principio de la comida labarte has las manos
y la boca, y donde te juntaras con otros á comer, no te sientes luego ; mas
antes tomáras el agua y la jicara para que se leben los otros, y echarles has
agua á los manos, y despues de esto, cojerá lo que sa ha caido por el suelo y
barrerás el lugar, de la comida y tambien despues de comer lavarás te las
manos y la boca, y limpiarás los dientes." Ibid., loc. cit.

smoke, which they frequently swallowed. Whether the women, who sat apart from the men at table, were allowed the indulgence of the fragrant weed, as in the most polished circles of modern Mexico, is not told us. It is a curious fact, that the Aztecs also took the dried leaf in the pulverized form of snuff.[42]

The table was well provided with substantial meats, especially game ; among which the most conspicuous was the turkey, erroneously supposed, as its name imports, to have come originally from the East.[43] These more solid dishes were flanked by others of vegetables and fruits, of every delicious variety found on the North American continent. The different viands were prepared in various ways, with delicate sauces and seasoning, of which the Mexicans were very fond. Their palate was still further regaled by confections and pastry, for which their maize-flour and sugar supplied ample materials. One other dish, of a disgusting nature, was sometimes added to the feast, especially when the celebration partook of a religious character. On such occasions a slave was sacrificed, and his flesh, elaborately

---

[42] Rel. d'un gent., ap. Ramusio, tom. III. fol. 306.—Sahagun, Hist. de Nueva España, lib. 4, cap. 37.—Torquemada, Monarch. Ind., lib. 13, cap. 23.—Clavigero, Stor. del Messico, tom. II. p. 227.

The Aztecs used to smoke after dinner, to prepare for the *siesta*, in which they indulged themselves as regularly as an old Castilian.—Tobacco, in Mexican *yetl*, is derived from a Haytian word, *tabaco*. The natives of Hispaniola, being the first with whom the Spaniards had much intercourse, have supplied Europe with the names of several important plants.—Tobacco, in some form or other, was used by almost all the tribes of the American continent, from the North-west Coast to Patagonia. (See McCulloh, Researches, pp. 91-94.) Its manifold virtues, both social and medicinal, are profusely panegyrized by Hernandez, in his Hist. Plantarum, lib. 2, cap. 109.

[43] This noble bird was introduced into Europe from Mexico. The Spanish called it *gallopavo*, from its resemblance to the peacock. See Rel. d'un gent., ap. Ramusio, (tom. III. fol. 306) ; also Oviedo, (Rel. Sumaria, cap. 38,) the earliest naturalist who gives an account of the bird, which he saw soon after the Conquest, in the West Indies, whither it had been brought, as he says, from New Spain. The Europeans, however, soon lost sight of its origin, and the name "turkey" intimated the popular belief of its Eastern origin. Several eminent writers have maintained its Asiatic or African descent ; but they could not impose on the sagacious and better instructed Buffon. (See Histoire Naturelle, Art. *Dindon*.) The Spaniards saw immense numbers of turkeys in the domesticated state, on their arrival in Mexico, where they were more common than any other poultry. They were found wild, not only in New Spain, but all along the continent, in the less frequented places, from the North-western territory of the United States to Panama. The wild turkey is larger, more beautiful, and every way an incomparably finer bird, than the tame. Franklin, with some point, as well as pleasantry, insists on its preference to the bald eagle, as the national emblem. (See his Works, vol. X. p. 63, in Sparks's excellent edition.) Interesting notices of the history and habits of the wild turkey may be found in the Ornithology both of Buonaparte and of that enthusiastic lover of nature, Audubon, *vox Meleagris Gallopavo*.

dressed, forme⸱ ⸱n⸱ ⸱f the chief ornaments of the banquet. Can‐
nibalism, in the guise of an Epicurean science, becomes even
the more revolting.[44]

The meats were kept warm by chafing-dishes. The table was
ornamented with vases of silver, and sometimes gold, of delicate
workmanship. The drinking cups and spoons were of the same
costly materials, and likewise of tortoise-shell. The favorite
beverage was the *Chocolatl*, flavored with vanilla and different
spices. They had a way of preparing the froth of it, so as to
make it almost solid enough to be eaten, and took it cold.[45] The
fermented juice of the maguey, with a mixture of sweets and
acids, supplied, also, various agreeable drinks, of different de‐
grees of strength, and formed the chief beverage of the elder
part of the company.[46]

As soon as they had finished their repast, the young people
rose from the table, to close the festivities of the day with dancing.
They danced gracefully, to the sound of various instruments,
accompanying their movements with chants, of a pleasing, though
somewhat plaintive character.[47] The older guests continued at

---

[44] Sahagun, Hist. de Nueva España, lib. 4, cap. 37 ; lib. 8, cap. 13 ; 9,
cap. 10–14.—Torquemada, Monarch. Ind., lib. 13, cap. 23.—Rel. d' un
gent., ap. Ramusio, tom. III. fol. 306.
Father Sahagun has gone into many particulars of the Aztec *cuisine*, and
the mode of preparing sundry savory messes, making, altogether, no despic‐
able contribution to the noble science of gastronomy,

[45] The froth, delicately flavored with spices and some other ingredients,
was taken cold by itself. It had the consistency almost of a solid ; and the
" Anonymous Conqueror," is very careful to inculcate the importance of
" opening the mouth wide, in order to facilitate deglutition, that the foam
may dissolve gradually, and descend imperceptibly, as it were, into the
stomach." It was so nutritious that a single cup of it was enough to sus‐
tain a man through the longest day's march. (Fol. 306.) The old soldier
discusses the beverage *con amore*.

[46] Sahagun, Hist. de Nueva España, lib. 4, cap. 37; lib, 8, cap. 13.—Tor‐
quemada, Monarch. Ind., lib. 13, cap. 23.—Rel. d' un gent., ap. Ramusio,
tom. III. fol. 306.

[47] Herrera, Hist. General, dec. 2, lib. 7, cap. 8.—Torquemada, Monarch.
Ind., lib. 14, cap. 11,
The Mexican nobles entertained minstrels in their houses, who composed
ballads suited to the times, or the achievements of their lord, which they
chanted, to the accompaniment of instruments, at the festivals and dances.
Indeed, their was more or less dancing at most of the festivals, and it was
performed in the court-yards of the houses, or in the open squares of the
city. (Ibid., ubi supra.) The principal men had, also, buffoons and jug‐
glers in there service, who amused them, and astonished the Spaniards by
their feats of dexterity and strength; (Acosta, lib. 6, cap. 28;) also Clavi‐
gero, Stor. del Messico, tom. II. pp. 179–186,) who has designed several rep‐
resentations of their exploits, truly surprising. It is natural that a people
of limited refinement should find their enjoyment in material, rather than in‐
tellectual pleasures, and, consequently, should excel in them. The Asiati⸱ na⸱

table, sipping *pulque*, and gossiping about other times, till the virtues of the exhilarating beverage put them in good-humor with their own. Intoxication was not rare in this part of the company, and, what is singular, was excused in them, though severely punished in the younger. The entertainment was concluded by a liberal distribution of rich dresses and ornaments among the guests, when they withdrew, after midnight, "some commending the feast, and others condemning the bad taste or extravagance of their host ; in the same manner," says an old Spanish writer, " as with us."[48] Human nature is, indeed, much the same all the world over.

In this remarkable picture of manners, which I have copied faithfully from the records of earliest date after the Conquest, we find no resemblance to the other races of North American Indians. Some resemblance we may trace to the general style of Asiatic pomp and luxury. But, in Asia, woman, far from being admitted to unreserved intercourse with the other sex, is too often jealously immured within the walls of the harem. European civilization, which accords to this loveliest portion of creation her proper rank in the social scale, is still more removed from some of the brutish usages of the Aztecs. That such usages should have existed with the degree of refinement they showed in other things is almost inconceivable. It can only be explained as the result of religious superstition ; superstition which clouds the moral perception, and perverts even the natural senses, till man, civilized man, is reconciled to the very things which are most revolting to humanity. Habits and opinions founded on religion must not be taken as conclusive evidence of the actual refinement of a people.

The Aztec character was perfectly original and unique. It was made up of incongruities apparently irreconcilable. It blended into one the marked peculiarities of different nations, not only of the same phase of civilization, but as far removed from each other as the extremes of barbarism and refinement. It may find a fitting parallel in their own wonderful climate, capable of producing, on a few square leagues of surface, the boundless variety of vegetable forms, which belong to the frozen regions of the North, the temperate zone of Europe, and the burning skies of Arabia and Hindostan !

tions, as the Hindoos and Chinese, for example, surpass the more polished Europeans in displays of agility and legerdemain.

[48] " V de esta manera pasaban gran rato de la noche, y se despedian, é iban á sus casas, unos alabando la fiesta, y otros murmurando de las demasías, y excesos; cosa mui ordinaria en los que á semejantes actos se juntan." Torquemada, Monarch. Ind., lib. 13, cap. 23.—Sahagun, Hist. de Nueva España, lib. 9, cap. 10–14.

One of the works repeatedly consulted and referred to in this Introduction is Boturini's *Idea de una nueva Historia General de la América Septentrional.* The singular persecutions sustained by its author, even more than the merits of his book, have associated his name inseparably with the literary history of Mexico. The Chevalier Lorenzo Boturini Benaduci was a Milanese by birth, of an ancient family, and possessed of much learning. From Madrid, where he was residing, he passed over to New Spain, in 1735, on some business of the Countess of Santibañez, a lineal descendant of Montezuma. While employed on this, he visited the celebrated shrine of Our Lady of Guadaloupe, and, being a person of devout and enthusiastic temper, was filled with the desire of collecting testimony to establish the marvellous fact of her apparition. In the course of his excursions, made with this view, he fell in with many relics of Aztec antiquity, and conceived—what to a Protestant, at least, would seem much more rational—the idea of gathering together all the memorials he could meet with of the primitive civilization of the land.

In pursuit of this double object, he penetrated into the remotest parts of the country, living much with the natives, passing his nights sometimes in their huts, sometimes in caves, and the depths of the lonely forests. Frequently months would elapse, without his being able to add anything to his collection; for the Indians had suffered too much, not to be very shy of Europeans. His long intercourse with them, however, gave him ample opportunity to learn their language and popular traditions, and in the end, to amass a large stock of materials, consisting of hieroglyphical charts on cotton, skins, and the fibre of the maguey; besides a considerable body of Indian manuscripts, written after the Conquest. To all these must be added the precious documents for placing beyond controversy the miraculous apparition of the Virgin. With this treasure he returned, after a pilgrimage of eight years, to the capital.

His zeal, in the meanwhile, had induced him to procure from Rome a bull authorizing the coronation of the sacred image at Guadaloupe. The bull, however, though sanctioned by the Audience of New Spain, had never been approved by the Council of the Indies. In consequence of this informality, Boturini was arrested in the midst of his proceedings, his papers were taken from him, and, as he declined to give an inventory of them, he was thrown into prison, and confined in the same apartment with two criminals! Not long afterward he was sent to Spain. He there presented a memorial to the Council of the Indies, setting forth his manifold grievances, and soliciting redress. At the same time, he drew up his " Idea," above noticed, in which he displayed the catalogue of his *museum* in New Spain, declaring, with affecting earnestness, that " he would not exchange these treasures for all the gold and silver, diamonds and pearls, in the New World."

After some delay, the Council gave an award in his favor; acquitting him of any intentional violation of the law, and pronouncing a high encomium on his deserts. His papers, however, were not restored. But his Majesty was graciously pleased to appoint him Historiographer General of the Indies, with a salary of one thousand dollars *per annum.* The stipend was too small to allow him to return to Mexico. He remained in Madrid, and completed there the first volume of a " General History of North America," in 1749. Not long after this event, and before the publication of the work, he died. The same injustice was continued to his heirs; and, notwithstanding repeated applications in their behalf, they were neither put in possession of their unfortunate kinsman's collection, nor received a remuneration for it. What was worse,—as far as the public was concerned,—the collection itself was deposited in apartments of the Vice-regal palace at Mexico, so damp, that they gradually fell to pieces, and the few remaining were still further diminished by the pilfering of *the curious.* When Baron Humboldt visited Mexico, not one eighth of this inestimable treasure was in existence !

I have been thus particular in the account of the unfortunate Boturini, as affording. on the whole, the most remarkable example of the serious obstacles and persecutions, which literary enterprise, directed in the path of the national antiquities, has, from some cause or other. been exposed to in New Spain.

Boturini's manuscript volume was never printed, and probably never will be, if, indeed, it is in existence. This will scarcely prove a great detriment to science, or to his own reputation. He was a man of a zealous temper, strongly inclined to the marvellous, with little of that acuteness requisite for penetrating the tangled mazes of antiquity, or of the philosophic spirit fitted for calmly weighing its doubts and difficulties. His "Idea" affords a sample of his peculiar mind. With abundant learning, ill-assorted and ill-digested, it is a jumble of fact and puerile fiction, interesting details, crazy dreams and fantastic theories. But it is hardly fair to judge by the strict rules of criticism a work, which, put together hastily, as a catalogue of literary treasures, was designed by the author rather to show what might be done, than that he could do it himself.—It is rare that talents for action and contemplation are united in the same individual. Boturini was eminently bualified, by his enthusiasm and perseverance, for collecting the materials necessary to illustrate the antiquities of the country. It requires a more highly gifted mind to avail itself of them.

CHAPTER VI.

TEZCUCANS.— THEIR GOLDEN AGE.— ACCOMPLISHED PRINCES.—
DECLINE OF THEIR MONARCHY.

THE reader would gather but an imperfect notion of the civilization of Anahuac, without some account of the Acolhuans, or
Tezcucans, as they are usually called; a nation of the same
great family with the Aztecs, whom they rivalled in power, and
surpassed in intellectual culture and the art of social refinement.
Fortunately, we have ample materials for this in the records left
by Ixtlilxochitl, a lineal descendant of the royal line of Tezcuco,
who flourished in the century of the Conquest.   With every opportunity for information he combined much industry and talent,
and, if his narrative bears the high coloring of one who would
revive the faded glories of an ancient, but dilapidated house, he
has been uniformly commended for his fairness and integrity, and
has been followed without misgiving by such Spanish writers as
could have access to his manuscripts.[1]   I shall confine myself
to the prominent features of the two reigns which may be said
to embrace the golden age of Tezcuco ; without attempting to
weigh the probability of the details, which I will leave to be
settled by the reader, according to the measure of his faith.
    The Acolhuans came into the Valley, as we have seen, about
the close of the twelfth century, and built their capital of Tezcuco
on the eastern borders of the lake, opposite to Mexico.   From
this point they gradually spread themselves over the northern
portion of Anahuac, when their career was checked by an invasion of a kindred race, the Tepanecs, who, after a desperate
struggle, succeded in taking their city, slaying their monarch,
and entirely subjugating his kingdom.[2]   This event took place
about 1418 ; and the young prince, Nexahualcoyotl, the heir to
the crown, then fifteen years old, saw his father butchered before his eyes, while he himself lay concealed among the friendly
branches of a tree, which overshadowed the spot.[8]   His subse-

---

[1] For a criticism on this writer, see the Postscript to this Chapter.
[2] See Chapter First of this Introduction, p. 15.
[8] Ixtlilxochitl, Relaciones, MS., No. 9.— Idem, Hist. Chich., MS.,
cap. 19.

quent history is as full of romantic daring, and perilous escapes, as that of the renowned Scanderbeg, or of the "young Chevalier."[4]

Not long after his flight from the field of his father's blood, the Tezcucan prince sell into the hands of his enemies, was borne off in triumph to his city, and was thrown into a dungeon. He effected his escape, however, through the connivance of the governor of the fortress, an old servant of his family, who took the place of the royal fugitive, and paid for his loyalty with his life. He was at length permitted, through the intercession of the reigning family in Mexico, which was allied to him, to retire to that capital, and subsequently to his own, where he found a shelter in his ancestral palace. Here he remained unmolested for eight years, pursuing his studies under an old preceptor, who had had the care of his early youth, and who instructed him in the various duties befitting his princely station.[5]

At the end of this period the Tepanec usurper died, bequeathing his empire to his son, Maxtla, a man of fierce and suspicious temper. Nezahualcoyotl hastened to pay his obeisance to him, on his accession. But the tyrant refused to receive the little present of flowers which he laid at his feet, and turned his back on him in presence of his chieftains. One of his attendants, friendly to the young prince, admonished him to provide for his own safety, by withdrawing, as speedily as possible, from the palace, where his life was in danger. He lost no time, consequently, in retreating from the inhospitable court, and returned to Tezcuco. Maxtla, however, was bent on his destruction. He saw with jealous eye the opening talents and popular manners of his rival, and the favor he was daily winning from his ancient subjects.[6]

He accordingly laid a plan for making way with him at an evening entertainment. It was defeated by the vigilance of the prince's tutor, who contrived to mislead the assassins, and to substitute another victim in the place of his pupil.[7] The baffled tyrant now threw off all disguise, and sent a strong party

---

[4] The adventures of the former hero are told with his usual spirit by Sismondi (Républiques Italiennes, chap. 79). It is hardly necessary, for the latter, to refer the English reader to Chambers's " History of the Rebellion of 1745 " ; a work which proves how thin is the partition in human life, which divides romance from reality.

[5] Ixtlilxochitl, Relaciones, MS., No. 10.

[6] Idem, Relaciones, MS., No. 10.—Hist. Chich., MS., cap. 20-24.

[7] Idem, Hist. Chich., MS., cap. 25. The contrivance was effected by means of an extraordinary personal resemblance of the parties; a fruitful source of comic,—as every reader of the drama knows,—though rarely of tragic interest.

of soldiers to Tezcuco. with orders to enter the place, seize the person of Nezahualcoyotl, and slay him on the spot. The prince, who became acquainted with the plot through the watchfulness of his preceptor, instead of flying, as he was counselled, resolved to await his enemy. They found him playing at ball, when they arrived, in the court of his palace. He received them courteously, and invited them in, to take some refreshments after their journey. While they were occupied in this way, he passed into an adjoining saloon, which excited no suspicion, as he was still visible through the open doors by which the apartments communicated with each other. A burning censer stood in the passage, and, as it was fed by the attendants, threw up such clouds of incense as obscured his movements from the soldiers. Under this friendly veil he succeeded in making his escape by a secret passage, which communicated with a large earthen pipe formerly used to bring water to the palace.[8] Here he remained till night-fall, when, taking advantage of the obscurity, he found his way into the suburbs, and sought a shelter in the cottage of one of his father's vassals.

The Tepanec monarch, enraged at this repeated disappointment, ordered instant pursuit. A price was set on the head of the royal fugitive. Whoever should take him, dead or alive, was promised, however humble his degree, the hand of a noble lady, and an ample domain along with it. Troops of armed men were ordered to scour the country in every direction. In the course of the search, the cottage, in which the prince had taken refuge, was entered. But he fortunately escaped detection by being hid under a heap of maguey fibres used for manufacturing cloth. As this was no longer a proper place of concealment, he sought a retreat in the mountainous and woody district lying between the borders of his own state and Tlascala.[9]

Here he led a wretched, wandering life, exposed to all the inclemencies of the weather, hiding himself in deep thickets and caverns, and stealing out, at night, to satisfy the cravings of appetite ; while he was kept in constant alarm by the activity of his pursuers, always hovering on his track. On one occasion he sought refuge from them among a small party of soldiers, who proved friendly to him, and concealed him in a large drum

[8] It was customary, on entering the presence of a great lord, to throw aromatics into the censer. "Hecho en el brasero incienso, y copal, que era uso y costumbre donde estaban los Reyes y Señores, cada vez que los criados entraban con mucha reverencia y acamiento echaban sahumerio en el brasero ; y así con este perfume se obscurecia algo la sala." Ixtlilxochitl, Relaciones, MS., No. 11.

[9] Idem, Hist. Chich., MS., cap. 26—Relaciones, MS., No. 11.—Veytia, Hist. Antig., lib 2, cap. 47.

around which they were dancing. At another time, he was just able to turn the crest of a hill, as his enemies were climbing it on the other side, when he fell in with a girl who was reaping *chiân*— a Mexican plant, the seed of which was much used in the drinks of the country. He persuaded her to cover him up with the stalks she had been cutting. When his pursuers came up, and inquired if she had seen the fugitive, the girl coolly answered that she had, and pointed out a path as the one he had taken. Notwithstanding the high rewards offered, Nezahualcoyotl seems to have incurred no danger from treachery, such was the general attachment felt to himself and his house. " Would you not deliver up the prince, if he came in your way?" he inquired of a young peasant who was unacquainted with his person. " Not I," replied the other. " What, not for a fair lady's hand, and a rich dowry beside?" rejoined the prince. At which the other only shook his head and laughed.[10] On more than one occasion, his faithful people submitted to torture, and even to lose their lives, rather than disclose the place of his retreat.[11]

However gratifying such proofs of loyalty might be to his feelings, the situation of the prince in these mountain solitudes became every day more distressing. It gave a still keener edge to his own sufferings to witness those of the faithful followers who chose to accompany him in his wanderings. " Leave me," he would say to them, " to my fate! Why should you throw away your own lives for one whom fortune is never weary of persecuting?" Most of the great Tezcucan chiefs had consulted their interests by a timely adhesion to the usurper. But some still clung to their prince, preferring proscription, and death itself, rather than desert him in his extremity.[12]

In the meantime, his friends at a distance were active in measures for his relief. The oppressions of Maxtla, and his growing empire, had caused general alarm in the surrounding states, who recalled the mild rule of the Tezcucan princes. A coalition was formed, a plan of operations concerted, and, on the day appointed for a general rising, Nezahualcoyotl found himself at the head of a force sufficiently strong to face his Tepanec adversaries. An engagement came on, in which the

[10] ' Nezahualcoiotzin le dixo, que si viese á quien buscaban, si lo iria á denunciar? respondí, que no; tornándole á replicar diciéndole, que haria mui mal en perder una muger hermosa, y lo demas, que el rey Maxtla prometia, el mancebo se rió de todo, no haciendo caso ni de lo uno, ni de lo otro." Ixtlilxochitl, Hist. Chich., MS., cap. 27.

[11] Ibid., MS., cap. 26, 27.—Relaciones. MS., No. 11.—Veytia, Hist. Antig., lib. 2, cap. 47, 48.

[12] Ixtlilxochitl, MSS., ubi supra.—Veytia, ubi supra.

latter were totally discomfited ; and the victorious prince, receiving everywhere on his route the homage of his joyful subjects,
entered his capital, not like a proscribed outcast, but as the
rightful heir, and saw himself once more enthroned in the halls
of his fathers.

Soon after, he united his forces with the Mexicans, long disgusted with the arbitrary conduct of Maxtla.   The allied powers,
after a series of bloody engagements with the usurper, routed
him under the walls of his own capital.   He fled to the baths,
whence he was dragged out, and sacrificed with the usual cruel
ceremonies of the Aztecs ; the royal city of Azcapozalco was
razed to the ground, and the wasted territory was henceforth reserved as the great slave-market for the nations of Anahuac.[18]

These events were succeeded by the remarkable league
among the three powers of Tezcuco, Mexico, and Tlacopan, of
which some account has been given in a previous chapter.[14] Historians are not agreed as to the precise terms of it ; the writers
of the two former nations, each, insisting on the paramount
authority of his own in the coalition.   All agree in the subordinate position of Tlacopan, a state, like the others, bordering on
the lake.   It is certain, that in their subsequent operations,
whether of peace or war, the three states shared in each other's
councils, embarked in each other's enterprises, and moved in
perfect concert together, till just before the coming of the Spaniards.

The first measure of Nezahualcoyotl, on returning to his
dominions, was a general amnesty.   It was his maxim, " that a
monarch might punish, but revenge was unworthy of him." [15] In
the present instance, he was averse even to punish, not only
freely pardoned his rebel nobles, but conferred on some, who
had most deeply offended, posts of honor and confidence.
Such conduct was doubtless politic, especially as their alienation was owing, probably, much more to fear of the usurper,
than to any disaffection towards himself.   But there are some
acts of policy which a magnanimous spirit only can execute.

The restored monarch next set about repairing the damages
sustained under the late misrule, and reviving, or rather re-
modelling, the various departments of government.   He framed
a concise, but comprehensive, code of laws, so well suited, it
was thought, to the exigencies of the times, that it was adopted

---

[18] Ixtlilxochitl, Hist. Chich., MS., cap. 28–31.—Relaciones, MS., No. 11.
—Veytia, Hist Antig., lib. 2, cap. 51–54.

[14] See page 18 of this volume.

[15] " Que venjanza no es justo la procuren los Reyes, sino castigar al que
lo mereciere."—MS. de Ixtlilxochitl.

as their own by the two other members of the triple alliance. It was written in blood, and entitled the author to be called the Draco, rather than "the Solon of Anahuac," as he is fondly styled by his admirers.[16] Humanity is one of the best fruits of refinement. It is only with increasing civilization, that the legislator studies to economize human suffering, even for the guilty; to devise penalties, not so much by way of punishment for the past, as of reformation for the future.[17]

He divided the burden of government among a number of departments, as the council of war, the council of finance, the council of justice. This last was a court of supreme authority, both in civil and criminal matters, receiving appeals from the lower tribunals of the provinces, which were obliged to make a full report, every four months, or eighty days, of their own proceedings to this higher judicature. In all these bodies, a certain number of citizens were allowed to have seats with the nobles and professional dignitaries. There was, however, another body, a council of state, for aiding the king in the despatch of business, and advising him in matters of importance, which was drawn altogether from the highest order of chiefs. It consisted of fourteen members; and they had seats provided for them at the royal table.[18]

Lastly, there was an extraordinary tribunal, called the council of music, but which, differing from the import of its name, was devoted to the encouragement of science and art. Works on astronomy, chronology, history, or any other science, were required to be submitted to its judgment, before they could be made public. This censorial power was of some moment, at least with regard to the historical department, where the wilful perversion of truth was made a capital offence by the bloody code of Nezahualcoyotl. Yet a Tezcucan author must have been a bungler, who could not elude a conviction under the cloudy veil of hieroglyphics. This body, which was drawn from the

---

[16] See Clavigero, Stor. del Messico, tom. I. p. 247.
Nezahualcoyotl's code consisted of eighty laws, of which thirty-four only have come down to us, according to Veytia. (Hist. Antig., tom. III. p. 224, nota.) Ixtlilxochitl enumerates several of them. Hist. Chich., MS., cap. 38, and Relaciones, MS., Ordenanzas.

[17] Nowhere are these principles kept more steadily in view than in the various writings of our adopted countryman, Dr. Lieber, having more or less to do with the theory of legislation. Such works could not have been produced before the nineteenth century.

[18] Ixtlilxochitl, Hist. Chich., MS., cap. 36.—Veytia, Hist. Antig., lib. 3, cap. 7.
According to Zurita, the principal judges, at their general meetings every four months, constituted also a sort of parliament or cortes, for advising the king on matters of state. See his Rapport, p. 106; also Ante. p. 30.

best instructed persons in the kingdom, with little regard to rank, had supervision of all the productions of art, and of the nicer fabrics. It decided on the qualifications of the professors in the various branches of science, on the fidelity of their instructions to their pupils, the deficiency of which was severely punished, and it instituted examinations of these latter. In short, it was a general board of education for the country. On stated days, historical compositions, and poems treating of moral or traditional topics, were recited before it by their authors. Seats were provided for the three crowned heads of the empire, who deliberated with the other members on the respective merits of the pieces, and distributed prizes of value to the successful competitors.[19]

Such are the marvellous accounts transmitted to us of this institution ; an institution certainly not to have been expected among the Aborigines of America. It is calculated to give us a higher idea of the refinement of the people, than even the noble architectural remains, which still cover some parts of the continent. Architecture is, to a certain extent, a sensual gratification. It addresses itself to the eye, and affords the best scope for the parade of barbaric pomp and splendor. It is the form in which the revenues of a semi-civilized people are most likely to be lavished. The most gaudy and ostentatious specimens of it, and sometimes the most stupendous, have been reared by such hands. It is one of the first steps in the great march of civilization. But the institution in question was evidence of still higher refinement. It was a literary luxury ; and argued the existence of a taste in the nation, which relied for its gratification on pleasures of a purely intellectual character.

The influence of this academy must have been most propitious to the capital, which became the nursery, not only of such sciences as could be compassed by the scholarship of the period, but of various useful and ornamental arts. Its historians, orators, and poets were celebrated throughout the country.[20] Its

[19] Ixtlilxochitl, Hist. Chich., MS., cap. 36—Clavigero, Stor. del Messico, tom. II. p. 137.—Veytia, Hist. Antig., lib. 3, cap. 7.
"Concurrian á este consejo las tres cabezas del imperio, en ciertos dias, á oir cantar las poesías históricas antiguas y modernas, para instruise de toda su historia, y tambien cuando habia algun nuevo invento en cualquiera facultad, para examinarlo, aprobarlo, ó reprobarlo. Delante de las sillas de los reyes habia una gran mesu cargada de joyas de oro y plata, pedrería, plumas, y otras cosas estimables, y en los rincones de la sala muchas de mantas de todas calidades, para premios de las habilidades y estimulo de los profesores, las cuales alhajas repartian los reyes, en los dias que concurrian, á los que se aventajaban en el ejercicio de sus facultades." Ibid.
[20] Veytia, Hist. Antig., lib. 3, cap. 7.—Clavigero, Stor. del Messico, tom. I. p. 247.

archives, for which accommodations were provided in the royal palace, were stored with the records of primitive ages.[21] Its idiom, more polished than the Mexican, was, indeed, the purest of all the Nahuatlac dialects ; and continued, long after the Conquest, to be that in which the best productions of the native races we.e composed. Tezcuco claimed the glory of being the Athens of the Western World.[22]

Among the most illustrious of her bards was the emperor himself,—for the Tezcucan writers claim this title for their chief, as head of the imperial alliance. He, doubtless, appeared as a competitor before that very academy where he so often sat as a critic. Many of his odes descended to a late generation, and are still preserved, perhaps, in some of the dusty repositories of Mexico or Spain.[23] The historian, Ixtlilxochitl, has left a translation, in Castilian, of one of the poems of his royal ancestor. It is not easy to render his version into corresponding English rhyme, without the perfume of the original escaping in this double filtration.[24] They remind one of the rich breathings of Spanish-Arab poetry, in which an ardent imagination is tempered by a not unpleasing and moral melancholy.[25] But, though sufficiently florid in diction, they are generally free from the meretricious ornaments and hyperbole with which the minstrelsy of

The latter author enumerates four historians, some of much repute, of the royal house of Tezcuco, descendants of the great Nezahualcoyotl. See his Account of writers, tom. I. pp. 6-21.

[21] " En la ciudad de Tezcuco estaban los Archivos Reales de todas las cosas referidas, por haver sido la Metrópoli de todas las ciencias, usos, y buenas costumbres. porque los Reyes que fuéron de ella se preciaron de esto." (Ixtlilxochitl, Hist. Chich., MS., Prólogo.) It was from the poor wreck of these documents, once so carefully preserved by his ancestors, that the historian gleaned the materials, as he informs us, for his own works.

[22] "Aunque es tenida la lengua Mejicana por materna, y la Tezcucana por mas cortesana y pulida." (Camargo, Hist. de Tlascala, MS.) "Tezcuco," says Boturini, "donde los Senores de la Tierra embiaban a sus hijos para aprehender *lo mas pulido de la Lengua Náhuatl,* la Poesía, Filosofía Moral, la Theología Gentílica, la Astronomia, Medicina, y la Historia." Idea, p. 142.

[23] "Compuso LX. cantares," says the author last quoted, "que quizas tambien havran perecido en las manos incendiarias de los ignorantes." (Idea, p. 79.) Boturini had translations of two of these in his museum, (Catálogo, p. 8.) and another has since come to light.

[24] Difficult as the task may be, it has been executed by the hand of a fair friend, who while she has adhered to the Castilian with singular fidelity, has shown a grace and flexibility in her poetical movements, which the Castilian version, and probably the Mexican original, cannot boast. See both translations in *Appendix, Part 2, No. 2.*

[25] Numerous specimens of this may be found in Condé's "Dominacion de los Arábes en España." None of them are superior to the plaintive strains of the royal Abderahman on the solitary palm-tree, which reminded him of the pleasant land of his birth. See Parte 2, cap. 9.

the East is usually tainted. They turn on the vanities and mutability of human life; a topic very natural for a monarch who had himself experienced the strangest mutations of fortune. There is mingled in the lament of the Tezcucan bard, however, an Epicurean philosophy, which seeks relief from the fears of the future in the joys of the present. "Banish care," he says, if there are bounds to pleasure, the saddest life must also have an end. Then weave the chaplet of flowers, and sing thy songs in praise of the all-powerful God; for the glory of this world soon fadeth away. Rejoice in the green freshness of thy spring: for the day will come when thou shalt sigh for these joys in vain; when the sceptre shall pass from thy hands, thy servants shall wander desolate in thy courts, thy sons, and the sons of thy nobles, shall drink the dregs of distress, and all the pomp of thy victories and triumphs shall live only in their recollection. Yet the remembrance of the just shall not pass away from the nations, and the good thou hast done shall ever be held in honor. The goods of this life, its glories and its riches, are but lent to us, its substance is but an illusory shadow and the things of to-day shall change on the coming of the morrow. Then gather the fairest flowers from thy gardens, to bind round thy brow, and seize the joys of the present, ere they perish." [26]

[26] " Io tocaré cantando
　　El músico instrumento sonoroso
　　Tufide flores gozando
　　Danza, y festeja á Dios que es poderoso:—
　　O gozemos de esta gloria,
　　Porque la humana vida es transitoria."
　　　　　　　　　　　MS. DE IXTLILXOCHITL.

The sentiment, which is common enough, is expressed with uncommon beauty by the English poet, Herrick:

" Gather the rosebud while you may,
　　Old Time is still a flying;
　　The fairest flower that blooms to-day,
　　To-morrow may be dying."

And with still greater beauty, perhaps by Racine;

" Rions, chantons, dit cette troupe impie;
　　De fleurs en fleurs, de plaisirs en plaisirs,
　　　　　　Promenons nos désirs.
　　Sur l'avenir insense qui se fie.
　　De nos ans passagers le nombre est incertain.
　　Hatons-nous aujourd'hui de jouir de la vie;
　　Qui sait si nous serons demain ?"
　　　　　　　　　　　ATHALIE. Acte 2.

It is interesting to see under what different forms the same sentiment, is developed by different races, and in different languages. It is an Epicurean sentiment, indeed, but its universality proves its truth to nature.

But the hours of the Tezcucan monarch were not all passed in idle dalliance with the Muse, nor in the sober contemplations of philosophy, as at a later period. In the freshness of youth and early manhood he led the allied armies in their annual expeditions, which were certain to result in a wider extent of territory to the empire.[27] In the intervals of peace he fostered those productive arts which are the surest sources of public prosperity. He encouraged agriculture above all ; and there was scarcely a spot so rude, or a steep so inaccessible, as not to confess the power of cultivation. The land was covered with a busy population, and towns and cities sprung up in places since deserted, or dwindled into miserable villages.[28]

From resources thus enlarged by conquest and domestic industry, the monarch drew the means for the large consumption of his own numerous household,[29] and for the costly works which he executed for the convenience and embellishment of the capital. He filled it with stately edifices for his nobles, whose constant attendance he was anxious to secure at his court.[30] He erected a magnificent pile of buildings which might serve both for a royal reisdence and for the public offices. It extended,

[27] Some of the provinces and places thus conquered were held by the allied powers in common ; Tlacopan, however, only receiving one fifth of the tribute. It was more usual to annex the vanquished territory to that one of the two great states, to which it lay nearest. See Ixtlilxochitl, Hist. Chich., MS., cap. 38.—Zurita Rapport, p. 11.

[28] Ixtlilxochitl, Hist. Chich., MS., cap. 41. The same writer, in another work, calls the population of Tezcuco, at this period, double of what it was at the Conquest; founding his estimate on the royal registers, and on the numerous remains of edifices still visible in his day, in places now depopulated. " Parece en las historias que en este tiempo, antes que se destruyesen, havia doblado mas gente de la que halló al tiempo que vino Cortes, y los demas Españoles; porque yo hallo en los padrones reales, que el menor pueblo tenia 1100 vecinos, y de alli para arriba, y ahora no tienen 200 vecinos, y aun en algunas partes de todo punto se han acabado. . . . . . Como se hecha de ver en las ruinas, hasta los mas altos montes y sierras tenian sus sementeras, y casas principales para vivir y morar." Relaciones, MS., No. 9.

[29] Torquemada has extracted the particulars of the yearly expenditure of the palace from the royal account book, which came into the historian's possession. The following are some of the items, namely : 4,900,300 fanegas of maize ; (the *fanega* is equal to about one hundred pounds;) 2,744,000 fanegas of cacao; 8000 turkeys; 1300 baskets of salt : besides an incredible quantity of game of every kind, vegetables, condiments, &c. (Monarch. Ind., lib. 2, cap. 53.) See, also, Ixtlilxochitl, Hist. Chich., MS., cap. 35.

[30] There were more than four hundred of these lordly residences. " Así mismo hizo edificar muchas casas y palacios para los señores y cavalleros, que asistian en su corte, cada uno conforme á la calidad y méritos de su persona, las quales llegáron á ser mas de quatrocientas casas de señores y cavalleros de solar conocido." Ibid., cap. 38.

from east to west, twelve hundred and thirty-four yards, and from north to south, nine hundred and seventy-eight. It was encompassed by a wall of unburnt bricks and cement, six feet wide and nine high, for one half of the circumference, and fifteen feet high for the other half. Within this inclosure were two courts. The outer one was used as the great market-place of the city; and continued to be so until long after the Conquest, —if, indeed, it is not now. The interior court was surrounded by the council-chambers and halls of justice. There were also accommodations there for the foreign ambassadors ; and a spacious saloon, with apartments opening into it, for men of science and poets, who pursued their studies in this retreat, or met together to hold converse under its marble porticos. In this quarter, also, were kept the public archives ; which fared better under the Indian dynasty, than they have since under their European successors.[31]

Adjoining this court were the apartments of the king, including those for the royal harem, as liberally supplied with beauties as that of an Eastern sultan. Their walls were incrusted with alabasters, and richly tinted stucco, or hung with gorgeous tapestries of variegated feather-work. They led through long arcades, and through intricate labyrinths of shrubbery, into gardens, where baths and sparkling fountains were overshadowed by tall groves of cedar and cypress. The basins of water were well stocked with fish of various kinds, and the aviaries with birds glowing in all the gaudy plumage of the tropics. Many birds and animals, which could not be obtained alive, were represented in gold and silver so skilfully as to have furnished the great naturalist, Hernandez, with models for his work.[32]

[31] Ibid., cap. 36. "Esta plaza cercada de portales, y tenia así mismo por la parte del poniente otra sala grande, y muchos quartos á la redonda, que era la universidad, en donde asistian todos los poetas, históricos, y philósophos del reyno, divididos en sus claves, y academias, conforme era la facultad de cada uno, y así mismo estaban aquí los archivos reales."

[32] This celebrated naturalist was sent by Philip II. to New Spain, and he employed several years in compiling a voluminous work on its various natural productions, with drawings illustrating them. Although the government is said to have expended sixty thousand ducats in effecting this great object, the volumes were not published till long after the author's death. In 1651 a mutilated edition of the part of the work relating to medical botany appeared at Rome. The original MSS. were supposed to have been destroyed by the great fire in the Escurial, not many years after. Fortunately, another copy, in the author's own hand, was detected by the indefatigable Muñoz, in the library of the Jesuits' College at Madrid, in the latter part of the last century ; and a beautiful edition, from the famous press of Ibara, was published in that capital, under the patronage of government, in 1790. (Hist. Plantarum, Præfatio.—Nic. Antonio, Bibliotheca Hispana Nova, (Matriti, 1790,) tom. II. p. 432.)

Accommodations on a princely scale were provided for the sovereigns of Mexico and Tlacopan, when they visited the court. The whole of this lordly pile contained three hundred apartments, some of them fifty yards square.[33] The height of the building is not mentioned. It was probably not great; but supplied the requisite room by the immense extent of ground which it covered. The interior was doubtless constructed of light materials, especially of the rich woods, which, in that country, are remarkable, when polished, for the brilliancy and variety of their colors. That the more solid materials of stone and stucco were also liberally employed is proved by the remains at the present day; remains, which have furnished an inexhaustible quarry for the churches and other edifices since erected by the Spaniards on the site of the ancient city.[34]

We are not informed of the time occupied in building this palace. But two hundred thousand workmen, it is said, were employed on it![35] However this may be, it is certain that the Tezcucan monarchs, like those of Asia, and ancient Egypt, had the control of immense masses of men, and would sometimes turn the whole population of a conquered city, including the women, into the public works.[36]—The most gigantic monuments of architecture which the world has witnessed would never have been reared by the hands of freemen.

Adjoining the palace were buildings for the king's children, who, by his various wives, amounted to no less than sixty sons and fifty daughters.[37] Here they were instructed in all the ex-

The work of Hernandez is a monument of industry and erudition, the more remarkable, as being the first on this difficult subject. And after all the additional light from the labors of later naturalists, it still holds its place as a book of the highest authority, for the perspicuity, fidelity, and thoroughness, with which the multifarious topics in it are discussed.

[33] Ixtlilxochitl, Hist. Chich., MS., cap. 36.

[34] "Some of the terraces on which it stood," says Mr. Bullock, speaking of this palace, "are still entire, and covered with cement, very hard, and equal in beauty to that found in ancient Roman buildings...... The great church, which stands close by, is almost entirely built of the materials taken from the palace, many of the sculptured stones from which may be seen in the walls, though most of the ornaments are turned inwards. Indeed, our guide informed us, that whoever built a house at Tezcuco made the ruins of the palace serve as his quarry." (Six Months in Mexico, chap. 26.) Torquemada notices the appropriation of the materials to the same purpose. Monarch. Ind., lib. 2, cap. 45.

[35] Ixtlilxochitl, MS., ubi supra.

[36] Thus, to punish the Chalcas for their rebellion, the whole population were compelled, women as well as men, says the chronicler so often quoted. to labor on the royal edifices, for four years together; and large granaries were provided with stores for their maintenance, in the mean time. Idem, Hist. Chich., MS., cap. 46.

[37] If the people in general were not much addicted to polygamy, the sover-

ercises and accomplishments suited to their station ; comprehending, what would scarcely find a place in a royal education on the other side of the Atlantic, the arts of working in metals, jewelry, and feather-mosaic.   Once in every four months, the whole household, not excepting the youngest, and including all the officers and attendants on the king's person, assembled in a grand saloon of the palace, to listen to a discourse from an orator, probably one of the priesthood.   The princes, on this occasion, were all dressed in *nequen*, the coarsest manufacture of the country.   The preacher began by enlarging on the obligations of morality, and of respect for the gods, especially important in persons whose rank gave such additional weight to example.   He occasionally seasoned his homily with a pertinent application to his audience, if any member of it had been guilty of a notorious delinquency.   From this wholesome admonition the monarch himself was not exempted, and the orator boldly reminded him of his paramount duty to show respect for his own laws.   The king, so far from taking umbrage, received the lesson with humility ; and the audience, we are assured, were often melted into tears by the eloquence of the preacher.[38]   This curious scene may remind one of similar usages in the Asiatic and Egyptian despotisms, where the sovereign occasionally condescended to stoop from his pride of place, and allow his memory to be refreshed with the conviction of his own mortality.[39]   It soothed the feelings of the subject, to find himself thus placed, though but for a moment, on a level with his king ; while it cost little to the latter, who was removed too far from his people, to suffer any thing by this short-lived familiarity. It is probable that such an act of public humiliation would have found less favor with a prince less absolute.

Nezahualcoyotl's fondness for magnificence was shown in his numerous villas, which were embellished with all that could make a rural retreat delightful.   His favorite residence was at Tezcotzinco ; a conical hill about two leagues from the capital.[40] It was laid out in terraces, or hanging gardens, having a flight of steps five hundred and twenty in number, many of them hewn

eign it must be confessed,—and it was the same, we shall see, in Mexico,—made ample amends for any self-denial on the part of his subjects.

[38] Ixtlilxochitl, Hist. Chich., MS., cap. 37.

[39] The Egyptian priests managed the affair in a more courtly style, and, while they prayed that all sorts of kingly virtues might descend on the prince, they threw the blame of actual delinquencies on his ministers ; thus, "not by the bitterness of reproof," says Diodorus, "but by the allurements of praise, enticing him to an honest way of life."   Lib. 1, cap. 70.

[40] Ixtlilxochitl, Hist. Chich., MS., cap. 42.—See *Appendix, Part 2, No 3,* for the original description of this royal residence.

in the natural porphyry.[41] In the garden on the summit was a reservoir of water, fed by an aqueduct that was carried over hill and valley, for several miles, on huge buttresses of masonry. A large rock stood in the midst of this basin, sculptured with the hieroglyphics representing the years of Nezahualcoyotl's reign and his principal achievements in each.[42] On a lower level were three other reservoirs, in each of which stood a marble statue of a woman, emblematic of the three states of the empire. Another tank contained a winged lion, (?) cut out of the solid rock, bearing in his mouth the portrait of the emperor.[43] His likeness had been executed in gold, wood, feather-work, and stone, but this was the only one which pl ased him.

From these copious basins the water was distributed in numerous channels through the gardens, or was made to tumble over the rocks in cascades, shedding refreshing dews on the flowers and odoriferous shrubs below. In the depths of this fragrant wilderness, marble porticos and pavilions were erected, and baths excavated in the solid porphyry, which are still shown by the ignorant natives, as the " Baths of Montezuma "![44] The visitor descended by steps cut in the living stone, and polished so bright as to reflect like mirrors.[45] Towards the base of the hill, in the midst of cedar groves, whose gigantic branches threw a refreshing coolness over the verdure in the

[41] "Quinientos y veynte escalones." Davilla Padilla, Historia de la Provincia de Santiago, (Madrid, 1596,) lib. 2, cap. 81.

This writer who lived in the sixteenth century, counted the steps himself. Those which were not cut in the rock were crumbling into ruins, as indeed, every part of the establishment was even then far gone to decay.

[42] On the summit of the mount, according to Padilla, stood an image of a *coyotl*,—an animal resembling a fox,—which, according to tradition, represented an Indian famous for his fasts. It was destroyed by that stanch iconoclast, Bishop Zummarraga as a relic of idolatry. (Hist. de Santiago, lib. 2, cap. 81.) This figure was, no doubt, the emblem of Nezahualcoytl himself, whose name, as elsewhere noticed, signified "hungry fox."

[43] " Hecho de una peña un leon de mas de dos brazas de largo con sus alas y plumas : estaba hechado y mirando á la parte del oriente, en cuia boca asomaba un rostro, que era el mismo retrato del Rey." Ixtlilxochitl, Hist. Chich., MS., cap. 42.

[44] Bullock speaks of a " beautiful basin, twelve feet long by eight wide, having a well five feet by four deep in the centre," &c., &c. Whether truth lies in the bottom of this well is not so clear. Latrobe describes the baths as " two singular basins, perhaps two feet and a half in diameter, not large enough for any monarch bigger than Oberon to take a duck in." (Comp. Six Months in Mexico, chap. 26; and Rambler in Mexico, let. 7.) Ward speaks much to the same purpose, (Mexico in 1827, (London,) 1828, vol. II. p. 296,) which agrees with verbal accounts I have received of the same spot.

[45] Gradas hechas de la misma peña tan bien gravadas y lizas que parecian espejos." (Ixtlilxochitl, MS., ubi supra.) The travellers just cited notice the beautiful polish still visible in the porphyry.

sultriest seasons of the year,[46] rose the royal villa, with its light
arcades and airy halls, drinking in the sweet perfumes of the
gardens.   Here the monarch often retired, to throw off the burden of state, and refresh his wearied spirits in the society of his
favorite wives, reposing during the noontide heats in the em-
bowering shades of his paradise, or mingling, in the cool of the
evening, in their festive sports and dances.   Here he entertained his imperial brothers of Mexico and Tlacopan, and followed the hardier pleasures of the chase in the noble woods
that stretched for miles around his villa, flourishing in all their
primeval majesty.   Here, too, he often repaired in the latter
days of his life, when age had tempered ambition and cooled
the ardor of his blood, to pursue in solitude the studies of philosophy and gather wisdom from meditation.

The extraordinary accounts of the Tezcucan architecture are
confirmed, in the main, by the relics which still cover the hill of
Tezcotzinco, or are half buried beneath its surface.   They attract
little attention, indeed, in the country, where their true history
has long since passed into oblivion ; [47] while the traveller, whose
curiosity leads him to the spot, speculates on their probable
origin, and, as he stumbles over the huge fragments of sculptured porphyry and granite, refers them to the primitive races
who spread their colossal architecture over the country, long before the coming of the Acolhuans and the Aztecs.[48]

---

[46] Padilla saw entire pieces of cedar among the ruins, ninety feet long, and four
in diameter. Some of the massive portals, he observed, were made of a single
stone. (Hist. de Santiago, lib. 11, cap. 81.)   Peter Martyr notices an enormous wooden beam, used in the construction of the palaces of Tezcuco, which
was one hundred and twenty feet long, by eight feet in diameter!   The accounts of this and similar huge pieces of timber were so astonishing, he adds,
that he could not have received them except on the most unexceptionable testimony. De Orbe Novo, dec. 5, cap. 10.

[47] It is much to be regretted that the Mexican government should not
take a deeper interest in the Indian antiquities. What might not be effected
by a few hands draw from the idle garrisons of some of the neighboring towns,
and employed in excavating this ground, "the Mount Palatine" of Mexico !
But, unhappily, the age of violence has been succeeded by one of apathy.

[48] "They are, doubtless," says Mr. Latrobe, speaking of what he calls,
"these inexplicable ruins,"—"rather of Toltec than Aztec origin, and, perhaps, with still more probability, attributable to a people of an age yet more
remote." (Rambler in Mexico, let. 7.)   "I am of opinion," says Mr.
Bullock, "that these were antiquities prior to the discovery of America, and
erected by a people whose history was lost even before the building of the
city of Mexico.—Who can solve this difficulty?" (Six months in Mexico,
ubi supra.)   The reader who takes Ixtlilxochitl for his guide will have no
great trouble in solving it.   He will find here, as he might, probably, in
some other instances, that one need go little higher than the Conquest, for
the origin of antiquities, which claim to be coeval with Phœnicia and
Ancient Egypt.

The Tezcucan princes were used to entertain a great number of concubines. They had but one lawful wife, to whose issue the crown descended.[49] Nezahualcoyotl remained unmarried to a late period. He was disappointed in an early attachment, as the princess, who had been educated in privacy to be the partner of his throne, gave her hand to another. The injured monarch submitted the affair to the proper tribunal. The parties, how‑ever, were proved to have been ignorant of the destination of the lady, and the court, with an independence which reflects equal honor on the judges who could give, and the monarch who could receive the sentence, acquitted the young couple. This story is sadly contrasted by the following.[50]

The king devoured his chagrin in the solitude of his beautiful villa of Tezcotzinco, or sought to divert it by travelling. On one of his journeys he was hospitably entertained by a potent vassal, the old lord of Tepechpan, who, to do his sovereign more honor, caused him to be attended at the banquet by a noble maiden, betrothed to himself, and who, after the fashion of the country, had been educated under his own roof. She was of the blood royal of Mexico, and nearly related, moreover, to the Tezcucan monarch. The latter, who had all the amorous temperament of the South, was captivated by the grace and personal charms of the youthful Hebe, and conceived a violent passion for her. He did not disclose it to any one, however, but, on his return home, resolved to gratify it, though at the expense of his own honor, by sweeping away the only obstacle which stood in his path.

He accordingly sent an order to the chief of Tepechpan to take command of an expedition set on foot against the Tlasca-lans. At the same time he instructed two Tezcucan chiefs to keep near the person of the old lord, and bring him into the thickest of the fight, where he might lose his life. He assured them, this had been forfeited by a great crime, but that, from regard for his vassal's past services, he was willing to cover up his disgrace by an honorable death.

The veteran, who had long lived in retirement on his estates, saw himself, with astonishment, called so suddenly and need-lessly into action, for which so many younger men were better fitted. He suspected the cause, and, in the farewell entertain-ment to his friends, uttered a presentiment of his sad destiny. His predictions were too soon verified ; and a few weeks placed the hand of his virgin bride at her own disposal.

Nezahualcoyotl did not think it prudent to break his passion publicly to the princess, so soon after the death of his victim.

[49] Zurita, Rapport, p. 12.
[50] Ixtlilxochitl. Hist, Chich. MS., cap. 42.

He opened a correspondence with her through a female relative, and expressed his deep sympathy for her loss. At the same time, he tendered the best consolation in his power, by an offer of his heart, and hand. Her former lover had been too well stricken in years for the maiden to remain long inconsolable. She was not aware of the perfidious plot against his life ; and, after a decent time, she was ready to comply with her duty, by placing herself at the disposal of her royal kinsman.

It was arranged by the king, in order to give a more natural aspect to the affair, and prevent all suspicion of the unworthy part he had acted, that the princess should present herself in his grounds at Tezcotzinco, to witness some public ceremony there. Nezahualcoyotl was standing in a balcony of the palace, when she appeared, and inquired, as if struck with her beauty for the first time, "who the lovely young creature was, in his garden." When his courtiers had acquainted him with her name and rank, he ordered her to be conducted to the palace, that she might receive the attentions due to her station. The interview was soon followed by a public declaration of his passion ; and the marriage was celebrated not long after, with great pomp, in the presence of his court, and of his brother monarchs of Mexico and Tlacopan.[61]

This story, which furnishes so obvious a counterpart to that of David and Uriah, is told with great circumstantiality, both by the king's son and grandson, from whose narratives Ixtlilxochitl derived it.[62] They stigmatize the action as the basest in their great ancestor's life. It is indeed too base not to leave an indelible stain on any character, however pure in other respects, and exalted.

The king was strict in the execution of his laws, though his natural disposition led him to temper justice with mercy. Many anecdotes are told of the benevolent interest he took in the concerns of his subjects, and of his anxiety to detect and reward merit, even in the most humble. It was common for him to ramble among them in disguise, like the celebrated caliph in the "Arabian Nights," mingling freely in conversation, and ascertaining their actual condition with his own eyes.[63]

On one such occasion, when attended only by a single lord, he met with a boy who was gathering sticks in a field for fuel.

---

[61] Idem, Hist. Chich., MS., cap. 43.

[62] Idem, ubi supra.

[63] " En traje de cazador, (que lo acostumbraba á hacer muy de ordinario,) saliendo á solas, y disfrazado para que no fuese conocido, á reconocer las faltas y necesidad que havia en la república para remediarlas." Idem, Hist. Chich., MS., cap. 46.

He inquired of him "why he did not go into the neighboring forest, where he would find a plenty of them." To which the lad answered, "It was the king's wood and he would punish him with death, if he trespassed there." The royal forests were very extensive in Tezcuco, and were guarded by laws full as severe as those of the Norman tyrants in England. "What kind of man is your king?" asked the monarch, willing to learn the effect of these prohibitions on his own popularity. "A very hard man," answered the boy, "who denies his people what God has given them." [54] Nezahualcoyotl urged him not to mind such arbitrary laws, but to glean his sticks in the forest, as there was no one present who would betray him. But the boy sturdily refused, bluntly accusing the disguised king, at the same time, of being a traitor, and of wishing to bring him into trouble.

Nezahualcoyotl, on returning to his palace, ordered the child and his parents to be summoned before him. They received the orders with astonishment, but, on entering the presence, the boy at once recognized the person with whom he had discoursed so unceremoniously, and he was filled with consternation. The good-natured monarch, however, relieved his apprehensions, by thanking him for the lesson he had given him, and, at the same time, commended his respect for the laws, and praised his parents for the manner in which they had trained their son. He then dismissed the parties with a liberal largess ; and afterwards mitigated the severity of the forest laws, so as to allow persons to gather any wood they might find on the ground, if they did not meddle with the standing timber.[55]

Another adventure is told of him, with a poor woodman and his wife, who had brought their little load of billets for sale to the market-place of Tezcuco. The man was bitterly lamenting his hard lot, and the difficulty with which he earned a wretched subsistence, while the master of the palace before which they were standing lived an idle life, without toil, and with all the luxuries in the world at his command.

He was going on in his complaints, when the good woman stopped him, by reminding him he might be overheard. He was so, by Nezahualcoyotl himself, who, standing, screened from observation, at a latticed window, which overlooked the market, was amusing himself, as he was wont, with observing the common people chaffering in the square. He immediately ordered the querulous couple into his presence. They appeared trembling and conscience-struck before him. The king gravely in-

[54] Un hombresillo miserable, pues quita á los hombres lo que Dios á manos llenas les da." Ibid., loc. cit.

[55] Ibid., cap. 46.

quired what they had said. As they answered him truly, he told
them they should reflect, that, if he had great treasures at his
command, he had still greater calls for them ; that, far from
leading an easy life, he was oppressed with the whole burden of
government ; and concluded by admonishing them "to be more
cautious in future, as walls had ears." [56]   He then ordered his
officers to bring a quantity of cloth, and a generous supply of
cacao, (the coin of the country,) and dismissed them. "Go,"
said he ; "with the little you now have, you will be rich ; while
with all my riches, I shall still be poor.[57]

It was not his passion to hoard. He dispensed his revenues
munificently, seeking out poor, but meritorious objects, on whom
to bestow them. He was particularly mindful of disabled
soldiers, and those who had in any way sustained loss in the public service ; and, in case of their death, extended assistance to
their surviving families. Open mendicity was a thing he would
never tolerate, but chastized it with exemplary rigor.[58]

It would be incredible, that a man of the enlarged mind and
endowments of Nezahualcoyotl should acquiesce in the sordid
superstitions of his countrymen, and still more in the sanguinary
rites borrowed by them from the Aztecs. In truth, his humane
temper shrunk from these cruel ceremonies, and he strenuously
endeavored to recall his people to the more pure and simple
worship of the ancient Toltecs. A circumstance produced a
temporary change in his conduct.

He had been married some years to the wife he had so un-
righteously obtained, but was not blessed with issue. The
priests represented that it was owing to his neglect of the gods
of his country, and that his only remedy was, to propitiate them
by human sacrifice. The king reluctantly consented, and the
altars once more smoked with the blood of slaughtered captives.
But it was all in vain ; and he indignantly exclaimed, "These
idols of wood and stone can neither hear nor feel; much less
could they make the heavens, and the earth, and man, the lord
of it. These must be the work of the all-powerful, unknown
God, Creator of the universe, on whom alone I must rely for
consolation and support.[59]

[56] " Porque las paredes oian." (Ibid.) A European proverb among the
American Aborigines looks too strange, not to make one suspect the land of
the chronicler.

[57] " Le dijo, que con aquello poco le bastaba, y viviria bien aventurado ,
y él con toda la máquina que le parecia que tenia arto, r ʼenia nada; y asi
lo despidió." Ibid.

[58] Ibid.

[59] " Verdaderamente los Dioses que lo adoro, que son ídolos depirdra que
no hablen, ni sienten, no pudiéron hacer ni formar la hermosura del cielo, el

He then withdrew to his rural palace of Tezcotzinco, where he remained forty days, fasting and praying at stated hours, and offering up no other sacrifice, than the sweet incense of copal, and aromatic herbs and gums. At the expiration of this time, he is said to have been comforted by a vision assuring him of the success of his petition. At all events, such proved to be the fact ; and this was followed by the cheering intelligence of the triumph of his arms in a quarter where he had lately experienced some humiliating reverses.[60]

Greatly strengthened in his former religious convictions, he now openly professed his faith, and was more earnest to wean his subjects from their degrading superstitions, and to substitute nobler and more spiritual conceptions of the Deity. He built a temple in the usual pyramidal form, and on the summit a tower nine stories high, to represent the nine heavens ; a tenth was surmounted by a roof painted black, and profusely gilded with stars, on the outside, and incrusted with metals and precious stones within. He dedicated this to "*the unknown God, the Cause of causes.*"[61] It seems probable, from the emblem on the tower, as well as from the complexion of his verses, as we shall see, that he mingled with his reverence for the Supreme the astral worship which existed among the Toltecs.[62] Various musical instruments were placed on the top of the tower, and the sound of them, accompanied by the ringing of a sonorous metal struck by a mallet, summoned the worshipers to prayers, at regular seasons.[63] No image was allowed in the edifice, as unsuited to

---

sol, luna, y estrellas que lo hermosean, y dan luz á la tierra, rios, aguas, y fuentes, árboles, y plantas que la hermosean, las gentes que la poseen, y todo lo criado; algun Dios muy poderoso, oculto, y no conocido es el Criador de todo el universo. El solo es él que puede consolarme en mi afliccion, y socorrerme en tan grande angustia como mi corazon siente." MS. de Ixtlilxochitl.

[60] MS. de Ixtlilxochitl.

The manuscript here quoted is one of the many left by the author on the antiquities of his country, and forms part of a voluminous compilation made in Mexico by father Vega, in 1792, by order of the Spanish government. See *Appendix, Part 2, No. 1.*

[61] " Al Dios no conocido, causa de las causas." MS. de Ixtlilxochitl.

[62] Their earliest temples were dedicated to the Sun. The Moon they worshipped as his wife, and the Stars as his sisters. (Veytia, Hist. Antig., tom, I, cap. 25.) The ruins still existing at Teotihuacan, about seven leagues from Mexico, are supposed to have been temples, raised by this ancient people, in honor of the two great deities. Boturini, Idea, p. 42.

[63] MS. de Ixtlilxochitl.

" This was evidently a *gong*," says Mr. Ranking, who treads with enviable confidence over the " suppositos cineres," in the path of the antiquary. See his Historical Researches on the Conquest of Peru, Mexico, &c., by the Mongols, (London, 1827,) p. 310.

the " invisible God " ; and the people were expressly prohibited from profaning the altars with blood, or any other sacrifices than that of the perfume of flowers and sweet-scented gums.

The remainder of his days was chiefly spent in his delicious solitudes of Tezcotzinco, where he devoted himself to astronomical and, probably, astrological studies, and to meditation on his immortal destiny,—giving utterance to his feelings in songs, or rather hymns, of much solemnity and pathos. An extract from one of these will convey some idea of his religious speculations. The pensive tenderness of the verses quoted in a preceding page is deepened here into a mournful, and even gloomy coloring ; while the wounded spirit, instead of seeking relief in the convivial sallies of a young and buoyant temperament, turns for consolation to the world beyond the grave.

" All things on earth have their term, and, in the most joyous career of their vanity and splendor, their strength fails, and they sink into the dust. All the round world is but a sepulchre ; and there is nothing, which lives on its surface, that shall not be hidden and entombed beneath it. Rivers, torrents, and streams move onward to their destination. Not one flows back to its pleasant source. They rush onward, hastening to bury themselves in the deep bosom of the ocean. The things of yesterday are no more to-day ; and things of to-day shall cease, perhaps, on the morrow.[64] The cemetery is full of the loathsome dust of bodies once quickened by living souls, who occupied thrones, presided over assemblies, marshalled armies, subdued provinces, arrogated to themselves worship, were puffed up with vainglorious pomp, and power, and empire.

" But these glories have all passed away, like the fearful smoke that issues from the throat of Popocatepetl, with no other memorial of their existence than the record on the page of the chronicler.

" The great, the wise, the valiant, the beautiful,—alas ! where are they now ?—They are all mingled with the clod ; and· that which has befallen them shall happen to us, and to those that come after us. Yet let us take courage, illustrious nobles and chieftains, true friends and loyal subjects,—*let us aspire to that heaven, where all is eternal, and corruption cannot come.*[65] The

---

[64] Toda la redondez de la tierra es un sepulcro: no hay cosa que sustente que con título de piedad no la esconda y entierre. Corren los rios, los arroyos, las fuentes, y las aguas, ningunas retroceden para sus alegros nacimientos: aceleranse con ansa para los vastos dominios de Tlulóca [Neptuno], y cuanto mas se arriman á sus dilatadas márgenes, tanto mas van lobarando las melancólicas urnas para sepultarse. Lo que fué ayer no es hoy, ni lo de hoy se afianza que sera mañana "

[65] " Aspiremos al cielo, que allí todo es eterno y nada se corrompe."

horrors of the tomb are but the cradle of the Sun, and the dark shadows of death are brilliant lights for the stars."[66] The mystic import of the last sentence seems to point to that superstition respecting the mansions of the Sun, which forms so beautiful a contrast to the dark features of the Aztec mythology.

At length, about the year 1470,[67] Nezahuacoyotl, full of years and honors, felt himself drawing near his end. Almost half a century had elapsed since he mounted the throne of Tezcuco, He had found his kingdom dismembered by faction, and bowed to the dust beneath the yoke of a foreign tyrant, He had broken that yoke; had breathed new life into the nation, renewed its ancient institutions, extended wide its domain; had seen it flourishing in all the activity of trade and agriculture, gathering strength from its enlarged resources, and daily advancing higher and higher in the great march of civilization. All this he had seen, and might fairly attribute no small portion of it to his own wise and beneficent rule. His long and glorious day was now drawing to its close; and he contemplated the event with the same serenity, which he had shown under the clouds of its morning and in its meridian splendor.

A short time before his death, he gathered around him those of his children in whom he most confided, his chief counsellors, the ambassador of Mexico, and Tlacopan, and his little son, the heir to the crown, his only offspring by the queen. He was then not eight years old; but had already given, as far as so tender a blossom might, the rich promise of future excellence.[68]

---

[66] " El horror del sepulcro es lisongera cuna para él, las funestas sombras, brillantes luces para los astros."

The original text and a Spanish translation of this poem first appeared, I believe, in a work of Granados y Galvez. (Tardes Americanas, (México, 1778,) p. 90 et seq.) The original is in the Otomie tongue, and both, together with a French version, have been inserted by M. Ternaux-Compans in the Appendix to his translation of Ixtlilxochitl's Hist. des Chichiméques (tom. I. pp. 359-367.) Bustamante, who has, also, published the Spanish version in his Galería de Antiguos Príncipes Mejicanos, (Puebla, 1821. (pp. 16, 17).) calls it the " Ode of the Flower," which was recited at a banquet of the great Tezcucan nobles. If this last, however, be the same mentioned by Torquemada, (Monarch. Ind., lib. 2, cap, 45,) it must have been written in the Tezcucan tongue; and, indeed, it is not probable that the Otomie, an Indian dialect, so distinct from the languages of Anahuac, however well understood by the royal poet, could have been comprehended by a miscellaneous audience of his countrymen.

[67] An approximation to a date is the most one can hope to arrive at with Ixtlilxochitl, who has entangled his chronology in a manner beyond my skill to unravel. Thus, after telling us that Nezahualcoyotl was fifteen years old when his father was slain in 1418, he says he died at the age of seventy-one in 1462. *Instar omnium.* Comp. Hist. Chich., MS., cap. 18, 19, 49.

[68] MS. de Ixtlilxochitl,—also, Hist. Chich., MS., cap. 49.

After tenderly em'..acing the child, the dying monarch threw over him the robes of sovereignty. He then gave audience to the ambassadors, and when they had retired, made the boy repeat the substance of the conversation. He followed this by such counsels as were suited to his comprehension, and which, when remembered through the long vista of after years, would serve as lights to guide him in his government of the kingdom. He besought him not to neglect the worship of "the unknown God," regretting that he himself had been unworthy to know him, and intimating his conviction that the time would come when he should be known and worshipped throughout the land.[69]

He next addressed himself to that one of his sons, in whom he placed the greatest trust, and whom he had selected as the guardian of the realm. " From this hour," said he to him, " you will fill the place that I have filled, of father to this child ; you will teach him to live as he ought ; and by your counsels he will rule over the empire. Stand in his place, and be his guide, till he shall be of age to govern for himself." Then, turning to his other children, he admonished them to live united with one another, and to show all loyalty to their prince, who, though a child, already manifested a discretion far above his years. " Be true to him," he added, "and he will maintain you in your rights and dignities." [70]

Feeling his end approaching, he exclaimed, " Do not bewail me with idle lamentations. But sing the song of gladness, and show a courageous spirit, that the nations I have subdued may not believe you disheartened, but may feel that each one of you is strong enough to keep them in obedience ! " The undaunted spirit of the monarch shone forth even in the agonies of death. That stout heart, however, melted, as he took leave of his children and friends, weeping tenderly over them, while he bade each a last adieu. When they had withdrawn, he ordered the officers of the palace to allow no one to enter it again. Soon after, he expired, in the seventy-second year of his age, and the forty-third of his reign.[71]

Thus died the greatest monarch, and, if one foul blot could be effaced, perhaps the best, who ever sat upon an Indian throne. His character is delineated with tolerable impartiality by his

---

[69] " No consentiendo que haya sacrificios de gente humana, que Dios se enoja de ello, castigando con rigor á los que lo hicieren ; que el dolor que llevo es no tener luz, ni conocimiento, ni ser merecedor de conocer tan gran Dios, el qual tengo por cierto que ya que los presentes no lo conozcan, *ha de venir tiempo en que sea conocido y adorado en esta tierra.*" MS. de Ixtlilxochitl.

[70] Idem, ubi supra; also Hist. Chich., cap. 49.

[71] Hist. Chich., cap. 49.

MEXICAN PEONS

kinsman, the Tezcucan chronicler. "He was wise, valiant, liberal ; and, when we consider the magnanimity of his soul, the grandeur and success of his enterprises, his deep policy, as well as daring, we must admit him to have far surpassed every other prince and captain of this New World. He had few failings himself, and rigorously punished those of others. He preferred the public to his private interest; was most charitable in his nature, often buying articles, at double their worth, of poor and honest persons, and giving them away again to the sick and infirm. In seasons of scarcity he was particularly bountiful, remitting the taxes of his vassals, and supplying their wants from the royal granaries. He put no faith in the idolatrous worship of the country. He was well instructed in moral science, and sought, above all things, to obtain light for knowing the true God. He believed in one God only, the Creator of heaven and earth, by whom we have our being, who never revealed himself to us in human form, nor in any other; with whom the souls of the virtuous are to dwell after death, while the wicked will suffer pains unspeakable. He invoked the Most High, as ' He by whom we live,' and ' Who has all things in himself.' He recognized the Sun for his father, and the Earth for his mother. He taught his children not to confide in idols, and only to conform to the outward worship of them from deference to public opinion. [72] If he could not entirely abolish human sacrifices, derived from the Aztecs, he, at least, restricted them to slaves and captives." [73]

I have occupied so much space with this illustrious prince, that but little remains for his son and successor, Nezahualpilli. I have thought it better, in our narrow limits, to present a complete view of a single epoch, the most interesting in the Tezcucan annals, than to spread the inquiries over a broader, but comparatively barren field. Yet Nezahualpilli, the heir to the crown, was a remarkable person, and his reign contains many incidents, which I regret to be obliged to pass over in silence. [74]

[72] " Solia amonestar á sus hijos en secreto bue no adorasen á aquellas figuras de Idolos, y que aquello que hiciesen en público fuese *solo por cumplimiento.*" Ibid.

[73] Idem, ubi supra.

[74] The name *Nezahualpilli* signifies "the prince for whom one has fasted," —in allusion, no doubt, to the long fast of his father previous to his birth. (See Ixtlilxochitl, Hist. Chich., MS., cap. 45.) I have explained the meaning of the equally euphonious name of his parent, Nezahualcoyotl. (Ante, ch. 4.) If it be true, that

Cæsar or Epaminondas
Could ne'er without names have been known to us,"

It is no less certain that such names as those of the two Tezcucan princes, so difficult to be pronounced or remembered by a European, are most unfavorable to immortality.

He had, in many respects, a taste similar to his father's, and, like him, displayed a profuse magnificence in his way of living and in his public edifices. He was more severe in his morals; and, in the execution of justice, stern even to the sacrifice of natural affection. Several remarkable instances of this are told; one, among others, in relation to his eldest son, the heir to the crown, a prince of great promise. The young man entered into a poetical correspondence with one of his father's concubines, the lady of Tula, as she was called, a woman of humble origin, but of uncommon endowments. She wrote verses with ease, and could discuss graver matters with the king and his ministers. She maintained a separate establishment, where she lived in state, and acquired, by her beauty and accomplishments, great ascendancy over her royal lover.[75] With this favorite the prince carried on a correspondence in verse,—whether of an amorous nature does not appear. At all events, the offence was capital. It was submitted to the regular tribunal, who pronounced sentence of death on the unfortunate youth; and the king, steeling his heart against all entreaties and the voice of nature, suffered the cruel judgment to be carried into execution. We might, in this case, suspect the influence of baser passions on his mind, but it was not a solitary instance of his inexorable justice towards those most near to him. He had the stern virtue of an ancient Roman, destitute of the softer graces which make virtue attractive. When the sentence was carried into effect, he shut himself up in his palace for many weeks, and commanded the doors and windows of his son's residence to be walled up, that it might never again be occupied.[76]

Nezahualpilli resembled his father in his passion for astronomical studies, and is said to have had an observatory on one of

---

[75] " De las concubinas la que mas privó con el rey, fué la que llamaban la Señora de Tula, no por linage, sino porque era hija de un mercader, y era tan sabia que competia con el rey y con los mas sabios de su reyno, y era en la poesía muy aventajada, que con estas gracias y dones naturales tenia al rey muy sugeto á su voluntad de tal manera que lo que queria alcanzaba de él, y así vivia sola por sí con grande aparato y magestad en unos palaciós que el rey le mandó edificar." Ixtlilxochitl, Hist. Chich., MS., cap. 57.

[76] Ibid., cap. 67.
The Tezcucan historian records several appalling examples of this severity; —one in particular, in relation to his guilty wife. The story, reminding one of the tales of an Oriental harem, has been translated for the *Appendix, Part 2, No.* 4. See also Torquemada, (Monarch. Ind., lib. cap. 66,) and Zurita (Rapport, pp. 108, 109.) He was the terror, in particular, of all unjust magistrates. They had little favor to expect from the man who could stifle the voice of nature in his own bosom, in obedience to the laws. As Suetonius said of a prince who had not his virtue, " Vehemens et in coercendis quidem delictis immodicus." Vita Galbæ, sec. 9.

his palaces.[77] He was devoted to war in his youth, but, as he
advanced in years, resigned himself to a more indolent way of
life, and sought his chief amusement in the pursuit of his favorite
science, or in the soft pleasures of the sequestered gardens of
Tezcotzinco. This quiet life was ill suited to the turbulent temper of the times, and of his Mexican rival, Montezuma. The
distant provinces fell off from their allegiance ; the army relaxed
its discipline ; disaffection crept into its ranks ; and the wily
Montezuma, partly by violence, and partly by stratagems unworthy of a king, succeeded in plundering his brother monarch
of some of his most valuable domains. Then it was, that he
arrogated to himself the title and supremacy of emperor, hitherto
borne by the Tezcucan princes, as head of the alliance. Such is
the account given by the historians of that nation, who, in this
way, explain the acknowledged superiority of the Aztec sovereign,
both in territory and consideration, on the landing of the Span-
:ards.[78]

These misfortunes pressed heavily on the spirits of Nezahualpilli. Their effect was increased by certain gloomy prognostics
of a near calamity which was to overwhelm the country.[79] He
withdrew to his retreat, to brood in secret over his sorrows. His
health rapidly declined ; and in the year 1515, at the age of fifty-
two, he sunk into the grave ;[80] happy at least, that, by this timely
death, he escaped witnessing the fulfilment of his own predictions,
in the ruin of his country, and the extinction of the Indian dyn-
asties, forever.[81]

In reviewing the brief sketch here presented of the Tezcucan
monarchy, we are strongly impressed with the conviction of its

[77] Torquemada saw the remains of this, *or what passed for such*, in his day.
Monarch. Ind., lib. 2, cap. 64.

[78] Ixtlilxochitl, Hist. Chich., MS., cap. 73, 74.
This sudden transfer of empire from the Tezcucans, at the close of the reigns
of two of their ablest monarchs, is so improbable, that one cannot but doubt
if they ever possessed it—at least, to the extent claimed by the patriotic historian. See Ante, Chap. 1, note 25, and the corresponding text.

[79] Ixtlilxochitl, Hist. Chich., MS., cap. 72.
The reader will find a particular account of these prodigies, better authen-
ticated than most miracles, in a future page of this History.

[80] Ibid., cap. 75.—Or rather at the age of fifty, if the historian is right, in
placing his birth, as he does in a preceding chapter, in 1465. (See cap. 46.)
It is not easy to decide what is true, when the writer does not take the trouble
to be true to himself.

[81] His obsequies were celebrated with sanguinary pomp. Two hundred
male and one hundred female slaves were sacrificed at his tomb. His body
was consumed, amidst a heap of jewels, precious stuffs, and incense, on a
funeral pile ; and the ashes, deposited in a golden urn, were placed in the
great temple of Huitzilopotchli, for whose worship the king notwithstanding
the lessons of his father, had some partiality. Ibid.

superiority, in all the great features of civilization, over the rest of Anahuac. The Mexicans showed a similar proficiency, no doubt in the mechanic arts, and even in mathematical science. But in the science of government, in legislation, in speculative doctrines of a religious nature, in the more elegant pursuits of poetry, eloquence, and whatever depended on refinement of taste and a polished idiom, they confessed themselves inferior by resorting to their rivals for instruction, and citing their works as the masterpieces of their tongue. The best histories, the best poems, the best code of laws, the purest dialect, were all allowed to be Tezcucan. The Aztecs rivalled their neighbors in splendor of living, and even in the magnificence of their structures. They displayed a pomp and ostentatious pageantry, truly Asiatic. But this was the development of the material, rather than the intellectual principle. They wanted the refinement of manners essential to a continued advance in civilization, An insurmountable limit was put to theirs, by that bloody mythology, which threw its withering taint over the very air that they breathed.

The superiority of the Tezcucans was owing, doubtless, in a great measure, to that of the two sovereigns whose reigns we have been depicting. There is no position, which affords such scope for ameliorating the condition of man, as that occupied by an absolute ruler over a nation imperfectly civilized. From his elevated place, commanding all the resources of his age, it is in his power to diffuse them far and wide among his people. He may be the copious reservoir on the mountain top, drinking in the dews of heaven, to send them in fertilizing streams along the lower slopes and valleys, clothing even the wilderness in beauty. Such were Nezahualcoyotl, and his illustrious successor, whose enlightened policy, extending through nearly a century, wrought a most salutary revolution in the condition of their country. It is remarkable that we, the inhabitants of the same continent, should be more familiar with the history of many a barbarian chief, both in the Old and New World, than with that of these truly great men, whose names are identified with the most glorious period in the annals of the Indian races.

What was the actual amount of the Tezcucan civilization, it is not easy to determine, with the imperfect light afforded us It was certainly far below anything, which the word conveys measured by a European standard. In some of the arts, and in any walk of science, they could only have made, as it were, a beginning. But they had begun in the right way, and already showed a refinement in sentiment and manners, a capacity for receiving instruction, which, under good auspices, might have led them on to indefinite improvement. Unhappily, they were fast falling under the dominion of the warlike Aztecs. And that people repaid the benefits received from their more polished neighbors by imparting to them their own ferocious superstition, which, falling like a mildew on the land, would soon have blighted its rich blossoms of promise, and turned even its fruits to dust and ashes.

Fernando de Alva Ixtlilxochitl, who flourished in the beginning of the sixteenth century, was a native of Tezcuco, and descended in a direct line from the sovereigns of that kingdom. The royal posterity became so numerous in a few generations, that it was common to see them reduced to great poverty, and earning a painful subsistence by the most humble occupations. Ixtlilxochitl who was descended from the principal wife or queen of Nezahualapilli, maintained a very respectable position. He filled the office of interpreter to the viceroy, to which he was recommended by his acquaintance with the ancient hieroglyphics, and his knowledge of the Mexican and Spanish languages. His birth gave him access to persons of the highest rank in his own nation, some of whom occupied important civil posts under the new government, and were thus enabled to make large collections of Indian manuscripts, which were liberally opened to him. He had an extensive library of his own, also, and with these means diligently pursued the study of the Tezcucan antiquities. He deciphered the hieroglyphics, made himself master of the songs and traditions and fortified his narrative by the oral testimony of some very aged persons, who had themselves been acquainted with the Conquerors. From such authentic sources he composed various works in the Castilian, on the primitive history of the Toltec and the Tezcucan races, continuing it down to the subversion of the empire by Cortés. These various accounts, compiled under the title of *Relaciones*, are, more or less, repetitions and abridgements of each other; nor is it easy to understand why they were thus composed. The *Historia Chichemeca* is the best digested and most complete of the whole series; and as such has been the most frequently consulted, for the preceding pages.

Ixtlilxochitl's writings have many of the defects belonging to his age. He often crowds the page with incidents of a trivial and sometimes improbable character. The improbability increases with the distance of the period; for distance, which diminishes objects to the natural eye, exaggerates them to the mental. His chronology, as I have more than once noticed, is inextricably entangled. He has often lent a too willing ear to traditions and reports which would startle the more sceptical criticism of the present time. Yet there is an appearance of good faith and simplicity in his writings, which may convince the reader, that, when he errs, it is from no worse cause than national partiality. And surely such partiality is excusable in the descendant of a proud line, shorn of its ancient splendors, which it was soothing to his own feelings to revive again,—though with something more than their legitimate lustre,—on the canvas of history. It should also be considered, that, if his narrative is sometimes startling, his researches penetrate into the mysterious depths of antiquity, where light and darkness meet and melt into each other; and when everything is still further liable to distortion, as seen through the misty medium of hieroglyphics.

With these allowances, it will be found that the Tezcucan historian has just claims to our admiration for the compass of his inquiries, and the sagacity with which they have been conducted. He has introduced us to the knowledge of the most polished people of Anahuac, whose records, if preserved, could not, at a much later period, have been comprehended; and he has thus afforded a standard of comparison, which much raises our ideas of American civilization. His language is simple, and, occasionally, eloquent and touching. His descriptions are highly picturesque. He abounds in familiar anecdote ; and the natural graces of his manner, in detailing the more striking events of history, and the personal adventures of his heroes, entitle him to the name of the Livy of Anahuac.

I shall be obliged to enter hereafter into his literary merits, in connection with the narrative of the Conquest ; for which he is a prominent authority. His earlier annals—though no one of his manuscripts has been printed—have been diligently studied by the Spanish writers in Mexico and liberally transferred to their pages ; and his reputation, like Sahagun's, has doubtless suffered by the process. His *Historia Chichemeca* is now turned into French by M. Ternaux-Compans, forming part of that inestimable series of translations from unpublished documents, which have so much enlarged our acquaintance with the early American history. I have had ample opportunity of proving the merits of his version of Ixtlilxochitl ; and am happy to bear my testimony to the fidelity and elegance with which it is executed.

NOTE. It was my intention to conclude this Introductory portion of the work with an inquiry into the *Origin of the Mexican Civilization.* "But the general question of the origin of the inhabitants of a continent," says Humdoldt, "is beyond the limits prescribed to history; perhaps it is not even a philosophic uestion." For the majority of readers," says Livy, "the origin and remote antiquities of a nation can have comparatively little interest." The criticism of these great writers is just and pertinent; and, on further consideration, I have thrown the observations on this topic, prepared with some care, into the *Appendix Part* IV); to which those, who feel sufficient curiosity in the discussion, can turn before entering on the narrative of the Conquest.

BOOK SECOND.

DISCOVERY OF MEXICO

BOOK II.

CHAPTER I.

SPAIN UNDER CHARLES V.—PROGRESS OF DISCOVERY.—COLONIAL POLICY.—CONQUEST OF CUBA.—EXPEDITIONS TO YUCATAN.

1516—1518.

IN the beginning of the sixteenth century, Spain occupied perhaps the most prominent position on the theatre of Europe. The numerous states, into which she had been so long divided, were consolidated into one monarchy. The Moslem crescent, after reigning there for eight centuries, was no longer seen on her borders. The authority of the crown did not, as in later times, overshadow the inferior orders of the state. The people enjoyed the inestimable privilege of political representation, and exercised it with manly independence. The nation at large could boast as great a degree of constitutional freedom, as any other, at that time, in Christendom. Under a system of salutary laws and an equitable administration, domestic tranquility was secured, public credit established, trade, manufactures, and even the more elegant arts, began to flourish; while a higher education called forth the first blossoms of that literature, which was to ripen into so rich a harvest before the close of the century. Arms abroad kept pace with arts at home. Spain found her empire suddenly enlarged by important acquisitions both in Europe and Africa, while a New World beyond the waters poured into her lap treasures of countless wealth, and opened an unbounded field for honorable enterprise.

Such was the condition of the kingdom at the close of the long and glorious reign of Ferdinand and Isabella, when, on the 23d of January, 1516, the sceptre passed into the hands of their daughter Joanna, or rather their grandson, Charles the Fifth, who alone ruled the monarchy during the long and imbecile existence of his unfortunate mother.   During the two years follow-ing Ferdinand's death, the regency, in the absence of Charles, was held by Cardinal Ximenes, a man whose intrepidity, extraordinary talents, and capacity for great enterprises were accompanied by a haughty spirit, which made him too indifferent as to the means of their execution. His administration, therefore, notwithstanding the uprightness of his intentions, was, from his total disregard of forms, unfavorable to constitutional liberty; for respect for forms is an essential element of freedom. With all his faults, however, Ximenes was a Spaniard, and the object he had at heart was the good of his country.

It was otherwise on the arrival of Charles, who, after a long absence, came as a foreigner into the land of his fathers   (November, 1517.) His manners, sympathies, even his language, were foreign, for he spoke the Castilian with difficulty. He knew little of his native country, of the character of the people or their institutions. He seemed to care still less for them, while his natural reserve precluded that freedom of communication, which might have counteracted, to some extent, at least, the errors of education. In everything, in short, he was a foreigner, and resigned himself to the direction of his Flemish counsellors with a docility that gave little augury of his future greatness.

On his entrance into Castile, the young monarch was accompanied by a swarm of courtly sycophants, who settled, like locusts, on every place of profit and honor throughout the kingdom. A Fleming was made grand chancellor of Castile; another Fleming was placed in the archiepiscopal see of Toledo. They even ventured to profane the sanctity of the cortes, by intruding themselves on its deliberations. Yet that body did not tamely submit to these usurpations, but gave vent to its indignation in tones becoming the representatives of a free people.[1]

The deportment of Charles, so different from that to which the Spaniards had been accustomed under the benign adminis-

---

[1] The following passage—one among many—from that faithful mirror of the times, Peter Martyr's correspondence, does ample justice to the intemperance, avarice, and intolerable arrogance of the Flemings. The testimony is worth the more, as coming from one who, though resident in Spain, was not a Spaniard. "Crumenas auro fulcire inhiant; huic uni studio invigilant. Nec detrectat juvenis Rex. Farcit quacunque posse datur; non satiat tamen. Quæ qualisve sit gens hæc, depingere adhuc nescio. Insufflat vulgus hic in omne genus hominum non arctoum. Minores faciunt Hispanos, quam si nati essent inter eorum cloacas. Rugiunt jam Hispani, labra mordent, submurmurant taciti, fatorum vices tales esse conqueruntur, quod ipsi domitores regnorum ita floccifiant ab his, quorum Deus unicus (sub rege temperato) Bacchus est cum Citherea." Opus Epistolarum, (Amstelodami, 1610,) op. 608.

tration of Ferdinand and Isabella, closed all hearts against him; and, as his character came to be understood, instead of the spontaneous outpourings of loyalty, which usually greet the accession of a new and youthful sovereign, he was everywhere encountered by opposition and disgust. In Castile, and afterwards in Aragon, Catalonia, and Valencia, the commons hesitated to confer on him the title of *King* during the lifetime of his mother, and, though they eventually yielded this point, and associated his name with hers in the sovereignty, yet they reluctantly granted the supplies he demanded, and, when they did so, watched over their appropriation with a vigilance which left little to gratify the cupidity of the Flemings. The language of the legislature on these occasions, though temperate and respectful, breathes a spirit of resolute independence not to be found, probably, on the parliamentary records of any other nation at that period. No wonder that Charles should have early imbibed a disgust for these popular assemblies,—the only bodies whence truths so unpalatable could find their way to the ears of the sovereign![2] Unfortunately, they had no influence on his conduct; till the discontent, long allowed to fester in secret, broke out into that sad war of the *comunidades*, which shook the state to its foundations, and ended in the subversion of its liberties.

The same pestilent foreign influence was felt, though much less sensibly, in the Colonial administration. This had been placed, in the preceding reign, under the immediate charge of the two great tribunals, the Council of the Indies, and the *Casa de Contratacion*, or India House, at Seville. It was their business to further the progress of discovery, watch over the infant settlements, and adjust the disputes which grew up in them. But the licenses granted to private adventurers did more for the cause of discovery, than the patronage of the crown or its officers. The long peace, enjoyed with slight interruption by Spain in the early part of the sixteenth century, was most auspicious for this; and the restless cavalier, who could no longer win laurels on the fields of Africa or Europe, turned with eagerness to the brilliant career opened to him beyond the ocean.

It is difficult for those of our time, as familiar from childhood with the most remote places on the globe as with those in their

<hr>

[2] Yet, the nobles were not all backward in manifesting their disgust. When Charles would have conferred the famous Burgundian order of the Golden Fleece on the Count of Benavente, that lord refused it, proudly telling him, "I am a Castilian. I desire no honors but those of my own country, in my opinion, quite as good as—indeed, better than those of any other." Sandoval, Historia de la Vida y Hechos del Emperador Cárlos V., (Amberes, 1681,) tom. I. p. 102.

own neighborhood, to picture to themselves the feelings of the men who lived in the sixteenth century. The dread mystery, which had so long hung over the great deep, had, indeed, been removed. It was no longer beset with the same undefined horrors as when Columbus launched his bold bark on its dark and unknown waters. A new and glorious world had been thrown open. But as to the precise spot where that world lay, its extent, its history, whether it were island or continent,—of all this, they had very vague and confused conceptions. Many, in their ignorance, blindly adopted the erroneous conclusion into which the great Admiral had been led by his superior science,—that the new countries were a part of Asia ; and, as the mariner wandered among the Bahamas, or steered his caravel across the Caribbean seas, he fancied he was inhaling the rich odors of the spice-islands in the Indian Ocean. Thus every fresh discovery, interpreted by this previous delusion, served to confirm him in his error, or, at least, to fill his mind with new perplexities.

The career thus thrown open had all the fascinations of a desperate hazard, on which the adventurer 'taked all his hopes of fortune, fame, and life itself. It was not often, indeed, that he won the rich prize which he most coveted ; but then he was sure to win the meed of glory, scarcely less dear to his chivalrous spirit ; and, if he survived to return to his home, he had wonderful stories to recount, of perilous chances among the strange people he had visited, and the burning climes, whose rank fertility and magnificence of vegetation so far surpassed anything he had witnessed in his own. These reports added fresh fuel to imaginations already warmed by the study of those tales of chivalry which formed the favorite reading of the Spaniards, at that period. Thus romance and reality acted on each other, and the soul of the Spaniard was exalted to that pitch of enthusiasm, which enabled him to encounter the terrible trials that lay in the path of the discovery. Indeed, the life of the cavalier of that day was romance put into action. The story of his adventures in the New World forms one of the most remarkable pages in the history of man.

Under this chivalrous spirit of enterprise, the progress of discovery had extended, by the beginning of Charles the Fifth's reign, from the bay of Honduras, along the winding shores of Darien, and the South American continent, to the Rio de la Plata. The mighty barrier of the Isthmus had been climbed, and the Pacific descried, by Nuñez de Balboa, second only to Columbus in this valiant band of " ocean chivalry." The Bahamas and Caribbee Islands had been explored, as well as the Peninsula of Florida on the northern continent. To this latter point Sebastian Cabot had arrived in his descent along the coast from Labrador, in 1497. So that before 1518, the period when our narrative begins, the eastern borders of both the great continents had been surveyed through nearly their whole extent. The shores of the great Mexican Gulf, however, sweeping with a wide circuit far into the interior, remained still concealed, with the rich realms that lay beyond, from the eye of the navigator. The time has now come for their discovery.

The business of colonization had kept pace with that of discovery. In several of the islands, and in various parts of Terra Firma, and in Darien, settlements had been established, under the control of governors who affected the state and authority of viceroys. Grants of land were assigned to the colonists, on which they raised the natural products of the soil, but gave still more attention to the sugar-cane, imported from the Canaries. Sugar, indeed, together with the beautiful dye-woods of the country and the precious metals, formed almost the only articles of export in the infancy of the colonies, which had not yet introduced those other staples of the West Indian commerce, which, in our day, constitute its principal wealth. Yet the precious metals, painfully gleaned from a few scanty sources, would have made poor returns, but for the gratuitous labor of the Indians.

The cruel system of *repartimientos*, or distribution of the Indians as slaves among the conquerors, had been suppressed by Isabella. Although subsequently countenanced by the government, it was under the most careful limitations. But it is impossible to license crime by halves,—to authorize injustice at all, and hope to regulate the measure of it. The eloquent remonstrances of the Dominicans,—who devoted themselves to the good work of conversion in the New World with the same zeal that they showed for persecution in the Old,—but, above all, those of Las Casas, induced the regent, Ximenes, to send out a commission with full powers to inquire into the alleged grievances, and to redress them. It had authority, moreover, to investigate the conduct of the civil officers, and to reform any abuses in their administration. This extraordinary commission consisted of three Hieronymite friars and an eminent jurist, all men of learning and unblemished piety.

They conducted the inquiry in a very dispassionate manner; but, after long deliberation, came to a conclusion most unfavorable to the demands of Las Casas, who insisted on the entire freedom of the natives. This conclusion they justified on the grounds that the Indians would not labor without compulsion, and that, unless they labored, they could not be brought into

communication with the whites, nor be converted to Christianity. Whatever we may think of this argument, it was doubtless
urged with sincerity by its advocates, whose conduct through
their whole administration places their motives above suspicion.
They accompanied it with many careful provisions for the protection of the natives. But in vain. The simple people, accustomed all their days to a life of indolence and ease, sunk under
the oppressions of their masters, and the population wasted
away with even more frightful rapidity than did the Aborigines
in our own country, under the operation of other causes. It is
not necessary to pursue these details further, into which I have
been led by the desire to put the reader in possession of the
general policy and state of affairs in the New World, at the
period when the present narrative begins.[3]

Of the islands, Cuba was the second discovered ; but no attempt had been made to plant a colony there during the lifetime
of Columbus ; who, indeed, after skirting the whole extent of its
southern coast, died in the conviction that it was part of the continent.[4]   At length, in 1511, Diego the son and successor of
the "Admiral," who still maintained the seat of the government
in Hispaniola, finding the mines much exhausted there, proposed to occupy the neighboring island of Cuba, or Fernandina, as
it was called, in compliment to the Spanish monarch.[5]   He
prepared a small force for the conquest, which he placed under
the command of Don Diego Velasquez ; a man described by a
contemporary, as "possessed of considerable experience in military affairs, having served seventeen years in the European
wars ; as honest, illustrious by his lineage and reputation, covetous of glory and somewhat more covetous of wealth." [6]   The portrait sketched by no unfriendly hand.

Valasquez, or rather, his lieutenant, Narvaez, who took the of-

---

[3] I will take the liberty to refer the reader, who is desirous of being more
minutely acquainted with the Spanish colonial administration and the state
of discovery previous to Charles V., to the "History of the Reign of Ferdinand and Isabella," (Part 2, ch. 9, 26,) where the subject is treated *in
extenso*.

[4] See the curious document attesting this, and drawn up by order of
Columbus, ap. Navarrete, Coleccion de los Viages y de Descubrimientos,
(Madrid, 1825,) tom. II. Col. Dip., No. 76.

[5] The island was originally called by Columbus, Juana, in honor of prince
John, heir to the Castilian crown.   After his death it received the name of
Fernandina, at the king's desire.   The Indian name has survived both.   Her-
rera, Hist. General, Descrip., cap. 6.

[6] "Erat Didacus, ut hoc in loco de eo semel tantum dicamus, veteranus
miles, rei militaris gnarus, quippe qui septem et decem annos in Hispania
militiam exercitus fuerat, homo probus, opibus genere et fama clarus, honoris
cupidus, pecuniæ aliquanto cupidior." De Rebus Gestis Ferdinandi Cortesii,
MS.

fiee on himself of scouring the country, met with no serious opposition from the inhabitants, who were of the same family with the effeminate natives of Hispaniola. The conquest, through the merciful interposition of Las Casas, "the protector of the Indians," who accompanied the army in its march, was affected without much bloodshed. One chief, indeed, named Hatuey, having fled originally from St. Domingo to escape the oppression of its invaders, made a desperate resistance, for which he was condemned by Velasquez to be burned alive. It was he, who made that memorable reply, more eloquent than a volume of invective. When urged at the stake to embrace Christianity, that his soul might find admission into heaven, he inquired if the white men would go there. On being answered in the affirmative, he exclaimed, "Then I will not be a Christian ; for I would not go again to a place where I must find men so cruel ! " [7]

After the conquest, Velasquez, now appointed governor, diligently occupied himself with measures for promoting the prosperity of the Island. He formed a number of settlements, bearing the same names with the modern towns, and made St. Jago, on the south-east corner, the seat of government. [8]

He invited settlers by liberal grants of land and slaves. He encouraged them to cultivate the soil, and gave particular attention to the sugar-cane, so profitable an article of commerce in later times. He was, above all, intent on working the gold mines, which promised better returns than those in Hispaniola. The affairs of his government did not prevent him, meanwhile, from casting many a wistful glance at the discoveries going forward on the continent, and he longed for an opportunity to embark in these golden adventures himself. Fortune favored him the occasion he desired.

An *hidalgo* of Cuba, named Hernandez de Cordova, sailed with three vessels on an expedition to one of the neighboring Bahama Islands, in quest of Indian slaves. (February 8, 1517.) He encountered a succession of heavy gales which drove him far out of his course, and at the end of three weeks he found himself on a strange and unknown coast. On landing and asking the name of the country, he was answered by the natives, " *Tectetan*," meaning " I do not understand you,"—but which the

---

[7] The story is told by Las Casas in his appalling record of the cruelties of of his countrymen in the New World, which charity—and common sense— may excuse us for believing the good father has greatly overcharged. Brevissima Relacion de la Destruycion de las Indias, (Venetia, 1643) p. 28.

[8] Among the most ancient of these establishments we find the Havana, Puerto del Principe, Trinidad, St. Salvador, Matanzas, or *the Slaughter*, so called from a massacre of the Spaniards there by the Indians. Bernal Diaz Hist. de la Conquista, cap. 8.

Spaniards, misinterpreting into the name of the place, easily cor.
rupted into Yucatan. Some writers give a different etymology.[9]
Such mistakes, however, were not uncommon with the early discoverers, and have been the origin of many a name on the American continent. [10]

Cordova had landed on the north-eastern end of the peninsula,
at cape Catoche. He was astonished at the size and solid
materials of the buildings constructed of stone and lime, so different from the frail tenements of reeds and rushes which formed
the habitations of the islanders. He was struck, also with the
higher cultivation of the soil, and with the delicate texture of the
cotton garments and gold ornaments of the natives. Every thing
indicated a civilization far superior to any thing he had before
witnessed in the New World. He saw the evidence of a different
race, moreover, in the warlike spirit of the people. Rumors of
the Spaniards had perhaps, preceded them, as they were repeatedly asked if they came from the east ; and, wherever they
landed, they were met with the most deadly hostility. Cordova
himself, in one of his skirmishes with the Indians, received more
than a dozen wounds, and one only of his party escaped unhurt.
At length, when he had coasted the peninsula as far as Campeachy, he returned to Cuba, which he reached after an absence
of several months, having suffered all the extremities of ill, which
these pioneers of the ocean were sometimes called to endure,
and which none but the most courageous spirit could have survived. As it was, half the original number, consisting of one
hundred and ten men, perished, including their brave commander,
who died soon after his return. The reports he had brought
back of the country, and, still more, the specimens of curiously
wrought gold, convinced Velasquez of the importance of this
discovery, and he prepared with all despatch to avail himself
of it.[11]

He accordingly fitted out a little squadron of four vessels for
the newly discovered lands, and placed it under the command

---

[9] Gormara, Historia de las Indias, cap. 52, ap Barcia, tom. II.
Bernal Diaz says the word came from the vegetable *yuca* and tale the name
for a hillock in which it is planted. (Hist. de la Conquista, cap. 6.) M.
Waldeck finds a much more plausible derivation in the Indian word *Ouyouck-*
atan, " listen to what they say." Voyage Pittoresque, p. 25.

[10] Two navigators, Solís and Pinzon, had described the coast as far back
as 1506, according to Herrera, though they had not taken possession of it.
(Hist. General, dec. 1, lib. 6. cap. 17.) It is indeed remarkable it should so
long have eluded discovery, considering that it is but two degrees distant
from Cuba.

[11] Oviedo, General y Natural Historia de las Indias, MS , lib. 33, cap. 1.—
De Rebus Gestis, MS.—Carta del Cabildo de Vera Cruz, (July 10, 1519,)
MS.

of his nephew, Juan de Grijalva, a man on whose probity, prudence, and attachment to himself he knew he could rely. The fleet left the port of St. Jago de Cuba, May 1, 1518.[12] It took the course pursued by Cordova, but was driven somewhat to the south, the first land that it made being the island of Cozumel. From this quarter Grijalva soon passed over to the continent and coasted the peninsula, touching at the same places as his predecessor. Everywhere he was struck, like him, with the evidence of a higher civilization, especially in the architecture ; as he well might be, since this was the region of those extraordinary remains which have become recently the subject of so much speculation. He was astonished, also at the sight of large stone crosses, evidently objects of worship, which he met with in various places. Reminded by these circumstances of his own country, he gave the peninsula the name of " New Spain," a name since appropriated to a much wider extent of territory.[13]

Wherever Grijalva landed, he experienced the same unfriendly reception as Cordova, though he suffered less, being better prepared to meet it. In the *Rio de Tabasco*, or *Grijalva*, as it is often called, after him, he held an amicable conference with a chief who gave him a number of gold plates fashioned into a sort of armor. As he wound round the Mexican coast, one of his captains, Pedro de Alvarado, afterwards famous in the Conquest, entered a river, to which he, also, left his own name. In a neighboring stream, called the *Rio de Vanderas*, or " River of Banners," from the ensigns displayed by the natives on its borders, Grijalva had the first communication with the Mexicans themselves.

The cacique who ruled over this province had received notice of the approach of the Europeans, and of their extraordinary appearance. He was anxious to collect all the information he could respecting them and the motives of their visit, that he might transmit them to his master, the Aztec emperor.[14] A

Bernal Diaz denies that the original object of the expedition, in which he took part, was to procure slaves, though Valasquez had proposed it. (Hist. de la Conquista, cap. 2.) But he is contradicted in this by the other contemporary records above cited.

[12] Itinerario de la isola de Iuchathan, novamente ritrovata per il signor Joan de Grijalva, per il suo capellano, MS.

The chaplain's word may be taken for the date, which is usually put at the eighth of April.

[13] De Rubus Gestis, MS.—Itinerario del Capellano, MS.

[14] According to the Spanish authorities, the cacique was sent with these presents from the Mexican sovereign, who had received previous tidings of the approach of the Spaniards. I have followed Sahagun, who obtained his intelligence directly from the natives. Historia de la Conquista, MS., cap. 2.

friendly conference took place between the parties on shore, where Grijalva landed with all his force, so as to make a suitable impression on the mind of the barbaric chief. The interview lasted some hours, though, as there was no one on either side to interpret the language of the other, they could communicate only by signs. They, however, interchanged presents, and the Spaniards had the satisfaction of receiving, for a few worthless toys and trinkets, a rich treasure of jewels, gold ornaments and vessels, of the most fantastic forms and workmanship.[15]

Grijalva now thought that in this successful traffic—successful beyond his most sanguine expectations — he had accomplished the chief object of his mission. He steadily refused the solicitations of his followers to plant a colony on the spot,—a work of no little difficulty in so populous and powerful a country as this appeared to be. To this, indeed, he was inclined, but deemed it contrary to his instructions, which limited him to barter with the natives. He therefore despatched Alvarado in one of the caravels back to Cuba, with the treasure and such intelligence as he had gleaned of the great empire in the interior, and then pursued his voyage along the coast.

He touched at San Juan de Ulua, and at the *Isla de los Sacrificios*, so called by him from the bloody remains of human victims found in one of the temples. He then held on his course as far as the province of Panuco, where finding some difficulty in doubting a boisterous headland, he returned on his track, and, after an absence of nearly six months, reached Cuba in safety. Grijalva has the glory of being the first navigator who set foot on the Mexican soil, and opened an intercourse with the Aztecs.[16]

On reaching the island, he was surprised to learn, that another and more formidable armament had been fitted out to follow up his own discoveries, and to find orders, at the same time, from the governor, couched in no very courteous language, to repair at once to St. Jago. He was received by that personage, not merely with coldness, but with reproaches for having neglected so fair an opportunity of establishing a colony in the country he had visited. Velasquez was one of those captious spirits, who, when things do not go exactly to their minds, are sure to shift the responsibility of the failure from their own shoulders, where it should lie, to those of others. He had an ungenerous nature

---

[15] Gomara has given the *per contra* of this negotation, in which gold and jewels, of the value of fifteen or twenty thousand *pesos de oro*, were exchanged for glass beads, pins, scissors, and other trinkets common in an assorted cargo for savages. Crónica, cap. 6.

[16] Itinerario del Capellano, MS.—Carta de Vera Cruz, MS.

says an old writer, and credulous, easily moved to suspicion.[17] In the present instance it was most unmerited. Grijalva, natu· rally a modest, unassuming person, had acted in obedience to the instructions of his commander, given before sailing ; and had done this in opposition to his own judgment and the importunities of his followers. His conduct merited anything but censure from his employer.[18]

When Alvarado had returned to Cuba with his golden freight, and the accounts of the rich empire of Mexico which he had gathered from the natives, the heart of the governor swelled with rapture as he saw his dreams of avarice and ambition so likely to be realized. Impatient of the long absence of Grijalva, he despatched a vessel in search of him under the command of Olid, a cavalier who took an important part afterwards in the Conquest. Finally he resolved to fit out another armament on a sufficient scale to insure the subjugation of the country.

He previously solicited authority for this from the Hieronymite commission in St. Domingo. He then despatched his chaplain to Spain with the royal share of the gold brought from Mexico, and a full account of the intelligence gleaned there. He set forth his own manifold services, and solicited from the court full powers to go on with the conquest and colonization of the newly discovered regions.[19] Before receiving an answer, he began his preparations for the armament, and, first of all, endevored to find a suitable person to share the expense of it, and to take the command. Such a person he found, after some difficulty and delay, in Hernando Cortés ; the man of all others best calculated to achieve this great enterprise,—the last man, to whom Velasquez, could he have foreseen the results, would have confided it.

[17] " Hombre de terrible condicion," says Herrera, citing the good Bishop of Chiapa, " para los que le servian, i aiudaban, i que facilmente se indignaba contra aquellos." Hist. General, dec. 2, lib. 3, cap. 10.

[18] At least, such is the testimony of Las Casas, who knew both the parties well, and had often conversed with Grijalva upon his voyage. Historia General de las Indias, MS., lib. 3, cap. 113.

[19] Itinerario del Capellano, MS.—Las Casas, Hist. de las Indias, MS., lib. 3, cap. 113.

The most circumstantial account of Grijalva's expedition is to be found in the *Itinerary* of his chaplain above quoted. The original is lost, but an indifferent Italian version was published at Venice, in 1522. A copy which belonged to Ferdinand Columbus, is still extant in the library of the great church of Seville. The book had become so exceedingly rare, however, that the historiographer, Muñoz, made a transcript of it with his own hand, and from his manuscript that in my possession was taken.

CHAPTER II.

HERNANDO CORTES.—HIS EARLY LIFE.—VISITS THE NEW WORLD.
—HIS RESIDENCE IN CUBA.—DIFFICULTIES WITH VELASQUEZ.
—ARMADA INTRUSTED TO CORTES.

1518.

HERNANDO CORTES was born at Medellin, a town in the south-east corner of Estremadura, in 1485.[1] He came of an ancient and respectable family ; and historians have gratified the national vanity by tracing it up to the Lombard kings, whose descendants crossed the Pyrenees, and established themselves in Aragon under the Gothic monarchy.[2] This royal genealogy was not found out till Cortés had acquired a name which would confer distinction on any descent, however noble. His father, Martin Cortés de Monroy, was a captain of infantry, in moderate circumstances, but a man of unblemished honor ; and both he and his wife, Doña Catalina Pizarro Altamirano, appear to have been much regarded for their excellent qualities.[3]

In his infancy Cortés is said to have had a feeble constitution, which strengthened as he grew older. At fourteen, he was sent to Salamanca, as his father, who conceived great hopes from his quick and showy parts, proposed to educate him for the law, a

---

[1] Gomara, Crónica, cap. 1.—Bernal Diaz, Hist. de la Conquista, cap. 203. I find no more precise notice of the date of his birth; except, indeed, by Pizarro y Orellana, who tells us " that Cortés came into the world the same day that that *infernal beast, the false heretic Luther,* went out of it,—by way of compensation, no doubt, since the labors of the one to pull down the true faith were counterbalanced by those of the other to maintain and extend it ! " (Varones Illustres del Nuevo Mundo, (Madrid, 1639,) p. 66.) But this statement of the good cavalier, which places the birth of our hero in 1483, looks rather more like a zeal for " the true faith," than for historic.

[2] Argensola, in particular, has bestowed great pains on the *prosapia* of the house of Cortés; which he traces up, nothing doubting, to Narnes Cortés, king of Lombardy and Tuscany. Anales de Aragon, (Zaragoza, 1630,) pp. 621-625.—Also, Caro de Torres, Historia de las Ordenes Militares, (Madrid, 1629,) fol. 103.

[3] De Rebus Gestis, MS.
Las Casas, who knew the father, bears stronger testimony to his poverty than to his noble birth. " Un escudero," he says of him, " que yo conocí harto pobre y humilde, aunque Christiano, viejo *y dizen que hidalgo.*" Hist. de las Indias, MS., lib. 3, cap. 27.

profession which held out better inducements to the young as-pirant than any other. The son, however, did not conform to these views. He showed little fondness for books, and, after loitering away two years at college, returned home, to the great chagrin of his parents. Yet his time had not been wholly mis-spent, since he had laid up a little store of Latin, and learned to write good prose, and even verses " of some estimation, con-sidering "—as an old writer quaintly remarks—" Cortés as the author."[4] He now passed his days in the idle, unprofitable manner of one who, too wilful to be guided by others, proposes no object to himself. His buoyant spirits were continually break-ing out in troublesome frolics and capricious humors, quite at variance with the orderly habits of his father's household. He showed a particular inclination for the military profession, or rather for the life of adventure to which in those days it was sure to lead. And when, at the age of seventeen, he proposed to enrol himself under the banners of the Great Captain, his parents, probably thinking a life of hardship and hazard abroad preferable to one of idleness at home, made no objection.

The youthful cavalier, however, hesitated whether to seek his fortunes under that victorious chief, or in the New World, where gold as well as glory was to be won, and where the very dangers had a mystery and romance in them inexpressibly fascinating to a youthful fancy. It was in this direction, accordingly, that the hot spirits of that day found a vent, especially from that part of the country where Cortés lived, the neighborhood of Seville and Cádiz, the focus of nautical enterprise. He decided on this latter course, and an opportunity offered in the splendid arma-ment fitted out under Don Nicolas de Ovando, successor to Columbus. An unlucky accident defeated the purpose of Cortés.[6]

As he was scaling a high wall, one night, which gave him access to the apartment of a lady with whom he was engaged in an intrigue, the stones gave way, and he was thrown down with much violence and buried under the ruins. A severe contusion, though attended with no other serious consequences, confined him to his bed till after the departure of the fleet.[6]

---

[4] Argensola, Anales, p. 220.

Las Casas and Bernal Diaz both state that he was Bachelor of Laws at Sal-amanca. (Hist. de las Indias, MS., ubi supra.—Hist. de la Conquista, cap. 203.) The degree was given probably in later life, when the University might feel a pride in claiming him among her sons.

[5] De Rebus Gestis, MS.—Gomara, Crónica, cap. 1

[6] De Rebus Gestis, MS.—Gomara, Ibid.

Argensola states the cause of his detention concisely enough : " Suspendió el viaje, *por enamorado y por quartanario.*" Anales, p. 621.

Two years longer he remained at home, profiting little, as it would seem, from the lesson he had received.   At length he availed himself of another opportunity presented by the departure of a small squadron of vessels bound to the Indian islands.   He was nineteen years of age, when he bade adieu to his native shores in 1504,—the same year in which Spain lost the best and greatest in her long line of princes, Isabella the Catholic.

The vessel in which Cortés sailed was commanded by one Alonso Quintero.   The fleet touched at the Canaries, as was common in the outward passage.   While the other vessels were detained there taking in supplies, Quintero secretly stole out by night from the island, with the design of reaching Hispaniola, and securing the market, before the arrival of his companions. A furious storm, which he encountered, however, dismasted his ship, and he was obliged to return to port and refit.   The convoy consented to wait for their unworthy partner, and after a short detention they all sailed in company again.   But the faithless Quintero, as they drew near the Islands, availed himself once more of the darkness of the night, to leave the squadron with the same purpose as before.   Unluckily for him, he met with a succession of heavy gales and head winds, which drove him from his course, and he wholly lost his reckoning.   For many days the vessel was tossed about, and all on board were filled with apprehensions, and no little indignation against the author of their calamities.   At length they were cheered one morning with the sight of a white dove, which, wearied by its flight, lighted on the topmast.   The biographers of Cortés speak of it as a miracle.[7]   Fortunately it was no miracle, but a very natural occurrence, showing incontestably that they were near land.   In a short time, by taking the direction of the bird's flight, they reached the island of Hispaniola ; and, on coming into port, the worthy master had the satisfaction to find his companions arrived before him, and their cargoes already sold.[8]

Immediately on landing, Cortés repaired to the house of the governor, to whom he had been personally known in Spain. Ovando was absent on an expedition into the interior, but the young man was kindly received by the secretary, who assured him there would be no doubt of his obtaining a liberal grant of

[7] Some thought it was the Holy Ghost in the form of this dove; "Sanctum esse Spiritum, qui, in illius alitis specie, ut mœstos et afflictos solaretur, venire erat dignatus"; (De Rebus Gestis, MS.;) a conjecture which seems very reasonable to Pizarro y Orellana, since the expedition was to "redound so much to the spread of the Catholic faith, and the Castilian monarchy"; Varones Illustres, p. 70.

[8] Gomara, Crónica, cap. 2.

land to settle on. "But I came to get gold," replied Cortés, "not to till the soil, like a peasant."

On the governor's return, Cortés consented to giving up his roving thoughts, at least for a time, as the other labored to convince him that he would be more likely to realize his wishes from the slow, indeed, but sure, returns of husbandry, where the soil and the laborers were a free gift to the planter, than by taking his chance in the lottery of adventure, in which there were so many blanks to a prize. He accordingly received a grant of land, with a *repartimiento* of Indians, and was appointed notary of the town or settlement of Açua. His graver pursuits, however, did not prevent his indulgence of the amorous propensities which belong to the sunny clime where he was born; and this frequently involved him in affairs of honor, from which, though an expert swordsman, he carried away scars that accompanied him to his grave.[9] He occasionally, moreover, found the means of breaking up the monotony of his way of life by engaging in the military expeditions, which, under the command of Ovando's lieutenant, Diego Velasquez, were employed to suppress the insurrections of the natives. In this school the young adventurer first studied the wild tactics of Indian warfare; he became familiar with toil and danger, and with those deeds of cruelty which have too often, alas! stained the bright scutcheons of the Castilian chivalry in the New World. He was only prevented by illness—a most fortunate one, on this occasion—from embarking in Nicuessa's expedition, which furnished a tale of woe, not often matched in the annals of Spanish discovery. Providence reserved him for higher ends.

At length, in 1511, when Velasquez undertook the conquest of Cuba, Cortés willingly abandoned his quiet life for the stirring scenes there opened, and took part in the expedition. He displayed, throughout the invasion, an activity and courage that won him the approbation of the commander; while his free and cordial manners, his good-humor, and lively sallies of wit made him the favorite of the soldiers. "He gave little evidence," says a contemporary "of the great qualities which he afterwards showed." It is probable these qualities were not known to himself; while to a common observer his careless manners and jocund repartees might well seem incompatible with any thing serious or profound; as the real depth of the current is not suspected under the light play and sunny sparkling of the surface.[11]

[9] Bernal Diaz, Hist. de la Conquista, cap. 203.
[11] De Rebus Gestis, MS —Gomara, Crónica, cap. 3, 4.—Las Casas, Hist de las Indias, MS., lib. 3, cap. 27.

After the reduction of the island, Cortés seems to have been held in great favor by Velasquez, now appointed its governor. According to Las Casas, he was made one of his secretaries.[11] He still retained the same fondness for gallantry, for which his handsome person afforded obvious advantages, but which had more than once brought him into trouble in earlier life.   Among the families who had taken up their residence in Cuba was one of the name of Xuarez, from Granada in Old Spain,   It consisted of a brother, and four sisters remarkable for their beauty.   With one of them, named Catalina, the susceptible heart of the young soldier became enamoured.[12] How far the intimacy was carried is not quite certain.   But it appears he gave his promise to marry her,—a promise, which, when the time came, and reason, it may be, had got the better of passion, he showed no alacrity in keeping.   He resisted, indeed, all remonstrances to this effect, from the lady's family, backed by the governor, and somewhat sharpened, no doubt, in the latter by the particular interest he took in one of the fair sisters, who is said not to have repaid it with ingratitude.

Whether the rebuke of Velasquez, or some other cause of disgust, rankled in the breast of Cortéz, he now became cold toward his patron, and connected himself with a disaffected party tolerably numerous in the island.   They were in the habit of meeting at his house and brooding over their causes of discontent, chiefly founded, it would appear, on what they conceived an ill requital of their services in the distribution of lands and offices.   It may well be imagined, that it could have been no easy task for the ruler of one of these colonies, however discreet and well intentioned, to satisfy the indefinite cravings of speculators and adventurers, who swarmed, like so many famished harpins, in the track of discovery in the New World.[13]

The malcontents determined to lay their grievances before the higher authorities in Hispaniola, from whom Velasquez had received his commission.   The voyage was one of some hazard, as it was to be made in an open boat, across an arm of the sea

[11] Hist. de las Indias, MS., loc. cit.

" Res omnes arduas difficilesque per Cortesium, quem in dies magis magisque amplectebatur, Velasquius agit.   Ex eo ducis favore et gratiâ magnâ Cortesio invidia est orta."   De Rebus Gestis, MS.

[12] Solís has found a patent of nobility for this lady also,—" doncella noble y recatada." (Historia de la Conquista de Méjico, (Paris, 1838,) lib 1, cap. 9.)   Las Casas treats her with less ceremony.   " Una hermana de *un* Juan Xuarez, *gente pobre.*"   Hist. de las Indias, MS., lib. 3, cap. 17.

[13] Gomara, Crónica, cap. 4.—Las Casas, His. de las Indias, MS., ubi supra. —De Rebus Gestis, MS.—Memorial de Benito Martinez, capellan de D. Velasquez, contra H. Cortés, MS.

eighteen leguer wide.; and they fixed on Cortés, with whose fearless spirit they were well acquainted, as the fittest man to undertake it. The conspiracy got wind, and came to the governor's ear before the departure of the envoy, whom he instantly caused to be seized, loaded with fetters, and placed in strict confinement. It is even said, he would have hung him, but for the interposition of his friends.[14] The fact is not incredible. The governors of these little territories, having entire control over the fortunes of their subjects, enjoyed an authority far more despotic than that of the sovereign himself. They were generally men of rank and personal consideration ; their distance from the mother country withdrew their conduct from searching scrutiny, and, when that did occur, they usually had interest and means of corruption at command, sufficient to shield them from punishment. The Spanish colonial history, in its earlier stages, affords striking instances of the extraordinary assumption and abuse of powers by these petty potentates ; and the sad fate of Vasquez Nuñez de Balboa, the illustrious discoverer of the Pacific, though the most signal, is by no means a solitary example, that the greatest services could be requited by persecution and an ignominious death.

The governor of Cuba, however, although irascible and suspicious in his nature, does not seem to have been vindictive, nor particularly cruel. In the present instance, indeed, it may well be doubted whether the blame would not be more reasonably charged on the unfounded expectations of his followers than on himself.

Cortés did not long remain in durance. He contrived to throw back one of the bolts of his fetters ; and, after extricating his limbs, succeeded in forcing open a window with the irons so as to admit of his escape, He was lodged on the second floor of the building, and was able to let himself down to the pavement without injury, and unobserved. He then made the best of his way to a neighboring church, where he claimed the privilege of sanctuary.

Velasquez, though incensed at his escape, was afraid to violate the sanctity of the place by employing force. But he stationed a guard in the neighborhood, with orders to seize the fugitive, if he should forget himself so far as to leave the sanctuary. In a few days this happened. As Cortes was carelessly standing without the walls in front of the building, an *alguacil* suddenly sprung on him from behind and pinioned his arms, while others rushed in and secured him. This man, whose

---

[14] Las Casas, Hist. de las Indias, MS., ubi supra.

name was Juan ⸍scudero, was afterwards hung by Cortes for some offence in New Spain.[15]

The unlucky prisoner was again put in irons, and carried on board a vessel to sail the next morning for Hispaniola, there to undergo his trial. Fortune favored him once more. He suc·ceeded, after much difficulty and no little pain, in passing his feet through the rings which shackled them. He then came cautiously on deck, and, covered by the darkness of the night, stole quietly down the side of the ship into a boat that lay floating below. He pushed off from the vessel with as little noise as possible. As he drew near the shore, the stream be·came rapid and turbulent. He hesitated to trust his boat to it ; and as he was an excellent swimmer prepared to breast it himself, and boldly plunged into the water. The current was strong, but the arm of a man struggling for life was stronger ; and after buffeting the waves till he was nearly exhausted, he succeeded in gaining a landing ; when he sought refuge in the same sanctuary which had protected him before. The facility with which Cortés a second time effected his escape may lead one to doubt the fidelity of his guards ; who perhaps looked on him as the victim of persecution, and felt the influence of those popular manners which seem to have gained him friends in every society into which he was thrown.[16]

For some reason not explained,—perhaps from policy,—he now relinquished his objections to the marriage with Catalina Xuarez. He thus secured the good offices of her family. Soon afterwards the governor himself relented, and became recon·ciled to his unfortunate enemy. A strange story is told in connexion with this event. It is said, his proud spirit refused to accept the proffers of reconciliation made him by Velasquez ; and that one evening, leaving the sanctuary, he presented himself unexpectedly before the latter in his own quarters, when on a military excursion at some distance from the capital. The governor, startled by the sudden apparition of his enemy completely armed before him, with some dismay in·quired the meaning of it. Cortés answered by insisting on a full explanation of his previous conduct. After some hot discus·sion the interview terminated amicably ; the parties embraced, and, when a messenger arrived to announce the escape of Cortés,

---

[15] Las Casas, Hist. de la Indias, MS. loc. cit.—Memorial de Martinez, MS.
[16] Gomara, Crónica, cap. 4.

Herrera tells a silly story of his being unable to swim, and throwing him·self on a plank, which, after being carried out to sea, was washed ashore with him at flood tide. Hist. General, dec. 1, lib. 9, cap. 8.

he found him in the apartments of his Excellency, where, having retired to rest, both were actually sleeping in the same bed! The anecdote is repeated without distrust by more than one biographer of Cortés.[17] It is not very probable, however, that a haughty, irascible man like Velasquez should have given such uncommon proofs of condescension and familiarity to one, so far beneath him in station, with whom he had been so recently in deadly feud ; nor, on the other hand, that Cortés should have had the silly temerity to brave the lion in his den, where a single nod would have sent him to the gibbet,—and that, too, with as little compunction or fear of consequences, as would have attended the execution of an Indian slave.[18]

The reconciliation with the governor, however brought about, was permanent. Cortés, though not reëstablished in the office of secretary, received a liberal *repartimiento* of Indians, and an ample territory in the neighborhood of St. Jago, of which he was soon after made *alcalde*. He now lived almost wholly on his estate, devoting himself to agriculture with more zeal than formerly. He stocked his plantation with different kinds of cattle, some of which were first introduced by him into Cuba.[19] He wrought, also, the gold mines which fell to his share, and which in this island promised better returns than those in Hispaniola. By this course of industry he found himself, in a few years, master of some two or three thousand *castellanos*, a large sum for one in his situation. "God, who alone knows at what cost of Indian lives it was obtained," exclaims Las Casas, " will take account of it!"[20] His days glided smoothly away in these tranquil pursuits, and in the society of his beautiful wife, who, however ineligible as a connexion, from the inferiority of her condition, appears to have fulfilled all the relations of a faithful and affectionate partner. Indeed, he was often heard to say at this time, as the good bishop above quoted remarks, "that he

[17] Gomara, Crónica, cap. 4.
" Cœnat cubatque Cortesius cum Velasquio eodem in lecto. Qui postero die fugæ Cortesii nuntius venerat, Velasquium et Cortesium juxta accubantes intuitus, miratur." De Rebus Gestis, MS.

[18] Las Casas, who remembered Cortes at this time "so poor and lowly that he would have gladly received any favor from the least of Velasquez' attendants," treats the story of the bravado with contempt. " Por lo qual si él [Velasquez] sintiera de Cortés una puncta de alfiler de cerviguillo ó presuncion, ó lo ahorcara ó á lomenos lo echara de la tierra y lo sumiera en ella sin que alzara cabeza en su vida." Hist. de las Indias, MS. lib. 3. cap 27.

[19] " Pecuariam primus quoque habuit, in insulamque induxit, omni pecorum genere ex Hispania petito." De Rebus Gestis, MS.

[20] " Los que por sacarle el oro muriéron Dios abrá tenido mejor cuenta que yo." Hist. de las Indias, MS., lib 3, cap. 27. The text is a free translation.

lived as happily with her as if she had been the daughter of a duchess." Fortune gave him the means in after life of verifying the truth of his assertion.[21]

Such was the state of things, when Alvarada returned with the tidings of Grijalva's discoveries, and the rich fruits of his traffic with the natives. The news spread like wildfire throughout the island; for all saw in it the promise of more important results than any hitherto obtained. The governor, as already noticed, resolved to follow up the track of discovery with a more considerable armament; and he looked around for a proper person to share the expense of it, and to take the command.

Several hidalgos presented themselves, whom, from want of proper qualifications, or from his distrust of their assuming an independence of their employer, he, one after another, rejected. There were two persons in St. Jago in whom he placed great confidence,—Amador de Lares, the *contador* or royal treasurer,[22] and his own secretary, Andres de Duero. Cortés was also in close intimacy with both these persons; and he availed himself of it to prevail on them to recommend him as a suitable person to be intrusted with the expedition. It is said, he reinforced the proposal, by promising a liberal share of the proceeds of it. However this may be, the parties urged his selection by the governor, with all the eloquence of which they were capable. That officer had had ample experience of the capacity and courage of the candidate. He knew, too, that he had acquired a fortune which would enable him to coöperate materially in fitting out the armament. His popularity in the island would speedily attract followers to his standard.[23] All past animosities had long since been buried in oblivion, and the confidence he was now to repose in him would insure his fidelity and gratitude. He lent a willing ear, therefore, to the recommendation of his counsellors, and, sending for Cortés, announced his purpose of making him Captain-General of the Armada.[24]

---

[21] " Estando commigo, me lo dixo que estava tan contento con ella como si fuera hija de una Duquessa." Hist. de las Indias, MS., ubi supra.—Gomara, Crónica, cap. 4.

[22] The treasurer used to boast he had passed some two and twenty years in the wars of Italy. He was a shrewd personage, and Las Casas, thinking that country a slippery school for morals, warned the governor, he says, more than once "to beware of the twenty-two years in Italy." Hist. de las Indias, MS., lib. 3, cap. 113.

[23] " Si él no fuera por Capitan, que no fuera la tercera, parte de la gente que con el fué." Declaracion de Puertocarrero, MS. (Coruña, 30 de Abril, 1520.)

[24] Bernal Diaz, Hist. de la Conquista, cap. 19.—De Rebus Gestis, MS.—Gomara, Crónica, cap. 7.—Las Casas, Hist. General de las Indias, MS., lib. 3, cap. 113.

Cortés had now attained the object of his wishes,—the object for which his soul had panted, ever since he had set foot in the New World. He was no longer to be condemned to a life of mercenary drudgery; nor to be cooped up within the precincts of a petty island. But he was to be placed on a new and independent theatre of action, and a boundless perspective was opened to his view, which might satisfy not merely the wildest cravings of avarice, but, to a bold, aspiring spirit like his, the far more importunate cravings of ambition. He fully appreciated the importance of the late discoveries, and read in them the existence of the great empire in the far West, dark hints of which had floated, from time to time, to the Islands, and of which more certain glimpses had been caught by those who had reached the continent. This was the country intimated to the "Great Admiral" in his visit to Honduras in 1502, and which he might have reached, had he held on a northern course, instead of striking to the south in quest of an imaginary strait. As it was, "he had but opened the gate," to use his own bitter expression, "for others to enter." The time had at length come, when they were to enter it; and the young adventurer, whose magic lance was to dissolve the spell which had so long hung over these mysterious regions, now stood ready to assume the enterprise.

From this hour the deportment of Cortés seemed to undergo a change. His thoughts, instead of evaporating in empty levities or idle flashes of merriment, were wholly concentrated on the great object to which he was devoted. His elastic spirits were shown in cheering and stimulating the companions of his toilsome duties, and he was roused to a generous enthusiasm, of which even those who knew him best had not conceived him capable. He applied at once all the money in his possession to fitting out the armament. He raised more by the mortgage of his estates, and by giving his obligations to some wealthy merchants of the place, who relied for their reimbursement on the success of the expedition; and, when his own credit was exhausted, he availed himself of that of his friends.

The funds thus acquired he expended in the purchase of vessels, provisions, and military stores, while he invited recruits by offers of assistance to such as were too poor to provide for themselves, and by the additional promise of a liberal share of the anticipated profits.[26]

All was now bustle and excitement in the little town of St.

---

[26] Declaracion de Puertocarrero, MS.—Carta de Vera Cruz, MS.—Probanza en la Villa Segura, MS. (4 de Oct., 1520.)

Jago. Some were busy in refitting the vessels and getting them ready for the voyage, some in providing naval stores; others in converting their own estates into money in order to equip themselves; every one seemed anxious to contribute in some way or other to the success of the expedition. Six ships, some of them of a large size, had already been procured; and three hundred recruits enrolled themselves in the course of a few days, eager to seek their fortunes under the banner of this daring and popular chieftain.

How far the governor contributed towards the expenses of the outfit is not very clear. If the friends of Cortés are to be believed, nearly the whole burden fell on him; since, while he supplied the squadron without remuneration, the governor sold many of his own stores at an exorbitant profit.[26] Yet it does not seem probable that Velasquez, with such ample means at his command, should have thrown on his deputy the burden of the expedition, nor that the latter—had he done so—could have been in a condition to meet these expenses, amounting, as we are told, to more than twenty thousand gold ducats. Still it cannot be denied that an ambitious man like Cortes, who was to reap all the glory of the enterprise, would very naturally be less solicitous to count the gains of it, than his employer, who, inactive at home, and having no laurels to win, must look on the pecuniary profits as his only recompense. The question gave rise, some years later, to a furious litigation between the parties, with which it is not necessary at present to embarrass the reader.

It is due to Velasquez to state that the instructions delivered by him for the conduct of the expedition cannot be charged with a narrow or mercenary spirit. The first object of the voyage was to find Grijalva, after which the two commanders were to proceed in company together. Reports had been brought back by Cordova, on his return from the first visit to Yucatan, that six Christians were said to be lingering in captivity in the interior

---

[26] The letter from the Municipality of Veia Cruz, after stating that Velasquez bore only one third of the original expense, adds, "Y sepan Vras. Magestades que la mayor parte de la dicha tercia parte que el dicho Diego Velasquez gastó en hacer la dicha armada fué, emplear sus dineros en vinos y en ropas, y en otras cosas de poco valor para nos lo vender acá en mucha mas cantidad de lo que á èl le costó, por manera que podemos decir que entre nosotros los Españoles vasallos de Vras. Reales Altezas ha hecho Diego Velasquez su rescate y granosea de sus dineros cobrándolos muy bien." (Carta de Vera Cruz, MS.) Puertocarrero and Montejo, also, in their depositions taken in Spain, both speak of Cortés' having furnished two thirds of the cost of the flotilla. (Declaracion de Puertocarrero, MS.—Declaracion de Montejo, MS. (29 de Abril, 1520.).) The letter from Vera Cruz, however, was prepared under the eye of Cortés; and the two last were his confidential officers

of the country. It was supposed they might belong to the party of the unfortunate Nicuessa, and orders were given to find them out, if possible, and restore them to liberty. But the great object of the expedition was barter with the natives. In pursuing this, special care was to be taken that they should receive no wrong, but be treated with kindness and humanity. Cortés was to bear in mind, above all things, that the object which the Spanish monarch had most at heart was the conversion of the Indians. He was to impress on them the grandeur and goodness of his royal master, to invite them "to give in their allegiance to him, and to manifest it by regaling him with such comfortable presents of gold, pearls, and precious stones as, by showing their own good-will, would secure his favor and protection." He was to make an accurate survey of the coast, sounding its bays and inlets for the benefit of future navigators. He was to acquaint himself with the natural products of the country, with the character of its different races, their institutions and progress in civilization; and he was to send home minute accounts of all these, together with such articles as he should obtain in his intercourse with them. Finally, he was to take *the most careful care* to omit nothing that might redound to the service of God or his sovereign.[27]

Such was the general tenor of the instructions given to Cortés, and they must be admitted to provide for the interests of science and humanity, as well as for those which had reference only to a commercial speculation. It may seem strange, considering the discontent shown by Velasquez with his former captain, Grijalva, for not colonizing, that no directions should have been given to that effect here. But he had not yet received from Spain the warrant for investing his agents with such powers; and that which had been obtained from the Hieronymite fathers In Hispaniola conceded only the right to traffic with the natives. The commission at the same time recognized the authority of Cortés as Captain-General of the expedition.[28]

---

[27] The instrument, in the original Castilian, will be found in *Appendix, Part 2, No. 5.* It is often referred to by writers who never saw it, as the Agreement between Cortés and Velasquez. It is, in fact, only the instructions given by this latter to his officer, who was no party to it.

[28] Declaracion de Puertocarrero, MS.—Gomara, Crónica, cap. 7.

Velasquez soon after obtained from the crown authority to colonize the new countries, with the title of *adelantado* over them. The instrument was dated at Barcelona, Nov. 13th, 1518. (Herrera, Hist. General. dec. 2, lib. 3, cap 8.) Empty privileges! Las Casas gives a caustic etymology of the title of *adelantado*, so often granted to the Spanish discoverers. "Adelantados porque se adelantaran en hazer males y daños tan gravisimos á gentes pacificas." Hist. de las Indias, MS., lib. 3, cap. 117

CHAPTER III.

JEALOUSY OF VELASQUEZ.—CORTES EMBARKS.—EQUIPMENT OF HIS FLEET.—HIS PERSON AND CHARACTER.—RENDEZVOUS AT HAVANA.—STRENGTH OF HIS ARMAMENT.

1519.

THE importance given to Cortés by his new position, and, perhaps, a somewhat more lofty bearing, gradually gave uneasiness to the naturally suspicious temper of Velasquez, who became apprehensive that his officer, when away where he would have the power, might also have the inclination, to throw off his dependence on him altogether. An accidental circumstance at this time heightened these suspicions. A mad fellow, his jester, one of those crack-brained wits, — half wit, half fool, — who formed in those days a common appendage to every great man's establishment, called out to the governor, as he was taking his usual walk one morning with Cortés towards the port, " Have a care, master Velasquez, or we shall have to go a hunting, some day or other, after this same captain of ours !" " Do you hear what the rogue says ?" exclaimed the governor to his companion. " Do not heed him," said Cortés, "he is a saucy knave, and deserves a good whipping." The words sunk deep, however, in the mind of Velasquez,—as, indeed, true jests are apt to stick.

There were not wanting persons about his Excellency, who fanned the latent embers of jealousy into a blaze. These worthy gentlemen, some of them kinsmen of Velasquez, who probably felt their own deserts somewhat thrown into the shade by the rising fortunes of Cortés, reminded the governor of his ancient quarrel with that officer, and of the little probability that affronts so keenly felt at the time could ever be forgotten. By these and similar suggestions, and by misconstructions of the present conduct of Cortés, they wrought on the passions of Velasquez to such a degree, that he resolved to intrust the expedition to other hands.[1]

---

[1] " Deterrebat," says the anonymous biographer, " eum Cortesii natura imperii avida, fiducia sui ingens, et nimius sumptus in classe parandâ. Timere itaque Velasquius cœpit, si Cortesius cum eâ classe iret, nihil ad se

He communicated his design to his confidential advisers, Lares and Duero, and these trusty personages reported it without delay to Cortés, although, " to a man of half his penetration," says Las Casas, " the thing would have been readily divined from the governor's altered demeanor." [2] The two functionaries advised their friend to expedite matters as much as possible, and to lose no time in getting his fleet ready for sea, if he would retain the command of it. Cortés showed the same prompt decision on this occasion, which more than once afterwards in a similar crisis gave the direction to his destiny.

He had not yet got his complement of men, nor of vessels; and was very inadequately provided with supplies of any kind. But he resolved to weigh anchor that very night. He waited on his officers, informed them of his purpose, and probably of the cause of it ; and at midnight, when the town was hushed in sleep, they all went quietly on board, and the little squadron dropped down the bay. First, however, Cortés had visited the person whose business it was to supply the place with meat, and relieved him of all his stock on hand, notwithstanding his complaint that the city must suffer for it on the morrow, leaving him, at the same time, in payment, a massive gold chain of much value, which he wore round his neck.[3]

Great was the amazement of the good citizens of St. Jago, when, at dawn, they saw that the fleet, which they knew was so ill prepared for the voyage, had left its moorings and was busily getting under way. The tidings soon came to the ears of his Excellency, who, springing from his bed, hastily dressed himself, mounted his horse, and, followed by his retinue, galloped down to the quay. Cortés, as soon as he described their approach, entered an armed boat, and came within speaking distance of the shore. "And is it thus you part from me ! " exclaimed Velasquez ; "a courteous way of taking leave, truly ! " " Pardon me," answered Cortés, " time presses, and there are some things that should be done before they are even thought of. Has your Excellency any commands ? " But the mortified governor had no commands to give ; and Cortés, politely waving his hand, returned to his vessel, and the little fleet instantly made sail for the port of Macaca, about fifteen leagues distant.

vel honoris vel lucri rediturum." De Rebus Gestis, MS.—Bernal Diaz, Hist. de la Conquista, cap. 19.—Las Casas, Hist. de las Indias, MS., cap. 114.

[2] "Cortés no avia menester mas para entendello de mirar el gesto a Diego Velasquez segun su astuta viveza y mundana sabiduria." Hist. de las Indias, MS., cap. 114.

[3] Las Casas had the story from Cortés' own mouth. Hist. de las Indias, MS., cap. 114.—Gomara, Crònica, cap. 7.—De Rebus Gestis, MS.

(November 18, 1518.) Velasquez rode back to his house to
digest his chagrin as he best might; satisfied, probably, that he
had made at least two blunders; one in appointing Cortés to
the command,—the other in attempting to deprive him of it.
For, if it be true, that, by giving our confidence by halves, we
can scarcely hope to make a friend, it is equally true, that, by
withdrawing it when given, we shall make an enemy.[4]

This clandestine departure of Cortés has been severely criticised by some writers, especially by Las Casas.[5] Yet much
may be urged in vindication of his conduct. He had been
appointed to the command by the voluntary act of the governor,
and this had been fully ratified by the authorities of Hispaniola. He had at once devoted all his resources to the undertaking, incurring, indeed, a heavy debt in addition. He was
now to be deprived of his commission, without any misconduct
having been alleged or at least proved against him. Such an
event must overwhelm him in irretrievable ruin, to say nothing
of the friends from whom he had so largely borrowed, and the
followers who had embarked their fortunes in the expedition on
the faith of his commanding it. There are few persons, probably, who, under these circumstances, would have felt called
tamely to acquiesce in the sacrifice of their hopes to a ground-
less and arbitrary whim. The most to have been expected from
Cortés was, that he should feel obliged to provide faithfully for
the interests of his employer in the conduct of the enterprise.
How far he felt the force of this obligation will appear in the
sequel.

From Macaca, where Cortés laid in such stores as he could
obtain from the royal farms, and which, he said, he considered
as "a loan from the king," he proceeded to Trinidad; a more
considerable town, on the southern coast of Cuba. Here he
landed, and, erecting his standard in front of his quarters, made
proclamation, with liberal offers to all who would join the expedition. Volunteers came in daily, and among them more

---

[4] Las Casas, Hist. de las Indias, MS., cap. 114.—Herrera, Hist. General,
dec. 2, lib. 3, cap. 12.

Solís, who follows Bernal Diaz is saying that Cortés parted openly and
amicably from Velasquez, seems to consider it a great slander on the character of the former to suppose that he wanted to break with the governor so
soon, when he had received so little provocation. (Conquista, lib. 1, cap.
10.) But it is not necessary to suppose that Cortés intended a rupture with
his employer by this clandestine movement; but only to secure himself in the
command. At all events, the text conforms in every particular to the statement of Las Casas, who, as he knew both the parties well, and resided on the
island at the time, had ample means of information.

[5] Hist. de las Indias, MS., cap. 114.

than a hundred of Grijalva's men, just returned from their voyage, and willing to follow up the discovery under an enterprising leader. The fame of Cortés attracted, also, a number of cavaliers of family and distinction, some of whom, having accompanied Grijalva, brought much information valuable for the present expedition. Among these hidalgos may be mentioned Pedro de Alvarado and his brothers, Cristóval de Olid, Alonso de Avila, Juan Velasquez de Leon, a near relation of the governor, Alonso Hernandez de Puertecarrero, and Gonzalo de Sandoval,—all of them men who took a most important part in the Conquest. Their presence was of great moment, as giving consideration to the enterprise ; and, when they entered the little camp of the adventurers, the latter turned out to welcome them amidst lively strains of music and joyous salvos of artillery.

Cortés meanwhile was active in purchasing military stores and provisions. Learning that a trading vessel laden with grain and other commodities for the mines was off the coast, he ordered out one of his caravels to seize her and bring her into port. He paid the master in bills for both cargo and ship, and even persuaded this man, named Seldeño, who was wealthy, to join his fortunes to the expedition. He also despatched one of his officers, Diego de Ordaz, in quest of another ship, of which he had tidings, with instructions to seize it in like manner, and to meet him with it off Cape St. Antonio, the westerly point of the island.[6] By this he effected another object, that of getting rid of Ordaz, who was one of the governor's household, and an inconvenient spy on his own actions.

While thus occupied, letters from Velasquez were received by the commander of Trinidad, requiring him to seize the person of Cortés and to detain him, as he had been deposed from the command of the fleet, which was given to another. This functionary communicated his instructions to the principal officers in the expedition, who counselled him not to make the attempt, as it would undoubtedly lead to a commotion among the soldiers, that might end in laying the town in ashes. Verdugo thought it prudent to conform to this advice.[7]

As Cortés was willing to strengthen himself by still further reinforcements, he ordered Alvarado with a small body of men

<hr/>

[6] Las Casas had this, also, from the lips of Cortés in later life. "Todo esto me dixo el mismo Cortes, con otras cosas çerca dello despues de Marques; . . . . . reindo y mofando é conestas formales palabras, *A la mi fé anduhe por alll como un gentil cosario.*" Hist. de las Indias, MS., cap. 115.

[7] De Rebus Gestis, MS.—Gomara, Crónica, cap. 6.—Las Casas, Hist. de las Indias, MS., cap. 114, 115.

to march across the country to the Havana, while he himself would sail round the westerly point of the island, and meet him there with the squadron. In this port he again displayed his standard, making the usual proclamation. He caused all the large guns to be brought on shore, and, with the small arms and crossbows, to be put in order. As there was abundance of cotton raised in this neighborhood, he had the jackets of the soldiers thickly quilted with it, for a defence against the Indian arrows, from which the troops in the former expeditions had grievously suffered. He distributed his men into eleven companies, each under the command of an experienced officer ; and it was observed, that, although several of the cavaliers in the service were the personal friends and even kinsmen of Velasquez, he appeared to treat them all with perfect confidence.

His principal standard was of black velvet embroidered with gold, and emblazoned with a red cross amidst flames of blue and white, with this motto in Latin beneath ; " Friends, let us follow the Cross ; and under this sign, if we have faith, we shall conquer." He now assumed more state in his own person and way of living, introducing a greater number of domestic and officers into his household, and placing it on a footing becoming a man of high station. This state he maintained through the rest of his life.[8]

Cortés at this time was thirty-three, or perhaps thirty-four years of age. In stature he was rather above the middle size. His complexion was pale ; and his large dark eye gave an expression of gravity to his countenance, not to have been expected in one of his cheerful temperament. His figure was slender, at least until later life ; but his chest was deep, his shoulders broad, his frame muscular and well proportioned. It presented the union of agility and vigor which qualified him to excel in fencing, norsemanship, and the other generous exercises of chivalry. In his diet he was temperate, careless of what he ate, and drinking little ; while to toil and privation he seemed perfectly indifferent. His dress, for he did not disdain the impression produced by such adventitious aids, was such as to set off his handsome person to advantage ; neither gaudy nor striking, but rich. He wore few ornaments, and usually the same ; but those were of great price. His manners, frank and soldierlike, concealed a most cool and calculating spirit. With his gayest humor there mingled a settled air of resolution, which

---

[8] Bernal Diaz, Hist. de la Conquista, cap. 24.—De Rebus Gestis, MS.— Gomara, Crónica, cap. 8—Las Casas, Hist. de las Indias, MS., cap. 115.
  The legend on the standard was, doubtless, suggested by that on the *labarum*,—the sacred banner of Constantine.

made those who approached him feel they must obey; and which infused something like awe into the attachment of his most devoted followers. Such a combination, in which love was tempered by authority, was the one probably best calculated to inspire devotion in the rough and turbulent spirits among whom his lot was to be cast.

The character of Cortés seemed to have undergone some change with change of circumstances; or, to speak more correctly, the new scenes in which he was placed called forth qualities which before lay dormant in his bosom. There are some hardy natures that require the heats of excited action to unfold their energies; like the plants, which, closed to the mild influence of a temperate latitude, come to their full growth, and give forth their fruits, only in the burning atmosphere of the tropics.—Such is the portrait left to us by his contemporaries of this remarkable man; the instrument selected by Providence to scatter terror among the barbarian monarchs of the Western World, and lay their empires in the dust.[9]

Before the preparations were fully completed at the Havana, the commander of the place, Don Pedro Barba, received despatches from Velasquez ordering him to apprehend Cortés, and to prevent the departure of his vessels; while another epistle from the same source was delivered to Cortés himself, requesting him to postpone his voyage till the governor could communicate with him, as he proposed, in person. " Never," exclaimed Las Casas, " did I see so little knowledge of affairs shown, as in this letter of Diego Velasquez,—that he should have imagined, that a man, who had so recently put such an affront on him, would defer his departure at his bidding!"[10] It was indeed, hoping to stay the flight of the arrow by a word, after it had left the bow.

The Captain-General, however, during his short stay, had entirely conciliated the good-will of Barba. And, if that officer had had the inclination, he knew he had not the power, to enforce his principal's orders, in the face of a resolute soldiery, incensed at this ungenerous persecution of their commander, and " all of whom," in the words of the honest chronicler who bore part in the expedition, " officers and privates, would have cheerfully laid down their lives for him."[11] Barba contented himself, therefore, with explaining to Velasquez the impractica-

---

[9] The most minute notices of the person and habits of Cortés are to be gathered from the narrative of the old cavalier Bernal Diaz, who served so long under him, and from Gomara, the general's chaplain. See in particular the last chapter of Gomara's Crónica, and cap. 203 of .e Hist. de la Conquista.

[10] Las Casas, Hist. de las Indias, MS., cap. 115.

[11] Bernal Diaz, Hist. de la Conquista, cap. 24.

bility of the attempt, and at the same time endeavored to tranquillize his apprehensions by asserting his own confidence in the
fidelity of Cortés. To this the latter added a communication of
his own, couched "in the soft terms he knew so well how to
use," [12] in which he implored his Excellency to rely on his devotion to his interests, and concluded with the comfortable assurance that he and the whole fleet, God willing, would sail on
the following morning.

Accordingly on the 10th of February, 1519, the little squadron
got under way, and directed its course towards Cape St. Antonio,
the appointed place of rendezvous. When all were brought together, the vessels were found to be eleven in number ; one of
them, in which Cortés himself went, was of a hundred tons'
burden, three others were from seventy to eighty tons ; the remainder were caravels and open brigantines. The whole was
put under the direction of Antonio de Alaminos, as chief pilot ;
a veteran navigator, who had acted as pilot to Columbus in his
last voyage, and to Cordova and Grijalva in the former expeditions to Yucatan.

Landing on the Cape and mustering his forces, Cortés found
they amounted to one hundred and ten mariners, five hundred
and fifty-three soldiers, including thirty-two crossbowmen, and
thirteen arquebusiers, besides two hundred Indians of the island,
and a few Indian women for menial offices. He was provided
with ten heavy guns, four lighter pieces called falconets, and
with a good supply of ammunition.[13] He had besides sixteen
horses. They were not easily procured ; for the difficulty of
transporting them across the ocean in the flimsy craft of that
day made them rare and incredibly dear in the Islands.[14] But

[12] Ibid., loc. cit.

[13] Bernal Diaz, Hist. de la Conquista, cap. 26.

There is some discrepancy among authorities, in regard to the numbers of
the army. The letter from Vera Cruz, which should have been exact, speaks
in round terms of only four hundred soldiers. (Carta de Vera Cruz, MS.)
Velasquez himself, in a communication to the Chief Judge of Hispaniola,
states the number at six hundred. (Carta de Diego Velasquez al Lic. Figueroa, MS.) I have adopted the estimates of Bernal Diaz, who, in his long
service, seems to have become intimately acquainted with every one of his
comrades, their persons, and private history.

[14] Incredibly dear indeed, since, from the statements contained in the depositions at Villa Segura, it appears that the cost of the horses for the expedition was from four to five hundred *pesos de oro* each ? "Si saben que de
caballos que el dicho Señor Capitan General Hernando Cortés ha comprado
para servir en la dicha Conquista, que son diez é ocho, que le han costado á
quatrocientos cinquenta é á quinientos pesos ha pagado, é que deve mas de
ocho mil pesos de oro dellos." (Probanza en Villa Segura, MS.) The estimation of these horses is sufficiently shown by the minute information Bernal
Diaz has thought proper to give of every one of them ; minute enough for the
pages of a sporting calendar. See Hist. de la Conquista, cap. 23.

Cortés rightfully estimated the importance of cavalry, however small in number, both for their actual service in the field, and for striking terror into the savages. With so paltry a force did he enter on a Conquest which even his stout heart must have shrunk from attempting with such means, had he but foreseen half its real difficulties!

Before embarking, Cortés addressed his soldiers in a short but animated harangue. He told them that they were about to enter on a noble enterprise, one that would make their name famous to after ages. He was leading them to countries more vast and opulent than any yet visited by Europeans. "I hold out to you a glorious prize," continued the orator, "but it is to be won by incessant toil. Great things are achieved only by great exertions, and glory was never the reward of sloth.[16] If I have labored hard and staked my all on this undertaking, it is for the love of that renown, which is the noblest recompense of man. But, if any among you covet riches more, be but true to me, as I will be true to you and to the occasion, and I will make you masters of such as our countrymen have never dreamed of! You are few in number, but strong in resolution; and, if this does not falter, doubt not but that the Almighty, who has never deserted the Spaniard in his contest with the infidel, will shield you, though encompassed by a cloud of enemies; for your cause is a *just cause*, and you are to fight under the banner of the Cross. Go forward, then," he concluded, "with alacrity and confidence, and carry to a glorious issue the work so auspiciously begun."[16]

The rough eloquence of the general, touching the various chords of ambition, avarice and religious zeal, sent a thrill through the bosoms of his martial audience; and receiving it with acclamations, they seemed eager to press forward under a chief who was to lead them not so much to battle, as to triumph.

Cortés was well satisfied to find his own enthusiasm so largely shared by his followers. Mass was then celebrated with the solemnities usual with the Spanish navigators, when entering on their voyages of discovery. The fleet was placed under the immediate protection of St. Peter, the patron saint of Cortés; and

---

[16] " Io vos propongo grandes premios, mas embueltos en grandes trabajos pero la virtud no quiere ociosidad." (Gomara, Crónica, cap. 9.) It is the thought so finely expressed by Thomson:

> " For sluggard's brow the laurel never grows;
> Renown is not the child of indolent re-----"

[16] The text is a very condensed abridgement of th original speech of Cortés —or of his chaplain, as the case may be. See it, in Gomara, Crónica, cap. 9.

weighing anchor, took its departure on the eighteenth day of February, 1519, for the coast of Yucatan.[17]

[17] Las Casas, Hist. de las Indias, MS., cap. 115.—Gomara, Cronica, cap. 10.—De Rebus Gestis, MS.

"Tantus fuit armorum apparatus," exclaims the author of the last work, "quo alterum terrarum orbem bellis Cortesius concutit; extam parvis opibus. tantum imperium Carolo facit; aperitque omnium primus Hispanæ genti Hispaniam novam!" The author of this work is unknown. It seems to have been part of a great compilation "De Orbe Novo," written, probably, on the plan of a series of biographical sketches, as the introduction speaks of a life of Columbus preceding this of Cortés. It was composed, as it states, while many of the old Conquerors were still surviving, and is addressed to the son of Cortés. The historian, therefore, had ample means of verifying the truth of his own statements, although they too often betray, in his partiality for his hero, the influence of the patronage under which the work was produced. It runs into a prolixity of detail, which, however tedious, has its uses in a contemporary document. Unluckily, only the first book was finished, or, at least, has survived; terminating with the events of this Chapter. It is written in Latin, in a pure and perspicuous style; and is conjectured with some plausibility to be the work of Calvet de Estrella, Chronicler of the Indies. The original exists in the Archives of Simancas, where it was discovered and transcribed by Muñoz, from whose copy that in my library wa taken.

CHAPTER IV.

VOYAGE TO COZUMEL.—CONVERSION OF THE NATIVES.—JERÓN
IMO DE AGUILAR.—ARMY ARRIVES AT TABASCO.—GREAT
BATTLE WITH THE INDIANS.—CHRISTIANITY INTRODUCED.

1519.

ORDERS were given for the vessels to keep as near together as possible, and to take the direction of the *capitania,* or admiral's ship, which carried a beacon light in the stern during the night. But the weather, which had been favorable, changed soon after their departure, and one of those tempests set in which at this season are often found in the latitudes of the West Indies. It fell with terrible force on the little navy, scattering it far asunder, dismantling some of the ships, and driving them all considerably south of their proposed destination.

Cortés, who had lingered behind to convoy a disabled vessel, reached the island of Cozumel last. On landing, he learned that one of his captains, Pedro de Alvarado, had availed himself of the short time he had been there, to enter the temples, rifle them of their few ornaments, and by his violent conduct, so far to terrify the simple natives, that they had fled for refuge into the interior of the island. Cortés, highly incensed at these rash proceedings, so contrary to the policy he had proposed, could not refrain from severely reprimanding his officer in the presence of the army. He commanded two Indian captives, taken by Alvarado, to be brought before him, and explained to them the pacific purpose of his visit. This he did through the assistance of his interpreter, Melchorejo, a native of Yucatan, who had been brought back by Grijalva, and who, during his residence in Cuba, had picked up some acquaintance with the Castilian. He then dismissed them loaded with presents, and with an invitation to their countrymen to return to their homes without fear of further annoyance. This humane policy succeeded. The fugitives, reassured, were not slow in coming back; and an amicable intercourse was established, in which Spanish cutlery and trinkets were exchanged for the gold ornaments of the natives; a traffic in which each party congratulated itself—a philosopher might think with equal reason—on outwitting the other.

The first object of Cortés was, to gather tidings of the unfortunate Christians who were reported to be still lingering in captivity on the neighboring continent. From some traders in the island, he obtained such a confirmation of the report, that he sent Diego de Ordaz with two brigantines to the opposite coast of Yucatan, with instructions to remain there eight days. Some Indians went as messengers in the vessels, who consented to bear a letter to the captives informing them of the arrival of their countrymen in Cozumel, with a liberal ransom for their release. Meanwhile the general proposed to make an excursion to the different parts of the island, that he might give employment to the restless spirits of the soldiers, and ascertain the resources of the country.

It was poor and thinly peopled. But everywhere he recognized the vestiges of a higher civilization than what he had before witnessed in the Indian islands. The houses were some of them large, and often built of stone and lime. He was particularly struck with the temples, in which were towers constructed of the same solid materials, and rising several stories in height. In the court of one of these he was amazed by the sight of a cross, of stone and lime, about ten palms high. It was the emblem of the God of rain. Its appearance suggested the wildest conjectures, not merely to the unlettered soldiers, but subsequently to the European scholar, who speculated on the character of the races that had introduced there the sacred symbol of Christianity. But no such inference, as we shall see hereafter, could be warranted.[1] Yet it must be regarded as a curious fact, that the Cross should have been venerated as the object of religious worship both in the New World, and in regions of the Old, where the light of Christianity had never risen.[2]

[1] See *Appendix, Part 1, Note* 27.

[2] Carta de Vera Cruz, MS.—Bernal Diaz, Hist. de la Conquista, cap. 25, et seq.—Gomara, Crónica, cap. 10, 15.—Las Casas, Hist. de las Indias, MS., lib. 3, cap. 115.—Herrera, Hist. General, dec. 2, lib. 4, cap. 6—Martyr de Insulis nuper inventis, (Coloniæ, 1574,) p. 344.

While these pages were passing through the press, but not till two years after they were written, Mr. Stephens' important and interesting volumes appeared, containing the account of his second expedition to Yucatan. In the latter part of the work, he describes his visit to Cozumel, now an uninhabited island covered with impenetrable forests. Near the shore he saw the remains of ancient Indian structures, which he conceives may possibly have been the same that met the eyes of Grijalva and Cortés, and which suggest to him some important inferences. He is led into further reflections on the existence of the cross as a symbol of worship among the islanders. (Incidents of Travel in Yucatan, (New York, 1843,) vol. II. chap. 20.) As the discussion of these matters would lead me too far from the track of our narrative, I shall take occasion to return to them hereafter, when I treat of the architectural remains of the country.

The first object of Cortés was to reclaim the natives from their gross idolatry and to substitute a purer form of worship. In accomplishing this he was prepared to use force, if milder measures should be ineffectual. There was nothing which the Spanish government had more earnestly at heart, than the conversion of the Indians. It forms the constant burden of their instructions, and gave to the military expeditions in this western hemisphere somewhat of the air of a crusade. The cavalier who embarked in them entered fully into these chivalrous and devotional feelings. No doubt was entertained of the efficacy of conversion, however sudden might be the change, or however violent the means. The sword was a good argument, when the tongue failed ; and the spread of Mahometanism had shown that seeds sown by the hand of violence, far from perishing in the ground, would spring up and bear fruit to after time. If this were so in a bad cause, how much more would it be true in a good one. The Spanish cavalier felt he had a high mission to accomplish as a soldier of the Cross. However unauthorized or unrighteous the war into which he had entered may seem to us, to him it was a holy war. He was in arms against the infidel. Not to care for the soul of his benighted enemy was to put his own in jeopardy. The conversion of a single soul might cover a multitude of sins. It was not for morals that he was concerned but for *the faith.* This though understood in its most literal and limited sense, comprehended the whole scheme of Christian morality. Whoever died in the faith, however immoral had been his life, might be said to die in the Lord. Such was the creed of the Castilian knight of that day, as imbibed from the preachings of the pulpit, from cloisters and colleges at home, from monks and missionaries abroad,—from all save one, whose devotion, kindled at a purer source, was not, alas! permitted to send forth its radiance far into the thick gloom by which he was encompassed.[1]

No one partook more fully of the feelings above described than Hernan Cortés. He was, in truth, the very mirror of the times in which he lived, reflecting its motley characteristics, its speculative devotion and practical license,—but with an intensity all his own. He was greatly scandalized at the exhibition of the idolatrous practices of the people of Cozumel, though untainted, as it would seem, with human sacrifices. He endeavored to persuade them to embrace a better faith, through the agency of two ecclesiastics who attended the expedition,—the licentiate Juan Diaz and father Bartolomé de Olmedo. The latter of these godly men afforded the rare example—rare in any age—of the

---

[1] See the biographical sketch of the good bishop Las Casas, the " Protector of the Indians," in the Postcript at the close of the present Book.

union of fervent zeal with charity, while he beautifully illustrated in his own conduct the precepts which he taught.   He remained with the army through the whole expedition, and by his wise and benevolent counsels was often enabled to mitigate the cruelties of the Conquerors, and to turn aside the edge of the sword from the unfortunate natives.

These two missionaries vainly labored to persuade the people of Cozumel to renounce their abominations, and to allow the Indian idols, in which the Christians recognized the true lineaments of Satan,[4] to be thrown down and demolished.   The simple natives, filled with horror at the proposed profanation, exclaimed that these were the gods who sent them the sunshine and the storm, and, should any violence be offered, they would be sure to avenge it by sending their lightnings on the heads of its perpetrators.

Cortéz was probably not much of a polemic.   At all events, he preferred on the present occasion action to argument; and thought that the best way to convince the Indians of their error was to prove the falsehood of the prediction.   He accordingly, without further ceremony, caused the venerated images to be rolled down the stairs of the great temple, amidst the groans and lamentations of the natives.   An altar was hastily constructed, an image of the Virgin and Child placed over it, and mass was performed by father Olmedo and his reverend companion for the first time within the w. ils of a temple in New Spain.   The patient ministers tried once more to pour the light of the gospel into the benighted understandings of the islanders, and to expound the mysteries of the Catholic faith.   The Indian interpreter must have afforded rather a dubious channel for the transmission of such abstruse doctrines.   But they at length found favor with their auditors, who, whether overawed by the bold bearing of the invaders, or convinced of the impotence of deities that could not shield their own shrines from violation, now con sented to embrace Christianity.[5]

[4] "Fuese que el Demonio se les aparecia como es, y dejaba en su imaginacion aquellas especies; con que seria primorosa imitacion del artifice la fealdad del simulacro."   Solís, Conquista, p. 39.

[5] Carta de Vera Cruz, MS.—Gomara, Crónica, cap. 13.—Herrera, Hist. General. dec. 2, lib. 4, cap. 7.—Ixtlilxochitl, Hist. Chich., MS., cap. 78.

Las Casas, whose enlightened views in religion would have done honor the present age, insists on the futility of these forced conversions, by which it is proposed in a few days to wean men from the idolatry which they had been taught to reverence from the cradle.   "The only way of doing this," he says, "is, by long, assiduous, and faithful preaching, until the heathen shall gather some ideas of the true nature of the Deity and of the doctrines they are to embrace.   Above all, the lives of the Christians should be such as to exemplify the truth of these doctrines, that, seeing this, the poor Indian may

While Cortéz was thus occupied with the triumphs of the Cross, he received intelligence that Ordaz had returned from Yucatan without tidings of the Spanish captives. Though much chagrined, the general did not choose to postpone longer his departure from Cozumel. The fleet had been well stored with provisions by the friendly inhabitants, and, embarking his troops, Cortéz, in the beginning of March, took leave of its hospitable shores. The squadron had not proceeded far, however, before a leak in one of the vessels compelled them to return to the same port. The detention was attended with important consequences; so much so, indeed that a writer of the time discerns in it " a great mystery and a miracle."[6]

Soon after landing, a canoe, with several Indians was seen making its way from the neighboring shores of Yucatan. On reaching the island, one of the men inquired, in broken Castilian, " if he were among Christians "; and, being answered in the affirmative, threw himself on his knees and returned thanks to Heaven for his delivery. He was one of the unfortunate captives for whose fate so much interest had been felt. His name was Jerónimo de Aguilar, a native of Ecija, in old Spain, where he had been regularly educated for the church. He had been established with the colony at Darien, and on a voyage from that place to Hispaniola, eight years previous, was wrecked near the coast of Yucatan. He escaped with several of his companions in the ship's boat, where some perished from hunger and exposure, while others were sacrificed, on their reaching land, by the cannibal natives of the peninsula. Aguilar was preserved from the same dismal fate by escaping into the interior, where he fell into the hands of a powerful cacique, who, though he spared his life, treated him at first with great rigor. The patience of the captive, however, and his singular humility, touched the better feelings of the chieftain, who would have persuaded Aguilar to take a wife among his people, but the ecclesiastic steadily refused, in obedience to his vows. This admirable constancy excited the distrust of the cacique, who put his virtue to a severe test by various temptations, and much of the same sort as those with which the Devil is said to have assailed St. Anthony.[7]

---

glorify the Father, and acknowledge him, who has such worshippers, for the true and only God." See the original remarks, which I quote *in extenso*, as a good specimen of the Bishop's style, when kindled by his subject into eloquence, in *Apendix Part* 2, *No.* 6.

[6] " Muy gran misterio y milagro de Dios." Carta de Vera Cruz, MS.

[7] They are enumerated by Herrera with a minute, ess which may claim, at least, the merit of giving a much higher notion of Aguilar's virtue than the barren generalities of the text. (Hist. General, dec. 2, lib. 1, cap. 6-8.) The

From all these fiery trials, however, like his ghostly predecessor, he came out unscorched. Continence is too rare and difficult a virtue with barbarians, not to challenge their veneration, and the practice of it has made the reputation of more than one saint in the Old as well as the New World. Aguilar was now intrusted with the care of his master's household and his numerous wives. He was a man of discretion, as well as virtue; and his counsels were found so salutary, that he was consulted on all important matters. In short, Aguilar became a great man among the Indians.

It was with much regret, therefore, that his master received the proposals for his return to his countrymen, to which nothing but the rich treasure of glass beads, hawk-bells, and other jewels of like value, sent for his ransom, would have induced him to consent. When Aguilar reached the coast, there had been so much delay, that the brigantines had sailed, and it was owing to the fortunate return of the fleet to Cozumel, that he was enabled to join it.

On appearing before Cortéz, the poor man saluted him in the Indian style, by touching the earth with his hand, and carrying it to his head. The commander, raising him up, affectionately embraced him, covering him at the same time with his own cloak, as Aguilar was simply clad in the habiliments of the country, somewhat too scanty for a European eye. It was long, indeed, before the tastes which he had acquired in the freedom of the forest could be reconciled to the constraints either of dress or manners imposed by the artificial forms of civilization. Aguilar's long residence in the country had familiarized him with the Mayan dialects of Yucatan, and, as he gradually revived his Castilian, he became of essential importance as an interpreter. Cortez saw the advantage of this from the first, but he could not fully estimate all the consequences that were to flow from it.[8]

The repairs of the vessels being at length completed, the Spanish commander once more took leave of the friendly natives of Cozumel, and set sail on the 4th of March. Keeping as near as possible to the coast of Yucatan, he doubled Cape Catoche, and with flowing sheets swept down the broad bay of Campeachy, fringed with the rich dye-woods which have since furnished so important an article of commerce to Europe. He passed Po-

story is prettily told by Washington Irving. Voyages and discoveries of the Companions of Columbus, (London, 1833,) p. 263, et seq.

[8] Camargo, Historia de Tlascala, MS.—Oviedo, His. de las Ind., MS., lib. 33, cap. 1.—Martyr, De Insulis, p. 347.—Bernal Diaz, Hist. de la Conquista, cap. 29.—Carta de Vera Cruz, MS.—Las Casas, Hist. de las Indias, MS, lib. 3, cap. 115, 116.

tonchan, where Cordova had experienced a rough reception from the natives ; and soon after reached the mouth of the *Rio de Tabasco,* or *Grijalva,* in which that navigator had carried on so lucrative a traffic. Though mindful of the great object of his voyage,—the visit to the Aztec territories,—he was desirous of acquainting himself with the resources of this country, and determined to ascend the river and visit the great town on its borders.

The water was so shallow, from the accumulation of sand at the mouth of the stream, that the general was obliged to leave the ships at anchor, and to embark in the boats with a part only of his forces. The banks were thickly studded with mangrove trees, that, with their roots shooting up and interlacing one another, formed a kind of impervious screen or net-work, behind which the dark forms of the natives were seen glancing to and fro with the most menacing looks and gestures. Cortez, much surprised at these unfriendly demonstrations, so unlike what he had had reason to expect, moved cautiously up the stream. When he had reached an open place, where a large number of Indians were assembled, he asked, through his interpreter, leave to land, explaining at the same time his amicable intentions. But the Indians, brandishing their weapons, answered only with gestures of angry defiance. Though much chagrined, Cortez thought it best not to urge the matter further that evening, but withdrew to a neighboring island, where he disembarked his troops, resolved to effect a landing on the following morning.

When day broke, the Spaniards saw the opposite banks lined with a much more numerous array than on the preceding evening, while the canoes along the shore were filled with bands of armed warriors, Cortés now made his preparations for the attack. He first landed a detachment of a hundred men under Alonso de Avila, at a point somewhat lower down the stream, sheltered by a thick grove of palms, from which a road, as he knew, led to the town of Tabasco, giving orders to his officer to march at once on the place, while he himself advanced to assault it in front.[9]

Then embarking the remainder of his troops, Cortes crossed the river in face of the enemy ; but, before commencing hostilities, that he might " act with entire regard to justice, and in obedience to the instructions of the Royal Council." [10] he first

[9] Bernal Diaz, Hist. de la Conquista, cap. 31.—Carta de Vera Cruz. MS. —Gomara, Crónica, cap. 18.—Las Casas, Hist. de las Indias, MS., lib. 3 cap. 118.—Martyr, De Insulis, p. 348.

There are some discrepancies between the statements of Bernal Diaz, and the Letter from Vera Cruz ; both by parties who were present.

[10] Carta de Vera Cruz, MS.—Bernal Diaz, Hist. de la Conquista, cap. 31.

caused proclamation to be made through the interpreter, that he desired only a free passage for his men; and that he proposed to revive the friendly relations which had formerly subsisted between his countrymen and the natives. He assured them that if blood were spilt, the sin would lie on their heads, and that resistance would be useless, since he was resolved at all hazards to take up his quarters that night in the town of Tabasco. This proclamation, delivered in lofty tone, and duly recorded by the notary, was answered by the Indians—who might possibly have comprehended one word in ten of it—with shouts of defiance and a shower of arrows.[11] Cortés, having now complied with all the requisitions of a loyal cavalier, and shifted the responsibility from his own shoulders to those of the Royal Council, brought his boats alongside of the Indian canoes. They grappled fiercely together, and both parties were soon in the water, which rose above the girdle. The struggle was not long, though desperate. The superior strength of the Europeans prevailed, and they forced the enemy back to land. Here, however, they were supported by their countrymen, who showered down darts, arrows, and blazing billets of wood on the heads of the invaders. The banks were soft and slippery, and it was with difficulty the soldiers made good their footing. Cortés lost a sandal in the mud, but continued to fight barefoot, with great exposure of his person, as the Indians, who soon singled out the leader called to one another, "Strike at the chief!"

At length the Spaniards gained the bank, and were able to come into something like order, when they opened a brisk fire from their arquebuses and crossbows. The enemy, astounded by the roar and flash of the fire-arms, of which they had had no experience, fell back, and retreated behind a breastwork of timber thrown across the way. The Spaniards, hot in the pursuit, soon carried these rude defences, and drove the Tabascans

---

[11] "See," exclaims the Bishop of Chiapa, in his caustic vein, "the reasonableness of this requisition," or, to speak more correctly, the folly and insensibility of the Royal Council, who could find, in the refusal of the Indians to receive it, a good pretext for war." (Hist. de las Indias, MS., lib. 3, cap. 118.) In another place, he pronounces an animated invective against the iniquity of those who covered up hostilities under this empty form of words, the import of which was utterly incomprehensible to the barbarians. (Ibid., lib. 3, cap. 57.) The famous formula, used by the Spanish conquerors on this occasion, was drawn up by Dr. Palacios Reubios, a man of letters, and a member of the King's council. "But I laugh at him and his letters," exclaims Oviedo, "if he thought a word of it could be comprehended by the untutored Indians!" (Hist. de las Ind., MS., lib. 29, cap. 7.) The regular Manifesto, *requirimiento*, may be found translated in the concluding pages of Irving's "Voyages of the Companions of Columbus."

before them towards the town, where they again took shelter behind their palisades.

Meanwhile Avila had arrived from the opposite quarter, and
the natives taken by surprise made no further attempt at resistance, but abandoned the place to the Christians. They had
previously removed their families and effects. Some provisions fell into the hands of the victors, but little gold, "a circumstance," says Las Casas, "which gave them no particular
satisfaction."[12] It was a very populous place. The houses
were mostly of mud ; the better sort of stone and lime ; affording
proofs in the inhabitants of a superior refinement to that found
in the Islands, as their stout resistance had given evidence of
superior valor.[13]

Cortés, having thus made himself master of the town, took
formal possession of it for the crown of Castile. He gave
three cuts with his sword on a large *ceiba* tree, which grew in
the place, and proclaimed aloud, that he took possession of the
city in the name and behalf of the Catholic sovereigns, and
would maintain and defend the same with sword and buckler
against all who should gainsay it. The same vaunting declaration was also made by the soldiers, and the whole was duly recorded and attested by the notary. This was the usual simple,
but chivalric form, with which the Spanish cavaliers asserted
the royal title to the conquered territories in the New World.
It was a good title, doubtless, against the claims of any other
European potentate.

The general took up his quarters that night in the court-yard
of the principal temple. He posted his sentinels, and took all
the precautions practised in wars with a civilized foe. Indeed,
there was reason for them. A suspicious silence seemed to
reign through the place and its neighborhood ; and tidings
were brought that the interpreter, Melchorejo, had fled, leaving
his Spanish dress hanging on a tree. Cortés was disquieted by

---

[12] "Halláronlas llenas de maizé gallinas y otros vastimentos, oro ninguno,
de lo que ellos no rescivièron mucho plazer." Hist. de las Ind., MS., ubi
supra.

[13] Peter Martyr gives a glowing picture of this Indian capital. "Ad flumi-
nis ripam protentum dicunt esse oppidum, quantum non ausim dicere : mille
quingentorum passuum, ait Alaminus nauclerus, et domorum quinque ac vig-
inti milium: strigunt alii, iniens tamen falentur et celebre. Hortis inter-
secantur domus, quæ sunt *egregiè lapidibus et calce fabrefactæ, maximâ industriâ et architectorum arte.*" (De Insulis, p. 349.) With his usual inquisitive
spirit, he gleaned all the particulars from the old pilot Alaminos, and from
two of the officers of Cortés who revisited Spain in the course of that year.
Tabasco was in the neighborhood of those ruined cities of Yucatan, which
have lately been the theme of so much speculation. The encomiums of Martyr
are not so remarkable as the apathy of other contemporary chroniclers.

the desertion of this man, who would not only inform his countrymen of the small number of the Spaniards, but dissipate any illusions that might be entertained of their superior natures.

On the following morning, as no traces of the enemy were visible, Cortés ordered out a detachment under Alvarado, and another under Francisco de Lujo, to reconnoitre. The latter officer had not advanced a league, before he learned the position of the Indians, by their attacking him in such force, that he was fain to take shelter in a large stone building, where he was closely besieged. Fortunately the loud yells of the assailants, like most barbarous nations seeking to strike terror by their ferocious cries, reached the ears of Alvarado and his men, who, speedily advancing to the relief of their comrades, enabled them to force a passage through the enemy. Both parties retreated, closely pursued, on the town, when Cortés, marching out to their support, compelled the Tabascans to retire.

A few prisoners were taken in this skirmish. By them Cortés found his worst apprehensions verified. The country was everywhere in arms. A force consisting of many thousands had assembled from the neighboring provinces, and a general assault was resolved on for the next day. To the general's inquiries why he had been received in so different a manner from his predecessor, Grijalva, they answered, that " the conduct of the Tabascans then had given great offence to the other Indian tribes, who taxed them with treachery and cowardice ; so that they had promised, on any return of the white men, to resist them in the same manner that their neighbors had done." [14]

Cortés might now well regret that he had allowed himself to diviate from the direct object of his enterprise, and to become entangled in a doubtful war which could lead to no profitable result. But it was too late to repent. He had taken the step, and had no alternative but to go forward. To retreat would dishearten his own men at the outset, impair their confidence in him as their leader, and confirm the arrogance of his foes, the tidings of whose success might precede him on his voyage, and prepare the way for greater mortifications and defeats. He did not hesitate as to the course he was to pursue ; but, calling his officers together, announced his intention to give battle the following morning. [15]

[14] Bernal Diaz, Hist. de la Conquista, cap. 31, 32.—Gomara, Crónica, cap. 18.—Las Casas, Hist. de las Indias, MS., lib. 3, cap. 118, 119.— Ixtlilxochitl, Hist. Chich., MS., cap. 78, 79.

[15] According to Solís, who quotes the address of Cortés on the occasion,

He sent back to .ie vessels such as were disabled by their wounds, and ordered the remainder of the forces to join the camp. Six of the heavy guns were also taken from the ships, together with all the horses. The animals were stiff and torpid from long confinement on board; but a few hours' exercise restored them to their strength and usual spirit. He gave the command of the artillery—if it may be dignified with the name —to a soldier named Mesa, who had acquired some experience as an engineer in the Italian wars. The infantry he put under the orders of Diego de Ordaz, and took charge of the cavalry himself. It consisted of some of the most valiant gentlemen of his little band, among whom may be mentioned Alvarado, Velasquez de Leon, Avila, Puertocarrero, Olid, Montejo. Having thus made all the necessary arrangements, and settled his plan of battle, he retired to rest,—but not to slumber. His feverish mind, as may well be imagined, was filled with anxiety for the morrow, which might decide the fate of his expedition; and, as was his want on such occasions. he was frequently observed, during the night, going the rounds. and visiting the sentinels, to see that no one slept upon his post.

At the first glimmering of light he mustered his army, and declared his purpose not to abide, cooped up in the town, the assault of the enemy, but to march at once against him. For he well knew that the spirits rise with action, and that the attacking party gathers a confidence from the very movement, which is not felt by the one who is passively, perhaps anxiously, awaiting the assault. The Indians were understood to be encamped on a level ground a few miles distant from the city, called the plain of Ceutla. The general commanded that Ordaz should march with the foot, including the artillery, directly across the country, and attack them in front, while he himself would fetch a circuit with the horse, and turn their flank when thus engaged, or fall upon their rear.

These dispositions being completed, the little army heard mass and then sallied forth from the wooden walls of Tabasco. It was Lady-day, the twenty-fifth of March,—long memorable in the annals of New Spain. The district around the town was checkered with patches of maize, and, on the lower level, with plantations of cacao,—supplying the beverage, and perhaps the coin of the country, as in Mexico. These plantations, requiring constant irrigation, were fed by numerous canals and reservoirs of water, so that the country could not be traversed

be summoned a council of his captains to advise him as to the course he should pursue. (Conquista, cap. 19.) It is possible; but I find no warrant for it anywhere.

without great toil and difficulty. It was, however, intersected by a narrow path or causeway, over which the cannon could be dragged.

The troops advanced more than a league on their laborious march, without descrying the enemy. The weather was sultry, but few of them were embarrassed by the heavy mail worn by the European cavaliers at that period. Their cotton jackets, thickly quilted, afforded a tolerable protection against the arrows of the Indians, and allowed room for the freedom and activity of movements essential to a life of rambling adventure in the wilderness.

At length they came in sight of the broad plains of Ceutla, and beheld the dusky lines of the enemy stretching, as far as the eye could reach, along the edge of the horizon. The Indians had shown some sagacity in the choice of their position; and, as the weary Spaniards came slowly on, floundering through the morass, the Tabascans set up their hideous battle-cries, and discharged volleys of arrows, stones, and other missiles, which rattled like hail on the shields and helmets of the assailants. Many were severely wounded, before they could gain the firm ground, where they soon cleared a space for themselves, and opened a heavy fire of artillery and musketry on the dense columns of the enemy, which presented a fatal mark for the balls. Numbers were swept down at every discharge; but the bold barbarians, far from being dismayed, threw up dust and leaves to hide their losses, and, sounding their war instruments, shot off fresh flights of arrows in return.

They even pressed closer on the Spaniards, and, when driven off by a vigorous charge, soon turned again, and, rolling back like the waves of the ocean, seemed ready to overwhelm the little band by weight of numbers. Thus cramped, the latter had scarcely room to perform their necessary evolutions, or even to work their guns with effect.[16]

The engagement had now lasted more than an hour, and the Spaniards, sorely pressed, looked with great anxiety for the arrival of the horse,—which some unaccountable impediments must have detained,—to relieve them from their perilous position. At this crisis, the furtherest columns of the Indian army were seen to be agitated and thrown into a disorder that rapidly spread through the whole mass. It was not long before the ears of the Christians were saluted with the cheering war-cry of " San

[16] Las Casas, Hist. de las Indias, MS., lib. 3, cap. 119.—Gomara. Crònica, cap. 19, 20.—Herrera, Hist. General, dec. 2, lib. 4, cap. 11.—Martyr, De Insulis p. 350.—Ixtlilxochitl, Hist. Chich., MS., cap. 79—Bernal Diaz, Hist. de la Conquista, cap. 33, 36.—Carta de Vera Cruz, MS.

Jago and San Pedro !" and they beheld the bright helmets and swords of the Castilian chivalry flashing back the rays of the morning sun, as they dashed through the ranks of the enemy, striking to the right and left, and scattering dismay around them. The eye of faith, indeed, could discern the patron Saint of Spain, himself, mounted on his gray war-horse, heading the rescue and trampling over the bodies of the fallen infidels ! [17]

The approach of Cortés had been greatly retarded by the broken nature of the ground. When he came up, the Indians were so hotly engaged, that he was upon them before they observed his approach. He ordered his men to direct their lances at the faces of their opponents, [18] who, terrified at the monstrous apparition,—for they supposed the rider and the horse, which they had never before seen to be one and the same, [19]—were seized with a panic. Ordaz availed himself of it to command a general charge along the line, and the Indians, many of them throwing away their arms, fled without attempting further resistance.

Cortés was too content with the victory, to care to follow it up by dipping his sword in the blood of the fugitives. He drew off his men to a copse of palms which skirted the place, and under their broad canopy the soldiers offered up thanksgivings to the Almighty for the victory vouchsafed them. The field of battle was made the site of a town, called in honor of the day on which the action took place, *Santa Maria da la Vitoria*, long afterwards the capital of the Province. [20] The number of those who fought or fell in the engagement is altogether doubtful. Nothing, indeed, is more uncertain than numerical estimates of barbarians. And they gain nothing in probability, when they come, as in the present instance, from the reports of their enemies. Most accounts, however, agree that the Indian force consisted of five

[17] Ixtlilxochitl, Hist. Chich., MS., cap. 79.

"Cortés supposed it was his own tutelar saint, St. Peter," says Pizarro y Orllana ; " but the common and indubitable opinion is, that it was our glorious apostle St. James, the bulwark and safeguard of our nation." (Varonas Ilustres, p. 73.) "Sinner that I am," exclaimed honest Bernal Diaz, in a more sceptical vein, "it was not permitted to me to see either the one or the other of the Apostles on this occasion." Hist. de la Conquista, cap 34.

[18] It was the order—as the reader may remember—given by Cæsar to his follwers in his battle with Pompey;

"Adversosque jubet ferro confundere vultus."
        LUCAN, Pharsalia, lib. 7, v. 575.

[19] "Equites," says Paolo Giovio, " unum integram Centaurorum specie animal esse existimarent." Elogia Virorum Illustrium, (Basil, 1696,) lib. 6, p. 229.

[20] Clavigero, Stor. del Messico, tom. III. p. 11.

squadrons of eight thousand men each. There is more discrepancy as to the number of slain, varying from one to thirty thousand! In this monstrous discordance, the common disposition
to exaggerate may lead us to look for truth in the neighborhood
of the smallest number. The loss of the Christians was inconsiderable; not exceeding—if we receive their own report, probably, from the same causes, much diminishing the truth—two
killed and less than a hundred wounded! We may readily comprehend the feelings of the conquerors, when they declared that
"Heaven must have fought on their side, since their own
strength could never have prevailed against such a multitude of
enemies!"[21]

Several prisoners were taken in the battle, among them two
chiefs. Cortés gave them their liberty, and sent a message by
them to their countrymen, "that he would overlook the past, if
they would come in at once, and tender their submission. Otherwise he would ride over the land, and put every living thing
in it, man, woman and child, to the sword!" With this formidable menace ringing in their ears, the envoys departed.

But the Tabascans had no relish for further hostilities. A
body of inferior chiefs appeared the next day, clad in dark
dresses of cotton, intimating their abject condition, and implored
leave to bury their dead. It was granted by the general, with
many assurances of his friendly disposition; but at the same
time he told them, he expected their principal caciques, as he
would treat with none other. These soon presented themselves, attended by a numerous train of vassals, who followed
with timid curiosity to the Christian camp. Among their pro-
pitiatory gifts were twenty female slaves, which, from the character of one of them, proved of infinitely more consequence
than was anticipated by either Spaniards or Tabascans. Confidence was soon restored; and was succeeded by a friendly intercourse, and the interchange of Spanish toys for the rude commodities of the country, articles of food, cotton, and a few gold
ornaments of little value. When asked where the precious metal was procured, they pointed to the west and answered "Cul-
hua," "Mexico." The Spaniards saw this was no place for
them to traffic, or to tarry in.—Yet here, they were not many

---

[21] "Crean Vras. Reales Altezas por cierto, que esta battalla fué vencida
mas por voluntad de Dios que por nras, fuerzas, porque para con quarente
mil hombres de guerra, poca defensa fuera quatrozientos que nostros eramos."
(Carta de Vera Cruz, MS.—Gomara, Crónica, cap. 20—Bernal Diaz, Hist.
de la Conquista, cap. 35.) It is Las Casas, who, regulating his mathematics.
as usual, by his feelings, rates the Indian loss at the exorbitant amount cited
in the text. "This," he concludes dryly, "was the first preaching of the
Gospel by Cortés in New Spain!" Hist. de las Indias, MS., lib. 3, cap. 119.

leagues distant from a potent and opulent city, or what once had been so, the ancient Palenque. But its glory may have even then passed away, and its name have been forgotten by the surrounding nations.

Before his departure the Spanish commander did not omit to provide for one great object of his expedition, the conversion of the Indians. He first represented to the caciques, that he had been sent thither by a powerful monarch on the other side of the water, to whom he had now a right to claim their allegiance. He then caused the reverend fathers Olmedo and Diaz to enlighten their minds, as far as possible, in regard to the great truths of revelation, urging them to receive these in place of their own heathenish abominations. The Tabascans, whose perceptions were no doubt materially quickened by the discipline they had undergone, made but a faint resistance to either proposal. The next day was Palm Sunday, and the general resolved to celebrate their conversion by one of those pompous ceremonials of the Church, which should make a lasting impression on their minds.

A solemn procession was formed of the whole army with the ecclesiastics at their head, each soldier bearing a palm-branch in his hand. The concourse was swelled by thousands of Indians of both sexes, who followed in curious astonishment at the spectacle. The long files bent their way through the flowery savannas that bordered the settlement, to the principal temple, where an altar was raised, and the image of the presiding deity was deposed to make room for that of the Virgin with the infant Saviour. Mass was celebrated by father Olmedo, and the soldiers who were capable joined in the solemn chant. The natives listened in profound silence, and, if we may believe the chronicler of the event who witnessed it, were melted into tears; while their hearts were penetrated with reverential awe for the God of those terrible beings who seemed to wield in their own hand the thunder and the lightning.[22]

The Roman Catholic communion has it must be admitted, some decided advantages over the Protestant, for the purposes of proselytism. The dazzling pomp of its service and its touching appeal to the sensibilities affect the imagination of the rude child of nature much more powerfully than the cold abstractions of Protestantism, which, addressed to the reason, demand a degree of refinement and mental culture in the audience to comprehend them. The respect, moreover. .own by the Catholic for the material representations of Divinity, greatly facilitates

[22] Gomara, Crónica, cap. 21, 22.—Carta de Vera Cruz., MS.—Martyr, De Insulis, p. 351. Las Casas, Hist. de las Indias, MS., ubi supra.

the same object. It is true, such representations are used by him only as incentives, not as the objects of worship. But this distinction is lost on the savage, who finds such forms of adoration too analogous to his own to impose any great violence on his feelings. It is only required of him to transfer his homage from the image of Quetzalcoatl, the benevolent deity who walked among men, to that of the Virgin or the Redeemer; from the Cross, which he has worshipped as the emblem of the God of rain, to the same Cross, the symbol of salvation.

These solemnities concluded, Cortés prepared to return to his ships, well satisfied with the impression made on the new converts, and with the conquests he had thus achieved for Castile and Christianity. The soldiers, taking leave of their Indian friends, entered the boats with the palm-branches in their hands, and descending the river reëmbarked on board their vessels, which rode at anchor at its mouth. A favorable breeze was blowing, and the little navy, opening its sails to receive it, was soon on its way again to the golden shores of Mexico.

CHAPTER V.

VOYAGE ALONG THE COAST.—DONA MARINA.—SPANIARDS LAND IN MEXICO.—INTERVIEW WITH THE AZTECS.

1519.

THE fleet held its course so near the shore, that the inhabitants could be seen on it; and, as it swept along the winding borders of the Gulf, the soldiers, who had been on the former expedition with Grijalva, pointed out to their companions the memorable places on the coast. Here was the *Rio de Alvarado*, named after the gallant adventurer, who was present, also, in this expedition; there the *Rio de Vanderas*, in which Grivalja had carried on so lucrative a commerce with the Mexicans; and there the *Isla de los Sacrificios*, where the Spaniards first saw the vestiges of human sacrifice on the coast. Puertocarrero, as he listened to these reminiscences of the sailors, repeated the words of the old ballad of Montesinos, " Here is France, there is Paris, and there the waters of the Duero,"[1] &c. " But I advise you," he added, turning to Cortés, " to look out only for the rich lands, and the best way to govern them." " Fear not," replied his commander, " if Fortune but favors me as she did Orlando, and I have such gallant gentlemen as you for my companions, I shall understand myself very well."[2]

The fleet had now arrived off San Juan de Ulua, the island so named by Grijalva. The weather was temperate and serene, and crowds of natives were gathered on the shore of the main land, gazing at the strange phenomenon, as the vessels glided along under easy sail on the smooth bosom of the waters. It was the evening of Thursday in Passion Week. The air came

[1] " Cata Francia, Montesino,
Cata Paris la ciudad,
Cata las aguas de Duero
Do van á dar en la mar."

They are the words of the popular old ballad, first published, I believe, in the Rómancero de Ambéres, and lately by Duran, Romances Caballerescos é Históricus, Parte I, p. 82.

[2] Bernal Diaz, Hist. de la Conquista, cap. 37.

pleasantly off the shore, and Cortés, liking the spot, thought he might safely anchor under the lee of the island, which would shelter him from the *nortes* that sweep over these seas with fatal violence in the winter, sometimes é even late in the spring.

The ships had not been long at anchor, when a light pirogue, filled with natives, shot off from the neighboring continent, and steered for the general's vessel, distinguished by the royal ensign of Castile floating from the mast. The Indians came on board with a frank confidence, inspired by the accounts of the Spaniards spread by their countrymen who had traded with Grijalva. They brought presents of fruits and flowers and little ornaments of gold, which they gladly exchanged for the usual trinkets. Cortés was baffled in his attempts to hold a conversation with his visiters by means of the interpreter, Aguilar, who was ignorant of the language ; the Mayan dialects, with which he was conversant, bearing too little resemblance to the Aztec. The natives supplied the deficiency, as far as possible, by the uncommon vivacity and significance of their gestures,—the hieroglyphics of speech,—but the Spanish commander saw with chagrin the embarrassment' he must encounter in future for want of a more perfect medium of communication.[8] In this dilemma, he was informed that one of the female slaves given to him by the Tabascan chiefs was a native Mexican, and understood the language. Her name— that given to her by the Spaniards—was Marina ; and, as she was to exercise a most important influence on their fortunes, it is necessary to acquaint the reader with something of her character and history.

She was born at Painalla, in the province of Coatzacualco, on the south-eastern borders of the Mexican empire. Her father, a rich and powerful cacique, died when she was very young. Her mother married again, and, having a son, she conceived the infamous idea of securing to this offspring of her second union Marina's rightful inheritance.

She accordingly feigned that the latter was dead, but secretly delivered her into the hands of some itinerant traders of Xical-lanco. She availed herself, at the same time, of the death of a child of one of her slaves, to substitute the corpse for that of her own daughter, and celebrated the obsequies with mock solemnity. These particulars are related by the honest old soldier, Bernal Diaz, who knew the mother, and witnessed the generous treat-

---

[8] Las Casas notices the significance of the Indian gestures as implying a most active imagination. "Señates é meneos con que los Yndios mucho mas que otras generaciones entienden y se dan á entender, por tener muy bivos los sentidos exteriores y tambien los interiores, mayormente ques adtrable su imaginacion." Hist. de las Indias, MS., lib. 3, cap. 120.

ment of her afterwards by Marina.   By the merchants the Indian maiden was again sold to the cacique of Tabasco, who delivered her, as we have seen, to the Spaniards.

From the place of her birth she was well acquainted with the Mexican tongue, which indeed, she is said to have spoken with great elegance.   Her residence in Tabasco familiarized her with the dialect of that country, so that she could carry on a conversation with Aguilar, which he in turn rendered into the Castilian. Thus a certain, though somewhat circuitous channel was opened to Cortés for communicating with the Aztecs; a circumstance of the last importance to the success of his enterprise.   It was not very long, however, before Marina, who had a lively genius, made herself so far mistress of the Castilian as to supersede the necessity of any other linguist.   She learned it the more readily, as it was to her the language of love.

Cortés, who appreciated the value of her services from the first made her his interpreter, then his secretary, and, won by her charms, his mistress.   She had a son by him, Don Martin Cortés, *comendador* of the Military order of St. James, less distinguished by his birth than his unmerited persecutions.

Marina was at this time in the morning of life.   She is said to have possessed uncommon personal attractions,[4] and her open, expressive features indicated her generous temper.   She always remained faithful to the countrymen of her adoption ; and her knowledge of the language and customs of the Mexicans, and often of their designs, enable her to extricate the Spaniards, more than once, from the most embarrassing and perilous situations.   She had her errors, as we have seen.   But they should be rather charged to the defects of early education, and to the evil influence of him to whom in the darkness of her spirit she looked with simple confidence for the light to guide her.   All agree that she was full of excellent qualities, and the

---

[4] " Hermosa como Diosa," *beautiful as a goddess,* says Camargo of her. (Hist. de Tlascala, MS.)   A modern poet pays her charms the following not inelegant tribute ;

> " Admira tan lúcida cabalgada
> Y espectáculo tal Doña Marina,
> India noble al caudillo presentada,
> De fortuna y belleza peregrina.
>
> Con despejado espíritu y viveza
> Gira la vista en el concurso mudo ;
> Rico manto de extrema sutileza
> Con chapas de oro autorizarla pudo,
> Prendió con bizarra gentileza
> Sobre los pechos en airoso nudo ;
> Reyna parece de la India Zara,
> Varonil y hermosísima Amazona "
>
> Moratin, Las Naves de Cortes Destruidas.

important services which she rendered the Spaniards have made
her memory deservedly dear to them ; while the name of Malinche — the name by which she is still known in Mexico—was
pronounced with kindness by the conquered races, with whose
misfortunes she showed an invariable sympathy.[5]

With the aid of his two intelligent interpreters, Cortés entered
into conversation with his Indian visitors.   He learned that they
were Mexicans, or rather subjects of the great Mexican empire,
of which their own province formed one of the comparatively recent conquests.   The country was ruled by a powerful monarch
called Moctheuzoma, or by Europeans more commonly Montezuma,[6] who dwelt on the mountain plains of the interior,
nearly seventy leagues from the coast; their own province was
governed by one of his nobles, named Teuhtlile, whose residence
was eight leagues distant.   Cortés acquainted them in turn
with his own friendly views in visiting their country, and with
his desire of an interview with the Aztec governor.   He then
dismissed them loaded with presents, having first ascertained
that there was abundance of gold in the interior, like the specimens they had brought.

Cortés, pleased with the manners of the people, and the goodly
reports of the land, resolved to take up his quarters here for the
present.   The next morning, April 21, being Good Friday, he
landed, with all his force, on the very spot where now stands
the modern city of Vera Cruz.   Little did the Conqueror imagine that the desolate beach, on which he first planted his foot,
was one day to be covered by a flourishing city, the great mart
of European and Oriental trade, the commercial capital of
New Spain.[7]

[5] Las Casas, Hist. de las Indias, MS., lib. 3, cap. 120.—Gomara, Crónica
cap. 25, 26.—Clavigero, Stor. del Messico, tom. III. pp. 12-14.—Oviedo,
Hist. de las Ind., MS., lib 33, cap 1, — Ixtlilxochitl Hist. Chich., MS.,
cap. 79.—Camargo, Hist. de Tlascala, MS.—Bernal Diaz, Hist. de la Conquista, cap. 37, 38.
    There is some discordance in the notices of the early life of Marina.   I
have followed Bernal Diaz,—from his means of observation, the best authority.   There is happily no difference in the estimate of her singular merits
and services.
    [6] The name of the Aztec monarch, like those of most persons and places
in New Spain, has been twisted into all possible varieties of orthography.
Modern Spanish historians usually call him Montezuma.   But as there is
no reason to suppose that this is correct, I have preferred to conform to the
name by which he is usually known to English readers.   It is the one adopted
by Bernal Diaz, and by no other contemporary, as far as I know.
    [7] Ixtlilxochitl, Hist. Chich., MS., cap. 79.—Clavigero, Stor. del Messico,
tom. III. p. 16.
    New Vera Cruz, as the present town is called, is distinct, as we shall see
hereafter, from that established by Cortés, and was not founded till the close

It was a wide and level plain, except where the sand had been drifted into hillocks by the perpetual blowing of the *norte*. On these sand-hills he mounted his little battery of guns, so as to give him the command of the country. He then employed the troops in cutting down small trees and bushes which grew near, in order to provide a shelter from the weather. In this he was aided by the people of the country, sent, as it appeared, by the governor of the district to assist the Spaniards. With their help stakes were firmly set in the earth, and covered with boughs, and with mats and cotton carpets, which the friendly natives brought with them. In this way they secured, in a couple of days, a good defence against the scorching rays of the sun, which beat with intolerable fierceness on the sands. The place was surrounded by stagnant marshes, the exhalations from which, quickened by the heat into the pestilent malaria, have occasioned in later times wider mortality to Europeans than all the hurricanes on the coast. The bilious disorders, now the terrible scourge of the *tierra caliente*, were little known before the Conquest. The seeds of the poison seem to have been scattered by the hand of civilization ; for it is only necessary to settle a town and draw together a busy European population, in order to call out the malignity of the venom which had before lurked innoxious in the atmosphere.[8]

While these arrangments were in progress, the natives flocked in from the adjacent district, which was tolerably populous in the interior, drawn by a natural curiosity to see the wonderful strangers. They brought with them fruits, vegetables, flowers in abundance, game, and many dishes cooked after the fashion of the country, with little articles of gold and other ornaments. They gave away some as presents, and bartered others for the wares of the Spaniards ; so that the camp, crowded with a motley throng of every age and sex, wore the appearance of a fair. From

of the sixteenth century, by the Conde de Monterey, viceroy of Mexico. It received its privileges as a city from Philip III. in 1615. Ibid., tom. III. p. 30, nota.

[8] The epidemic of the *matlazahuatl*, so fatal to the Aztecs, is shown by M. de Humboldt to be essentially different from the *vómito*, or bilious fever of our day. Indeed, this disease is not noticed by the early conquerors and colonists; and Clavigero asserts was not known in Mexico, till 1725. (Stor. del Messico, tom. I. p. 117, nota.) Humboldt, however, arguing that the same physical causes must have produced similar results, carries the disease back to a much higher antiquity, of which he discerns some traditional and historic vestiges. "Il ne faut pas confondre l'époque," he remarks with his usual penetration, "à laquelle une maladie a été décrite pour la première fois, parce qu'elle a fait de grands ravages dans un court espace de temps, avec l'époque de sa première apparition." Essai Polique, tom. IV. p. 161 et seq., and 179.

some of the visiters Cortés learned the intention of the governor to wait on him the following day.

This was Easter. Teuhtlile arrived, as he had announced, before noon. He was attended by a numerous train, and was met by Cortés, who conducted him with much ceremony to his tent, where his principal officers were assembled. The Aztec chief returned their salutations with polite, though formal courtesy. Mass was first said by father Olmedo, and the service was listened to by Teuhtlile and his attendants with decent reverence. A collation was afterwards served, at which the general entertained his guest with Spanish wines and confections. The interpreters were then introduced, and a conversation commenced between the parties.

The first inquiries of Teuhtlile were respecting the country of the strangers, and the purport of their visit. Cortés told him, that " he was the subject of a potent monarch beyond the seas, who ruled over an immense empire, and had kings and princes for his vassals ; that, acquainted with the greatness of the Mexican emperor, his master had desired to enter into a communication with him, and had sent him as his envoy to wait on Montezuma with a present in token of his good-will, and a message which he must deliver in person." He concluded by inquiring of Teuhtlile when he could be admitted to his sovereign's presence.

To this the Aztec noble somewhat haughtily replied, " How is it, that you have been here only two days, and demand to see the emperor ?" He then added, with more courtesy, that " he was surprised to learn there was another monarch as powerful as Montezuma ; but that, if it were so, he had no doubt his master would be happy to communicate with him. He would send his couriers with the royal gift brought by the Spanish commander, and, so soon as he had learned Montezuma's will, would communicate it."

Teuhtlile then commanded his slaves to bring forward the present intended for the Spanish general. It consisted of ten loads of fine cottons, several mantles of that curious featherwork whose rich and delicate dyes might vie with the most beautiful painting, and a wicker basket filled with ornaments of wrought gold, all calculated to inspire the Spaniards with high ideas of the wealth and mechanical ingenuity of the Mexicans.

Cortés received these presents with suitable acknowledgments, and ordered his own attendants to lay before the chief the articles designed for Montezuma. These were an arm-chair richly carved and painted, a crimson cap of cloth, having a gold medal emblazoned with St. George and the dragon, and a quantity of collars, bracelets and other ornaments of cut glass, which in a country where glass was not to be had, might claim to have the value of real gems, and no doubt passed for such with the inexperienced Mexican. Teuhtlile observed a soldier in the camp with a shining gilt helmet on his head, which he said reminded him of one worn by the god Quetzalcoatl in Mexico ; and he showed a desire that Montezuma should see it. The coming of the Spaniards, as the reader will soon see, was associated with some traditions of this same deity. Cortés expressed his willingness that the casque should be sent to the emperor, intimating a hope that it would be returned filled with the gold dust of the country, that he might be able to compare its quality with that in his own ! He further told the governor, as we are informed by his chaplain, " that the Spaniards were troubled with a disease of the heart, for which gold was a specific remedy " ![9] " In short," says Las Casas, " he contrived to make his want of gold very clear to the governor." [10]

While these things were passing, Cortes observed one of Teuhtlile's attendants busy with a pencil, apparently delineating some object. On looking at his work, he found that it was a sketch on canvas of the Spaniards, their costumes, arms, and, in short, different objects of interest, giving to each its appropriate form and color. This was the celebrated picture-writing of the Aztecs, and, as Teuhtlile informed him, this man was employed in portraying the various objects for the eye of Montezuma, who would thus gather a more vivid notion of their appearance than from any description by words. Cortés was pleased with the idea ; and, as he knew how much the effect would be heightened by converting still life into action, he ordered out the cavalry on the beach, the wet sands of which afforded a firm footing for the horses. The bold and rapid movements of the troops, as they went through their military exercises ; the apparent ease with which they managed the fiery animals on which they were mounted ; the glancing of their weapons, and the shrill cry of the trumpet, all filled the spectators with astonishment ; but when they heard the thunders of the cannon, which Cortés ordered to be fired at the same time, and witnessed the volumes of smoke and flame issuing from these terrible engines, and the rushing sound of the balls, as they dashed through the trees of the neighboring forest, shivering their branches into fragments, they were filled with consternation, from which the Aztec chief himself was not wholly free.

[9] Gomara, Crónica, cap. 26.
[10] Las Casas, Hist. de las Ind'is, MS., lib. 3, cap. 119.

Nothing of all this was lost on the painters, who faithfully recorded, after their fashion, every particular ; not omitting the ships, " the water-houses,"—as they called them,—of the strangers, which, with their dark hulls and snow-white sails reflected from the water, were swinging lazily at anchor on the calm bosom of the bay. All was depicted with a fidelity, that excited in their turn the admiration of the Spaniards, who, doubtless unprepared for this exhibition of skill, greatly overestimated the merits of the execution.

These various matters completed, Teuhtlile with his attendants withdrew from the Spanish quarters, with the same ceremony with which he had entered them ; leaving orders that his people should supply the troops with provisions and other articles requisite for their accommodation, till further instructions from the capital.[11]

---

[11] Ixtlilxochitl, Relaciones, MS., No. 13.—Idem, Hist. Chich., MS., cap. 79.—Gomara, Crónica, cap. 25, 26.—Bernal Diaz, Hist. de la Conquista, cap. 38.—Herrera, Hist. General, dec. lib. 5, cap. 4.—Carta de Vera Cruz, MS.—Torquemada, Monarch. Ind., lib. 4, cap. 13-15.—Tezozomoc, Crón. Mexicana, MS., cap. 107.

CHAPTER VI.

ACCOUNT OF MONTEZUMA.—STATE OF HIS EMPIRE.—STRANGE PROGNOSTICS.—EMBASSY AND PRESENTS.—SPANISH ENCAMPMENT.

1519.

WE must now take leave of the Spanish camp in the *tierra caliente*, and transport ourselves to the distant capital of Mexico, where no little sensation was excited by the arrival of the wonderful strangers on the coast. The Aztec throne was filled at that time by Montezuma the Second, nephew of the last, and grandson of a preceding monarch. He had been elected to the regal dignity in 1502, in preference to his brothers, for his superior qualifications, both as a soldier and a priest,—a combination of offices sometimes found in the Mexican candidates, as it was, more frequently, in the Egyptian. In early youth, he had taken an active part in the wars of the empire, though of late he had devoted himself more exclusively to the services of the temple ; and he was scrupulous in his attentions to all the burdensome ceremonial of the Aztec worship. He maintained a grave and reserved demeanor, speaking little and with prudent deliberation. His deportment was well calculated to inspire ideas of superior sanctity.[1]

When his election was announced to him, he was found sweeping down the stairs in the great temple of the national war-god. He received the messengers with a becoming humility, professing his unfitness for so responsible a station. The address delivered as usual on the occasion was made by his relative Nezahualpilli, the wise king of Tezcuco.[2] It has fortunately been preserved, and presents a favorable specimen of Indian eloquence. Towards the conclusion, the orator exclaims, " who can doubt that the Aztec empire has reached the zenith of its greatness, since the Almighty has placed over it one whose very presence fills every

---

[1] His name suited his nature; Montezuma, according to Las Casas, signifying, in the Mexican, "sad or severe man." Hist. de las Indias, MS., lib. 3, cap. 120.—Ixtlilxochitl, Hist. Chich., MS., cap. 70.—Acosta, lib. 7, cap. 20—Col de Mendoza, pp. 13-16; Codex Tel. Rem., p. 143, ap. Antiq. of Mexico, vol. VI.

[2] For a full account of this prince, see Book I., chap. 6.

beholder with reverence ?   Rejoice, happy people, that you have
now a sovereign who will be to you a steady column of support ;
a father in distress, a more than brother in tenderness and sym·
pathy ; one whose aspiring soul will disdain all the profligate
pleasures of the senses, and the wasting indulgence of sloth.
And thou, illustrious youth, doubt not that the Creator, who has
laid on thee so weighty a charge, will also give strength to sustain it ; that he who has been so liberal in times past, will shower
yet more abundant blessings on thy head, and keep thee firm in
thy royal seat through many long and glorious years."—These
golden prognostics, which melted the royal auditor into tears,
were not destined to be realized.[8]

Montezuma displayed all the energy and enterprise in the
commencement of his reign, which had been anticipated from
him.   His first expedition against a rebel province in the neighborhood was crowned with success, and he led back in triumph
a throng of captives for the bloody sacrifice that was to grace his
coronation.   This was celebrated with uncommon pomp.   Games
and religious ceremonies continued for several days, and among
the spectators who flocked from distant quarters were some noble
Tlascalans, the hereditary enemies of Mexico.   They were in
disguise, hoping thus to elude detection.   They were recognized,
however, and reported to the monarch.   But he only availed himself of the information to provide them with honorable entertainment, and a good place for witnessing the games.   This was a
magnanimous act, considering the long cherished hostility between the nations.

In his first years, Montezuma was constantly engaged in war,
and frequently led his armies in person.   The Aztec banners
were seen in the furthest provinces of the Gulf of Mexico, and
the distant regions of Nicaragua and Honduras.   The expeditions
were generally successful ; and the limits of the empire were
more widely extended than at any preceding period.

Meanwhile the monarch was not inattentive to the interior
concerns of the kingdom.   He made some important changes
in the courts of justice ; and carefully watched over the execu·
tion of the laws, which he enforced with stern severity.   He was
in the habit of patrolling the streets of his capital in disguise, to
make himself personally acquainted with the abuses in it.   And
with more questionable policy, it is said, he would sometimes try
the integrity of his judges by tempting them with large bribes

---

[8] The address is fully reported by Torquemada, (Monarch. Ind., lib. 3,
cap. 68.) who came into the country little more than half a century after its
delivery.   It has been recently republished by Bustamante.   **Tezcuco en los
Ultimos** Tiempos, (México, 1826,) pp. 256–258.

to swerve from their duty, and then call the delinquent to strict account for yielding to the temptation.

He liberally recompensed all who served him. He showed a similar munificent spirit in his public works, constructing and embellishing the temples, bringing water into the capital by a new channel, and establishing a hospital, or retreat for invalid soldiers, in the city of Colhuacan.

These acts, so worthy of a great prince, were counterblanced by others of an opposite complexion. The humility, displayed so ostentatiously before his elevation, gave way to an intolerable arrogance. In his pleasure-houses, domestic establishment, and way of living, he assumed a pomp unknown to his predecessors. He secluded himself from public observation, or, when he went abroad, exacted the most slavish homage ; while in the palace he would be served only, even in the most menial offices, by persons of rank. He, further, dismissed several plebeians, chiefly poor soldiers of merit, from the places they had occupied near the person of his predecessor, considering their attendance a dishonor to royalty. It was in vain that his oldest and sagest counsellors remonstrated on a conduct so impolitic.

While he thus disgusted his subjects by his haughty deportment, he alienated their affections by the imposition of grievous taxes. These were demanded by the lavish expenditure of his court. They fell with peculiar heaviness on the conquered cities. This oppression led to frequent insurrection and resistance ; and the latter years of his reign present a scene of unintermitting hostility, in which the forces of one half of the empire were employed in suppressing the commotions of the other. Unfortunately there was no principle of amalgamation by which the new acquisitions could be incorporated into the ancient monarchy, as parts of one whole. Their interests, as well as sympathies, were different. Thus the more widely the Aztec empire was extended, the weaker it became ; resembling some vast and ill-proportioned edifice, whose disjointed materials, having no principle of cohesion, and tottering under their own weight, seem ready to fall before the first blast of the tempest.

In 1516, died the Tezcucan king, Nezahualpilli; in whom Montezuma lost his most sagacious counsellor. The succession was contested by his two sons, Cacama and Ixtlilxochitl. The former was supported by Montezuma. The latter, the younger of the princes, a bold, aspiring youth, appealing to the patriotic sentiment of his nation, would have persuaded them that his

<hr/>

[4] Acosta, lib. 7, cap. 22—Sahagun, Hist. de Nueva España, lib. 8, Prólogo, et cap. 1.—Torquemada, Monarch. Ind., lib. 3, cap. 73, 74, 81, - Col. de Mendoza, pp. 14, 85, ap. Antiq. of Mexico, vol. VI.

brother was too much in the Mexican interests to be true to his own country. A civil war ensued, and ended by a compromise, by which one half of the kingdom, with the capital, remained to Cacama, and the northern portion to his ambitious rival. Ixtlilxochitl became from that time the mortal foe of Montezuma.[5]

A more formidable enemy still was the little republic of Tlascala, lying midway between the Mexican Valley and the coast. It had maintained its independence for more than two centuries against the allied forces of the empire. Its resources were unimpaired, its civilization scarcely below that of its great rival states, and for courage and military prowess it had established a name inferior to none other of the nations of Anahuac.

Such was the condition of the Aztec monarchy, on the arrival of Cortés ;—the people disgusted with the arrogance of the sovereign ; the provinces and distant cities outraged by fiscal exactions ; while potent enemies in the neighborhood lay watching the hour when they might assail their formidable rival with advantage. Still the kingdom was strong in its internal resources, in the will of its monarch, in the long habitual deference to his authority,—in short, in the terror of his name, and in the valor and discipline of his armies, grown gray in active service, and well drilled in all the tactics of Indian warfare. The time had now come, when these imperfect tactics and rude weapons of the barbarian were to be brought into collision with the science and enginery of the most civilized nations of the globe.

During the latter years of his reign, Montezuma had rarely taken part in his military expeditions, which he left to his captains, occupying himself chiefly with his sacerdotal functions. Under no prince had the priesthood enjoyed greater consideration and immunities. The religious festivals and rites were celebrated with unprecedented pomp. The oracles were consulted on the most trivial occasions ; and the sanguinary deities were propitiated by hetacombs of victims dragged in triumph to the capital from the conquered or rebellious provinces. The religion, or, to speak correctly, the superstition of Montezuma proved a principal cause of his calamities. In a preceding chapter I have noticed the popular traditions respecting Quetzalcoatl, that deity with a fair complexion and flowing beard, so unlike the Indian physiognomy, who, after fulfilling his mission of benevolence among the Aztecs, embarked on the Atlantic Sea for the mysterious shores of Tlapallan.[6] He promised, on his departure, to return at some future day with his posterity, and resume the pos-

[5] Clavigero, Stor. del Messico, tom. I. pp. 267, 274, 275.—Ixtlilxochitl, Hist Chich., MS., cap. 70-76.—Acosta, lib. 7, cap, 21.

[6] Ante, Book I., chap. 3, pp. 59, 60, and note 6.

session of his empire. That day was looked forward to with hope or with apprehension, according to the interest of the believer, but with general confidence throughout the wide borders of Anahuac. Even after the Conquest, it still lingered among the Indian races, by whom it was as fondly cherished, as the advent of their king Sebastian continued to be by the Portuguese, or that of the Messiah by the Jews.[7]

A general feeling seems to have prevailed in the time of Montezuma, that the period for the return of the deity, and the full accomplishment of his promise, was near at hand. This conviction is said to have gained ground from various preternatural occurrences, reported with more or less detail by all the most ancient historians.[8] In 1510, the great lake of Tezcuco, without the occurrence of a tempest, or earthquake, or any other visible cause, became violently agitated, overflowed its banks, and, pouring into the streets of Mexico, swept off many of the buildings by the fury of the waters. In 1511, one of the turrets of the great temple took fire, equally without any apparent cause, and continued to burn in defiance of all attempts to extinguish it. In the following years, three comets were seen ; and not long before the coming of the Spaniards a strange light broke forth in the east. It spread broad at its base on the horizon, and rising in a pyramidal form tapered off as it approached the zenith. It resembled a vast sheet or flood of fire, emitting sparkles, or, as an old writer expresses it, " seemed thickly powdered with stars."[9] At the same time, low voices were heard in the air, and doleful wailings, as if to announce some strange, mysterious calamity ! The Aztec monarch, terrified at the apparitions in the heavens, took counsel of Nezahualpilli, who was a great proficient in the subtle science of astrology. But the royal sage cast a deeper cloud over his spirit by reading in these prodigies the speedy downfall of the empire.[10]

[7] Tézozomoc, Crón. Mexicana, MS., cap 107.—Ixtlilxochitl, Hist. Chich., MS., cap. 1.—Torquemada, Monarch. Ind., lib. 4, cap. 14 ; lib. 6, cap. 24.—Codex Vaticanus, Antiq. of Mexico, vol. VI. Sahagun, Hist. de Nuevo España, lib. 8, cap. 7.—Ibid., MS., lib. 12, cap. 3, 4.

[8] " Tenia por cierto," says Las Casas of Montezuma, " segun sus próphetas agoreros le avian certificado, que su estado é rriquezas y prosperidad avia de perezer dentro de pocos años por çiertas gentes que avian de venir en sus dias, que de su felicidad lo derrocase, y por esto vivia siempre con temor y en tristeça y sobresaltado." Hist. de las Indias, MS., lib. 3, cap. 120.

[9] Camargo, Hist. de Tlascala, MS.—The Interpreter of the Codex Tel.-Rem. intimates that this scintillating phenomenon was probably nothing more than an eruption of one of the great volcanoes of Me~ico. Antiqu. of Mexico, vol. VI. p. 144.

[10] Sahagun, Hist. de Nueva España, MS., lib. 12, cap. 1.—Camargo, Hist. de Tlascala, MS.—Acosta, lib. 7, cap. 23.—Herrera, Hist. General, dec. 2 lib. 5, cap. 5.—Ixtlilxochitl, Hist. Chich., MS. cap. 74.

Such are the strange stories reported by the chroniclers, in which it is not impossible to detect the glimmerings of truth.[11] Nearly thirty years had elapsed since the discovery of the Islands by Columbus, and more than twenty since his visit to the American continent. Rumors, more or less distinct, of this wonderful appearance of the white men, bearing in their hands the thunder and the lightning, so like in many respects to the traditions of Quetzalcoatl, would naturally spread far and wide among the Indian nations. Such rumors, doubtless, long before the landing of the Spaniards in Mexico, found their way up the grand plateau, filling the minds of men with anticipations of the near coming of the period when the great deity was to return and receive his own again. In the excited state of their imaginations, prodigies became a familiar occurrence. Or rather, events not very uncommon in themselves, seen through the discolored medium of fear, were easily magnified into prodigies; and the accidental swell of the lake, the appearance of a comet, and the conflagration of a building were all interpreted as the special annunciations of Heaven.[12] Thus it happens in those great political convulsions which shake the foundations of society,—the mighty events that cast their shadows before them in their coming. Then it is that the atmosphere is agitated with the low, prophetic murmurs, with which Nature, in the moral as in the physical world, announces the march of the hurricane;

> " When from the shores
> And forest-rustling mountains comes a voice,
> That, solemn sounding, bids the world prepare ! "

When tidings were brought to the capital, of the landing of Grijalva on the coast, in the preceding year, the heart of Montezuma was filled with dismay. He felt as if the destinies which had so long brooded over the royal line of Mexico were to be accomplished, and the sceptre was to pass away from his house

[11] I omit the most extraordinary miracle of all,—though legal attestations of its truth were furnished the Court of Rome, (see Clavigero, Stor. del Messico, tom I. p. 289,)—namely, the ressurection of Montezuma's sister, Papantzin, four days after her burial, to warn the monarch of the approaching ruin of his empire. It finds credit with one writer at least, in the nineteenth century! See the note of Sahagun's Mexican editor, Bustamante, Hist. de Nueva España, tom. II. p. 270.

[12] Lucan gives a fine enumeration of such prodigies witnessed in the Roman capital in a similar excitement. (Pharsalia, lib. 1, v. 523. et seq.) Poor human nature is much the same everywhere. Machiavelli has thought the subject worthy of a separate chapter in his Discourses. The philosopher intimates a belief even in the existence of beneficent intelligences who send those portents as a sort of *premonitories*, to warn mankind of the coming tempest. Discorsi sopra Tito Livio, lib. 1, cap. 56.

forever. Though somewhat relieved by the departure of the Spaniards, he caused sentinels to be stationed on the heights; and, when the Europeans returned under Cortés, he doubtless received the earliest notice of the unwelcome event. It was by his orders, however, that the provincial governor had prepared so hospitable a reception for them. The hieroglyphical report of these strange visitors, now forwarded to the capital, revived all his apprehensions. He called, without delay, a meeting of his principal counsellors, including the kings of Tezcuco and Tlacopan, and laid the matter before them. [18]

There seems to have been much division of opinion in that body. Some were for resisting the strangers, at once, whether by fraud or by open force. Others contended, that, if they were supernatural beings, fraud and force would be alike useless. If they were, as they pretended, ambassadors from a foreign prince, such a policy would be cowardly and unjust. That they were not of the family of Quetzalcoatl was argued from the fact, that they had shown themselves hostile to his religion; for tidings of the proceedings of the Spaniards in Tabasco, it seems, had already reached the capital. Among those in favor of giving them a friendly and honorable reception was the Tezcucan king, Cacama.

But Montezuma, taking counsel of his own ill-defined apprehensions, preferred a half-way course,—as usual, the most impolitic. He resolved to send an embassy, with such a magnificent present to the strangers, as should impress them with high ideas of his grandeur and resources; while, at the same time, he would forbid their approach to the capital. This was to reveal, at once, both his wealth and his weakness. [14]

While the Aztec court was thus agitated by the arrival of the Spaniards, they were passing their time in the *tierra caliente*, not a little annoyed by the excessive heats and suffocating atmosphere of the sandy waste on which they were encamped. They experienced every alleviation that could be derived from the attentions of the friendly natives. These, by the governor's command, had constructed more than a thousand huts or booths of branches and matting, which they occupied in the neighborhood of the camp. Here they prepared various articles of food for the tables of Cortés and his officers, without any recompense; while the common soldiers easily obtained a supply for them-

---

[18] Las Casas, Hist. de las Indias, MS., lib. 3, cap. 120.—Ixtlilxochitl, Hist. Chich., MS., cap. 80.—Idem, Relaciones, MS.—Sahagun, Hist. de Nueva España, MS., lib. 12, cap. 3, 4.—Tezozomoc, Crón. Mexicana, MS., cap. 108.

[14] Tezozomoc, Crón. Mexicana MS., loc. cit.—Camargo, Hist. de Tlascala, MS., Ixtlilxochitl, Hist. Chich., MS., cap. 80.

selves, in exchange for such trifles as they brought with them for barter Thus the camp was liberally provided with meat and fish dressed in many savory ways, with cakes of corn, bananas, pine-apples, and divers luscious vegetables of the tropics, hitherto unknown to the Spaniards. The soldiers contrived, moreover, to obtain many little bits of gold, of no great value, indeed, from the natives ; a traffic very displeasing to the partisans of Velasquez, who considered it an invasion of his rights. Cortés, however, did not think it prudent, in this matter, to balk the inclinations of his followers.[15]

At the expiration of seven, or eight days at most, the Mexican embassy presented itself before the camp. It may seem an incredibly short space of time, considering the distance of the capital was near seventy leagues. But it may be remembered that tidings were carried there by means of posts, as already noticed, in the brief space of four and twenty hours ; [16] and four or five days would suffice for the descent of the envoys to the coast, accustomed as the Mexicans were to long and rapid travelling. At all events, no writer states the period, occupied by the Indian emissaries on this occasion, as longer than that men tioned.

The embassy, consisting of two Aztec nobles, was accompanied by the governor, Teuhtlile, and by a hundred slaves, bearing the princely gifts of Montezuma. One of the envoys had been selected on account of the great resemblance which, as appeared from the painting representing the camp, he bore to the Spanish commander. And it is a proof of the fidelity of the painting, that the soldiers recognized the resemblance, and always distinguished the chief by the name of the "Mexican Cortés.'

On entering the general's pavilion, the ambassadors saluted him and his officers with the usual signs of reverence to persons of great consideration, touching the ground with their hands and then carrying them to their heads, while the air was filled with clouds of incense, which rose up from the censers borne by their attendants. Some delicately wrought mats of the country (*petates*) were then unrolled, and on them the slaves displayed the various articles they had brought. They were of the most miscellaneous kind ; shields, helmets, cuirasses, embossed with plates and ornaments of pure gold ; collars and bracelets of the same metal, sandals, fans, *panaches* and crests of variegated feathers, intermingled with gold and silver threads and sprinkled with pearls and precious stones ; imitations of birds and animals

[15] Bernal Diaz, Hist. de la Conquista, cap. 39.—Gomara, Crônica, cap. 27.—ap. Barcia, tom. II.
[16] Ante, Book 1, Chap. 2. p 42.

in wrought and cast gold and silver, of exquisite workmanship; curtains, coverlets, and robes of cotton, fine as silk, of rich and various dyes, interwoven with feather-work that rivalled the delicacy of painting.[17] There were more than thirty loads of cotton cloth in addition. Among the articles was the Spanish helmet sent to the capital, and now returned filled to the brim with grains of gold. But the things which excited the most admiration were two circular plates of gold and silver, " as large as carriage-wheels." One, representing the sun, was richly carved with plants and animals,—no doubt, denoting the Aztec century. It was thirty palms in circumference, and was valued at twenty thousand *pesos de oro*. The silver wheel, of the same size, weighed fifty marks.[18]

The Spaniards could not conceal their rapture at the exhibition of treasures which so far surpassed all the dreams in which

[17] From the checkered figure of some of these colored cottons, Peter Martyr infers, the Indians were acquainted with chess I He notices a curious fabric made of the hair of animals, feathers, and cotton thread, interwoven together. "Plumas illas et concinnant inter cuniculorum villos interque gosampij stamina ordiuntur, et intexunt operose adeo, ut quo pacto id facient non bene intellexerimus." De Orbe Novo, (Parisiis, 1587.) dec. 5. cap. 10.

[18] Bernal Diaz, Hist. de la Conquista, cap. 39—Oviedo, Hist. de las. Ind., MS., lib. 33, cap. 1.—Las Casas Hist. de las Indies, MR.. lib. 3, cap. 120.— Gomara, Crónica, cap. 27, ap. Barcia, tom. II,—Carta de Vera Cruz, MS.— Herrera, Hist. General, dec. 2, lib. 5, cap. 5.

Robertson cites Bernal Diaz as reckoning the value of the silver plate at 20,000 *pesos*, or about £5,000. (History of America, Vol. II. note 75.) But Bernal Diaz speaks only of the value of the gold plate, which he estimates at 20,000 *pesos de oro*, a different affair from the *pesos*, dollars, or ounces of silver, with which the historian confounds them. As the mention of the *peso de oro* will often recur in these pages, it will be well to make the reader acquainted with its probable value.

Nothing is more difficult than to ascertain the actual value of the currency of a distant age ; so many circumstances occur to embarrass the calculation, besides the general depreciation of the precious metals, such as the adulteration of specific coins, and the like.

Señor Clemencin, the Secretary of the Royal Academy of History, in the sixth volume of its *Memorias*, has computed with great accuracy the value of the different denominations of the Spanish currency at the close of the fifteenth century, the period just preceding that of the conquest of Mexico. He makes no mention of the *peso de oro* in his tables. But he ascertains the precise value of the gold ducat, which will answer our purpose as well. (Memorias de la Real Academia de Historia, (Madrid, 1821,) tom. VI. Ilust. 20.) Oviedo, a contemporary of the Conquerors, informs us that the *peso de oro* and the *castellano* were of the same value, and that was precisely one third greater than the value of the ducat. (Hist. del Ind., lib. 6. cap. 8, ap. Ramusio, Navigationi et Viaggi, (Venetia, 1565.) tom. III. Now the ducat, as appears from Clemencin, reduced to our own currency, would be equal to eight dollars and seventy-five cents. *The peso de oro, therefore, was equal to eleven dollars and sixty-seven cents or two pounds twelve shillings and sixpence sterling*. Keeping this in mind, it will be easy for the reader to determine the actual value, in *pesos de oro*, of any sum that may be hereafter mentioned.

they had indulged. For, rich as were the materials, they were exceeded—according to the testimony of those who saw these articles afterwards in Seville, where they could coolly examine them—by the beauty and richness of the workmanship.[19]

When Cortés and his officers had completed their survey, the ambassadors courteously delivered the message of Montezuma. "It gave their master great pleasure," they said, "to hold this communication with so powerful a monarch as the King of Spain, for whom he felt the most profound respect. He regretted much that he could not enjoy a personal interview with the Spaniards, but the distance of his capital was too great; since the journey was beset with difficulties, and with too many dangers from formidable enemies, to make it possible. All that could be done, therefore, was for the strangers to return to their own land, with the proofs thus afforded them of his friendly disposition."

Cortés though much chagrined at this decided refusal of Montezuma to admit his visit, concealed his mortification as he best might, and politely expressed his sense of the emperor's munificence. "It made him only the more desirous," he said, "to have a personal interview with him. He should feel it, indeed, impossible to present himself again before his own sovereign, without having accomplished this great object of his voyage; and one, who had sailed over two thousand leagues of ocean, held lightly the perils and fatigues of so short a journey by land." He once more requested them to become the bearers of his message to their master, together with a slight additional token of his respect.

This consisted of a few fine Holland shirts, a Florentine goblet, gilt and somewhat curiously enamelled, with some toys of little value,—a sorry return for the solid magnificence of the royal present. The ambassadors may have thought as much. At least, they showed no alacrity in charging themselves either with the present or the message; and, on quitting the Castilian

---

[19] "Cierto cosas de ver!" exclaims Las Casas, who saw them with the Emperor Charles V. in Seville, in 1520. "Quedáron todos los que viéron aquestas cosas tan ricas y tan bien artifiçiadas y ermosísimas como de cosas nunca vistas," &c. (Hist. de las Indias, MS., lib. 3, cap. 120.) "Muy hermosas"; says Oviedo, who saw them in Valladolid, and describes the great wheels more minutely; "todo era mucho de ver!" "Hist. de las Indias, MS., loc. cit.) The inquisitive Martyr, who examined them carefully, remarks, yet more emphatically, "Si quid unquam honoris humana ingenia in huiuscemodi artibus sunt adepta, principatum iure merito ista consequentur. Aurum, gemmasque non admiror quidem, quâ industriâ, quóve studio superet opus materiam, stupeo. Mille figuras et facies mille prospexi quæ scribere nequeo. Quid oculos hominum suâ pulchritudine æque possit alicere meo iudicio vidi nunquam." De Orbe Novo, dec. 4, cap. 9.

quarters, repeated their assurance that the general's application would be unavailing.[20]

The splendid treasure, which now lay dazzling the eyes of the Spaniards, raised in their bosoms very different emotions, according to the difference of their characters. Some it stimulated with the ardent desire to strike at once into the interior, and possess themselves of a country which teemed with such boundless stores of wealth. Others looked on it as the evidence of a power altogether too formidable to be encountered with their present insignificant force. They thought, therefore, it would be most prudent to return and report their proceedings to the governor of Cuba, where preparations could be made commensurate with so vast an undertaking. There can be little doubt as to the impression made on the bold spirit of Cortés, on which difficulties ever operated as incentives, rather than discouragements, to enterprise. But he prudently said nothing,—at least in public,—preferring that so important a movement should flow from the determination of his whole army, rather than from his own individual impulse.

Meanwhile the soldiers suffered greatly from the inconveniences of their position amidst burning sands and the pestilent effluvia of the neighboring marshes, while the venomous insects of these hot regions left them no repose, day or night. Thirty of their number had already sickened and died; a loss that could ill be afforded by the little band. To add to their troubles, the coldness of the Mexican chiefs had extended to their followers; and the supplies for the camp were not only much diminished, but the prices set on them were exorbitant. The position was equally unfavorable for the shipping, which lay in an open roadstead, exposed to the fury of the first *norte* which should sweep the Mexican Gulf.

The general was induced by these circumstances to dispatch two vessels, under Francisco de Montejo, with the experienced Alaminos for his pilot, to explore the coast in a northerly direction, and see if a safer port and more commodious quarters for the army could not be found there.

After the lapse of ten days the Mexican envoys returned. They entered the Spanish quarters with the same formality as on the former visit, bearing with them an additional present of rich stuffs and metallic ornaments, which, though inferior in value to those before brought, were estimated at three thousand ounces of gold. Besides these, there were four precious stones

[20] **Las Casas, Hist. de las Indias,** MS., lib. 3, cap. 121.—**Bernal Diaz, Hist de la Conquista,** cap. 39.—**Ixtlilxochitl, Hist. Chich.,** MS., cap 80.— **Gomara. Crónica,** cap 27, cap. **Barcia,** tom. II.

of considerable size, resembling emeralds, called by the natives *chalchuites*, each of which, as they assured the Spaniards, was worth more than a load of gold, and was designed as a mark of particular respect for the Spanish monarch.[21] Unfortunately they were not worth as many loads of earth in Europe.

Montezuma's answer was in substance the same as before. It contained a positive prohibition for the strangers to advance nearer to the capital ; and expressed the confidence, that, now they had obtained what they had most desired, they would return to their own country without unnecessary delay. Cortés received this unpalatable response courteously, though somewhat coldly, and, turning to his officers, exclaimed, " This is a rich and powerful prince indeed ; yet it shall go hard, but we will one day pay him a visit in his capital ! "

While they were conversing, the bell struck for vespers. At the sound, the soldiers, throwing themselves on their knees, offered up their orisons before the large wooden cross planted in the sands. As the Aztec chiefs gazed with curious surprise, Cortés thought it a favorable occasion to impress them with what he conceived to be a principal object of his visit to the country. Father Olmedo accordingly expounded, as briefly and clearly as he could, the great doctrines of Christianity, touching on the atonement, the passion, and the resurrection, and concluding with assuring his astonished audience, that it was their intention to extirpate the idolatrous practices of the nation, and to substitute the pure worship of the true God. He then put into their hands a little image of the Virgin with the infant Redeemer, requesting them to place it in their temples instead of their sanguinary deities. How far the Aztec lords comprehended the mysteries of the faith, as conveyed through the double version of Aguilar and Marina, or how well they perceived the subtle distinctions between their own images and those of the Roman Church, we are not informed. There is reason to fear, however, that the seed fell on warren ground ; for, when the homily of the good father ended, they withdrew with an air of dubious reserve very different from their friendly manners at the first interview. The same night every hut was deserted by the natives, and the Spaniards saw themselves suddenly cut off from supplies in the midst of a desolate wilderness. The move-

---

[21] Bernal Diaz, Hist. de la Conquista, cap. 40.

Father Sahagun thus describes these stones, so precious in Mexico that the use of them was interdicted to any but the nobles. " Las *chalchuites* son verdes y no transparentes mezcladas de blanco, usanlas mucho los principales, trayendolas á las muñecas atadas en hilo, y aquello es señal de que es persona noble el que las trae." Hist. de Nueva España, lib. 11, cap. 8.

ment had so suspicious an appearance, that Cortés apprehended an attack would be made on his quarters, and took precautions accordingly. But none was meditated.

The army was at length cheered by the return of Montejo from his exploring expedition, after an absence of twelve days. He had run down the Gulf as far as Panuco, where he experienced such heavy gales, in attempting to double that headland, that he was driven back, and had nearly foundered. In the whole course of the voyage he had found only one place tolerably sheltered from the north winds. Fortunately, the adjacent country, well watered by fresh, running streams, afforded a favorable position for the camp; and thither, after some deliberation, it was determined to repair.[22]

[22] Camargo, Hist. de Tlascala, MS.—Las Casas, Hist de las Indias, MS., lib. 3, cap. 121.—Bernal Diaz, Hist. de la Conquista, cap. 40, 41.—Herrera, Hist. General, dec. 2, lib. 5. cap. 6.—Gomara. Crónica, cap. 29, ap. Barcia, tom. II.

CHAPTER VII.

TROUBLES IN THE CAMP.—PLAN OF A COLONY.—MANAGEMENT
OF CORTES.—MARCH TO CEMPOALLA.—PROCEEDINGS WITH THE
NATIVES.—FOUNDATION OF VERA CRUZ.

1519.

THERE is no situation which tries so severely the patience and
discipline of the soldier, as a life of idleness in camp, where his
thoughts, instead of being bent on enterprise and action, are
fastened on himself and the inevitable privations and dangers
of his condition.   This was particularly the case in the present
instance, where, in addition to the evils of a scanty subsistence,
the troops suffered from excessive heat, swarms of venomous
insects, and the other annoyances of a sultry climate. They were,
moreover, far from possessing the character of regular forces,
trained to subordination under a commander whom they had
long been taught to reverence and obey.   They were soldiers of
fortune, embarked with him in an adventure in which all seem
to have an equal stake, and they regarded their captain—the
captain of a day—as little more than an equal.

There was a growing discontent among the men at their longer
residence in this strange land. They were still more dissatisfied
on learning the general's intention to remove to the neighborhood of the port discovered by Montejo. "It was time to return," they said, "and report what had been done to the governor
of Cuba, and not to linger on these barren shores until they had
brought the whole Mexican empire on their heads !" Cortés
evaded their importunities as well as he could, assuring them
there was no cause for despondency. "Everything so far had
had gone on prosperously, and, when they had taken up a more
favorable position, there was no reason to doubt they might still
continue the same profitable intercourse with the natives."

While this was passing, five Indians made their appearance
in the camp one morning, and were brought to the general's
tent. Their dress and whole appearance were different from
those of the Mexicans. They wore rings of gold, and gems of
a bright blue stone in their ears and nostrils, while a gold leaf
delicately wrought was attached to the under lip. Marina was

unable to comprehend their language, but on her addressing them in Aztec, two of them, it was found, could converse in that tongue They said they were natives of Cempoalla, the chief town of the Totonacs, a powerful nation who had come upon the great plateau many centuries back, and, descending its eastern slope, settled along the sierras and broad plains which skirt the Mexican Gulf towards the north. Their country was one of the recent conquests of the Aztecs, and they experienced such vexatious oppressions from their conquerors as made them very impatient of the yoke. They informed Cortés of these and other particulars. The fame of the Spaniards had reached their master, who sent these messengers to request the presence of the wonderful strangers in his capital.

This communication was eagerly listened to by the general, who, it will be remembered, was possessed of none of those facts, laid before the reader, respecting the internal condition of the kingdom, which he had no reason to suppose other than strong and united. An important truth now flashed on his mind ; as his quick eye described in this spirit of discontent a potent lever, by the aid of which he might hope to overturn this barbaric empire. — He received the mission of the Totonacs most graciously, and, after informing himself, as far as possible, of their dispositions and resources, dismissed them with presents, promising soon to pay a visit to their lord.[1]

Meanwhile, his personal friends, among whom may be particularly mentioned Alonso Hernandez Puertocarrero, Christoval de Olid, Alonso de Avila, Pedro de Alvarado and his brothers, were very busy in persuading the troops to take such measures as should enable Cortés to go forward in those ambitious plans, for which he had no warrant from the powers of Velasquez. "To return now," they said, "was to abandon the enterprise on the threshold, which, under such a leader, must conduct to glory and incalculable riches. To return to Cuba would be to surrender to the greedy governor the little gains they had already got. The only way was to persuade the general to establish a permanent colony in the country, the government of which would take the conduct of matters into its own hands, and provide for the interests of its members. It was true, Cortés had no such authority from Velasquez. But the interests of the sovereigns, which were paramount to every other, imperatively demanded it."

These conferences could not be conducted so secretly, though held by night, as not to reach the ears of the friends of Velasquez.[2]

---

[1] Bernal Diaz, Hist. de la Conquista, cap. 41.—Las Casas, Hist. de las Indias, MS., lib. 3, cap 121.—Gomara, Crónica, cap. 28.

[2] The letter from the *cabildo* of Vera Cruz says nothing of these midnight

They remonstrated against the proceedings, as insidious and disloyal. They accused the general of instigating them; and, calling on them to take measures without delay for the return of the troops to Cuba, announced their own intention to depart, with such followers as still remained true to the governor.

Cortés, instead of taking umbrage at this high-handed proceeding, or even answering in the same haughty tone, mildly replied, "that nothing was further from his desire than to exceed his instructions. He, indeed, preferred to remain in the country, and continue his profitable intercourse with the natives. But, since the army thought otherwise, he should defer to their opinion, and give orders to return, as they desired." On the following morning, proclamation was made for the troops to hold themselves in readiness to embark at once on board the fleet, which was to sail for Cuba.[8]

Great was the sensation caused by their general's order. Even many of those before clamorous for it, with the usual caprice of men whose wishes are too easily gratified, now regretted it. The partisans of Cortes were loud in their remonstrances. "They were betrayed by the general," they cried, and, thronging round his tent, called on him to countermand his orders. "We came here," said they, "expecting to form a settlement, if the state of the country authorized it. Now it seems you have no warrant from the governor to make one. But there are interests, higher than those of Velasquez, which demand it. These territories are not his property, but were discovered for the Sovereigns;[4] and it is necessary to plant a colony to watch over their interests, instead of wasting time in idle barter, or, still worse, of

conferences. Bernal Diaz, who was privy to them, is a sufficient authority. See Hist. de la Conquista, cap. 42.

[8] Gomara, Crónica, cap. 30.—Las Casas, Hist. de las Indias. MS., lib. 3 cap. 121.—Ixtlilxochitl, Hist. Chich., MS., cap. 80.—Bernal Diaz, Ibid., loc. cit.—Declaracion de Puertocarrero, MS.

The deposition of a respectable person like Puertocarrero, taken in the course of the following year after his return to Spain, is a document of such authority, that I have transferred it entire, in the original, to the *Appendix*, Part 2, No. 7.

[4] Sometimes we find the Spanish writers referring to "the sovereigns," sometimes to "the emperor"; in the former case, intending queen Joanna, the crazy mother of Charles V., as well as himself. Indeed, all public acts and ordinances ran in the name of both. The title of "Highness," which, until the reign of Charles V., had usually—not uniformly, as Robertson imagines (History of Charles V., vol. II. p. 59)—been applied to the sovereign, now gradually gave way to that of "Majesty," which Charles affected after his election to the imperial throne. The same title is occasionally found in the correspondence of the Great Captain, and other courtiers of the reign of Ferdinand and Isabella.

returning, in the present state of affairs, to Cuba. If you re-fuse," they concluded, "we shall protest against your conduct as disloyal to their Highnesses."

Cortés received this remonstrance with the embarrassed air of one by whom it was altogether unexpected. He modestly requested time for deliberation, and promised to give his answer on the following day. At the time appointed, he called the troops together, and made them a brief address. "There was no one," he said, "if he knew his own heart, more deeply devoted than himself to the welfare of his sovereigns, and the glory of the Spanish name. He had not only expended his all, but incurred heavy debts, to meet the charges of this expedition, and had hoped to reimburse himself by continuing his traffic with the Mexicans. But if the soldiers thought a different course advisable, he was ready to postpone his own advantage to the good of the state." [5] He concluded by declaring his willingness to take measures for settling a colony *in the name of the Spanish sovereigns*, and to nominate a magistracy to preside over it.[6]

For the *alcaldes* he selected Puertocarrero and Montejo, the former cavalier his fast friend, and the latter the friend of Velas-quez, and chosen for that very reason ; a stroke of policy which perfectly succeeded. The *regidores, alguacil*, treasurer, and other functionaries, were then appointed, all of them his personal friends and adherents. They were regularly sworn into office, and the new city received the title of *Villa Rica de Vera Cruz*, "The Rich Town of the True Cross"; a name which was con-sidered as happily intimating that union of spiritual and temporal interests to which the arms of the Spanish adventurers in the New World were to be devoted.[7] Thus, by a single stroke of the pen, as it were, the camp was transformed into a civil com-

---

[5] According to Robertson, Cortés told his men that he had proposed to establish a colony on the coast, before marching into the country ; but he abandoned his design, at their entreaties to set out at once on the expedition In the very next page, we find him organizing this same colony. (History of America, vol. II. pp. 241. 242.) The historian would have been saved this inconsistency, if he had followed either of the authorities whom he cites, Bernal Diaz and Herrera, or the letter from Vera Cruz, of which he had a copy. They all concur in the statement in the text.

[6] Las Casas, Hist. de las Indias, MS., lib. 3, cap. 122.—Carta de Vera Cruz, MS.—Declaracion de Montejo, MS.—Declaracion de Puertocarrero, MS.

"Our general, after some urging, acquiesced," says the blunt old soldier, Bernal Diaz; "for, as the proverb says, 'You ask me to do what I have al-ready made up my mind to.'" *Tu me lo ruegas é yo me lo quiero.* Hist. de la Conquista, cap. 42.

[7] According to Bernal Diaz, the title of "Vera Cruz" was intended to com-memorate their landing on Good Friday. Hist. de la Conquista, cap. 42.

munity, and the whole frame-work and even title of the city were arranged, before the site of it had been settled.

The new municipality were not slow in coming together ; when Cortés presented himself, cap in hand, before that august body, and, laying the powers of Velasquez on the table, respectfully tendered the resignation of his office of Captain-General, " which, indeed," he said, " had necessarily expired, since the authority of the governor was now superseded by that of the magistracy of Villa Rica de Vera Cruz." He then, with a profound obeisance, left the apartment.[8]

The council, after a decent time spent in deliberation, again requested his presence. "There was no one," they said, "who, on mature reflection, appeared to them so well qualified to take charge of the interests of the community, both in peace and in war, as himself ; and they unanimously named him, in behalf of their Catholic Highnesses, Captain General and Chief Justice of the colony." He was further empowered to draw, on his own account, one fifth of the gold and silver which might hereafter be obtained by commerce or conquest from the natives.[9] Thus clothed with supreme civil and military jurisdiction, Cortés was not backward in exerting his authority. He found speedy occasion for it.

The transactions above described had succeeded each other so rapidly, that the governor's party seemed to be taken by surprise, and had formed no plan of opposition. When the last measure was carried, however, they broke forth into the most indignant and opprobrious invectives, denouncing the whole as a systematic conspiracy against Velasquez. These accusations led to recrimination from the soldiers of the other side, until from words they nearly proceeded to blows. Some of the principal cavaliers, among them Velasquez de Leon, a kinsman of the governor, Escobar, his page, and Diego de Ordaz, were so active in instigating these turbulent movements, that Cortés took

---

[8] Solís, whose taste for speech-making might have satisfied even the Abbé Mably, (See his Treatise, " De la Manière d'écrire l'Histoire,") has put a very flourishing harangue on this occasion into the mouth of his hero, of which there is not a vestige in any contemporary account. (Conquista, lib. 2, cap. 7.) Dr. Robertson has transferred it to his own eloquent pages, without citing his author, indeed who, considering he came a century and a half after the Conquest, must be allowed to be not the best, especially when the only voucher for a fact.

[9] " Lo peor de todo que le otorgámos." says Bernal Diaz, somewhat peevishly, was, " que la dariamos el quinto del oro de lo que se huuiesse, despues de sacado el Real quinto." (Hist. de la Conquista, cap 42.) The letter from Vera Cruz says nothing of this fifth. The reader, who would see the whole account of this remarkable transaction in the original, may find it in *Appendix, Part 2, No. 8.*

the bold measure of putting them all in irons, and sending them on board the vessels. He then dispersed the common file by detaching many of them with a strong party under Alvarado to forage the neighboring country, and bring home provisions for the destitute camp.

During their absence, every argument that cupidity or ambition could suggest was used to win the refractory to his views. Promises, and even gold, it is said, were liberally lavished ; till, by degrees, their understandings were opened to a clearer view of the merits of the case. And when the foraging party reappeared with abundance of poultry and vegetables, and the cravings of the stomach—that great laboratory of disaffection, whether in camp or capital—were appeased, good-humor returned with good cheer, and the rival factions embraced one another as companions in arms, pledged to a common cause. Even the high-mettled hidalgos on board the vessels did not long withstand the general tide of reconciliation, but one by one gave in their adhesion to the new government. What is more remarkable is that this forced conversion was not a hollow one, but from this time forward several of these very cavaliers became the most steady and devoted partisans of Cortés.[19]

Such was the address of this extraordinary man, and such the ascendency which in a few months he had acquired over these wild and turbulent spirits ! By this ingenious transformation of a military into a civil community, he had secured a new and effectual basis for future operations. He might now go forward without fear of check or control from a superior,—at least from any other superior than the Crown, under which alone he held his commission. In accomplishing this, instead of incurring the charge of usurpation, or of transcending his legitimate powers, he had transferred the responsibility, in a great measure, to those who had imposed on him the necessity of action. By this step, moreover, he had linked the fortunes of his followers indissolubly

---

[19] Carta de Vera Cruz, MS.—Gomara, Crónica, cap. 30, 31.—Las Casas, Hist. de las Indias, MS., lib. 3, cap. 122.—Ixtlilxochitl, Hist. Chich., MS., cap. 80.—Bernal Diaz, Hist. de la Conquista, cap. 42.—Declaraciones de Montejo y Puertocarrero, MSS.

In the process of Narvaez against Cortés, the latter is accused of being possessed with the Devil, as only Lucifer could have gained him thus the affections of the soldiery. (Demanda de Narvaez, MS.) Solis, on the other hand, sees nothing but good faith and loyalty in the conduct of the general, who acted from a sense of duty ! (Conquista, lib. 2, cap. 6, 7.) Solis is even a more steady apologist for his hero, than his own chaplain, Gomara, or the worthy magistrates of Vera Cruz. A more impartial testimony than either, probably, may be gathered from honest Bernal Diaz, so often quoted. A hearty champion of the cause, ho was by no means blind to the defects nor the merits of his leader.

with his own. They had taken their chance with him, and,
whether for weal or for woe, must abide the consequences. He
was no longer limited to the narrow concerns of a sordid traffic,
but, sure of their coöperation, might now boldly meditate, and
gradually disclose, those lofty schemes which he had formed in
his own bosom for the conquest of an empire.[11]

Harmony being thus restored, Cortés sent his heavy guns on
board the fleet, and ordered it to coast along the shore to the
north as far as Chiahuitztla, the town near which the destined
port of the new city was situated ; proposing, himself, at the head
of his troops, to visit Cempoalla, on the march. The road lay
for some miles across the dreary plains in the neighborhood of
the modern Vera Cruz. In this sandy waste no signs of vegetation met their eyes, which, however, were occasionally refreshed by glimpses of the blue Atlantic, and by the distant view
of the magnificent Orizaba, towering, with his spotless diadem
of snow, far above his colossal brethren of the Andes.[12] As they
advanced, the country gradually assumed a greener and richer
aspect. They crossed a river, probably a tributary of the *Rio de
la Antigua*, with difficulty, on rafts, and on some broken canoes
that were lying on the banks. They now came in view of very
different scenery,—wide-rolling plains covered with a rich carpet
of verdure, and overshadowed by groves of cocoas and feathery
palms, among whose tall, slender stems were seen deer and various wild animals with which the Spaniards were unacquainted.
Some of the horsemen gave chase to the deer, and wounded, but

---

[11] This may appear rather indifferent logic to those who consider that
Cortés appointed the very body, who, in turn, appointed him to the command.
But the affectation of legal forms afforded him a thin varnish for his proceedings, which served his purpose, for the present at least, with the troops.
For the future, he trusted to his good star,—in other words, to the success
of his enterprise,— to vindicate his conduct to the Emperor. He did not
miscalculate.

[12] The name of the mountain is not given, and probably was not known,
but the minute description in the MS. of Vera Cruz leaves no doubt that it
was the one mentioned in the text. " Entre las quales así una que. excede
en mucha altura á todas las otras y de ella se vee y descubre gran parte de
la mar y de la tierra, y es tan alta, que si el dia no es bien claro, no se puede
de divisar ni ver lo alto de ella, porque de la mitad arriba está toda cubierta
de nubes: y algunos veces, cuando hace muy claro dia, se vee por cima de
las dichas nubes lo alto de ella, y esta tan blanco, que lo jusgamos por nieve."
(Carta de Vera Cruz, MS.) This huge volcano was called *Citlaltepetl*, or
" Star-mountain," by the Mexicans,—perhaps from the fire which once
issued from its conical summit, far above the clouds. It stands in the in-
tendancy of Vera Cruz, and rises, according to Humboldt's measurement, to
the enormous height of 17, 368 feet above the ocean. (Essai Politique, tom.
I. p. 265.) It is the highest peak but one in the whole range of the Mexican
Cordilleras.

did not succeed in killing them. They saw also, pheasants and other birds; among them the wild turkey, the pride of the American forest, which the Spaniards described as a species of peacock.[18]

On their route they passed through some deserted villages, in which were Indian temples, where they found censers, and other sacred utensils, and manuscripts of the *agave* fibre, containing the picture-writing, in which, probably, their religious ceremonies were recorded. They now beheld, also, the hideous spectacle, with which they became afterwards familiar, of the mutilated corpses of victims who had been sacrificed to the accursed deities of the land. The Spaniards turned with loathing and indignation from a display of butchery, which formed so dismal a contrast to the fair scenes of nature by which they were surrounded.

They held their course along the banks of the river, towards its source, when they were met by twelve Indians, sent by the cacique of Cempoalla to show them the way to his residence. At night they bivouacked in an open meadow, where they were well supplied with provisions by their new friends. They left the stream on the following morning, and, striking northerly across the country, came upon a wide expanse of luxuriant plains and woodland, glowing in all the splendor of tropical vegetation. The branches of the stately trees were gayly festooned with clustering vines of the dark-purple grape, variegated convolvuli, and other flowering parasites of the most brilliant dyes. The undergrowth of prickly aloe, matted with wild rose and honeysuckle, made in many places an almost impervious thicket. Amid this wilderness of sweet-smelling buds and blossoms, fluttered numerous birds of the parrot tribe, and clouds of butterflies, whose gaudy colors, nowhere so gorgeous as in the *tierra caliente*, rivalled those of the vegetable creation; while birds of exquisite song, the scarlet cardinal, and the marvellous mocking-bird, that comprehends in his own notes the whole music of a forest, filled the air with delicious melody.—The hearts of the stern Conquerors were not very sensible to the beauties of nature. But the magical charms of the scenery drew forth unbounded expressions of delight, and as they wandered through this "terrestrial paradise," as they called it, they fondly compared it to the fairest regions of their own sunny land.[14]

[18] Carta de Vera Cruz. MS.—Bernal Diaz, Hist. de la Conquista, cap. 44.

[14] Gomara, Crónica, cap. 32, ap. Barcia, tom. II.—Herrera, Hist General, dec. 2, lib. 5, cap. 8.—Oviedo, Hist. de las Ind., MS, lib. 33, cap. 1.

"Mui hermosas vegas y riberas tales y tan hermosas que en toda España no pueden ser mejores an sí de apaçibles á la vista como de fructíferas."

As they approached the Indian city, they saw abundant signs of cultivation, in the trim gardens and orchards that lined both sides of the road. They were now met by parties of the natives of either sex, who increased in numbers with every step of their progress. The women, as well as men, mingled fearlessly among the soldiers, bearing bunches and wreaths of flowers, with which they decorated the neck of the general's charger, and hung a chaplet of roses about his helmet. Flowers were the delight of this people. They bestowed much care in their cultivation, in which they were well seconded by a climate of alternate heat and moisture, stimulating the soil to the spontaneous production of every form of vegetable life. The same refined taste, as we shall see, prevailed among the warlike Aztecs, and has survived the degradation of the nation in their descendants of the present day.[15]

Many of the women appeared, from their richer dress and numerous attendants, to be persons of rank. They were clad in robes of fine cotton, curiously colored, which reached from the neck—in the inferior orders, from the waist—to the ankles. The men wore a sort of mantle of the same material, *á la Morisca*, in the Moorish fashion, over their shoulders, and belts or sashes about the loins. Both sexes had jewels and ornaments of gold round their necks, while their ears and nostrils were perforated with rings of the same metal.

(Carta de Vera Cruz, MS.) The following poetical apostrophe, by Lord Morpeth, to the scenery of Cuba, equally applicable to that of the *tierra caliente*, will give the reader a more animated picture of the glories of these sunny climes, than my own prose can. The verses, which have never been published, breathe the generous sentiment characteristic of their noble author.

> " Ye tropic forests of unfaded green,
>   Where the palm tapers and the orange glows,
> Where the light bamboo weaves her feathery screen,
>   And her far shade the matchless *ceiba* throws !

> " Ye cloudless ethers of unchanging blue,
>   Save where the rosy streaks of eve give way
> To the clear sapphire of your midnight hue,
>   The burnished azure of your perfect day !

> " Yet tell me not my native skies are bleak,
>   That flushed with liquid wealth no cane fields wave ;
> For Virtue pines and Manhood dares not speak,
>   And Nature's glories brighten round the Slave."

"The same love of flowers," observes one of the most delightful of modern travellers, " distinguishes the natives now, as in the times of Cortés. And it presents a strange anomaly," she adds, with her usual acuteness; " this love of flowers having existed along with their sanguinary worship and barbarous sacrifices." Madame Calderon de la Barca, Life in Mexico, vol. I. let. 12.

Just before reaching the town, some horsemen who had rode in advance returned with the amazing intelligence, "that they had been near enough to look within the gates, and found the houses all plated with burnished silver!" On entering the place, the silver was found to be nothing more than a brilliant coating of stucco, with which the principal buildings were covered; a circumstance which produced much merriment among the soldiers at the expense of their credulous comrades. Such ready credulity is a proof of the exalted state of their imaginations, which were prepared to see gold and silver in every object around them.[16] The edifices of the better kind were of stone and lime, or bricks dried in the sun; the poorer were of clay and earth. All were thatched with palm-leaves, which, though a flimsy roof, apparently, for such structures, were so nicely interwoven as to form a very effectual protection against the weather.

The city was said to contain from twenty to thirty thousand inhabitants. This is the most moderate computation, and not improbable.[17] Slowly and silently the little army paced the narrow and now crowded streets of Cempoalla, inspiring the natives with no greater wonder than they themselves experienced at the display of a policy and refinement so far superior to anything they had witnessed in the New World.[18] The cacique came out in front of his residence to receive them. He was a tall and very corpulent man, and advanced leaning on two of his attendants. He received Cortés and his followers with great courtesy; and, after a brief interchange of civilities, assigned the army its quarters in a neighboring temple, into the spacious court-yard of which a number of apartments opened, affording excellent accommodations for the soldiery.

Here the Spaniards were well supplied with provisions, meat cooked after the fashion of the country, and maize made into bread-cakes. The general received, also, a present of considerable value from the cacique, consisting of ornaments of gold and fine cottons. Notwithstanding these friendly demonstrations, Cortés did not relax his habitual vigilance, nor neglect any of

---

[16] "Con la imaginacion que llevaban, i buenos deseos, todo se les antojaba plata i oro lo que relucia." Gomara, Crónica, cap. 32, ap. Barcia, tom. II.

[17] This is Las Casas' estimate. (Hist. de las Ind., MS., lib. 3, cap. 121.) Torquemada hesitates between twenty, fifty, and one hundred and fifty thousand, each of which he names at different times! (Clavigero, Stor. del Messico, tom. III. p. 26, nota.) The place was gradually abandoned, after the Conquest, for others, in a more favorable position, probably, for trade. Its ruins were visible at the close of the last century. See Lorenzana, Hist. de Nueva España, p. 39, nota.

[18] "Porque viven mas política y rasonablemente que ninguna de las gentes que hasta oy en estas partes se ha visto." Carta de Vera Cruz, MS.

the precautions of a good soldier. On his route, indeed, he had always marched in order of battle, well prepared against sur. prise. In his present quarters, he stationed his sentinels with like care, posted his small artillery so as to command the en. trance, and forbade any soldier to leave the camp without orders, under pain of death.[19]

The following morning, Cortés, accompanied by fifty of his men, paid a visit to the lord of Cempoalla in his own residence. It was a building of stone and lime, standing on a steep terrace of earth, and was reached by a flight of stone steps. It may have borne resemblance in its structure to some of the ancient buildings found in Central America. Cortés, leaving his soldiers in the court-yard, entered the mansion with one of his officers, and his fair interpreter, Doña Marina.[20] A long conference ensued, from which the Spanish general gathered much light respecting the state of the country. He first announced to the chief, that he was the subject of a great monarch who dwelt beyond the waters; that he had come to the Aztec shores, to abolish the in. human worship which prevailed there, and to introduce the knowledge of the true God. The cacique replied, that their gods, who sent them the sunshine and the rain, were good enough for them; that he was the tributary of a powerful mon. arch also, whose capital stood on a lake far off among the moun. tains; a stern prince, merciless in his exactions, and, in case of resistance, or any offence, sure to wreak his vengeance by carry. ing off their young men and maidens to be sacrificed to his dei. ties. Cortés assured him that he would never consent to such enormities; he had been sent by his sovereign to redress abuses and to punish the oppressor; [21] and, if the Totonacs would be true to him, he would enable them to throw off the detested yoke of the Aztecs.

The cacique added, that the Totonac territory contained about thirty towns and villages, which could muster a hundred thou. sand warriors,—a number much exaggerated.[22] There were other

---

[19] Las Casas, Hist. de las Indias, MS., lib. 3, cap. 121.—Carta de Vera Cruz, MS.—Gomara, Crónica, cap. 33, ap. Barcia, tom. II.—Oviedo, Hist. de las Ind., MS., lib 33, cap. I.

[20] The courteous title of *dona* is usually given by the Spanish chroniclers to this accomplished Indian.

[21] "No venia, sino á deshacer agravos, i favorecer los presos aiudar á los mezquinos, i quitar tiranías." (Gomara, Crónica, cap. 33, ap. Barcia, tom. II.) Are we reading the adventures—it is the language—of Don Quixote, or Amadis de Gaula?

[22] Ibid., cap. 36.
Cortés, in his Second Letter to the emperor Charles V., estimates the number of fighting men at 50,000. Relacion Segunda, ap. Lorenzana, p. 40.

provinces of the empire, he said, where the Aztec rule was equally odious; and between him and the capital lay the warlike republic of Tlascala, which had always maintained its independence of Mexico. The fame of the Spaniards had gone before them, and he was well acquainted with their terrible victory at Tabasco. But still he looked with doubt and alarm to a rupture with "the great Montezuma," as he always styled him; whose armies, on the least provocation, would pour down from the mountain regions of the West, and, rushing over the plains like a whirlwind, sweep off the wretched people to slavery and sacrifice!

Cortés endeavored to reassure him, by declaring that a single Spaniard was stronger than a host of Aztecs. At the same time, it was desirable, to know what nations would coöperate with him, not so much on his account, as theirs, that he might distinguish friend from foe, and know whom he was to spare in this war of extermination. Having raised the confidence of the admiring chief by this comfortable and politic vaunt, he took an affectionate leave, with the assurance that he would shortly return and concert measures for their future operations, when he had visited his ships in the adjoining port, and secured a permanent settlement there.[23]

The intelligence gained by Cortés gave great satisfaction to his mind. It confirmed his former views, and showed, indeed, the interior of the monarchy to be in a state far more distracted than he had supposed. If he had before scarcely shrunk from attacking the Aztec empire in the true spirit of a knight-errant, with his single arm, as it were, what had he now to fear, when one half of the nation could be thus marshalled against the other? In the excitement of the moment, his sanguine spirit kindled with an enthusiasm which overleaped every obstacle. He communicated his own feelings to the officers about him, and, before a blow was struck, they already felt as if the banners of Spain were waving in triumph from the towers of Montezuma! But many a bloody field was to be fought, many a peril and privation to be encountered, before that consummation could be attained.

Taking leave of the hospitable Indian, on the following day, the Spaniards took the road to Chiahuitztla,[24] about four leagues distant, near which was the port discovered by Montejo, where

[23] Las Casas, Hist. de las Indias, MS., lib. 3, cap. 121.—Ixtlilxochitl, Hist. Chich., MS., cap. 81.—Oviedo, Hist. de las Ind., MS., lib. 33, cap. 1.
[24] The historian, with the aid of Clavigero, himself a Mexican, may rectify frequent blunders of former writers, in the orthography of Aztec names. Both Robertson and Solís spell the name of this place *Quiabislan.* Blunders in such a barbarous nomenclature must be admitted to be very pardonable.

their ships were now riding at anchor. They were provided by the cacique with four hundred Indian porters, *tamanes*, as they were called, to transport the baggage. These men easily carried fifty pounds' weight, five or six leagues in a day. They were in use all over the Mexican empire, and the Spaniards found them of great service, henceforth, in relieving the troops from this part of their duty. They passed through a country of the same rich, voluptuous character as that which they had lately traversed; and arrived early next morning at the Indian town, perched like a fortress on a bold, rocky eminence that commanded the Gulf. Most of the inhabitants had fled, but fifteen cf the principal men remained, who received them in a friendly manner, offering the usual compliments of flowers and incense. The people of the place, losing their fears, gradually returned. While conversing with the chiefs, the Spaniards were joined by the worthy cacique of Cempoalla, borne by his men on a litter. He eagerly took part in their deliberations. The intelligence gained here by Cortés confirmed the accounts already gathered of the feelings and resources of the Totonac nation.

In the midst of their conference, they were interrupted by a movement among the people, and soon afterwards five men entered the great square or market-place, where they were standing. By their lofty port, their peculiar and much richer dress, they seemed not to be of the same race as these Indians. Their dark, glossy hair was tied in a knot on the top of the head. They had bunches of flowers in their hands, and were followed by several attendants, some bearing wands with cords, others fans, with which they brushed away the flies and insects from their lordly masters. As these persons passed through the place, they cast a haughty look on the Spaniards, scarcely deigning to return their salutations. They were immediately, joined, in great confusion, by the Totonac chiefs, who seemed anxious to conciliate them by every kind of attention.

The general, much astonished, inquired of Marina, what it meant. She informed him, they were Aztec nobles, empowered to receive the tribute for Montezuma. Soon after, the chiefs returned with dismay painted on their faces. They confirmed Marina's statement, adding, that the Aztecs greatly resented the entertainment afforded the Spaniards without the Emperor's permission; and demanded in expiation twenty young men and women for sacrifice to the gods. Cortés showed the strongest indignation at this insolence. He required the Totonacs not only to refuse the demand, but to arrest the persons of the collectors, and throw them into prison. The chiefs hesitated, but he insisted on it so peremptorily, that they at length complied, and the Aztecs were seized, bound hand and foot, and placed under a guard.

In the night, the Spanish general procured the escape of two of them, and had them brought secretly before him. He expressed his regret at the indignity they had experienced from the Totonacs; told them, he would provide means for their flight, and to-morrow would endeavor to obtain the release of their companions. He desired them to report this to their master, with assurances of the great regard the Spaniards entertained for him, notwithstanding his ungenerous behavior in leaving them to perish from want on his barren shores. He then sent the Mexican nobles down to the port, whence they were carried to another part of the coast by water, for fear of the violence of the Totonacs. These were greatly incensed at the escape of the prisoners, and would have sacrificed the remainder, at once, but for the Spanish commander, who evinced the utmost horror at the proposal, and ordered them to be sent for safe custody on board the fleet. Soon after, they were permitted to join their companions.— This artful proceeding, so characteristic of the policy of Cortés, had, as we shall see, hereafter, all the effect intended on Montezuma. It cannot be commended, certainly, as in the true spirit of chivalry. Yet it has not wanted its panegyrist among the national historians![26]

By order of Cortés, messengers were despatched to the Totonac towns, to report what had been done, calling on them to refuse the payment of further tribute to Montezuma. But there was no need of messengers. The affrighted attendants of the Aztec lords had fled in every direction, bearing the tidings, which spread like wildfire through the country, of the daring insult offered to the majesty of Mexico. The astonished Indians, cheered with the sweet hope of regaining their ancient liberty, came in numbers to Chiahuitztla, to see and confer with the formidable strangers. The more timid, dismayed at the thoughts of encountering the power of Montezuma, recommended an embassy to avert his displeasure by timely concessions. But the dexterous management of Cortés had committed them too far to allow any reasonable expectation of indulgence from this quarter. After some hesitation, therefore, it was determined to embrace the protection of the Spaniards, and to make one bold effort for the recovery of freedom. Oaths of allegiance were taken by the chiefs to the Spanish sovereigns, and duly recorded by Godoy, the royal notary. Cortés, satisfied with the important acquisi-

---

[26] "Grande artífice," exclaims Solís, " de medir lo que disponia con lo que recelaba; y prudente capitan él que sabe caminar en alcance de las contingencias"! Conquista, lib. 2, cap. 9.

tion of so many vassels to the crown set out soon after for the destined port, having first promised to revisit Cempoalla, where his business was but partially accomplished.[26]

The spot selected for the new city was only half a league dis-tant, in a wide and fruitful plain, affording a tolerable haven for the shipping. Cortés was not long in determining the circuit of the walls, and the sites of the fort, granary, town-house, temple, and other public buildings. The friendly Indians eagerly assist-ed, by bringing materials, stone, lime, wood, and bricks dried in the sun. Every man put his hand to the work. The general labored with the meanest of the soldiers, stimulating their exer-tions by his example, as well as voice. In a few weeks, the task was accomplished, and a town rose up, which, if not quite worthy of the aspiring name it bore, answered most of the pur-poses for which it was intended. It served as a good *point d'ap-pui* for future operations; a place of retreat for the disabled, as well as for the army in case of reverses; a magazine for stores, and for such articles as might be received from or sent to the mother country; a port for the shipping; a position of sufficient strength to overawe the adjacent country.[27]

It was the first colony—the fruitful parent of so many others —in New Spain. It was hailed with satisfaction by the simple natives, who hoped to repose in safety under its protecting shad-ow. Alas! they could not read the future, or they would have found no cause to rejoice in this harbinger of a revolution more tremendous than any predicted by their bards and prophets. It was not the good Quetzalcoatl, who had returned to claim his own again, bringing peace, freedom, and civilization in his train. Their fetters, indeed, would be broken; and their wrongs be amply avenged on the proud head of the Aztec. But it was to

---

[26] Ixtlilxochitl, Hist. Chich., MS., cap. 81.—Rel. Seg. de Cortés, ap. Lorenzana, p. 40.—Gomara, Crónica, cap. 34–36, ap. Barcia, tom. II.— Bernal Diaz, Conquista, cap. 46, 47.—Herrera, Hist. General, dec. 2, lib. 5, cap. 10, 11.

[27] Carta de Vera Cruz, MS.—Bernal Diaz, Conquista, cap. 48.—Oviedo, Hist. de las Ind., MS., lib. 33, cap. 1.—Declaracion de Montejo, MS.

Notwithstanding the advantages of its situation, La Villa Rica was aban-doned in a few years for a neighboring position to the south, not far from the mouth of the Antigua. This second settlement was known by the name of *Vera Cruz Vieja,* "Old Vera Cruz." Early in the 17th century this place, also, was abandoned for the present city, *Nueva Vera Cruz,* or New Vera Cruz, as it is called. (See Ante, chap. 5, note 7.) Of the true cause of these successive migrations we are ignorant. If, as is pretended, it was on account of the *vómito,* the inhabitants, one would suppose, can have gained little by the exchange. (See Humboldt, Essai Politique, tom. II. p. 210.) A want of attention to these changes has led to much confusion and inaccuracy in the ancient maps. Lorenzana has not escaped them in his chart and topographical account of the route of Cortés.

be by that strong arm, which should bow down equally the oppressor and the oppressed. The light of civilization would be poured on their land. But it would be the light of a consuming fire, before which their barbaric glory, their institutions, their very existence and name as a nation, would wither and become extinct ! Their doom was sealed, when the white man had set his foot on their soil

CHAPTER VIII.

ANOTHER AZTEC EMBASSY.—DESTRUCTION OF THE IDOLS.—DE-
SPATCHES SENT TO SPAIN.—CONSPIRACY IN THE CAMP.—THE
FLEET SUNK.

1519.

WHILE the Spaniards were occupied with their new settlement, they were surprised by the presence of an embassy from Mexico. The account of the imprisonment of the royal collectors had spread rapidly through the country. When it reached the capital, all were filled with amazement at the unprecedented daring of the strangers. In Montezuma every other feeling, even that of fear, was swallowed up in indignation; and he showed his wonted energy in the vigorous preparations which he instantly made, to punish his rebellious vassals, and to avenge the insult offered to the majesty of the empire. But when the Aztec officers liberated by Cortés reached the capital, and reported the courteous treatment they had received from the Spanish commander, Montezuma's anger was mitigated, and his superstitious fears, getting the ascendency again, induced him to resume his former timid and conciliatory policy. He accordingly sent an embassy, consisting of two youths, his nephews, and four of the ancient nobles of his court, to the Spanish quarters. He provided them, in his usual munificent spirit, with a princely donation of gold, rich cotton stuffs, and beautiful mantles of the *plumaje*, or feather embroidery. The envoys, on coming before Cortés, presented him with the articles, at the same time offering the acknowledgments of their master for the courtesy he had shown in liberating his captive nobles. He was surprised and afflicted, however, that the Spaniards should have countenanced his faithless vassals in their rebellion. He had no doubt they were the strangers whose arrival had been so long announced by the oracles, and of the same lineage with himself.[1] From deference to them he would spare the Totonacs, while they were present. But the time for vengeance would come.

[1] "Teniendo respeto á que tiene por cierto, que somos los que sus antepassados les auian dicho, que auian de venir á sus tierras, é que deuemos de ser de sus linajes." Bernal Diaz, Hist. de la Conquista, cap. 48.

Cortes entertained the Indian chieftains with frank hospitality. At the same time, he took care to make such a display of his resources, as, while it amused theirminds, should leave a deep impression of his power. He then after a few trifling gifts, dismissed them with a conciliatory message to their master, and the assurance that he should soon pay his respects to him in his capital, where all misunderstanding between them would be readily adjusted.

The Totonac allies could scarcely credit their senses, when they gathered the nature of this interview. Notwithstanding the presence of the Spaniards, they had looked with apprehension to the consequences of their rash act ; and their feelings of admiration where heightened into awe, for the strangers who, at this distance, could exercise so mysterious an influence over the terrible Montezuma.[2]

Not long after, the Spaniards received an application from the cacique of Cempoalla to aid him in a dispute in which he was engaged with a neighboring city. Cortés marched with a party of his forces to his support. On the route, one Morla, a common soldier, robbed a native of a couple of fowls. Cortés, indignant at this violation of his orders before his face, and aware of the importance of maintaining a reputation for good faith with his allies, commanded the man to be hung up, at once, by the roadside, in face of the whole army. Fortunately for the poor wretch, Pedro de Alvarado, the future conqueror of Quiché, was present, and ventured to cut down the body, while there was yet life in it. He, probably, thought enough had been done for example, and the loss of a single life, unnecessarily, was more than the little band could afford. The anecdote is characteristic, as showing the strict discipline maintained by Cortés over his men, and the freedom assumed by his captains, who regarded him on terms nearly of equality,—as a fellow-adventurer with themselves. This feeling of companionship led to a spirit of insubordination among them. which made his own post as commander the more delicate and difficult.

On reaching the hostile city, but a few leagues from the coast, they were received in an amicable manner ; and Cortes, who was accompanied by his allies, had the satisfaction of reconciling these different branches of the Totonac family with each other, without bloodshed. He then returned to Cempoalla, where he was welcomed with joy by the people, who were now impressed with as favorable an opinion of his moderation and justice, as they had before been of his valor. In token of his

*Gomara, Crónica, cap. 37.—Ixtlilxochitl, Hist. Chich., MS , cap 82.

gratitude, the Indian cacique delivered to the general eight Indian maidens, richly dressed, wearing collars and ornaments of gold, with a number of female slaves to wait on them. They were daughters of the principal chiefs, and the cacique requested that the Spanish captains might take them as their wives. Cortés received the damsels courteously, but told the cacique they must first be baptized, as the sons of the Church could have no commerce with idolaters.[3] He then declared that it was a great object of his mission to wean the natives from their heathenish abominations, and besought the Totonac lord to allow his idols to be cast down, and symbols of the true faith to be erected in their place.

To this the other answered as before, that his gods were good enough for him ; nor could all the persuasions of the general, nor the preaching of father Olmedo, induce him to acquiesce. Mingled with his polytheism, he had conceptions of a Supreme and Infinite Being, Creator of the Universe, and his darkened understanding could not comprehend how such a Being could condescend to take the form of humanity, with its infirmities and ills, and wander about on earth, the voluntary victim of persecution from the hands of those whom his breath had called into existence.[4] He plainly told the Spaniards that he would resist any violence offered to his gods, who would indeed avenge the act themselves, by the instant destruction of their enemies.

But the zeal of the Christians had mounted too high to be cooled by remonstrance or menace. During their residence in the land, they had witnessed more than once the barbarous rites of the natives, their cruel sacrifices of human victims, and their disgusting cannibal repasts.[5] Their souls sickened at these

---

[3] " De buena gana recibirian las Doncellas como fuesen Christianos ; porque de otra manera, no era permitido á hombres, hijos de la Iglesia de Dios, tener comercio con idolatras." Herrera Hist. General, dec. 2, lib. 5, cap. 13.

[4] Ibid., dec. 2, lib. 5, cap. 13.—Las Casas, Hist. de las Indias, MS., lib. 3, cap. 122.

Herrera has put a very edifying harangue, on this occasion, into the mouth of Cortés, which savors much more of the priest than the soldier. Does he not confound him with father Olemedo ?

[5] "Esto habemos visto." says the Letter of Vera Cruz, "algunos de nosotros, y los que lo han visto dizen qué es la mas terrible y la mas espantosa cosa de ver que jamas han visto." Still more strongly speaks Bernal Diaz. (Hist. de la Conquista, cap. 51.) The Letter computes that there were fifty or sixty persons thus butchered in each of the *teocallis* every year, giving an annual consumption, in the countries which the Spaniards had then visited, of three or four thousand victims ! (Carta de Vera Cruz, MS.) However loose this arithmetic may be, the general fact is appalling.

abominations, and they agreed with one voice to stand by their general, when he told them, that "Heaven would never smile on their enterprise, if they countenanced such atrocities, and that, for his own part, he was resolved the Indian idols should be demolished that very hour, if it cost him his life." To postpone the work of conversion was a sin. In the enthusiasm of the moment, the dictates of policy and ordinary prudence were alike unheeded.

Scarcely waiting for his commands, the Spaniards moved towards one of the principal *teocallis*, or temples, which rose high on a pyramidal foundation, with a steep ascent of stone steps in the middle. The cacique, divining their purpose, instantly called his men to arms. The Indian warriors gathered from all quarters, with shrill cries and clashing of weapons; while the priests, in their dark cotton robes, with dishevelled tresses matted with blood, flowing wildly over their shoulders, rushed frantic among the natives, calling on them to protect their gods from violation! All was now confusion, tumult, and warlike menace, where so lately had been peace and the sweet brotherhood of nations.

Cortés took his usual prompt and decided measures. He caused the cacique and some of the principal inhabitants and priests to be arrested by his soldiers. He then commanded them to quiet the people, for, if an arrow was shot against a Spaniard, it should cost every one of them his life. Marina, at the same time, represented the madness of resistance, and reminded the cacique, that, if he now alienated the affections of the Spaniards, he would be left without a protector against the terrible vengeance of Montezuma. These temporal considerations seem to have had more weight with the Totonac chieftain, than those of a more spiritual nature. He covered his face with his hands, exclaiming, that the gods would avenge their own wrongs.

The Christians were not slow in availing themselves of his tacit acquiescence. Fifty soldiers, at a signal from their general, sprang up the great stairway of the temple, entered the building on the summit, the walls of which were black with human gore, tore the huge wooden idols from their foundations, and dragged them to the edge of the terrace. Their fantastic forms and features, conveying a symbolic meaning, which was lost on the Spaniards, seemed in their eyes only the hideous lineaments of Satan. With great alacrity they rolled the colossal monsters down the steps of the pyramid, amidst the triumphant shouts of their own companions, and the groans and lamentations of the natives. They then consummated the

whole by burning them in the presence of the assembled mul
titude.

The same effect followed as in Cozumel. The Totonacs,
finding their deities incapable of preventing or even punishing
this profanation of their shrines, conceived a mean opinion of
their power, compared with that of the mysterious and formidable strangers. The floor and walls of the *teocalli* were then
cleansed, by command of Cortés, from their foul impurities ; a
fresh coating of stucco was laid on them by the Indian masons ;
and an altar was raised, surmounted by a lofty cross, and hung
with garlands of roses. A procession was next formed, in
which some of the principal Totonac priests, exchanging their
dark mantles for robes of white, carried lighted candles in their
hands ; while an image of the Virgin, half smothered under the
weight of flowers, was borne aloft, and, as the procession
climbed the steps of the temple, was deposited above the altar.
Mass was performed by father Olmedo, and the impressive
character of the ceremony and the passionate eloquence of the
good priest touched the feelings of the motley audience, until
Indians as well as Spaniards, if we may trust the chronicler,
were melted into tears and audible sobs. The Protestant missionary seeks to enlighten the understanding of his convert by
the pale light of reason. But the bolder Catholic, kindling the
spirit by the splendor of the spectacle and by the glowing portrait of an agonized Redeemer, sweeps along his hearers in a
tempest of passion, that drowns everything like reflection. He
has secured his convert, however, by the hold on his affections,
—an easier and more powerful hold with the untutored savage,
than reason.

An old soldier named Juan de Torres, disabled by bodily
infirmity, consented to remain and watch over the sanctuary,
and instruct the natives in its services. Cortés then, embracing
his Totonac allies, now brothers in religion as in arms, set out
once more for the Villa Rica, where he had some arrangements
to complete, previous to his departure for the capital.[6]

He was surprised to find that a Spanish vessel had arrived
here in his absence, having on board twelve soldiers and two
horses. It was under the command of a captain named Sau-
cedo, a cavalier of the ocean, who had followed in the track of
Cortés in quest of adventure. Though a small, they afforded a
very seasonable body of recruits for the little army. By these
men, the Spaniards were informed that Velasquez, the governor

[6] Las Casas, Hist. de las Indias, MS., lib. 3, cap. 122.—Bernal Diaz, Hist.
de la Conquista, cap. 51, 52.—Gomara, Crónica, cap. 43.—Herrera, Hist.
General, dec. 2, lib. 5, cap. 13, 14.—Ixtlilxochitl, Hist. Chich., MS., cap. 83

of Cuba, had lately received a warrant from the Spanish government to establish a colony in the newly discovered countries.

Cortés now resolved to put a plan in execution which he had been some time meditating. He knew that all the late acts of the colony, as well as his own authority, would fall to the ground without the royal sanction. He knew, too, that the interest of Velasquez, which was great at court, would, so soon as he was acquainted with his secession, be wholly employed to circumvent and crush him. He resolved to anticipate his movements, and to send a vessel to Spain, with despatches addressed to the emperor himself, announcing the nature and extent of his discoveries, and to obtain, if possible, the confirmation of his proceedings. In order to conciliate his master's good-will, he further proposed to send him such a present, as should suggest lofty ideas of the importance of his own services to the crown. To effect this, the royal fifth he considered inadequate. He conferred with his officers and persuaded them to relinquish their share of the treasure. At his instance, they made a similar application to the soldiers ; representing that it was the earnest wish of the general, who set the example by resigning his own fifth, equal to the share of the crown. It was but little that each man was asked to surrender, but the whole would make a present worthy of the monarch for whom it was intended. By this sacrifice, they might hope to secure his indulgence for the past, and his favor for the future ; a temporary sacrifice, that would be well repaid by the security of the rich possessions which awaited them in Mexico. A paper was then circulated among the soldiers, which, all who were disposed to relinquish their shares, were requested to sign. Those who declined should have their claims respected, and receive the amount due to them. No one refused to sign ; thus furnishing another example of the extraordinary power obtained by Cortés over these rapacious spirits, who, at his call, surrendered up the very treasures which had been the great object of their hazardous enterprise ![7]

---

[7] Bernal Diaz, Hist. de la Conquista, cap. 53.—Ixtlilochitl, Hist. Chich. MS., cap. 82 —Carta de Vera Cruz, MS.

A complete inventory of the articles received from Montezuma is contained in the *Carta de Vera Cruz.*—The following are a few of the items.

Two collars made of gold and precious stones.

A hundred ounces of gold ore, that their Highnesses might see in what state the gold came from the mines.

Two birds made of green feathers, with feet, beaks, and eyes of gold,—and, in the same piece with them, animals of gold, resembling snails.

A large alligator's head of gold.

He accompanied this present with a letter to the emperor, in which he gave a full account of all that had befallen him since his departure from Cuba ; of his various discoveries, battles, and traffic with the natives ; their conversion to Christianity ; his strange perils and sufferings ; many particulars respecting the lands he had visited, and such as he could collect in regard to the great Mexican monarchy and its sovereign. He stated his difficulties with the governor of Cuba, the proceedings of the army in reference to colonization, and besought the emperor to confirm their acts, as well as his own authority, expressing his entire confidence, that he should be able, with the aid of his brave followers, to place the Castilian crown in possession of this great Indian empire.[8]

This was the celebrated *First Letter*, as it is called, of Cortés which has hitherto eluded every search that has been made for it in the libraries of Europe.[9] Its existence is fully established by

A bird of green feathers, with feet, beak, and eyes of gold.

Two birds made of thread and feather-work having the quills of their wings and tails, their feet, eyes, and the ends of their beaks, of gold,—standing upon two reeds covered with gold, which are raised on balls of feather-work and gold embroidery, one white and the other yellow, with seven tassels of feather-work hanging from each of them,

A large wheel of silver weighing forty marks, and several smaller ones of the same metal.

A box of feather-work embroidered on leather, with a large plate of gold, weighing seventy ounces, in the midst.

Two pieces of cloth woven with feathers; another with variegated colors; and another worked with black and white figures.

A large wheel of gold, with figures of strange animals on it, and worked with tufts of leaves; weighing three thousand, eight hundred ounces.

A fan of variegated feather-work, with thirty-seven rods plated with gold.

Five fans of variegated feathers,—four of which have ten, and the other thirteen, rods embossed with gold.

Sixteen shields of precious stones, with feathers of various colors hanging from their rims.

Two pieces of cotton very richly wrought with black and white embroidery.

Six shields, each covered with a plate of gold, with something resembling a golden mitre in the centre.

[8] " Una muy larga Carta," says Gomara, in his loose analysis of it. Crónica cap. 40.

[9] Dr. Robertson states that the Imperial Library at Vienna was examined for this document, at his instance, but without success. (History of America, vol. II. note 70.) I have not been more fortunate in the researches made for me in the British Museum, the Royal Library of Paris, and that of the Academy of History at Madrid. The last is a great depository for the colonial historical documents ; but a very thorough inspection of its papers makes it certain that this is wanting to the collection. As the emperor received it on the eve of his embarkation for Germany, and the Letter of Vera Cruz, forwarded at the same time, is in the library of Vienna, this would seem, after all, to be the most probable place of its retreat.

references to it, both in his own subsequent letters, and in the writings of contemporaries.[10] Its general purport is given by his chaplain, Gomara. The importance of the document has doubtless been much overrated ; and, should it ever come to light, it will probably be found to add little of interest to the matter contained in the letter from Vera Cruz, which has formed the basis of the preceding portion of our narrative. He had no sources of information beyond those open to the authors of the latter document. He was even less full and frank in his communications, if it be true, that he suppressed all notice of the discoveries of his two immediate predecessors.[11]

The magistrates of the Villa Rica, in their epistle, went over the same ground with Cortés concluding with an emphatic representation of the misconduct of Valasquez, whose venality, extortion, and selfish devotion to his personal interests, to the exclusion of those of his sovereigns as well as of his own followers, they placed in a most clear and unenviable light.[12] They implored the government not to sanction his interference with the new colony, which would be fatal to its welfare, but to commit the undertaking to Hernando Cortés, as the man most capable, by his experience and conduct, of bringing it to a glorious termination.[13]

[10] " En una nao,"says Cortés, in the very first sentence of his Second Letter to the emperor, "que de esta Nueva España de Vuestra Sacra Magestad despaché á 16 de Julio de el año 1519 embié á Vuestra Alteza muy larga y particular Relacion de las cosas hasta aquella sazon despues que yo á ella vine en ella sucedidas." (Rel. Seg. de Cortés, ap. Lorenzana, p. 38.) "Cortés escriuió," says Bernal Diaz, " segun él nos dixo, correcta relacion, mas no vímos su carta." Hist. de la Conquista, cap. 53. (Also, Oviedo, Hist. de las Ind., MS., lib. 33, cap. 1, and Gomara, ut supra.) Were it not for these positive testimonies, one might suppose that the Carta de Vera Cruz had suggested an imaginary letter of Cortés. Indeed, the copy of the former document, belonging to the Spanish Academy of History,—and perhaps the original at Vienna,—bears the erroneous title of Primera Relacion de Cortes."

[11] This is the imputation of Bernal Diaz, reported on hearsay. as he admits he never saw the letter himself. Ibid., cap. 54.

[12] " Fingiendo mill cautelas," says Las Casas, politely, of this part of the letter, " y afirmando otras muchas falsedades é mentiras " ! Hist. de las Indias, MS., lib. 3, cap. 122.

[13] This document is of the greatest value and interest, coming as it does from the best instructed persons in the camp. It presents an elaborate record of all then known of the countries they had visited, and of the principal movements of the army, to the time of the foundation of the Villa Rica. The writers conciliate our confidence by the circumspect tone of their narration. "Querer dar," they say, "á Vuestra Magestad todas las particularidades de esta tierra y gente de ella, podria ser que en algo se errase la relacion, porque muchas de ellas no se han visto mas de por informaciones de los naturales de ella, y por esto no nos entremetemos á dar mas de aquello que por muy cierto y verdadero Vras. Reales Altezas podrán mandar tener •

With this letter went also another in the name of the citizen-soldiers of Villa Rica, tendering their dutiful submission to the sovereigns, and requesting the confirmation of their proceedings, above all, that of Cortés as their general.

The selection of the agents for the mission was a delicate matter, as on the result might depend the future fortunes of the colony and its commander. Cortés intrusted the affair to two cavaliers on whom he could rely; Francisco de Montejo, the ancient partisan of Velasquez, and Alonso Hernandez de Puerto-carrero. The latter officer was a near kinsman of the count of Medellin, and it was hoped his high connections might secure a favorable influence at court.

Together with the treasure, which seemed to verify the assertion that "the land teemed with gold as abundantly as that whence Solomon drew the same precious metal for his temple,"[14] several Indian manuscripts were sent. Some were of cotton, others of the Mexican *agave*. Their unintelligible characters, says a chronicler, excited little interest in the Conquerors. As evidence of intellectual culture, however, they formed higher objects of interest to a philosophic mind, than those costly fabrics which attested only the mechanical ingenuity of the nation.[15] Four Indian slaves were added as specimens of the natives. They had been rescued from the cages in which they were confined for sacrifice. One of the best vessels of the fleet was selected for the voyage, manned by fifteen seamen, and placed under the direction of the pilot Alaminos. He was directed to hold his course through the Bahama channel, north of Cuba, or Fernandina, as it was then called, and on no account to touch at that island or any other in the Indian ocean. With these instructions, the good ship took its departure on the 26th of July, freighted with the treasures and the good wishes of the community of the Villa Rica de Vera Cruz.

After a quick run the emissaries made the island of Cuba, and, in direct disregard of orders, anchored before Marien, on the

---

The account given of Velasquez, however, must be considered as an *ex parte* testimony, and, as such admitted with great reserve. It was essential to their own vindication, to vindicate Cortés. The letter has never been printed. The original exists, as above stated, in the Imperial Library at Vienna. The copy in my possession, covering more than sixty pages folio, is taken from that of the Academy of History at Madrid.

[14] "A nuestra parecer se debe creer, que ai en esta tierra tanto quanto en aquella de donde se dize aver llevado Salomon el oro para el templo." Carta de Vera Cruz, MS.

[15] Peter Martyr, preëminent above his contemporaries for the enlightened views he took of the new discoveries, devotes half a chapter to the Indian manuscripts, in which he recognized the evidence of a civilization analogous to the Egyptian. De Orbe Novo. dec. 4, cap. 8.

northern side of the island. This was done to accommodate Montejo, who wish to visit a plantation owned by him in the neighborhood. While off the port, a sailor got on shore, and, crossing the island to St. Jago, the capital, spread everywhere tidings of the expedition, until they reached the ears of Velasquez. It was the first intelligence which had been received of the armament since its departure; and, as the governor listened to the recital, it would not be easy to paint the mingled emotions of curiosity, astonishment, and wrath which agitated his bosom. In the first sally of passion, he poured a storm of invective on the heads of his secretary and treasurer, the friends of Cortés, who had recommended him as the leader of the expedition. After somewhat relieving himself in this way, he despatched two fast-sailing vessels to Marien with orders to seize the rebel ship, and in case of her departure, to follow and overtake her.

But before the ships could reach that port, the bird had flown, and was far on her way across the broad Atlantic. Stung with mortification at this fresh disappointment, Velasquez wrote letters of indignant complaint to the government at home, and to the fathers of St. Jerome, in Hispaniola, demanding redress. He obtained little satisfaction from the last. He resolved, however, to take it into his own hands, and set about making formidable preparations for another squadron, which should be more than a match for that under his rebellious officer. He was indefatigable in his exertions, visiting every part of the island, and straining all his resources to effect his purpose. The preparations were on a scale that necessarily consumed many months.

Meanwhile the little vessel was speeding her prosperous way across the waters; and, after touching at one of the Azores, came safely into the harbor of St. Lucar, in the month of October. However long it may appear, in the more perfect nautical science of our day, it was reckoned a fair voyage for that. Of what befell the commissioners on their arrival, their reception at court, and the sensation caused by their intelligence, I defer the account to a future chapter.[16]

Shortly after the departure of the commissioners, an affair occurred of a most unpleasant nature. A number of persons, with the priest Juan Diaz at their head, ill-affected, from some cause or other, towards the administration of Cortés, or not relishing

---

[16] Bernal Diaz, Hist. de la Conquista, cap. 54-57.—Gomara, Crónica, cap. 40.—Herrera, Hist. General, dec. 2, lib. 5, cap. 14.— Carta de Vera Cruz, MS.

Martyr's copious information was chiefly derived from his conversations with Alaminos and the two envoys, on their arrival at court. De Orbe Novo, dec. 4, cap. 6, et alibi; also Idem, Opus Epistolarum, (Amstelodami, 1670,) ep. 650.

the hazardous expedition before them, laid a plan to seize one of the vessels, make the best of their way to Cuba, and report to the governor the fate of the armament.   It was conducted with so much secrecy, that the party had got their provisions, water, and everything necessary for the voyage, on board, without detection ; when the conspiracy was betrayed, on the very night they were to sail, by one of their own number, who repented the part he had taken in it.   The general caused the persons implicated to be instantly apprehended.   An examination was instituted.   The guilt of the parties was placed beyond a doubt. Sentence of death was passed on two of the ringleaders ; another, the pilot, was condemned to lose his feet, and several others to be whipped.   The priest, probably the most guilty of the whole, claiming the usual benefit of clergy, was permitted to escape.   One of those condemned to the gallows was named Escudero, the very alguacil who, the reader may remember, so stealthily apprehended Cortés before the sanctuary in Cuba.[17] The general, on signing the death-warrants, was heard to exclaim, " Would that I had never learned to write ! "   It was not the first time, it was remarked, that the exclamation had been uttered in similar circumstances.[18]

The arrangements being now finally settled at the Villa Rica, Cortés, sent forward Alvarado, with a large part of the army, to Cempoalla, where he soon after joined them with the remainder. The late affair of the conspiracy seems to have made a deep impression on his mind.   It showed him, that there were timid spirits in the camp on whom he could not rely, and who, he feared, might spread the seeds of disaffection among their companions. Even the more resolute, on any occasion of disgust or disappointment hereafter, might falter in purpose, and, getting possession of the vessels, abandon the enterprise.   This was already too vast, and the odds were too formidable, to authorize expectation of success with diminution of numbers.   Experience showed that this was always to be apprehended, while means of escape were at hand.[19]   The best chance for success was to cut off these

---

[17] See Ante, p. 176.

[18] Bernal Diaz, Hist. de la Conquista, cap. 57.—Oviedo, Hist de las Ind., MS., lib. 33, cap. 2.—Las Casas, Hist. de las Indias, MS., lib. 3, cap. 122. —Demanda de Narvaez, MS.—Rel. Seg. de Cortès, ap. Lorenzana, p. 41.

It was the exclamation of Nero, as reported by Suetonius. " Etcum de supplicio cujusdam capite damnati ut ex more subscriberet, admoneretur, ' Quam vellem,' inquit, ' nescire literas ! '"   Lib. 6. cap. 10.

[19] " Y porque," says Cortés, " demas de los que por ser criados y amigos de Diego Velasquez tenian voluntad de salir de la Tierra, habia otros, que por verla tan grande, y de tanta gente, y tal, y ver los pocos Españoles que eramos, estaban del mismo propósito; creyendo, que si allí los navios de

means.—He came to the daring resolution to destroy the fleet, without the knowledge of his army.

When arrived at Cempoalla, he communicated his design to a few of his devoted adherents, who entered warmly into his views. Through them he readily persuaded the pilots, by means of those golden arguments which weigh more than any other with ordinary minds, to make such a report of the condition of the fleet as suited his purpose. The ships, they said, were grievously racked by the heavy gales they had encountered, and, what was worse, the worms had eaten into their sides and bottoms until most of them were not sea-worthy, and some, indeed, could scarcely now be kept afloat.

Cortés received the communication with surprise; "for he could well dissemble," observes Las Casas, with his usual friendly comment, "when it suited his interests." "If it be so," he exclaimed, "we must make the best of it! Heaven's will be done!"[20] He then ordered five of the worst conditioned to be dismantled, their cordage, sails, iron, and whatever was movable, to be brought on shore, and the ships to be sunk. A survey was made of the others, and, on a similar report, four more were condemned in the same manner. Only, one small vessel remained!

When the intelligence reached the troops in Cempoalla, it caused the deepest consternation. They saw themselves cut off by a single blow from friends, family, country! The stoutest hearts quailed before the prospect of being thus abandoned on a hostile shore, a handful of men arrayed against a formidable empire. When the news arrived of the destruction of the five vessels first condemned, they had acquiesced in it as a necessary measure, knowing the mischievous activity of the insects in these tropical seas. But, when this was followed by the loss of the remaining four, suspicions of the truth flashed on their minds. They felt they were betrayed. Murmurs, at first deep, swelled louder and and louder, menacing open mutiny. "Their general," they said, "had led them like cattle to be butchered in the shambles!"[21] The affair wore a most alarming aspect.

---

jasse, se me alzarian con ellos, y yéndose todos los que de esta voluntad estavan, yo quedara casi solo."

[20] "Mostró quando se lo dixéron mucho sentimiento Cortés, porque savie bien hacer fingimientos quando le era provechoso, y rrespondióles que mirasen vien en ello, é que si no estavan para navegar que diesen gracias á Dios por ello, pues no se podia hacer mas." Las Casas. Hist. de las Indias. MS., lib. 3, cap. 122.

[21] "Decian, que los queria meter en el matadero." Gomara, Crónica, cap. 42.

In no situation was Cortés ever exposed to greater danger from his soldiers.[22]

His presence of mind did not desert him at this crisis. He called his men together, and, employing the tones of persuasion rather than authority, assured them, that a survey of the ships showed they were not fit for service. If he had ordered them to be destroyed, they should consider, also, that his was the greatest sacrifice, for they were his property,—all, indeed, he possessed in the world. The troops, on the other hand, would derive one great advantage from it, by the addition of a hundred able-bodied recruits, before required to man the vessels. But, even if the fleet had been saved, it could have been of little service in their present expedition; since they would not need it if they succeeded, while they would be too far in the interior to profit by it if they failed. He besought them to turn their thoughts in another direction. To be thus calculating chances and means of escape was unworthy of brave souls. They had set their hands to the work ; to look back, as they advanced, would be their ruin. They had only to resume their former confidence in themselves and their gent   and success was certain. "As for me," he concluded, "I ave chosen my part. I will remain here, while there is one to bear me company. If there be any so craven, as to shrink from sharing the dangers of our glorious enterprise, let them go home, in God's name. There is still one vessel left. Let them take that and return to Cuba. They can tell there, how they have deserted their commander and their comrades, and patiently wait till we return loaded with the spoils of the Aztecs." [23]

The politic orator had touched the right chord in the bosoms of the soldiers. As he spoke, their resentment gradually died away. The faded visions of future riches and glory, rekindled by his eloquence, again floated before their imaginations. The first shock over, they felt ashamed of their temporary distrust. The enthusiasm for their leader revived, for they felt that under his banner only they could hope for victory ; and as he concluded,

[22] "Al cavo lo oviéron de sentir la gente y ayna se le amotinaran muchos, ʋ esta fué uno de los peligros que pasáron por Cortés de muchos que para matallo de los mismos Españoles estuvo." Las Casas, Hist. de las Indias, MS., lib. 3, cap. 122.

[23] "Que ninguno seria tan cobarde y tan pusilánime que queria estimar su vida mas que la suya, ni de tan debil corazon que dudase de ir con él á México, donde tanto bien le estaba aparejado, y que si acaso se determinaba alguno de dejar de hacer este se podia ir bendito de Dios á Cuba en el navío que habia dexado, de que antes de mucho se arrepentiria, y pelaria ias barbas, viendo ia buena **ventura que** esperaba le sucederia." Ixtlilxochitl, Hist. Chich., MS., cap 82.

they testified the revulsion of their feelings by making the air ring with their shouts, "To Mexico! to Mexico!"

The destruction of his fleet by Cortés is, perhaps, the most remarkable passage in the life of this remarkable man. History, indeed, affords examples of a similar expedient in emergencies somewhat similar; but none where the chances of success were so precarious, and defeat would be so disastrous.[24] Had he failed, it might well seem an act of madness. Yet it was the fruit of deliberate calculation. He had set fortune, fame, life itself, all upon the cast, and must abide the issue. There was no alternative in his mind but to succeed or perish. The measure he adopted greatly increased the chance of success. But to carry it into execution, in the face of an incensed and desperate soldiery, was an act of resolution that has few parallels in history.[25]

[24] Perhaps the most remarkable of these examples is that of Julian, who, in his unfortunate Assyrian invasion, burnt the fleet which had carried him up the Tigris. The story is told by Gibbon, who shows very satisfactorily that the fleet would have proved a hinderance rather than a help to the emperor in his further progress. See History of the Decline and Fall, (vol. IX. p. 177,) of Milman's excellent edition.

[25] The account given in the text of the destruction of the fleet is not that of Bernal Diaz, who states it to have been accomplished, not only with the knowledge, but entire approbation of the army, though at the suggestion of Cortés. (Hist. de la Conquista, cap. 58). This version is sanctioned by Dr. Robertson (History of America, vol. II. pp. 253, 254). One should be very slow to depart from the honest record of the old soldier, especially when confirmed by the discriminating judgment of the Historian of America. But Cortés expressly declares in his letter to the emperor, that he ordered the vessels to be sunk, without the knowledge of his men, from the apprehension, that, if the means of escape were open, the timid and disaffected might, at some future time, avail themselves of them. (Rel. Seg. de Cortés, ap. Lorenzana. p. 41.) The cavaliers Montejo y Puertocarrero, on their visit to Spain, stated in their depositions, that the general destroyed the fleet on information received from the pilots. (Declaraciones, MSS.) Narvaez in his accusation of Cortés, and Las Casas, speak of the act in terms of unqualified reprobation, charging him, moreover, with bribing the pilots to bore holes in the bottoms of the ships, in order to disable them. (Demanda de Narvaez, MS.,—Hist. de las Indias, MS., lib. 3, cap. 122.) The same account of the transaction, though with a very different commentary as to its merits, is repeated by Oviedo. Hist. de las Ind., MS., lib. 33, cap. 2.) Gomara, (Crónica, cap. 42,) and Peter Martyr, (De Orbe Novo, dec. 5, cap. 1,) all of whom had access to the best sources of information.

The affair, so remarkable as the act of one individual, becomes absolutely incredible, when considered as the result of so many independent wills. It is not improbable, that Bernal Diaz, from his known devotion to the cause, may have been one of the few to whom Cortés confided his purpose. The veteran, in writing his narrative, many years after, may have mistaken a part for the whole, and in his zeal to secure to the army a full share of the glory of the expedition, too exclusively appropriated by the general, (a great object, as he tells us, of his history,) may have distributed among his comrades the credit of an exploit which, in this instance, at least, properly belonged to their commander.—Whatever be the cause of the discrepancy, his solitary testimony can hardly be sustained against the weight of contemporary evidence from such competent sources.

Fray Bartolomé de las Casas, bishop of Chiapa, whose "History of the Indies" forms an important authority for the preceding pages, was one of the most remarkable men of the sixteenth century. He was born at Seville in 1474. His father accompanied Columbus, as a common soldier, in his first voyage to the New World; and he acquired wealth enough by his vocation to place his son at the University of Salamanca. During his residence there, he was attended by an Indian page, whom his father had brought with him from Hispaniola. Thus the uncompromising advocate for freedom began his career as the owner of a slave himself. But he did not long remain so, for his slave was one of those subsequently liberated by the generous commands of Isabella.

In 1498, he completed his studies in law and divinity, took his degree of licentiate, and, in 1502, accompanied Oviedo, in the most brilliant armada which had been equipped for the Western World. Eight years after, he was admitted to priest's orders in St. Domingo, an event somewhat memorable, since he was the first person consecrated in that holy office in the colonies. On the occupation of Cuba by the Spaniards, Las Casas passed over to that island, where he obtained a curacy in a small settlement. He soon, however made himself known to the governor, Velasquez, by the fidelity with which he discharged his duties, and especially by the influence which his mild and benevolent teaching obtained for him over the Indians. Through his intimacy with the governor, Las Casas had the means of ameliorating the condition of the conquered race, and from this time he may be said to have consecrated all his energies to this one great object. At this period, the scheme of *repartimientos*, introduced soon after the discoveries of Columbus, was in full operation, and the Aboriginal population of the Islands was rapidly melting away under a system of oppression which has been seldom paralleled in the annals of mankind. Las Casas, outraged at the daily exhibition of crime and misery, returned to Spain to obtain some redress from government. Ferdinand died soon after his arrival. Charles was absent, but the reins were held by Cardinal Ximenes, who listened to the complaints of the benevolent missionary, and, with his characteristic vigor, instituted a commission of three Hieronomite friars, with full authority, as already noticed in the text, to reform abuses. Las Casas was honored, for his exertions, with the title of "Protector General of the Indians."

The new commissioners behaved with great discretion. But their office was one of consummate difficulty, as it required time to introduce important changes in established institutions. The ardent and impetuous temper of Las Casas, disdaining every consideration of prudence, overleaped all these obstacles, and chafed under what he considered the lukewarm and temporizing policy of the commissioners. As he was at no pains to conceal his disgust, the parties soon came to a misunderstanding with each other; and Las Casas again returned to the mother country, to stimulate the government, if possible, to more effectual measures for the protection of the natives.

He found the country under the administration of the Flemings, who discovered from the first a wholesome abhorrence of the abuses practised in the colonies, and who, in short, seemed inclined to tolerate no peculation or extortion, but their own. They acquiesced, without much difficulty, in the recommendations of Las Casas, who proposed to relieve the natives by sending but Castilian laborers, and by importing Negro slaves into the Islands. This last proposition has brought heavy obloquy on the head of its author, who has been freely accused of having thus introduced Negro slavery into the New World. Others, with equal groundlessness, have attempted to vindicate his memory from the reproach of having recommended the measure at all. Unfortunately for the latter assertion, Las Casas, in his History of the Indies, confesses, with deep regret and humiliation, his advice on this occasion, founded on the most erroneous views, as he frankly states; since, to use his own words, "the same law applies equally to the Negro as to the Indian." But so far from having introduced slavery by this measure into the Islands, the importation of blacks there dates from the beginning of the century. It was recommended by some of the wisest and most benevolent persons in the colony, as the means of diminishing the amount of human suffering; since the African was more fitted by his constitution to endure the climate and the severe toil imposed on the slave than the feeble and effeminate islander. It was a suggestion of humanity, however mistaken, and considering the circumstances under which it occurred, and the age, it may well be forgiven in Las Casas, especially taking into view, that, as he became more enlightened himself, he was so ready to testify his regret at having unadvisedly countenanced the measure.

The experiment recommended by Las Casas was made, but through the apathy of Fonseca, president of the Indian Council, not heartily,—and it failed. The good missionary now proposed another, and much bolder scheme. He requested that a large tract of country in Tierra Firme, in the neighborhood of the famous pearl fisheries, might be ceded to him for the purpose of planting a colony there, and of converting the natives to Christianity. He required that none of the authorities of the Islands, and no military force, especially, should be allowed to interfere with his movements. He pledged himself by peaceful means alone to accomplish all that had been done by violence in other quarters. He asked only that a certain number of laborers should attend him, invited by a bounty from government, and that he might further be accompanied by fifty Dominicans, who were to be distinguished like himself by a peculiar dress, that should lead the natives to suppose them a different race of men from the Spaniards. This proposition was denounced as chimerical and fantastic by some, whose own opportunities of observation entitled their judgment to respect. These men declared the Indian, from his nature, incapable of civilization. The question was one of such moment, that Charles the Fifth ordered the discussion to be conducted before him. The opponent of Las Casas was first heard, when the good missionary, in answer, warmed by the noble cause he was to maintain, and nothing daunted by the august presence in which he stood, delivered himself with a fervent eloquence that went directly to the hearts of his auditors. "The Christian religion," he concluded, "is equal in its operation, and is accommodated to every nation on the globe. It robs no one of his freedom, violates none of his inherent rights, on the ground that he is a slave by nature, as pretended; and it well becomes your Majesty to banish so monstrous an oppression from your kingdoms in the beginning of your reign, that the Almighty may make it long and glorious."

In the end Las Casas prevailed. He was furnished with the men and means for establishing his colony; and, in 1520, embarked for America. But the result was a lamentable failure. The country assigned to him lay in the neighborhood of a Spanish settlement, which had already committed some acts of violence on the natives. To quell the latter, now thrown into commotion, an armed force was sent by the young " Admiral" from Hispaniola. The very people, among whom Las Casas was to appear as the messenger of peace, were thus involved in deadly strife with his countrymen. The enemy had been before him in his own harvest. While waiting for the close of these turbulent scenes, the laborers, whom he had taken out with him, dispersed.

m despair of effecting their object. And after an attempt to pursue, with his faithful Dominican brethren, the work of colonization further, other untoward circumstances compelled them to abandon the project altogether. Its unfortunate author, overwhelmed with chagrin, took refuge in the Dominican monastery in the island of Hispaniola.—The failure of the enterprise should, no doubt, be partly ascribed to circumstances beyond the control of its projector. Yet it is impossible not to recognize, in the whole scheme, and in the conduct of it, the hand of one much more familiar with books than men, who, in the seclusion of the cloister, had meditated and matured his benevolent plans, without fully estimating the obstacles that lay in their way, and who counted too confidently on meeting the same generous enthusiasm in others, which glowed in his own bosom.

He found, in his disgrace, the greatest consolation and sympathy from the brethren of St. Dominic, who stood forth as the avowed champions of the Indians on all occasions, and showed themselves as devoted to the cause of freedom in the New World, as they had been hostile to it in the Old. Las Casas soon became a member of their order, and, in his monastic retirement, applied himself for many years to the performance of his spiritual duties, and the composition of various works, all directed, more or less, to vindicate the rights of the Indians. Here, too, he commenced his great work, the "Historia General de las Indias," which he pursued, at intervals of leisure, from 1527 till a few years before his death. His time, however, was not wholly absorbed by these labors; and he found means to engage in several laborious missions. He preached the gospel among the natives of Nicaragua, and Guatemala; and succeeded in converting and reducing to obedience some wild tribes in the latter province, who had defied the arms of his countrymen. In all these pious labors, he was sustained by his Dominican brethren. At length, in 1539, he crossed the waters again, to seek further assistance and recruits among the members of his order.

A great change had taken place in the board that now presided over the colonial department. The cold and narrow-minded Fonseca, who, during his long administration, had, it may be truly said, shown himself the enemy of every great name and good measure connected with the Indians, had died. His place, as president of the Indian Council, was filled by Loaysa, Charles's confessor. This functionary, general of the Dominicans, gave ready audience to Las Casas, and showed a good-will to his proposed plans of reform. Charles, too, now grown older, seemed to feel more deeply the responsibility of his station, and the necessity of redressing the wrongs, too long tolerated, of his American subjects. The state of the colonies became a common topic of discussion, not only in the council, but in the court; and the representations of Las Casas made an impression that manifested itself in the change of sentiment more clearly every day. He promoted this by the publication of some of his writings at this time, and especially of his "Brevisima Relacion," or short Account of the Destruction of the Indies, in which he sets before the reader the manifold atrocities committed by his countrymen in different parts of the New World in the prosecution of their conquests. It is a tale of woe. Every line of the work may be said to be written in blood. However good the motives of its author, we may regret that the book was ever written. He would have been certainly right not to spare his countrymen; to exhibit their misdeeds in their true colors, and by this appalling picture—for such it would have been—to have recalled the nation, and those who governed it, to a proper sense of the iniquitous career it was pursuing on the other side of the water. But, to produce a more striking effect, he has lent a willing ear to every tale of violence and rapine, and magnified the amount to a degree which borders on the ridiculous. The wild extravagance of his numerical estimates is of itself sufficient to shake confidence in the accuracy of his statements generally. Yet the naked truth was too startling in itself to demand the aid of exaggeration. The book found great favor with foreigners; was rapidly translated into various languages, and ornamented with characteristic designs, which seemed to put into action all the recorded atrocities of the text. It excited somewhat different feelings in his own countrymen, particularly the people of the colonies, who considered themselves the subjects of a gross, however undesigned, misrepresentation; and, in his future intercourse with them, it contributed, no doubt, to diminish his influence and consequent usefulness, by the spirit of alienation, and even resentment, which it engendered.

Las Casas' honest intentions, his enlightened views and long experience, gained him deserved credit at home. This was visible in the important regulations made at this time for the better government of the colonies, and particularly in respect to the Aborigines. A code of laws, *Las Nuevas Leyes*, was passed, having for their avowed object the enfranchisement of this unfortunate race; and, in the wisdom and humanity of its provisions, it is easy to recognize the hand of the Protector of the Indians. The history of Spanish colonial legislation is the history of the impotent struggles of the government in behalf of the natives, against the avarice and cruelty of its subjects. It proves that an empire powerful at home—and Spain then was so—may be so widely extended, that its authority shall scarcely be felt in its extremities.

The government testified their sense of the signal services of Las Casas, by promoting him to the bishopric of Cuzco, one of the richest sees in the colonies. But the disinterested soul of the missionary did not covet riches or preferment. He rejected the proffered dignity without hesitation. Yet he could not refuse the bishopric of Chiapa, a country, which, from the poverty and ignorance of its inhabitants, offered a good field for his spiritual labors. In 1544, though at the advanced age of seventy, he took upon himself these new duties, and embarked, for the fifth and last time, for the shores of America. His fame had preceded him. The colonists looked on his coming with apprehension, regarding him as the real author of the new code, which struck at their ancient immunities, and which he would be likely to enforce to the letter. Everywhere he was received with coldness. In some places his person was menaced with violence. But the venerable presence of the prelate, his earnest expostulations, which flowed so obviously from conviction, and his generous self-devotion, so regardless of personal considerations, preserved him from this outrage. Yet he showed no disposition to conciliate his opponents by what he deemed an unworthy concession; and he even stretched the arm of authority so far as to refuse the sacraments to any, who still held an Indian in bondage. This high-handed measure not only outraged the planters, but incurred the disapprobation of his own brethren in the Church. Three years were spent in disagreeable altercation without coming to any decision. The Spaniards, to borrow their accustomed phraseology on these occasions, "obeying the law, but not fulfilling it," applied to the Court for further instructions; and the bishop, no longer supported by his own brethren, thwarted by the colonial magistrates, and outraged by the people, relinquished a post where his presence could be no further useful, and returned to spend the remainder of his days in tranquillity at home.

Yet, though withdrawn to his Dominican convent, he did not pass his hours in slothful seclusion. He again appeared as the champion of Indian freedom in the famous controversy with Sepulveda, one of the most astute scholars of the time, and far surpassing Las Casas in elegance and correctness of composition. But the bishop of Chiapa was his superior in argument, at least in this discussion, where he had right and reason on his side. In his "Thirty Propositions," as they are called, in which he sums up the several points of his case, he maintains, that the circumstance of infidelity in religion cannot deprive a nation of its political rights; that the Holy See, in its grant of the New World to the Catholic sovereigns, designed only to confer the right of converting its inhabitants to Christianity, and of thus winning a peaceful authority over them; and that no authority could be valid, which rested on other foundations. This was striking at the root of the colonial empire, as assumed by Castile. But the disinterested views of Las Casas, the respect entertained for his principles, and the general conviction, it may be, of the force of his arguments, prevented the Court from taking umbrage at their import, or from pressing them to their legitimate conclusion. While the writings of his adversary were interdicted from publication, he had the satisfaction to see his own printed and circulated in every quarter.

From this period his time was distributed among his religious duties, his studies, and the composition of his works, especially his History. His constitution, naturally excellent, had been strengthened by a life of temperance and toil; and he retained his faculties unimpaired to the last. He died after a short illness, July, 1566, at the great age of ninety-two, in his monastery of Atocha, at Madrid.

The character of Las Casas may be inferred from his career. He was one of those, to whose gifted minds are revealed those glorious moral truths, which, like the lights of heaven, are fixed and the same forever; but which, though now familiar, were hidden from all but a few penetrating intellects by the general darkness of the time in which he lived. He was a reformer, and had the virtues and errors of a reformer. He was inspired by one great and glorious idea. This was the key to all his thoughts, all that he said and wrote, to every act of his long life. It was this which urged him to lift the voice of rebuke in the presence of princes, to brave the menaces of an infuriated populace, to cross seas, to traverse mountains and deserts, to incur the alienation of friends, the hostility of enemies, to endure obloquy, insult, and persecution. It was this, too, which made him reckless of obstacles, led him to count too confidently on the coöperation of others, animated his discussion, sharpened his invective, too often steeped his pen in the gall of personal vituperation, led him into gross exaggeration and over-coloring in his statements, and a blind credulity of evil that rendered him unsafe as a counsellor, and unsuccessful in the practical concerns of life. His motives were pure and elevated. But his manner of enforcing them was not always so commendable. This may be gathered not only from the testimony of the colonists generally, who, as parties interested, may be supposed to have been prejudiced; but from that of the members of his own profession, persons high in office, and of integrity beyond suspicion, not to add that of missionaries engaged in the same good work with himself. These, in their letters and reported conversations, charged the Bishop of Chiapa with an arrogant, uncharitable temper, which deluded his judgment, and vented itself in unwarrantable crimination against such as resisted his projects, or differed from him in opinion. Las Casas, in short, was a man. But, if he had the errors of humanity, he had virtues that rarely belong to it. The best commentary on his character is the estimation which he obtained in the court of his sovereign. A liberal pension was settled on him after his last return from America, which he chiefly expended on charitable objects. No measure of importance, relating to the Indians, was taken without his advice. He lived to see the fruits of his efforts in the positive amelioration of their condition, and in the popular admission of those great truths which it had been the object of his life to unfold. And who shall say how much of the successful efforts and arguments since made in behalf of persecuted humanity may be traced to the example and the writings of this illustrious philanthropist?

His compositions were numerous, most of them of no great length. Some were printed in his time: others have since appeared, especially in the French translation of Llorente. His great work, which occupied him at intervals for more than thirty years, the *Historia General de las Indias*, still remains in manuscript. It is in three volumes, divided into as many parts, and embraces the colonial history from the discovery of the country by Columbus to the year 1520. The style of the work, like that of all his writings, is awkward, disjointed, and excessively diffuse; abounding in repetitions, irrelevant digressions, and pedantic citations. But it is sprinkled over with passages of a different kind; and, when he is roused by the desire to exhibit some gross wrong to the natives, his simple language kindles into eloquence, and he expounds those great and immutable principles of natural justice, which in his own day, were so little understood. His defect as a historian is, that he wrote history, like everything else, under the influence of one dominant idea. He is always pleading the cause of the persecuted native. This gives a coloring to events which passed under his own eyes, and filled him with a too easy confidence in those which he gathered from the reports of others. Much of the preceding portion of our narrative which relates to affairs in Cuba must have come under his personal observation. But he seems incapable of shaking off his early deference to Velasquez, who, as we have noticed, treated him, while a poor curate in the island, with peculiar confidence, For Cortés, on the other hand, he appears to have felt a profound contempt. He witnessed the commencement of his career, when he was standing, cap in hand, as it were, at the proud governor's door, thankful even for a smile of recognition. Las Casas remembered all this, and, when he saw the Conqueror of Mexico rise into a glory and renown, that threw his former patron into the shade,—and most unfairly, as Las Casas deemed, at the expense of that patron,—the good bishop could not withhold his indignation; nor speak of him otherwise than with a sneer, as a mere upstart adventurer.

It was the existence of defects like these, and the fear of the misconception likely to be produced by them, that have so long prevented the publication of his history. At his death, he left it to the convent of San Gregorio, at Valladolid, with directions that it should not be printed for forty years, nor be seen during that time by any layman or member of the fraternity. Herrera, however was permitted to consult it, and he liberally transferred its contents to his own volumes, which appeared in 1601. The Royal Academy of History revised the first volume of Las Casas some years since, with a view to the publication of the whole work. But the indiscreet and imaginative style of the composition, according to Navarrete, and the consideration that its most important facts were already known through other channels, induced that body to abandon the design. With deference to their judgment, it seems to me a mistake. Las Casas with every deduction is one of the great writers of the nation; great from the important truths which he discerned when none else could see them, and from the courage with which he proclaimed them to the world. They are scattered over his History as well as his other writings. They are not however, the passages transcribed by Herrera. In the statement of fact, too, however partial and prejudiced, no one will impeach his integrity ; and as an enlightened contemporary, his evidence is of undeniable value. It is due to the memory of Las Casas, that if his work be given to the public at all, it should not be through the garbled extracts of one who was no fair interpreter of his opinions. Las Casas does not speak for himself in the courtly pages of Herrera. Yet the History should not be published without a suitable commentary to enlighten the student, and guard him against any undue prejudices in the writer. We may hope that the entire manuscript will one day be given to the world under the auspices of that distinguished body, which has already done so much in this way for the illustration of the national annals.

The life of Las Casas has been several times written. The two memoirs most worthy of notice are that by Llorente, late secretary of the Inquisition, prefixed to his French translation of the Bishop's controversial writings, and that by Quintana, in the third volume of his " Españoles Célebres," where it presents a truly noble specimen of biographical composition, enriched by a literary criticism as acute as it is candid.—I have gone to the greater length in this notice, from the interesting character of the man, and the little that is known of him to the English reader. I have also transferred a passage from his work in the original to the Appendix, that the Spanish scholar may form an idea of his style of composition. He ceases to be an authority for us hereafter, as his account of the expedition of Cortés terminates with the destruction of the navy.

BOOK THE THIRD

MARCH TO MEXICO.

BOOK III.

MARCH TO MEXICO.

CHAPTER I.

PROCEEDINGS AT CEMPOALLA.—THE SPANIARDS CLIMB THE TABLE-LAND.—PICTURESQUE SCENERY.—TRANSACTIONS WITH THE NATIVES.—EMBASSY TO TLASCALA.

1519.

WHILE at Cempoalla, Cortes received a message from Escalante, his commander at Villa Rica, informing him there were four strange ships hovering off the coast, and that they took no notice of his repeated signals. This intelligence greatly alarmed the general, who feared they might be a squadron sent by the governor of Cuba, to interfere with his movements. In much haste, he set out at the head of a few horsemen, and, ordering a party of light infantry to follow, posted back to Villa Rica. The rest of the army he left in charge of Alvarado and of Gonzalo de Sandoval, a young officer, who had begun to give evidence of the uncommon qualities which have secured to him so distinguished a rank among the conquerors of Mexico.

Escalante would have persuaded the general, on his reaching the town, to take some rest, and allow him to go in search of the strangers. But Cortés replied with the homely proverb, "A wounded hare takes no nap," [1] and, without stopping to refresh himself or his men, pushed on three or four leagues to the north, where he understood the ships were at anchor. On the way, he fell in with three Spaniards, just landed from them. To his eager inquiries whence they came, they replied, that they belonged to a squadron fitted out by Francisco de Garay, governor of Jamaica. This person, the year previous, had visited the Florida coast, and obtained from Spain — where he had some interest at court —authority over the countries he might discover in that vicinity. The three men, consisting of a notary and two witnesses, had been sent on shore to warn their countrymen under Cortés to desist from what was considered an encroachment on the ter-

---

[1] "Cabra coxa no tenga siesta."

ritories of **Garay.** Probably neither the governor of Jamaica, nor his officers, had any very precise notion of the geography and limits of these territories.

Cortés saw at once there was nothing to apprehend from this quarter. He would have been glad, however, if he could, by any means, have induced the crews of the ships to join his expedition. He found no difficulty in persuading the notary and his companions. But when he came in sight of the vessels, the people on board, distrusting the good terms on which their comrades appeared to be with the Spaniards, refused to send their boat ashore. In his dilemma, Cortés had recourse to a stratagem.

He ordered three of his own men to exchange dresses with the new comers. He then drew off his little band in sight of the vessels, affecting to return to the city. In the night, however, he came back to the same place, and lay in ambush, directing the disguised Spaniards, when the morning broke, and they could be discerned, to make signals to those on board. The artifice succeeded. A boat put off, filled with armed men, and three or four leaped on shore. But they soon detected the deceit, and Cortés, springing from his ambush, made them prisoners. Their comrades in the boat, alarmed, pushed off, at once, for the vessels, which soon got underway, leaving those on shore to their fate. Thus ended the affair. Cortés returned to Cempoalla, with the addition of half a dozen able-bodied recruits, and, what was of more importance, relieved in his own mind from the apprehension of interference with his operations.[2]

He now made arrangements for his speedy departure from the Totonac capital. The forces reserved for the expedition amounted to about four hundred foot and fifteen horse, with seven pieces of artillery. He obtained, also, thirteen hundred Indian warriors, and a thousand *tamanes*, or porters, from the cacique of Cempoalla, to drag the guns, and transport the baggage. He took forty more of their principal men as hostages, as well as to guide him on the way, and serve him by their counsels among the strange tribes he was to visit. They were, in fact, of essential service to him throughout the march.[3]

The remainder of his Spanish force he left in garrison at Villa

[2] Oviedo, Hist. de las Ind., MS., lib. 33. cap. 1.—Rel. Seg. de Cortés, ap-Lorenzana, pp. 42–45.—Bernal Diaz, Hist. de la conquista, cap, 59, 60.

[3] Gomara, Crónica cap. 44.—Ixtlilxochitl, Hist. Chich., MS., cap. 83.—Bernal Diaz, Hist. de la Conquista, cap. 61.

The number of the Indian auxiliaries stated in the text is " uch larger than that allowed by either Cortés or Diaz. Both these actors in the drama show too obvious a desire to magnify their own prowess, by exaggerating the numbers of their foes, and diminishing their own, to be entitled to much confidence in their estimates.

Rica de Vera Cruz, the command of which he had intrusted to the alguacil, Juan de Escalante, an officer devoted to his interests. The selection was judicious. It was important to place there a man who would resist any hostile interference from his European rivals, on the one hand, and maintain the present friendly relations with the natives, on the other. Cortés recommended the Totonac chiefs to apply to this officer, in case of any difficulty, assuring them, that, so long as they remained faithful to their new sovereign and religion, they should find a sure protection in the Spaniards.

Before marching, the general spoke a few words of encouragement to his own men. He told them, they were now to embark, in earnest, on an enterprise which had been the great object of their desires ; and that the blessed Saviour would carry them victorious through every battle with their enemies. "Indeed," he added, "this assurance must be our stay, for every other refuge is now cut off, but that afforded by the Providence of God, and your own stout hearts."[4] He ended by comparing their achievements to those of the ancient Romans, "in phrases of honeyed eloquence far beyond anything I can repeat," says the brave and simple-hearted chronicler who heard them. Cortés was, indeed, master of that eloquence which went to the soldiers' hearts. For their sympathies were his, and he shared in that romantic spirit of adventure which belonged to them. "We are ready to obey you," they cried as with one voice. "Our fortunes, for better or worse, are cast with yours."[6] Taking leave, therefore, of their hospitable Indian friends, the little army, buoyant with high hopes and lofty plans of conquest, set forward on the march to Mexico.

It was the sixteenth of August, 1519. During the first day, their road lay through the *tierra caliente*, the beautiful land where they had been so long lingering ; the land of the vanilla, cochineal, cacao, (not till later days of the orange and the sugar-cane,) products which, indigenous to Mexico, have now become the luxuries of Europe ; the land where the fruits and the flowers chase one another in unbroken circle through the year ; where the gales are loaded with perfumes till the sense aches at their sweetness ; and the groves are filled with many-colored birds, and insects whose enamelled wings glisten like diamonds in the bright sun of the tropics. Such are the magical splendors of this paradise of the senses. Yet Nature, who generally works in a

---

[4] " No teniamos otro socorro, ni ayuda sino el de Dios ; porque ya no teniamos naufos para ir á Cuba, salvo nuestro buen pelear, y coraçones fuertes." Bernal Diaz, Hist. de la Conquista, cap. 59.

[6] " Y todos á vna le respondimos, que hariamos lo que ordenasse, que echada estaua la suerte de la buena, ó mala ventura." Loc. cit.

spirit of compensation, has provided one here; since the same burning sun, which quickens into life these glories of the vege· table and animal kingdoms, calls forth the pestilent *malaria*, with its train of bilious disorders, unknown to the cold skies of the North. The season in which the Spaniards were there, the rainy months of summer, was precisely that in which the *vómito* rages with greatest fury; when the European stranger hardly ventures to set his foot on shore, still less to linger there a day. We find no mention made of it in the records of the Conquerors, nor any notice, indeed, of an uncommon mortality. The fact doubtless corroborates the theory of those who postpone the appearance of the yellow fever till long after the occupation of the country by the whites. It proves, at least, that, if existing be· fore it must have been in a very much mitigated form.

After some leagues of travel over roads made nearly impas- sable by the summer rains, the troops began the gradual ascent —more gradual on the eastern than the western declivities of the Cordilleras—which leads up to the table-land of Mexico. At the close of the second day, they reached Xalapa, a place still retaining the same Aztec name, that it has communicated to the drug raised in its environs, the medicinal virtues of which are now known throughout the world.[6] This town stands mid· way up the long ascent, at an elevation where the vapors from the ocean, touching in their westerly progress, maintain a rich verdure throughout the year. Though somewhat infected with these marine fogs, the air is usually bland and salubrious. The wealthy resident of the lower regions retires here for safety in the heats of summer, and the traveller hails its groves of oak with delight, as announceing that he is above the deadly influ- ence of the *vómito*.[7] From this delicious spot, the Spaniards enjoyed one of the grandest prospects in nature. Before them was the steep ascent,—much steeper after this point,—which they were to climb. On the right rose the *Sierra Madre*, girt with its dark belt of pines, and its long lines of shadowy hills stretching away in the distance. To the south, in brilliant con- trast, stood the mighty Orizaba, with his white robes of snow descending far down his sides, towering in solitary grandeur, the giant spectre of the Andes. Behind them, they beheld, unrolled at their feet, the magnificent *tierra caliente*, with its gay

---

[6] Jalap, *Convolvulus jalapæ.* The *x* and *j* are convertible consonants in the Castilian.

[7] The heights of Xalapa are crowned with a convent dedicated to St. Francis, erected in later days by Cortés, showing, in its solidity, like others of the period built under the same auspices, says an agreeable traveller, a military as well as religious design. Tudor's Travels in⚫North America, (London, 1834.) vol. II. p. 186.

confusion of meadows, streams, and flowering forests, sprinkled over with shining Indian villages; while a faint line of light on the edge of the horizon told them that there was the ocean, beyond which were the kindred and country—they were many of them never more to see.

Still winding their way upward, amidst scenery as different as was the temperature from that of the regions below, the army passed through settlements containing some hundreds of inhabitants each, and on the fourth day reached a "strong town," as Cortés terms it, standing on a rocky eminence, supposed to be that now known by the Mexican name of Naulinco. Here they were hospitably entertained by the inhabitants, who were friends of the Totonacs. Cortés endeavored, through father Olmedo, to impart to them some knowledge of Christian truths, which were kindly received, and the Spaniards were allowed to erect a cross in the place, for the future adoration of the natives. Indeed, the route of the army might be tracked by these emblems of man's salvation, raised wherever a willing population of Indians invited it, suggesting a very different idea from what the same memorials intimate to the traveller in these mountain solitudes in our day.[8]

The troops now entered a rugged defile, the Bishop's Pass,[9] as it is called, capable of easy defense against an army. Very soon they experienced a most unwelcome change of climate. Cold winds from the mountains, mingled with rain, and, as they rose still higher, with driving sleet and hail, drenched their garments, and seemed to penetrate to their very bones. The Spaniards, indeed, partially covered by their armor and thick jackets of quilted cotton, were better able to resist the weather, though their long residence in the sultry regions of the valley made them still keenly sensible to the annoyance. But the poor Indians, natives of the *tierra caliente*, with little protection in the way of covering, sunk under the rude assault of the elements, and several of them perished on the road.

The aspect of the country was as wild and dreary as the climate. Their route wound along the spur of the huge Cofre

---

[8] Oviedo, Hist. de las Ind., MS., lib. 33, cap. 1.—Rel. Seg. de Cortés, ap. Lorenzana, p. 40.—Gomara, Crónica, cap. 44.—Ixtlilxochitl, Hist. Chich., M S., cap 83.

"Every hundred yards of our route." says the traveller last quoted, speaking of this very region, "was marked by the melancholy erection of a wooden cross, denoting, according to the custom of the country, the commission of some horrible murder on the spot where it was planted." Travels in North America, vol. II. p. 188.

[9] *El paso del Obispo.* Cortés named it *Puerto del Nombre de Dios.* Viaje, ap. Lorenzana, p. il.

de Perote, which borrows its name, both in Mexican and Castilian, from the coffer-like rock on its summit.[10]   It is one of the
great volcanoes of New Spain.   It exhibits now, indeed, no
vestage of a crater on its top, but abundant traces of volcanic
action at its base, where acres of lava, blackened scoriæ, and
cinders, proclaim the convulsions of nature, while numerous
shrubs and mouldering trunks of enormous trees, among the
crevices, attest the antiquity of these events.   Working their
toilsome way across this scene of desolation, the path often
led them along the borders of precipices, down whose sheer
depths of two or three thousand feet the shrinking eye might
behold another climate, and see all the glowing vegetation
of the tropics choking up the bottom of the ravines.

After three days of this fatiguing travel, the way-worn army
emerged through another defile, the *Sierra del Agua*.[11]   They
soon came upon an open reach of country, with a genial climate,
such as belongs to the temperate latitudes of southern Europe.
They had reached the level of more than seven thousand feet
above the ocean, where the great sheet of table-land spreads out
for hundreds of miles along the crests of the Cordilleras.   The
country showed signs of careful cultivation, but the products
were, for the most part, not familiar to the eyes of the Spaniards.   Fields and hedges of the various tribes of the cactus,
the towering organum, and plantations of aloes with rich yellow
clusters of flowers on their tall stems, affording drink and
clothing to the Aztec, were everywhere seen.   The plants of the
torrid and temperate zones had disappeared, one after another,
with the ascent into these elevated regions.   The glossy and
dark-leaved banana, the chief, as it is the cheapest, aliment of
the countries below, had long since faded from the landscape.
The hardy maize, however, still shone with its golden harvests
in all the pride of cultivation, the great staple of the higher,
equally with the lower terraces of the plateau.

Suddenly the troops came upon what seemed the environs of
a populous city, which, as they entered it, appeared to surpass
even that of Cempoalla in the size and solidity of its structures.[12]

---

[10] The Aztec name is Nauhcampatepetl, from *nauhcampa*, "any thing
square," and *tepetl*, "a mountain."—Humboldt, who waded through forests
and snows to its summit, ascertained its height to be 4,089 metres=13,414
feet, above the sea.   See his Vues des Cordillères, p, 234, and Essai Politique,
vol. I. p. 266.

[11] The same mentioned in Cortés' Letter as the *Puerto de la Leña*.   Viaje,
ap. Lorenzana, p. iii.

[12] Now known by the euphonious Indian name of Tlatlauquitepec.   (Viaje,
ap. Lorenzana, p. iv.)   It is the *Cocotlan* of Bernal Diaz.   (Hist. de la Conquista, cap. 61.)   The old Conquerors made sorry work with the Aztec names

These were of stone and lime, many of them spacious and tolerably high. There were thirteen *teocallis* in the place; and in the
suburbs they had seen a receptacle, in which, according to Bernal
Diaz, were stored a hundred thousand skulls of human victims,
all piled and ranged in order! He reports the number as one
he had ascertained by counting them himself.[13] Whatever faith
we may attach to the precise accuracy of his figures, the result
is almost equally startling. The Spaniards were destined to become familiar with this appalling spectacle, as they approached
nearer to the Aztec capital.

The lord of the town ruled over twenty thousand vassals. He
was tributary to Montezuma, and a strong Mexican garrison was
quartered in the place. He had probably been advised of the
approach of the Spaniards, and doubted how far it would be
welcome to his sovereign. At all events, he gave them a cold
reception, the more unpalatable after the extraordinary sufferings of the last few days. To the inquiry of Cortés, whether he
were subject to Montezuma, he answered, with real or affected
surprise, "Who is there that is not a vassal to Montezuma?"[14]
The general told him, with some emphasis, that he was not.
He then explained whence and why he came, assuring him that
he served a monarch who had princes for his vassals as powerful
as the Aztec monarch himself.

The cacique in turn fell nothing shorter of the Spaniard, in
the pompous display of the grandeur and resources of the Indian
emperor. He told his guest that Montezuma could muster thirty
great vassals, each master of a hundred thousand men![15] His
revenues were immense, as every subject, however poor, paid
something. They were all expended on his magnificent state,
and in support of his armies. These were continually in the
field, while garrisons were maintained in most of the large cities
of the empire. More than twenty thousand victims, the fruit of
his wars, were annually sacrificed on the altars of his gods!

both of places and persons, for which they must be allowed to have had
ample apology.

[13] "Puestos tantos rimeros de calaueras de muertos, que se podian bien con-
tar, segun el concierto con que estauan puestas, que me parece que eran mas
de cien mil, y digo otra vez sobre cien mil." Ibid., ubi supra.

[14] "El qual casi admirado de lo que le preguntaba me respondió, diciendo:
¿que quien no era vasallo de Muctezuma? queriendo decir, que alli era Señor
del Mundo." Rel. Seg. de Cortés, ap. Lorenzana, p. 47.

[15] "Tiene mas de 30 Principes á sí subjectos, que cada uno dellos tiene
cient mill hombres é mas de pelea." (Oviedo, Hist. de las Ind., MS., lib. 33,
cap. 1.) This marvellous tale is gravely repeated by more than one Spanish
writer, in their accounts of the Aztec monarchy, not as the assertion of this
chief, but as a veritable piece of statistics. See among others, Herrera, Hist.
General, dec. 2, lib. 7, cap. 12.—Solis, Conquista, lib. 3, cap. 16.

His capital, the cacique said, stood in a lake, in the centre of a spacious valley. The lake was commanded by the emperor's vessels, and the approach to the city was by means of cause-ways, several miles long, connected in parts by wooden bridges, which, when raised, cut off all communication with the country. Some other things he added, in answer to queries of his guest, in which, as the reader may imagine, the crafty, or credulous cacique varnished over the truth with a lively coloring of romance. Whether romance, or reality, the Spaniards could not determine. The particulars they gleaned were not of a kind to tranquillize their minds, and might well have made bolder hearts than theirs pause, ere they advanced. But far from it. "The words which we heard," says the stout old cavalier, so often quoted, "however they may have filled us with wonder, made us — such is the temper of the Spaniard — only the more earnest to prove the adventure, desperate as it might appear." [16]

In a further conversation Cortes inquired of the chief, whether his country abounded in gold, and intimated a desire to take home some, as specimens to his sovereign. But the Indian lord declined to give him any, saying it might displease Montezuma. "Should he command it," he added, "my gold, my person, and all I possess, shall be at your disposal." The general did not press the matter further.

The curiosity of the natives was naturally excited by the strange dresses, weapons, horses and dogs of the Spaniards. Marina, in satisfying their inquiries, took occasion to magnify the prowess of her adopted countrymen, expatiating on their exploits and victories, and stating the extraordinary marks of respect they had received from Montezuma. This intelligence seemed to have had its effect; for soon after, the cacique gave the general some curious trinkets of gold, of no great value, indeed, but as a testimony of his good-will. He sent him, also, some female slaves to prepare bread for the troops, and supplied the means of refreshment and repose, more important to them, in the present juncture, than all the gold of Mexico.[17]

The Spanish general, as usual, did not neglect the occasion to inculcate the great truths of revelation on his host, and to display the atrocity of the Indian superstitions. The cacique listened with civil, but cold indifference. Cortés, finding him un-

[15] Bernal Diaz, Hist. de la Conquista, cap. 61.
There is a slight ground-swell of glorification in the Captain's narrative, which may provoke a smile, not a sneer, for it is mingled with too much real courag and simplicity of character.

[17] For the preceding pages, besides authorities cited in course, see Peter Martyr, De Orbe Novo, dec. 5, cap. 1,—Ixtlilxochitl, Hist. Chich., MS., cap. 83,—Gomara, Crónica, cap. 44.—Torquemada, Monarch. Ind., lib. 4, cap. 26.

moved, turned briskly round to his soldiers, exclaiming that now was the time to plant the Cross. They eagerly seconded his pious purpose, and the same scenes might have been enacted as at Cempoalla, with, perhaps, very different results, had not father Olmedo, with better judgment, interposed. He represented that to introduce the Cross among the natives, in their present state of ignorance and incredulity, would be to expose the sacred symbol to desecration, so soon as the backs of the Spaniards were turned. The only way was to wait patiently the season when more leisure should be afforded to instil into their minds a knowledge of the truth. The sober reasoning of the good father prevailed over the passions of the martial enthusiasts.

It was fortunate for Cortés that Olmedo was not one of those frantic friars, who would have fanned his fiery temper on such occasions into a blaze. It might have had a most disastrous influence on his fortunes; for he held all temporal consequences light in comparison with the great work of conversion, to effect which the unscrupulous mind of the soldier, trained to the stern discipline of the camp, would have employed force, whenever fair means were ineffectual.[18] But Olmedo belonged to that class, of benevolent missionaries—of whom the Roman Catholic church to its credit, has furnished many examples — who rely on spiritual weapons for the great work, inculcating those doctrines of love and mercy which can best touch the sensibilities and win the affections of their rude audience. These, indeed, are the true weapons of the Church, the weapons employed in the primitive ages, by which it has spread its peaceful banners over the farthest regions ot the globe. Such were not the means used by the conquerors of America, who, rather adopting the policy of the victorious Moslems in their early career, carried with them the sword in one hand and the Bible in the other. They imposed obedience in matters of faith, no less than of government, on the vanquished, little heeding whether the conversion were genuine, so that it conformed to the outward observances of the Church. Yet the seeds thus recklessly scattered must have perished but for the missionaries of their own nation, who, in later times, worked over the same ground, living among the Indians as brethren, and, by long and patient culture, enabling the germs of truth to take root and fructify in their hearts.

The Spanish commander remained in the city four or five days

---

[18] The general clearly belonged to the church militant, mentioned by Butler

" Such as do build their faith upon
The holy text of pike and gun ;
And prove their doctrines orthodox
By apostolic blows and knocks "

to recruit his fatigued and famished forces ; and the modern Indians still point out, or did at the close of the last century, a
venerable cypress, under the branches of which was tied the
horse of the *Conquistador*, — the Conqueror, as Cortés was styled,
par excellence.[19]   Their route now opened on a broad and verdant
valley, watered by a noble stream, — a circumstance of not too
frequent occurrence on the parched table-land of New Spain.
The soil was well protected by woods, a thing stil rarer at the
present day ; since the invaders, soon after the Conquest, swept
away the magnificent growth of timber, rivalling that of our
Southern and Western States in variety and beauty, which covered
the plateau under the Aztecs.[20]

All along the river, on both sides of it, an unbroken line of
Indian dwellings, " so near as almost to touch one another," extended for three or four leagues ; arguing a population much
denser than at present.[21]   On a rough and rising ground stood a
town, that might contain five or six thousand inhabitants, commanded by a fortress, which, with its walls and trenches, seemed to
the Spaniards quite "on a level with similar works in Europe."
Here the troops again halted, and met with friendly treatment.[22]

Cortés now determined his future line of march.   At the last
place he had been counselled by the natives to take the route of
the ancient city of Cholula, the inhabitants of which, subjects of
Montezuma, were a mild race, devoted to mechanical and other
peaceful arts, and would be likely to entertain him kindly.   Their
Cempoallan allies, however, advised the Spaniards not to trust
the Cholulans, "a false and perfidious people," but to take the
road to Tlascala, that valiant little republic, which had so long

---

[19] " Arbol grande, dicho *ahuehuete*." (Viaje, ap. Lorenzana, p. iii.)   The
cupressus disticha of Linnæus.   See Humboldt, Essai Politique, tom. II. p.
54, note.

[20] It is the same taste which has made the Castiles, the table-land of the
Peninsula, so naked of wood.   Prudential reasons, as well as taste, however,
seem to have operated in New Spain.   A friend of mine on a visit to a
noble *hacienda*, but uncommonly barren of trees, was informed by the proprietor that they were cut down to prevent the lazy Indians on the plantation
from wasting their time by loitering in their shade !

[21] It confirms the observations of M. de Humboldt.   "Sans doute lors de
la première arrivée des Espagnols, toute cette côte, depuis la rivière de Papal-
oapan (Alvarado) jusque'à Huaxtecapan, était plus habitée et mieux cultivée
qu'elle ne l'est aujourd'hui.   Cependant à mesure que les conquérans mon-
tèrent au plateau, ils trouvèrent les villages plus rapprochés les uns des autres,
les champs divisés en portions plus petites, le peuple plus policé."   Humboldt,
Essai Politique, tom. II. p. 202.

[22] The correct Indian name of the town, *Yxtacamaxtitlán*, *Yztacmastitan* of
Cortés, will hardly be recognized in the *Xalacingo* of Diaz.   The town was removed, in 1601, from the top of the hill to the plain.   On the original site are
still visible remains of carved stones of large dimensions, attesting the elegance
of the ancient fortress or palace of the cacique.   Viaje, ap. Lorenzana, p. v.

maintained its independence against the arms of Mexico. The people were frank as they were fearless, and fair in their dealings. They had always been on terms of amity with the Totomacs, which afforded a strong guaranty for their amicable disposition on the present occasion.

The arguments of his Indian allies prevailed with the Spanish commander, who resolved to propitiate the good-will of the Tlascalans by an embassy. He selected four of the principal Cempoallans for this, and sent by them a martial gift,—a cap of crimson cloth, together with a sword and a crossbow, weapons which it was observed, excited general admiration among the natives. He added a letter, in which he asked permission to pass through their country. He expressed his admiration of the valor of the Tlascalans, and of their long resistance to the Aztecs, whose proud empire he designed to humble.[23] It was not to be expected that this epistle, indited in good Castilian, would be very intelligible to the Tlascalans. But Cortés communicated its import to the ambassadors. Its mysterious characters might impress the natives with an idea of superior intelligence, and the letter serve instead of these hieroglyphical missives which formed the usual credentials of an Indian ambassador.[24]

The Spaniards remained three days in this hospitable place, after the departure of the envoys, when they resumed their progress. Although in a friendly country, they marched always as if in a land of enemies, the horse and light troops in the van, with the heavy-armed and baggage in the rear, all in battle array.

They were never without their armor, waking or sleeping, lying down with their weapons by their sides. This unintermitting and restless vigilance was, perhaps, more oppressive to the spirits than even bodily fatigue. But they were confident in their superiority in a fair field, and felt that the most serious danger they had to fear from Indian warfare was surprise. "We are few against many, brave companions," Cortés would say to them, "be prepared, then, not as if you was going to battle, but as if actually in the midst of it!"[25]

The road taken by the Spaniards was the same which at present leads to Tlascala; not that, however, usually followed in

---

[23] " Estas cosas y otras de gran persuasion contentla la carta, pero como no sabian leer no pudiéron entender lo que contenia." Camargo, Hist. de Tlasla, MS.

[24] For an account of the diplomatic usages of the people of Anahuac, see Ante, p. 44.

[25] "Mira, señores compañeros, ya veis que somos pocos, hemos de estar siempre tan apercebidos, y aparejados, como si aora viessemos venir los contrarios á pelear, y no solamente vellos venir, sino hazer cuenta que estamos ya en la batalla con ellos." Bernal Diaz, Hist. de la Conquista, cap. 62.

passing from Vera Cruz to the capital, which makes a circuit considerably to the south, towards Puebla, in the neighborhood of the ancient Cholula. They more than once forded the stream that rolls through this beautiful plain, lingering several days on the way, in hopes of receiving an answer from the Indian republic. The unexpected delay of the messengers could not be explained, and occasioned some uneasiness.

As they advanced into a country of rougher and bolder features, their progress was suddenly arrested by a remarkable fortification. It was a stone wall nine feet in height, and twenty in thickness, with a parapet, a foot and a half broad, raised on the summit for the protection of those who defended it. It had only one opening, in the centre, made by two semicircular lines of wall overlapping each other for the space of forty paces, and affording a passage-way between, ten paces wide, so contrived therefore, as to be perfectly commanded by the inner wall. This fortification, which extended more than two leagues, rested at either end on the bold natural buttresses formed by the sierra. The work was built of immense blocks of stones nicely laid together without cement ; [26] and the remains still existing, among which are rocks of the whole breadth of the rampart, fully attest its solidity and size.[27]

This singular structure marked the limits of Tlascala, and was intended, as the natives told the Spaniards, as a barrier against the Mexican invasions. The army paused, filled with amazement at the contemplation of this Cyclopean monument, which naturally suggested reflections on the strength and resources of the people who had raised it. It caused them, too, some painful solicitude as to the probable result of their mission to Talasca, and their own consequent reception there. But they were too sanguine to allow such uncomfortable surmises long to dwell in their minds. Cortés put himself at the head of his cavalry, and calling out, "Forward, soldiers, the Holy Cross is our banner, and under that we shall conquer," led his little army through the undefended passage, and in a few moments they trod the soil of the free republic of Tlascala.[28]

[26] According to the writer last cited, the stones were held by a cement so hard that the men could scarcely break it with their pikes. (Hist. de la Conquista, cap. 62.) But the contrary statement, in the general's letter is con firmed by the present appearance of the wall. Viaje, ap. Lorenzana, p. vii.

[27] Viaje, ap. Lorenzana, p. vii.
The attempts of the Archbishop to identify the route of Cortés have been very successful. It is a pity, that his map illustrating the itinerary should be so worthless.

[28] Camargo, Hist. de Tlaxcala, MS—Gomara, Crónica, cap. 44, 45—Ixtlil xochitl, Hist. Chich., MS., cap, 83.—Herrera, Hist. General, dec. 2, lib 6, cap. 3.—Oviedo, Hist. de las Ind., MS., lib. 33, cap. 2.—Peter Martyr, De Orbe Novo, dec. 5, cap. 1.

CHAPTER II.

REPUBLIC OF TLASCALA.—ITS INSTITUTIONS.—EARLY HISTORY.—
DISCUSSIONS IN THE SENATE.—DESPERATE BATTLES.

1519.

BEFORE advancing further with the Spaniards into the territory
of Tlascala, it will be well to notice some traits in the character
and institutions of the nation, in many respects, the most remarkable in Anahuac.　The Tlascalans belong to the same great
family with the Aztecs.[1]　They came on the grand plateau about
the same time with the kindred races, at the close of the twelfth
century, and planted themselves on the western borders of the
lake of Tezcuco.　Here they remained many years engaged in
the usual pursuits of a bold and partially civilized people.　From
some cause or other, perhaps their turbulent temper, they incurred the enmity of surrounding tribes.　A coalition was formed
against them ; and a bloody battle was fought on the plains of
Poyauhtlan, in which the Tlascalans were completely victorious.

Disgusted, however, with their residence among nations with
whom they found so little favor, the conquering people resolved
to migrate.　They separated into three divisions, the largest of
which, taking a southern course by the great *volcan* of Mexico,
wound round the ancient city of Cholula, and finally settled in
the district of country overshadowed by the sierra of Tlascala.
The warm and fruitful valleys, locked up in the embraces of
this rugged brotherhood of mountains, afforded means of subsistence for an agricultural people, while the bold eminences of
the sierra presented secure positions for their towns.

After the lapse of years, the institutions of the nation underwent an important change.　The monarchy was divided first
into two, afterwards into four separate states, bound together by

---

[1] The Indian chronicler, Camargo, considers his nation a branch of the
Chichemec.　(Hist. de Tlascala, MS.) So, also, Torquemada. (Monarch.
Ind., lib. 3, cap. 9.) Claviergo, who has carefully investigated the antiquities
of Anahuac, calls it one of the seven Nahuatlac tribes.　(Stor. del Messico,
tom. I. p. 153, nota.)　The fact is not of great moment, since they were all
cognate races, speaking the same tongue, and probably, migrated from their
country in the far north at nearly the same time.

a sort of fed⸗ a¹ compact, probably not very nicely defined. Each state, however, had its lord or supreme chief, independent in his own territories, and possessed of coördinate authority with the others in all matters concerning the whole republic. The affairs of government, especially all those relating to peace and war, were settled in a senate or council, consisting of the four lords with their inferior nobles.

The lower dignitaries held of the superior, each in his own district, by a kind of feudal tenure, being bound to supply his table, and enable him to maintain his state in peace, as well as to serve him in war.[2] In return, he experienced the aid and protection of his suzerain. The same mutual obligation existed between him and the followers among whom his own territories were distributed.[3] Thus a chain of feudal dependencies was established, which, if not contrived with all the art and legal refinements of analogous institutions in the Old World, displayed their most prominent characteristics in its personal relations, the obligations of military service on the one hand, and protection on the other. This form of government, so different from that of the surrounding nations, subsisted till the arrival of the Spaniards. And it is certainly evidence of considerable civilization, that so complex a polity should have so long continued, undisturbed by violence or faction in the confederate states, and should have been found competent to protect the people in their rights, and the country from foreign invasion.

The lowest order of the people, however, do not seem to have enjoyed higher immunities than under the monarchical government; and their rank was carefully defined by an appropriate

[2] The descendants of these petty nobles attached as great value to their pedigrees, as any Biscayan or Asturian in Old Spain. Long after the Conquest, they refused, however needy, to dishonor their birth by resorting to mechanical or other plebeian occupations, *oficios viles y bojos.* " Los descendientes de estos son estimados por hombres calificados, que aunque sean probrísimos no usan oficios mecánicos ni tratos bajos ni viles, ni jamas se permiten cargar ni cabar con coas y azadones, diciendo que son hijos Idalgos enque no han de aplicarse á estas cosas soeces y bajas, sino servir en guerras y fronteras, como Idalgos, y morir como hombres peleando." Camargo, Hist. de Tlascala, MS.

[3] " Cualquier Tecuhtli que formaba un Tecalli, que es casa de Mayorazgo, todas aquellas tierras que le caian en suerte de repartimiento, con montes, fuentes, rios, ó lagunas tomase para la casa principal la mayor y mejor suerte ó pagos de tierra y luego las demas que quedaban se partian por sus soldados amigos y parientes, igualmente, y todos estos están obligados á reconocer la casa mayor y acudir á ella á alzarla y repararla, y á ser continuos en reconocer á ella de aves, caza, flores, y ramos para el sustento de la casa del Mayorazgo, y el que lo es está obligado á sustentarlos ᵕ regalarlos como amigos de aquella casa y parientes de ella." Ibid., MS.

dress, and by their exclusion from the insignia of the aristocratic orders.[4]

The nation, agricultural in its habits, reserved its highes* honors, like most other rude—unhappily also, civilized—nations, for military prowess. Public games were instituted, and prizes decreed to those who excelled in such manly and athletic exercises, as might train them for the fatigues of war. Triumphs were granted to the victorious general, who entered the city, leading his spoils and captives in long procession, while his achievements were commemorated in national songs, and his effigy, whether in wood or stone, was erected in the temples. It was truly in the martial spirit of republican Rome.[5]

An institution not unlike knighthood was introduced, very similar to one existing also among the Aztecs. The aspirant to the honors of this barbaric chivalry watched his arms and fasted fifty or sixty days in the temple, then listened to a grave discourse on the duties of his new profession. Various whimsical ceremonies followed, when his arms were restored to him ; he was led in solemn procession through the public streets, and the inauguration was concluded by banquets and public rejoicings.—The new knight was distinguished henceforth by certain peculiar privileges, as well as by a badge intimating his rank. It is worthy of remark, that this honor was not reserved exclusively for military merit ; but was the recompense, also, of public services of other kinds, as wisdom in council, or sagacity and success in trade. For trade was held in as high estimation by the Tlascalans, as by the other people of Anahuac.[6]

The temperate climate of the table-land furnished the ready means for distant traffic. The fruitfulness of the soil was indicated by the name of the country,—*Tlascala* signifying the "land of bread." Its wide plains, to the slopes of its rocky hills, waved with yellow harvests of maize, and with the bountiful maguey, a plant, which, as we have seen, supplied the materials for some important fabrics. With these, as well as the products of agricultural industry, the merchant found his way down the sides of the Cordilleras, wandered over the sunny regions at

---

[4] Camargo, Hist. de Tlascala, MS.

[5] "Los grandes recibimientos que hacian á los capitanes que venian y alcanzaban victoria en las guerras, las fiestas y solenidades con que se solenizaban á menera de triunfo, que los metian en andas en su puebla, trayendo consigo á los vencidos ; y por eternizar sus hazañas se las cantaban publicamente, y ansi quedaban memoradas y con estatuas que les ponian en los templos." Ibid., MS.

[6] For the whole ceremony of inauguration,—though as it seems having especial reference to the merchant-knights,—see *Appendix, Part 2, No. 9,* where the original is given from Camargo.

their base, and brought back the luxuries which nature had denied to his own.[7]

The various arts of civilization kept pace with increasing wealth and public prosperity; at least, these arts were cultivated to the same limited extent, apparently, as among the other people of Anahuac. The Tlascalan tongue, says the national historian, simple as beseemed that of a mountain region, was rough compared with the polished Tezcucan, or the popular Aztec dialect, and, therefore, not so well fitted for composition. But they made like proficiency with the kindred nations in the rudiments of science. Their calendar was formed on the same plan. Their religion, their architecture, many of their laws and social usages were the same, arguing a common origin for all. Their tutelary deity was the same ferocious war-god as that of the Aztecs, though with a different name ; their temples, in like manner, were drenched with the blood of human victims, and their boards groaned with the same cannibal repasts.[8]

Though not ambitious of foreign conquest, the prosperity of the Tlascalans, in time, excited the jealousy of their neighbors, and especially of the opulent state of Cholula. Frequent hostilities arose between them, in which the advantage was almost always on the side of the former. A still more formidable foe appeared in later days in the Aztecs ; who could ill brook the independence of Tlascala, when the surrounding nations had acknowledged, one after another, their influence, or their empire. Under the ambitious Axayacatl, they demanded of the Tlascalans the same tribute and obedience rendered by other people of the country. If it were refused, the Aztecs would raze their cities to their foundations, and deliver the land to their enemies.

To this imperious summons, the little republic proudly replied, " Neither they nor their ancestors had ever paid tribute or homage to a foreign power, and never would pay it. If their country was invaded, thay knew how to defend it, and would pour out their blood as freely in defence of their freedom now, as their fathers did of yore, when they routed the Aztecs on the plains of Poyauhtlan ! "[9]

[7] " Ha bel paese," says the Anonymous Conqueror, speaking of Tlascala, at the time of the invasion, " di pianure et mōtagne, et é provincia popolosa et vi si raccoglie molto pane." Rel. d' un gent., ap. Ramusio, tom. III. p. 308.

[8] A full account of the manners, customs, and domestic policy of Tlascala is given by the national historian, throwing much light on the other states of Anahuac, whose social institutions seem to have been all cast in the same mould.

[9] Camargo, Hist. de Tlascala, MS.—Torquemada, Monarch. Ind., lib c, cap. 70.

This resolute answer brought on them the forces of the monarchy. A pitched battle followed, and the sturdy republicans were victorious. From this period, hostilities between the two nations continued with more or less activity, but with unsparing ferocity. Every captive was mercilessly sacrificed. The children were trained from the cradle to deadly hatred against the Mexicans ; and, even in the brief intervals of war, none of those intermarriages took place between the people of the respective countries, which knit together in social bonds most of the other kindred races of Anahuac.

In this struggle, the Tlascalans, received an important support in the accession of the Othomis, or Otomies,—as usually spelt by Castilian writers,—a wild and warlike race originally spread over the table-land north of the Mexican valley. A portion of them obtained a settlement in the republic, and were speedily incorporated in its armies. Their courage and fidelity to the nation of their adoption showed them worthy of trust, and the frontier places were consigned to their keeping. The mountain barriers, by which Tlascala is encompassed, afforded many strong natural positions for defence against invasion. The country was open toward the east, where a valley, of some six miles in breadth, invited the approach of an enemy. But here it was, that the jealous Tlascalans erected the formidable rampart which had excited the admiration of the Spaniards, and which they manned with the garrison of Otomies.

Efforts for their subjugation were renewed on a greater scale, after the accession of Montezuma. His victorious arms had spread down the declivities of the Andes to the distant provinces of Vera Paz and Nicaragua,[10] and his haughty spirit was chafed by the opposition of a petty state, whose territorial extent did not exceed ten leagues in breadth by fifteen in length.[11] He sent an army against them under the command of a favorite son. His troops were beaten, and his son was slain. The enraged and mortified monarch was roused to still greater preparations. He enlisted the forces of the cities bordering on his enemy, together with those of the empire, and with this formidable army swept over the devoted valleys of Tlascala. But the bold mountaineers withdrew into the recesses of their hills, and, coolly awaiting their opportunity, rushed like a torrent on the invaders,

---

[10] Camargo (Hist. de Tlascala, MS.) notices the extent of Montezuma's conquests,—a debatable ground for the historian.

[11] Torquemada, Monarch. Ind., lib. 3, cap. 16.—Solis says, " The Tlascalan territory was fifty leagues in circumference, ten long, from east to west, and four broad, from north to south." (Conquesta de Méjico, lib. 3, cap. 3.) It must have made a curious figure in geometry!

and drove them back, with dreadful slaughter, from their territories.

Still, notwithstanding the advantages gained over the enemy
in the field, the Tlascalans were sorely pressed by their long
hostilities with a foe so far superior to themselves in numbers
and resources. The Aztec armies lay between them and the
coast, cutting off all communication with that prolific region, and
thus limited their supplies to the products of their own soil and
manufacture. For more than half a century they had neither
cotton, nor cacao, nor salt. Indeed, their taste had been so
far affected by long abstinence from these articles, that it required the lapse of several generations after the Conquest, to
reconcile them to the use of salt at their meals.[12] During the
short intervals of war, it is said, the Aztec nobles, in the true
spirit of chivalry, sent supplies of these commodities as presents,
with many courteous expressions of respect, to the Tlascalan
chiefs. This intercourse, we are assured by the Indian chronicler, was unsuspected by the people. Nor did it lead to any
further correspondence, he adds, between the parties, prejudicial
to the liberties of the republic, " which maintained its customs
and good government inviolate, and the worship of its gods." [13]

Such was the condition of Tlascala, at the coming of the Spaniards ; holding, it might seem, a precarious existence under the
shadow of the formidable power which seemed suspended like
an avalanche over her head, but still strong in her own resources,
stronger in the indomitable temper of her people ; with a reputation established throughout the land, for good faith and moderation in peace, for valor in war, while her uncompromising spirit
of independence secured the respect even of her enemies. With
such qualities of character, and with an animosity sharpened by
long, deadly hostility with Mexico, her alliance was obviously of
the last importance to the Spaniards, in their present enterprise.
It was not easy to secure it.[14]

The Tlascalans had been made acquainted with the advance
and victorious career of the Christians, the intelligence of which

---

[12] Camargo, Hist. de Tlascala MS.

[13] " Los Señores Mejicanos y Tezcucanos entiempo que ponian treguas por
algunas temporadas embiaban á los Señores de Tlaxcalla grandes presents
y dádivas de oro, ropa, y cacao, y sal, y de todas las cosas de que carecian,
sin que la gente plebeya lo entendiese, y se saludaban secretamente, guar-
dándose eldecoro que se debian: mas con todos estos trabajos la orden de
su republica jamas se dejaba de gobernar con la rectitud de sus costumbres
guardando inviolablemente el culto de sus Dioses." Ibid., MS.

[14] The Tlascalan chronicler discerns in this deep-rooted hatred of Mexico
the hand of Providence, who wrought out of it an important means for sub-
verting the Aztec empire. Hist. de Tlascala MS.

had spread far and wide over the plateau. But they do not seem to have anticipated the approach of the strangers to their own borders. They were now much embarrassed by the embassy demanding a passage through their territories. The great council was convened, and a considerable difference of opinion prevailed in its members. Some, adopting the popular superstition, supposed the Spaniards might be the white and bearded men foretold by the oracles.[15] At all events, they were the enemies of Mexico, and as much might coöperate with them in their struggle with the empire. Others argued that the strangers could have nothing in common with them. Their march throughout the land might be tracked by the broken images of the Indian gods, and desecrated temples. How did the Tlascalans even know that they were foes to Montezuma? They had received his embassies, accepted his presents, and were now in the company of his vassals on the way to his capital.

These last were the reflections of an aged chief, one of the four who presided over the republic. His name was Xicotencatl. He was nearly blind, having lived, as it is said, far beyond the limits of a century.[16] His son, an impetuous young man of the same name with himself, commanded a powerful army of Tlascalan and Otomie warriors, near the eastern frontier. It would be best, the old man said, to fall with this force at once on the Spaniards. If victorious, the latter would then be in their power. If defeated, the senate could disown the act as that of the general, not of the republic.[17] The cunning counsel of the chief found favor with his hearers, though assuredly not in the spirit of chivalry, nor of the good faith for which his countrymen were celebrated. But with an Indian, force and stratagem, courage and deceit, were equally admissible in war, as they were among the barbarians of ancient Rome.[18]—The Cempoallan envoys were to be detained under pretence of assisting at a religious sacrifice.

[15] "Si bien os acordais, como tenemos de nuestra antiguedad como han de venir gentes á la parte donde sale el sol, y que han de emparentar con nosotros, y que hemos de ser todos unos; y que han de ser blancos y barbudos." Ibid., MS.

[16] To the ripe age of one hundred and forty! if we may credit Camargo. Solís, who confounds this veteran with his son, has put a flourishing harangue in the mouth of the latter, which would be a rare gem of Indian eloquence—were it not Castilian. (Conquista, lib. 2, cap. 16.

[17] Camargo, Hist. de Tlascala, MS.—Herrera, Hist. General, dec. 2, lib. 6, cap. 3.—Torquemado, Monarch. Ind., lib. 2, lib. 4, cap. 27.

There is sufficient contradiction, as well as obscurity, in the proceedings reported of the council, which it is not easy to reconcile altogether with subsequent events.

[18] "——Dolus an virtus, quis in hoste requirat?"

Meanwhile, Cortés and his gallant band, as stated in the preceding chapter, had arrived before the rocky rampart on the eastern confines of Tlascala. From some cause or other, it was not manned by its Otomie garrison, and the Spaniards passed in, as we have seen, without resistance. Cortés rode at the head of his body of horse, and, ordering the infantry to come on at a quick pace, went forward to reconnoitre. After advancing three or four leagues, he descried a small party of Indians, armed with sword and buckler, in the fashion of the country. They fled at his approach. He made signs for them to halt, but, seeing that they only fled the faster, he and his companions put spur to their horses, and soon came up with them. The Indians, finding escape impossible, faced round, and, instead of showing the accustomed terror of the natives at the strange and appalling aspect of a mounted trooper, they commenced a furious assault on the cavaliers. The latter, however, were too strong for them, and would have cut their enemy to pieces without much difficulty, when a body of several thousand Indians appeared in sight, and coming briskly on to the support of their countrymen.

Cortes, seeing them, despatched one of his party, in all haste, to accelerate the march of his infantry. The Indians, after discharging their missiles, fell furiously on the little band of Spaniards. They strove, to tear the lances from their grasp, and to drag the riders from the horses. They brought one cavalier to the ground, who afterwards died of his wounds, and they killed two of the horses, cutting through their necks with their stout broadswords—if we may believe the chronicler—at a blow![19] In the narrative of these campaigns, there is sometimes but one step—and that a short one—from history to romance. The loss of the horses, so important and so few in number, was seriously felt by Cortés, who could have better spared the life of the best rider in the troop.

The struggle was a hard one. But the odds were as overwhelming as any recorded by the Spaniards in their own romances, where a handful of knights is arrayed against legions of enemies. The lances of the Christians did terrible execution here also ; but they had need of the magic lance of Astolpho, that overturned myriads with a touch, to carry them safe through so unequal a contest. It was with no little satisfaction, therefore, that they beheld their comrades rapidly advancing to their support.

[19] " I les matáron dos Caballos, de dos cuchilladas, i segu . algunos, que lo viéron, cortáron à cercen de un golpe cada pescueço con riendas, i todas." Gomaro, Crónica, cap. 45.

No sooner had the main body reached the field of battle, than, hastily forming, they poured such a volley from their muskets and crossbows as staggered the enemy. Astounded, rather than intimidated, by the terrible report of the fire-arms, now heard for the first time in these regions, the Indians made no further effort to continue the fight, but drew off in good order, leaving the road open to the Spaniards. The latter, too well satisfied to be rid of the annoyance, to care to follow the retreating foe, again held on their way.

Their route took them through a country sprinkled over with Indian cottages, amidst flourishing fields of maize and maguey, indicating an industrious and thriving peasantry. They were met here by two Tlascalan envoys, accompanied by two of the Cempoallans. The former, presenting themselves before the general, disavowed the assault on his troops, as an unauthorized act, and assured him of a friendly reception at their capital. Cortés received the communication in a courteous manner, affecting to place more confidence in its good faith, than he probably felt.

It was now growing late, and the Spaniards quickened their march, anxious to reach a favorable ground for encampment before nightfall. They found such a spot on the borders of a stream that rolled sluggishly across the plain. A few deserted cottages stood along the banks, and the fatigued and famished soldiers ransacked them in quest of food. All they could find was some tame animals resembling dogs. These they killed and dressed without ceremony, and, garnishing their unsavory repast with the fruit of the *tuna*, the Indian fig, which grew wild in the neighborhood, they contrived to satisfy the cravings of appetite. A careful watch was maintained by Cortés, and companies of a hundred men each relieved each other in mounting guard through the night. But no attack was made. Hostilities by night were contrary to the system of Indian tactics.[20]

By break of day on the following morning, it being the second of September, the troops were under arms. Beside the Spaniards, the whole number of Indian auxiliaries might now amount to three thousand; for Cortés had gathered recruits from the friendly places on his route; three hundred from the last. After hearing mass, they resumed their march. They moved in close array; the general had previously admonished the men

---

[20] Rel. Seg. de Cortés, ap. Lorenzana, p. 50.—Camargo, Hist. de Tlascala, MS.—Bernal Diaz, Hist. de la Conquista, cap. 62.—Gomara, Crónica, cap. 45.—Oviedo, Hist. de las Ind., MS., lib. 33, cap. 3, 41.—Sahagun, Hist. de Nueva España, MS., lib. 12, cap. 10.

not to lag behind, or wander from the ranks a moment, as strag
glers would be sure to be cut off by their stealthy and vigilant
enemy.   The horsemen rode three abreast, the better to give
one another support; and Cortés instructed them, in the heat
of fight to keep together, and never to charge singly.   He
taught them how to carry their lances, that they might not be
wrested from their hands by the Indians, who constantly attempted it.   For the same reason, they should avoid giving
thrusts, but aim their weapons steadily at the faces of their
foes.[21]

They had not proceeded far, when they were met by the
two remaining Cempoallan envoys, who with looks of terror
informed the general that they had been treacherously seized
and confined, in order to be sacrificed at an approaching festival
of the Tlascalans, but in the night had succeeded in making
their escape.   They gave the unwelcome tidings, also, that a
large force of the natives was already assembled to oppose the
progress of the Spaniards.

Soon after, they came in sight of a body of Indians, about a
thousand, apparently, all armed and brandishing their weapons,
as the Christians approached, in token of defiance.   Cortés.
when he had come within hearing, ordered the interpreters to
proclaim that he had no hostile intentions; but wished only to
be allowed a passage through their country, which he had entered as a friend.   This declaration he commanded the royal
notary, Godoy, to record on the spot, that, if blood were shed,
it might not be charged on the Spaniards.   This pacific proclamation was met, as usual on such occasions, by a shower of darts,
stones, and arrows, which fell like rain on the Spaniards, rattling
on their stout harness, and in some instances penetrating to the
skin.   Galled by the smart of their wounds, they called on the
general to lead them on, till he sounded the well known battle-
cry, "St. Jago, and at them!"[22]

The Indians maintained their ground for a while with spirit,
when they retreated with precipitation, but not in disorder.[23]
The Spaniards, whose blood was heated by the encounter,
followed up their advantage with more zeal than prudence, suffering the wily enemy to draw them into a narrow glen or defile,
intersected by a little stream of water, where the broken ground

<hr>

[21] "Que quando rompiessemos por los esquadrones, que lleuassen las
lanças, por las caras, y no parassen á dar lançadas, porque no les echassen
mano dellas." Bernal Diaz, Hist. de la Conquista, cap. 62.

[22] "Entonces dixo Cortés, 'Santiago, y á ellos.'" Ibid., cap. 63.

[23] "Una gentil contienda," says Gomara of this skirmish.   Crónica
cap. 46.

was impracticable for artillery, as well as for the movements of cavalry. Pressing forward with eagerness, to extricate them-selves from their perilous position, to their great dismay, on turning an abrupt angle of the pass, they came in presence of a numerous army, choking up the gorge of the valley, and stretching far over the plains beyond. To the astonished eyes of Cortés, they appeared a hundred thousand men, while no account estimates them at less than thirty thousand.[24]

They presented a confused assemblage of helmets, weapons, and many-colored plumes, glancing bright in the morning sun, and mingled with banners, above which proudly floated one that bore as a device the heron on a rock. It was the well known ensign of the house of Titcala, and, as well as the white and yellow stripes on the bodies, and the like colors on the feather-mail of the Indians, showed that they were the warriors of Xicotencatl.[25]

As the Spaniards came in sight, the Tlascalans set up a hideous war-cry, or rather whistle, piercing the ear with its shrillness, and which, with the beat of their melancholy drums, that could be heard for half a league or more,[26] might well have filled the stoutest heart with dismay. This formidable host came rolling on towards the Christians, as if to everwhelm them by their very numbers. But the courageous band of warriors, closely serried together and sheltered under their strong pano-plies, received the shock unshaken, while the broken masses of the enemy, chafing and heaving tumultuously around them,

[24] Rel Seg. de Cortés, ap. Lorenzana, p. 51. According to Gomara, (Crónica, cap. 46,) the enemy mustered 80,000. So, also, Ixtlilxochitl. (Hist. Chich., MS., cap. 83.) Bernal Diaz says, more than 40,000, (Hist. de la Conquista, cap 63.) But Herrera (Hist. General, dec. 2, lib. 6, cap, 5) and Torquemada (Monarch. Ind., lib. 4, cap. 20) reduce them to 30,000. One might as easily reckon the leaves in a forest, as the numbers of a confused throng of barbarians. As this was only one of several armies kept on foot by the Tlascalans, the smallest amount is, probably, too large, The whole population of the state, according to Clavigero, who would not be likely to underrate it, did not exceed half a million at the time of the invasion. Stor. del Messico, tom. I. p. 156.

[25] " La divisa y armas de la casa y cabecera de Titcala es una garga blanca sobre un peñasco."(Camargo, Hist. de Tlascala, MS.) " El capitan general,' says Bernal Diaz, "que se dezia Xicotenga, y con sus diuisas de blanco y colorado, porque aquella diuisa y liberea era de aquel Xicotenga." Hist. de la Conquista, cap. 63.

[26] " Llaman Teponaztle ques de un trozo de madero concavado y de una pieza rollizo y, como decimos, hueco por de dentro, que suena algunas veces mas demedia legua y con el atambor hace estraña y suave consonancia." (Camargo, Hist. de Tlascala, MS.) Clavigero, who gives a drawing of this same drum, says it is still used by the Indians, and may be heard two or three miles. Stor. del Messico, tom. II. p. 179.

seemed to recede only to return with new and accumulated force.

Cortés, as usual, in the front of danger, in vain endeavored, at the head of the horse, to open a passage for the infantry. Still his men, both cavalry and foot, kept their array unbroken, offering no assailable point to their foe. A body of the Tlascalans, however, acting in concert, assaulted a soldier named Moran, one of the best riders in the troops. They succeeded in dragging him from his horse, which they despatched with a thousand blows. The Spaniards, on foot, made a desperate effort to rescue their comrade from the hands of the enemy,— and from the horrible doom of the captive. A fierce struggle now began over the body of the prostrate horse. Ten of the Spaniards were wounded, when they succeeded in retrieving the unfortunate cavalier from his assailants, but in so disastrous a plight that he died on the following day. The horse was borne off in triumph by the Indians, and his mangled remains were sent, a strange trophy, to the different towns of Tlascala. The circumstances troubled the Spanish commander, as it divested the animal of the supernatural terrors with which the superstition of the natives had usually surrounded it. To prevent such a consequence ; he had caused the two horses, killed on the preceding day, to be secretly buried on the spot.

The enemy now began to give ground gradually, borne down by the riders, and trampled under the hoofs of their horses. Through the whole of this sharp encounter, the Indian allies were of great service to the Spaniards. They rushed into the water, and grappled their enemies, with the desperation of men who felt that "their only safety was in the despair of safety."[27] "I see nothing but death for us," exclaimed a Cempoallan chief to Marina ; "we shall never get through the pass alive "The God of the Christians is with us," answered the intrepid woman ; "and He will carry us safely through."[28]

Amidst the din of battle, the voice of Cortes was heard, cheering on his soldiers. "If we fail now," he cried, "the cross of Christ can never be planted in the land. Forward, comrades ! When was it ever known that a Castilian turned his back on a foe ?"[29] Animated by the words and heroic bearing of their general, the soldiers, with desperate efforts, at length succeeded

---

[27] "Una illis fuit spes salutis, desperâsse de salute." (P. Martyr, De Orbe Novo, dec. 1, cap. 1.) It is said with the classic energy of Tacitus.

[28] "Respondióle Marina, que no tuviese miedo, porque el Dios de los Christianos, que es muy poderoso, i los queria mucho, los sacaria de peligro.' Herrera, Hist. General, dec. 2, lib. 6, cap. 5.

[29] Ibid., ubi supra.

in forcing a passage through the dark columns of the enemy, and emerged from the defile on the open plain beyond.

Here they quickly recovered their confidence with their superiority. The horse soon opened a space for the manœuvres of the artillery. The close files of their antagonists presented a sure mark ; and the thunders of the ordnance vomiting forth torrents of fire and sulphurous smoke, the wide desolation caused in their ranks, and the strangely mangled carcasses of the slain, filled the barbarians with consternation and horror. They had no weapons to cope with these terrible engines, and their clumsy missiles, discharged from uncertain hands, seemed to fall ineffectual on the charmed heads of the Christians. What added to their embarrassment was, the desire to carry off the dead and wounded from the field, a general practice among the people of Anahuac, but which necessarily exposed them, while thus employed, to still greater loss.

Eight of their principal chiefs had now fallen ; and Xicotencatl, finding himself wholly unable to make head against the Spaniards in the open field, ordered a retreat. Far from the confusion of a panic-struck mob, so common among barbarians, the Tlascalan force moved off the ground with all the order of a well disciplined army. Cortes as on the preceding day, was too well satisfied with his present advantage to desire to follow it up. It was within an hour of sunset, and he was anxious before nightfall to secure a good position, where he might refresh his wounded troops, and bivouac for the night.[30]

Gathering up his wounded, he held on his way, without loss of time ; and before dusk reached a rocky eminence, called *Tzompachtepetl*, or "the hill Tzompach." It was crowned by a sort of tower or temple, the remains of which are still visible.[31] His first care was given to the wounded, both men and horses. Fortunately, an abundance of provisions were found in some neighboring cottages ; and the soldiers, at least all who were not disabled by their injuries, celebrated the victory of the day with feasting and rejoicing.

As to the number of killed or wounded on either side, it is matter of loosest conjecture. The Indians must have suffered severely but the practice of carrying off the dead from the field made it impossible to know to what extent. The injury sustained by the Spaniards appears to have been principally in the number

[30] Oviedo, Hist. de las Ind., MS., lib. 33, cap. 3, 45.—Ixtlilxochitl, Hist. Chich., MS., cap. 83.—Rel. Seg. de Cortés, ap. Lorenzana, p. 51.—Bernal Diaz, Hist. de la Conquista, cap. 63.—Gomara, Crònica, cap. 40.

[31] Viaje de Cortés, ap. Lorenzana, p. lx.

of their wounded. The great object of the natives of Anahuac in their battles was, to make prisoners, who might grace their triumphs, and supply victims for sacrifice. To this brutal superstition the Christians were indebted, in no slight degree, for their personal preservation. To take the reports of the Conquerors, their own losses in action were always inconsiderable. But whoever has had occasion to consult the ancient chroniclers of Spain in relation to its wars with the infidel, whether Arab or American, will place little confidence in numbers.[82]

The events of the day had suggested many topics for painful reflection to Cortés. He had nowhere met with so determined a resistance within the borders of Anahuac ; nowhere had he encountered native troops so formidable for their weapons, their discipline, and their valor. Far from manifesting the superstitious terrors felt by the other Indians, at the strange arms and aspect of the Spaniards, the Tlascalans had boldly grappled with their enemy, and only yielded to the inevitable superiority of his military science. How important would the alliance of such a nation be in a struggle with those of their own race,—for example, with the Aztecs ! But how was he to secure this alliance ? Hitherto, all overtures had been rejected with disdain ; and it seemed probable, that every step of his progress in this populous land was to be fiercely contested. His army, especially the Indians, celebrated the events of the day with feasting and dancing, songs of merriment, and shouts of triumph. Cortés encouraged it, well knowing how important it was to keep up the spirits of his soldiers. But the sounds of revelry at length died away ; and in the still watches of the night, many an anxious thought must have crowded on the mind of the general, while his little army lay buried in slumber in its encampment around the Indian hill.

---

[82] According to Cortes not a Spaniard fell,—though many were wounded,—in this action so fatal to the infidel ! Diaz allows one. In the famous battle of Navas de Tolosa, between the Spaniards and Arabs, in 1212, equally matched in military science at that time, there were left 200,000 of the latter on the field; and, to balance this bloody roll, only five and twenty Christians ! See the estimate in Alfonso IX.'s veracious letter, ap. Mariana (Hist. de España, lib. 2, cap. 24). The official returns of the old Castilian crusaders, whether in the Old World or in the New, are scarcely more trustworthy than a French *imperial* bulletin in our day.

CHAPTER III.

DECISIVE VICTORY.—INDIAN COUNCIL.—NIGHT ATTACK.—NEGO-
TIATIONS WITH THE ENEMY.—TLASCALAN HERO.

519.

THE Spaniards were allowed to repose undisturbed the following day, and to recruit their strength after the fatigue and hard
fighting of the preceding. They found sufficient employment,
however, in repairing and cleaning their weapons, replenishing
their diminished stock of arrows, and getting every thing in
order for further hostilities, should the severe lesson they had inflicted on the enemy prove insufficient to discourage him. On
the second day, as Cortés received no overtures from the Tlascalans, he determined to send an embassy to their camp, proposing a cessation of hostilities, and expressing his intention to
visit their capital as a friend. He selected two of the principal
chiefs taken in the late engagement, as the bearers of the
message.

Meanwhile, averse to leaving his men longer in a dangerous
state of inaction, which the enemy might interpret as the result of
timidity or exhaustion, he put himself at the head of the cavalry
and such light troops as were most fit for service, and made a
foray into the neighboring country. It was a mountainous region,
formed by a ramification of the great sierra of Tlascaia, with
verdant slopes and valleys teeming with maize and plantations
of maguey, while the eminences were crowned with populous
towns and villages. In one of these, he tells us, he found three
thousand dwellings.[1] In some places he met with a resolute resistance, and on these occasions took ample vengeance by lay-

[1] Rel. Seg. de Cortés, ap. Lorenzana, p. 52.
Oviedo who made free use of the manuscripts of Cortés, writes thirty-nine
houses. (Hist. de las Ind., MS., lib. 33, cap. 3.) This may perhaps, be
explained by the sign for a thousand, in Spanish notation, bearing great
resemblance to the figure 9. Martyr, who had access, also, to the Conqueror's
manuscript, confirms the larger, and, *a priori*, less probable number.

ing the country waste with fire and sword. **After a successful** inroad he returned laden with forage and provisions, and driving before him several hundred Indian captives, He treated them kindly, however, when arrived in camp, endeavoring to make them understand that these acts of violence were not dictated by his own wishes, but by the unfriendly policy of their countrymen. In this way he hoped to impress the nation with the conviction of his power on the one hand, and of his amicable intentions, if met by them in the like spirit, on the other.

On reaching his quarters, he found the two envoys returned from the Tlascalan camp. They had fallen in with Xicotencatl at about two leagues' distance, where he lay encamped with a powerful force. The cacique gave them audience at the head of his troops. He told them to return with the answer, "That the Spaniards might pass on as soon as they chose to Tlascala; and, when they reached it, their flesh would be hewn from their bodies, for sacrifice to the gods ! If they preferred to remain in their own quarters, he would pay them a visit there the next day." [2] The ambassadors added, that the chief had an immense force with him, consisting of five battalions of ten thousand men each. They were the flower of the Tlascalan and Otomie warriors, assembled under the banners of their respective leaders, by command of the senate, who were resolved to try the fortunes of the state in a pitched battle, and strike one decisive blow for the extermination of the invaders.[3]

This bold defiance fell heavily on the ears of the Spaniards, not prepared for so pertinacious a spirit in their enemy. They had had ample proof of his courage and formidable prowess. They were now, in their crippled condition, to encounter him with a still more terrible array of numbers. The war, too, from the horrible fate with which it menaced the vanquished, wore a peculiarly gloomy aspect, that pressed heavily on their spirits. "We feared death," says the lion-hearted Diaz, with his usual simplicity, "for we were men." There was scarcely one in the army, that did not confess himself that night to the reverend father Olmedo, who was occupied nearly the whole of it with

2 "Que fuessemos á su pueblo adonde está su padre q alla harian las pazes cõ hartarse de nuestras carnes, y honrar sus dioses con nuestros coracones, y sangre, é que para otro dia de mañana veriamos su respuesta." Bernal Diaz, Hist. de la Conquista, cap. 64.

3 More than one writer repeats a story of the Tlascalan general's sending a good supply of provisions, at this time, to the famished army of the Spaniards; to put them in stomach. it may be, for the fight. (Gomara, Crónica, cap 46.—Ixlilxochitl, Hist. Chich., MS., cap. 83.) This ultra-chivalrous display from the barbarian is not very probable, and Cortés' own account of his successful foray may much better explain the abundance which reigned in his camp.

CAPTURE OF THE CITY OF MEXICO BY CORTES

administering absolution, and with the other solemn offices of the Church. Armed with the blessed sacraments, the Catholic soldier lay tranquilly down to rest, prepared for any fate that might betide him under the banner of the cross.[4]

As a battle was now inevitable, Cortés resolved to march out and meet the enemy in the field. This would have a show of confidence, that might serve the double purpose of intimidating the Tlascalans, and inspiriting his own men, whose enthusiasm might lose somewhat of its heat, if compelled to await the assault of their antagonists, inactive in their own intrenchments. The sun rose bright on the following morning, the 5th of September, 1519, an eventful day in the history of the Spanish Conquest. The general reviewed his army, and gave them, preparatory to marching, a few words of encouragement and advice. The infantry he instructed to rely on the point rather than the edge of their swords, and to endeavor to thrust their opponents through the body. The horsemen were to charge at half speed, with their lances aimed at the eyes of the Indians. The artillery, the arquebusiers, and crossbowmen, were to support one another, some loading while others discharged their pieces, that there should be an unintermitted firing kept up through the action. Above all, they were to maintain their ranks close and unbroken, as on this depended their preservation.

They had not advanced a quarter of a league, when they came in sight of the Tlascalan army. Its dense array stretched far and wide over a vast plain or meadow ground, about six miles square. Its appearance justified the report which had been given of its numbers.[5] Nothing could be more picturesque than the aspect of these Indian battalions, with the naked bodies of the common soldiers gaudily painted, the fantastic helmets of the chiefs glittering with gold and precious stones, and the glowing panoplies of feather-work, which decorated their persons.[6] Innumerable spears and darts tipped with points of

---

[4] Rel. Seg. de Cortés, ap. Lorenzana, p. 52.—Ixtlilxochitl, Hist. Chich., MS., cap. 83.—Gomara, Cronica, cap. 46, 47.—Oviedo, Hist. de las Ind., MS., lib. 33, cap. 3.—Bernal Diaz, Hist. de la Conquista, cap. 64.

[5] Through the magnifying lens of Cortés, they appeared to be 150,000 men; (Rel. Seg., ap. Lorenzana, p. 52;) a number usually preferred by succeeding writers.

[6] " Not half so gorgeous, for their May-day mirth
All wreathed and ribanded, our youths and maids,
As these stern *Tlascalans* in war attire !
The golden glitterance, and the feather-mail
More gay than glittering gold ; and round the helm
A coronal of high upstanding plumes,
Green as the spring grass in a sunny shower ;
Or scarlet bright, as in the wintry wood

transparent *itztli*, or fiery copper, sparkled bright in the morning sun, like the phosphoric gleams playing on the surface of a troubled sea, while the rear of the mighty host was dark with the shadows of banners, on which were emblazoned the armorial bearings of the great Tlascalan and Otomie chieftains.[1] Among these, the white heron on the rock, the cognizance of the house of Xicotencatl, was conspicuous, and, still more, the golden eagle with outspread wings, in the fashion of a Roman *signum*, richly ornamented with emeralds and silver-work, the great standard of the republic of Tlascala.[8]

The common file wore no covering except a girdle round the loins. Their bodies were painted with the appropriate colors of the chieftain whose banner they followed. The feather-mail of the higher class of warriors exhibited, also, a similar selection of colors for the like object, in the same manner as the color of the tartan indicates the peculiar clan of the Highlander.[9] The cacique and principal warriors were clothed in a quilted cotton tunic, two inches thick, which, fitting close to the body, protected, also, the thighs and the shoulders. Over this the wealthier Indians wore cuirasses of thin gold plate, or silver. Their legs were defended by leathern boots or sandals, trimmed

> The clustered holly; or of purple tint ;
> Whereto shall that be likened? to what gem
> Indiademed, what flower, what insect's wing?
> With war songs and wild music they came on ;
> We, the while kneeling, raised with one accord
> The hymn of supplication."
>
> Southey's Madoc, Part 1, canto 7.

[1] The standards of the Mexicans were carried in the centre, those of the Tlascalans in the rear of the army. (Clavigero, Stor. del Messico, vol. II. p. 145.) According to the Anonymous Conqueror, the banner staff was attached to the back of the ensign, so that it was impossible to be torn away. "Ha ogni cōpagnia il suo Alfiere con la sua insegna inhastata, et in tal modo ligata sopra el spalle, che non gli da alcun disturbo di poter combattere ne far ciò che vuole, et la porta cosi ligata bene al corpo, che se nō fanno del suo corpo pezzi, non se gli puo sligare, ne torgliela mai." Rel. d' un gent., ap. Ramusio, tom. III. fol. 305.

[8] Camargo, Hist. de Tlascala, MS.—Herrera, Hist. General. dec. 2, lib. 6, cap. 6.—Gomara, Crónica, cap. 46.—Bernal Diaz, Hist. de la Conquista, cap. 64.—Oviedo, Hist de las Ind., MS., lib. 33, cap. 45.

The two last authors speak of the device of "a white bird like an ostrich," as that of the republic. They have evidently confounded it with that of the Indian general. Camargo, who has given the heraldic emblems of the four great families of Tlascala, notices the white heron, as that of Xicotencatl.

[9] The accounts of the Tlascalan chronicler are confirmed by the Anonymous Conqueror and by Bernal Diaz, both eye-witnesses; though the latter frankly declares, that, had he not seen them with his own eyes, he should never have credited the existence of orders and badges among the barbarians, like those found among the civilized nations of Europe. Hist. de la Conquista, cap. 64, et alibi.—Camargo, Hist. de Tlascala, MS.—Rel. d' un gent., ap. Ramusio, tom. III. fol. 305.

with gold. But the most brilliant part of their costume was a rich mantle of the *plumaje* or feather-work, embroidered with curious art, and furnishing some resemblance to the gorgeous surcoat worn by the European knight over his armor in the Middle Ages. This graceful and picturesque dress was surmounted by a fantastic head-piece made of wood or leather, representing the head of some wild animal, and frequently displaying a formidable array of teeth. With this covering the warrior's head was enveloped, producing a most grotesque and hideous effect.[b] From the crown floated a splendid panache of the richly variegated plumage of the tropics, indicating, by its form and colors, the rank and family of the wearer. To complete their defensive armor, they carried shields or targets, made sometimes of wood covered with leather, but more usually of a light frame of reeds quilted with cotton, which were preferred, as tougher and less liable to fracture than the former. They had other bucklers, in which the cotton was covered with an elastic substance, enabling them to be shut up in a more compact form like a fan or umbrella. These shields were decorated with showy ornaments, according to the taste or wealth of the wearer, and fringed with a beautiful pendant of feather-work.

Their weapons were slings, bow and arrows, javelins, and darts. They were accomplished archers, and would discharge two or even three arrows at a time. But they most excelled in throwing the javelin. One species of this, with a thong attached to it, which remained in the slinger's hand, that he might recall the weapon, was especially dreaded by the Spaniards. These various weapons were pointed with bone, or the mineral *itztli,* (obsidian,) the hard vitreous substance, already noticed, as capable of taking an edge like a razor, though easily blunted. Their spears and arrows were also frequently headed with copper. Instead of a sword, they bore a two-handed staff, about three feet and a half long, in which, at regular distances, were inserted, transversely, sharp blades of *itztli.*—a formidable weapon, which, an eye-witness assures us, he had seen fell a horse at a blow.[11]

---

[10] "Portano in testa," says the Anonymous Conqueror, "per difesa una cosa come teste di serpeti, ò di tigri, ò di leoni, ò di lupi, che ha le mascelle, et è la testa dell' huomo messa nella testa di qsto animale come se lo volesse diuorare: sono di legno, et sopra vi é la pena, et di piastra d' oro et di pietre preciose copte, che è cosa marauigliosa da vedere." Rel. d' un gent., ap Ramusio, tom. III fol. 305.

[11] "Io viddi che cõbattédosi un dì, diede un Indiano una cortellata a un cauallo sopra il qual era un caualliero co chi cobatteua, nel petto, che glielo apaise fin alle Iteriora, et cadde icotanete morto, et il medesimo giorno viddi

Such was the costume of the Tlascalan warrior, and, indeed, of that great family of nations generally, who occupied the plateau of Anahuac. Some parts of it, as the targets and the cotton mail or *escauple*, as it was called in Castilian, were so excellent, that they were subsequently adopted by the Spaniards, as equally effectual in the way of protection, and superior, on the score of lightness and convenience, to their own. They were of sufficient strength to turn an arrow, or the stroke of a javelin, although impotant as a defence against fire-arms. But what armor is not? Yet it is probably no exaggeration to say, that, in convenience, gracefulness, and strength the arms of the Indian warrior were not very inferior to those of the polished nations of antiquity.[12]

As soon as the Castilians came in sight, the Tlascalans set up their yell of defiance, rising high above the wild barbaric ministrelsy of shell, atabal, and trumpet, with which they proclaimed their triumphant anticipations of victory over the paltry forces of the invaders. When the latter had come within bowshot, the Indians hurled a tempest of missiles, that darkened the sun for a moment as with a passing cloud, strewing the earth around with heaps of stones and arrows. Slowly and steadily the little band of Spaniards held on its way amidst this arrowy shower, until it had reached what appeared the proper distance for delivering its fire with full effect. Cortes then halted, and, hastily forming his troops, opened a general well-directed fire along the whole line. Every shot bore its errand of death; and the ranks of the Indians were mowed down faster than their comrades in the rear could carry off their bodies, according to custom, from the field. The balls in their passage through the crowded files, bearing splinters of the broken harness, and mangled limbs of the warriors, scattered havoc and desolation in their path. The mob of barbarians stood petrified with dismay, till, at length, galled to desperation by their intolerable suffering, they poured forth simultaneously their hideous war-shriek, and rushed impetuously on the Christians.

On they came like an avalanche, or mountain torrent, shaking

---

cne un altro Indiano diede un altra cortellata a un altro cauallo su il collo che se lo gettó morto a i piedi.'' Rel d' un gent., ap. Ramusio, tom. III. fol. 305.

[12] Particular notices of the military dress and appointments of the American tribes on the plateau may be found in the Camargo, Hist. de Tlascala, MS.,—Clavigero, Stor. del Messico, tom. II. p. 101, et seq.,—Acosta, lib. 6, cap. 26,—Rel. d' un gent., ap. Ramusio, tom. III. fol. 305, et auct. al.

[18] '' Que granizo de piedra de los honderos! Pues flechas todo el suelo hecho parva de varas todas de á dos galos, que passan qualquiera arma, y las entrañas adonde no ay defensa.'' Bernal Diaz, Hist. de la Conquista, cap. 65.

the solid earth, and sweeping away every obstacle in its path The little army of Spaniards opposed a bold front to the over. elming mass. But no strength could withstand it. They altered, gave way, were borne along before it, and their rauk were broken and thrown into disorder. It was in vain the general called on them to close again and rally. His voice was drowned by the din of fight and the fierce cries of the assailants. For a moment, it seemed that all was lost. The tide of battle had turned against them, and the fate of the Christians was sealed.

But every man had that within his bosom, which spoke louder than the voice of the general. Despair gave unnatural energy to his arm. The naked body of the Indian afforded no resistance to the sharp Toledo steel; and with their good swords, the Spanish infantry at length succeeded in staying the human torrent. The heavy guns from a distance thundered on the flank of the assailants, which, shaken by the iron tempest, was thrown into disorder. Their very numbers increased the confusion, as they were precipitated on the masses in front. The horse at the same moment, charging gallantly under Cortes, followed up the advantage, and at length compelled the tumultuous throng to fall back with greater precipitation and disorder than that with which they had advanced.

More than once in the course of the action, a similar assault was attempted by the Tlascalans, but each time with less spirit, and greater loss. They were too deficient in military science to profit by their vast superiority in number. They were distributed into companies, it is true, each serving under its own chieftain and banner. But they were not arranged by rank and file and moved in a confused mass, promiscuously heaped together. They knew not how to concentrate numbers on a given point, or even how to sustain an assault, by employing successive detachments to support and relieve one another. A very small part only of their array could be brought into contact with an enemy inferior to them in amount of forces. The remainder of the army, inactive and worse than useless, in the rear, served only to press tumultuously on the advance and embarrass its movements by mere weight of number, while on the least alarm, they were seized with a panic and threw the whole body into inextricable confusion. It was, in short, the combat of the ancient Greeks and Persians over again.

Still, the great numerical superiority of the Indians might have enabled them, at a severe cost of their own lives, indeed, to wear out, in time, the constancy of the Spaniards, disabled by wounds and incessant fatigue. But, fortunately for the latter, dissensions arose among their enemies. A Tlascalan chieftain, commanding one of the great divisions, had taken umbrage at the haughty demeanor of Xicotencatl, who had charged him with misconduct or cowardice in the late action. The injured cacique challenged his rival to single combat. This did not take place. But, burning with resentment, he chose the present occasion to indulge it, by drawing off his forces, amounting to ten thousand men, from the field. He also persuaded another of the commanders to follow his example.

Thus reduced to about half his original strength, and that greatly crippled by the losses of the day, Xicotencatl could no longer maintain his ground against the Spaniards. After disputing the field with admirable courage for four hours, he retreated and resigned it to the enemy. The Spaniards were too much jaded, and too many were disabled by wounds, to allow, them to pursue; and Cortes, satisfied with the decisive victory he had gained, returned in triumph to his position on the hill of Tzompach.

The number of killed in his own ranks had been very small, notwithstanding the severe loss inflicted on the enemy. These few he was careful to bury where they could not be discovered, anxious to conceal not only the amount of the slain, but the fact that the whites were mortal. But very many of the men were wounded, and all the horses. The trouble of the Spaniards was much enhanced by the want of many articles important to them in their present exigency. They had neither oil, nor salt, which, as before noticed, was not to be obtained in Tlascala. Their clothing, accommodated to a softer climate, was ill adapted to the rude air of the mountains; and bows and arrows, as Bernal Diaz sarcastically remarks, formed an indifferent protection against the inclemency of the weather.

Still, they had much to cheer them in the events of the day; and they might draw from them a reasonable ground for con-

---

[14] So says Bernal Diaz; who, at the same time, by the epithets, *los muertos, los cuerpos,* plainly contradicts his previous boast that only one Christian fell in the fight. (Hist. de la Conquista, cap. 65.) Cortés has not the grace to acknowledge that one.

[15] Oviedo, Hist. de las Ind., MS., lib. 33, cap. 3.—Rel. Seg. de Cortés, ap. Lorenzana, p. 52.—Herrera, Hist. General, dec. 2, lib. 6, cap. 6.—Ixtlilxochtil, Hist. Chich., MS., cap. 83.—Gomara Crónica, cap. 46.—Torquemada, Monarch. Ind., lib. 4, cap. 32.—Bernal Diaz, Hist. de la Conquista, cap. 65, 66

The warm, chivalrous glow of feeling, which colors the rude composition of the last chronicler, makes him a better painter than his more correct and classical rivals. And, if there is somewhat too much of the self-complacent tone of the *quorum pars magna fui* in his writing, it may be pardoned in the hero of more than a hundred battles, and almost as many wounds.

fidence in their own resources, such as no other experience could have supplied. Not that the results could authorize anything like contempt for their Indian foe. Singly and with the same weapons, he might have stood his ground against the Spaniard.[16] But the success of the day established the superiority of science and discipline over mere physical courage and numbers. It was fighting over again, as we have said, the old battle of the European and the Asiatic. But the handful of Greeks who routed the hosts of Xerxes and Darius, it must be remembered, had not so obvious an advantage on the score of weapons, as was enjoyed by the Spaniards in these wars. The use of firearms gave an ascendency which cannot easily be estimated ; one so great, that a contest between nations equally civilized, which should be similar in all other respects to that between the Spaniards and the Tlascalans, would probably be attended with a similar issue. To all this must be added the effect produced by the cavalry. The nations of Anahuac had no large domesticated animals, and were unacquainted with any beast of burden. Their imaginations were bewildered, when they beheld the strange apparition of the horse and his rider moving in unison and obedient to one impulse, as if possessed of a common nature ; and as they saw the terrible animal, with his "neck clothed in thunder," bearing down their squadrons and trampling them in the dust, no wonder they should have regarded him with the mysterious terror felt for a supernatural being. A very little reflection on the manifold grounds of superiority, both moral and physical, possessed by the Spaniards in this contest, will surely explain the issue, without any disparagement to the courage or capacity of their opponents.[17]

Cortés, thinking the occasion favorable, followed up the important blow he had struck by a new mission to the capital, bearing a message of similar import with that recently sent to the camp. But the senate was not yet sufficiently humbled. The late defeat caused, indeed, general consternation. Maxixcatzin, one of the four great lords who presided over the republic, reiterated with greater force the arguments before urged by him

---

[16] The Anonymous Conqueror bears emphatic testimony to the valor of the Indians, specifying instances in which he had seen a single warrior defend himself for a long time against two, three, and even four Spaniards ! " Sono fra loro di valetissimi huomini et che ossano morir ostinatissimamete. Et io ho veduto un d' essi difendersi valétmente da duoi caualli leggieri, et un altro da tre, et quattro." Rel. d'un gent., ap. Ramusio, tom. III. fol 305.

[17] The appalling effect of the cavalry on the natives reminds one of the confusion into which the Roman legions were thrown by the strange appearance of the elephants in their first engagements with Pyrrhus, as told by Plutarch in his life of that prince.

for embracing the proffered alliance of the strangers. The armies
of the state had been beaten too often to allow any reasonable
hope of successful resistance ; and he enlarged on the generosity
shown by the politic Conqueror to his prisoners,—so unusual in
Anahuac,—as an additional motive for alliance with men who
knew how to be friends as well as foes.

But in these views he was overruled by the war-party, whose
animosity was sharpened, rather than subdued, by the late dis-
comfiture.   Their hostile feelings were further exasperated by
the younger Xicotencatl, who burned for an opportunity to retrieve his disgrace, and to wipe away the stains which had fallen
for the first time on the arms of the republic.

In their perplexity, they called in the assistance of the priests,
whose authority was frequently invoked in the deliberations of
the American chiefs.   The latter inquired, with some simplicity,
of these interpreters of fate, whether the strangers were supernatural beings, or men of flesh and blood like themselves.   The
priests, after some consultation, are said to have made the strange
answer, that the Spaniards, though not gods, were children of the
Sun ; that they derived their strength from that luminary, and,
when his beams were withdrawn, their powers would also fail.
They recommended a night attack, therefore, as one which afforded the best chance of success. This apparently childish response may have had in it more of cunning than credulity.   It
was not improbably suggested by Xicotencatl himself, or by the
caciques in his interest, to reconcile the people to a measure,
which was contrary to the military usages,—indeed, it may be
said, to the public law of Anahuac.   Whether the fruit of artifice
or superstition, it prevailed and the Tlascalan general was empowered, at the head of a detachment of ten thousand warriors,
to try the effect of an assault by night on the Christian camp.

The affair was conducted with such secrecy, that it did not
reach the ears of the Spaniards.   But their general was not one
who allowed himself, sleeping or waking, to be surprised on his
post.   Fortunately, the night appointed was illuminated by the
full beams of an autumnal moon ; and one of the videttes perceived
by its light, at a considerable distance, a large body of Indians
moving towards the Christian lines.   He was not slow in giving
the alarm to the garrison.

The Spaniards slept, as has been said, with their arms by their
side ; while their horses, picketed near them, stood ready saddled,
with the bridle hanging at the bow.   In five minutes, the whole
camp was under arms ; when they beheld the dusky columns
of the Indians cautiously advancing over the plain, their heads
just peering above the tall maize with which the land was par-

tially covered. Cortés determined not to abide the assault in his intrenchments, but to sally out and pounce on the enemy when he had reached the bottom of the hill.

Slowly and stealthily the Indians advanced, while the Christian camp, hushed in profound silence, seemed to them buried in slumber. But no sooner had they reached the slope of the rising ground, than they were astounded by the deep battle-cry of the Spaniards, followed by the instantaneous apparition of the whole army, as they sallied forth from the works, and poured down the sides of the hill. Brandishing aloft their weapons, they seemed to the troubled fancies of the Tlascalans, like so many spectres or demons hurrying to and fro in mid air, while the uncertain light magnified their numbers, and expanded the horse and his rider into gigantic and unearthly dimensions.

Scarcely waiting the shock of their enemy, the panic-struck barbarians let off a feeble volley of arrows, and, offering no other resistance, fled rapidly and tumultuously across the plain. The horse easily overtook the fugitives, riding them down and cutting them to pieces without mercy, until Cortés, weary with slaughter, called off his men, leaving the field loaded with the bloody trophies of victory.[18]

The next day, the Spanish commander, with his usual policy after a decisive blow had been struck, sent a new embassy to the Tlascalan capital. The envoys received their instructions through the interpreter, Marina. That remarkable woman had attracted general admiration by the constancy and cheerfulness with which she endured all the privations of the camp. Far from betraying the natural weakness and timidity of her sex, she had shrunk from no hardship herself, and had done much to fortify the drooping spirits of the soldiers; while her sympathies, whenever occasion offered, had been actively exerted in mitigating the calamities of her Indian countrymen.[19]

Through his faithful interpreter, Cortés communicated the terms of his message to the Tlascalan envoys. He made the same professions of amity as before, promising oblivion of all past injuries; but, if this proffer were rejected, he would visit their capital a conqueror, raze every house in it to the ground, and

[18] Rel. Seg. de Cortés, ap. Lorenzana, pp. 53, 54.—Oviedo, Hist. de las Ind., MS., lib. 33, cap. 3.—P. Martyr, De Orbe Novo, dec 2, cap. 2.—Torquemada, Monarch. Ind., lib. 4, cap. 32.—Herrera, Hist. General, dec. 2, lib. 6. cap. 8.—Bernal Diaz, Hist. de la Conquista, cap. 66.

[19] "Digamos como Doña Marina, con ser muger de la tierra, que esfuerço tan varonil tenia, que con oir cada dia que nos auian de matar, y comer nuestras, carnes y auernos visto cercado en las batallas passadas, y que aora todos estauamos heridos, y dolientes, jamas vimos flaqueza en ella, sino muy mayor esfuerço que de muger." Bernal Diaz, Hist. de la Conquista, cap. 66.

put every inhabit⌐ it ⸍ ⸍ the sword ! He then dismissed the ambassadors with ⸗e ⸗ymbolical presents of a letter in one hand, and an arrow in the other.

The envoys obtained respectful audience from the council of Tlascala, whom they found plunged in deep dejection by their recent reverses. The failure of the night attack had extinguished every spark of hope in their bosoms. Their armies had been beaten again and again, in the open field and in secret ambush. Stratagem and courage, all their resources, had alike proved ineffectual against a foe whose hand was never weary, and whose eye was never closed. Nothing remained but to submit. They selected four principal caciques, whom they intrusted with a mission to the Christian camp. They were to assure the strangers of a free passage through the country, and a friendly reception in the capital. The proffered friendship of the Spaniards was cordially embraced, with many awkward excuses for the past. The envoys were to touch at the Tlascalan camp on their way, and inform Xicotencatl of their proceedings. They were to require him, at the same time, to abstain from all further hostilities, and to furnish the white men with an ample supply of provisions.

But the Tlascalan deputies, on arriving at the quarters of that chief, did not find him in the humor to comply with these instructions. His repeated collisions with the Spaniards, or, it may be, his constitutional courage, left him inaccessible to the vulgar terrors of his countrymen. He regarded the strangers not as supernatural beings, but as men like himself. The animosity of a warrior had rankled into a deadly hatred from the mortifications he had endured at their hands, and his head teemed with plans for recovering his fallen honors, and for taking vengeance on the invaders of his country. He refused to disband any of the force, still formidable, under his command ; or to send supplies to the enemy's camp. He further induced the ambassadors to remain in his quarters, and relinquish their visit to the Spaniards. The latter, in consequence, were kept in ignorance of the movements in their favor, which had taken place in the Tlascalan capital.[20]

The conduct of Xicotencatl is condemned by Castilian writers, as that of a ferocious and sanguinary barbarian. It is natural they should so regard it. But those, who have no national prejudice to warp their judgments, may come to a different conclusion. they may find much to admire in that high, unconquerable spirit, like some proud column, standing alone in its majesty

[20] Ibid., cap. 67.—Camargo, Hist. de Tlascala, MS.—Ixtlilxochitl, Hist. Chich., MS., cap. 83.

amid the fragments and ruins around it. They may see evidences of a clear-sighted sagacity, which, piercing the thin veil
of insidious friendship proffered by the Spaniards, and penetrating the future, discerned the coming miseries of his country ;
the noble patriotism of one who would rescue that country at any
cost, and, amidst the gathering darkness, would infuse his own
intrepid spirit into the hearts of his nation, to animate them to a
last struggle for independence.

CHAPTER IV.

DISCONTENTS IN THE ARMY.—TLASCALAN SPIES.—PEACE WITH
THE REPUBLIC.—EMBASSY FROM MONTEZUMA.

1519.

DESIROUS to keep up the terror of the Castilian name, by
leaving the enemy no respite, Cortés, on the same day that he
despatched the embassy to Tlascala, put himself at the head of
a small corps of cavalry and light troops to scour the neighboring country. He was at that time so ill from fever, aided by
medical treatment,[1] that he could hardly keep his seat in the
saddle. It was a rough country, and the sharp winds from the
frosty summits of the mountains pierced the scanty covering of
the troops, and chilled both men and horses. Four or five of
the animals gave out, and the general, alarmed for their safety,
sent them back to the camp. The soldiers, discouraged by this
ill omen, would have persuaded him to return. But he made
answer, " We fight under the banner of the Cross; God is
stronger than nature,"[2] and continued his march.

It led through the same kind of checkered scenery of rugged
hill and cultivated plain as that already described, well covered
with towns and villages, some of them the frontier posts occupied by the Otomies. Practising the Roman maxim of lenity to
the submissive foe, he took full vengeance on those who resisted,
and, as resistance too often occurred, marked his path with fire
and desolation. After a short absence, he returned in safety,
laden with the plunder of a successful foray. It would have
been more honorable to him, had it been conducted with less
rigor. The excesses are imputed by Bernal Diaz to the Indian
allies, whom in the heat of victory it was found impossible to

---

[1] The effect of the medicine—though rather a severe dose, according to
the precise Diaz—was suspended during the general's active exertions.
Gomara, however, does not consider this a miracle. (Crónica, cap. 49.)
Father Sandoval does. (Hist. de Cárlos Quinto, tom. I p. 127.) Solis,
after a conscientious inquiry into this perplexing matter, decides—strange
as it may seem—against the father! Conquista, lib. 2, cap. 20.

[2] " **Dios es sobre natura.**" Rel. Seg. de Cortès, ap. Lorenzana, p. 54.

restrain.⁰ On whose head soever they fall, they seem to have given little uneasiness to the general, who declares in his letter to the Emperor Charles the Fifth, " As we fought under the standard of the Cross,[1] for the true Faith, and the service of your Highness, Heaven crowned our arms with such success, that, while multitudes of the infidel were slain, little loss was suffered by the Castilians." [2]   The Spanish Conquerors, to judge from their writings, unconscious of any worldly motive lurking in the bottom of their hearts, regarded themselves as soldiers of the Church, fighting the great battle of Christianity ; and in the same edifying and comfortable light are regarded by most of the national historians of a later day.[3]

On his return to the camp, Cortés found a new cause of disquietude in discontents which had broken out among the soldiery. Their patience was exhausted by a life of fatigue and peril to which there seemed to be no end. The battles they had won against such tremendous odds had not advanced them a jot. The idea of their reaching Mexico, says the old soldier so often quoted, " was treated as a jest by the whole army ; " [4] and the indefinite prospect of hostilities with the ferocious people among whom they were now cast, threw a deep gloom over their spirits.

Among the malcontents were a number of noisy, vaporing persons, such as are found in every camp, who, like empty bubbles, are sure to rise to the surface and make themselves seen in seasons of agitation. They were, for the most part, of the old faction of Velasquez, and had estates in Cuba, to which they turned many a wistful glance as they receded more and more from the coast. They now waited on the general, not in a mutinous spirit of resistance, (for they remembered the lesson in Villa Rica,) but with the design of frank expostulation, as with a brother adventurer in a common cause.[6] The tone of

---

[1] Hist de la Conquista, cap. 64.
Not so Cortés, who says boldly, " Quemé mas de diez pueblos." (Ibid. p. 52.) His reverend commentator specifies the localities of the Indian towns destroyed by him, in his forays. Viaje, ap. Lorenzana, pp. ix.–xi.

[2] The famous banner of the Conqueror, with the Cross emblazoned on it, has been preserved in Mexico to our day.

[3] " E como trayamos la Bandera de la Cruz, y pufiabamos por nuestra Fe, y por servicio de Vuestra Sacra Magestad, en su muy Real ventura nos dió Dios tanta victoria, que les matamos mucha gente, sin que los nuestros recibiessen dano." Rel. Seg. de Cortés, ap. Lorenzana, p. 52.

[4] " Y fué cosa notable," exclaims Herrera, " con quanta humildad, i devocion, bolvian todos alabando a Dios, que tan milagrosas victorias les daba; de donde se conocia claro, que los favorecia con su Divina asistencia."

[6] " Porque entrar en México, teniamoslo por cosa de risa, a causa de sus grandes fuerças." Bernal Diaz, Hist. de la Conquista, cap. 66.

⁰ Diaz indignantly disclaims the idea of mutiny, which Gomara attached to

familiarity thus assumed was eminently characteristic of the footing of equality on which the parties in the expedition stood with one another.

Their sufferings, they told him, were too great to be endured. All the men had received one, most of them, two or three wounds. More than fifty had perished, in one way or another, since leaving Vera Cruz. There was no beast of burden but led a life preferable to theirs. For when the night came, the former could rest from his labors ; but they, fighting or watching, had no rest, day nor night. As to conquering Mexico, the very thought of it was madness. If they had encountered such opposition from the petty republic of Tlascala, what might they not expect from the great Mexican empire ? There was now a temporary suspension of hostilities. They should avail themselves of it, to retrace their steps to Vera Cruz. It is true, the fleet there was destroyed ; and by this act, unparalleled for rashness even in Roman annals, the general had become responsible for the fate of the whole army. Still there was one vessel left. That might be despatched to Cuba, for reinforcements and supplies ; and, when these arrived, they would be enabled to resume operations with some prospect of success.

Cortés listened to this singular expostulation with perfect composure. He knew his men, and, instead of rebuke or harsher measures, replied in the same frank and soldier-like vein which they had affected.

There was much truth, he allowed, in what they said. The sufferings of the Spaniards had been great ; greater than those recorded of any heroes in Greek or Roman story. So much the greater would be their glory. He had often been filled with admiration as he had seen his little host encircled by myriads of barbarians, and felt that no people but Spaniards could have triumphed over such formidable odds. Nor could they, unless the arm of the Almighty had been over them. And they might reasonably look for his protection hereafter ; for was it not in his cause they were fighting ? They had encountered dangers and difficulties, it was true. But they had not come here expecting a life of idle dalliance and pleasure. Glory, as he had told them at the outset, was to be won only by toil and danger. They would do him the justice to acknowledge, that he had never shrunk from his share of both.—This was a truth,

---

this proceeding. "**Las palabras** que le dezian era por via de acōsejarle, y porque les parecia que eran bien dichas y no por otra via. porque siempre la siguiéron muy bien. y lealmēte: y no es mucho que en los exércitos algunos buenos soldados aconsejen á su Capitan, y mas si se ven tan trabajados como nosotros andauamos." Ibid., cap. 71.

adds the honest chronicler who heard and reports the dialogue, which no one could deny.—But, if they had met with hardships, he continued, they had been everywhere victorious. Even now, they were enjoying the fruits of this, in the plenty which reigned in the camp. And they would soon see the Tlascalans, humbled by their late reverses, suing for peace on any terms. To go back now was impossible. The very stones would rise up against them. The Tlascalans would hunt them in triumph down to the water's edge. And how would the Mexicans exult at this miserable issue of their vainglorious vaunts! Their former friends would become their enemies ; and the Totonacs, to avert the vengeance of the Aztecs, from which the Spaniards could no longer shield them, would join in the general cry. There was no alternative, then, but to go forward in their career. And he besought them to silence their pusillanimous scruples, and, instead of turning their eyes toward Cuba, to fix them on Mexico, the great object of their enterprise.

While this singular conference was going on, many other soldiers had gathered round the spot ; and the discontented party, emboldened by the presence of their comrades, as well as by the general's forbearance, replied, that they were far from being convinced. Another such victory as the last would be their ruin. They were going to Mexico only to be slaughtered. Until at length, the general's patience being exhausted, he cut the argument short, by quoting a verse from an old song, implying that it was better to die with honor, than to live disgraced ; a sentiment which was loudly echoed by the greater part of his audience, who, notwithstanding their occasional murmurs, had no design to abandon the expedition, still less the commander, to whom they were passionately devoted. The malcontents, disconcerted by this rebuke, slunk back to their own quarters, muttering half-smothered execrations on the leader who had projected the enterprise, the Indians who had guided him, and their own countrymen who supported him in it.[9]

Such were the difficulties that lay in the path of Cortes, a wily and ferocious enemy ; a climate uncertain, often unhealthy, illness in his own person, much aggravated by anxiety as to the

---

[9] This conference is reported, with some variety, indeed, by nearly every historian. (Rel. Seg. de Cortés, ap. Lorenzana, p. 55.—Oviedo, Hist. de las Ind., MS., lib, 33, cap. 3.—Gomara, Cronica, cap 51, 52.—Ixtlilxochitl, Hist. Chich., MS., cap. 80.—Herrera, Hist. General, dec. 2, lib. 6, cap. 9. —P. Martyr, De Orbe Novo, dec. 5, cap. 2.) I have abridged the account given by Bernal Diaz, one of the audience, though not one of the parties to the dialogue,—for that reason, the better authority.

manner in which his conduct would be received by his sovereign; last, not least, disaffection among his soldiers, on whose constancy and union he rested for the basis of his operations,—the great lever by which he was to overturn the empire of Montezuma.

On the morning following this event, the camp was surprised by the appearance of a small body of Tlascalans, decorated with badges, the white color of which intimated peace. They brought a quantity of provisions, and some trifling ornaments, which, they said, were sent by the Tlascalan general, who was weary of the war, and desired an accommodation with the Spaniards. He would soon present himself to arrange this in person. The intelligence diffused general joy, and the emissaries received a friendly welcome.

A day or two elapsed, and while a few of the party left the Spanish quarters, the others, about fifty in number, who remained, excited some distrust in the bosom of Marina. She communicated her suspicions to Cortes that they were spies. He caused several of them, in consequence, to be arrested, examined separately, and ascertained that they were employed by Xicotencatl to inform him of the state of the Christian camp, preparatory to a meditated assault, for which he was mustering his forces, Cortes, satisfied of the truth of this, determined to make such an example of the delinquents, as should intimidate his enemy from repeating the attempt. He ordered their hands to be cut off, and in that condition sent them back to their countrymen, with the message, "that the Tlascalans might come by day or night; they would find the Spaniards ready for them.[10]   "

The doleful spectacle of their comrades returning in this mutilated state filled the Indian camp with horror and consternation. The haughty crest of their chief was humbled. From that moment, he lost his wonted buoyancy and confidence. His soldiers, filled with superstitious fear, refused to serve longer against a foe who could read their very thoughts, and divine their plans before they were ripe for execution.[11]

The punishment inflicted by Cortés may well shock the reader by its brutality. But it should be considered in mitigation, that

[10] Diaz says only seventeen lost their hands, the rest their thumbs. (Hist. de la Conquista, cap. 70.) Cortés does not flinch from confessing, the hands of the whole fifty. "Los mandé tomar á todos cincuenta, y cortarles las manos, y los embié, que dixessen a su Senor, que de noche, y de dia, y cada, y quando el viniesse, verian quien eramos." Rel. Seg. de Cortes, ap. Lorenzana, p. 53.

[11] "De que los Tlascaltecas se admiráron, entendiendo que Cortés las entendia sus pensamiendos." Ixtlilxochitl, Hist. Chich., MS., cap. 83.

the victims of it were spies, and, as such, by the laws of war, whether among civilized or savage nations, had incurred the penalty of death. The amputation of the limbs was a milder punishment, and reserved for inferior offences. If we revolt at the barbarous nature of the sentence, we should reflect that it was no uncommon one at that day ; not more uncommon, indeed, than whipping and branding with a hot iron were in our own country, at the beginning of the present century, or than cropping the ears was in the preceding one. A higher civilization, indeed, rejects such punishments, as pernicious in themselves, and degrading to humanity. But in the sixteenth century, they were openly recognized by the laws of the most polished nations in Europe. And it is too much to ask of any man, still less one bred to the iron trade of war, to be in advance of the refinement of his age. We may be content, if, in circumstances so unfavorable to humanity, he does not fall below it.

All thoughts of further resistance being abandoned, the four delegates of the Tlascalan republic were now allowed to proceed on their mission. They were speedily followed by Xicotencatl himself, attended by a numerous train of military retainers. As they drew near the Spanish lines, they were easily recognized by the white and yellow colors of their uniforms, the livery of the house of Titcala. The joy of the army was great at this sure intimation of the close of hostilities ; and it was with difficulty that Cortes was enabled to restore the men to tranquillity, and the assumed indifference which it was proper to maintain in presence of an enemy.

The Spaniards gazed with curious eye on the valiant chief who had so long kept his enemies at bay, and who advanced with the firm and fearless step of one who was coming rather to bid defiance than to sue for peace. He was rather above the middle size, with broad shoulders, and a muscular frame intimating great activity and strength. His head was large, and his countenance marked with the lines of hard service rather than of age, for he was but thirty-five. When he entered the presence of Cortes, he made the usual salutation, by touching the ground with his hand, and carrying it to his head ; while the sweet incense of aromatic gums rolled up in clouds from the censers carried by his slaves.

Far from a pusillanimous attempt to throw the blame on the senate, he assumed the whole responsibility of the war. He had considered the white men, he said, as enemies, for they came with the allies and vassals of Montezuma. He loved his country, and wished to preserve the independence which she had maintained through her long wars with the Aztecs. He had been beaten. They might be the strangers, who, it had been so long predicted, would come from the east, to take possession of the country. He hoped they would use their victory with moderation, and not trample on the liberties of the republic. He came now in the name of his nation, to tender their obedience to the Spaniards, assuring them they would find his countrymen as faithful in peace as they had been firm in war.

Cortes, far from taking umbrage, was filled with admiration at the lofty spirit which thus disdained to stoop beneath misfortunes. The brave man knows how to respect bravery in another. He assumed, however, a severe aspect, as he rebuked the chief for having so long persisted in hostilities. Had Xicotencatl believed the word of the Spaniards, and accepted their proffered friendship sooner, he would have spared his people much suffering, which they well merited by their obstinacy. But it was impossible, continued the general, to retrieve the past. He was willing to bury it in oblivion, and to receive the Tlascalans as vassals to the emperor, his master. If they proved true, they should find him a sure column of support: if false, he would take such vengeance on them as he had intended to take on their capital, had they not speedily given in their submission.—It proved an ominous menace for the chief to whom it was addressed.

The cacique then ordered his slaves to bring forward some trifling ornaments of gold and feather embroidery, designed as presents. They were of little value, he said, with a smile, for the Tlascalans were poor. They had little gold, not even cotton, nor salt. The Aztec emperor had left them nothing but their freedom and their arms. He offered this gift only as a token of his good-will. "As such I receive it," answered Cortes, "and, coming from the Tlascalans, set more value on it, than I should from any other source, though it were a house full of gold";—a politic, as well as magnanimous reply, for it was by the aid of this good-will, that he was to win the gold of Mexico.

Thus ended the bloody war with the fierce republic of Tlascala, during the course of which, the fortunes of the Spaniards, more than once, had trembled in the balance. Had it been persevered in but a little longer, it must have ended in their confusion and ruin, exhausted as they were by wounds, watching. and fatigues, with the seeds of disaffection rankling among them-

---

[12] Rel. Seg. de Cortés, ap. Lorenzana, pp. 56, 57.—Oviedo, Hist. de las Ind., MS., lib. 33, cap. 3.—Gomara, Crónica, cap. 53.—Bernal Diaz, Hist. de la Conquista, cap. 71, et seq.—Sahagun, Hist. de Nueva España, MS., lib. 12, cap. 11.

selves. As it was, they came out of the fearful contest with untarnished glory. To the enemy, they seemed invulnerable, bearing charmed lives, proof alike against the accidents of fortune and the assaults of man. No wonder that they indulged a similar conceit in their own bosoms, and that the humblest Spaniard should have fancied himself the subject of a special interposition of Providence, which shielded him in the hour of battle, and reserved him for a higher destiny.

While the Tlascalans were still in the camp, an embassy was announced from Montezuma. Tidings of the exploits of the Spaniards had spread far and wide over the plateau. The emperor, in particular, had watched every step of their progress, as they climbed the steeps of the Cordilleras, and advanced over the broad table-land, on their summit. He had seen them, with great satisfaction, take the road to Tlascala, trusting, that, if they were mortal men, they would find their graves there. Great was his dismay, when courier after courier brought him intelligence of their successes, and that the most redoubtable warriors on the plateau had been scattered like chaff, by the swords of this handful of strangers.

His superstitious fears returned in full force. He saw in the Spaniards " the men of destiny," who were to take possession of his sceptre. In his alarm and uncertainty, he sent a new embassy to the Christian camp. It consisted of five great nobles of his court, attended by a train of two hundred slaves. They brought with them a present, as usual, dictated partly by fear, and, in part, by the natural munificence of his disposition. It consisted of three thousand ounces of gold, in grains, or in various manufactured articles, with several hundred mantles and dresses of embroidered cotton, and the picturesque feather-work. As they laid these at the feet of Cortés, they told him they had come to offer the congratulations of their master on the late victories of the white men. The emperor only regretted that it would not be in his power to receive them in his capital, where the numerous population was so unruly, that their safety would be placed in jeopardy. The mere intimation of the Aztec emperor's wishes, in the most distant way, would have sufficed with the Indian nations. It had very little weight with the Spaniards; and the envoys, finding this puerile expression of them ineffectual, resorted to another argument, offering a tribute in their master's name to the Castilian sovereign, provided the Spaniards would relinquish their visit to his capital. This was a greater error; it was displaying the rich casket with one hand, which he was unable to defend with the other. Yet the author of this pusillanimous policy, the unhappy victim of superstition, was a monarch re-

nowned among the I ⎯⎯ian nations for his intrepidity and enterprise,—the terror of Anahuac !

Cortés, while he urged his own sovereign's commands as a
reason for disregarding the wishes of Montezuma, uttered expressions of the most profound respect for the Aztec prince, and
declared that if he had not the means of requiting his munificence, as he could wish, at present, he trusted *to repay him,
at some future day, with good works !* [13]

The Mexican ambassadors were not much gratified with finding the war at an end, and a reconciliation established between
their mortal enemies and the Spaniards. The mutual disgust of
the two parties with each other was too strong to be repressed
even in the presence of the general, who saw with satisfaction
the evidences of a jealousy, which, undermining the strength of
the Indian emperor, was to prove the surest source of his own
success.[14]

Two of the Aztec mission returned to Mexico, to acquaint
their sovereign with the state of affairs in the Spanish camp.
The others remained with the army, Cortés being willing that
they should be personal spectators of the deference shown him
by the Tlascalans. Still he did not hasten his departure for
their capital. Not that he placed reliance on the injurious
intimations of the Mexicans respecting their good faith. Yet
he was willing to put this to some longer trial, and, at the same
time, to reëstablish his own health more thoroughly, before
his visit. Meanwhile, messengers daily arrived from the city,
pressing his journey, and were finally followed by some of the
aged rulers of the republic, attended by a numerous retinue,
impatient of his long delay. They brought with them a body of
five hundred *tamanes*, or *men of burden*, to drag his cannon, and
relieve his own forces from this fatiguing part of their duty. It
was impossible to defer his departure longer ; and after mass,
and a solemn thanksgiving to the great Being who had crowned
their arms with triumph, the Spaniards bade adieu to the
quarters which they had occupied for nearly three weeks on the
hill of Tzompach. The strong tower, or *teocalli*, which commanded

---

[13] "Cortés recibió con alegría aquel presente, y dixo que se lo tenia en
merced, y que él lo pagaria al señor Moteçuma en buenas obras." Bernal
Diaz, Hist. de la Conquista, cap. 73.

[14] He dwells on it in his letter to the Emperor. "Vista la discordia y des-
conformidad de los unos y de los otros, no huve poco placer, porque me pareció hacer mucho á mi proposito, y que podria tener manera de mas ayna
sojuzgarlos, é aun acordéme de una autoridad Evangélica, que dice : *Omne
Regnum in seipsum divesum desolabitur :* y con los unos y con los otros man-
eaba, y á cadauno en secreto le agradecia el aviso, que me daba, y la daba
crédito de mas amistad que al otro." Rel. Seg. de Cortés, ap. Lorenzana, p. 61.

it was called, in commemoration of their residence, " the tower of victory " ; and the few stones, which still survive of its ruins, point out to the eye of the traveller a spot ever memorable in history for the courage and constancy of the early Conquerors.

[15] Herrera, Hist. General, dec. 2, lib. 6, cap. 10.—Oviedo, Hist. de las Ind., MS., lib. 33, cap. 4.—Gomara, Crónica, cap. 54.—Martyr, De Orbe Novo, dec. 5, cap. 2.—Bernal Diaz, Hist. de la Conquista, cap. 72-74.—Ixtlilxochitl, Hist. Chich., MS., cap. 83.

CHAPTER V.

Spaniards enter Tlascala.—Description of the Capital.—
Attempted Conversion.—Aztec Embassy.—Invited to
Cholula.

1519.

The city of Tlascala, the capital of the republic of the same
name, lay at the distance of about six leagues from the Spanish
camp. The road led into a hilly region, exhibiting in every
arable patch of ground the evidence of laborious cultivation.
Over a deep *barranca*, or ravine, they crossed on a bridge of
stone, which, according to tradition,—a slippery authority,—is
the same still standing, and was constructed originally for the
passage of the army.[1] They passed some considerable towns
on their route, where they experienced a full measure of Indian
hospitality. As they advanced, the approach to a populous city
was intimated by the crowds who flocked out to see and welcome
the strangers; men and women in their picturesque dress, with
bunches and wreaths of roses, which they gave to the Spaniards,
or fastened to the necks and caparisons of their horses, in the
same manner as at Cempoalla. Priests, with their white robes,
and long matted tresses floating over them, mingled in the crowd,
scattering volumes of incense from their burning censers. In
this way, the multitudinous and motley procession defiled though
the gates of the ancient capital of Tlascala. It was the twenty-
third of September, 1519, the anniversary of which is still celebrated by the inhabitants, as a day of jubilee.[2]

---

[1] "A distancia de un quarto de legua caminando á esta dicha ciudad se
encuentra una barranca honda, que tiene para passer *un Puente de cal y canto
de bóveda*, y es tradicion en el pueblo de San Salvador, que se hizo en aquellos
dias que estubo allí Cortés paraque pasasse." (Viaje, ap. Lorenzana, p. xi.)
If the antiquity of this *arched* stone bridge could be established, it would settle a point much mooted in respect to Indian architecture. But the construction of so solid a work in so short a time is a fact requiring a better voucher
than the villagers of San Salvador.

[2] Clavigero, Stor. del Messico, tom. III. p. 53.
"Recibimiento el mas solene y famoso que en el mundo se ha visto," exclaims the enthusiastic historian of the republic. He adds, that "more than
a hundred thousand men flocked out to receive the Spaniards; a thing that
appears impossible," *que parece cosa impossible!* It does indeed. Camargo,
Hist. de Tlascala, MS.

The press was now so great, that it was with difficulty the police of the city could clear a passage for the army ; while the *azeoteas*, or flat terraced roofs of the buildings, were covered with spectators, eager to catch a glimpse of the wonder- ful strangers. The houses were hung with festoons of flowers, and arches of verdant boughs, intertwined with roses and honeysuckle, were thrown across the streets. The whole population abandoned itself to rejoicing; and the air was rent with songs and shouts of triumph mingled with the wild music of the national instruments, that might have excited apprehen- sions in the breasts of the soldiery, had they not gathered their peaceful import from the assurance of Marina, and the joyous countenances of the natives.

With these accompaniments, the procession moved along the principal streets to the mansion of Xicotencatl, the aged father of the Tlascalan general, and one of the four rulers of the republic. Cortés dismounted from his horse, to receive the old chieftain's embrace. He was nearly blind ; and satisfied, as far as he could, a natural curiosity respecting the person of the Spanish general, by passing his hand over his features. He then led the way to a spacious hall in his palace, where a banquet was served to the army. In the evening, they were shown to their quarters, in the buildings and open ground surrounding one of the principal *teo- callis;* while the Mexican ambassadors, at the desire of Cortés, had apartments assigned them next to his own, that he might the better watch over their safety, in this city of their enemies.[3]

Tlascala was one of the most important and populous towns on the table-land. Cortés in his letter to the Emperor, compares it to Granada, affirming, that it was larger, stronger, and more pop- ulous than the Moorish capital, at the time of the conquest, and quite as well built.[4] But, notwithstanding we are assured by a most respectable writer at the close of the last century, that its remains justify the assertion,[6] we shall be slow to believe that its edifices could have rivalled those monuments of Oriental magnifi- cence, whose light, aërial forms still survive after the lapse of ages, the admiration of every traveller of sensibility and taste.

[3] Sahagun, Hist. de Nueva España, MS., lib. 12, cap. 11.—Rel. Seg. de Cortés, ap. Lorenzana, p. 59.—Camargo, Hist. de Tlascala, MS.—Gomara, Crónica, cap. 54.—Herrera, Hist. General, dec. 2, lib. 6, cap. 11.

[4] " La qual ciudad es tan grande, y de tanta admiracion, que aunque mucho de lo, que de ella podria decir, dexe, lo poco que diré creo es casi increible, porque es muy mayor que Granada, y muy mas fuerte, y de tan buenos Edi- ficios, y de muy mucha mas gente que Granada tenia al tiempo que se gané." Rel. Seg. de Cortés, ap. Lorenzana, p. 58.

[6] " En las Ruinas, que aun hoy se v n en Tlaxcala, se conoce, que no es ponderacion." Ibid., p. 58. Nota del editor, Lorenzana.

The truth is, that Cortés, like Columbus, saw objects through the warm medium of his own fond imagination, giving them a higher tone of coloring and larger dimensions than were strictly warranted by the fact. It was natural that the man who had made such rare discoveries should unconsciously magnify their merits to his own eyes, and to those of others.

The houses were built, for the most part, of mud or earth ; the better sort of stone and lime, or bricks dried in the sun. They were unprovided with doors or windows, but in the apertures for the former hung mats fringed with pieces of copper or something which, by its tinkling sound, would give notice of any one's entrance. The streets were narrow and dark. The population must have been considerable, if, as Cortés asserts, thirty thousand souls were often gathered in the market on a public day. These meetings were a sort of fairs, held, as usual in all the great towns, every fifth day, and attended by the inhabitants of the adjacent country, who brought there for sale every description of domestic produce and manufacture, with which they were acquainted. They peculiarly excelled in pottery, which was considered as equal to the best in Europe.[6] It is a further proof of civilized habits, that the Spaniards found barbers' shops, and baths both of vapor and hot water, familiarly used by the inhabitants. A still higher proof of refinement may be discerned in a vigilant police which repressed everything like disorder among the people.[7]

The city was divided into four quarters, which might rather be called so many separate towns, since they were built at different times, and separated from each other by high stone walls, defining their respective limits. Over each of these districts ruled one of the four great chiefs of the republic, occupying his own spacious mansion, and surrounded by his own immediate vassals. Strange arrangement,—and more strange, that it should have been compatible with social order and tranquillity ! The ancient capital, through one quarter of which flowed the rapid current of the Zahuatl, stretched along the summits and sides of hills, at whose base are now gathered the miserable remains of its once flourishing population.[8] Far beyond, to the south-east, extended

---

[6] "Nullum est fictile vas apud nos, quod arte superet ab illis vasa formata." Martyr, De Orbe Novo, dec. 5, cap. 2.

[7] Camargo, Hist. de Tlascala, MS.—Rel. Seg. de Cortés, ap. Lorenzana, p. 59.—Oviedo, Hist. de las Ind., MS., lib. 33, cap 4.—Ixtlilxochitl, Hist. Chich., MS., cap 83.

The last historian enumerates such a number of contemporary Indian authorities for his narrative, as of itself argues no inconsiderable degree of civilization in the people.

[8] Herrera, Hist. General, dec. 2, lib. 6, cap. 12.

the bold sierra of Tlascala, and the huge Malinche, crowned with the usual silver diadem of the highest Andes, having its shaggy sides clothed with dark-green forests of firs, gigantic sycamores, and oaks whose towering stems rose to the height of forty or fifty feet, unincumbered by a branch. The clouds, which sailed over from the distant Atlantic, gathered round the lofty peaks of the sierra, and, settling into torrents, poured over the plains in the neighborhood of the city, converting them, at such seasons, into swamps. Thunder storms, more frequent and terrible here, than in other parts of the table-land, swept down the sides of the mountains, and shook the frail tenements of the capital to their foundations. But, although the bleak winds of the sierra gave an austerity to the climate, unlike the sunny skies and genial temperature of the lower regions, it was far more favorable to the development of both the physical and moral energies. A bold and hardy peasantry was nurtured among the recesses of the hills, fit equally to cultivate the land in peace, and to defend it in war. Unlike the spoiled child of Nature, who derives such facilities of subsistence from her too prodigal hand, as supersede the necessity of exertion on his own part, the Tlascalan earned his bread—from a soil not ungrateful, it is true—by the sweat of his brow. He led a life of temperance and toil. Cut off by his long wars with the Aztecs from commercial intercourse, he was driven chiefly to agricultural labor, the occupation most propitious to purity of morals and sinewy strength of constitution. His honest breast glowed with the patriotism,—or local attachment to the soil, which is the fruit of its diligent culture; while he was elevated by a proud consciousness of independence, the natural birthright of the child of the mountains.—Such was the race with whom Cortés was now associated, for the achievement of his great work.

Some days were given by the Spaniards to festivity, in which they were successively entertained at the hospitable boards of the four great nobles, in their several quarters of the city. Amidst these friendly demonstrations, however, the general never relaxed for a moment his habitual vigilance, or the strict discipline of the camp; and he was careful to provide for the security of the citizens by prohibiting, under severe penalties, any soldier from leaving his quarters without express permission. Indeed, the severity of his discipline provoked the remonstrance of more than one of his officers, as a superfluous caution; and the Tlascalan

The population of a place, which Cortés could compare with Granada, had dwindled by the beginning of the present century to 3,400 inhabitants, of which less than a thousand were of the Indian stock. See Humboldt, Essai Politique, tom. II. p. 158.

chiefs took some exception at it, as inferring an unreasonable distrust of them.   But when Cortés explained it, as in obedience to
an established military system, they testified their admiration, and
the ambitious young general of the republic proposed to introduce
it, if possible, into his own ranks.[9]

The Spanish commander, having assured himself of the loyalty
of his new allies, next proposed to accomplish one of the great
objects of his new mission, their conversion to Christianity.   By
the advice of father Olmedo, always opposed to precipitate measures, he had deferred this till a suitable opportunity presented
itself for opening the subject.   Such a one occurred when the
chiefs of the state proposed to strengthen the alliance with the
Spaniards, by the intermarriage of their daughters with Cortés
and his officers.   He told them, this could not be, while they continued in the darkness of infidelity.   Then, with the aid of the
good friar, he expounded as well as he could the doctrines of the
Faith ; and, exhibiting the image of the Virgin with the infant
Redeemer, told them that there was the God, in whose worship
alone they would find salvation, while that of their own false
idols would sink them in eternal perdition.

It is unnecessary to burden the reader with a recapitulation of
his homily, which contained, probably, dogmas quite as incomprehensible to the untutored Indian, as any to be found in his own
rude mythology.   But, though it failed to convince his audience,
they listened with a deferential awe.   When he had finished, they
replied, they had no doubt that the God of the Christians must
be a good and a great God, and as such they were willing to give
him a place among the divinities of Tlascala.   The polytheistic
system of the Indians, like that of the ancient Greeks, was of that
accommodating kind which could admit within its elastic folds
the deities of any other religion, without violence to itself.[10]   But
every nation, they continued, must have its own appropriate and
tutelary deities.   Nor could they, in their old age, abjure the service of those who had watched over them from youth.   It would
bring down the vengeance of their gods, and of their own nation,
who were as warmly attached to their religion as their liberties,
and would defend both with the last drop of their blood !

---

[9] Sahagun, Hist. de Nueva España, MS., lib. 12, cap 11.—Camargo, Hist.,
de Tlascala, MS.—Comara, Crónica, cap. 54,   55.—Herrera, Hist. General,
dec, 2, lib. 6, cap, 13.—Bernal Diaz, Hist de la Conquista, cap. 75.

[10] Camargo notices this elastic property in the religions of Anahuac. " Este
modo de hablar y decir que les querrá dar otro Dios, es saber que cuando
estas gentes tenian noticia de algun Dios de buenas propiedades y costumbres,
que le rescibiesen admitiéndole por tal, porque otras gentes advenedizas
trujéron muchos ídolos que tubiéron por Dioses, y á este fin y propósito
decian, que Cortés les traia otro Dios."   Hist. de Tlascala, M S

It was clearly inexpedient to press the matter further, at present. But the zeal of Cortés, as usual, waxing warm by opposition, had now mounted too high for him to calcula' obstacles ; nor would he have shrunk, probably, from the crown of martyrdom in so good a cause. But, fortunately, at least for the success of his temporal cause, this crown was not reserved for him.

The good monk, his ghostly adviser, seeing the course things were likely to take, with better judgment interposed to prevent it. He had no desire, he said, to see the same scenes acted over again as at Cempoalla. He had no relish for forced conversions. They could hardly be lasting. The growth of an hour might well die with the hour. Of what use was it to overturn the altar, if the idol remained enthroned in the heart ? or to destroy the idol itself, if it were only to make room for another ? Better to wait patiently the effect of time and teaching to soften the heart and open the understanding, without which there could be no assurance of a sound and permanent conviction. These rational views were enforced by the remonstrances of Alvarado, Velasquez de Leon, and those in whom Cortés placed most confidence ; till, driven from his original purpose, the military polemic consented to relinquish the attempt at conversion, for the present, and to refrain from a repetition of the scenes, which, considering the different mettle of the population, might have been attended with very different results from those at Cozumel and Cempoalla.[11]

In the course of our narrative, we have had occasion to witness more than once the good effects of the interposition of father Olmedo. Indeed, it is scarcely too much to say, that his discretion in spiritual matters contributed as essentially to the success of the expedition, as did the sagacity and courage of Cortés in temporal. He was a true disciple in the school of Las Casas. His heart was unscathed by that fiery fanaticism which sears and hardens whatever it touches. It melted with the warm glow of Christian charity. He had come out to the New World, as a missionary among the heathen, and he shrunk from no sacrifice, but that of the welfare of the poor benighted

---

[11] Ixtlilxochitl, Hist. Chich., MS., cap. 84.—Gomara, Crónica, cap. 56—Bernal Diaz, Hist. de la Conquista, cap. 76, 77.

This is not the account of Camargo. According to him Cortés gained his point; the nobles led the way by embracing Christianity, and the idols were broken. (Hist. de Tlascala, MS.) But Camargo was himself a Christianized Indian, who lived in the next generation after the Conquest; and may very likely have felt as much desire to relieve his nation from the reproach of infidelity, as a modern Spaniard would to scour out the stain—*mala raza y mancha*—of Jewish or Moorish lineage, from his escutcheon.

flock to whom he had consecrated his days. If he followed the banners of the warrior, it was to mitigate the ferocity of war, and to turn the triumphs of the Cross to a good account for the natives themselves, by the spiritual labors of conversion. He afforded the uncommon example—not to have been looked for, certainly, in a Spanish monk of the sixteenth century—of enthusiasm controlled by reason, a quickening zeal tempered by the mild spirit of toleration.

But, though Cortés abandoned the ground of conversion for the present, he compelled the Tlascalans to break the fetters of the unfortunate victims reserved for sacrifice; an act of humanity unhappily only transient in its effects, since the prisons were filled with fresh victims, on his departure.

He also obtained permission for the Spaniards to perform the services of their own religion unmolested. A large cross was erected in one of the great courts or squares. Mass was celebrated every day in the presence of the army and of crowds of natives, who, if they did not comprehend its full import, were so far edified, that they learned to reverence the religion of their conquerors. The direct interposition of Heaven, however, wrought more for their conversion than the best homily of priest or soldier. Scarcely had the Spaniards left the city,—the tale is told on very respectable authority,—when a thin, transparent cloud descended and settled like a column on the cross, and, wrapping it round in its luminous folds, continued to emit a soft, celestial radiance through the night, thus proclaiming the sacred character of the symbol, on which was shed the halo of divinity ! [12]

The principle of toleration in religious matters being established, the Spanish general consented to receive the daughters of the caciques. Five or six of the most beautiful of the Indian maidens were assigned to as many of his principal officers, after they had been cleansed from the stains of infidelity by the waters of baptism. They received, as usual, on this occasion, good Castilian names, in exchange for the barbarous nomenclature of their own vernacular.[13] Among them, Xicotencatl's daughter, Doña Luisa, as she was called after her baptism, was a princess of the highest estimation and authority in Tlascala. She was given by her father to Alvarado, and their posterity intermarried

---

[12] The miracle is reported by Herrera, (Hist. General, dec. 2, lib. 6, cap. 15,) and *believed* by Solís. Conquista de Méjico, lib, 3, cap. 5.

[13] To avoid the perplexity of selection, it was common for the missionary to give the same names to all the Indians baptized on the same day. Thus, one day was set apart for the Johns, another for the Peters, and so on: an ingenious arrangement, much more for the convenience of the clergy, than of the converts. See Camargo, Hist. de Tlascala, MS.

with the noblest families of Castile. The frank and joyous manners of this cavalier made him a great favorite with the Tlascalans; and his bright, open countenance, fair complexion, and golden locks, gave him the name of *Tonatiuh*, the "Sun." The Indians often pleased their fancies by fastening a *sobriquet*, or some characteristic epithet on the Spaniards. As Cortés was always attended, on public occasions, by Doña Marina, or Malinche, as she was called by the natives, they distinguished him by the same name. By these epithets, originally bestowed in Tlascala, the two Spanish captains were popularly designated among the Indian nations.[14]

While these events were passing, another embassy arrived from the court of Mexico. It was charged, as usual, with a costly donative of embossed gold plate, and rich embroidered stuffs of cotton and feather-work. The terms of the message might well argue a vacillating and timid temper in the monarch, did they not mask a deeper policy. He now invited the Spaniards to his capital, with the assurance of a cordial welcome. He besought them to enter into no alliance with the base and barbarous Tlascalans; and he invited them to take the route of the friendly city of Cholula, where arrangements, according to his orders, were made for their reception.[16]

The Tlascalans viewed with deep regret the general's proposed visit to Mexico. Their reports fully confirmed all he had before heard of the power and ambition of Montezuma. His armies, they said, were spread over every part of the continent. His capital was a place of great strength, and as, from its insular position, all communication could be easily cut off with the adjacent country, the Spaniards, once entrapped there, would be at his mercy. His policy, they represented, was as insidious, as his ambition was boundless. "Trust not his fair words,"

---

[14] Ibid., MS.—Bernal Diaz, Hist. de la Conquista, cap. 74, 77.

According to Camargo, the Tlascalans gave the Spanish commander three hundred damsels to wait on Marina ; and the kind treatment and instruction they received led some of the chiefs, to surrender their own daughters, "con proposito de que *si acaso* algunas se empreñasen quedase entre ellos generacion de hombres tan valientes y temidos."

[16] Bernal Diaz. Hist. de la Conquista, cap. 80.—Rel. Seg. de Cortés, ap. Lorenzana, p. 60.—Martyr, De Orbe Novo, dec. 5, cap. 2.

Cortés notices only one Aztec mission, while Diaz speaks of three. The former, from brevity, falls so much short of the whole truth, and the latter, from forgetfulness perhaps, goes so much beyond it, that it is not always easy to decide between them. Diaz did not compile his narrative till some fifty years after the Conquest ; a lapse of time, which may excuse many errors, but must considerably impair our confidence in the minute accuracy of his details. A more intimate acquaintance with his chronicle does not strengthen this confidence.

they said, "his courtesies, and his gifts. His professions are hollow, and his friendships are false." When Cortés remarked, that he hoped to bring about a better understanding between the emperor and them, they replied, it would be impossible ; however smooth his words, he would hate them at heart.

They warmly protested, also against the general's taking the route of Cholula. The inhabitants, not brave in the open field, were more dangerous from their perfidy and craft. They were Montezuma's tools, and would do his bidding. The Tlascalans seemed to combine with this distrust a superstitious dread of the ancient city, the head-quarters of the religions of Anahuac. It was here that the god Quetzalcoatl held the pristine seat of his empire. His temple was celebrated throughout the land, and the priests were confidently believed to have the power, as they themselves boasted, of opening an inundation from the foundations of his shrine, which should bury their enemies in the deluge. The Tlascalans further reminded Cortés, that, while so many other and distant places had sent to him at Tlascala, to testify their good-will, and offer their allegiance to his sovereigns, Cholula, only six leagues distant, had done neither.—The last suggestion struck the general more forcibly than any of the preceding. He instantly despatched a summons to the city, requiring a formal tender of its submission.

Among the embassies from different quarters which had waited on the Spanish commander, while at Tlascala, was one from Ixtlilxochitl, son of the great Nezahualpilli, and an unsuccessful competitor with his elder brother—as noticed in a former part of our narrative—for the crown of Tezcuco.[16] Though defeated in his pretensions, he had obtained a part of the kingdom, over which he ruled with a deadly feeling of animosity towards his rival, and to Montezuma, who had sustained him. He now offered his services to Cortés, asking his aid, in return, to place him on the throne of his ancestors. The politic general returned such an answer to the aspiring young prince, as might encourage his expectations, and attach him to his interests. It was his aim to strengthen his cause, by attracting to himself every particle of disaffection that was floating through the land.

It was not long before deputies arrived from Cholula, profuse in their expressions of good-will, and inviting the presence of the Spaniards in their capital. The messengers were of low degree, far beneath the usual rank of ambassadors. This was pointed out by the Tlascalans ; and Cortés regarded it as a fresh indignity. He sent in consequence a new summons, declar-

[16] Ante, p. 217.

ıng, if they did not instantly send him a deputation of their principal men, he would deal with them as *rebels* to his own sovereign, the rightful lord of these realms![17] The menace had the desired effect. The Cholulans were not inclined to contest, at least, for the present, his magnificent pretensions. Another embassy appeared in the camp, consisting of some of the highest nobles; who repeated the invitation for the Spaniards to visit their city, and excused their own tardy appearance by apprehensions for their personal safety in the capital of their enemies. The explanation was plausible, and was admitted by Cortés.

The Tlascalans were now more than ever opposed to his projected visit. A strong Aztec force, they had ascertained, lay in the neighborhood of Cholula, and the people were actively placing their city in a posture of defence. They suspected some insidious scheme concerted by Montezuma to destroy the Spaniards.

These suggestions disturbed the mind of Cortés, but did not turn him from his purpose. He felt a natural curiosity to see the venerable city so celebrated in the history of the Indian nations. He had, besides, gone too far to recede, too far, at least, to do so without a show of apprehension, implying a distrust in his own resources, which could not fail to have a bad effect on his enemies, his allies, and his own men. After a brief consultation with his officers, he decided on the route to Cholula.[18]

It was now three weeks since the Spaniards had taken up their residence within the hospitable walls of Tlascala; and nearly six, since they entered her territory. They had been met on the threshold as an enemy, with the determined hostility. They were now to part with the same people, as friends and allies; fast friends, who were to stand by them, side by side, through the whole of their arduous struggle. The result of their visit, therefore, was of the last importance; since on the coöperation of these brave and warlike republicans, greatly depended the ultimate success of the expedition.

---

[17] " Si no viniessen, iria sobre ellos, y los destruira, y procederia contra ellos como contra personas rebeldes; diciéndoles, como todas estas Partes, y otras muy mayores Tierras, y Señorios eran de Vuestra Alteza." (Rel. Seg. de Cortés, ap. Lorenzana, p. 63.) " Rebellion " was a very convenient term, fastened in like manner by the countrymen of Cortés on the Moors for defending the possessions which they had held for eight centuries in the Peninsula. It justified very rigorous reprisals.—(See the History of Ferdinand and Isabella, Part. I. chap. 13, et alibi.)

[18] Rel. Seg. de Cortés, ap. Lorenzana, pp. 62, 63.—Oviedo, Hist. de las Ind., MS., lib 33, cap. 4.—Ixtlilxochitl, Hist. Chich., MS., cap. 84.—Gomara, Crónica, cap. 58.—Martyr, De Orbe Novo, dec, 5, cap. 2.—Herrera, Hist. General, dec. 2, lib. 6, cap. 18.—Sahagun, Hist. de Nueva España. MS., lib. 12. cap. 11.

CHAPTER VI.

CITY OF CHOLULA.—GREAT TEMPLE.—MARCH TO CHOLULA.—
RECEPTION OF THE SPANIARDS.—CONSPIRACY DETECTED.

1519.

THE ancient city of Cholula, capital of the republic of that name, lay nearly six leagues south of Tlascala, and about twenty east, or rather south-east, of Mexico. It was said by Cortés to contain twenty thousand houses within the walls, and as many more in the environs ;[1] though now dwindled to a population of less than sixteen thousand souls.[2] Whatever was its real number of inhabitants, it was unquestionably, at the time of the Conquest, one of the most populous and flourishing cities in New Spain.

It was of great antiquity, and was founded by the primitive races who overspread the land before the Aztecs.[3] We have few particulars of its form of government, which seems to have been cast on a republican model similar to that of Tlascala. This answered so well, that the state maintained its independence down to a very late period, when, if not reduced to vassalage by the Aztecs, it was so far under their control, as to enjoy few of the benefits of a separate political existence. Their connection with Mexico brought the Cholulans into frequent collision with their neighbors and kindred, the Tlascalans. But, although far superior to them in refinement and the various arts of civilization, they were no match in war for the bold mountaineers, the Swiss of Anahuac. The Cholulan capital was the great commercial

---

[1] Rel. Seg., ap. Lorenzana, p. 67.

According to Las Casas, the place contained 30,000 *vecinos* or about 150,000 inhabitants. (Brevissima Relatione della Distruttione dell' Indie Occidentale (Venetia, 1643).) This latter, being the smaller estimate, is *a priori* the most credible ; especially—a rare occurrence—when in the pages of the good bishop of Chiapa.

[2] Humboldt, Essai Politique, tom. III. p. 159.

[3] Veytia carries back the foundation of the city to the Ulmecs, a people who preceded the Toltecs. (Hist. Antig., tom., I. cap. 3, 20.) As the latter, after occupying the land several centuries, have left not a single written record, probably, of their existence, it will be hard to disprove the licentiate's assertion,—still harder to prove it.

emporium of the plateau. The inhabitants excelled in various mechanical arts, especially that of working in metals, the manufacture of cotton and agave cloths, and of a delicate kind of pottery, rivalling, it was said, that of Florence in beauty.[4] But such attention to the arts of a polished and peaceful community naturally indisposed them to war, and disqualified them for coping with those who made war the great business of life. The Cholulans were accused of effeminacy; and were less distinguished—it is the charge of their rivals—by their courage, than their cunning.[5]

But the capital, so conspicuous for its refinement and its great antiquity, was even more venerable for the religious traditions which invested it. It was here that the god Quetzalcoatl paused in his passage to the coast, and passed twenty years in teaching the Toltec inhabitants the arts of civilization. He made them acquainted with better forms of government, and a more spiritualized religion, in which the only sacrifices were the fruits and flowers of the season.[6] It is not easy to determine what he taught, since his lessons have been so mingled with the licentious dogmas of his own priests, and the mystic commentaries of the Christian missionary.[7] It is probable he was one of those rare and gifted beings, who, dissipating the darkness of the age by the illumination of their own genius, are deified by a grateful posterity, and placed among the lights of heaven. .

It was in honor of this benevolent deity, that the stupendous mound was erected, on which the traveller still gazes with admiration as the most colossal fabric in New Spain, rivalling in dimensions, and somewhat resembling in form, the pyramidal structures of ancient Egypt. The date of its erection is unknown; for it was found there when the Aztecs entered on the plateau. It had the form common to the Mexican *teocallis*, that of a truncated pyramid, facing with its four sides the cardinal points, and divided into the same number of terraces. Its original outlines, however, have been effaced by the action of time

---

[4] Herrera, Hist. General, dec. 2, lib. 7, cap. 2.

[5] Camargo, Hist. de Tlascala, MS.—Gomara Crónica, cap. 58.—Torquemada, Monarch. Ind., lib. 3, cap. 19.

[6] Veytia, Hist. Antig., tom. I. cap. 15, et seq.—Sahagun, Hist. de Nueva España, lib. 1, cap. 5; lib. 3.

[7] Later divines have found in these teachings of the Toltec god, or high priest, the germs of some of the great mysteries of the Christian faith, as those of the Incarnation, and the Trinity, for example. In the teacher himself, they recognize no less a person than St. Thomas the Apostle! See the Dissertation of the irrefragable Dr. Mier, with an edifying commentary by Señor Bustamante, ap. Sahagun. (Hist. de Nueva España, tom. I. Suplemento.) The reader will find farther particulars of this matter in *Appendix Part I*, of this History.

and of the elements, while the exuberant growth of shrubs and wild flowers, which have mantled over its surface, give it the appearance of one of those symmetrical elevations thrown up by the caprice of nature, rather than by the industry of man. It is doubtful, indeed, whether the interior be not a natural hill, though it seems not improbable that it is an artificial composition of stone and earth, deeply incrusted, as is certain, in every part, with alternate strata of brick and clay.[8]

The perpendicular height of the pyramid is one hundred and seventy-seven feet. Its base is one thousand four hundred and twenty three feet long, twice as long as that of the great pyramid of Cheops. It may give some idea of its dimensions to state, that its base, which is square, covers about forty-four acres, and the platform on its truncated summit embraces more than one. It reminds us of those colossal monuments of brick work, which are still seen in ruins on the banks of the Euphrates, and, in much higher preservation, on those of the Nile.[9]

On the summit stood a sumptuous temple, in which was the image of the mystic deity, " god of the air, " with ebon features, unlike the fair complexion which he bore upon earth, wearing a mitre on his head waving with *plumes of fire*, with a resplen·dent collar of gold round his neck, pendants of mosaic turquoise in his ears, a jewelled sceptre in one hand, and a shield curiously painted, the emblem of his rule over the winds, in the other.[10] The sanctity of the place, hallowed by hoary tradition, and the magnificence of the temple and its services, made it an object of veneration throughout the land, and pilgrims from the furthest corners of Anahuac came to offer up their devotions at the shrine

---

[8] Such, on the whole, seems to be the judgment of M. de Humboldt, who has examined this interesting monument with his usual care. (Vues des Cordiléres, p. 27, et seq. Essai Politique, tom. II. p. 150, et seq.) The opinion derives strong confirmation from the fact, that a road, cut some years since across the tumulus, laid open a large section of it, in which the alternate layers of brick and clay are distinctly visible. (Ibid., loc. cit.) The present appearance of this monument, covered over with the verdure and vegetable mould of centuries, excuses the scepticism of the more superficial traveller.

[9] Several of the pyramids of Egypt, and the ruins of Babylon, are, as is well known, of brick. An inscription on one of the former, indeed, celebrates this material as superior to stone. (Herodotus, Euterpe, sec. 136.)—Humboldt furnishes an apt illustration of the size of the Mexican *teocalli*, by comparing it to a mass of bricks covering a square four times as large as the *place Vendome*, and of twice the height of the Louvre. Essai Politique, tom. II. p. 152.

[10] A minute account of the costume and insignia of Quetzalcoatl is given by father Sahagun, who saw the Aztec gods before the arm of the Christian convert had tumbled them from " their pride of place." See Hist. de Nueva Espana, lib. 1, cap. 3.

of Quetzalcoatl.[11]   The number of these was so great, as to give an air of mendicity to the motley population of the city; and Cortés, struck with the novelty, tells us, that he saw multitudes of beggars, such as are to be found in the enlightened capitals of Europe,[12]—a whimsical criterion of civilization, which must place our own prosperous land somewhat low in the scale.

Cholula was not the resort only of the indigent devotee. Many of the kindred races had temples of their own in the city, in the same manner as some Christian nations have in Rome, and each temple was provided with its own peculiar ministers for the service of the deity to whom it was consecrated.   In no city was there seen such a concourse of priests, so many processions, such pomp of ceremonial, sacrifice, and religious festivals. Cholula was, in short, what Mecca is among Mahometans, or Jerusalem among Christians; it was the Holy City of Anahuac.[13]

The religious rites were not performed, however, in the pure spirit originally prescribed by its tutelary deity.   His altars, as well as those of the numerous Aztec gods, were stained with human blood; and six thousand victims *are said* to have been annually offered up at their sanguinary shrines![14]   The great number of these may be estimated from the declaration of Cortés, that he counted four hundred towers in the city;[15] yet no temple had more than two, many only one.   High above the rest rose the great "pyramid of Cholula," with its undying fires flinging their radiance far and wide over the capital, and proclaiming to the nations, that there was the mystic worship—alas! how corrupted by cruelty and superstition!—of the good deity who was one day to return and resume his empire over the land.

Nothing could be more grand than the view which met the eye from the area on the truncated summit of the pyramid. Toward the west stretched that bold barrier of porphyritic rock which nature has reared around the Valley of Mexico, with the

---

[11] They came from the distance of two hundred leagues, says Torquemada, Monarch. Ind., lib. 3, cap. 19.

[12] " Hay mucha gente pobre, y que piden entre los Ricos por las Calas y por las Casas, y Mercados, como hacen los Pobres en España, y en otras partes que hay *Gente de razon*." Rel. Seg., ap. Lorenzana, pp. 67, 68.

[13] Torquemada, Monarch. Ind., lib. 3. cap. 19.—Gomara, Crónica, cap. 61.—Camargo, Hist. de Tlascala, MS.

[14] Herrera, Hist. General, dec. 2, lib. 7, cap. 2.—Torquemada, Monarch. Ind., ubi supra.

[15] " E certifico á Vuestra Alteza, que yo conte desde una mezquita quatrocientas, y tantas Torres en la dicha Ciudad, y todas son de Mezquitas." Rel. Seg., ap. Lorenzana, p. 67.

huge Popocatepetl and Iztaccihuatl standing like two colossal sentinels to guard the entrance to the enchanted region. Far away to the east was seen the conical head of Orizaba soaring high into the clouds, and nearer, the barren, though beautifully shaped Sierra de Malinche, throwing its broad shadows over the plains of Tlascala. Three of these are volcanoes higher than the highest mountain peak in Europe, and shrouded in snows which never melt under the fierce sun of the tropics. At the foot of the spectator lay the sacred city of Cholula, with its bright towers and pinnacles sparkling in the sun, reposing amidst gardens and verdant groves, which then thickly studded the cultivated environs of the capital. Such was the magnificent prospect which met the gaze of the Conquerors, and may still, with slight change, meet that of the modern traveller, as from the platform of the great pyramid his eye wanders over the fairest portion of the beautiful plateau of Puebla.[16]

But it is time to return to Tlascala. On the appointed morning, the Spanish army took up its march to Mexico by the way of Cholula. It was followed by crowds of the citizens, filled with admiration at the intrepidity of men who, so few in number, would venture to brave the great Montezuma in his capital. Yet an immense body of warriors offered to share the dangers of the expedition ; but Cortés, while he showed his gratitude for their good-will, selected only six thousand of the volunteers to bear him company.[17] He was unwilling to encumber himself with

---

[16] The city of Puebla de los Angeles was found by the Spaniards soon after the Conquest, on the site of an insignificant village in the territory of Cholula, a few miles to the east of that capital. It, is, perhaps, the most considerable city in New Spain, after Mexico itself, which it rivals in beauty. It seems to have inherited the religious preëminence of the ancient Cholula, being distinguished, like her, for the number and splendor of its churches, the multitude of its clergy, and the magnificence of its ceremonies and festivals. These are fully displayed in the pages of travellers, who have passed through the place on the usual route from Vera Cruz to the capital. (See in particular, Bullock's Mexico, vol. I. chap. 6.) The environs of Cholula, still irrigated as in the days of the Aztecs, are equally remarkable for the fruitfulness of the soil. The best wheat lands, according to a very respectable authority, yield in the proportion of eighty for one. Ward's Mexico, vol. II. p. 270.—See, also, Humboldt, Essai Polique, tom. II. p. 158 ; tom. IV. p. 330.

[17] According to Cortes, a hundred thousand men offered their services on this occasion! " E puesto que yo ge lo defendiesse, y rogué que no fuessen, porque no habia necesidad, todavía me siguiéron hasta cien mil Hombres muy bien aderezados de Guerra, y llegáron con migo hasta dos leguas de la Ciudad: y desde allí por mucha importunidad mia se bolviéron, aunque todavía quedaron en mi compañia hasta cinco ó seis mil de ellos." Rel. Seg., ap. Lorenzana, p. 64.) This, which must have been nearly the whole fighting force of the republic, does not startle Oviedo, (Hist. de las Ind., MS, cap, 4;) nor Gomara, Crónica, cap. 58.

an unwieldy force that might impede his movements; and probably did not care to put himself so far in the power of allies, whose attachment was too recent to afford sufficient guaranty for their fidelity.

After crossing some rough and hilly ground, the army entered on the wide plain which spreads out for miles around Cholula. At the elevation of more than six thousand feet above the sea, they beheld the rich products of various climes growing side by side, fields of towering maize, the juicy aloe, the *chilli* or Aztec pepper, and large plantations of the cactus, on which the brilliant cochineal is nourished. Not a rood of land but was under cultivation;[18] and the soil—an uncommon thing on the table-land—was irrigated by numerous streams and canals, and well shaded by woods, that have disappeared before the rude axe of the Spaniards. Towards evening, they reached a small stream, on the banks of which Cortés determined to take up his quarters for the night, being unwilling to disturb the tranquillity of the city by introducing so large a force into it at an unseasonable hour.

Here he was soon joined by a number of Cholulan caciques and their attendants, who came to view and welcome the strangers. When they saw their Tlascalan enemies in the camp, however, they exhibited signs of displeasure, and intimated an apprehension that their presence in the town might occasion disorder. The remonstrance seemed reasonable to Cortés, and he accordingly commanded his allies to remain in their present quarters, and to join him as he left the city on the way to Mexico.

On the following morning, he made his entrance at the head of his army into Cholula, attended by no other Indians than those from Cempoalla, and a handful of Tlascalans, to take charge of the baggage. His allies, at parting, gave him many cautions respecting the people he was to visit, who, while they affected to despise them as a nation of traders, employed the dangerous arms of perfidy and cunning. As the troops drew near the city, the road was lined with swarms of people of both sexes and every age, old men tottering with infirmity, women with children in their arms, all eager to catch a glimpse of the strangers, whose persons, weapons, and horses were objects of intense curiosity to eyes which had not hitherto encountered them in battle. The Spaniards, in turn, were filled with admiration at the aspect of the Cholulans, much superior in dress and general appearance to the nations they had hitherto seen.

[18] The words of the *Conquistador* are yet stronger. " Ni un palmo de tierra hay que no este labrada." Rel. Seg., ap. Lorenzana, p. 67.

They were particularly struck with the costume of the higher classes, who wore fine embroidered mantles, resembling the graceful *albornoz*, or Moorish cloak, in their texture and fashion.[19] They showed the same delicate taste for flowers as the other tribes of the plateau, decorating their persons with them, and tossing garlands and bunches among the soldiers. An immense number of priests mingled with the crowd, swinging their aromatic censers, while music from various kinds of instruments gave a lively welcome to the visitors, and made the whole scene one of gay, bewildering enchantment. If it did not have the air of a triumphal procession so much as at Tlascala, where the melody of instruments was drowned by the shouts of the multitude, it gave a quiet assurance of hospitality and friendly feeling not less grateful.

The Spaniards were also struck with the cleanliness of the city, the width and great regularity of the streets, which seemed to have been laid out on a settled plan, with the solidity of the houses, and the number and size of the pyramidal temples. In the court of one of these, and its surrounding buildings, they were quartered.[20]

They were soon visited by the principal lords of the place, who seemed solicitous to provide them with accommodations. Their table was plentifully supplied, and, in short, they experienced such attentions as were calculated to dissipate their suspicions, and made them impute those of their Tlascalan friends to prejudice and old national hostility.

In a few days the scene changed. Messengers arrived from

[19] " Los honrados ciudadanos de ella todos trahen *albornoces*, encima de la otra ropa, aunque son diferenciados de los de Africa, porque tienen maneras; pero en la hechura y tela y los rapacejos son muy semejables." Rel. Seg. de Cortés, ap. Lorenzana, p. 67.

[20] Ibid., p. 67.—Ixtlilxochitl, Hist. Chich., MS., cap. 84.—Oviedo, Hist. de las Ind., MS., lib. 33, cap. 4.—Bernal Diaz, Hist, de la Conquista, cap. 82,

The Spaniards compared Cholula to the beautiful Valladolid, according to Herrera, whose description of the entry is very animated. " Saliéronle otro dia á recibir mas de diez mil ciudadanos en diversas tropas, con rosas, flores, pan, aves, i fruitas, i mucha música. Llegaba vn esquadron á dar la bien llegada á Hernando Cortés, i con buena órden se iba apartando, dando lugar á que otro llegase. . . . . En llegando á la ciudad, que pareció mucho á los Castellanos, en el asiento, i perspectiva, á Valladolid, salió la demas gente, quedando mui espantada de ver las figuras, talles, i armas de los Castellanos. Saliéron los sacerdotes con vestiduras blancas, como sobrepellices, i algunas cerradas por delante, los braços defuera, con fluecos de algoden en las orillas. Unos llevaban figuras de ídolos en las manos, otros sahumerios; otros tocaban cornetas, atabalejos, i diversas músicas, i todos iban cantando, i llegaban á encensar û los Castellanos. Con esta pompa entráron en Chulula." Hist. General, dec. 2, lib. 7, cap. 1.

Montezuma, who, after a short and unpleasant intimation to Cortés that his approach occasioned much disquietude to their master, conferred separately with the Mexican ambassadors still in the Castilian camp, and then departed, taking one of the latter along with them. From this time, the deportment of their Cholulan hosts underwent a visible alteration. They did not visit the quarters as before, and, when invited to do so, excused themselves on pretence of illness. The supply of provisions was stinted, on the ground that they were short of maize. These symptoms of alienation, independently of temporary embarrassment, caused serious alarm in the breast of Cortés, for the future. His apprehensions were not allayed by the reports of the Cempoallans, who told him, that in wandering round the city, they had seen several streets barricaded, the *azoteas*, or flat roofs of the houses, loaded with huge stones and other missiles, as if preparatory to an assault, and in some places they had found holes covered over with branches, and upright stakes planted within, as if to embarrass the movements of the cavalry.[21] Some Tlascalans coming in, also, from their camp, informed the general, that a great sacrifice, mostly of children, had been offered up in a distant quarter of the town, to propitiate the favor of the gods, apparently for some intended enterprise. They added, that they had seen numbers of the citizens leaving the city with their women and children, as if to remove them to a place of safety. These tidings confirmed the worst suspicions of Cortés, who had no doubt that some hostile scheme was in agitation. If he had felt any, a discovery by Marina, the good angel of the expedition, would have turned these doubts into certainty.

The amiable manners of the Indian girl had won her the regard of the wife of one of the caciques, who repeatedly urged Marina to visit her house, darkly intimating that in this way she would escape the fate that awaited the Spaniards. The interpreter, seeing the importance of obtaining further intelligence at once, pretended to be pleased with the proposal, and affected, at the same time, great discontent with the white men, by whom she was detained in captivity. Thus throwing the credulous Cholulan off her guard, Marina gradually insinuated herself into her confidence, so far as to draw from her the full account of the conspiracy.

[21] Cortés, indeed, noticed these same alarming appearances on his entering the city, thus suggesting the idea of a premeditated treachery. " Y en el camino topámos muchas señales, de las que los Naturales de esta Provincia nos habian dicho: por que hallamos el camino real cerrado, y hecho otro y algunos hoyos aunque no muchos, y algunas calles de la ciudad tapiadas, y muchas piedras en todas las Azoteas. Y con esto nos hicieron estar mas sobre aviso, y a mayor recaudo," Rel. Seg., ap. Lorenzana, p 64.

It originated, she said, with the Aztec emperor, who had sent rich bribes to the great caciques, and to her husband among others, to secure them in his views. The Spaniards were to t assaulted as they marched out of the capital, when entangled in its streets, in which numerous impediments had been placed to throw the cavalry into disorder. A force of twenty thousand Mexicans was already quartered at no great distance from the city; to support the Cholulans in the assault. It was confidently expected that the Spaniards, thus embarrassed in their movements, would fall an easy prey to the superior strength of their enemy. A sufficient number of prisoners was to be reserved to grace the sacrifices of Cholula; the rest were to be led in fetters to the capital of Montezuma.

While this conversation was going on, Marina occupied herself with putting up such articles of value and wearing apparel as she proposed to take with her in the evening, when she could escape unnoticed from the Spanish quarters to the house of her Cholulan friend, who assisted her in the operation. Leaving her visitor thus employed, Marina found an opportunity to steal away for a few moments, and, going to the general's apartment, disclosed to him her discoveries. He immediately caused the cacique's wife to be seized, and on examination, she fully confirmed the statement of his Indian mistress.

The intelligence thus gathered by Cortés filled him with the deepest alarm. He was fairly taken in the snare. To fight or to fly seemed equally difficult. He was in a city of enemies, where every house might be converted into a fortress, and where such embarrassments were thrown in the way, as might render the manœuvres of his artillery and horse nearly impracticable. In addition to the wily Cholulans, he must cope, under all these disadvantages, with the redoubtable warriors of Mexico. He was like a traveller who has lost his way in the darkness among precipices, where any step may dash him to pieces, and where to retreat or to advance is equally perilous.

He was desirous to obtain still further confirmation and particulars of the conspiracy. He accordingly induced two of the priests in the neighborhood, one of them a person of much influence in the place, to visit his quarters. By courteous treatment, and liberal largesses of the rich presents he had received from Montezuma,—thus turning his own gifts against the giver,—he drew from them a full confirmation of the previous report. The emperor had been in a state of pitiable vacillation since the arrival of the Spaniards. His first orders to the Cholulans were, to receive the strangers kindly. He had recently consulted his oracles anew, and obtained for answer, that Cholula would be the grave of his enemies; for the gods would be sure to support him in avenging the sacrilege offered to the Holy City. So confident were the Aztecs of success, that numerous manacles, or poles with thongs which served as such, were already in the place to secure the prisoners.

Cortés, now feeling himself fully possessed of the facts, dismissed the priests, with injunctions of secrecy, scarcely necessary. He told them it was his purpose to leave the city on the following morning, and requested that they would induce some of the principal caciques to grant him an interview in his quarters. He then summoned a council of his officers, though, as it seems, already determined as to the course he was to take.

The members of the council were differently affected by the startling intelligence, according to their different characters. The more timid, disheartened by the prospect of obstacles which seemed to multiply as they drew nearer the Mexican capital, where for retracing their steps, and seeking shelter in the friendly city of Tlascala. Others, more persevering, but prudent, were for taking the more northerly route, originally recommended by their allies. The greater part supported the general, who was ever of opinion that they had no alternative but to advance. Retreat would be ruin. Half-way measures were scarcely better; and would infer a timidity which must discredit them with both friend and foe. Their true policy was to rely on themselves; to strike such a blow, as should intimidate their enemies, and show them that the Spaniards were as incapable of being circumvented by artifice, as of being crushed by weight of numbers and courage in the open field.

When the caciques, persuaded by the priests, appeared before Cortés, he contented himself with gently rebuking their want of hospitality, and assured them the Spaniards would be no longer a burden to their city, as he proposed to leave it early on the following morning. He requested, moreover, that they would furnish a reinforcement of two thousand men to transport his artillery and baggage. The chiefs, after some consultation, acquiesced in a demand which might in some measure favor their own designs.

On their departure, the general summoned the Aztec ambassadors before him. He briefly acquainted them with his detection of the treacherous plot to destroy his army, the contrivance of which, he said, was imputed to their master, Montezuma. It grieved him much, he added, to find the emperor implicated in so nefarious a scheme, and that the Spaniards must now march as enemies against the prince, whom they had hoped to visit as a friend.

The ambassadors, with earnest protestations, asserted their entire ignorance of the conspiracy; and their belief that Monte-zuma was equally innocent of a crime, which they charged wholly on the Cholulans. It was clearly the policy of Cortés to keep on good terms with the Indian monarch; to profit as long as possible by his good offices; and to avail himself of his fancied security—such feelings of security as the general could inspire him with—to cover his own future operations. He affected to give credit, therefore, to the assertion of the envoys, and declared his unwillingness to believe, that a monarch, who had rendered the Spaniards so many friendly offices, would now consummate the whole by a deed of such unparalleled baseness. The discovery of their twofold duplicity, he added, sharpened his resentment against the Cholulans, on whom he would take such vengeance as should amply requite the injuries done both to Montezuma and the Spaniards. He then dismissed the ambassadors, taking care, notwithstanding this show of confidence, to place a strong guard over them, to prevent communication with the citizens.[22]

That night was one of deep anxiety to the army. The ground they stood on seemed loosening beneath their feet, and any moment might be the one marked for their destruction. Their vigilant general took all possible precautions for their safety, increasing the number of the sentinels, and posting his guns in such a manner as to protect the approaches to the camp. His eyes, it may well be believed, did not close during the night. Indeed, every Spaniard lay down in his arms, and every horse stood saddled and bridled, ready for instant service. But no assault was meditated by the Indians, and the stillness of the hour was undisturbed except by the occasional sounds heard in a populous city, even when buried in slumber, and by the hoarse cries of the priests from the turrets of the *teocallis*, proclaiming through their trumpets the watches of the night.[23]

[22] Bernal Diaz, Hist. de la Conquista, cap. 83.—Gomara, Crónica, cap. 59.—Rel. Seg. de Cortés, ap. Lorenzana, p. 65.—Torquemada, Monarch. Ind., lib. 4, cap. 39.—Oviedo, Hist. de las Ind., MS., lib. 83, cap. 4.—Martyr, De Orbe Novo, dec. 5, cap. 2.—Herrera, Hist. General, dec. 2, lib. 7 cap. 1.—Argensola, Anales, lib. 1, cap. 85.

[23] Las horas de la noche las regulaban por las estrellas, y tocaban los ministros del templo que estaban destinados para este fin, ciertos instrumentos como vocinas, con que hacian conocer all, pueblo el tiempo." Gama, Descr pcion, Parte I, p. 14.

CHAPTER VII.

TERRIBLE MASSACRE.—TRANQUILLITY RESTORED.—REFLECTIONS ON THE MASSACRE.—FURTHER PROCEEDINGS.—ENVOYS FROM MONTEZUMA.

1519.

WITH the first streak of morning light, Cortés was seen on horseback, directing the movements of his little band. The strength of his forces he drew up in the great square or court, surrounded partly by buildings, as before noticed, and, in part by a high wall. There were three gates of entrance, at each of which he placed a strong guard. The rest of his troops, with his great guns, he posted without the inclosure, in such a manner as to command the avenues and secure those within from interruption in their bloody work. Orders had been sent the night before to the Tlascalan chiefs to hold themselves ready, at a concerted signal, to march into the city and join the Spaniards.

The arrangements were hardly completed, before the Cholulan caciques appeared, leading a body of levies, *tamanes*, even more numerous than had been demanded. They were marched, at once, into the square, commanded, as we have seen, by the Spanish infantry which was drawn up under the walls. Cortés then took some of the caciques aside. With a stern air, he bluntly charged them with the conspiracy, showing that he was well acquainted with all the particulars. He had visited their city, he said, at the invitation of their emperor; had come as a friend; had respected the inhabitants and their property; and, to avoid all cause of umbrage, had left a great part of his forces without the walls. They had received him with a show of kindness and hospitality, and, reposing on this, he had been decoyed into the snare, and found this kindness only a mask to cover the blackest perfidy.

The Cholulans were thunderstruck at the accusation. An undefined awe crept over them, as they gazed on the mysterious strangers, and felt themselves in the presence of beings who seemed to have the power of reading the thoughts scarcely formed in their bosoms. There was no use in prevarication or

denial before such judges.   They confessed the whole, and endeavored to excuse themselves by throwing the blame on
Montezuma.   Cortés, assuming an air of higher indignation at
this, assured them that the pretence should not serve, since,
even if well founded, it would be no justification; and he would
now make such an example of them for their treachery, that the
report of it should ring throughout the wide borders of Anahuac !

The fatal signal, the discharge of an arquebuse, was then
given.   In an instant every musket and crossbow was levelled
at the unfortunate Cholulans in the court-yard, and a frightful
volley poured into them as they stood crowded together like a
herd of deer in the centre.   They were taken by surprise, for
they had not heard the preceding dialogue with the chiefs. They
made scarcely any resistance to the Spaniards, who followed up the
discharge of their pieces by rushing on them with their swords;
and as the half-naked bodies of the natives afforded no protection,
they hewed them down with as muc .ease as the reaper mows down
the ripe corn in harvest time.   Son ɔ endeavored to scale the walls,
but only afforded a surer mark to the arquebusiers and archers.
Others threw themselves into the gateways, but were received on
the long pikes of the soldiers who guarded them.   Some few had
better luck in hiding themselves under the heaps of slain with
which the ground was soon loaded.

While this work of death was going on, the countrymen of the
slaughtered Indians, drawn together by the noise of the massacre, had commenced a furious assault on the Spaniards from
without.   But Cortés had placed his battery of heavy guns in a
position that commanded the avenues, and swept off the files of
the assailants as they rushed on.   In the intervals between the
discharges, which, in the imperfect state of the science in that
day, were much longer than in ours, he forced back the press by
charging with the horse into the midst.   The steeds, the guns,
the weapons of the Spaniards were all new to the Cholulans.
Notwithstanding the novelty of the terrific spectacle, the flash of
of fire-arms mingling with the deafening roar of the artillery as
its thunders reverberated among the buildings, the despairing
Indians pushed on to take the places of their fallen comrades.

While this fierce struggle was going forward, the Tlascalans,
hearing the concerted signal, had advanced with quick pace into
the city.   They had bound, by order of Cortés, wreaths of sedge
round their heads, that they might the more surely be distinguished from the Cholulans.[1]   Coming up in the very heat of the

---

[1] " Usáron los de Tlaxcalla de un aviso muy bueno y les dió Hernando
Cortés porque fueran conocidos y no morir entre los enemigos por yerro,
porque sus armas y divisas eran casi de una manera. . . . . y ansí se pusiron,

engagement, they fell on the defenceless rear of the townsmen, who, trampled down under the heels of the Castilian cavalry on one side, and galled by their vindictive enemies on the other, could no longer maintain their ground. They gave way, some taking refuge in the nearest buildings, which, being partly of wood, were speedily set on fire. Others fled to the temples. One strong party, with a number of priests at its head, got possession of the great *teocalli.* There was a vulgar tradition, already alluded to, that on removal of part of the walls, the god would send forth an inundation to overwhelm his enemies. The superstitious Cholulans with great difficulty succeeded in wrenching away some of the stones in the walls of the edifice. But dust, not water, followed. Their false god deserted them in the hour of need. In despair they flung themselves into the wooden turrets that crowned the temple, and poured down stones, javelins, and burning arrows on the Spaniards, as they climbed the great staircase, which, by a flight of one hundred and twenty steps, scaled the face of the pyramid. But the fiery shower fell harmless on the steel bonnets of the Christians, while they availed themselves of the burning shafts to set fire to the wooden citadel, which was speedily wrapt in flames. Still the garrison held out, and though quarter, *it is said*, was offered, only one Cholulan availed himself of it. The rest threw themselves headlong from the parapet, or perished miserably in the flames.[2]

All was now confusion and uproar in the fair city which had so lately reposed in security and peace. The groans of the dying, the frantic supplications of the vanquished for mercy, were mingled with the loud battle-cries of the Spaniards as they rode down their enemy, and with the shrill whistle of the Tlascalans, who gave full scope to the long cherished rancor of ancient rivalry. The tumult was still further swelled by the incessant rattle of musketry, and the crash of falling timbers, which sent up a volume of flame that outshone the ruddy light of morning, making all together a hideous confusion of sights and sounds, that converted the Holy City into a Pandemonium. As resistance slackened, the victors broke into the houses and sacred places, plundering them of whatever valuables they contained, plate, jewels, which were found in some quantity, wearing apparel and provisions, the two last coveted even more than the former by the simple Tlascalans, thus facilitating a division of

en las cabezas unas guirnaldas de esparto á manera de torzales, y con esto eran conocidos los de nuestra parcialidad que no fué pequeño aviso." Camargo, Hist. de Tlascala, MS.

[2]Camargo, Hist. de Tlascala, MS.—Oviedo, Hist. de las Ind., MS., lib. 33, cap. 4, 45.—Torquemada, Monarch. Ind., lib. 4, cap. 40.—Ixtlilxochitl Hist. Chich., MS., cap. 84.—Gomara, Crónica, cap. 60.

the spoil much to the satisfaction of their Christian confederates. Amidst this universal license, it is worthy of remark, the commands of Cortés were so far respected that no violence was offered to women or children, though these, as well as numbers of the men, were made prisoners to be swept into slavery by the Tlascalans. These scenes of violence had lasted some hours, when Cortés, moved by the entreaties of some Cholulan chiefs, who had been reserved from the massacre, backed by the prayers of the Mexican envoys, consented, out of regard, as he said, to the latter, the representatives of Montezuma, to call off the soldiers, and put a stop, as well as he could, to further outrage. Two of the caciques were, also, permitted to go to their countrymen with assurances of pardon and protection to all who would return to their obedience.

These measures had their effect. By the joint efforts of Cortés and the caciques, the tumult was with much difficulty appeased. The assailants, Spaniards and Indians, gathered under their respective banners, and the Cholulans, relying on the assurance of their chiefs, gradually returned to their homes.

The first act of Cortés was, to prevail on the Tlascalan chiefs to liberate their captives.[4] Such was their deference to the Spanish commander that they acquiesced, though not without murmurs, contenting themselves, as they best could, with the rich spoil rifled from the Cholulans, consisting of various luxuries long since unknown in Tlascala. His next care was to cleanse the city from its loathsome impurities, particularly from the dead bodies which lay festering in heaps in the streets and great square. The general, in his letter to Charles the Fifth, admits three thousand slain, most accounts say six, and some swell the amount yet higher. As the eldest and principal cacique was among the number, Cortés assisted the Cholulans in installing a successor in his place.[5] By these pacific measures confidence was gradually restored. The people in the environs, reassured, flocked into the capital to supply the place of the diminished population. The markets were again opened; and the usual avocations of an orderly, industrious community were resumed. Still, the long piles of black and smouldering ruins proclaimed the hurricane which had so lately swept over the city, and the

---

[3] " Matáron casi seis mil personas sin tocar a niños ni mugeres, porque así se les ordenó." Herrera, Hist. General, dec. 2, lib. 7, cap. 2.

[4] Bernal Diaz, Hist. de la Conquista, cap. 83.—Ixtlilxochitl, Hist. Chich., MS., ubi supra.

[5] Bernal Diaz, Hist. de la Conquista, cap. 83.
The descendants of the principal Cholulan cacique are living at this day in Puebla, according to Bustamante. See Gomara, Crónica. *trad de Chimalpain.* (México, 1826,) tom. I. p. 98, nota.

walls surrounding the scene of slaughter in the great square, which were standing more than fifty years after the event, told the sad tale of the Massacre of Cholula.[6]

This passage in their history is one of those that have left a dark stain on the memory of the Conquerors. Nor can we contemplate at this day, without a shudder, the condition of this fair and flourishing capital thus invaded in its privacy, and delivered over to the excesses of a rude and ruthless soldiery. But, to judge the action fairly, we must transport ourselves to the age when it happened. The difficulty that meets us in the outset is, to find a justification of the right of conquest, at all. But it should be remembered, that religious infidelity, at this period, and till a much later, was regarded—no matter whether founded on ignorance or education, whether hereditary or acquired, heretical or Pagan—as a sin to be punished with fire and faggot in this world, and eternal suffering in the next. This doctrine, monstrous as it is, was the creed of the Romish, in other words, of the Christian Church,—the basis of the In-

---

[6] Rel. Seg. de Cortés, ap. Lorenzana, 66.—Camargo, Hist. de Tlascala, MS.—Ixtlilxochitl, Hist. Chich., MS., cap. 84.—Oviedo, Hist. de las Ind., MS., lib. 33, cap. 4, 45.—Bernal Diaz, Hist. de la Conquista, cap. 83.—Gomara, Crónica, cap. 60.—Sahagun, Hist. de Nueva España, MS., lib. 12, cap. 11.

Las Casas, in his printed treatise on the Destruction of the Indies, garnishes his account of these transactions with some additional and rather startling particulars. According to him Cortés caused a hundred or more of the caciques to be impaled or roasted at the stake! He adds the report, that, while the massacre in the court-yard was going on, the Spanish general repeated a scrap of an old *romance*, describing Nero as rejoicing over the burning ruins of Rome:

> "Mira Nero de Tarpeya,
> A Roma como se ardia.
> Gritos dan niños y viejos,
> Y él de nada se dolia."
> (Brevisima Relacion, p. 46.)

This is the first instance, I suspect, on record, of any person being ambitious of finding a parallel for himself in that emperor! Bernal Diaz, who had seen "the interminable narrative," as he calls it, of Las Casas, treats it with great contempt. His own version—one of those chiefly followed in the text—was corroborated by the report of the missionaries, who, after the Conquest, visited Cholula, and investigated the affair with the aid of the priests and several old survivors who had witnessed it. It is confirmed in its substantial details by the other contemporary accounts. The excellent bishop of Chiapa wrote with the avowed object of moving the sympathies of his countrymen in behalf of the oppressed natives; a generous object, certainly, but one that has too often warped his judgment from the strict line of historic impartiality. He was not an eye-witness of the transactions in New Spain, and was much too willing to receive whatever would make for his case, and to "over-red," if I may so say, his argument with such details of blood and slaughter, as, from their very extravagance, carry their own refutation with them.

quisition, and of those other species of religious persecutions, which have stained the annals, at some time or other, of nearly every nation in Christendom.[7] Under this code the territory of the heathen, wherever found, was regarded as a sort of religious waif, which, in default of a legal proprietor, was claimed and taken possession of by the Holy See, and as such was freely given away by the head of the Church, to any temporal potentate whom he pleased, that would assume the burden of conquest.[8] Thus, Alexander the Sixth generously granted a large portion of the Western hemisphere to the Spaniards, and of the Eastern to the Portuguese. These lofty pretensions of the successors of the humble fisherman of Galilee, far from being nominal, were acknowledged and appealed to as conclusive in controver· sies between nations.[9]

With the right of conquest, thus conferred, came, also, the obligation, on which it may be said to have been founded, to

---

[7] For an illustration of the above remark the reader is refered to the closing pages of chap. 7, Part II., of the "History of Ferdinand and Isabella," where I have taken some pains to show how deep settled were these convictions in Spain, at the period with which we are now occupied. The world had gained little in liberality since the age of Dante, who could coolly dispose of the great and good of Antiquity in one of the circles of Hell, because— no fault of theirs, certainly—they had come into the world too soon. The memorable verses, like many others of the immortal bard, are a proof at once of the strength and weakness of the human understanding. They may be cited as a fair exponent of the popular feeling at the beginning of the sixteenth century.

> " Ch'ei non peccaro, e s'egli hanno mercedi,
> Non basta, *perch' e' non ebber battesme,*
> Ch' è porta della fede che tu credi.
> E, se furon dinanzi al Cristianesmo,
> Non adorar debitamente Dio ;
> E di questi cotai son io medesmo.
> Per tai difetti, e non per altro rio,
> Semo perduti, e sol di tanto offesi
> Che sanza speme vivemo in disio.'
>   INFERNO, canto 4.

[8] It is in the same spirit that the laws of Oleron, the maritime code of so high authority in the Middle Ages, abandon the property of the infidel, in common with that of pirates, as fair spoil to the true believer! "S'ilz sont pyrates, pilleurs, ou escumeurs de mer, ou Turcs, *et autres contraires et ennemis de nos tredicte foy catholicque,* chascun peut prendre sur telles manieres de gens, *comme sur chiens, et peut l'on les desrobber et spolier de leurs biens sans pugnition.* C'est le jugement." Jugemens d'Oleron, Art. 45, ap. Collection de Lois Maritimes, par J. M. Pardessus, (ed. Paris, 1828,) tom. I. p. 351.

[9] The famous bull of partition became the basis of the treaty of Tordesillas, by which the Castilian and Portuguese governments determined the boundary line of their respective discoveries; a line that secured the vast empire of Brazil to the latter, which from priority of occupation should have belonged to their rivals. See the History of Ferdinand and Isabella, Part I., chap. 18; Part II., chap. 9,—the closing pages of each.

retrieve the nations sitting in darkness from eternal perdition. This obligation was acknowledged by the best and the bravest, the gownsman in his closet, the missionary, and the warrior in the crusade. However much it may have been debased by temporal motives and mixed up with worldly considerations of ambition and avarice, it was still active in the mind of the Christian conqueror. We have seen how far paramount it was to every calculation of personal interest in the breast of Cortés. The concession of the Pope, then, founded on, and enforcing, the imperative duty of conversion,[10] was the assumed basis—and, in the apprehension of that age, a sound one—of the right of conquest.[11]

This right could not, indeed, be construed to authorize any unnecessary act of violence to the natives. The present expedi-

---

[10] It is the condition, unequivocally expressed and reiterated, on which Alexander VI., in his famous bulls of May 3d and 4th, 1493, conveys to Ferdinand and Isabella full and absolute right over all such territories in the Western World, as may not have been previously occupied by Christian princes. See these precious documents *in extenso*, apud Navarrete, Coleccion de los Viages y Descubrimientos, (Madrid, 1825,) tom. II. Nos. 17, 18.

[11] The ground on which Protestant nations assert a natural right to the fruits of their discoveries in the New World is very different. They consider that the earth was intended for cultivation ; and that Providence never designed that hordes of wandering savages should hold a territory far more than necessary for their own maintenance, to the exclusion of civilized man. Yet it may be thought, as far as improvement of the soil is concerned, that this argument would afford us but an indifferent tenure for much of our own unoccupied and uncultivated territory, far exceeding what is demanded for our present or prospective support. As to a right founded on difference of civilization, this is obviously a still more uncertain criterion. It is to the credit of our Puritan ancestors, that they did not avail themselves of any such interpretation of the law of nature, and still less rely on the powers conceded by King James' patent, asserting rights as absolute, nearly, as those claimed by the Roman See. On the contrary, they established their title to the soil by fair purchase of the Aborigines ; thus forming an honorable contrast to the policy pursued by too many of the settlers on the American continents It should be remarked, that, whatever difference of opinion may have subsisted between the Roman Catholic,—or rather the Spanish and Portuguese nations, —and the rest of Europe, in regard to the true foundation of their titles in a moral view, they have always been content, in their controversies with one another, to rest them exclusively on priority of discovery. For a brief view of the discussion, see Vattel, (Droit des Gens, sec. 209,) and especially Kent, (Commentaries on American Law, vol. III. lec. 51,) where it is handled with much perspicuity and eloquence. The argument, as founded on the law of nations, may be found in the celebrated case of Johnson *v.* McIntosh. (Wheaton, Reports of Cases in the Supreme Court of the United States, vol. VIII. p. 543, et seq.) If it were not treating a grave discussion too lightly, I should crave leave to refer the reader to the renowned Diedrich Knickerbocker's History of New York, (book 1, chap. 5,) for a luminous disquisition on this knotty question. At all events, he will find there the popular arguments subjected to the test of ridicule ; a test, showing, more than any reasoning can, how much, or rather how little, they are really worth.

tion, up to the period of its history at which we are now arrived, had probably been stained with fewer of such acts than almost any similar enterprise of the Spanish discoverers in the New World. Throughout the campaign, Cortés had prohibited all wanton injuries to the natives, in person or property, and had punished the perpetrators of them with exemplary severity. He had been faithful to his friends, and, with perhaps a single exception, not unmerciful to his foes. Whether from policy or principle, it should be recorded to his credit; though, like every sagacious mind, he may have felt, that principle and policy go together.

He had entered Cholula as a friend, at the invitation of the Indian emperor, who had a real, if not avowed, control over the state. He had been received as a friend, with every demonstration of good-will; when, without any offence of his own or his followers, he found they were to be the victims of an insidious, plot,—that they were standing on a mine which might be sprung at any moment, and bury them all in its ruins. His safety, as he truly considered, left no alternative but to anticipate the blow of his enemies. Yet who can doubt that the punishment thus inflicted was excessive,—that the same end might have been attained by directing the blow against the guilty chiefs, instead of letting it fall on the ignorant rabble, who but obeyed the commands of their masters? But when was it ever seen, that fear, armed with power, was scrupulous in the exercise of it? or that the passions of a fierce soldiery, inflamed by conscious injuries, could be regulated in the moment of explosion?

We shall, perhaps, pronounce more impartially on the conduct of the Conquerors, if we compare it with that of our own contemporaries under somewhat similar circumstances. The atrocities at Cholula were not so bad as those inflicted on the descendants of these very Spaniards, in the late war of the Peninsula, by the most polished nations of our time; by the British at Badajoz, for example, — at Taragona, and a hundred other places, by the French. The wanton butchery, the ruin of property, and, above, all, those outrages worse than death, from which the female part of the population were protected at Cholula, show a catalogue of enormities quite as black as those imputed to the Spaniards, and without the same apology for resentment,—with no apology, indeed, but that afforded by a brave and patriotic resistance. The consideration of these events, which, from their familiarity, make little impression on our senses, should render us more lenient in our judgments of the past, showing, as they do, that man in a state of excitement, savage or civilized, is much the same in every age. It may teach us,—it is one of the best lessons of history,—that, since such are the *inevitable* evils of war, even among the most polished people, those who hold the destinies of nations in their hands, whether rulers or legislators, should submit to every sacrifice, save that of honor, before authorizing an appeal to arms. The extreme solicitude to avoid these calamities, by the aid of peaceful congresses and impartial mediation, is, on the whole, the strongest evidence, stronger than that afforded by the progress of science and art, of our boasted advance in civilization.

It is far from my intention to vindicate the cruel deeds of the old Conquerors. Let them lie heavy on their heads. They were an iron race, who periled life and fortune in the cause; and, as they made little account of danger and suffering for themselves, they had little sympathy to spare for their unfortunate enemies. But, to judge them fairly, we must not do it by the lights of our own age. We must carry ourselves back to theirs, and take the point of view afforded by the civilization of their time. Thus only can we arrive at impartial criticism in reviewing the generations that are past. We must extend to them the same justice which we shall have occasion to ask from Posterity, when, by the light of a higher civilization, it surveys the dark or doubtful passages in our own history, which hardly arrest the eye of the contemporary.

But, whatever be thought of this transaction in a moral view, as a stroke of policy, it was unquestionable. The nations of Anahuac had beheld, with admiration mingled with awe, the little band of Christian warriors steadily advancing along the plateau in face of every obstacle, overturning army after army with as much ease, apparently, as the good ship throws off the angry billows from her bows, or rather like the lava, which, rolling from their own volcanoes, holds on its course unchecked by obstacles, rock, tree, or building, bearing them along, or crushing and consuming them in its fiery path. The prowess of the Spaniards—"the white gods," as they were often called [12]—made them to be thought invincible. But it was not till their arrival at Cholula, that the natives learned how terrible was their vengeance,—and they trembled!

None trembled more than the Aztec emperor on his throne among the mountains. He read in these events the dark characters traced by the finger of Destiny.[13] He felt his empire

---

[12] *Los Dioses blancos.*—Camargo, Hist. de Tlascala, MS.—Torquemada, Monarch. Ind., lib. 4, cap. 40.

[13] Sahagun, Hist. de Nueva España, MS., lib. 12, cap. 11.

In an old Aztec harangue, made a a matter of form on the accession of a prince, we find the following remarkable prediction. "Perhaps ye are dismayed at the prospect of the terrible calamities that are one day to overwhelm

melting away like a morning mist. He might well feel so.
Some of the most important cities in the neighborhood of Cholula, intimidated by the fate of that capital, now sent their envoys to the Castilian camp, tendering their allegiance, and pro-
pitiating the favor of the strangers by rich presents of gold and
slaves.[14]   Montezuma, alarmed at these signs of defection, took
counsel again of his impotent deities ; but, although the altars
smoked with fresh hecatombs of human victims, he obtained no
cheering response. He determined, therefore, to send another
embassy to the Spaniards, disavowing any participation in the
conspiracy of Cholula.

Meanwhile Cortés was passing his time in that capital. He
thought that the impression produced by the late scenes, and by
the present restoration of tranquillity, offered a fair opportunity
for the good work of conversion. He accordingly urged the citizens to embrace the Cross, and abandon the false guardians who
had abandoned them in their extremity. But the traditions of
centuries rested on the Holy City, shedding a halo of glory
around it as " the sanctuary of the gods," the religious capital of
Anahuac. It was too much to expect that the people would
willingly resign this preëminence, and descend to the level of an
ordinary community. Still Cortés might have pressed the matter, however unpalatable, but for the renewed interposition of
the wise Olmedo, who persuaded him to postpone it till after
the reduction of the whole country.[15]

The Spanish general, however, had the satisfaction to break
open the cages in which the victims for sacrifice were confined,
and to dismiss the trembling inmates to liberty and life. He
also seized upon the great *teocalli,* and devoted that portion of
the building, which, being of stone, had escaped the fury of the
flames, to the purposes of a Christian church ; while a crucifix
of stone and lime, of gigantic dimensions, spreading out its arms
above the city, proclaimed that the population below was under
the protection of the Cross. On the same spot now stands a
temple overshadowed by dark cypresses of unknown antiquity,
and dedicated to Our Lady *de los Remedios.* An image of the
Virgin presides over it, *said* to have been left by the Conqueror

---

us, calamities foreseen and foretold, though not felt, by our fathers ! . . . . .
When the destruction and desolation of the empire shall come, when all shall
be plunged in darkness, when the hour shall arrive in which they shall make
us slaves throughout the land, and we shall be condemned to the lowest and
most degrading offices !'' (Ibid., lib. 6, cap 16.) This random shot of pro-
phecy, which I have rendered literally, shows how strong and settled was the
apprehension of some impending revolution.
[14] Herrera, Hist. General, dec. 2, lib. 7, cap. 3.
[15] Bernal Diaz, Hist. de la Conquista, cap. 83.

himself; [16] and an Indian ecclesiastic, a descendant of the ancient Cholulans, performs the peaceful services of the Roman Catholic communion, on the spot where his ancestors celebrated the sanguinary rites of the mystic Quetzalcoatl.[17]

During the occurrence of these events, envoys arrived from Mexico. They were charged, as usual, with a rich present of plate and ornaments of gold, among others, artificial birds in imitation of turkeys, with plumes of the same precious metal. To these were added fifteen hundred cotton dresses of delicate fabric. The emperor even expressed his regret at the catastrophe of Cholula, vindicated himself from any share in the conspiracy, which he said had brought deserved retribution on the heads of its authors, and explained the existence of an Aztec force in the neighborhood by the necessity of repressing some disorders there.[18]

One cannot contemplate this pusillanimous conduct of Montezuma without mingled feelings of pity and contempt. It is not easy to reconcile his assumed innocence of the plot with many circumstances connected with it. But it must be remembered here and always, that his history is to be collected solely from Spanish writers and such of the natives as flourished after the Conquest, when the country had become a colony of Spain. Not an Aztec record of the primitive age survives, in a form capable of interpretation.[19] It is the hard fate of this unfortunate monarch, to be wholly indebted for his portraiture to the pencil of his enemies.

More than a fortnight had elapsed since the entrance of the Spaniards into Cholula, and Cortés now resolved without loss of

---

[16] Veytia, Hist. Antig., tom. I cap. 13.

[17] Humboldt, Vues des Cordillères, p. 32.

[18] Rel. Seg. de Cortés, ap. Lorenzana, p. 69.—Gomara, Crónica, cap. 63.—Oviedo, Hist. de las Ind., MS., lib. 33, cap. 5.—Ixtlilxochitl, Hist. Chich., MS, cap. 84.

[19] The language of the text may appear somewhat too unqualified, considering that three Aztec codices exist with interpretations. (See Ante, Vol. I. pp. 103, 104.) But they contain very few and general allusions to Montezuma, and these strained through commentaries of Spanish monks, oftentimes manifestly irreconcilable with the genuine Aztec notions. Even such writers as Ixtlilxochitl and Camargo, from whom, considering their Indian descent, we might expect more independence, seem less solicitous to show this, than their loyalty to the new faith and country of their adoption. Perhaps the most honest Aztec record of the period is to be obtained from the volumes, the twelfth book, particularly, of father Sahagun, embodying the traditions of the natives soon after the Conquest. This portion of his great work was rewritten by its author, and considerable changes were made in it, at a later period of his life. Yet it may be doubted if the reformed version reflects the traditions of the country as faithfully as the original, which is still in manuscript, and which I have chiefly followed.

time to resume his march towards the capital. His rigorous reprisals had so far intimidated the Cholulans, that he felt assured he should no longer leave an active enemy in his rear, to annoy him in case of retreat. He had the satisfaction, before his departure, to heal the feud—in outward appearance, at least —that had so long subsisted between the Holy City and Tlascala, and which, under the revolution which so soon changed the destinies of the country, never revived.

It was with some disquietude that he now received an application from his Cempoallan allies to be allowed to withdraw from the expedition, and return to their own homes. They had incurred too deeply the resentment of the Aztec emperor, by their insults to his collectors, and by their coöperation with the Spaniards, to care to trust themselves in his capital. It was in vain Cortés endeavored to reassure them, by promises of his protection. Their habitual distrust and dread of "the great Montezuma" were not to be overcome. The general learned their determination with regret, for they had been of infinite service to the cause by their stanch fidelity and courage. All this made it the more difficult for him to resist their reasonable demand. Liberally recompensing their services, therefore, from the rich wardrobe and treasures of the emperor, he took leave of his faithful followers, before his own departure from Cholula. He availed himself of their return to send letters to Juan de Escalante, his lieutenant at Vera Cruz, acquainting him with the successful progress of the expedition. He rejoined on that officer to strengthen the fortifications of the place, so as the better to resist any hostile interference from Cuba,—an event for which Cortés was ever on the watch,—and to keep down revolt among the natives. He especially commended the Totonacs to his protection, as allies whose fidelity to the Spaniards exposed them, in no slight degree, to the vengeance of the Aztecs.[20]

[20] Bernal Diaz, Hist. de la Conquista, cap. 84, 85.—Rel. Seg. de Cortés, ap. Lorenzana, p. 67.—Gomara, Crónica, cap. 60.—Oviedo, Hist. de las Ind., MS., lib. 33, cap. 5.

CHAPTER VIII.

MARCH RESUMED.—ASCENT OF THE GREAT VOLCANO.—VALLEY OF MEXICO.—IMPRESSION ON THE SPANIARDS.—CONDUCT OF MONTEZUMA.—THEY DESCEND INTO THE VALLEY.

1519.

EVERYTHING being now restored to quiet in Cholula, the allied army of Spaniards and Tlascalans set forward in high spirits, and resumed the march on Mexico. The road lay through the beautiful savannas and luxuriant plantations that spread out for several leagues in every direction. On the march, they were met occasionally by embassies from the neighboring places, anxious to claim the protection of the white men, and to propitiate them by gifts, especially of gold, for which their appetite was generally known throughout the country.

Some of these places were allies of the Tlascalans, and all showed much discontent with the oppressive rule of Montezuma. The natives cautioned the Spaniards against putting themselves in his power, by entering his capital ; and they stated, as evidence of his hostile disposition, that he had caused the direct road to it to be blocked up, that the strangers might be compelled to choose another, which, from its narrow passes and strong positions, would enable him to take them at great disadvantage.

The information was not lost on Cortés, who kept a strict eye on the movements of the Mexican envoys, and redoubled his own precautions against surprise.[1] Cheerful and active, he was ever where his presence was needed, sometimes in the van, at others in the rear, encouraging the weak, stimulating the sluggish, and striving to kindle in the breasts of others the same courageous spirit which glowed in his own. At night he never omitted to go the rounds, to see that every man was at his post. On one occasion, his vigilance had well-nigh proved fatal to him. He approached so near a sentinel, that the man, unable to dis-

---

[1] Andauamos," says Diaz, in the homely, but expressive Spanish proverb, " la barba sobre el ombro." Hist. de la Conquista, cap. 86.

tinguish his person in the dark, levelled his crossbow at him, when fortunately an exclamation of the general, who gave the watch-word of the night, arrested a movement, which might else have brought the campaign to a close, and given a respite for some time longer to the empire of Montezuma.

The army came at length to the place mentioned by the friendly Indians, where the road forked, and one arm of it was found, as they had foretold, obstructed with large trunks of trees, and huge stones which had been strewn across it. Cortés inquired the meaning of this from the Mexican ambassadors. They said it was done by the emperor's orders, to prevent their taking a route which, after some distance, they would find nearly impracticable for the cavalry. They acknowledged, however, that it was the most direct road ; and Cortés, declaring that this was enough to decide him in favor of it, as the Spaniards made no account of obstacles, commanded the rubbish to be cleared away. Some of the timber might still be seen by the road-side, as Bernal Diaz tells us, many years after. The event left little doubt in the general's mind of the meditated treachery of the Mexicans. But he was too politic to betray his suspicions.[2]

They were now leaving the pleasant champaign country, as the road wound up the bold sierra which separates the great plateaus of Mexico and Puebla. The air, as they ascended, became keen and piercing ; and the blasts, sweeping down the frozen sides of the mountains, made the soldiers shiver in their thick harness of cotton, and benumbed the limbs of both men and horses.

They were passing between two of the highest mountains on the North American continent ; Popocatepetl, " the hill that smokes," and Iztaccihuatl, or " white woman,"[3]—a name suggested, doubtless, by the bright robe of snow spread over its broad and broken surface. A puerile superstition of the Indians regarded these celebrated mountains as gods, and Iztaccihuatl as the wife of her more formidable neighbor.[4] A tradition of a higher character described the northern volcano, as the abode of the departed spirits of wicked rulers, whose fiery agonies, in their prison-house, caused the fearful bellowings, and convulsions

[2] Ibid., ubi supra.—Rel. Seg. de Cortés, ap. Lorenzana, p. 70.—Torquemada, Monarch. Ind. lib. 4, cap., 41.

[3] " Llamaban al volcan Popocatépetl, y á la sierra nevada Iztaccihuatl, que quiere decir la sierra que humea, y la blanca muger." Camargo, Hist. de Tlascala, MS.

[4] " La Sierra nevada y el volcan los tenian por Dioses ; y que el volcan la Sierra nevada eran marido y muger." Ibid., MS.

In times of eruption. It was the classic fable of Antiquity.[6] These superstitious legends had invested the mountain with a mysterious horror, that made the natives shrink from attempting its ascent, which, indeed, was from natural causes a work of incredible difficulty.

The great *volcan*,[6] as Popocatepetl was called, rose to the enormous height of 17,852 feet above the level of the sea ; more than 2000 feet above the " monarch of mountains,"—the highest elevation in Europe.[7] During the present century, it has rarely given evidence of its volcanic origin, and " the hill that smokes" has almost forfeited its claim to the appellation. But at the time of the Conquest it was frequently in a state of activity, and raged with uncommon fury while the Spaniards were at Tlascala ; an evil omen it was thought, for the natives of Anahuac. Its head, gathered into a regular cone by the deposit of successive eruptions, wore the usual form of volcanic mountains, when not disturbed by the falling in of the crater. Soaring towards the skies, with its silver sheet of everlasting snow, it was seen far and wide over the broad plains of Mexico and Puebla, the first object which the morning sun greeted in his rising, the last where his evening rays were seen to linger, shedding a glorious effulgence over its head, that contrasted strikingly with the ruinous waste of sand and lava immediately below, and the deep fringe of funereal pines that shrouded its base.

The mysterious terrors which hung over the spot, and the wild love of adventure, made some of the Spanish cavaliers desirous to attempt the ascent, which the natives declared no man could accomplish and live. Cortés encouraged them in the enterprise, willing to show the Indians that no achievement was above the dauntless daring of his followers. One of his captains, accordingly, Diego Ordaz, with nine Spaniards, and several Tlascalans, encouraged by their example, undertook the ascent. It was attended with more difficulty than had been anticipated.

---

[6] Gomara, Crónica, cap. 62

> " Ætna Giganteos nunquam tactura triumphos,
> Enceladi bustum, qui saucia terga revinctus
> Spirat inexhaustum flagranti pectore sulphur."
> CLAUDIAN, De Rapt. Pros., lib. 1, v. 152

[6] The old Spaniards called any lofty mountain by that name, though never having given signs of combustion. Thus, Chimborazo was called *a volcan de nieve*, or "snow volcano"; (Humboldt, Essai Politique, tom. I. p. 162; and that enterprising traveller, Stephens, notices the *volcan de agua*, " water volcano," in the neighborhood of Antigua Guatemala. Incidents of Travel in Chiapas Central America, and Yucatan, (New York, 1841,) vol. I chap. 13.

[7] Mont Blanc, according to M. de Saussure, is 15,070 feet high. For the estimate of Popocatepetl, see an elaborate communication in the *Revista Mexicana*, tom. II. No. 4

The lower region was clothed with a dense forest, so thickly matted, that in some places it was scarcely possible to penetrate it.   It grew thinner, however, as they advanced, dwindling, by degrees, into a straggling. stunted vegetation, till, at the height of somewhat more than thirteen thousand feet, it faded away altogether.   The Indians who had held on thus far, intimidated by the strange subterraneous sounds of the volcano, even then in a state of combustion, now left them.   The track opened on a black surface of glazed volcanic sand and of lava, the broken fragments of which, arrested in its boiling progress in a thousand fantastic forms, opposed continual impediments to their advance.   Amidst these, one huge rock, the *Pico del Fraile,* a conspicuous object from below, rose to the perpendicular height of a hundred and fifty feet, compelling them to take a wide circuit. They soon came to the limits of perpetual snow, where new difficulties presented themselves, as the treacherous ice gave an imperfect footing, and a false step might precipitate them into the frozen chasms that yawned around.   To increase their distress, respiration in these aerial regions became so difficult, that every effort was attended with sharp pains in the head and limbs.   Still they pressed on, till, drawing nearer the crater, such volumes of smoke, sparks, and cinders were belched forth from its burning entrails, and driven down the sides of the mountain, as nearly suffocated and blinded them.   It was too much even for their hardy frames to endure, and, however reluctantly, they were compelled to abandon the attempt on the eve of its completion.   They brought back some huge icicles,— a curious sight in these tropical regions,—as a trophy of their achievement, which, however imperfect, was sufficient to strike the minds of the natives with wonder, by showing that with the Spaniards the most appalling and mysterious perils were only as pastimes.   The undertaking was eminently characteristic of the bold spirit of the cavalier of that day, who, not content with the dangers that lay in his path, seemed to court them from the mere Quixotic love of adventure.   A report of the affair was transmitted to the Emperor Charles the Fifth, and the family of Ordaz was allowed to commemorate the exploit by assuming a burning mountain on their escutcheon.[8]

The general was not satisfied with the result.   Two years

[8] Rel. Seg. de Cortés. ap. Lorenzana. p. 70.—Oviedo, Hist. de las Ind., MS., lib. 33. cap. 5.—Bernal Diaz, Hist. de la Conquista, cap. 78.

The latter writer speaks of the ascent as made when the army lay at Tlascala, and of the attempt as perfectly successful.   The general's letter, written soon after the event, with no motive for misstatement, is the better authority. See, also, Herrera, Hist. General, dec. 2, lib. 6, cap. 18.—Rel. d'un gent. ap. Ramusio, tom. III. p. 308.—Gomara, Crónica, cap. 62.

after, he sent up another party, under Francisco Montano, a cavalier of determined resolution. The object was to obtain sulphur to assist in making gunpowder for the army. The mountain was quiet at this time, and the expedition was attended with better success. The Spaniards, five in number, climbed to the very edge of the crater, which presented an irregular ellipse at its mouth, more than a league in circumference. Its depth might be from eight hundred to a thousand feet. A lurid flame burned gloomily at the bottom, sending up a sulphureous steam, which, cooling as it rose, was precipitated on the sides of the cavity. The party cast lots, and it fell on Montano himself, to descend in a basket into this hideous abyss, into which he was lowered by his companions to the depth of four hundred feet! This was repeated several times, till the adventurous cavalier had collected a sufficient quantity of sulphur for the wants of the army. This doughty enterprise excited general admiration at the time. Cortés concludes his report of it, to the emperor, with the judicious reflection, that it would be less inconvenient, on the whole, to import their powder from Spain.[9]

But it is time to return from our digression, which may, perhaps, be excused, as illustrating, in a remarkable manner, the chimerical spirit of enterprise,—not inferior to that in his own romances of chivalry,—which glowed in the breast of the Spanish cavalier in the sixteenth century.

The army held on its march through the intricate gorges of the sierra. The route was nearly the same as that pursued at the present day by the courier from the capital to Puebla, by the was of Mecameca. It was not that usually taken by travellers from Vera Cruz, who follow the more circuitous road round the northern base of Iztaccihuatl, as less fatiguing than the other, though inferior in picturesque scenery and romantic points of

---

[9] Rel. Ter. y Quarta de Cortés, ap. Lorenzana, pp. 318, 380.—Herrera, Hist. General, dec. 3, lib. 3, cap. 1.—Oviedo, Hist. de las Ind., MS., lib. 33, cap. 41.

M. de Humboldt doubts the fact of Montaño's descent into the crater, thinking it more probable that he obtained the sulphur through some lateral crevice in the mountain. (Essai Politique, tom 1. p. 164.) No attempt—at least, no successful one—has been made to gain the summit of Popocatepetl, since this of Montaño, till the present century. In 1827, it was reached in two expeditions, and again in 1833 and 1834. A very full account of the last, containing many interesting details and scientific observations, was written by Federico de Gerolt, one of the party, and published in the periodical already referred to. (Revista Mexicana, tom. I. pp 461-482.) The party from the topmast peak, which commanded a full view of the less elevated Iztaccihuatl saw no vestage of a crater in that mountain, contrary to the opinion usually received.

[10] Humboldt, Essai Politique, tom. IV p 17.

view. The icy winds, that now swept down the sides of the mountains, brought with them a tempest of arrowy sleet and snow, from which the Christians suffered even more than the Tlascalans, reared from infancy among the wild solitudes of their own native hills. As night came on, their sufferings would have been intolerable, but they luckily found a shelter in the commodious stone buildings which the Mexican government had placed at stated intervals along the roads for the accommodation of the traveller and their own couriers. It little dreamed it was providing a protection for its enemies.

The troops, refreshed by a night's rest, succeeded, early on the following day, in gaining the crest of the sierra of Ahualco, which stretches like a curtain between the two great mountains on the north and south. Their progress was now comparatively easy, and they marched forward with a buoyant step, as they felt they were treading the soil of Montezuma.

They had not advanced far, when, turning an angle of the sierra, they suddenly came on a view which more than compensated the toils of the preceding day. It was that of the Valley of Mexico, or Tenochtitlan, as more commonly called by the natives ; which, with its picturesque assemblage of water, woodland and cultivated plains, its shining cities and shadowy hills, was spread out like some gay and gorgeous panorama before them. In the highly rarefied atmosphere of these upper regions, even remote objects have a brilliancy of coloring and a distinctness of outline which seem to annihilate distance.[11] Stretching far away at their feet, were seen noble forests of oak, sycamore, and cedar, and beyond, yellow fields of maize and the towering maguey, intermingled with orchards and blooming gardens ; for flowers, in such demand for their religious festivals, were even more abundant in this populous valley than in other parts of Anahuac. In the centre of the great basin were beheld the lakes, occupying then a much larger portion of its surface than at present ; their borders thickly studded with towns and hamlets, and, in the midst,—like some Indian empress with her coronal of pearls,—the fair city of Mexico, with her white towers and pyramidal temples, reposing, as it were, on the bosom of the waters,—the far-famed " Venice of the Aztecs." High over all rose the royal hill of Chapoltepec, the residence of the Mexican monarchs, crowned with the same grove of gigantic cypresses, which at this day fling their broad shadows over the land. In the distance beyond the blue waters of the lake, and

[11] The lake of Tezcuco, on which stood the capital of Mexico, is 2277 metres, nearly 7500 feet, above the sea. Humboldt, Essai Politique, tom II. p. 45.

nearly screened by intervening foliage, was seen a shining speck, the rival capital of Tezcuco, and, still further on, the dark belt of porphyry, girdling the Valley around, like a rich setting which Nature had devised for the fairest of her jewels.

Such was the beautiful vision which broke on the eyes of the Conquerors. And even now, when so sad a change has come over the scene ; when the stately forests have been laid low, and the soil, unsheltered from the fierce radiance of a tropical sun, is in many places abandoned to sterility ; when the waters have retired, leaving a broad and ghastly margin white with the incrustation of salts, while the cities and hamlets on their borders have mouldered into ruins ;—even now that desolation broods over the landscape, so indestructible are the lines of beauty which Nature has traced on its features, that no traveller, how-ever cold, can gaze on them with any other emotions than those of astonishment and rapture.[12]

What, then, must have been the emotions of the Spaniards, when, after working their toilsome way into the upper air, the cloudy tabernacle parted before their eyes, and they beheld these fair scenes in all their pristine magnifience and beauty ! It was like the spectacle which greeted the eyes of Moses from the summit of Pisgah, and, in the warm glow of their feelings, they cried out, " It is the promised land ! " [13]

But these feelings of admiration were soon followed by others of a very different complexion ; as they saw in all this the evi-dences of a civilization and power far superior to anything they had yet encountered. The more timid, disheartened by the prospect, shrunk from a contest so unequal, and demanded, as they had done on some former occasions, to be led back again to Vera Cruz. Such was not the effect produced on the sanguine spirit of the general. His avarice was sharpened by the display of the dazzling spoil at his feet ; and, if he felt a natural anxiety at the formidable odds, his confidence was renewed, as he gazed on the lines of his veterans, whose weather-beaten visages and battered armor told of battles won and difficulties surmounted, while his bold barbarians, with appetites, whetted by the view of their enemies' country, seemed like eagles on the mountains, ready to pounce upon their prey. By argument, entreaty, and

[12] It is unnecessary to refer to the pages of modern travellers, who however they may differ in taste, talent, or feeling, all concur in the impressions pro-duced on them by the sight of this beautiful valley.

[13] Torquemada, Monarch Ind., lib. 4, cap. 41

It may call to the reader's mind the memorable view of the fair plains of Italy which Hannibal displayed to his hungry barbarians, after a similar march through the wild passes of the Alps, as reported by the prince of historic painters. Livy, Hist., lib. 21, cap. 35.

menace, he endeavored to restore the faltering courage of the soldiers, urging them not to think of retreat, now that they had reached the goal for which they had panted; and the golden gates were open to receive them.   In these efforts, he was well seconded by the brave cavaliers, who held honor as dear to them as fortune ; until the dullest spirits caught somewhat of the enthusiasm of their leaders, and the general had the satisfaction to see his hesitating columns, with their usual buoyant step, once more on their march down the slopes of the sierra.[14]

With every step of their progress, the woods became thinner ; patches of cultivated land more frequent ; and hamlets were seen in the green and sheltered nooks, the inhabitants of which, coming out to meet them, gave the troops a kind reception. Everywhere they heard complaints of Montezuma, especially of the unfeeling manner in which he carried off their young men to recruit his armies, and their maidens for his harem.   These symptoms of discontent were noticed with satisfaction by Cortés, who saw that Montezuma's "mountain-throne," as it was called, was, indeed, seated on a volcano, with the elements of combustion so active within, that it seemed as if any hour might witness an explosion.   He encouraged the disaffected natives to rely on his protection, as he had come to redress their wrongs.   He took advantage, moreover, of their favorable dispositions, to scatter among them such gleams of spiritual light as time and the preaching of father Olmedo could afford.

He advanced by easy stages, somewhat retarded by the crowd of curious inhabitants gathered on the highways to see the strangers, and halting at every spot of interest or importance.   On the road, he was met by another embassy from the capital.   It consisted of several Aztec lords, freighted, as usual, with a rich largess of gold, and robes of delicate furs and feathers. The message of the emperor was couched in the same deprecatory terms as before.   He even condescended to bribe the return of the Spaniards, by promising, in that event, four loads of gold to the general, and one to each of the captains,[15] with a yearly tribute to their sovereign.   So effectually had the lofty and naturally courageous spirit of the barbarian monarch been subdued by the influence of superstition !

But the man, whom the hostile array of armies could not daunt, was not to be turned from his purpose by a woman's

---

[14] Torquemada, Monarch. Ind., ubi supra.—Herrera, Hist. General, dec. 2, lib. 7, cap. 3—Gomara, Crónica, cap. 64—Oviedo, Hist. de las Ind., MS., lib. 33, cap. 5.

[15] A load for a Mexican *tamane* was about fifty pounds, or eight hundred ounces.   Clavigero, Stor. del. Messico, tom. III. p. 69, nota.

prayers. He received the embassy with his usual courtesy, declaring, as before, that he could not answer it to his own sovereign, if he were now to return without visiting the emperor in his capital. It would be much easier to arrange matters by a personal interview than by distant negotiation. The Spaniards came in the spirit of peace. Montezuma would so find it, but, should their presence prove burdensome to him, it would be easy for them to relieve him of it.[16]

The Aztec monarch, meanwhile, was a prey to the most dismal apprehensions. It was intended that the embassy above noticed should reach the Spaniards before they crossed the mountains. When he learned that this was accomplished, and that the dread strangers were on their march across the Valley, the very threshold of his capital, the last spark of hope died away in his bosom. Like one who suddenly finds himself on the brink of some dark and yawning gulf, he was too much bewildered to be able to rally his thoughts, or even to comprehend his situation. He was the victim of an absolute destiny; against which no foresight or precautions could have availed. It was as if the strange beings, who had thus invaded his shores, had dropped from some distant planet, so different were they from all he had ever seen, in appearance and manners; so superior—though a mere handful, in numbers –to the banded nations of Anahuac in strength and science, and all the fearful accompaniments of war! They were now in the Valley. The huge mountain screen, which nature had so kindly drawn around it, for its defence, had been overleaped. The golden visions of security and repose, in which he had so long indulged, the lordly sway descended from his ancestors, his broad imperial domain, were all to pass away. It seemed like some terrible dream,—from which he was now, alas! to awake to a still more terrible reality.

In a paroxysm of despair, he shut himself up in his palace, refused food, and sought relief in prayer and in sacrifice. But the oracles were dumb. He then adopted the more sensible expedient of calling a council of his principal and oldest nobles. Here was the same division of opinion which had before prevailed. Cacama, the young king of Tezcuco, his nephew, counselled him to receive the Spaniards courteously, as ambassadors, so styled by themselves, of a foreign prince. Cuitlahua, Montezuma's more warlike brother, urged him to muster his forces

---

[16] Sahagun, Hist. de Nueva España, MS., lib. 12, cap. 12.—Rel. Seg. de Cortés, ap. Lorenzana, p. 73.—Herrera, Hist. General, dec. 2, lib. 7, cap. 3. Bernal Diaz, Hist. de la Conquista, cap. 87.
Gomara, Crónica, cap. 64.—Oviedo, Hist. de las Ind. MS., lib. 33, cap. 5.

on the instant, and drive back the invaders from his capital, or
die in its defence.   But the monarch found it difficult to rally
his spirits for this final struggle.   With downcast eye and dejected mien, he exclaimed, "Of what avail is resistance, when
the gods have declared themselves against us![17]   Yet I mourn
most for the old and infirm, the women and children, too feeble
to fight or to fly.   For myself and the brave men around me, we
must bare our breasts to the storm, and meet it as we may!"
Such are the sorrowful and sympathetic tones in which the Aztec
emperor is said to have uttered the bitterness of his grief.   He
would have acted a more glorious part, had he put his capital in
a posture of defence, and prepared, like the last of the Palæo-
logi, to bury himself under its ruins.[18]

He straightway prepared to send a last embassy to the Spaniards, with his nephew, the lord of Tezcuco, at his head, to welcome them to Mexico.

The Christian army, meanwhile, had advanced as far as
Amaquemecan, a well built town of several thousand inhabitants.
They were kindly received by the cacique, lodged in large, commodious, stone buildings, and at their departure presented, among
other things, with gold to the amount of three thousand *castellanos.*[19]   Having halted there a couple of days, they descended
among flourishing plantations of maize, and of maguey, the latter of which might be called the Aztec vineyards, towards the
lake of Chalco.   Their first resting-place was Ajotzinco, a town
of considerable size, with a great part of it then standing on
piles in the water.   It was the first specimen which the Spaniards had seen of this maritime architecture.   The canals which
intersected the city, instead of streets, presented an animated
scene, from the number of barks which glided up and down
freighted with provisions and other articles for the inhabitants.
The Spaniards were particularly struck with the style and commodious structure of the houses, built chiefly of stone, and with
the general aspect of wealth and even elegance which prevailed
there.

Though received with the greatest show of hospitality, Cortés

---

[17] This was not the sentiment of the Roman hero.

> " Victrix causa Diis placuit, sed victa Catoni!"
> LUCAN, lib. 1, v. 128.

[18] Sahagun, Hist. de Nueva España, MS., lib. 12, cap. 13.—Torquemada
Monarch. Ind., lib. 4, cap. 44.—Gomara, Crónica, cap. 63.

[19] " El señor de esta provincia y pueblo me dió hasta quarenta esclavas, y
tres mil castellanos; y dos dias que alli estuve nos proveyó muy cumplid-
amente de todo lo necessario para nuestra comida." Rel. Seg. de Cortés, ap.
Lorenzana, p 74.

;ound some occasion for distrust in the eagerness manifested by the people to see and approach the Spaniards.[20] Not content with gazing at them in the roads, some even made their way stealthily into their quarters, and fifteen or twenty unhappy Indians were shot down by the sentinels as spies. Yet there appears, as well as we can judge, at this distance of time, to have been no real ground for such suspicion. The undisguised jealousy of the Court, and the cautions he had received from his allies, while they very properly put the general on his guard, seem to have given an unnatural acuteness, at least in the present instance, to his perceptions of danger.[21]

Early on the following morning, as the army was preparing to leave the place, a courier came, requesting the general to postpone his departure till after the arrival of the king of Tezcuco, who was advancing to meet him. It was not long before he appeared, borne in a palanquin or litter, richly decorated with plates of gold and precious stones, having pillars curiously wrought, supporting a canopy of green plumes, a favorite color with the Aztec princes. He was accompanied by a numerous suite of nobles and inferior attendants. As he came into the presence of Cortés, the lord of Tezcuco descended from his palanquin, and the obsequious officers swept the ground before him as he advanced. He appeared to be a young man of about twenty-five years of age, with a comely presence, erect and stately in his deportment. He made the Mexican salutation usually addressed to persons of high rank, touching the earth with his right hand, and raising it to his head. Cortés embraced him as he rose, when the young prince informed him that he came as the representative of Montezuma, to bid the Spaniards welcome to his capital. He then presented the general with three pearls of uncommon size and lustre. Cortés, in return, threw over Cacama's neck a chain of cut glass, which, where glass was as rare as diamonds, might be admitted to have a value as real as the latter. After this interchange of courtesies, and the most friendly and respectful assurances on the part of

---

[20] " De todas partes era infinita la gente que de un cabo é de otro concurrian á mirar á los Españoles, é maravillébanse mucho de los ver. Tenian grande espacio é atenci onen mirar los caballos; decian, ' Estos son Teules,' que quiere decir Demonios." Oviedo, Hist. de las Ind., MS., lib. 33, cap. 45.

[21] Cortés tells the affair coolly enough to the emperor. " E aquella noche tuve tal guarda, que assí de espías, que venian por el agua en canoas, como de otras, que por la sierra abajaban, á ver si habia aparejo para executar su voluntad, amaneciéron casi quince, ó veinte, que las nuestras las habian tomado, y muerto. Por manera que pocas bolviéron á dar su respuesta de el aviso que venian á tomar." Rel. Seg. de Cortés, ap. Lorenzana, p. 74.

Cortés, the Indian prince withdrew, leaving the Spaniards strongly impressed with the superiority of his state and bearing over anything they had hitherto seen in the country.[22]

Resuming its march, the army kept along the southern borders of the lake of Chalco, overshadowed, at that time, by noble woods, and by orchards glowing with autumnal fruits of unknown names, but rich and tempting hues. More frequently it passed through cultivated fields waving with the yellow harvest, and irrigated by canals introduced from the neighboring lake ; the whole showing a careful and economical husbandry, essential to the maintenance of a crowded population.

Leaving the main land, the Spaniards came on the great dike or causeway, which stretches some four or five miles in length, and divides lake Chalco from Xochicalco on the west. It was a lance in breadth in the narrowest part, and in some places wide enough for eight horsemen to ride abreast. It was a solid structure of stone and lime, running directly through the lake, and struck the Spaniards as one of the most remarkable works which they had seen in the country.

As they passed along, they beheld the gay spectacle of multitudes of Indians darting up and down in their light pirogues, eager to catch a glimpse of the strangers, or bearing the products of the country to the neighboring cities. They were amazed, also, by the sight of the *chinampas*, or floating gardens, —those wandering islands of verdure, to which we shall have occasion to return hereafter,—teeming with flowers and vegetables, and moving like rafts over the water. All around the margin and occasionally far in the lake, they beheld little towns and villages, which, half concealed by the foliage, and gathered in white clusters round the shore, looked in the distance like companies of wild swans riding quietly on the waves. A scene so new and wonderful filled their rude hearts with amazement. It seemed like enchantment ; and they could find nothing to compare it with, but the magical pictures in the " Amadis de Gaula." [23] Few pictures, indeed, in that or any other legend of

---

[22] Rel. Seg. de Cortés, ap. Lorenzana, p. 75.—Gomara, Crónica, cap. 64. —Ixtlilxochitl, Hist. Chich., MS., cap. 85.—Oviedo, Hist. de las Ind., MS. lib. 33, cap. 5.

" Llegó con el mayor fausto, y grandeza que ningun señor de los Mexicanos auiamos visto traer, ... y lo tuuímos por muy gran cosa: y platicámos entre nosotros, que quando aquel Cacique traia tanto triunfo, que haria el gran Monteçuma?" Bernal Diaz, Hist. de la Conquista, cap. 87.

[23] " Nos quedámos admirados," exclaims Diaz, with simple wonder, "y deziamos que parecia á las casas de encantamento, que cuentan en el libro de Amadis !" (Ibid., loc. cit.) An edition of this celebrated romance in its Castilian dress had appeared before this time, as the prologue to the

chivalry, could surpass the realities of their own experience. The life of the adventurer in the New World was romance put into action. What wonder, then, if the Spaniard of that day, feeding his imagination with dreams of enchantment at home, and with its realities abroad, should have displayed a Quixotic enthusiasm,—a romantic exultation of character, not to be comprehended by the colder spirits of other lands !

Midway across the lake the army halted at the town of Cuitlahuac, a place of moderate size, but distinguished by the beauty of the buildings,—the most beautiful, according to Cortés, that he had yet seen in the country.[24] After taking some refreshment at this place, they continued their march along the dike. Though broader in this northern section, the troops found themselves much embarrassed by the throng of Indians, who, not content with gazing on them from the boats, climbed up the causeway, and lined the sides of the road. The general, afraid that his ranks might be disordered, and that too great familiarity might diminish a salutary awe in the natives, was obliged to resort not merely to command, but menace, to clear a passage. He now found, as he advanced, a considerable change in the feelings shown towards the government. He heard only of the pomp and magnificence, nothing of the oppressions, of Montezuma. Contrary to the usual fact, it seemed that the respect for the court was greatest in its immediate neighborhood.

From the causeway, the army descended on that narrow point of land which divides the waters of the Chalco from the Tezcucan lake, but which in those days was overflowed for many a mile now laid bare.[25] Traversing this peninsula, they entered the royal residence of Iztapalapan, a place containing twelve or fifteen thousand houses, according to Cortés.[26] It was governed

second edition of 1512 speaks of a former one in the reign of the " Catholic Sovereigns." See Cervantes, Don Quixote, ed. Pellicer, (Madrid, 1797,) tom. I., Discurso Prelim.

[24] " Una ciudad, la mas hermosa, aunque pequeña, que hasta entonces habiamos visto, assí de muy bien obradas Casas, y Torres, como de la buena órden, que en el fundamento de ella habia por ser armada toda sobre Agua." (Rel. Seg. de Cortés, ap. Lorenzana, p. 76.) The Spaniards gave this aquatic city the name of Venezuela, or little Venice. Toribio, Hist. de los Indios, MS., Parte 2, cap. 4.

[25] M. de Humboldt has dotted the *conjectural* limits of the ancient lake in his admirable chart of the Mexican Valley. (Atlas Géographique et Physique de la Nouvelle Espagne, (Paris, 1811,) carte 3.) Notwithstanding his great care, it is not easy always to reconcile his topography with the itineraries of the Conquerors, so much has the face of the country been changed by natural and artificial causes. It is still less possible to reconcile their narratives with the maps of Clavigero, Lopez, Robertson, and others, defying equally topography and history.

[26] Several writers notice a visit of the Spaniards to Tezcuco on the way to

by Cuitlahua, the emperor's brother, who, to do greater honor to the general, had invited the lords of some neighboring cities, of the royal house of Mexico, like himself, to be present at the interview. This was conducted with much ceremony, and, after the usual present of gold and delicate stuffs,[27] a collation was served to the Spaniards in one of the great halls of the palace. The excellence of the architecture here, also, excited the admiration of the general, who does not hesitate, in the glow of his enthusiasm, to pronounce some of the buildings equal to the best in Spain.[28] They were of stone, and the spacious apartments had roofs of odorous cedar-wood, while the walls were tapestried with fine cottons stained with brilliant colors.

But the pride of Iztapalapan, on which its lord had freely lavished his care and his revenues, was its celebrated gardens. They covered an immense tract of land ; were laid out in regular squares, and the paths intersecting them were bordered with trellises, supporting creepers and aromatic shrubs that loaded the air with their perfumes. The gardens were stocked with fruit-trees, imported from distant places, and with the gaudy family of flowers which belong to the Mexican Flora, scientifically arranged, and growing luxuriant in the equable temperature of the table-land. The natural dryness of the atmosphere was counteracted by means of aqueducts and canals that carried water into all parts of the grounds.

In one quarter was an aviary, filled with numerous kinds of birds, remarkable in this region both for brilliancy of plumage and of song. The gardens were intersected by a canal communicating with the lake of Tezcuco, and of sufficient size for barges to enter from the latter. But the most elaborate piece of work was a huge reservoir of stone, filled to a considerable height with water well supplied with different sorts of fish. This basin was sixteen hundred paces in circumference, and was surrounded by a walk, made also of stone, wide enough for four persons

the capital. (Torquemada, Monarch. Ind., lib. 4 cap. 42.—Solís, Conquista, lib. 3, cap. 9.—Herrera, Hist. General, dec. 2, lib. 7, cap. 4.—Clavigero, Stor. del Messico, tom. III. p. 74.) This improbable episode—which it may be remarked, has led these authors into some geographical perplexities, not to say blunders—is altogether too remarkable to have been passed over in silence, in the minute relation of Bernal Diaz, and that of Cortés neither of whom alludes to it.

[27] " E me diéron," says Cortés, " hasta tres, ó quarto mil Castellanos, y algunas Esclavas, y Ropa, é me hiciéron muy buen acogimiento " Rel. Seg., ap. Lorenzana, p. 76.

[28] " Tiene eí Señor de ella unas Casas nuevas, que aun no están acabadas, que son tan buenas como las mejores de España, digo de grandes y bien labradas." Ibid., p. 77.

to go abreast. The sides were curiously sculptured, and a flight of steps led to the water below, which fed the aqueducts above noticed, or, collected into fountains, diffused a perpetual moisture.

Such are the accounts transmitted of these celebrated gardens, at a period when similar horticultural establishments were unknown in Europe; [29] and we might well doubt their existence in this semi-civilized land, were it not a matter of such notoriety at the time, and so explicitly attested by the invaders. But a generation had scarcely passed after the Conquest, before a sad change came over these scenes so beautiful. The town itself was deserted, and the shore of the lake was strewed with the wreck of buildings which once were its ornament and its glory. The gardens shared the fate of the city. The retreating waters withdrew the means of nourishment, converting the flourishing plains into a foul and unsightly morass, the haunt of loathsome reptiles; and the water-fowl built her nest in what had once been the palaces of princes! [30]

In the city of Iztapalapan, Cortés took up his quarters for the night. We may imagine what a crowd of ideas must have pressed on the mind of the Conqueror, as, surrounded by these evidences of civilization, he prepared with his handful of followers to enter the capital of a monarch who, as he had abundant reason to know, regarded him with distrust and aversion. This capital was now but a few miles distant, distinctly visible from Iztapalapan. And as its long lines of glittering edifices, struck by the rays of the evening sun, trembled on the dark-blue waters of the lake, it looked like a thing of fairy creation, rather than the work of mortal hands. Into this city of enchantment Cortés prepared to make his entry on the following morning. [31]

---

[29] The earliest instance of a Garden of Plants in Europe is said to have been at Padua, in 1545. Carli, Lettres Américaines, tom. I. let. 21.

[30] Rel. Seg. de Cortés, ubi supra.—Herrera, Hist. General, dec. 2 lib. 7, cap. 44.—Sahagun, Hist. de Nueva España, MS., lib. 12 cap. 13.—Oviedo, Hist. de las Ind., MS., lib. 33, cap. 5.—Bernal Diaz, Hist. de la Conquista, cap. 87.

[31] "There Aztlan stood upon the farther shore;
Amid the shade of trees its dwellings rose,
Their level roofs with turrets set around,
And battlements all burnished white, which shone
Like silver in the sunshine. I beheld
The imperial city, her far-circling walls,
Her garden groves and stately palaces,
Her temples mountain size, her thousand roofs;
And when I saw her might and majesty,
My mind misgave me then"
Southey's Madoc, Part 1, canto 6.

CHAPTER IX.

Environs of Mexico.—Interview with Montezuma.—Entrance into the Capital.—Hospitable Reception.—Visit to the Emperor.

519.

With the first faint streak of dawn, the Spanish general was up, mustering his followers. They gathered, with beating hearts, under their respective banners, as the trumpet sent forth its spirit-stirring sounds across water and woodland, till they died away in distant echoes among the mountains. The sacred flames on the altars of numberless *teocallis*, dimly seen through the gray mists of morning, indicated the site of the capital, till temple, tower and palace were fully revealed in the glorious illumination which the sun, as he arose above the eastern barrier, poured over the beautiful Valley. It was the eighth of November, 1519; a conspicuous day in history, as that on which the Europeans first set foot in the capital of the Western World.

Cortés with his little body of horse formed a sort of advance guard to the army. Then came the Spanish infantry, who in a summer's campaign had acquired the discipline, and the weather-beaten aspect, of veterans. The baggage occupied the centre; and the rear was closed by the dark files of Tlascalan warriors. The whole number must have fallen short of seven thousand; of which less than four hundred were Spaniards.[1]

For a short distance, the army kept along the narrow tongue of land that divides the Tezcucan from the Chalcan waters, when it entered on the great dike, which, with the exception of an angle near the commencement, stretches in a perfectly straight line across the salt floods of Tezcuco to the gates of the capital. It was the same causeway, or rather the basis of that, which

---

[1] He took about 6000 warriors from Tlascala; and some few of the Cempoallan and other Indian allies continued with him. The Spanish force on leaving Vera Cruz amounted to about 400 foot and 15 horse. In the remonstrance of the disaffected soldiers, after the murderous Tlascalan combats, they speak of having lost fifty of their number since the beginning of the campaign. Ante, Vol. I. p. 458.

still form the great southern avenue of Mexico.[2] The Spaniards had occasion more than ever to admire the mechanical science of the Aztecs, in the geometrical precision with which the work was executed, as well as the solidity of its construction. It was composed of huge stones well laid in cement ; and wide enough, throughout its whole extent, for ten horsemen to ride abreast.

They saw, as they passed along, several large towns, resting on piles, and reaching far into the water,—a kind of architecture which found great favor with the Aztecs, being in imitation of that of their metropolis.[3] The busy population obtained a good subsistence from the manufacture of salt, which they extract- ed from the waters of the great lake. The duties on the traffic in this article were a considerable source of revenue to the crown.

Everywhere the Conquerors beheld the evidence of a crowded and thriving population, exceeding all they had yet seen. The temples and principal buildings of the cities were covered with a hard white stucco, which glistened like enamel in the level beams of the morning. The margin of the great basin was more thickly gemmed, than that of Chalco, with towns and hamlets.[4] The water was darkened by swarms of canoes filled with In- dians,[5] who clambered up the sides of the causeway, and gazed with curious astonishment on the strangers. And here, also, they beheld those fairy islands of flowers, overshadowed occasion- ally by trees of considerable size, rising and falling with the gentle undulation of the billows. At the distance of half a league, from the capital, they encountered a solid work or curtain

---

[2] "La calzada d'Iztapalapan est fondée sur cette même digue ancienne, sur laquelle Cortéz fit des prodiges de valeur dans ses rencontres avec les assiéges." Humboldt, Essai Politique, tom. II. p. 57.

[3] Among these towns were several containing from three to five or six thousand dwellings, according to Cortès, whose barbarous orthography in proper names will not easily be recognized by Mexican or Spaniard. Rel. Seg., ap. Lorenzana, p. 78.

[4] Father Toribio Benavente does not stint his panegyric in speaking of the neighborhood of the capital, which he saw in its glory. "Creo, que en toda nuestra Europa hay pocas ciudades que tengan tal asiento y tal comarca, con tantos pueblos á la redonda de sí y tan bien asentados." Hist. de los In- dios, MS., Parte 3, cap. 7.

[5] It is not necessary, however, to adopt Herrera's account of 50.000 canoes, which, he says, were constantly employed in supplying the capital with pro- visions! (Hist. General, dec. 2, lib. 7, cap. 14.) The poet-chronicler Saavedra is more modest in his estimate.

> "Dos mil y mas canoas cada dia.
> Basteren el gran pueblo Mexicano
> De la mas y la menos ninería
> Que es necessario al alimento humano."
> El Peregrino Indiano, canto 11.

of stone, which traversed the dike. It was twelve feet high, was strengthened by towers at the extremities, and in the centre was a battlemented gateway, which opened a passage to the troops. It was called the Fort of Xoloc, and became memorable in aftertimes as the position occupied by Cortés in the famous siege of Mexico.

Here they were met by several hundred Aztec chiefs, who came out to announce the approach of Montezuma, and to welcome the Spaniards to his capital. They were dressed in the fanciful gala costume of the country, with the *maxtlatl*, or cotton sash, around their loins, and a broad mantle of the same material, or of the brilliant feather-embroidery, flowing gracefully down their shoulders. On their necks and arms they displayed collars and bracelets of turquoise mosaic, with which delicate plumage was curiously mingled, while their ears, under-lips, and occasionally their noses, were garnished with pendants formed of precious stones, or crescents of fine gold. As each cacique made the usual formal salutation of the country separately to the general, the tedious ceremony delayed the march more than an hour. After this, the army experienced no further interruption till it reached a bridge near the gates of the city. It was built of wood, since replaced by one of stone, and was thrown across an opening of the dike, which furnished an outlet to the waters, when agitated by the winds, or swollen by a sudden influx in the rainy season. It was a drawbridge; and the Spaniards, as they crossed it, felt how truly they were committing themselves to the mercy of Montezuma, who, by thus cutting off their communications with the country, might hold them prisoners in his capital.[7]

In the midst of these unpleasant reflections, they beheld the glittering retinue of the emperor emerging from the great street which led then, as it still does, through the heart of the city.[8] Amidst a

[6] "Usaban unos brazaletes de musaico, hechos de turquezas con unas plumas ricas que salian de ellos, que eran mas altas que la cabeza, y bordadas con plumas ricas y con oro y unas bandas de oro, que subian con las plumas." Sahagun, Hist. de Nueva España, lib. 8, cap. 9.
[7] Gonzalo de las Casas, Defensa, MS., Parte 1, cap. 24.—Gomara, Crónica, cap. 65.—Bernal Diaz, Hist. de la Conquista, cap. 88.—Oviedo, Hist. de las Ind., MS., lib. 33, cap. 5.—Rel. Seg. de Cortés, ap Lorenzana, pp. 78, 79.—Ixtlilxochitl, Hist. Chich., MS., cap. 85.
[8] Cardinal Lorenzana says, the street intended, probably, was that crossing the city from the Hospital of San Antonio. (Rel. Seg. de Cortés, p. 79, nota.) This is confirmed by Sahagun. "Y así en aquel trecho que está desde la Iglesia de San Antonio (que ellos llaman Xuluco) que va por cave las casas de Alvarado, hacia el Hospital de la Concepcion, salió Moctezuma á recibir de paz á D. Hernando Cortéz." Hist. de Nueva España, MS., lib. 12, cap. 16.

crowd of Indian nobles, preceded by three officers of state, bearing golden wands,[9] they saw the royal palanquin blazing with burnished gold. It was borne on the shoulders of nobles, and over it a canopy of gaudy feather-work, powdered with jewels, and fringed with silver, was supported by four attendants of the same rank. They were bare-footed, and walked with a slow, measured pace, and with eyes bent on the ground. When the train had come within a convenient distance, it halted, and Montezuma, descending from his litter, came forward leaning on the arms of the lords of Tezcuco and Iztapalapan, his nephew and brother, both of whom, as we have seen, had already been made known to the Spaniards. As the monarch advanced under the canopy, the obsequious attendants strewed the ground with cotton tapestry, that his imperial feet might not be contaminated by the rude soil. His subjects of high and low degree, who lined the sides of the causeway, bent forward with their eyes fastened on the ground as he passed, and some of the humbler class prostrated themselves before him.[10] Such was the homage paid to the Indian despot, showing that the slavish forms of Oriental adulation were to be found among the rude inhabitants of the Western World.

Montezuma wore the girdle and ample square cloak, *tilmatli*, of his nation. It was made of the finest cotton, with the embroidered ends gathered in a knot round his neck. His feet were defended by sandals having soles of gold, and the leathern thongs which bound them to his ankles were embossed with the same metal. Both the cloak and sandals were sprinkled with pearls and precious stones, among which the emerald and the *chalchivitl*—a green stone of higher estimation than any other among the Aztecs—were conspicuous. On his head he wore no other ornament than a *panache* of plumes of the royal green which floated down his back, the badge of military, rather than of regal, rank.

He was at this time about forty years of age. His person was tall and thin, but not ill-made. His hair, which was black and straight, was not very long ; to wear it short was considered unbecoming persons of rank. His beard was thin ; his complexion somewhat paler than is often found in his dusky, or rather copper-colored race. His features, though serious in their expression, did not wear the look of melancholy, indeed, of

---

[9] Carta del Lic. Zuazo, MS.

[10] "Toda la gente que estaba en las calles se le humiliaban y hacian profunda reverencia y grande acatamiento sin levantar los ojos á le mirar, sino que todos estaban hasta que él era pasado, *tan inclinados como frayles en Gloria Patri.*" Toribio, Hist. de los Indios, MS., Parte 3, cap. 7.

dejection, which characterizes his portrait, and which may well
have settled on them at a later period. He moved with dignity,
and his whole demeanor, tempered by an expression of benignity
not to have been anticipated from the reports circulated of his
character, was worthy of a great prince.—Such is the portrait left
to us of the celebrated Indian emperor, in this his first interview
with the white men.[11]

The army halted as he drew near. Cortés, dismounting, threw
his reins to a page, and, supported by a few of the principal
cavaliers, advanced to meet him. The interview must have
been one of uncommon interest to both. In Montezuma, Cortés
beheld the lord of the broad realms he had traversed, whose
magnificence and power had been the burden of every tongue.
In the Spaniard, on the other hand, the Aztec prince saw the
strange being whose history seemed to be so mysteriously connected with his own ; the predicted one of his oracles ; whose
achievements proclaimed him something more than human. But,
whatever may have been the monarch's feelings, he so far suppressed them as to receive his guest with princely courtesy, and
to express his satisfaction at personally seeing him in his capital.[12] Cortés, responded by the most profound expressions of
respect, while he made ample acknowledgments for the substantial proofs which the emperor had given the Spaniards of
his munificence. He then hung round Montezuma's neck a
sparkling chain of colored crystal, accompanying this with a
movement as if to embrace him, when he was restrained by the
two Aztec lords shocked at the menaced profanation of the

---

[11] For the preceding account of the equipage and appearance of Montezu-
ma, see Bernal Diaz, Hist. de la Conquista, cap. 88,—Carta de Zuazo,
MS.,—Ixtlilxochitl, Hist. Chich., MS., cap. 85,—Gomara, Crónica, cap. 65.
—Oviedo, Hist. de las Ind., MS., ubi supra, et cap. 45,—Acosta, lib. 7,
cap. 22,—Sahagun, Hist. de Neuva España, MS., lib. 12, cap. 16,—Toribio,
Hist. de los Indios, MS., Parte 3, cap. 7.

The noble Castilian, or rather Mexican bard, Saavedra, who belonged to
the generation after the Conquest, has introduced most of the particulars in
his rhyming chronicle. The following specimen will probably suffice for the
reader.

> ' Yva el gran Moteçuma atauiado
> De manta açul y blanca con gran falda,
> De algodon muy sutil y delicado,
> Y al remate vna concha de esmeralda :
> En la parte que el nudo tiene dado,
> Y una tiara á modo de guirnalda,
> Zapatos que de oro son las suelas
> Asidos con muy ricas correhuelas.''
>   EL PEREGRINO, INDIANO, canto 11.

[12] Satis vultu læto.'' says Martyr, "an stomacho sedatus, et an hospites
per vim quis unquam libens susceperit experti loquantur.'' De Orbe Novo
dec. 5, cap. 3.

sacred person of their master.[13] After the interchange of these civilities, Montezuma appointed his brother to conduct the Spaniards to their residence in the capital, and again entering his litter was borne off amidst prostrate crowds in the same state in which he had come. The Spaniards quickly followed, and with colors flying and music playing soon made their entrance into the southern quarter of Tenochtitlan.[14]

Here, again, they found fresh cause for admiration in the grandeur of the city, and the superior style of its architecture. The dwellings of the poorer class were, indeed, chiefly of reeds and mud. But the great avenue through which they were now marching was lined with the houses of the nobles, who were encouraged by the emperor to make the capital their residence. They were built of a red porous stone drawn from quarries in the neighborhood, and, though they rarely rose to a second story, often covered a large space of ground. The flat roofs, *azoteas*, were protected by stone parapets, so that every house was a fortress. Sometimes these roofs resembled parterres of flowers, so thickly were they covered with them, but more frequently these were cultivated in broad terraced gardens, laid out between the edifices.[15] Occasionally a great square or market-place intervened, surrounded by its porticos of stone and stucco; or a pyramidal temple reared its colossal bulk, crowned with its tapering sanctuaries, and altars blazing with inextinguishable fires. The great street facing the southern causeway, unlike most others in the place, was wide, and extended some miles in nearly a straight line, as before noticed, through the centre of the city. A spectator standing at one end of it, as his eye ranged along the deep vista of temples, terraces, and gardens, might clearly discern the other, with the blue mountains in the distance, which, in the transparent atmosphere of the table-land, seemed almost in contact with the buildings.

But what most impressed the Spaniards was the throngs of people who swarmed through the streets and on the canals, filling every door-way and window, and clustering on the roofs of the buildings. "I well remember the spectacle," exclaims Bernal Diaz; "it seems now, after so many years, as present to my mind, as if it were but yesterday."[16] But what must have

---

[13] Rel. Seg. de Cortés, ap. Lorenzana, p. 79.

[14] "Entráron en la ciudad de Méjico á punto de guerra, tocando los atamboros, y con banderas desplegadas," &c. Sahagun, Hist. de Nueva España, MS., lib. 12, cap. 15.

[16] "Et giardini alti et bassi, che era cosa maravigliosa da vedore." Rel. d' un gent., ap. Ramusio, tom. III. fol. 309.

[1] "Quien podrá," exclaims the old soldier, "dezir la multitud de hombres, y mugeres, muchachos, que estauan en las calles, é açuteas, y en Canoas

been the sensations of the Aztecs themselves, as they looked on the portentous pageant! as they heard, now for the first time, the well-cemented pavement ring under the iron tramp of the horses,—the strange animals which fear had clothed in such supernatural terrors; as they gazed on the children of the East, revealing their celestial origin in their fair complexions; saw the bright falchions and bonnets of steel, a metal to them unknown, glancing like meteors in the sun, while sounds of unearthly music—at least, such as their rude instruments had never wakened—floated in the air! But every other emotion was lost in that of deadly hatred, when they beheld their detested enemy, the Tlascalan, stalking, in defiance, as it were, through their streets, and staring around with looks of ferocity and wonder, like some wild animal of the forest, who had strayed by chance from his native fastnesses into the haunts of civilization.[17]

As they passed down the spacious street, the troops repeatedly traversed bridges suspended above canals, along which they saw the Indian barks gliding swiftly with their little cargoes of fruits and vegetables for the markets of Tenochtitlan.[18] At length, they halted before a broad area near the centre of the city, where rose the huge pyramidal pile dedicated to the patron war-god of the Aztecs, second only, in size, as well as sanctity, to the temple of Cholula, and covering the same ground now in part occupied by the great cathedral of Mexico.

Facing the western gate of the inclosure of the temple, stood a low range of stone buildings, spreading over a wide extent of ground, the palace of Axayacatl, Montezuma's father, built by that monarch about fifty years before.[19] It was appropriated as the barracks of the Spaniards. The emperor himself was in the courtyard, waiting to receive them. Approaching Cortés, he took from a vase of flowers, borne by one of his slaves, a massy

---

en aquellas acequias, que nos salian á mirar? Era cosa de notar, que agora que lo estoy escriuiendo, se me representa todo delante de mis ojos, como si ayer fuera quando esto passó." Hist. de la Conquista, cap. 88.

[17] "Ad spectaculum," says the penetrating Martyr, "tandem Hispanis placidum, quia diu optatum, Tenustiatanis prudentibus forte aliter, quia verentur fore, vt hi hospites quietem suam Elysiam veniant perturbaturi; de populo secus, qui nil sentit æque delectabile, quàm res novas ante oculos in presentiarum habere, de futuro nihil anxius." De Orbe Novo, dec. 5, cap. 3.

[18] The euphonious name of *Tenochtitlan* is commonly derived from Aztec words signifying "the *tuno*, or cactus, on a rock," the appearance of which, as the reader may remember, was to determine the site of the future capital. (Toribio, Hist. de los Indios, Parte 3, cap. 7.—Esplic. de la Colec: de Mendoza, ap. Antiq. of Mexico, vol. IV.) Another etymology derives the word from *Tenoch*, the name of one of the founders of the monarchy.

[19] Clavigero, Stor. del Messico, tom. III. p. 78.

collar, in which the shell of a species of craw-fish, much prized by the Indians, was set in gold, and connected by heavy links of the same metal. From this chain depended eight ornaments, also of gold, made in resemblance of the same shell-fish, a span in length each, and of delicate workmanship;[2] for the Aztec goldsmiths were confessed to have shown skill in their craft, not inferior to their brethren of Europe.[21] Montezuma, as he hung the gorgeous collar round the general's neck, said, " This palace belongs to you, Malinche,"[22] (the epithet by which he always addressed him,) "and your brethren. Rest after your fatigues, for you have much need to do so, and in a little while I will visit you again." So saying, he withdrew with his attendants, evincing, in this act, a delicate consideration not to have been expected in a barbarian.

Cortés' first care was to inspect his new quarters. The building, though spacious, was low, consisting of one floor, except, indeed, in the centre, where it rose to an additional story. The apartments were of great size, and afforded accommodations, according to the testimony of the Conquerors themselves, for the whole army![23] The hardy mountaineers of Tlascala were, probably, not very fastidious, and might easily find a shelter in the out-buildings, or under temporary awnings in the ample court-yards. The best apartments were hung with gay cotton draperies, the floors covered with mats or rushes. There were, also, low stools made of single pieces of wood elaborately carved, and in most of the apartments beds made of the palm-leaf, woven into a thick mat, with coverlets, and sometimes canopies of cotton. These mats were the only beds used by the natives, whether of high or low degree.[24]

After a rapid survey of this gigantic pile, the general assigned

It occupied what is now the corner of the streets, " Del Indio Triste " and " Tacuba." Humboldt, Vues des Cordillères, p. 7, et seq.

[2] Rel. Seg. de Cortés, ap. Lorenzana, p. 88.—Gonzalo de las Casas, Defensa, MS., Parte 1, cap. 24.

[21] Boturini says, greater, by the acknowledgment of the goldsmiths themselves. "Los plateros de Madrid, viendo algunas Piezas, y Brazaletes de oro, con que se armaban en guerra los Reyes, y Capitanes Indianos, confessáron, que eran inimitables en Europa." (Idea, p. 78.) And Oviedo, speaking of their work in jewelry, remarks, " Io vi algunas piedras jaspes, calcidonias, jacintos, corniolas, é plasmas de esmeraldas, é otras de otras especies labradas é fechas, cabezas de Aves, é otras hechas animales é otras figuras, que dudo haber en España ni en Italia quien las supiera hacer con tanta perficion." Hist. de las Ind., MS., lib 33, cap. 11.

[22] Ante, Vol. I. p. 483.

[23] Bernal Diaz, Hist. de la Conquista, cap. 88.—Rel. Seg. de Cortés, ap. Lorenzana, p. 80.

[24] Bernal Diaz, Ibid., loc. cit.—Oviedo, Hist. de las Ind., MS., lib. 33, cap. 5.—Sahagun, Hist. de Nueva España, MS., lib. 12, cap. 16.

his troops their respective quarters, and took as vigilant precautions for security, as if he had anticipated a siege, instead of a friendly entertainment. The place was encompassed by a stone wall of considerable thickness, with towers or heavy buttresses at intervals, affording a good means of defence. He planted his cannon so as to command the approaches, stationed his sentinels along the works, and, in short, enforced in every respect as strict military discipline as had been observed in any part of the march. He well knew the importance to his little band, at least for the present, of conciliating the good-will of the citizens; and, to avoid all possibility of collision, he prohibited any soldier from leaving his quarters without orders, under pain of death. Having taken these precautions, he allowed his men to partake of the bountiful collation which had been prepared for them.

They had been long enough in the country to become reconciled to, if not to relish, the peculiar cooking of the Aztecs. The appetite of the soldier is not often dainty, and on the present occasion it cannot be doubted that the Spaniards did full justice to the savory productions of the royal kitchen. During the meal they were served by numerous Mexican slaves, who were, indeed, distributed through the palace, anxious to do the bidding of the strangers. After the repast was concluded, and they had taken their *siesta*, not less important to a Spaniard than food itself, the presence of the emperor was again announced.

Montezuma was attended by a few of his principal nobles. He was received with much deference by Cortés; and, after the parties had taken their seats, a conversation commenced between them, through the aid of Doña Marina, while the cavaliers and Aztec chieftains stood around in respectful silence.

Montezuma made many inquiries concerning the country of the Spaniards, their sovereign, the nature of his government, and especially their own motives in visiting Anahuac. Cortés explained these motives by the desire to see so distinguished a monarch, and to declare to him the true Faith professed by the Christians. With rare discretion, he contented himself with dropping this hint, for the present, allowing it to ripen in the mind of the emperor, till a future conference. The latter asked, whether those white men, who in the preceding year had landed on the eastern shores of his empire, were their countrymen. He showed himself well informed of the proceedings of the Spaniards from their arrival in Tabasco to the present time, information of which had been regularly transmitted in the hieroglyphical paintings. He was curious, also, in regard to the rank of his visitors in their own country; inquiring, if they were the kinsmen of the sovereign. Cortés replied, they were kinsmen of one another, and subjects of their great monarch, who held them all in peculiar estimation. Before his departure, Montezuma made himself acquainted with the names of the principal cavaliers, and the position they occupied in the army.

At the conclusion of the interview, the Aztec prince commanded his attendants to bring forward the presents prepared for his guests. They consisted of cotton dresses, enough to supply every man, it is said, including the allies, with a suit ![26] And he did not fail to add the usual accompaniment of gold chains and other ornaments, which he distributed in profusion among the Spaniards. He then withdrew with the same ceremony with which he had entered, leaving every one deeply impressed with his munificence, and his affability so unlike what they had been taught to expect, by, what they now considered, an invention of the enemy.[26]

That evening, the Spaniards celebrated their arrival in the Mexican capital by a general discharge of artillery. The thunders of the ordnance reverberating among the buildings and shaking them to their foundations, the stench of the sulphureous vapor that rolled in volumes above the walls of the encampment, reminding the inhabitants of the explosions of the great *volcan*, filled the hearts of the superstitious Aztecs with dismay. It proclaimed to them, that their city held in its bosom those dread beings whose path had been marked with desolation, and who could call down the thunderbolts to consume their enemies! It was doubtless the policy of Cortés to strengthen this superstitious feeling as far as possible, and to impress the natives, at the outset, with a salutary awe of the supernatural powers of the Spaniards.[27]

[26] " Muchas y diversas Joyas de Oro, y Plata, y Plumajes, y con fasta cinco ó seis mil Piezas de Ropa de Algodon muy ricas, y de diversas maneras texida, y labrada." (Rel. Seg. de Cortés, ap. Lorenzana, p. 80.) Even this falls short of truth, according to Diaz. " Tenia apercebido el gran Monteçuma muy ricas joyas de oro, y de muchas hechuras, que dió á nuestro Capitan, é assí mismo á cada vno de nuestros Capitanes dió cositas de oro, y tres cargas de mantas de labores ricas de pluma, y entre todos los soldados tambien nos dió á cada vno a dos cargas de mantas, con alegría, y en todo parecia gran señor." (Hist. de la Conquista, cap. 89.) " Sex millia vestium, aiunt, que eas vidêre." Martyr, De Orbe Novo, dec. 5, cap. 3.

[26] Ixtlilxochitl. Chich., MS., cap. 85.—Gomara, Crónica, cap. 66.—Herrera, Hist. General, dec. 2, lib. 7, cap. 6.—Bernal Diaz, Ibid., ubi upra.—Oviedo, Hist. de las Ind., MS., lib. 33, cap. 5.

[27] " La noche siguiente jugáron la artillería por la solemnidad de haber llegado sin daño á donde deseaban ; pero los Indios como no usados á los truenos de la artillería, mal edor de la pólvora, recibiéron grande alteraciou

On the following morning, the general requested permission to return the emperor's visit, by waiting on him in his palace. This was readily granted, and Montezuma sent his officers to conduct the Spaniards to his presence. Cortés dressed himself in his richest habit, and left the quarters attended by Alvarado, Sandoval, Velasquez, and Ordaz, together with five or six of the common file.

The royal habitation was at no great distance. It stood on the ground, to the south-west of the cathedral, since covered in part by the *Casa del Estado,* the palace of the dukes of Monteleone, the descendants of Cortés.[28] It was a vast, irregular pile of low stone buildings, like that garrisoned by the Spaniards. So spacious was it, indeed, that, as one of the Conquerors assures us, although he had visited it more than once, for the express purpose, he had been too much fatigued each time by wandering through the apartments ever to see the whole of it.[29] It was built of the red porous stone of the country, *tetzontli,* was ornamented with marble, and on the façade over the principal entrance were sculptured the arms or device of Montezuma, an eagle bearing an ocelot in his talons.[30]

In the courts through which the Spaniards passed, fountains of crystal water, were playing, fed from the copious reservoir on the distant hill of Chapoltepec, and supplying in their turn more than a hundred baths in the interior of the palace. Crowds of Aztec nobles were sauntering up and down in these squares, and in the outer halls, loitering away their hours in attendance on the court. The apartments were of immense size, though not lofty. The ceilings were of various sorts of odoriferous wood ingeniously carved ; the floors covered with mats

y miedo toda aquella noche." Sahagun, Hist. de Nueva España, MS., lib. 12, cap. 17.

[28] "C'est là que la famille construisit le bel édifice dans lequel se trouvent les archives del Estado, et qui est passé avec tout l'héritage au duc Napolitain de Monteleone." (Humboldt, Essai Politique, tom. II. p. 72.) The inhabitants of modern Mexico have large obligations to this inquisitive traveller, for the care he has taken to identify the memorable localities of their capital. It is not often that a philosophical treatise is, also, a good *manuel du voyageur.*

[29] "Et io entrai più di quattro volte in una casa del gran Signor non per altro effetto che per vederla, et ogni volta vi camminauo tanto che mi stancauo, et mai la fini di vedere tutta." Rel. d' un gent., ap. Ramusio, tom III. fol. 309.

[30] Gomara, Crónica, cap. 71.—Herrera, Hist. General, dec. 2, lib. 7, cap: 9.

The authorities call it "tiger," an animal not known in America. I have ventured to substitute, the "ocelotl," *tlalocelotl* of Mexico, a native animal, which, being of the same family, might easily be confounded by the Spaniards with the tiger of the Old Continent.

of the palm-leaf. The walls were hung with cotton richly stained, with the skins of wild animals, or gorgeous draperies of feather-work wrought in imitation of birds, insects, and flowers, with the nice art and glowing radiance of colors that might compare with the tapestries of Flanders. Clouds of incense rolled up from censers, and diffused intoxicating odors through the apartments. The Spaniards might well have fancied themselves in the voluptuous precincts of an Eastern harem, instead of treading the halls of a wild barbaric chief in the Western World.[31]

On reaching the hall of audience, the Mexican officers took off their sandals, and covered their gay attire with a mantle of *nequen*, a coarse stuff made of the fibres of the maguey, worn only by the poorest classes. This act of humiliation was imposed on all, except the members of his own family, who approached the sovereign.[32] Thus bare-footed, with down-cast eyes, and formal obeisance, they ushered the Spaniards into the royal presence.

They found Montezuma seated at the further end of a spacious saloon, and surrounded by a few of his favorite chiefs. He received them kindly, and very soon Cortés, without much ceremony, entered on the subject which was uppermost in his thoughts. He was fully aware of the importance of gaining the royal convert, whose example would have such an influence on the conversion of his people. The general, therefore, prepared to display the whole store of his theological science, with the most winning arts of rhetoric he could command, while the interpretation was conveyed through the silver tones of Marina, as inseparable from him, on these occasions, as his shadow.

He set forth, as clearly as he could, the ideas entertained by the Church in regard to the holy mysteries of the Trinity, the Incarnation, and the Atonement. From this he ascended to the origin of things, the creation of the world, the first pair, paradise, and the fall of man. He assured Montezuma, that the idols he

---

[31] Toribio, Hist. de los Indios, MS., Parte 3. cap. 7.—Herrera, Hist. General, dec. 2, lib. 7, cap. 9.—Gomara, Crónica, cap. 71.—Bernal Diaz, Hist. de la Conquista, cap. 91.—Oviedo, Hist. de las Ind., MS., lib. 33. cap. 5, 46.—Rel. Seg. de Cortés, ap. Lorenzana, pp. 111-114.

[32] " Para entrar en su palacio, á que ellos llaman Tecpa, todos se descalzaban, y los que entraban á negociar con él habian de llevar mantas gróseras encima de si, y si eran grandes señores ó en tiempo de frio, sobre las mantas buenas que llevaban vestidas, ponian una manta grosera y pobre ; y para hablarle, estaban muy humiliados y sin levantar los ojos." (Toribio, Hist. de los Indios, MS., Parte 3, cap. 7.) There is no better authority than this worthy missionary, for the usages of the ancient Aztecs, of which he had such large personal knowledge.

worshipped were Satan under different forms. A sufficient proof of it was the bloody sacrifices they imposed, which he contrasted with the pure and simple rite of the mass. Their worship would sink him in perdition. It was to snatch his soul, and the souls of his people, from the flames of eternal fire by opening to them a purer faith, that the Christians had come to his land. And he earnestly besought him not to neglect the occasion, but to secure his salvation by embracing the Cross, the great sign of human redemption.

The eloquence of the preacher was wasted on the insensible heart of his royal auditor. It, doubtless, lost somewhat of its efficacy, strained through the imperfect interpretation of so recent a neophyte as the Indian damsel. But the doctrines were too abstruse in themselves to be comprehended at a glance by the rude intellect of a barbarian. And Montezuma may have, perhaps, thought it was not more monstrous to feed on the flesh of a fellow-creature, than on that of the Creator himself.[83] He was, besides, steeped in the superstitions of his country from his cradle. He had been educated in the straitest sect of her religion; had been himself a priest before his election to the throne; and was now the head both of the religion and the state. Little probability was there that such a man would be open to argument or persuasion, even from the lips of a more practised polemic than the Spanish commander. How could he abjure the faith that was intertwined with the dearest affections of his heart, and the very elements of his being? How could he be false to the gods who had raised him to such prosperity and honors and whose shrines were intrusted to his especial keeping?

He listened, however, with silent attention, until the general had concluded his homily. He then replied, that he knew the Spaniards had held this discourse wherever they had been. He doubted not their God was, as they said, a good being. His gods, also, were good to him. Yet what his visitor said of the creation of the world was like what he had been taught to believe.[84] It was not worth while to discourse further of the matter. His ancestors, he said, were not the original proprietors of the land They had occupied it but a few ages, and had been led there by a great Being, who, after giving them laws and ruling

---

[83] The ludicrous effect—if the subject be not too grave to justify the expression--of a literal belief in the doctrine of Transubstantiation in the mother country, even at this day, is well illustrated by Blanco White, Letters from Spain, (London, 1822,) let. 1.

[84] "Y en esso de la creacion del mundo assí lo tenemos nosotros creido muchos tiempos passados." (Bernal Diaz, Hist. de la Conquista, cap. 90.) For some points of resemblance between the Aztec and Hebrew traditions, see Book 1, Ch. 3, and *Appendix Part* 1, of this History.

over the nation for a time, had withdrawn to the regions where the sun rises. He had declared, on his departure, that he or his descendants would again visit them and resume his empire.[85] The wonderful deeds of the Spaniards, their fair complexions, and the quarter whence they came, all showed they were his descendants. If Montezuma had resisted their visit to his capital, it was because he had heard such accounts of their cruelties, — that they sent the lightning to consume his people or crushed them to pieces under the hard feet of the ferocious animals on which they rode. He was now convinced that these were idle tales ; that the Spaniards were kind and generous in their natures ; they were mortals, of a different race, indeed, from the Aztecs, wiser, and more valiant,—and for this he honored them.

" You, too," he added, with a smile, " have been told, perhaps, that I am a god, and dwell in palaces of gold and silver.[n] But you see it is false. My houses, though large, are of stone and wood like those of others ; and as to my body," he said, baring his tawny arm, " you see it is flesh and bone like yours. It is true, I have a great empire inherited from my ancestors ; lands, and gold, and silver. But your sovereign beyond the waters is, I know, the rightful lord of all. I rule in his name. You, Malinche, are his ambassador ; you and your brethren shall share these things with me. Rest now from your labors. You are here in your own dwellings, and everything shall be provided for your subsistence. I will see that your wishes shall be obeyed in the same way as my own."[87] As the monarch concluded these words, a few natural tears suffused his eyes, while the image of ancient independence, perhaps, flitted across his mind.[88]

[85] " E siempre hemos tenido, que de los que de él descendiessen habin de venir á sojuzgar esta tierra, y á nosotros como á sus Vasallos." Rel. Seg de Cortés ap. Lorenzana, p. 81.

[86] " Y luego Monteçuma dixo riendo, porque en toda era muy regozijado en su hablar de gran señor : Malinche, bien sé que te han dicho essos de Tlascala, con quien tanta amistad aueis tomado que yo que soy como Dios, ó Teule, que quanto ay en mis casas es todo oro é plata, y piedras ricas." Bernal Diaz, Ibid., ubi supra.

[87] " E por tanto Vos sed cierto, que os obedecerémos, y ternémos por señor en lugar de esse gran señor, que decis, y que en ello no habia falta, ni engaño ; alguno é bien podeis en toda la tierra, digo que en la que yo en mi Señorio poseo, mandar á vuestra voluntad, porque sera obedecido y fecho, y todo lo que nosotros tenemos es para lo que Vos de ello quisieredes disponer." Rel. Seg. de Cortes, ubi supra.

[88] Martyr, De Orbe Novo, dec. 5, cap. 3.—Gomara, Cronica, cap. 66—Oviedo, Hist. de las Ind., MS., lib. 33, cap. 5.—Gonzalo de las Casas, MS., Parte 1, cap. 24.

Cortes, in his brief notes of this proceeding, speaks only of the interview

Cortés, while he encouraged the idea that his own sovereign was the great Being indicated by Montezuma, endeavored to comfort the monarch by the assurance that his master had no desire to interfere with his authority, otherwise than, out of pure concern for his welfare, to effect his conversion and that of his people to Christianity. Before the emperor dismissed his visitors he consulted his munificent spirit, as usual, by distributing rich stuffs and trinkets of gold among them, so that the poorest soldier, says Bernal Diaz, one of the party, received at least two heavy collars of the precious metal for his share. The iron hearts of the Spaniards were touched with the emotion displayed by Montezuma, as well as by his princely spirit of liberality. As they passed him, the cavaliers, with bonnet in hand, made him the most profound obeisance, and " on the way home," continues the same chronicler, " we could discourse of nothing but the gentle breeding and courtesy of the Indian monarch, and of the respect we entertained for him." [39]

Speculations of a graver complexion must have pressed on the mind of the general, as he saw around him the evidences of a civilization, and consequently power, for which even the exaggerated reports of the natives—discredited from their apparent exaggeration—had not prepared him. In the pomp and burdensome ceremonial of the court, he saw that nice system of subordination and profound reverence for the monarch which characterize the semi-civilized empires of Asia. In the appearance of the capital, its massy, yet elegant architecture, its luxurious social accommodations, its activity in trade, he recognized the proofs of the intellectual progress, mechanical skill, and enlarged resources of an old and opulent community ; while the swarms in the streets attested the existence of a population capable of turning these resources to the best account.

In the Aztec he beheld a being unlike either the rude republican Tlascalan, or the effeminate Cholulan ; but combining the courage of the one with the cultivation of the other. He was in the heart of a great capital, which seemed like an extensive fortification, with its dikes and its draw-bridges, where every house might be easily converted into a castle. Its insular

---

with Montezuma in the Spanish quarters, which he makes the scene of the preceding dialogue.—Bernal Diaz transfers this to the subsequent meeting in the palace. In the only fact of importance, the dialogue itself, both substantially agree.

[39] " Assí nos despedímos con grandes cortesías del, y nos fuymos á nuestros aposentos, e ibamos platicando de la buena manera é criança que en todo tenia é que nosotres en todo le tuuiessemos mucho acato, é con las gorras de armas colchadas quitadas, quando delante dél passassemos." Bernal Diaz, Hist. de la Conquista, cap. 90.

position removed it from the continent, from which, at the mere nod of the sovereign, all communication might be cut off, and the whole warlike population be at once precipitated on him and his handful of followers. What could superior science avail against such odds? [40]

As to the subversion of Montezuma's empire, now that he had seen him in his capital, it must have seemed a more doubtful enterprise than ever. The recognition which the Aztec prince had made of the feudal supremacy, if I may so say, of the Spanish sovereign, was not to be taken too literally. Whatever show of deference he might be disposed to pay the latter, under the influence of his present—perhaps temporary—delusion, it was not to be supposed that he would so easily relinquish his actual power and possessions, or that his people would consent to it. Indeed, his sensitive apprehensions in regard to this very subject, on the coming of the Spaniards, were sufficient proof of the tenacity with which he clung to his authority. It is true that Cortés had a strong lever for future operations in the superstitious reverence felt for himself both by prince and people. It was undoubtedly his policy to maintain this sentiment unimpaired in both, as far as possible. [41] But, before settling any plan of operations, it was necessary to make himself personally acquainted with the topography and local advantages of the capital, the character of its population, and the real nature and amount of its resources. With this view, he asked the emperor's permission to visit the principal public edifices.

[40] " Y assí," says Toribio de Benavente, "estaba tan fuerte esta ciudad, que parecia no bastar poder humano para ganarla ; porque ademas de su fuerza y municion que tenia, era cabeza y Señoría de todo la tierra, y el Señor de ella (Moteczuma) gloriábase en su silla y en la fortaleza de su ciudad, y en la muchedumbre de sus vassallos." Hist. de los Indios, MS., Parte 3, cap. 8.

[41] "Many are of opinion," says Father Acosta, " that if the Spaniards had continued the course they began, they might easily have disposed of Montezuma and his kingdom, and introduced the law of Christ, without much bloodshed." Lib. 7, cap. 25.

Antonio de Herrera, the celebrated chronicler of the Indies, was born of a respectable family at Cuella in Old Spain, in 1549. After passing through the usual course of academic discipline in his own country, he went to Italy, to which land of art and letters the Spanish youth of that time frequently resorted to complete their education. He there became acquainted with Vespasian Gonzaga, brother of the duke of Mantua, and entered into his service. He continued with this prince after he was made viceroy of Navarre, and was so highly regarded by him, that, on his death-bed Gonzaga earnestly commended him to the protection of Philip the Second. This penetrating monarch soon discerned the excellent qualities of Herrera and raised him to the post of Historiographer of the Indies,—an office for which Spain is indebted to Philip. Thus provided with a liberal salary, and with every facility for pursuing the historical researches to which his inclination led him, Herrera's days glided peacefully away in the steady but silent, occupations of a man of letters. He continued to hold the office of historian of the colonies through Philip the Second's reign, and under his successors, Philip the Third, and the Fourth ; till in 1625 he died at the advanced age of seventy six, leaving behind him a high character for intellectual and moral worth.

Herrera wrote several works, chiefly historical. The most important, that on which his reputation rests, is his *Historia General de las Indias Occidentales.* It extends from the year 1492, the time of the discovery of America, to 1554, and is divided into eight decades. Four of them were published in 1601, and the remaining four in 1615, making in all five volumes in folio. The work was subsequently republished in 1730, and has been translated into most of the languages of Europe. The English translator, Stevens, has taken great liberties with his original, in the way of abridgment and omission but the execution of his work is on the whole superior to that of most of the old English versions of the Castilian chroniclers.

Herrera's vast subject embraces the whole colonial empire of Spain in the New World. The work is thrown into the form of annals, and the multifarious occurrences in the distant regions of which he treats are all marshalled with exclusive reference to their chronology, and made to move together *pari passu.* By means of this tasteless arrangement the thread of interest is perpetually snapped, the reader is hurried from one scene to another, without the opportunity of completing his survey of any. His patience is exhausted and his mind perplexed with partial and scattered glimpses, instead of gathering new light as he advances from the skilful development of a continuous and well digested narrative. This is the great defect of a plan founded on a slavish adherence to chronology. The defect becomes more serious, when the work, as in the present instance, is of vast compass and embraces a great variety of details, having little relation to each other. In such a work we feel the superiority of a plan like that which Robertson has pursued in his " History of America," where every subject is allowed to occupy its own independent place, proportioned to its importance, and thus to make a distinct and individual impression on the reader.

Herrera's position gave him access to the official returns from the colonies, state-papers, and whatever documents existed in the public offices for the illustration of the colonial history. Among these sources of information were some manuscripts, with which it is now not easy to meet; as, for example, the memorial of Alonso de Ojeda, one of the followers of Cortés, which has eluded my researches both in Spain and Mexico. Other writings, as those of father Sahagun, of much importance in the history of Indian civilization, were unknown to the historian. Of such manuscripts as fell into his hands, Herrera made the freest use. From the writings of Las Casas, in particular, he borrowed without ceremony. The bishop had left orders that his " History of the Indies " should not be published till at least forty years after his death. Before that period had elapsed, Herrera had entered on his labors, and as he had access to the papers of Las Casas, he availed himself of it to transfer whole pages, nay, chapters, of his narrative in the most unscrupulous manner to his own work. In doing this, he made a decided improvement on the manner of his original, reduced his cumbrous and entangled sentences to pure Castilian, omitted his turgid declamation and his unreasonable invectives. But, at the same time, he also excluded the passages that bore hardest on the conduct of his countrymen, and those bursts of indignant eloquence, which showed a moral sensibility in the bishop of

Chiapa that raised him so far above his age. By this sort of metempsychosis, if one may so speak, by which the letter and not the spirit of the good missionary was transferred to Herrera's pages, he rendered the publication of Las Casas' history, in some measure, superfluous; and this circumstance has, no doubt, been one reason for its having been so long detained in manuscript.

Yet, with every allowance for the errors incident to rapid composition, and to the pedantic chronological system pursued by Herrera, his work must be admitted to have extraordinary merit. It displays to the reader the whole progress of Spanish conquest and colonization in the New World, for the first sixty years after the discovery. The individual actions of his complicated story, though unskilfully grouped together, are unfolded in a pure and simple style, well suited to the gravity of his subject. If at first sight he may seem rather too willing to magnify the merits of the early discoverers, and to throw a veil over their excesses, it may be pardoned, as flowing not from moral insensibility, but from the patriotic sentiment which made him desirous, as far as might be, to wipe away every stain from the escutcheon of his nation, in the proud period of her renown. It is natural that the Spaniard, who dwells on this period, should be too much dazzled by the display of her gigantic efforts, scrupulously to weigh their moral character, or the merits of the cause in which they were made. Yet Herrera's national partiality never makes him the apologist of crime; and, with the allowances fairly to be conceded, he may be entitled to the praise so often given him of integrity and candor.

It must not be forgotten, that, in addition to the narrative of the early discoveries of the Spaniards, Herrera has brought together a vast quantity of information in respect to the institutions and usages of the Indian nations, collected from the most authentic sources. This gives his work a completeness, beyond what is to be found in any other on the same subject. It is, indeed, a noble monument of sagacity and erudition; and the student of history, and still more the historical compiler, will find himself unable to advance a single step among the early colonial settlements of the New World without reference to the pages of Herrera.

Another writer on Mexico, frequently consulted in the course of the present narrative, is Toribio de Benavente, or *Motolinia*, as he is still more frequently called, from his Indian cognomen. He was one of the twelve Franciscan missionaries who, at the request of Cortés, were sent out to New Spain immediately after the Conquest, in 1523. Toribio's humble attire, naked feet, and, in short, the poverty-stricken aspect which belongs to his order, frequently drew from the natives the exclamation of *Motolinia*, or "poor man." It was the first Aztec word, the signification of which the missionary learned, and he was so much pleased with it, as intimating his own condition, that he henceforth assumed it as his name. Toribio employed himself zealously with his brethren in the great object of their mission. He travelled on foot over various parts of Mexico, Guatemala, and Nicaragua. Wherever he went, he spared no pains to wean the natives from their dark idolatry, and to pour into their minds the light of revelation. He showed even a tender regard for their temporal as well as spiritual wants, and Bernal Diaz testifies that he has known him to give away his own robe to clothe a destitute and suffering Indian. Yet this charitable friar, so meek and conscientious in the discharge of his Christian duties, was one of the fiercest opponents of Las Casas, and sent home a remonstrance against the bishop of Chiapa, couched in terms the most opprobrious and sarcastic. It has led the bishops's biographer, Quintana, to suggest that the friar's threadbare robe may have covered somewhat of worldly pride and envy. It may be so. Yet it may also lead us to distrust the discretion of Las

Casas himself, who could carry measures with so rude a hand as to provoke such unsparing animadversions from his fellow-laborers in the vineyard.

Toribio was made guardian of a Franciscan convent at Tezcuco. In this situation he continued active in good works, and, at this place, and in his different pilgrimages, is stated to have baptized more than four hundred thousand natives. His efficacious piety was attested by various miracles. One of the most remarkable was, when the Indians were suffering from great drought, which threatened to annihilate the approaching harvests. The good father recommended a solemn procession of the natives to the church of Santa Cruz, with prayers and a vigorous flagellation. The effect was soon visible in such copious rains as entirely relieved the people from their apprehensions, and in the end made the season uncommonly fruitful. The counterpart to this prodigy was afforded a few years later, while the country was laboring under excessive rains ; when, by a similar remedy, the evil was checked, and a like propitious influence exerted on the season as before. The exhibition of such miracles greatly edified the people, says his biographer, and established them firmly in the Faith. Probably Toribio's exemplary life and conversation, so beautifully illustrating the principles which he taught, did quite as much for the good cause as his miracles.

Thus passing his days in the peaceful and pious avocations of the Christian missionary, the worthy ecclesiastic was at length called from the scene of his earthly pilgrimage, in what year is uncertain, but at an advanced age, for he survived all the little band of missionaries who had accompanied him to New Spain. He died in the convent of San Francisco at Mexico, and his panegyric is thus emphatically pronounced by Torquemada, a brother of his own order : " He was a truly apostolic man, a great teacher of Christianity, beautiful in the ornament of every virtue, jealous of the glory of God, a friend of evangelical poverty, most true to the observance of his monastic rule, and zealous in the conversion of the heathen."

Father Toribio's long personal intercourse with the Mexicans, and the knowledge of their language, which he was at much pains to acquire, opened to him all the sources of information respecting them and their institutions, which existed at the time of the Conquest. The results he carefully digested in the work so often cited in these pages, the *Historia de los Indios de Nueva España,* making a volume of manuscript in folio. It is divided into three parts. 1. The religion, rites, and sacrifices of the Aztecs. 2. Their conversion to Christianity, and their manner of celebrating the festivals of the Church. 3. The genius and character of the nation, their chronology and astrology, together with notices of the principal cities and the staple productions of the country. Notwithstanding the methodical arrangement of the work, it is written in the rambling unconnected manner of a common-place book, into which the author has thrown at random his notices of such matters as most interested him in his survey of the country. His own mission is ever before his eyes, and the immediate topic of discussion, of whatever nature it may be, is at once abandoned to exhibit an event or an anecdote that can illustrate his ecclesiastical labors. The most startling occurrences are recorded with all the credulous gravity which is so likely to win credit from the vulgar ; and a stock of miracles is duly attested by the historian, of more than sufficient magnitude to supply the wants of the infant religious communities of New Spain.

Yet, amidst this mass of pious *incredibilia,* the inquirer into the Aztec antiquities will find much curious and substantial information. Toribio's long and intimate relations with the natives put him in possession of their whole stock of theology and science ; and as his manner, though somewhat discursive, is plain and unaffected, there is no obscurity in the communication of his ideas. His inferences, colored by the superstitions of the age, and the peculiar nature of his profession, may be often received with distrust. But, as his integrity and his means of information were unquestionable, his work becomes of the first authority in relation to the antiquities of the country, and its condition at the period of the Conquest. As an educated man, he was enabled to penetrate deeper than the illiterate soldiers of Cortés, men given to action rather than to speculation.—Yet Toribio's manuscript, valuable as it is to the historian, has never been printed, and has too little in it of popular interest probably, ever to be printed. Much that it contains has found its way, in various forms, into subsequent compilations. The work itself is very rarely to be found. Dr. Robertson had a copy, as it seems from the catalogue of MSS. published with his "History of America"; though the author's name is not prefixed to it. There is no copy, I believe, in the library of the Academy of History at Madrid ; and for that in my possession I am indebted to the kindness of that curious bibliographer, Mr. O. Rich, now consul for the United States at Minorca.

Pietro Martire de Angleria, or Peter Martyr, as he is called by English writers, belonged to an ancient and highly respectable family of Arona in the north of Italy. In 1487 he was induced by the count of Tendilla, the Spanish ambassador at Rome, to return with him to Castile. He was graciously received by Queen Isabella, always desirous to draw around her enlightened foreigners, who might exercise a salutary influence on the rough and warlike nobility of Castile. Martyr, who had been educated for the Church, was persuaded by the queen to undertake the instruction of the young nobles at the court. In this way he formed an intimacy with some of the most illustrious men of the nation, who seem to have cherished a warm personal regard for him through the remainder of his life. He was employed by the Catholic sovereigns in various concerns of public interest, was sent on a mission to Egypt, and was subsequently raised to a distinguished post in the cathedral of Granada. But he continued to pass much of his time at court, where he enjoyed the confidence of Ferdinand and Isabella, and of their successor, Charles the Fifth, till in 1525 he died, at the age of seventy.

Martyr's character combined qualities not often found in the same individual,—an ardent love of letters, with a practical sagacity that can only result from familiarity with men and affairs. Though passing his days in the gay and dazzling society of the capital, he preserved the simple tastes and dignified temper of a philosopher. His correspondence, as well as his more elaborate writings, if the term elaborate can be applied to any of his writings, manifests an enlightened and oftentimes independant spirit ; though one would have been better pleased, had he been sufficiently independent to condemn the religious intolerance of the government. But Martyr, though a philosopher, was enough of a courtier to look with a lenient eye on the errors of princes, Though deeply imbued with the learning of Antiquity, and a scholar at heart, he had none of the feelings of the recluse, but took the most lively interest in the events that were passing around him. His various writings, including his copious correspondence, are for this reason the very best mirror of the age in which he lived.

His inquisitive mind was particularly interested by the discoveries that were going on in the New World. He was allowed to be present at the sittings of the Council of the Indies, when any communication of importance was made to it ; and he was subsequently appointed a member of that body. All that related to the colonies passed through his hands. The correspondence of Columbus, Cortés, and the other discoverers, with the Court of Castile was submitted to his perusal. He became personally acquainted with these illustrious persons, on their return home, and frequently, as we find from his own letters, entertained them at his own table. With these advantages, his testimony becomes but one degree removed from that of the actors themselves in the great drama. In one respect it is of a higher kind, since it is free from the prejudice and passion, which a personal interest in events is apt to beget. The testimony of Martyr is that of a philosopher, taking a clear and comprehensive survey of the ground, with such lights of previous knowledge to guide him, as none of the actual discoverers and conquerors could pretend to. It is true, this does not prevent his occasionally falling into errors ; the errors of credulity,—not, however, of the credulity founded on superstition, but that which arises from the uncertain nature of the subject, where phenomena, so unlike any thing with which he had been familiar, were now first disclosed by the revelation of an unknown world.

He may be more fairly charged with inaccuracies of another description, growing out of haste and inadvertence of composition. But even here we should be charitable. For he confesses his sins with a candor that disarms criticism. In truth, he wrote rapidly, and on the spur of the moment, as occasion served. He shrunk from the publication of his writings, when it was urged on him, and his Decades *De Orbe Novo*, in which he embodied the results of his researches in respect to the American discoveries, were not published entire till after his death. The most valuable and complete edition of this work—the one referred to in the present pages—is the edition of Hakluyt, published at Paris, in 1587.

Martyr's works are all in Latin. and that not the purest : a circumstance rather singular, considering his familiarity with the classic models of Antiquity. Yet he evidently handled the dead languages with the same facility as the living. Whatever defects may be charged on his manner, in the selection and management of his topics he shows the superiority of his genius. He passes over the trivial details, which so often encumber the literal narratives of the Spanish voyagers, and fixes his attention on the great results of their discoveries,—the products of the country, the history and institutions of the races, their character and advance in civilization. In one respect his writings are of peculiar value. They show the state of feeling which existed at the Castilian court during the progress of discovery. They furnish, in short, the reverse side of the picture; and, when we have followed the Spanish conquerors in their wonderful career of adventure in the New World, we have only to turn to the pages of Martyr to find the impression produced by them on the enlightened minds of the Old. Such a view is necessary to the completeness of the historical picture.

If the reader is curious to learn more of this estimable scholar, he will find the particulars given in " The History of Ferdinand and Isabella," (Part I. chap. 14, postscript, and chap. 19,) for the illustration of whose reign his voluminous correspondence furnish the most authentic materials.

BOOK FOURTH

RESIDENCE IN MEXICO.

BOOK IV.

RESIDENCE IN MEXICO.

CHAPTER I.

TEZCUCAN LAKE.—DESCRIPTION OF THE CAPITAL.—PALACES AND
MUSEUMS.—ROYAL HOUSEHOLD.—MONTEZUMA'S WAY OF LIFE.

(1519.)

THE ancient city of Mexico covered the same spot occupied
by the modern capital. The great causeways touched it in the
same points; the streets ran in much the same direction, nearly
from north to south and from east to west; the cathedral in the
plaza mayor stands on the same ground that was covered by the
temple of the Aztec war-god; and the four principal quarters of
the town are still known among the Indians by their ancient
names. Yet an Aztec of the days of Montezuma, could he be
hold the modern metropolis, which has risen with such phœnix-
like splendor from the ashes of the old, would not recognize its
site as that of his own Tenochtitlan. For the latter was encompassed by the salt floods of Tezcuco, which flowed in ample
canals through every part of the city; while the Mexico of our
day stands high and dry on the main land, nearly a league distant, at its centre, from the water. The cause of this apparent
change in its position is the diminution of the lake, which, from
the rapidity of evaporation in these elevated regions, had become perceptible before the Conquest, but which has since been
greatly accelerated by artificial causes.[1]

The average level of the Tezcucan lake, at the present day,
is but four feet lower than the great square of Mexico.[2] It is

---

[1] The lake, it seems, had perceptibly shrunk before the Conquest, from
the testimony of Motilinia, who entered the country soon after. Toribio,
Hist. de los Indios, MS., Parte 3, cap. 6.

[2] Humboldt, Essai Politique, tom. II. p. 95.

Cortés supposes there were regular tides in this lake. (Rel. Seg., ap
Lorenzana, p. 101.) This sorely puzzles the learned Martyr; (De Orbe
Novo, dec. 5, cap. 3;) as it has more than one philosopher since, whom it
has led to speculate on a subterraneous communication with the ocean!

considerably lower than the other great basins of water which are found in the Valley. In the heavy swell sometimes caused by long and excessive rains, these latter reservoirs anciently overflowed into the Tezcuco, which, rising with the accumulated volume of waters, burst through the dikes, and, pouring into the streets of the capital, buried the lower part of the buildings under a deluge. This was comparatively a light evil, when the houses stood on piles so elevated that boats might pass under them; when the streets were canals, and the ordinary mode of communication was by water. But it became more disastrous, as these canals, filled up with the rubbish of the ruined Indian city, were supplanted by streets of solid earth, and the foundations of the capital were gradually reclaimed from the watery element. To obviate this alarming evil, the famous drain of Huehuetoca was opened, at an enormous cost, in the beginning of the seventeenth century, and Mexico, after repeated inundations, has been at length placed above the reach of the flood.[3] But what was gained to the useful, in this case, as in some others, has been purchased at the expense of the beautiful. By this shrinking of the waters, the bright towns and hamlets once washed by them have been removed some miles into the interior, while a barren strip of land, ghastly from the incrustation of salts formed on the surface, has taken place of the glowing vegetation which once enamelled the borders of the lake, and of the dark groves of oak, cedar, and sycamore which threw their broad shadows over its bosom.

The *chinampas,* that archipelago of wandering islands, to which our attention was drawn in the last chapter, have, also, nearly disappeared. These had their origin in the detached masses of earth, which, loosening from the shores, were still held together by the fibrous roots with which they were penetrated. The primitive Aztecs, in their poverty of land, availed themselves of the hint thus afforded by nature. They constructed rafts of reeds, rushes, and other fibrous materials, which, tightly knit together, formed a sufficient basis for the sediment that they drew up from the bottom of the lake. Gradually islands were formed, two or three hundred feet in length, and three or four feet in depth, with a rich stimulated soil, on which the economical Indian raised his vegetables and flowers

---

What the general called "tides" was probably the periodical swells caused by the prevalence of certain regular winds.

  [3] Humboldt has given a minute account of this tunnel, which he pronounces one of the most stupendous hydraulic works in existence, and the completion of which, in its present form, does not date earlier than the latter part of the last century. See his Essai Politique, tom. II. p. 105, et seq.

for the markets of Tenochtitlan. Some of these *chinampas* were even firm enough to allow the growth of small trees, and to sustain a hut for the residence of the person that had charge of it, who with a long pole, resting on the sides or the bottom of the shallow basin, could change the position of his little territory at pleasure, which with its rich freight of vegetable stores was seen moving like some enchanted island over the water.[4]

The ancient dikes were three in number. That of Iztapalapan, by which the Spaniards entered, approaching the city from the south. That of Tepejacac, on the north, which, continuing the principal street, might be regarded, also, as a continuation of the first causeway. Lastly, the dike of Tlacopan, connecting the island-city with the continent on the west. This last causeway, memorable for the disastrous retreat of the Spaniards, was about two miles in length. They were all built in the same substantial manner, of lime and stone, were defended by drawbridges, and were wide enough for ten or twelve horsemen to ride abreast.[5]

The rude founders of Tenochtitlan built their frail tenements of reeds and rushes on the group of small islands in the western part of the lake. In process of time, these were supplanted by more substantial buildings. A quarry in the neighborhood, of a red porous amygdaloid, *tetzontli*, was opened, and a light, brittle stone drawn from it and wrought with little difficulty. Of this their edifices were constructed, with some reference to architectural solidity, if not elegance. Mexico, as already noticed, was the residence of the great chiefs, whom the sovereign encouraged, or rather compelled, from obvious motives of policy, to spend part of the year in the capital. It was also the temporary abode of the great lords of Tezcuco and Tlacopan, who shared, nominally, at last, the sovereignty of the empire.[6] The mansions of these dignitaries, and of the principal nobles, were on a scale of rude magnificence corresponding with their state. They were low, indeed; seldom of more than one floor, never exceeding two. But they spread over a wide extent of ground; were arranged in a quadrangular form, with a court in the centre, and were surrounded by porticos embellished with porphyry and jasper, easily found in the neighborhood, while not unfrequently a

[4] Ibid., tom. II. p. 87, et seq.—Clavigero, Stor. del Messico, tom. II. p. 153.

[5] Toribio, Hist. de los Indos, MS., Parte 3, cap. 8.

Cortés, indeed, speaks of four causeways. (Rel. Seg., ap. Lorenzana, p. 102.) He may have reckoned an arm of the southern one leading to Cojohuacan, or possibly the great aqueduct of Chapoltepec.

[6] Ante, Vol. I. p. 18

fountain of crystal water in the centre shed a grateful coolness over the atmosphere. The dwellings of the common people were also placed on foundations of stone, which rose to the height of a few feet, and were then succeeded by courses of un-baked bricks, crossed occasionally by wooden rafters.[7] Most of the streets were mean and narrow. Some few, however, were wide and of great length. The principal street, conducting from the great southern causeway, penetrated in a straight line the whole length of the city, and afforded a noble vista, in which the long lines of low stone edifices were broken occasionally by interven·ing gardens, rising on terraces, and displaying all the pomp of Aztec horticulture.

The great streets, which were coated with a hard cement, were intersected by numerous canals. Some of these were flanked by a solid way, which served as a foot-walk for passen-gers, and as a landing-place where boats might discharge their cargoes. Small buildings were erected at intervals, as stations for the revenue officers who collected the duties on different articles of merchandise. The canals were traversed by numer-ous bridges, many of which could be raised, affording the means of cutting off communication between different parts of the city.[8]

From the accounts of the ancient capital, one is reminded of those aquatic cities in the Old World, the positions of which have been selected from similar motives of economy and de-fence ; above all, of Venice,[9]—if it be not rash to compare the rude architecture of the American Indian with the marble palaces and temples—alas, how shorn of their splendor !—which crowned the once proud mistress of the Adriatic.[10] The example

[7] Martyr gives a particular account of these dwellings, which shows that even the poorer classes were comfortably lodged. " Populares vero domus cingulo virili tenus lapideæ sunt et ipsæ, ob lacunæ incrementum per fluxum aut fluviorum in ea labentium alluvies. Super fundamentis illis magnis, lateribus tum coctis, tum æstivo sole siccatis, immixtis trabibus reliquam molem construunt; uno sunt communes domus contentæ tabulato. In solo parum hospitantur propter humiditatem, tecta non tegulis sed bitumine quo-dam terreo vestiunt ; ad solem captandum commodior est ille modus, breviore tempore consumi debere credendum est." De Orbe Novo, dec. 5, cap. 10.

[8] Toribio, Hist. de los Indios, MS., Parte 3, cap. 8.—Rel. Seg. de Cortés, ap. Lorenzana, p. 108.—Oviedo, Hist. de las Ind., MS., lib. 33, cap. 10, 11. —Rel. d'un gent., ap. Ramusio, tom. III. fol. 309.

[9] Martyr was struck with the resemblance. " Uti de illustrissima civitate Venetiarum legitur, ad tumulum in ea sinus Adriatici parte visum, fuisse constructam." Martyr, De Orbe Novo, dec. 5, cap. 10.

[10] May we not apply, without much violence, to the Aztec capital, Gio-vanni della Casa's spirited sonnet, contrasting the origin of Venice with its meridian glory?

" Questi Palazzi e queste logge or colte
D'ostro, di marmo e di figure elette,

of the metropolis was soon followed by the other towns in the vicinity. Instead of resting their foundations on *terra firma*, they were seen advancing far into the lake, the shallow waters of which in some parts do not exceed four feet in depth.[11] Thus an easy means of intercommunication was opened, and the surface of this inland " sea," as Cortés styles it, was darkened by thousands of canoes [12]—an Indian term—industriously engaged in the traffic between these little communities. How gay and picturesque must have been the aspect of the lake in those days, with its shining cities, and flowering islets rocking, as it were, at anchor on the fair bosom of its waters !

The population of Tenochtitlan, at the time of the Conquest, is variously stated. No contemporary writer estimates it at less than sixty thousand houses, which, by the ordinary rules of reckoning, would give three hundred thousand souls.[13] If a dwelling often contained, as is asserted, several families, it would swell the amount considerably higher.[14] Nothing is more un-

Fur poche e basse case insieme accolte,
Deserti lidi e povere Isolette.
Ma genti ardite d'ogni vizio sciolte
Premeano il mar con picciole barchette,
Che qui non per domar provincie molte,
Ma fuggir servitus' eran ristrette.
on era ambizion ne' petti loro ;
Ma'l mentire abborrian più che la **morte,**
Nè vi regnava ingorda fame d'oro.
Se'l Ciel v' ha dato più beata sorte,
Non sien quel e virtù che tanto onoro,
Dalle nuove ricchezze oppresse emorte."

[11] " Le lac de Tezcuco n'a généralement que trois à cinq mètres de profondeur. Dans quelques endroits le fond se trouve même déjà à moins d'un mètre." Humboldt, Essai Politique, tom. II. p. 49.

[12] " Y cada dia entran gran multitud de Indios cargados de Bastimentos y tributos, así por tierra como por agua, en acales ó barcas, que *en lengua de las Islas llaman Canoas.*" Toribio, Hist. de los Indios, MS., Parte 3. cap. 6

[13] " Esta la cibdad de Méjico ó *Teneztatan,* que será de sesenta mil vecinos." (Carta de Lic. Zuazo, MS.) " Tenustitanam ipsam inquiunt sexaginta circites esse millium domorum." (Martyr, De Orbe Novo, dec. 5. cap. 3.) " Era Méjico, quando Cortés entró, pueblo de sesenta mil casas." (Gomara, Crónica, cap. 78.) Toribio says, vaguely, " Los moradores y gente era innumerable." (Hist. de los Indios, MS., Parte 3, cap. 8.) The Italian translation of the " Anonymous Conqueror," who survives only in translation, says, indeed, "meglio di sessanta mila *habitatori*"; (Rel. d'un gent., ap. Ramusio, tom. III. fol. 309;) owing, probably, to a blunder in rendering the word *vecinos,* the ordinary term in Spanish statistics, which, signifying *householders,* corresponds with the Italian *fuochi.* See, also, Clavigera. (Stor. del Messico, tom. III. p. 86, nota.) Robertson rests *exclusively* on this Italian translation for his estimate. (History of America. vol. II. p. 281.) He cites, indeed, two other authorities on the same connection ; Cortés, who says nothing of the population, and Herrera, who confirms the popular statement of " sesenta mil casas." (Hist. General, dec. 2, lib. 7, cap. 13.) The fact is of some importance.

[14] " En las casas, por pequeñas que eran, pocas veces dexaban de mora

certain than estimates of numbers among barbarous communities, who necessarily live in a more confused and promiscuous manner than civilized, and among whom no regular system is adopted for ascertaining the population. The concurrent testimony of the Conquerors ; the extent of the city, which was said to be nearly three leagues in circumference ; [15] the immense size of its great market-place ; the long lines of edifices, vestiges of whose ruins may still be found in the suburbs, miles from the modern city ; [16] the fame of the metropolis throughout Anahuac, which, however, could boast many large and populous places ; lastly, the economical husbandry and the ingenious contrivances to extract aliment from the most unpromising sources,[17] —all attest a numerous population, far beyond that of the present capital. [18]

A careful police provided for the health and cleanliness of the city. A thousand persons are said to have been daily employed in watering and sweeping the streets,[19] so that a man— to borrow the language of an old Spaniard —" could walk through them with as little danger of soiling his feet as his hands." [20] The water, in a city washed on all sides by the salt floods, was extremely brackish. A liberal supply of the pure element, however, was brought from Chapoltepec, " the grasshopper's hill," less than a league distant. It was brought through an earthen pipe, along a dike constructed for the purpose. That there might be no failure in so essential an article, when repairs were going on, a double course of pipes was laid. In this way a column of water of the size of a man's body was

dos, quatro, y seis vecinos." Herrera, Hist. General, dec. 2, lib. 7, cap. 13.

[15] Rel. d'un gent., ap. Ramusio, tom. III. fol. 309.

[16] "C'est sur le chemin qui mène à Tanepantla et aux Ahuahuetes que l'on peut marcher plus d'une heure entre les ruines de l'ancienne ville. On y reconnaît, ainsi que sur la route de Tacuba et d'Iztapalapan, combien Mexico rebâti par Cortéz, est plus petit que l'était Tenochtitlan sous le dernier des Montezuma. L'énorme grandeur du marché de Tlatelolco, dont on reconnaît encore les limites, prouve combien la population de l'ancienne ville doit avoir été considérable." Humboldt, Essai Politique, tom II. p. 43.

[17] A common food with the lower classes was a glutinous scum found in the lakes, which, they made into a sort of cake, having a savor not unlike cheese. (Bernal Diaz, Hist. de la Conquista, cap. 92.)

[18] One is confirmed in this inference by comparing the two maps at the end of the first edition of Bullock's " Mexico" ; one of the modern City, the other of the ancient, taken from Boturini's museum, and showing its regular arrangement of streets and canals ; as regular, indeed, as the squares on a chessboard.

[19] Clavigero, Stor. del Messico, tom. I. p. 274.

[20] " Era tan barrido y el suelo tan asentado y liso, que aunque la planta del pie fuera tan delicada como la de la mano no recibiera el pie detrimento ninguno en andar descalzo." Toribio, Hist. de los Indios, MS., Parte 3, cap. 7.

conducted into the heart of the capital, where it fed the fountains and reservoirs of the principal mansions. Openings were made in the aqueduct as it crossed the bridges, and thus a supply was furnished to the canoes below, by means of which it was transported to all parts of the city.[21]

While Montezuma encouraged a taste for architectural magnificence in his nobles, he contributed his own share towards the embellishment of the city. It was in his reign that the famous calendar stone, weighing, probably, in its primitive state, nearly fifty tons, was transported from its native quarry, many leagues distant, to the capital, where it still forms one of the most curious monuments of Aztec science. Indeed, when we reflect on the difficulty of hewing such a stupendous mass from its hard basaltic bed without the aid of iron tools, and that of transporting it such a distance across land and water without the help of animals, we may well feel admiration at the mechanical ingenuity and enterprise of the people who accomplished it.[22]

Not content with the spacious residence of his father, Montezuma erected another on a yet more magnificent scale. It occupied, as before mentioned, the ground partly covered by the private dwellings on one side of the *plaza mayor* of the modern city. This building, or, as it might more correctly be styled, pile of buildings, spread over an extent of ground so vast, that, as one of the Conquerors assures us, its terraced roof might have afforded ample room for thirty knights to run their courses in a regular tourney.[23] I have already noticed its interior decorations, its fanciful draperies, its roofs inlaid with cedar and other odoriferous woods, held together without a nail, and, probably, without a knowledge of the arch,[24] its numerous and spacious apartments, which Cortés, with enthusiastic hyperbole, does not hesitate to declare superior to anything of the kind in Spain.[25]

---

[21] Rel. Seg. de Cortes, ap. Lorenzana. p. 10S —Carta del Lic. Zuazo, MS., —Rel. d' un gent., ap. Ramusio, tom. III. fol. 309.

[22] These immense masses, according to Martyr, who gathered his information from eye-witnesses, were transported by means of long files of men, who dragged them with ropes over huge wooden rollers. (De Orbe Novo, dec. 5, cap. 10.) It was the manner in which the Egyptians removed their enormous blocks of granite, as appears from numerous reliefs sculptured on their buildings.

[23] Rel. d' un gent., ap. Ramusio, tom. III. fol. 309.

[24] " Ricos edificios," says the Licentiate Zuazo, speaking of the buildings in Anahuac generally, " ecepto que no se halla alguno con *boveda.*" (Carta, MS.) The writer made large and careful observations, the year after the Conquest. His assertion, if it be received, will settle a question much mooted among antiquaries.

[25] " Tenia dentro de la ciudad sus Casas de Aposentamiento, tales y tan

Adjoining the principal edifice were others devoted to various objects. One was an armory, filled with the weapons and military dresses worn by the Aztecs, all kept in the most perfect order, ready for instant use. The emperor was himself very expert in the management of the *maquahuitl,* or Indian sword, and took great delight in witnessing athletic exercises, and the mimic representation of war by his young nobility. Another building was used as a granary, and others as warehouses for the different articles of food and apparel contributed by the districts charged with the maintenance of the royal household.

There were, also, edifices appropriated to objects of quite another kind. One of these was an immense aviary, in which birds of splendid plumage were assembled from all parts of the empire. Here was the scarlet cardinal, the golden pheasant, the endless parrot-tribe with their rainbow hues, (the royal green predominant,) and that miniature miracle of nature, the humming-bird, which delights to revel among the honeysuckle bowers of Mexico.[26] Three hundred attendants had charge of this aviary, who made themselves acquainted with the appropriate food of its inmates, oftentimes procured at great cost, and in the moulting season were careful to collect the beautiful plumage, which, with its many-colored tints, furnished the materials for the Aztec painter.

A separate building was reserved for the fierce birds of prey the voracious vulture-tribes and eagles of enormous size, whose home was in the snowy solitudes of the Andes. No less than five hundred turkeys, the cheapest meat in Mexico, were allowed for the daily consumption of these tyrants of the feathered race.

Adjoining this aviary was a menagerie of wild animals, gathered from the mountain forests, and even from the remote swamps of the *tierra caliente.* The resemblance of the different species to those in the Old World, with which no one of them, however, was identical, led to a perpetual confusion in the

maravillosas, que me pareceria casi imposible poder decir la bondad y grandeza de ellas. E por tanto, no me porné en expresar cosa de ellas, mas de que en España no hay su semejable." Rel. Seg., ap. Lorenzana p. 111.

[26] Herrera's account of these feathered insects, if one may so style them, shows the fanciful errors into which even men of science were led in regard to the new tribes of animals discovered in America. "There are some birds in the country of the size of butterflies, with long beaks, brilliant plumage, much esteemed for the curious works made of them. Like the bees they live on flowers, and the dew which settles on them ; and when the rainy season is over, and the dry weather sets in, they fasten themselves to the trees by their beaks and soon die. But in the following year, when the new rains come, they come to life again "! Hist. General, dec. 2, lib. 10. cap. 21.

nomenclature of the Spaniards, as it has since done in that of better instructed naturalists. The collection was still further swelled by a great number of reptiles and serpents remarkable for their size and venomous qualities, among which the Spaniards beheld the fiery little animal " with the castanets in his tail," the terror of the American wilderness.[27] The serpents were confined in long cages lined with down or feathers, or in troughs of mud and water. The beasts and birds of prey were provided with apartments large enough to allow of their moving about, and secured by a strong lattice-work, through which light and air were freely admitted. The whole was placed under the charge of numerous keepers, who acquainted themselves with the habits of their prisoners, and provided for their comfort and cleanliness. With what deep interest would the enlightened naturalist of that day—an Oviedo, or a Martyr, for example—have surveyed this magnificent collection, in which the various tribes which roamed over the Western wilderness, the unknown races of an unknown world, were brought into one view ! How would they have delighted to study the peculiarities of these new species, compared with those of their own hemisphere, and thus have risen to some comprehension of the general laws by which Nature acts in all her works ! The rude followers of Cortés did not trouble themselves with such refined speculations. They gazed on the spectacle with a vague curiosity not unmixed with awe ; and, as they listened to the wild cries of the ferocious animals and the hissings of the serpents, they almost fancied themselves in the infernal regions.[28]

I must not omit to notice a strange collection of human monsters, dwarfs, and other unfortunate persons, in whose organization Nature had capriciously deviated from her regular laws. Such hideous anomalies were regarded by the Aztecs as a suitable appendage of state. It is even said, they were in some cases the result of artificial means, employed by unnatural parents desirous to secure a provision for their offspring by thus qualifying them for a place in the royal museum![29]

---

[27] " Pues mas tenian," says the honest Captain Diaz, " en aquella maldita casa muchas Viboras, y Culebras emponçoñadas que traen en las colas vnos que suenan como cascabeles ; estas son las peores Viboras de todas." Hist. de la Conquista, cap. 91.

[28] " Digamos aora," exclaims Captain Diaz, "las cosas infernales que hazian, quando bramauan los Tigres y Leones, y aullauan los Adiues y Zorros, y silbauan las Sierpes, era grima oirlo, y parecia infierno." Ibid., loc. cit.

[29] Ibid., ubi supra.—Rel. Seg. de Cortés, ap. Lorenzana, pp. 111-113.—Carta del Lic. Zuazo, MS.—Toribio, Hist. de los Indios, MS., Parte 3, cap. 7.—Oviedo, Hist. de las Ind., MS., lib. 33, cap. 11, 46.

Extensive gardens were spread out around these buildings, filled with fragrant shrubs and flowers, and especially with medicinal plants.[30] No country has afforded more numerous species of these last, than New Spain; and their virtues were perfectly understood by the Aztecs, with whom medical botany may be said to have been studied as a science. Amidst this labyrinth of sweet-scented groves and shrubberies, fountains of pure water might be seen throwing up their sparkling jets, and scattering refreshing dews over the blossoms. Ten large tanks, well stocked with fish, afforded a retreat on their margins to various tribes of water-fowl, whose habits were so carefully consulted, that some of these ponds were of salt water, as that which they most loved to frequent. A tessellated pavement of marble inclosed the ample basins, which were overhung by light and fanciful pavilions, that admitted the perfumed breezes of the gardens, and offered a grateful shelter to the monarch and his mistresses in the sultry heats of summer.[31]

But the most luxurious residence of the Aztec monarch, at that season, was the royal hill of Chapoltepec, a spot consecrated, moreover, by the ashes of his ancestors. It stood in a westerly direction from the capital, and its base was, in his day, washed by the waters of the Tezcuco. On its lofty crest of porphyritic rock, there now stands the magnificent, though desolate, castle erected by the young viceroy Galvez, at the close of the seventeenth century. The view from its windows is one of the finest in the environs of Mexico. The landscape is not disfigured here, as in many other quarters, by the white and barren patches, so offensive to the sight; but the eye wanders over an unbroken expanse of meadows and cultivated fields, waving with rich harvests of European grain. Montezuma's gardens stretched for miles around the base of the hill. Two statues of that monarch and his father, cut in *bas relief* in the porphyry, were spared till the middle of the last century;[32] and the grounds are still shaded by gigantic cypresses, more than fifty feet in circumfer-

---

[30] Montezuma, according to Gomara, would allow no fruit-trees, considering them as unsuitable to pleasure-grounds. (Crónica, cap. 75.) Toribio says, to the same effect, "Los Indios Señores no procuran árboles de fruta, porque se la traen sus vasallos, sino árboles de floresta, de donde cojan rosas, y adonde se crian aves, así para gozar del canto, como para las tirar con Cerbatana, de la cual son grandes tiradores." Hist. de los Indios, MS., Parte 3, cap. 6.

[31] Ibid., loc. cit.—Rel. Seg. de Cortés, ubi supra.—Oviedo, Hist. de las Ind., MS., lib. 33, cap. 11.

[32] Gama, a competent critic, who saw them just before their destruction, praises their execution. Gama, Descripcion, Parte 2, pp. 81-83.—Also Ante, Vol. 1. p. 115.

ence, which were centuries old at the time of the Conquest. The place is now a tangled wilderness of wild shrubs where the myrtle mingles its dark, glossy leaves with the red berries and delicate foliage of the pepper-tree. Surely, there is no spot better suited to awaken meditation on the past; none, where the traveller, as he sits under those stately cypresses gray with the moss of ages, can so fitly ponder on the sad destinies of the Indian races and the monarch who once held his courtly revels under the shadow of their branches.

The domestic establishment of Montezuma was on the same scale of barbaric splendor as everything else about him. He could boast as many wives as are found in the harem of an Eastern sultan.[31] They were lodged in their own apartments, and provided with every accommodation, according to their ideas, for personal comfort and cleanliness. They passed their hours in the usual feminine employments of weaving and embroidery, especially in the graceful feather-work, for which such rich materials were furnished by the royal aviaries. They conducted themselves with strict decorum, under the supervision of certain aged females, who acted in the respectable capacity of duennas, in the same manner as in the religious houses attached to the *teocallis*. The palace was supplied with numerous baths, and Montezuma set the example, in his own person, of frequent ablutions. He bathed at least once, and changed his dress four times, it is said, every day.[34] He never put on the same apparel a second time, but gave it away to his attendants. Queen Elizabeth, with a similar taste for costume, showed a less princely spirit in hoarding her discarded suits. Her wardrobe was, probably, somewhat more costly than that of the Indian emperor

Besides his numerous female retinue, the halls and antechambers were filled with nobles in constant attendance on his person, who served also as a sort of body-guard. It had been usual for plebeians of merit to fill certain offices in the palace. But the haughty Montezuma refused to be waited upon by any but men of noble birth. They were not unfrequently the sons of the great chiefs, and remained as hostages in the absence of their fathers; thus serving the double purpose of security and state.[35]

---

[35] No less than one thousand, if we believe Gomara; who adds the edifying intelligence, "que huvo vez, que tuvo ciento i cincuenta preñadas á un tiempo!"

[34] "Vestíase todos los dias quatro maneras de vestiduras todas nuevas, y nunca mas se las vestia otra vez." Rel. Seg. de Cortés, ap Lorenzana, p. 114.

[35] Bernal Diaz, Hist. de la Conquista, cap. 91.—Gomara, Crónica, cap

His meals the emperor took alone. The well-matted floor of a large saloon was covered with hundreds of dishes.[36] Sometimes Montezuma himself, but more frequently his steward, indicated those which he preferred, and which were kept hot by means of chafing-dishes.[37]. The royal bill of fare comprehended, besides domestic animals, game from the distant forests, and fish which, the day before, was swimming in the Gulf of Mexico! They were dressed in manifold ways, for the Aztec *artists*, as we have already had occasion to notice, had penetrated deep into the mysteries of culinary science.[38]

The meats were served by the attendant nobles, who then resigned the office of waiting on the monarch to maidens selected for their personal grace and beauty. A screen of richly gilt and carved wood was drawn around him, so as to conceal him from vulgar eyes during the repast. He was seated on a cushion, and the dinner was served on a low table covered with a delicate cotton cloth. The dishes were of the finest ware of Cholula. He had a service of gold, which was reserved for religious celebrations. Indeed, it would scarcely have comported with even his princely revenues to have used it on ordinary occasions, when his table equipage was not allowed to appear a second time, but was given away to his attendants. The saloon was lighted by torches made of a resinous wood, which sent forth a sweet odor and, probably, not a little smoke, as they burned. At his meal, he was attended by five or six of his ancient counsellors, who stood at a respectful distance, answering his ques-

---

67, 71, 76.—Rel. Seg. de Cortés, ap. Lorenzana, pp. 113, 114. Toribio, Hist. de los Indios, MS., Parte 3, cap. 7.

"A la puerta de la sala estaba vn patio mui grande en que habia cien aposentos de 25 ó 30 pies de largo cada vno sobre sí en torno de dicho patio, é allí estaban los Señores principales aposentados como guardas del palacio ordinarias, y estos tales aposentos se llaman galpones, los quales á la contina ocupan mas de 600 hombres, que jamas se quitaban de allí, é cada vno de aquellos tenian mas de 30 servidores, de manera que á lo menos nunca faltaban 3000 hombres de guerra en esta guarda cotediana del palacio." (Oviedo, Hist. de las Ind., MS., lib. 33, cap. 46.) A very curious and full account of Montezuma's household is given by this author, as he gathered it from the Spaniards who saw it in its splendor. As Oviedo's history still remains in manuscript, I have transferred the chapter in the original Castilian to *Appendix*, *Part 2 No.* 10.

[35] Bernal Diaz, Ibid., loc. cit.—Rel. Seg. de Cortés, ubi supra.

[37] " Y porque la Tierra es fria, trahian debaxo de cada plato y escudilla de manjar un braserico con brasa, porque no se enfriasse." Rel. Seg. de Cortés, ap. Lorenzana, p. 113.

[38] Bernal Diaz has given us a few items of the royal *carte*. The first cover is rather a startling one, being a fricassee or stew of little children ! "*carnes de muchachos de poca edad.*" He admits, however, that this is somewhat apocryphal. Ibid., ubi supra.

tions, and occasionally rejoiced by some of the viands with which he complimented them from his table.

This course of solid dishes was succeeded by another of sweetmeats and pastry, for which the Aztec cooks, provided with the important requisites of maize-flour, eggs, and the rich sugar of the aloe, were famous. Two girls were occupied at the further end of the apartment, during dinner, in preparing fine rolls and wafers, with which they garnished the board from time to time. The emperor took no other beverage than the *chocolatl*, a potation of chocolate, flavored with vanilla and other spices, and so prepared as to be reduced to a froth of the consistency of honey, which gradually dissolved in the mouth. This beverage, if so it could be called, was served in golden goblets, with spoons of the same metal or of tortoise-shell finely wrought. The emperor was exceedingly fond of it, to judge from the quantity,—no less than fifty jars or pitchers being prepared for his own daily consumption.[39] Two thousand more were allowed for that of his household.[40]

The general arrangement of the meal seems to have been not very unlike that of Europeans. But no prince in Europe could boast a dessert which could compare with that of the Aztic emperor. For it was gathered fresh from the most opposite climes ; and his board displayed the products of his own temperate region, and the luscious fruits of he tropics, plucked, the day previous, from the green groves of the *tierra caliente*, and transmitted with the speed of steam, by means of couriers, to the capital. It was as if some kind fairy should crown our banquets with the spicy products that but yesterday were growing in a sunny isle of the far-off Indian seas !

After the royal appetite was appeased, water was handed to him by the female attendants, in a silver basin, in the same manner as had been done before commencing his meal ! for the Aztecs were as constant in their ablutions, at these times, as any nation of the East. Pipes were then brought, made of a varnished and richly gilt wood, from which he inhaled, sometimes through the nose, at others though the mouth, the fumes of an intoxicating weed, " called *tobacco*," [41] mingled with liquid-amber. While

[39] " *Lo que yo vi*," says Diaz, speaking from his own observation, " que traian sobre cincuenta jarros grandes hechos de buen cacao con su espuma, y de lo que bebia." Ibid., cap. 91.

[40] Ibid., ubi supra.—Rel. Seg. de Cortés, ap. Lorenzana, pp. 113, 114.—Oviedo, Hist. de las Ind., MS., lib. 33, cap. 11, 46.—Gomara, Crónica, cap. 67.

[41] " Tambien le ponian en la mesa tres cañutos muy pintados, y dorados, y dentro traian liquidámbar, rebuelto con vnas yervas *que se dize tabaco*." Bernal Diaz, Hist. de la Conquista, cap. 91.

this soothing process of fumigation was going on, the emperor enjoyed the exhibitions or his mountebanks and jugglers, of whom a regular corps was attached to the palace. No people, not even those of China or Hindostan, surpassed the Aztecs in feats of agility and ledgerdemain.[42]

Sometimes he amused himself with his jester; for the Indian monarch had his jesters, as well as his more refined brethren of Europe, at that day. Indeed, he used to say, that more in-struction was to be gathered from them than from wiser men, for they dared to tell the truth. At other times, he witnessed the graceful dances of his women, or took delight in listening to music,—if the rude minstrelsy of the Mexicans deserve that name,—accompanied by a chant, in slow and solemn cadence, celebrating the heroic deeds of great Aztic warriors, or of his own princely line.

When he had sufficiently refreshed his spirits with these diver-sions, he composed himself to sleep, for in his *siesta* he was as regular as a Spaniard. On awaking, he gave audience to am-bassadors from foreign states, or his own tributary cities, or to such caciques as had suits to prefer to him. They were intro-duced by the young nobles in attendance, and, whatever might be their rank, unless of the blood royal, they were obliged to submit to the humiliation of shrouding their rich dresses under the coarse mantel of *nequen*, and entering barefooted, with down-cast eyes into his presence. The emperor addressed few and brief remarks to the suitors, answering them generally by his secretaries; and the parties retired with the same reveren-tial obeisance, taking care to keep their faces turned towards the monarch. Well might Cortés exclaim, that no court whether of the Grand Seignior or any other infidel ever displayed so pom-pous and elaborate a ceremonial![43]

Besides the crowd of retainers already noticed, the royal household was not complete without a host of artisans constantly employed in the erection or repair of buildings, besides a great number of jewellers and persons skilled in working metals, who found abundant demand for their trinkets among the dark-eyed beauties of the harem. The imperial mummers and jugglers were also very numerous, and the dancers belonging to the

---

[42] The feats of jugglers and tumblers were a favorite diversion with the Grand Khan of China, as Sir John Maundeville informs us. (Voiage and Travaille, chap. 22.) The Aztec mountebanks had such repute, that Cortés send two of them to Rome to amuse his Holiness, Clement VII. Clavigero, Stor. del Messico, tom. II. p. 186.

[43] " Ninguno de los Soldanes, ni otro ningun señor infiel, de los que hasta agora se tiene noticia, no creo, que tantas, ni tales ceremonias en servicie tengan." Rel. Seg. de Cortés, ap. Lorenzana, p. 115.

palace occupied a particular district of the city, appropriated exclusively to them.

The maintenance of this little host, amounting to some thousands of individuals, involved a heavy expenditure, requiring accounts of a complicated, and, to a simple people, it might well be, embarrassing nature. Everything, however was conducted with perfect order; and all the various receipts and disbursements were set down in the picture-writing of the country. The arithmetical characters were of a more refined and conventional sort than those for narrative purposes; and a separate apartment was filled with hieroglyphical ledgers, exhibiting a complete view of the economy of the palace. The care of all this was intrusted to a treasurer, who acted as a sort of major-domo in the household, having a general superintendence over all its concerns. This responsible office, on the arrival of the Spaniards, was in the hands of a trusty cacique named Tapia.[44]

Such is the picture of Montezuma's domestic establishment and way of living, as delineated by the Conquerors and their immediate followers, who had the best means of information ;[45] too highly colored, it may be, by the proneness to exaggerate, which was natural to those who first witnessed a spectacle so striking to the imagination, so new and unexpected. I have thought it best to present the full details, trivial though they may seem to the reader, as affording a curious picture of manners, so superior in point of refinement to those of the other Aboriginal tribes on the North American continent. Nor are they, in fact, so trivial, when we reflect, that, in these details of private life, we possess a surer measure of civilization, than in those of a public nature.

In surveying them we are strongly reminded of the civilization of the East; not of that higher intellectual kind which belonged to the more polished Arabs and the Persians, but that semi-civilization which has distinguished, for example, the Tartar races, among whom art, and even science, have made, indeed, some progress in their adaptation to material wants and sensual gratification, but little in reference to the higher and more ennobling interests of humanity. It is characteristic of such a people to find a puerile pleasure in a dazzling and ostentatious pageantry ;

[44] Bernal Diaz, Hist. de la Conquista, cap. 91.—Carta del Lic. Zuazo, MS.—Oviedo, Hist. de las Ind., MS., ubi supra.—Toribio, Hist. de los Indios, MS., Parte 3, cap. 7.—Rel. Seg. de Cortés, ap. Lorenzana, pp. 110 115.—Rel. d' un gent., ap. Ramusio, tom. III. fol. 306.
[45] If the historian will descend but a generation later for his authorities, he may find materials for as good a chapter as any in Sir John Maundeville or the Arabian Nights.

to mistake show for substance; vain pomp for power; to hedge round the throne itself with a barren and burdensome ceremonial, the counterfeit of real majesty.

Even this, however, was an advance in refinement, compared with the rude manners of the earlier Aztecs. The change may, doubtless, be referred in some degree to the personal influence of Montezuma. In his younger days, he had tempered the fierce habits of the soldier with the milder profession of religion. In later life, he had withdrawn himself still more from the brutalizing occupations of war, and his manners acquired a refinement tinctured, it may be added, with an effeminacy, unknown to his martial predecessors.

The condition of the empire, too, under his reign was favorable to this change. The dismemberment of the Tezcucan kingdom, on the death of the great Nezahualpilli, had left the Aztec monarchy without a rival; and it soon spread its colossal arms over the furthest limits of Anahuac. The aspiring mind of Montezuma rose with the acquisition of wealth and power; and he displayed the consciousness of new importance by the assumption of unprecedented state. He affected a reserve unknown to his predecessors; withdrew his person from the vulgar eye, and fenced himself round with an elaborate and courtly etiquette. When he went abroad, it was in state, on some public occasion, usually to the great temple, to take part in the religious services; and, as he passed along, he exacted from his people, as we have seen, the homage of an adulation worthy of an Oriental despot.[46] His haughty demeanor touched the pride of his more potent vassals, particularly those who, at a distance, felt themselves nearly independent of his authority. His exactions, demanded by the profuse expenditure of his palace, scattered broad-cast the seeds of discontent; and, while the empire seemed towering in its most palmy and prosperous state, the canker had eaten deepest into its heart.

---

[46] "Referre in tanto rege piget superbam mutationem vestis, et desideratas humi jacentium adulationes." (Livy, Hist., lib. 9, cap. 18.) The remarks of the Roman historian in reference to Alexander, after he was infected by the manners of Persia, fit equally well the Aztec emperor.

CHAPTER II.

MARKET OF MEXICO.—GREAT TEMPLE.—INTERIOR SANCTUARIES. SPANISH QUARTERS.

1519.

FOUR days had elapsed since the Spaniards made their entry into Mexico. Whatever schemes their commander may have revolved in his mind, he felt that he could determine on no plan of operations till he had seen more of the capital, and ascertained by his own inspection the nature of its resources. He accordingly, as was observed at the close of the last Book, sent to Montezuma, asking permission to visit the great *teocalli*, and some other places in the city.

The friendly monarch consented without difficulty. He even prepared to go in person to the great temple to receive his guests there,—it may be, to shield the shrine of his tutelar deity from any attempted profanation. He was acquainted, as we have already seen, with the proceedings of the Spaniards on similar occasions in the course of their march.—Cortés put himself at the head of his little corps of cavalry, and nearly all the Spanish foot, as usual, and followed the caciques sent by Montezuma to guide him. They proposed first to conduct him to the great market of Tlateloco in the western part of the city.

On the way, the Spaniards were struck, in the same manner as they had been on entering the capital, with the appearance of the inhabitants, and their great superiority in the style and quality of their dress, over the people of the lower countries.[1] The *tilmatli* or cloak thrown over the shoulders and tied round the neck, made of cotton of different degrees of fineness, according to the condition of the wearer, and the ample sash around the loins, were often wrought in rich and elegant figures, and edged with a deep fringe or tassel. As the weather

---

[1] "La Gente de esta Ciudad es de mas manera y primor en su vestido, y servicio, que no la otra de estas otras Provincias, y Ciudades: porque como allí estaba siempre este Señor Moteczuma, y todos los Señores sus Vasallos ocurrian siempre á la Ciudad, habia en ella mas manera, y policia en todas las cosas." Rel. Seg., ap. Lorenzana, p. 109.

was now growing cool, mantles of fur or of the gorgeous feather-work were sometimes substituted. The latter combined the advantage of great warmth with beauty.[2] The Mexicans had also the art of spinning a fine thread of the hair of the rabbit and other animals, which they wove into a delicate web that took a permanent dye.

The women, as in other parts of the country, seemed to go about as freely as the men. They wore several skirts or petticoats of different lengths, with highly ornamented borders, and sometimes over them loose flowing robes, which reached to the ankles. These, also, were made of cotton, for the wealthier classes, of a fine texture, prettily embroidered.[3] No veils were worn here, as in some other parts of Anahuac, where they were made of the aloe thread, or of a light web of hair, above noticed. The Aztec women had their faces exposed; and their dark, raven tresses floated luxuriantly over their shoulders, revealing features, which, although of a dusky or rather cinnamon hue, were not unfrequently pleasing, while touched with the serious, even sad expression characteristic of the national physiognomy.[4]

On the drawing near to the *tianguez,* or great market, the Spaniards were astonished at the throng of people pressing towards it, and, on entering the place, their surprise was still further heightened by the sight of the multitudes assembled there, and the dimensions of the inclosure, thrice as large as the celebrated square of Salamanca.[5] Here were met together traders from all parts, with the products and manufactures peculiar to their countries; the goldsmiths of Azcapozalco; the potters and jewellers of Cholula, the painters of Tezcuco, the stone-cutters of Tenajocan, the hunters of Xilotepec, the fishermen of Cuitlahuac, the fruiterers of the warm countries, the mat and chairmakers of Quauhtitlan, and the florists of Xochimilco,—all busily engaged in recommending their respective wares, and in chaffering with purchasers.[6]

---

[2] Zuazo, speaking of the beauty and warmth of this national fabric, says, "Ví muchas mantas de á dos haces labrades de plumas de papos de aves tan suaves, que trayendo la mano por encima, á pelo y á pospelo, no era mas que vna manta zebellina muí bien adobada: hice pesar vna dellas no peso mas de seis onzas. Dicen que en el tiempo del Ynbierno una abasta para encima de la camisa sin otro cobertor ni mas ropa encima de la cama." Carta, MS.

[3] "Sono lunghe & large, lauorate di bellisimi, & molto gentili lauori sparsi per esse, cō le loro frangie, ò orletti ben lauorati che compariscono benissimo." Rel. d'un gent., ap. Ramusio, tom. III. fol. 305.

[4] Ibid., fol. 305.

[5] Ibid., fol. 309.

[6] "Quivi concorrevano i Pentolai, ed i Giojellieri di Cholulla, gli Orefici

The market-place was surrounded by deep porticos, and the several articles had each its own quarter allotted to it. Here might be seen cotton piled up in bales, or manufactured into dresses and articles of domestic use, as tapestry, curtains, coverlets and the like. The richly stained and nice fabrics reminded Cortés of the *alcaycería*, or silk-market of Granada. There was the quarter assigned to the goldsmiths, where the purchaser might find various articles of ornament or use formed of the precious metals, or curious toys, such as we have already had occasion to notice, made in imitation of birds and fishes, with scales and feathers alternately of go'd and silver, and with movable heads and bodies. These fantastic little trinkets were often garnished with precious stones, and showed a patient, puerile ingenuity in the manufacture, like that of the Chinese.[7]

In an adjoining quarter were collected specimens of pottery coarse and fine, vases of wood elaborately carved, varnished or gilt, of curious and sometimes graceful forms. There were also hatchets made of copper alloyed with tin, the substitute, and, as it proved, not a bad one, for iron. The soldier found here all the implements of his trade. The casque fashioned into the head of some wild animal, with its grinning defences of teeth, and bristling crest dyed with the rich tint of the cochineal;[8]

---

d' Azcapozalco, i Pittori di Tezcuco, gli Scarpellini di Tenajocan, i Cacciatori di Xilotepec, i Pescatori di Cuitlahuac, i fruttajuoli de' paesi caldi, gli artefici di stuoje, e di scranne di Quauhtitlan ed i coltivatori de' fiori di Xochimilco." Clavigero, Stor. del Messico, tom. II. p. 165,

[7] "Oro y plata, piedras de valor, con otros plumajes é argenterías maravillosas, y con tanto primor fabricadas que excede todo ingenio humano para comprenderlas y alcanzarlas," (Carta del Lic. Zuazo, MS.) The licentiate then enumerates several of these elegant pieces of mechanism. Cortés is not less emphatic in his admiration ; "Contrahechas de oro, y plata, y piedras y plumas, tan al natural lo de Oro, y Plata, que no hay Platero en el Mundo que mejor lo hiciesse, y lo de las Piedras, que no baste juicio comprehender con que Instrumentos se hiciesse tan perfecto, y lo de Pluma, que ni de Cera, ni en ningun broslado se podria hacer tan maravillosamente." (Rel. Seg., ap. Lorenzana, p. 110.) Peter Martyr, a less prejudiced critic than Cortés, and who saw and examined many of these golden trinkets afterwards in Castile, bears the same testimony to the exquisite character of the workmanship, which, he says, far surpassed the value of the material. De Orbe Novo, dec. 5, cap. 10.

[8] Herrera makes the unauthorized assertion, repeated by Solís, that the Mexicans were unacquainted with the value of the cochineal, till it was taught them by the Spaniards. (Herrera, Hist. General, dec. 4, lib 8, cap. 11.) The natives, on the contrary, took infinite pains to rear the insect on plantations of the cactus, and it formed one of the staple tributes to the crown from certain districts. See the tribute-rolls, ap. Lorenzana, Nos. 23, 24.—Hernandez, Hist. Plantarum, lib. 6 cap. 116.—Also, Clavigero, St r. del Messico, tom. I. p. 114, nota.

the *escaupil,* or quilted doublet of cotton, the rich surcoat of
feather-mail, and weapons of all sorts, copper-headed lances
and arrows, and the broad *maquahuitl,* the Mexican sword, with
its sharp blades of *itztli.*   Here were razors and mirrors of this
same hard and polished mineral which served so many of the
purposes of steel with the Aztecs.[9]   In the square were also to
be found booths occupied by barbers, who used these same
razors in their vocation.   For the Mexicans, contrary to the
popular and erroneous notions respecting the Aborigines of the
New World, had beards, though scanty ones.   Other shops or
booths were tenanted by apothecaries, well provided with drugs,
roots, and different medicinal preparations.   In other places,
again, blank books or maps for the hieroglyphical picture-writing were to be seen, folded together like fans, and made of
cotton, skins, or more commonly the fibres of the agave, the
Aztec papyrus.

Under some of the porticos they saw hides raw and dressed,
and various articles for domestic or personal use made of the
leather.   Animals, both wild and tame, were offered for sale,
and near them, perhaps, a gang of slaves, with collars round
their necks, intimating they were likewise on sale,—a spectacle
unhappily not confined to the barbarian markets of Mexico,
though the evils of their condition were aggravated there by the
conciou.ness that a 'ife of degradation might be consummated
at any moment by the dreadful doom of sacrifice.

The heavier materials for building, as stone, lime, timber,
were considered too bulky to be allowed a place in the square,
and were deposited in the adjacent streets on the borders of
the canals.   It would be tedious to enumerate all the various
articles, whether for luxury or daily use, which were collected
from all quarters in this vast bazaar.   I must not omit to mention, however, the display of provisions, one of the most attractive features of the *tianguez ;* meats of all kinds, domestic
poultry, game from the neighboring mountains, fish from the
lakes and streams, fruits in all the delicious abundance of these
temperate regions, green vegetables, and the unfailing maize.
There was many a viand, too, ready dressed, which sent up its
savory streams provoking the appetite of the idle passenger ;
pastry, bread of the Indian corn, cakes, and confectionery.[10]

[9] Ante, Vol. I. p. 115.

[10] Zuazo, who seems to have been nice in these matters, concludes a paragraph of dainties with the following tribute to the Aztec *cuisine.*   "Vendense
huebos asados, crudos, en tortilla, è diversidad de guisados que se suelen
guisar, con otras cazuelas y parteles, que en el mal cocinado de Medina, ni
en otros lugares de Tlamencos dicen que hai ni se pueden hallar tales truja-
manes," Carta, M.S.

Along with these were to be seen cooling or stimulating beverages, the spicy foaming *chocolatl*, with its delicate aroma of vanilla, and the inebriating *pulque*, the fermented juice of the aloe. All these commodities, and every stall and portico, were set out, or rather smothered, with flowers, showing, on a much greater scale, indeed, a taste similar to that displayed in the markets of modern Mexico. Flowers seem to be the spontaneous growth of this luxuriant soil ; which, instead of noxious weeds, as in other regions, is ever ready, without the aid of man, to cover up its nakedness with this rich and variegated livery of Nature.[11]

I will spare the reader the repetition of all the particulars enumerated by the bewildered Spaniards, which are of some interest as evincing the various mechanical skill and the polished wants, resembling those of a refined community, rather than of a nation of savages. It was the *material* civilization, which belongs neither to the one nor the other. The Aztec had plainly reached that middle station, as far above the rude races of the New World as it was below the cultivated communities of the Old.

At to the numbers assembled in the market, the estimates differ, as usual. The Spaniards often visited the place, and no one states the amount at less than forty thousand ! Some carry it much higher.[12] Without relying too much on the arithmetic of the Conquerors, it is certain that on this occasion, which occurred every fifth day, the city swarmed with a motley crowd of strangers, not only from the vicinity, but from many leagues around ; the causeways were thronged, and the lake was darkened by canoes filled with traders flocking to the great *tianguez*. It resembled, indeed, the perodical fairs in Europe, not as they exist now, but as they existed in the Middle Ages, when, from the difficulties of intercommunication, they served is the great central marts for commercial intercourse,

---

[11] Ample details—many more than I have thought it necessary to give—of the Aztec market of Tlatelolco may be found in the writings of all the old Spaniards who visited the capital. Among others, see Rel. Seg. de Cortes, ap. Lorenzana, pp. 103-105.—Toribio, Hist. de los Indios, MS., Parte 3, cap) 7.—Carta del Lic. Zuazo, MS.—Rel. d'un gent., ap. Ramusio, tom. III. fol. 309.—Bernal Diaz, Hist. de la Conquista, cap. 92.

[12] Zuazo raises it to 80,000! (Carta, MS.) Cortes to 60,000. (Rel. Seg., ubi supra.) The most modest computation is that of the "Anonymous Conqueror," who says from 40,000 to 50,000. " Et il giorno del mercato, che si fa di cinque in cinque giorni, vi sono da quaranta ò cinquanta mila persone "; (Rel. d'un gent., ap. Ramusio, tom. III. fol. 309.) a confirmation, by the by, of the supposition that the estimated population of the capital, found in the Italian version of this author, is a misprint. (See the preceding chapter, note 13.) He would hardly have crowded an amount equal to the whole of it into the market.

exercising a most important and salutary influence on the com munity.

The exchanges were conducted partly by barter, but more usually in the currency of the country. This consisted of bits of tin stamped with a character like a T, bags of cacao, the value of which was regulated by their size, and lastly quills filled with gold dust. Gold was part of the regular currency, it seems, in both hemispheres. In their dealings it is singular that they should have had no knowledge of scales and weights. The quan‐ tity was determined by measure and number.[13]

The most perfect order reigned throughout this vast assembly. Officers patrolled the square, whose business it was to keep the peace, to collect the duties imposed on the different articles of merchandise, to see that no false measures or fraud of any kind were used, and to bring offenders at once to justice. A court of twelve judges sat in one part of the *tianguez,* clothed with those ample and summary powers, which, in despotic countries, are often delegated even to petty tribunals. The extreme severity with which they exercised these powers, in more than one in‐ stance, proves that they were not a dead letter.[14]

The *tianguez* of Mexico was naturally an object of great inter‐ est, as well as wonder, to the Spaniards. For in it they saw converged into one focus, as it were, all the rays of civilization scattered throughout the land. Here they beheld the various evidences of mechanical skill, of domestic industry, the multiplied resources, of whatever kind, within the compass of the natives. It could not fail to impress them with high ideas of the magni‐ tude of these resources, as well as of the commercial activity and social subordination by which the whole community was knit together ; and their admiration is fully evinced by the min‐ uteness and energy of their description.[15]

From this bustling scene, the Spaniards took their way to the great *teocalli,* in the neighborhood of their own quarters. It covered, with the subordinate edifices, as the reader has already seen, the large tract of ground now occupied by the cathedral, part of the market-place, and some of the adjoining streets.[16] It was the spot which had been consecrated to the same object,

[13] Ante, Vol. I. p. 145.

[14] Toribio, Hist. de los Indios, MS., Parte 3, cap. 7.—Rel. Seg., ap. Lor‐ enzana, p. 104.—Oviedo, Hist. de las Ind., MS., lib. 33, cap. 10.—Bernal Diaz, Hist. de la Conquista, loc, cit.

[15] "Entre nosotros," says Diaz, "huuo soldados que auian estado en muchas partes del mundo, y en Constantinopla, y en toda Italia, y Roma, y dixéron, que plaça tan bien compassada, y con tanto concierto, y tamaña, y llena de tanta gente, no la auian visto." Ibid., ubi **supra.**

[16] Clavigero, Stor. del Messico, tom. II. p. 27.

probably, ever since the foundation of the city. The present building, however, was of no great antiquity, having been constructed by Ahuitzotl, who celebrated its dedication in 1486, by that hecatomb of victims, of which such incredible reports are to be found in the chronicles.[17]

It stood in the midst of a vast area, encompassed by a wall of stone and lime, about eight feet high, ornamented on the outer side by figures of serpents, raised in relief, which gave it the name of the *coatepantli*, or "wall of serpents." This emblem was a common one in the sacred sculpture of Anahuac, as well as of Egypt. The wall, which was quadrangular, was pierced by huge battlemented gateways, opening on the four principal streets of the capital. Over each of the gates was a kind of arsenal, filled with arms and warlike gear; and, if we may credit the report of the Conquerors, there were barracks adjoining, garrisoned by ten thousand soldiers, who served as a sort of military police for the capital, supplying the emperor with a strong arm in case of tumult or sedition.[18]

The *teocalli* itself was a solid pyramidal structure of earth and pebbles, coated on the outside with hewn stones probably of the light, porous kind employed in the buildings of the city.[19] It was probably square, with its sides facing the cardinal points.[20] It was divided into five bodies or stories, each one receding so as to be of smaller dimensions than that immediately below it; the usual form of the Aztec *teocallis*, as already described, and bearing obvious resemblance to some of the primitive pyramidal structures in the Old World.[21] The ascent was by a flight of steps on the outside, which reached to the narrow terrace or platform at the base of the second story, passing quite round the

---

[17] Ante, Vol. I. p. 80.

[18] " Et di più v' hauea vna guarnigione di dieci mila huomini di guerra, tutti eletti per huomini valenti, & questi accompagnauano & guardauano la sua persona, & quando si facea qualche rumore ò ribellione nella città ò nel paese circumuicino, andauano questi, ò parte d' essi per Capitani.' Rel. d' un gent., ap. Ramusio, tom. III. fol. 309.

[19] Humboldt, Essai Politique, tom. II. p. 40.

On paving the square, not long ago, round the modern cathedral, there were found large blocks of sculptured stone buried between thirty and forty feet deep in the ground. Ibid., loc. cit.

[20] Clavigero calls it oblong, on the alleged authority of the " Anonymous Conqueror." (Stor. del Messico, tom. II. p. 27, nota.) But the latter says not a word of the shape, and his contemptible woodcut is too plainly destitute of all proportion, to furnish an inference of any kind. (Comp. Rel. d' un gent., ap. Ramusio, tom. III. fol. 307.) Torquemada and Gomara both say, it was square; (Monarch. Ind., lib. 8, cap. 11;—Crónica, cap. 80;) and Toribio de Benavente, speaking generally of the Mexican temples, says, they had that form. Hist. de los. Ind., MS., Parte 1, cap. 12

[21] See *Appendix, Part 1.*

building, when a second stairway conducted to a similar landing at the base of the third. The breadth of this walk was just so much space as was left by the retreating story next above it. From this construction the visitor was obliged to pass round the whole edifice four times, in order to reach the top. This had a most imposing effect in the religious ceremonials, when the pomp ous procession of priests with their wild minstrelsy came sweep ing round the huge sides of the pyramid, as they rose higher and higher, in the presence of gazing multitudes, towards the sum mit.

The dimensions of the temple cannot be given with any cer tainty. The Conquerors judged by the eye, rarely troubling themselves with anything like an accurate measurement. It was, probably, not much less than three hundred feet square at the base ; [22] and, as the Spaniards counted a hundred and four. teen steps, was probably, less than one hundred feet in height.[23]

When Cortés arrived before the *teocalli*, he found two priests and several caciques commissioned by Montezuma to save him the fatigue of the ascent by bearing him on their shoulders, in the same manner as had been done to the emperor. But the gen eral declined the compliment, preferring to march up at the head of his men. On reaching the summit, they found it a vast area, paved with broad flat stones. The first object that met their view was a large block of jasper, the peculiar shape of which showed it was the stone on which the bodies of the un happy victims were stretched for sacrifice. Its convex surface, by raising the breast, enabled the priest to perform his diabolical

[22] Clavigero, calling it oblong, adopts Torquemada's estimate,—not Saha gun's, as he pretends, which he never saw, and who gives no measurement of the building,—for the length, and Gomara's estimate, which is somewhat less, for the breadth. (Stor. del. Messico, tom. II. p. 28, nota.) As both his authorities make the building square, this spirit of accommodation is whimsical enough. Toribio, who did measure a *teocalli* of the usual con struction in the town of Tenayuca, found it to be forty *brazas*, or two hun dred and forty feet square. (Hist. de los Ind., MS., Parte 1, cap. 12.) The great temple of Mexico was undoubtedly larger, and, in the want of better authorities, one may accept Torquemado, who makes it a little more than three hundred and sixty Toledan, equal to three hundred and eight French feet, square. (Monarch, Ind., lib. 8, cap. 11.) How can M. de Humboldt speak of the "great concurrence of testimony" in regard to the dimensions of the temple? (Essai Politique, tom. II. p. 41.) No two authorities agree.

[23] Bernal Diaz says he counted one hundred and fourteen steps. (Hist. de la Conquista, cap. 92.) Toribio says that more than one person who had numbered them told him they exceeded a hundred. (Hist. de los Indios, MS., Parte 1, cap. 12.) The steps could hardly have been less than eight or ten inches high, each ; Clavigero assumes that they were a foot, and that the building, therefore, was a hundred and fourteen feet high, precisely. (Stor. del Messico, tom. II. pp. 28, 29.) It is seldom safe to use anything stronger than *probably* in history.

task more easily, of removing the heart. At the other end of the area were two towers or sanctuaries, consisting of three stories, the lower one of stone and stucco, the two upper of wood elaborately carved. In the lower division stood the images of their gods; the apartments above were filled with utensils for their religious services, and with the ashes of some of their Aztec princes, who had fancied this airy sepulchre. Before each sanctuary stood an altar with that undying fire upon it, the extinction of which boded as much evil to the empire, as that of the Vestal flame would have done in ancient Rome. Here, also, was the huge cylindrical drum made of serpents' skins, and struck only on extraordinary occasions, when it sent forth a melancholy sound that might be heard for miles,—a sound of woe in after-times to the Spaniards.

Montezuma, attended by the high-priest, came forward to receive Cortés as he mounted the area. "You are weary, Malinche," said he to him, "with climbing up our great temple." But Cortés, with a politic vaunt, assured him "the Spaniards were never weary"! Then, taking him by the hand, the emperor pointed out the localities of the neighborhood. The temple on which they stood, rising high above all other edifices in the capital, afforded the most elevated as well as central point of view. Below them, the city lay spread out like a map, with its streets and canals intersecting each other at right angles, its terraced roofs blooming like so many parterres of flowers. Every place seemed alive with business and bustle; canoes were glancing up and down the canals, the streets, were crowded with people in their gay, picturesque costumes, while from the market-place, they had so lately left, a confused hum of many sounds and voices rose upon the air.[24] They could distinctly trace the symmetrical plan of the city, with its principal avenues issuing, as it were, from the four gates of the *coatepantli*; and connecting themselves with the causeways, which formed the grand entrances to the capital. This regular and beautiful arrangement was imitated in many of the inferior towns, where the great roads converged towards the chief *teocalli*, or cathedral, as to a common focus.[25] They could discern the insular position of the me-

---

[24] "Tornámos á ver la gran plaça, y la multitud de gente que en ella auia, vnos comprädos, y otros vendiendo, que solamente el rumor, y zumbido de las vozes, y palabras que allí auia, sonaua mas que de vna legua!" Bernal Diaz, Hist. de la Conquista, cap. 92.

[25] "Y por honrar mas sus templos sacaban los caminos muy derechos por cordel de una y de dos leguas que era cosa harto de ver, desde lo Alto del principal templo, como venian de todos los pueblos menores y barrios; salian los caminos muy derechos y iban á dar al patio de los teocallis." Toribio, Hist. de los Indios, MS., Parte 1, cap. 12.

tropolis, bathed on all sides by the salt floods of the Tezcuco, and in the distance the clear fresh waters of the Chalco; far beyond stretched a wide prospect of fields and waving woods, with the burnished walls of many a lofty temple rising high above the trees, and crowning the distant hill-tops.[26] The view reached in an unbroken line to the very base of the circular range of mountains, whose frosty peaks glittered as if touched with fire in the morning ray; while long, dark wreaths of vapor, rolling up from the hoary heard of Popocatepetl, told that the destroy-ing element was, indeed, at work in the bosom of the beautiful Valley.

Cortés was filled with admiration at this grand and glorious spectacle, and gave utterance to his feelings in animated lan-guage to the emperor, the lord of these flourishing domains. His thoughts, however, soon took another direction; and, turn-ing to father Olmedo, who stood by his side, he suggested that the area would afford a most conspicuous position for the Christian Cross, if Montezuma would but allow it to be planted there. But the discreet ecclesiastic, with the good sense which on these occasions seems to have been so lamentably deficient in his commander, reminded him, that such a request, at present, would be exceedingly ill-timed, as the Indian monarch had shown no dispositions as yet favorable to Christianity.[27]

Cortés then requested Montezuma to allow him to enter the sanctuaries, and behold the shrines of his gods. To this the latter, after a short conference with the priests, assented, and conducted the Spaniards into the building. They found them-selves in a spacious apartment incrusted on the sides with stucco, on which various figures were sculptured, representing the Mexican calendar, perhaps, or the priestly ritual. At one end of the saloon was a recess with a roof of timber richly carved and gilt. Before the altar in this sanctuary, stood the colossal image of Huitzilopotchli, the tutelary deity and war-god of the Aztecs. His countenance was distorted into hideous lineaments of symbolical import. In his right hand he wielded a bow, and in his left a bunch of golden arrows, which a mystic legend had connected with the victories of his people. The huge folds of a

---

[26] "No se contentaba el Demonio con los [Teucales] ya dichos, sino que en cada pueblo, en cada barrio, y á cuarto de legua, tenian otros patios pequeños adonde habia tres ó cuatro teocallis, y en algunos mas, en otras partes solo uno, y en cada Mogote ó Cerrejon uno ó dos, y por los caminos y entre los Maizales, habia otros muchos pequeños, y todos estaban blancos y encalados, que parecian y abultaban mucho, que en la tierra bien poblada parecia que todo estaba lleno de casas, en especial de los patios del Demonio, que eran muy de ver." Toribio, Hist. de los Indios, MS., ubi supra.

[27] Bernal Diaz. Hist. de la Conquista, ubi supra.

serpent, consisting of pearls and precious stones, were coiled round his waist, and the same rich materials were profusely sprinkled over his person. On his left foot were the delicate feathers of the humming-bird, which, singularly enough, gave its name to the dread deity.[28] The most conspicuous ornament was a chain of gold and silver hearts alternate, suspended round his neck, emblematical of the sacrifice in which he most delighted. A more unequivocal evidence of this was afforded by three human hearts smoking and almost palpitating, as if recently torn from the victims, and now lying on the altar before him !

The adjoining sanctuary was dedicated to a milder deity. This was Tezcatlipoca, next in honor to that invisible Being the Supreme God, who was represented by no image, and confined by no temple. It was Tezcatlipoca who created the world, and watched over it with a providential care. He was represented as a young man, and his image, of polished black stone, was richly garnished with gold plates and ornaments ; among which a shield, burnished like a mirror, was the most characteristic emblem, as in it he saw reflected all the doings of the world. But the homage to this god was not always of a more refined or merciful character than that paid to his carnivorous brother ; for five bleeding hearts were also seen in a golden platter on his altar.

The walls of both these chapels were stained with human gore. "The stench was more intolerable," exclaims Diaz, "than that of the slaughter-houses in Castile !" And the frantic forms of the priests, with their dark robes clotted with blood, as they flitted to and fro, seemed to the Spaniards to be those of the very ministers of Satan ![29]

From this foul abode they gladly escaped into the open air; when Cortés, turning to Montezuma, said, with a smile, "I do not comprehend how a great and wise prince, like you, can put faith in such evil spirits as these idols, the representatives of the Devil ! If you will but permit us to erect here the true Cross and place the images of the blessed Virgin and her Son in your sanctuaries, you will soon see how your false gods will shrink before them !"

Montezuma was greatly shocked at this sacrilegious address. "These are the gods," he answered, "who have led the Aztecs

<hr />

[28] Ante, Vol. I. p. 63.

[29] " Y tenia en las paredes tantas costras de sangre, y el suelo todo bañado dello, que en los mataderos de Castilla no auia tanto hedor." Bernal Diaz, Hist. de la Conquista. ubi supra.—Rel. Seg. de Cortés, ap. Lorenzana, pp. 105, 106.—Carta del Lic. Zuazo, MS.—See, also, for notices of these deities, Sahagun, lib. 3, cap. 1, et seq.,—Torquemada. Monarch. Ind., lib. 6, cap. 20, 21,—Acosta, lib. 5, cap. 9.

on to victory since they were a nation, and who send the seed-time and harvest in their seasons. Had I thought you would have offered them this outrage, I would not have admitted you into their presence."

Cortés, after some expressions of concern at having wounded the feelings of the emperor, took his leave. Montezuma remained, saying that he must expiate, if possible, the crime of exposing the shrines of the divinities to such profanation by the strangers.[30]

On descending to the court, the Spaniards took a leisurely survey of the other edifices in the inclosure. The area was protected by a smooth stone pavement, so polished, indeed, that it was with difficulty the horses could keep their legs. There were several other *teocallis*, built generally on the model of the great one, though of much inferior size, dedicated to the different Aztec deities.[31] On their summits were the altars crowned with perpetual flames, which, with those on the numerous temples in others quarters of the capital, shed a brilliant illumination over its streets, through the long nights.[32]

Among the *teocallis* in the inclosure was one consecrated to Quetzalcoatl, circular in its form, and having an entrance in imitation of a dragon's mouth, bristling with sharp fangs, and dropping with blood. As the Spaniards cast a furtive glance into the throat of this horrible monster, they saw collected there implements of sacrifice and other abominations of fearful import. Their bold hearts shuddered at the spectacle, and they designated the place not inaptly as the " Hell."[33]

One other structure may be noticed as characteristic of the

---

[30] Bernal Diaz, Ibid., ubi supra.

Whoever examines Cortés great letter to Charles V. will be surprised to find it stated, that, instead of any acknowledgment to Montezuma, he threw down his idols and erected the Christian emblems in their stead. (Rel. Seg., ap. Lorenzana, p. 106.) This was an event of much later date. The *Conquistador* wrote his despatches too rapidly and concisely to give heed always to exact time and circumstance. We are quite as likely to find them attended to in the long-winded, gossiping,—inestimable chronicle of Diaz.

[31] " Quarent a torres muy altas y bien obradas." Rel. Seg. de Cortés, ap. Lorenzana, p. 105.

[32] " Delante de todos estos altares habia braçeros que todo la noche hardian, y en las salas tambien tenian sus fuegos." Toribio, Hist. de los Indios, MS., Parte I, cap. 12.

[33] Bernal Diaz, Ibid., ubi supra.

Toribio, also, notices this temple with the same complimentary epithet.

" La boca hecha como de infierno y en ella pintada la boca de una temerosa Sierpe con terribles colmillos y dientes, y en algunas de'estas los colmillos eran de bulto, que verlo y entrar dentro ponia gran temor y grima, en especial el infierno que estaba en México, que parecia traslado del verdadero infierno." Hist. de los Indies, MS., Parte I, cap. 4.

brutish nature of their religion. This was a pyramidal mound or tumulus, having a complicated frame-work of timber on its broad summit. On this was strung an immense number of human skulls, which belonged to the victims, mostly prisoners of war, who had perished on the accursed stone of sacrifice. one of the soldiers had the patience to count the number of these ghastly trophies, and reported it to be one hundred and thirty-six thousand ![34] Belief might well be staggered, did not the Old World present a worthy counterpart in the pyramidal Golgothas which commemorated the triumphs of Tamerlane.[35]

There were long ranges of buildings in the inclosure, appropriated as the residence of the priests and others engaged in the offices of religion. The whole number of them was said to amount to several thousand. Here were, also, the principal seminaries for the instruction of youth of both sexes, drawn chiefly from the higher and wealthier classes. The girls were taught by elderly women who officiated as priestesses in the temples, a custom familiar, also, to Egypt. The Spaniards admit that the greatest care for morals, and the most blameless deportment, were maintained in these institutions. The time of the pupils was chiefly occupied, as in most monastic establishments, with the minute and burdensome ceremonial of their religion. The boys were likewise taught such elements of science as were known to their teachers, and the girls initiated in the mysteries of embroidery and weaving, which they employed in decorating the temples. At a suitable age they generally went forth into the world to assume the occupations fitted to their condition, though some remained permanently devoted to the services of religion.[36]

The spot was also covered by edifices of a still different character. There were granaries filled with the rich produce of the church-lands, and with the first-fruits and other offerings of the faithful. One large mansion was reserved for strangers of emi-

[34] Bernal Diaz, ubi supra.

"Andres de Tapia, *que me lo dijo*, i Gonçalo de Umbria, las contáron vn Dia, i halláron ciento i treinta i seis mil Calaberas, en las Vigas, i Gradas." Gomara, Crónica, cap. 82.

[35] Three collections, thus fancifully disposed, of these grinning horrors— In all 230,000—are noticed by Gibbon! (Decline and Fall, ed. Milman, vol. I. p. 52; vol. XII. p. 45.) A *European* scholar commends "the conqueror's piety, his moderation, and his justice"! Rowe's Dedication of "Tamerlane."

[36] Ante, Vol. I. pp. 69, 70.

The desire of presenting the reader with a complete view of the actual state of the capital, at the time of its occupation by the Spaniards, has led me in this and the preceding chapter into a few repetitions of remarks on the Aztec institutions in the Introductory Book of this History.

nence, who were on a pilgrimage to the great *teocalli.* The in-closure was ornamented with gardens, shaded by ancient trees and watered by fountains and reservoirs from the copious streams of Chapoltepec. The little community was thus provided with almost everything requisite for its own maintenance, and the services of the temple.[37]

It was a microcosm of itself, a city within a city; and according to the assertion of Cortés, embraced a tract of ground large enough for five hundred houses.[38] It presented in this brief compass the extremes of barbarism, blended with a certain civilization, altogether characteristic of the Aztecs. The rude Conquerors saw only the evidence of the former. In the fantastic and symbolical features of the deities, they beheld the literal lineaments of Satan ; in the rites and frivolous ceremonial, his own especial code of damnation ; and in the modest deportment and careful nurture of the inmates of the seminaries, the snares by which he was to beguile his deluded victims ![39] Before a century had elapsed, the descendants of these same Spaniards discerned in the mysteries of the Aztec religion the features, obscured and defaced, indeed, of the Jewish and Christian revelations ![40] Such were the opposite conclusions of the unlettered soldier and of the scholar. A philosopher, untouched by superstition, might well doubt which of the two was the most extraordinary.

The sight of the Indian abominations seems to have kindled in the Spaniards a livelier feeling for their own religion ; since, on the following day, they asked leave of Montezuma to convert one of the halls in their residence into a chapel, that they might celebrate the services of the Church there. The monarch, in whose bosom the feelings of resentment seem to have soon subsided, easily granted their request, and sent some of his own artisans to aid them in the work.

While it was in progress, some of the Spaniards observed what appeared to be a door recently plastered over. It was a common rumor that Montezuma still kept the treasures of his father, King Axayacatl, in this ancient palace. The Spaniards, acquainted with this fact, felt no scruple in gratifying their curiosity

---

[37] Toribio, Hist. de los Indios, MS., Parte 1, cap. 12.—Gomara, Crónica, cap. 80.—Rel. d'un gent., ap. Ramusia, tom. III. fol. 309.

[38] " Es tan grande que dentro del circuito de ella, que es todo cercado de Muro muy alto, se podia muy bien facer una Villa de quinientos Vecinos." Rel. Seg., ap. Lorenzana, p. 105.

[39] " Todas estas mugeres," says father Toribio, " estaban aquí sirviendo al demonio por sus propios intereses; las unas porque el Demonio las hiciese modestas," etc. Hist. de los Indios, MS., Parte 1, cap. 9.

[40] See *Appendix Part* 1.

by removing the plaster. As was anticipated, it concealed a door. On forcing this, they found the rumor was no exaggeration. They beheld a large hall filled with rich and beautiful stuffs, articles of curious workmanship of various kinds, gold and silver in bars and in the ore, and many jewels of value. It was the private hoard of Montezuma, the contributions, it may be, of tributary cities, and once the property of his father. " I was a young man," says Diaz, who was one of those that obtained a sight of it, " and it seemed to me as if all the riches of the world were in that room ! " [41] The Spaniards, notwithstanding their elation at the discovery of this precious deposit, seem to have felt some commendable scruples as to appropriating it to their own use,—at least for the present. And Cortés, after closing up the wall as it was before, gave strict injunctions that nothing should be said of the matter, unwilling that the knowledge of its existence by his guests should reach the ears of Montezuma.

Three days sufficed to complete the chapel ; and the Christians had the satisfaction to see themselves in possession of a temple where they might worship God in their own way, under the protection of the Cross, and the blessed Virgin. Mass was regularly performed by the fathers Olmedo and Diaz, in the presence of the assembled army, who were most earnest and exemplary in their devotions, partly, says the chronicler above quoted, from the propriety of the thing, and partly for its edifying influence on the benighted heathen.[42]

[41] " Y luego lo supímos entre todos los demas Capitanes, y soldados, y lo entrámos á ver muy secretamente, y como yo lo ví, digo que me admiré, é como en aquel tiempo era mancebo, y no auia visto en mi vida riquezas como aquellas, tuue por cierto, que en el mundo no deuiera auer otras tantas !" Hist. de la Conquista cap. 93

[42] Ibid., loc. cit.

CHAPTER III.

ANXIETY OF CORTES.—SEIZURE OF MONTEZUMA.—HIS TREAT-
MENT BY THE SPANIARDS.—EXECUTION OF HIS OFFICERS.—
MONTEZUMA IN IRONS.—REFLECTIONS.

1519.

THE Spaniards had been now a week in Mexico. During this
time, they had experienced the most friendly treatment from the
emperor. But the mind of Cortés was far from easy. He felt
that it was quite uncertain how long this amiable temper would
last. A hundred circumstances might occur to change it. He
might very naturally feel the maintenance of so large a body too
burdensome on his treasury. The people of the capital might
become dissatisfied at the presence of so numerous an armed
force within their walls. Many causes of disgust might arise
betwixt the soldiers and the citizens. Indeed, it was scarcely
possible that a rude, licentious soldiery, like the Spaniards, could
be long kept in subjection without active employment.[1] The
danger was even greater with the Tlascalans, a fierce race now
brought into daily contact with the nation who held them in
loathing and detestation. Rumors were already rife among the
allies, whether well-founded or not, of murmurs among the
Mexicans, accompanied by menaces of raising the bridges.[2]

Even should the Spaniards be allowed to occupy their present
quarters unmolested, it was not advancing the great object of
the expedition. Cortés was not a whit nearer gaining the
capital, so essential to his meditated subjugation of the country;

---

[1] "Los Españoles," says Cortés frankly, of his countrymen, "somos algo
incomportables, é importunos." Rel. Seg., ap. Lorenzana, p. 84.

[2] Gomara, Crónica, cap. 83.

There is a reason to doubt the truth of these stories. "Segun una carta
original que tengo en mi poder firmada de las tres cabezas de la Nueva
España en donde escriben á la Magestad del Emperador Nuestro Señor (que
Dios tenga en su Santo Reyno) disculpan en ella á Motecuhzoma y á los
Mexicanos de eso, y de lo demas que se les argulló, que lo cierto era que
fué invencion de los Tlascaltecas, y de algunos de los Españoles que veian
la hora de salirse de miedo de la Ciudad, y poner en cobro innumerables
riquezas que habian venido á sus manos." Ixtlilxochitl, Hist. Chich., MS.,
cap. 85.

and any day he might receive tidings that the Crown, or, what he most feared, the governor of Cuba, had sent a force of superior strength to wrest from him a conquest but half achieved. Disturbed by these anxious reflections, he resolved to extricate himself from his embarrassment by one bold stroke. But he first submitted the affair to a council of the officers in whom he most confided, desirous to divide with them the responsibility of the act, and, no doubt, to interest them more heartily in its execution, by making it in some measure the result of their combined judgments.

When the general had briefly stated the embarrassments of their position, the council was divided in opinion. All admitted the necessity of some instant action. One party were for retiring secretly from the city, and getting beyond the causeways before their march could be intercepted. Another advised that it should be done openly, with the knowledge of the emperor, of whose good-will they had had so many proofs. But both these measures seemed alike impolitic. A retreat under these circumstances, and so abruptly made, would have the air of a flight. It would be construed into distrust of themselves ; and any thing like timidity on their part would be sure not only to bring on them the Mexicans, but the contempt of their allies, who would, doubtless, join in the general cry.

As to Montezuma, what reliance could they place on the protection of a prince so recently their enemy, and who, in his altered bearing, must have taken counsel of his fears, rather than his inclinations ?

Even should they succeed in reaching the coast, their situation would be little better. It would be proclaiming to the world, that, after all their lofty vaunts, they were unequal to the enterprise. Their only hopes of their sovereign's favor, and of pardon for their irregular proceedings, were founded on success. Hitherto, they had only made the discovery of Mexico ; to retreat would be to leave conquest and the fruits of it to another. —In short, to stay and to retreat seemed equally disastrous.

In this perplexity, Cortés proposed an expedient, which none but the most daring spirit, in the most desperate extremity, would have conceived. This was, to march to the royal palace, and bring Montezuma to the Spanish quarters, by fair means if they could persuade him, by force if necessary,—at all events, to get possession of his person. With such a pledge, the Spaniards would be secure from the assault of the Mexicans, afraid by acts of violence to compromise the safety of their prince. If he came by his own consent, they would be deprived of all apology for doing so. As long as the emperor remained among the Spaniards, it would be easy, by allowing him a show of sovereignty, to rule in his name, until they had taken measures for securing their safety, and the success of their enterprise. The idea of employing a sovereign as a tool for the government of his own kingdom, if a new one in the age of Cortés, is certainly not so in ours.[8]

A plausible pretext for the seizure of the hospitable monarch—for the most barefaced action seeks to veil itself under some show of decency—was afforded by a circumstance of which Cortés had received intelligence at Cholula.[4] He had left, as we have seen, a faithful officer, Juan de Escalante, with a hundred and fifty men in garrison at Vera Cruz, on his departure for the capital. He had not been long absent, when his lieutenant received a message from an Aztec chief named Quauhpopoca, governor of a district to the north of the Spanish settlement, declaring his desire to come in person and tender his allegiance to the Spanish authorities at Vera Cruz. He requested that four of the white men might be sent to protect him against certain unfriendly tribes through which his road lay. This was not an uncommon request and excited no suspicion in Escalante. The four soldiers were sent ; and on their arrival two of them were murdered by the false Aztec. The other two made their way back to the garrison.[5]

---

[8] Rel. Seg. de Cortés, ap. Lorenzana, p. 84.—Ixtlilxochitl, Hist. Chich., MS., cap. 85.—P. Martyr, De Orbe Novo, dec. 5, cap. 3.—Oviedo, Hist. de las Ind., MS., lib. 33, cap. 6.
Bernal Diaz gives a very different report of this matter. According to him, a number of officers and soldiers, of whom he was one, suggested the capture of Montezuma to the general, who came into the plan with hesitation. (Hist. de la Conquista, cap. 93.) This is contrary to the character of Cortés, who was a man to lead, not to be led, on such occasions. It is contrary to the general report of historians, though these, it must be confessed, are mainly built on the general's narrative. It is contrary to anterior probability; since, if the conception seems almost too desperate to have seriously entered into the head of any one man, how much more improbable is it, that it should have originated with a number! Lastly, it is contrary to the positive written statement of Cortés to the Emperor, publicly known and circulated, confirmed in print by his chaplain, Gomara, and all this when the thing was fresh, and when the parties interested were alive to contradict it. We cannot but think that the captain here, as in the case of the burning of the ships, assumes rather more for himself and his comrades, than the facts will strictly warrant, an oversight, for which the lapse of half a century—to say nothing of his avowed anxiety to show up the claims of the latter—may furnish some apology.
[4] Even Gomara has the candor to style it a " pretext "—*achaque* Crónica, cap. 83.
[5] Bernal Diaz states the affair, also, differently. According to him, the Aztec governor was enforcing the payment of the customary tribute from the Totonacs, when Escalante, interfering to protect his allies, now subjects of

The commander marched at once with fifty of his men and several thousand Indian allies to take vengeance on the cacique. A pitched battle followed, The allies fled from the redoubted Mexicans. The few Spaniards stood firm and with the aid of their fire-arms and the blessed Virgin who was distinctly seen hovering over their ranks in the van, they made good the field against the enemy. It cost them dear, however; since seven or eight Christians were slain, and among them the gallant Escalante himself who died of his injuries soon after his return to the fort. The Indian prisoners captured in the battle spoke of the whole proceeding as having taken place at the instigation of Montezuma. One of the Spaniards fell into the hands of the natives, but soon after perished of his wounds. His head was cut off and sent to the Aztec emperor. It was uncommonly large and covered with hair; and, as Montezuma gazed on the ferocious features, rendered more horrible by death, he seemed to read in them the dark lineaments of the destined destroyers of his house. He turned from it with a shudder and commanded that it should be taken from the city, and not offered at the shrine of any of his gods.

Although Cortés had received intelligence of this disaster at Cholula, he had concealed it within his own breast, or communicated it to very few only of his most trusty officers, from apprehension of the ill effect it might have on the spirits of the common soldiers.

The cavaliers whom Cortés now summoned to the council were men of the same mettle with their leader. Their bold, chivalrous spirits seemed to court danger for its own sake. If one or two, less adventurous, were startled by the proposal he made, they were soon overruled by the others, who, no doubt, considered that a desperate disease required as desperate a remedy.

That night, Cortés was heard pacing his apartment to and fro, like a man oppressed by thought, or agitated by strong emotion. He may have been ripening in his mind the daring scheme

---

Spain, was slain in an action with the enemy. (Hist. de la Conquista, cap, 93.) Cortés had the best means of knowing the facts, and wrote at the time. He does not usually shrink from avowing his policy, however severe, towards the natives ; and I have thought it fair to give him the benefit of his own version of the story.

[6] Oviedo, Hist. de las Ind., MS., lib. 33, cap. 5.—Rel. Seg. de Cortes, ap. Lorenzana, pp. 83, 84.

The apparition of the Virgin was seen only by the Aztecs, who, it is true had to make out the best case for their defeat they could to Montezuma ; a suspicious circumstance, which, however, did not stagger the Spaniards. " Y ciertamente, todos, los soldados que passámos con Cortés tenemos muy creido, è assí es verdad, que la misericordia divina, y Nuestra Señora la Vírgen Maria siempre era con nosotros." Bernal Díaz, Hist. de la Conquista, cap. 94.

for the morrow.[7]   In the morning the soldiers heard mass as usual, and father Olmedo invoked the blessing of Heaven on their hazardous enterprise.   Whatever might be the cause in which he was embarked, the heart of the Spaniard was cheered with the conviction that the Saints were on his side![8]

Having asked an audience from Montezuma, which was readily granted, the general made the necessary arrangements for his enterprise.   The principal part of his force was drawn up in the courtyard, and he stationed a considerable detachment in the avenues leading to the palace, to check any attempt at rescue by the populace.   He ordered twenty-five or thirty of the soldiers to drop in at the palace, as if by accident, in groups of three or four at a time, while the conference was going on with Montezuma.   He selected five cavaliers, in whose courage and coolness he placed most trust, to bear him company ; Pedro de Alvarado, Gonzalo de Sandoval, Francisco de Lujo, Velasquez de Leon, and Alonso de Avila,—brilliant names in the annals of the Conquest.   All were clad, as well as the common soldiers, in complete armor, a circumstance of too familiar occurrence to excite suspicion.

The little party were graciously received by the emperor, who soon, with the aid of the interpreters, became interested in a sportive conversation with the Spaniards, while he indulged his natural munificence by giving them presents of gold and jewels. He paid the Spanish general the particular compliment of offering him one of his daughters as his wife; an honor which the latter respectfully declined, on the ground that he was already accommodated with one in Cuba, and that his religion forbade a plurality.

When Cortés perceived that a sufficient number of his soldiers were assembled, he changed his playful manner, and with a serious tone briefly acquainted Montezuma with the treacherous proceedings in the *tierra caliente*, and the accusation of him as their author.   The emperor listened to the charge with surprise; and disavowed the act, which he said could only have been imputed to him by his enemies.   Cortés expressed his belief in his declaration, but added, that, to prove it true, it would be necessary to send for Quauhpopoca, and his accomplices, that they might be examined and dealt with according to their deserts. To this Montezuma made no objection.   Taking from his wrist,

---

[7] " Paseóse vn gran rato solo, ' cuidadoso de aquel gran hecho, que emprendia, i que aun á él mesmo le parecia temerario, pero necesario para su intento, andando."   Gomara, Crónica, cap. 83.

[8] Diaz says, they were at prayer all night.   " Toda la noche estuuimos en oracion con el Padre de la Merced, rogando á Dios que fuesse de tal modo, que redundasse para su santo servicio."   Hist. de la Conquista, cap. 95.

to which it was attached, a precious stone, the royal signet, on which was cut the figure of the War-god,[9] he gave it to one of his nobles, with orders to show it to the Aztec governor, and required his instant presence in the capital, together with all those who had been accessory to the murder of the Spaniards. If he resisted, the officer was empowered to call in the aid of the neighboring towns, to enforce the mandate.

When the messenger had gone, Cortés assured the monarch that this prompt compliance with his request convinced him of his innocence. But it was important that his own sovereign should be equally convinced of it. Nothing would promote this so much as for Montezuma to transfer his residence to the palace occupied by the Spaniards, still on the arrival of Quauhpopoca the affair could be fully investigated. Such an act of condescension would, of itself, show a personal regard for the Spaniards, incompatible with the base conduct alleged against him, and would fully absolve him from all suspicion![10]

Montezuma listened to this proposal, and the flimsy reasoning with which it was covered, with looks of profound amazement. He became pale as death; but in a moment, his face flushed with resentment, as, with the pride of offended dignity he exclaimed, "When was it ever heard that a great prince, like myself, voluntarily left his own palace to become a prisoner in in the hands of strangers!"

Cortés assured him he would not go as a prisoner. He would experience nothing but respectful treatment from the Spaniards; would be surrounded by his own household, and hold intercourse with his people as usual. In short, it would be but a change of residence, from one of his palaces to another, a circumstance of frequent occurrence with him.—It was in vain. "If I should consent to such a degradation," he answered," my subjects never would!"[11] When further pressed, he offered to give up one of his sons and of his daughters to remain as hostages with the Spaniards, so that he might be spared this disgrace.

Two hours passed in this fruitless discussion, till a high-mettled cavalier, Valasquez de Leon, impatient of the long delay, and seeing that the attempt, if not the deed, must ruin them, cried out, "Why do we waste words on this barbarian? We have gone too far to recede now. Let us seize him, and, if he resists,

---

[9] According to Ixtlilxochitl, it was his own portrait. "Se quitó del brazo una rica piedra, donde está esculpido su rostro (que era lo mismo que un sello Real)." Hist. Chich., MS., cap. 85.

[10] Rel. Seg. de Cortés ap. Lorenzana, p. 86.

[11] "Quando lo lo consintiera, los mios no pasarian por ello." Ixtlilxochitl Hist. Chich., MS., cap. 85.

plunge our swords into his body!"[12] The fierce tone and menacing, with which this was uttered, alarmed the monarch, who inquired of Marina what the angry Spaniard said. The interpreter explained it in as gentle a manner as she could, beseeching him " to accompany the white men to their quarters, where he would be treated with all respect and kindness, while to refuse them would but expose himself to violence, perhaps to death." Marina, doubtless, spoke to her sovereign as she thought, and no one had better opportunity of knowing the truth than herself.

This last appeal shook the resolution of Montezuma. It was in vain that the unhappy prince looked around for sympathy or support. As his eyes wandered over the stern visages and iron forms of the Spaniards, he felt that his hour was indeed come ; and, with a voice scarcely audible from emotion he consented to accompany the strangers,—to quit the palace, whither he was never more to return. Had he possessed the spirit of the first Montezuma, he would have called his guards around him, and left his life blood on the threshold sooner than have been dragged a dishonored captive across it. But his courage sunk under circumstances. He felt he was the instrument of an irresistible Fate ![18]

No sooner had the Spaniards got his consent, than orders were given for the royal litter. The nobles, who bore and attended it, could scarcely believe their senses, when they learned their master's purpose. But pride now came to Montezuma's aid, and, since he must go, he preferred that it should appear to be with his own free will. As the royal retinue, escorted by the Spaniards, marched through the street with downcast eyes and dejected mien, the people assembled in crowds, and a rumor ran among then, that the emperor was carried off by force to the quarters of the white men. A tumult would have soon arisen but for the

<hr>

[12] " ¿Que haze v. m. ya con tantas palabras ? O le lleuemos preso, ó le darémos de estocadas, por esso tornadle á dezir, que si da vozes, o haze alboroto, que le mataréis, porque mas vale que desta vez asseguremos nuestras vidas, ó las perdamos." Bernal Diaz, Hist. de la Conquista, cap. 95.

[18] Oviedo has some doubts whether Montezuma's conduct is to be viewed as pusillanimous or as prudent. "Al coronista le parece, segun lo que se puede colegir de esta materia, que Montezuma era, o mui falto de animo, o pusilanimo, mui prudente, aunque en muchas cosas, los que le viéron lo loan de mui señor y mui liberal; y en sus razonamientos mostraba ser de buen juicio." He strikes the balance, however, in favor of pusillanimity. " Un Príncipe tan grande como Montezuma no se habia de dexar incurrir en tales terminos, ni consentir ser detenido de tan poco número de Españoles, ni de otra generacion alguna ; mas como Dios tiene ordenado lo que ha de ser, ninguno puede huir de su, juicio." Hist. de las Ind.. MS., lib. **33** cap. 6.

intervention of Montezuma himself who called out to the people to disperse, as he was visiting his friends of his own accord; thus sealing his ignominy by a declaration which deprived his subjects of the only excuse for resistance. On reaching the quarters, he sent out his nobles with similar assurances to the mob, and renewed orders to return to their homes.[14]

He was received with ostentatious respect by the Spaniards, and selected the suite of apartments which best pleased him. They were soon furnished with fine cotton tapestries, feather-work, and all the elegancies of Indian upholstery. He was attended by such of his household as he chose, his wives and his pages, and was served with his usual pomp and luxury at his meals. He gave audience, as in his own palace, to his subjects, who were admitted to his presence, few, indeed, at a time, under the pretext of greater order and decorum. From the Spaniards themselves he met with a formal deference. No one, not even the general himself, approached him without doffing his casque, and rendering the obeisance due to his rank. Nor did they ever sit in his presence, without being invited by him to do so.[15]

With all this studied ceremony and show of homage, there was one circumstance which too clearly proclaimed to his people that their sovereign was a prisoner. In the front of the palace a patrol of sixty men was established, and the same number in the rear. Twenty of each corps mounted guard at once, maintaining a careful watch, day and night.[16] Another body, under command of Velasquez de Leon, was stationed in the royal antechamber. Cortés punished any departure from duty, or relaxation of vigilance, in these sentinels, with the utmost severity.[17] He felt, as, indeed, every Spaniard must have felt, that the escape of the emperor now would be their ruin. Yet the task of this unintermitting watch sorely added to their fatigues. "Better this dog of a king should die," cried a soldier

---

[14] The story of the seizure of Montezuma may be found, with the usual discrepancies in the details, in Rel. Seg. de Cortes, ap. Lorenzana, pp. 84-86,—Bernal Diaz. Hist. de la Conquista, cap. 95,—Ixtlilxochitl, Hist. Chich., MS., cap. 85,—Oviedo, Hist de las Ind., MS., lib. 33, cap. 6.—Gomara, Cronica, cap. 83,—Herrera, Hist. General, dec. 2, lib. 8, cap. 2, 3.—Martyr, De Orbe Novo, dec. 5, cap. 3.

[15] "Siempre que ante el passauamos, y aunque fuesse Cortes, le quitauamos los bonetes de armas ò cascos, que siempre estauamos armados, y el nos hazia gran mesura, y honra á todos. . . . . . Digo que no se sentauan Cortes, ni ningun Capitan, hasta que el Montecuma les mandaua dar sus assentaderos ricos, y les mandaua assentar." Bernal Diaz, Hist. de la Conquista, cap. 95, 100.

[16] Herrera, Hist. General, dec. 2, lib. 8, cap. 3.

[17] On one occasion, three soldiers, who left their post without orders, were sentenced to run the gantlet,—a punishment little short of death. Ibid. ubi supra.

one day, " than that we should wear out our lives in this manner." The words were uttered in the hearing of Montezuma, who gathered something of their import, and the offender was severely chastised by order of the general.[18] Such instances of disrespect, however, were very rare. Indeed, the amiable deportment of the monarch, who seemed to take pleasure in the society of his jailers, and who never allowed a favor or at tention from the meanest soldier to go unrequited, inspired the Spaniards with as much attachment as they were capable of feeling—for a barbarian.

Things were in this posture, when the arrival of Quauhpopoca from the coast was announced. He was accompanied by his son and fifteen Aztec chiefs. He had travelled all the way, borne, as became his high rank, in a litter. On entering Montezuma's presence, he threw over his dress the coarse robe of *nequen*, and made the usual humiliating acts of obeisance. The poor parade of courtly ceremony was the more striking, when placed in contrast with the actual condition of the parties.

The Aztec governor was coldly received by his master, who referred the affair (had he the power to do otherwise?) to the examination of Cortés. It was, doubtless, conducted in a sufficiently summary manner. To the general's query, whether the cacique was the subject of Montezuma, he replied, " And what other sovereign could I serve?" implying that his sway was universal.[19] He did not deny his share in the transaction, nor did he seek to shelter himself under the royal authority, till sentence of death was passed on him and his followers, when they all laid the blame of their proceedings on Montezuma.[20] They were condemned to be burnt alive in the area before the palace. The funeral piles were made of heaps of arrows, javelins, and other weapons, drawn by the emperor's permission from the arsenals round the great *teocalli*, where they hăd been stored to supply means of defence in times of civic tumult or insurrection. By this politic precaution, Cortés proposed to remove a ready means of annoyance in case of hostilities with the citizens.

To crown the whole of these extraordinary proceedings, Cortés,

[18] Bernal Diaz, Hist de la Conquista, cap. 97.

[19] " Y despues que confesáron haber muerto los Españoles, les hice interrogar si ellos eran Vasallés de Muteczuma? Y el dicho Qualpopoca respondio, que si habia otro Señor, de quien pudiesse serlo? casi diciendo, que no habia otro, y que si eran." Rel. Seg. de Cortés, ap. Lorenzana. p. 87.

[20] " E assimismo les pregunte, si lo que allí se habia hecho si habia sido poe su mandado? y dijéron que no aunque despues, al tiempo que en ellos se executo la sentencia, que fuessen quemados, todos á una voz dijéron, que era verdad que el dicho Muteczuma se lo habia embiado a mandar, y que por su mandado lo habian hecho." Ibid., loc. cit.

while preparations for the execution were going on, entered the emperor's apartment, attended by a soldier bearing fetters in his hands. With a severe aspect, he charged the monarch with being the original contriver of the violence offered to the Spaniards, as was now proved by the declaration of his own Instruments. Such a crime, which merited death in a subject, could not be atoned for, even by a sovereign, without some punishment. So saying, he ordered the soldier to fasten the fetters on Montezuma's ankles. He coolly waited till it was done ; then, turning his back on the monarch, quitted the room.

Montezuma was speechless under the infliction of this last insult. He was like one struck down by a heavy blow, that deprives him of all his faculties. He offered no resistance. But, though he spoke not a word, low, ill-suppressed moans, from time to time, intimated the anguish of his spirit. His attendants, bathed in tears, offered him their consolations. They tenderly held his feet in their arms, and endeavored, by inserting their shawls and mantles, to relieve them from the pressure of the iron. But they could not reach the iron which had penetrated into his soul. He felt that he was no more a king.

Meanwhile, the execution of the dreadful doom was going forward in the courtyard. The whole Spanish force was under arms, to check any interruption that might be offered by the Mexicans. But none was attempted. The populace gazed in silent wonder, regarding it as the sentence of the emperor. The manner of the execution, too excited less surprise, from their familiarity with similar spectacles, aggravated, indeed, by additional horrors, in their own diabolical sacrifices. The Aztec lord and his companions ; bound hand and foot to the blazing piles, submitted without a cry or a complaint to their terrible fate. Passive fortitude is the virtue of the Indian warrior; and it was the glory of the Aztec, as of the other races on the North American continent, to show how the spirit of the brave man may triumph over torture and the agonies of death.

When the dismal tragedy was ended, Cortés réntered Montezuma's apartment. Kneeling down, he unclasped his shackles with his own hand expressing at the same time his regret that so disagreeable a duty as that of subjecting him to such a punishment had been imposed on him. This last indignity had entirely crushed the spirit of Montezuma; and the monarch, whose frown, but a week since, would have made the nations of Anahuac tremble to their remotest borders, was now craven enough to thank his deliverer for his freedom, as for a great and unmerited boon.[21]

[21] Gomara, Cronica, cap. 89.— Oviedo, Hist. de las Ind., MS., lb. 33, cap. 6.—Bernal Diaz, Hist. de la Conquista, cap. 95

Not long after, the Spanish general, conceiving that his royal captive was sufficiently humbled, expressed his willingness that he should return, if he inclined, to his own palace. Montezuma declined it; alleging, it is said, that his nobles had more than once importuned him to resent his injuries by taking arms against the Spaniards; and that, were he in the midst of them, it would be difficult to avoid it, or to save his capital from bloodshed and anarchy.[22] The reason did honor to his heart, if it was the one which influenced him. It is probable that he did not care to trust his safety to those haughty and ferocious chieftains, who had witnessed the degradation of their master, and must despise his pusillanimity, as a thing unprecedented in an Aztec monarch. It is also said, that, when Marina conveyed to him the permi sion of Cortés, the other interpreter, Aguilar, gave him to understand the Spanish officers never would consent that he should avail himself of it.[23]

Whatever were his reasons, it is certain that he declined the offer ; and the general, in a well feigned, or real ecstasy, embraced him, declaring, " that he loved him as a brother, and that every Spaniard would be zealously devoted to his interests, since he had shown himself so mindful of theirs ! " Honeyed words, "which," says the shrewd old chronicler who was present, Monte-zum was wise enough to know the worth of."

The events recorded in this chapter are certainly some of the most extraordinary on the page of history. That a small body of men, like the Spaniards, should have entered the palace of a mighty prince, have seized his person in the midst of his vassals, have borne him off a captive to their quarters,——that they should have put to an ignominious death before his face his high officers, for executing, probably, his own commands, and have crowned the whole by putting the monarch in irons like a common male-factor,——that this should have been done, not to a drivelling dotard in the decay of his fortunes, but to a proud monarch in the plentitude of his power, in the very heart of his capital, sur-rounded by thousands and tens of thousands, who trembled at his nod, and would have poured out their blood like water in his defence,—that all this should have been done by a mere handful

---

One may doubt whether pity or contempt predominates in Martyr's notice of this event. "Infelix tunc Muteczumo re adeo noua perculsus, formidine repletur, decidit animo, neque iam erigere caput audet, aut suorum auxilia implorare. Ille vero pœnam se meruisse fassus est, vti agnus mitis. Æquo animo pati videtur has regulas grammaticalibus duriores, imberbibus pueris dictatas, omnia placide fert, ne seditio ciuium et procerum oriatur " De Orbe Novo, dec. 5, cap. 3.

[22] Rel. Seg. de Cortes, ap. Lorenzana, p. 88.
[23] Bernal Diaz, Ibid., ubi supra.

of adventurers, is a thing too extravagant, altogether too improbable, for the pages of romance ! It is, nevertheless, literally
true.   Yet we shall not be prepared to acquiesce in the judgments
of contemporaries who regarded these acts with admiration.
We may well distrust any grounds on which it is attempted to
justify the kidnapping of a friendly sovereign,—by those very
persons, too, who were reaping the full benefit of his favors.

To view the matter differently, we must take the position of
the Conquerors, and assume with them the original right of conquest.   Regarded from this point of view, many difficulties van-
ish.   If conquest were a duty, whatever was necessary to effect
it was right also.   Right and expedient become convertible
terms.   And it can hardly be denied, that the capture of the
monarch was expedient, if the Spaniards would maintain their
hold on the empire.[24]

The execution of the Aztec governor suggests other considerations.   If he were really guilty of the perfidious act imputed
to him by Cortés and if Montezuma disavowed it, the governor
deserved death, and the general was justified by the law of
nations in inflicting it.[62]   It is by no means so clear, however, why
he should have involved so many in this sentence ; most, perhaps
all, of whom must have acted under his authority.   The cruel
manner of the death will less startle those who are familiar with
the established penal codes in most civilized nations in the sixteenth century.

But, if the governor deserved death, what pretence was there
for the outrage on the person of Montezuma ?   If the former
was guilty, the latter surely was not.   But, if the cacique only
acted in obedience to orders, the responsibility was transferred
to the sovereign who gave the orders.   They could not both stand
in the same category.

It is vain, however, to reason on the matter, on any abstract
principles of right and wrong, or to suppose that the Conquerors
troubled themselves with the refinements of casuistry.   Their
standard of right and wrong, in reference to the natives, was a
very simple one.   Despising them as an outlawed race, without
God in the world, they, in common with their age, held it to be

[24] Archbishop Lorenzana, as late as the close of the last century, finds
good Scripture warrant for the proceeding of the Spaniards.   " Fué grande
prudencia, y Arte militar haber asegurado á el Emperador, porque sino
quedaban expuestos Hernan Cortés, y sus soldados á perecer á traycion, y
teniendo seguro á el Emperador se aseguraba á sí mismo, pues los Españoles
no se confian ligeramente : Jónathas fué muerto, y sorprendido por haberse
confiado de Triphon."   Rel. Seg. de Cortés, p. 84, nota.
[62] See Puffendorf, De Jure Naturæ et Gentium, lib. 8, cap. 6, sec. 10 —
Vattel, Law of Nations, book 3, chap. 8, sec. 141.

their " mission " (to borrow the cant phrase of our own day) to conquer and to convert. The measures they adopted certainly facilitated the first great work of conquest. By the execution of the caciques, they struck terror not only into the capital, but throughout the country. It proclaimed that not a hair of a Spaniard was to be touched with impunity! By rendering Monte-zuma contemptible in his own eyes and those of his subjects, Cortés deprived him of the support of his people, and forced him to lean on the arm of the stranger. It was a politic proceed-ing, — to which few men could have been equal, who had a touch of humanity in their natures.

A good criterion of the moral sense of the actors in these events is afforded by the reflections of Bernal Diaz, made some fifty years, it will be remembered, after the events themselves, when the fire of youth had become extinct, and the eye, glancing back through the vista of half a century, might be supposed to be unclouded by the passions and prejudices which throw their mist over the present. "Now that I am an old man," says the veteran, " I often entertain myself with calling to mind the hero-ical deeds of early days, till they are as fresh as the events of yesterday. I think of thes eizure of the Indian monarch, his confinement in irons, and the execution of his officers, till all these things seem actually passing before me. And, as I ponder on our exploits, I feel that it was not of ourselves that we per-formed them, but that it was the providence of God which guided us. Much food is there here for meditation!"[26] There is so, indeed, and for a meditation not unpleasing, as we reflect on the advance, in speculative morality, at least, which the nineteenth century has made over the sixteenth. But should not the consciousness of this teach us charity? . Should it not make us the more distrustful of applying the standard of the present to measure the actions of the past?

---

[26] " Osar quemar sus Capitanes delante de sus Palacios, y echalle grillos entre tanto que se hazia la Justicia, que muchas vezes aora que soy viejo me paro á considerar las cosas heroicas que en aquel tiempo passámos, que me parece las veo presentes : Y digo que nuestros hechos, que no los hazia-mos nosotros, sino que venian todos encaminados por Dios. . . . . . Porque ay mucho que ponderar en ello." Hist. de la Conquista, **cap.** 95.

CHAPTER IV.

Montezuma's Deportment.—His Life in the Spanish Quarters.—Meditated Insurrection.—Lord of Tezcuco seized.—Further Measures of Cortes.

1520.

THE settlement of La Villa Rica de Vera Cruz was of the last importance to the Spaniards. It was the port by which they were to communicate with Spain, the strong post on which they were to retreat in case of disaster, and which was to bribe their enemies and give security to their allies; the *point d' appui* for all their operations in the country. It was of great moment, therefore, that the care of it should be intrusted to proper hands.

A cavalier, named Alonso de Grado, had been sent by Cortes to take the place made vacant by the death of Escalante. He was a person of greater repute in civil than military matters, and would be more likely, it was thought, to maintain peaceful relations with the natives, than a person of more belligerent spirit. Cortes made—what was rare with him—a bad choice. He soon received such accounts of troubles in the settlement from the exactions and negligence of the new governor, that he resolved to supersede him.

He now gave the command to Gonzalo de Sandoval, a young cavalier, who had displayed, through the whole campaign singular intrepidity united with sagacity and discretion; while the good-humor with which he bore every privation, and his affable manners, made him a favorite with all, privates, as well as officers. Sandoval accordingly left the camp for the coast. Cortes did not mistake his man a second time.

Notwithstanding the actual control exercised by the Spaniards through their royal captive, Cortes felt some uneasiness, when he reflected that it was in the power of the Indians, at any time, to cut off his communications with the surrounding country, and hold him a prisoner in the capital. He proposed, therefore, to build two vessels of sufficient size to transport his forces across the lake, and thus to render himself independent of the cause ways. Montezuma was pleased with the idea of seeing those wonderful, " water-houses," of which he had heard so much, and, readily gave permission to have the timber in the royal forests felled for the purpose. The work was placed under the direction of Martin Lopez, an experienced ship-builder. Orders were also given to Sandoval to send up from the coast a supply of cordage, sails, iron, and other necessary materials, which had been judiciously saved on the destruction of the fleet.[1]

The Aztec emperor, meanwhile, was passing his days in the Spanish quarters in no very different manner from what he had been accustomed to in his own palace. His keepers were too well aware of the value of their prize, not to do everything which could make his captivity comfortable, and disguise it from himself. But the chain will gall, though wreathed with roses. After Montezuma's breakfast, which was a light meal of fruits or vegetables, Cortés or some of his officers usually waited on him, to learn if he had any commands for them. He then devoted some time to business. He gave audience to those of his subjects who had petitions to prefer, or suits to settle. The statement of the party was drawn upon the hieroglyphic scrolls which were submitted to a number of counsellors or judges, who assisted him with their advice on these occasions. Envoys from foreign states or his own remote provinces and cities were also admitted, and the Spaniards were careful that the same precise and punctilious etiquette should be maintained towards the royal puppet as when in the plenitude of his authority.

After business was dispatched, Montezuma often amused himself with seeing the Castilian troops go through their military exercises. He, too, had been a soldier, and in his prouder days had led armies in the field. It was very natural he should take an interest in the novel display of European tactics and discipline. At other times, he would challenge Cortés or his officers to play at some of the national games. A favorite one was called *totoloque*, played with golden balls aimed at a target or mark of the same metal. Montezuma usually staked something of value,—precious stones or ingots of gold. He lost with good-humor ; indeed, it was of little consequence whether he won or lost, since he generally gave away his winnings to his attendants.[2] He had, in truth, a most munificent spirit. His enemies accused him of avarice. But, if he were avaricious, it could have been only that he might have the more to give away.

Each of the Spaniards had several Mexicans, male and female, who attended to his cooking and various other personal offices.

---

[1] Bernal Diaz, Hist. de la Conquista, cap. 96.
[2] Ibid., cap. 97.

Cortés, considering that the maintenance of this host of menials, was a heavy tax on the royal exchequer, ordered them to be dismissed excepting one to be retained for each soldier. Montezuma, on learning this, pleasantly remonstrated with the general on his careful economy, as unbecoming a royal establishment, and, countermanding the order, caused additional accommodations to be provided for the attendants, and their pay to be doubled.

On another occasion a soldier purloined some trinkets of gold from the treasure kept in the chamber, which, since Montezuma's arrival in the Spanish quarters, had been reopened. Cortés would have punished the man for the theft, but the emperor interfering said to him, " Your countrymen are welcome to the gold and other articles, if you will but spare those belonging to the gods." Some of the soldiers, making the most of his permission, carried off several hundred loads of fine cotton to their quarters. When this was represented to Montezuma, he only replied, "What I have once given, I never take back again." [3]

While thus indifferent to his treasures, he was keenly sensitive to personal slight or insult. When a common soldier once spoke to him angrily, the tears came into the monarch's eyes, as it made him feel the true character of his impotent condition. Cortés, on becoming acquainted with it, was so much incensed, that he ordered the soldier to be hanged ; but, on Montezuma's intercession, commuted this severe sentence for a flogging. The general was not willing that any one but himself should treat his royal captive with indignity. Montezuma was desired to procure a further mitigation of the punishment. But he refused, saying, " that, if a similar insult had been offered by any one of his subjects to Malinche, he would have resented it in like manner." [4]

Such instances of disrespect were very rare. Montezuma's amiable and inoffensive manners, together with his liberality, the most popular of virtues with the vulgar, made him generally beloved by the Spaniards.[5] The arrogance, for which he had been so distinguished in his prosperous days, deserted him in his fallen fortunes. His character in captivity seems to have undergone something of that change which takes place in the wild animals of the forest, when caged within the walls of the menagerie.

The Indian monarch knew the name of every man in the army,

[3] Gomara, Crónica, cap. 84.—Herrera, Hist. General, dec. 2, lib. 8, cap. 4
[4] Ibid., dec. 2, lib. 8, cap. 5.
[5] " En esto era tan bien mirado, que todos le queriamos con gran amor, porque verdaderamente era gran señor en todas las cosas que le viamos hazer." Bernal Diaz, Hist. de la Conquista, cap. 100.

and was careful to discriminate his proper rank.[6] For some he showed a strong partiality. He obtained from the general a favorite page, named Orteguilla, who, being in constant attendance on his person, soon learned enough of the Mexican language to be of use to his countrymen. Montezuma took great pleasure, also, in the society of Velasquez de Leon, the captain of his guard, and Pedro de Alvarado, *Tonatiuh,*or "the Sun," as he was called by the Aztecs, from his yellow hair and sunny countenance. The sunshine, as events afterwards showed, could sometimes be the prelude to a terrible tempest.

Notwithstanding the care taken to cheat him of the tedium of captivity, the royal prisoner cast a wistful glance, now and then, beyond the walls of his residence to the ancient haunts of business or pleasure. He intimated a desire to offer up his devotions at the great temple, where he was once so constant in his worship. The suggestion startled Cortés. It was too reasonable, however, for him to object to it, without wholly discarding the appearances which he was desirous to maintain. But he secured Montezuma's return by sending an escort with him of a hundred and fifty soldiers under the same resolute cavaliers who had aided in his seizure. He told him, also, that, in case of any attempt to escape, his life would instantly pay the forfeit. Thus guarded, the Indian prince visited the *teocalli*, where he was received with the usual state, and, after performing his devotions, he returned again to his quarters.[7]

It may well be believed that the Spaniards did not neglect the opportunity afforded by his residence with them, of instilling into him some notions of the Christian doctrine. Fathers Diaz and Olmedo exhausted all their battery of logic and persuasion, to shake his faith in his idols, but in vain. He, indeed, paid a most edifying attention, which gave promise of better things. But the conferences always closed with the declaration, that "the God of the Christians was good, but the gods of his own country were the true gods for him."[8] It is said, however, they extorted a promise from him, that he would take part in no more human sacrifices. Yet such sacrifices were of daily occurrence in the great temples of the capital; and the people were too blindly

---

[6] " Y él bien conocia á todos, y sabia nuestros nombres, y aun calidades, y era tan bueno, que á todos nos daua joyas, á otros mantas é Indias hermosas." Ibid., cap. 97,

[7] Ibid., cap. 98.

[8] According to Solís, the Devil closed his heart against these good men : though, in the historian's opinion, there is no evidence that this evil counsellor actually appeared and conversed with Montezuma, after the Spaniards had displayed the Cross in Mexico. Conquista, lib. 3, cap. 20.

attached to their bloody abominations, for the Spaniards to deem it safe, for the present at least, openly to interfere.

Montezuma showed, also, an inclination to engage in the pleasures of the chase, of which he once was immoderately fond. He had large forests reserved for the purpose on the other side of the lake. As the Spanish brigantines were now completed, Cortés proposed to transport him and his suite across the water in them. They were of a good size, strongly built. the largest was mounted with four falconets, or small guns. It was protected by a gayly-colored awning stretched over the deck, and the royal ensign of Castile floated proudly from the mast. On board of this vessel, Montezuma, delighted with the opportunity of witnessing the nautical skill of the white men, embarked with a train of Aztec nobles and a numerous guard of Spaniards. A fresh breeze played on the waters, and the vessel soon left behind it the swarms of light pirogues which darkened their surface. She seemed like a thing of life in the eyes of the astonished natives, who saw her, as if disdaining human agency, sweeping by with snowy pinions as if on the wings of the wind, while the thunders from her sides, now for the first time breaking on the silence of this "inland sea," showed that the beautiful phantom was clothed in terror.[9]

The royal chase was well stocked with game ; some of which the emperor shot with arrows, and others were driven by the numerous attendants into nets.[10] In these woodland exercises, while he ranged over his wild domain, Montezuma seemed to enjoy again the sweets of liberty. It was but the shadow of liberty, however ; as in his quarters, at home, he enjoyed but the shadow of royalty. At home or abroad, the eye of the Spaniard was always upon him.

But while he resigned himself without a struggle to his inglorious fate, there were others who looked on it with very different emotions. Among them was his nephew, Cacama, lord of Tezcuco, a young man not more than twenty-five years of age, but who enjoyed great consideration from his high personal qualities, especially his intrepidity of character. He was the same prince who had been sent by Montezuma to welcome the Spaniards on their entrance into the Valley ; and, when the question of their reception was first debated in the council, he had advised to admit them honorably as ambassadors of a foreign

---

[9] Bernal Diaz, Hist de la Conquista, cap. 99.—Rel Seg de Cortés ap. Lorenzana, p. 88.

[10] He sometimes killed his game with a tube, a sort of air-gun, through which he blew little balls at birds and rabbits. "La Caça á que Monteçuma iba por la Laguna, era á tirar á Pàjaros, i á Conejos, con Cobratana, de la qual era diestro." Herrera, Hist. General, dec. 2, lib. 8, cap 4.

prince, and, if they should prove different from what they pretended, it would be time enough then to take up arms against them. That time, he thought, had now come.

In a former part of this work, the reader has been made acquainted with the ancient history of the Acolhuan or Tezcucan monarchy, once the proud rival of the Aztec in power, and greatly its superior in civilization.[11] Under its last sovereign, Nezahualpilli, its territory is said to have been grievously clipped by the insidious practices of Montezuma, who fomented dissen-sions and insubordination among his subjects. On the death of the Tezcucan prince, the succession was contested, and a bloody war ensued between his eldest son, Cacama, and an ambitious younger brother, Ixtlilxochitl. This was followed by a partition of the kingdom, in which the latter chieftain held the mountain districts north of the capital, leaving the residue to Cacama. Though shorn of a large part of his hereditary domain, the city was itself so important, that the lord of Tezcuco still held a high rank among the petty princes of the Valley. His capital, at the time of the Conquest, contained, according to Cortés, a hundred and fifty thousand inhabitants.[12] It was embellished with noble buildings, rivalling those of Mexico itself, and the ruins still to be met with on its ancient site attest that it was once the abode of princes.[13]

The young Tezcucan chief beheld, with indignation, and no slight contempt, the abject condition of his uncle. He endeav-ored to rouse him to manly exertion, but in vain. He then set about forming a league with several of the neighboring caciques to rescue his kinsman, and to break the detested yoke of the strangers. He called on the lord of Iztapalapan, Montezuma's

---

[11] Ante, Book I. Chap. 6.

[12] " E llámase esta Ciudad Tezcuco, y será de hasta treinta mil Vecinos." (Rel. Seg., ap. Lorenzana, p. 94.) According to the licentiate Zuazo, double that number,—*sesenta mil Vecinos.* (Carta, MS.) Scarcely probable, as Mexico had no more. Toribio speaks of it as covering a league one way by six another! (Hist. de los Indios, MS., Parte 3, cap. 7.) This must include the environs to a considerable extent. The language of the old chroniclers is not the most precise.

[13] A description of the capital in its glory is thus given by an eye-witness. " Esta Ciudad era la segunda cosa principal de la tierra, y así habia en Tezcuco muy grandes edificios de templos del Demonio, y muy gentiles casas y aposentos de Señores, entre los cuales, fué muy cosa de ver la casa del Señor principal, así la vieja con su huer ta cercada de mas de mil cedros muy grandes y muy hermosos, de los cuales hoy dia están los mas en pie, aunque la casa está asolada, otra casa tenia que se podia aposentar en ella un egército, con muchos jardines, y un muy grande estanque, que por debajo de tierra solian entrar á él con barcas." (Toribio, Hist. de los Indios, MS., Parte 3, cap. 7.) The last relics of this palace were employed in the fortifi-cations of the city in the revolutionary war of 1810. (Ixtlilxochitl, Venida

brother, the lord of Tlacopan, and some others of most authority all of whom entered heartily into his views. He then urged the Aztec nobles to join them, but they expressed an unwilling- ness to take any step not first sanctioned by the emperor.[14] They entertained, undoubtedly, a profound reverence for their master; but it seems probable that jealousy of the personal views of Cacama had its influence on their determination. Whatever were their motives, it is certain, that, by this refusal, they relinquished the best opportunity ever presented for retrieving their sovereign's independence, and their own.

These intrigues could not be conducted so secretly as not to reach the ears of Cortés, who, with his characteristic promptness, would have marched at once on Tezcuco, and trodden out the spark of "rebellion,"[15] before it had time to burstinto a flame. But from this he was dissuaded by Montezuma, who represented that Cacama was a man of resolution, backed by a powerful force, and not to be put down without a desperate struggle. He consented, therefore, to negotiate, and sent a message of amica- ble expostulation to the cacique. He received a haughty answer in return. Cortés rejoined in a more menacing tone, asserting the supremacy of his own sovereign, the emperor of Castile. To this Cacama replied, " He acknowledged no such authority; he knew nothing of the Spanish sovereign nor his people, nor did he wish to know anything of them."[16] Montezuma was not

de los Esp., p. 78. nota.) Tezcuco is now an insignificant little place, with a population of a few thousand inhabitants. Its architectural remains, as still to be discerned, seem to have made a stronger impression on Mr. Bul- lock than on most travellers. Six Months in Mexico, chap. 27.

[14] " Cacama reprehendió asperamente á la Nobleza Mexicana porque con- sentia hacer semejantes desacatos á quatro Estrangeros y que no les mataban se escusaban con decirles les iban á la mano y no les consentian tomar las Armas para libertarlo, y tomar sí una tan gran deshonra como era la que los Estrangeros les habian hecho en prender á su señor, y quemar á Quauhpo- pocatzin, los demas sus Hijos y Deudos sin culpa, con las Armas y Municion que tenian para la defenza y guarda de la ciudad, y de su autoridad tomar para sí los tesoros del Rey y de los Dioses y otras libertades y desvergüenzas que cada dia pasaban, y aunque todo esto vehian lo disimulaban por no enojar á Motecuhzoma que tan amigo y casado estaba con ellos." Ixtlilxo- chitl, Hist. Chich., MS., cap. 86.

[16] It is the language of Cortés. " Y esta señor *se rebeló*, assi contra el servicio de Vuestra Alteza, á quien se habia ofrecido, como contra el dicho Muteczuma." Rel. Seg., ap. Lorenzana, p. 95.—Voltaire, with his quick eye for the ridiculous, notices this arrogance in his tragedy of Alzire.

> Tu vois de ces tyrans la fureur despotique;
> Ils pensent que pour eux le Ciel fit l'Amérique,
> Qu'ils en sont nés les Rois; et Zamore à leurs yeux,
> Tout souverain qu'il fut, n'est qu'un séditieux."
>
> ALZIRE, Act 4, sc. 3.

[16] Gomara, Crónica, cap. 91.

more successful in his application to Cacama to come to Mexico, and allow him to mediate his differences with the Spaniards, with whom he assured the prince he was residing as a friend. But the young lord of Tezcuco was not to be so duped. He understood the position of his uncle, and replied, "that, when he did visit his capital it would be to rescue it, as well as the emperor himself, and their common gods, from bondage. He should come, not with his hand in his bosom, but on his sword,—to drive out the detested strangers who had brought such dishonor on their country !" [17]

Cortés, incensed at this tone of defiance, would again have put himself in motion to punish it, but Montezuma interposed with his more politic arts. He had several of the Tezcucan nobles, he said, in his pay ; [18] and it would be easy, through their means, to secure Cacama's person, and thus break up the confederacy, at once, without bloodshed. The maintaining of a corps of stipendiaries in the courts of neighboring princes was a refinement which showed that the Western barbarian understood the science of political intrigue, as well as some of his royal brethren on the other side of the water.

By the contrivance of these faithless nobles, Cacama was induced to hold a conference, relative to the proposed invasion, in a villa which overhung the Tezcucan lake, not far from his capital. Like most of the principal edifices, it was raised so as to admit the entrance of boats beneath it. In the midst of the conference, Cacama was seized by the conspirators, hurried on board a bark in readiness for the purpose, and transported to Mexico. When brought into Montezuma's presence, the high-spirited chief abated nothing of his proud and lofty bearing. He taxed his uncle with his perfidy, and a pusillanimity, so unworthy of his former character, and of the royal house from which he was descended. By the emperor he was referred to Cortés, who, holding royalty but cheap in an Indian prince, put him in fetters.[19]

---

[17] " I que para reparar la Religion, í restituir los Dioses, guardar el Reino, cobrar la fama, i libertad á él, í á México, iria de mui buena gana, mas no las manos en el seno, sino en la Espada, para matar los Españoles, que tanta mengua, i afrenta havian hecho á la Nacion de Culhúa." Ibid., cap. 91.

[18] " Pero que él tenia en su Tierra de el dicho Cacamazin muchas Personas Principales, que vivian con él, y les daba su salario." Rel. Seg. de Cortés, ap. Lorenzana, p. 95.

[19] Ibid., pp. 95, 96.—Oviedo, Hist. de las Ind., MS., lib. 33, cap. 8.— Ixtlilxochitl, Hist. Chich., MS., cap. 86.

The latter author dismisses the capture of Cacama with the comfortable reflection, "that it saved the Spaniards much embarrassment, and greatly facilitated the introduction of the Catholic faith."

THE TEMPLE OF THE SUN

There was at this time in Mexico a brother of Cacama, a stripling much younger than himself. At the instigation of Cortés, Montezuma, pretending that his nephew had forfeited the sovereignty by his late *rebellion*, declared him to be deposed, and appointed Cuicuitzca in his place. The Aztec sovereigns had always been allowed a paramount authority in questions relating to the succession. But this was a most unwarrantable exercise of it. The Tezcucans acquiesced, however, with a ready ductility, which showed their allegiance hung but lightly on them, or, what is more probable, that they were greatly in awe of the Spaniards ; and the new prince was welcomed with acclamations to his capital.[20]

Cortés still wanted to get into his hands the other chiefs who had entered into the confederacy with Cacama. This was no difficult matter. Montezuma's authority was absolute, every-where but in his own palace. By his command, the Caciques were seized, each in his own city, and brought in chains to Mexico, where Cortés placed them in strict confinement with their leader.[21]

He had now triumphed over all his enemies. He had set his feet on the necks of princes ; and the great chief of the Aztec empire was but a convenient tool in his hands, for accomplishing his purposes. His first use of this power was, to ascertain the actual resources of the monarchy. He sent several parties of Spaniards, guided by the natives, to explore the regions where gold was obtained. It was gleaned mostly from the beds of rivers, several hundred miles from the capital.

His next object was, to learn if there existed any good natural harbor for shipping on the Atlantic coast, as the road of Vera Cruz left no protection against the tempests that at certain seasons swept over these seas. Montezuma showed him a chart on which the shores of the Mexican Gulf were laid down with tolerable accuracy.[22] Cortés, after carefully inspecting it, sent

---

[20] Cortés calls the name of this prince Cucuzca. (Rel. Seg. ap. Lorenzana, p. 66.) In the orthography of Aztec words, the general was governed by his ear ; and was wrong nine times out of ten.—Bustamante, in his catalogue of Tezcucan monarchs, omits him altogether. He probably regards him as an intruder, who had no claim to be reckoned among the rightful sovereigns of the land. (Galería de Antiguos Príncipes, (Puebla, 1821,) p. 21.) Sahagun has, in like manner, struck his name from the royal roll of Tezcuco. Hist. de Nueva España, lib. 8, cap. 3.

[21] The exceeding lenity of the Spanish commander, on this occasion, excited general admiration, if we are to credit Solís, throughout the Aztec empire! "Tuvo notable aplauso en todo el imperio este género de castigo sin sangre, que se atribuyó al superior juicio de los Españoles, porque no esperaban de Motezuma semejante moderacion." Conquista, lib. 4, cap. 2.

[22] Rel. Seg. de Cortés, ap. Lorenzana, p. 91.

a commission consisting of ten Spaniards, several of them pilots, and some Aztecs, who descended to Vera Cruz, and made careful survey of the coast for nearly sixty leagues south of that settlement, as far as the great river Coatzacualco which seemed to offer the best, indeed, the only, accommodations for a safe and suitable harbor. A spot was selected as the site of a fortified post, and the general sent a detachment of a hundred and fifty men under Velasquez de Leon to plant a colony there.

He also obtained a grant of an extensive tract of land, in the fruitful province of Oaxaca, where he proposed to lay out a plantation for the Crown. He stocked it with the different kind of domesticated animals peculiar to the country, and with such indigenous grains and plants as would afford the best articles for export. He soon had the estate under such cultivation, that he assured his master, the emperor, Charles the Fifth, it was worth twenty thousand ounces of gold.[23]

---

[23] " Damus quæ dant," says Martyr, briefly, in reference to this valuation. (De Orbe Novo, dec. 5, cap. 3.) Cortés notices the reports made by his people, of large and beautiful edifices in the province of Oaxaca. (Rel. Seg., ap. Lorenzana, p. 89.) It is here, also, that some of the most elaborate specimens of Indian architecture are still to be seen, in the ruins of Mitla.

CHAPTER V.

MONTEZUMA SWEARS ALLEGIANCE TO SPAIN.—ROYAL TREASURES —THEIR DIVISION.—CHRISTIAN WORSHIP IN THE TEOCALLI.—DISCONTENTS OF THE AZTECS.

1520.

CORTES now felt his authority sufficiently assured to demand from Montezuma a formal recognition of the supremacy of the Spanish emperor. The Indian monarch had intimated his willingness to acquiesce in this, on their very first interview. He did not object, therefore, to call together his principal caciques for the purpose. When they were assembled, he made them an address, briefly stating the object of the meeting. They were all acquainted, he said, with the ancient tradition, that the great Being, who had once ruled over the land, had declared, on his departure, that he should return at some future time and resume his sway. That time had now arrived. The white men have come from the quarter where the sun rises, beyond the ocean, to which the good deity had withdrawn. They were sent by their master to reclaim the obedience of his ancient subjects. For himself he was ready to acknowledge his authority. "You have been faithful vassals of mine," continued Montezuma, "during the many years that I have sat on the throne of my fathers. I now expect that you will show me this last act of obedience by acknowledging the great king beyond the waters to be your lord, also, and that you will pay him tribute in the same manner as you have hitherto done to me."[1] As he concluded, his voice was nearly stifled by his emotion, and the tears fell fast down his cheeks.

His nobles, many of whom, coming from a distance, had not kept pace with the changes which had been going on in the capital, were filled with astonishment, as they listened to his

---

[1] "Y mucho os ruego, pues á todos os es notorio todo esto, que assí como hasta aquí á mí me habeis tenido, y obedecido por Señor vuestro, de aquí adelante tengais, y obedescais á este Gran Rey, pues él es vuestro natural Señor y en su lugar tengais á este su Capitan : y todos los Tributos, y Servicios, que fasta aquí á mí me haciades, los haced, y dad á él, porque yo assimismo tengo de contribuir, y servir con todo lo que me mandaré." Rel. Seg. de Cortés, ap. Lorenzana, p. 97.

words, and beheld the voluntary abasement of their master, whom they had hitherto reverenced as the omnipotent lord of Anahuac. They were the more affected, therefore, by the sight of his distress.[2] His will, they told him, had always been their law. It should be so now, and, if he thought the sovereign of the strangers was the ancient lord of their country, they were willing to acknowledge him as such still. The oaths of allegiance were then administered with all due solemnity, attested by the Spaniards present, and a full record of the proceedings was drawn up by the royal notary, to be sent to Spain.[3] There was something deeply touching in the ceremony by which an independent and absolute monarch, in obedience less to the dictates of fear than of conscience, thus relinquished his hereditary rights in favor of an unknown and mysterious power. It even moved those hardy men who were thus unscrupulously availing themselves of the confiding ignorance of the natives ; and, though " it was in the regular way of their own business," says an old chronicler, " there was not a Spaniard who could look on the spectacle with a dry eye" ![4]

[2] " Lo qual todo les dijo llorando, con las mayores lágrimas, y suspiros, que un hombre podia manifestar ; é assimismo todos aquellos Señores, que le estaban oiendo, lloraban tanto, que en gran rato no le pudiéron responder." Ibid., loc. cit.

[3] Solís regards this ceremony as supplying what was before defective in the title of the Spaniards to the country. The remarks are curious, even from a professed casuist. " Y siendo una como insinuacion misteriosa del título que se debió despues al derecho de las armas, sobre justa provocacion, como lo verémos en su lugar : circumstancia particular, que concurrió en la conquista de Méjico para mayor justificacion de aquel dominio, sobre las demas consideraciones generales que no solo hiciéron lícita la guerra en otras partes, sino legítima y razonable siempre que se puso en términos de medio necesario para la introduccion del Evangelio." Conquista. lib. 4, cap. 3.

[4] Bernal Diaz, Hist. de la Conquista, cap. 101.—Solís, Conquista, loc. cit. —Herrera, Hist. General, dec. 2, lib. 9, cap. 4.—Ixtlilxochitl, Hist. Chich., MS., cap. 87.

Oviedo considers the grief of Montezuma as sufficient proof that his homage, far from being voluntary, was extorted by necessity. The historian appears to have seen the drift of events more clearly than some of the actors in them. " Y en la verdad si como Cortés lo dice, ó escrivió, pasó en efecto, mui gran coso me parece la conciencia y liberalidad de Montezuma en esta su restitucion é obediencia al Rey de Castilla, por la simple ó cautelosa informacion de Cortés, que le podia hacer para ello ; Mas aquellas lágrimas con que dice, que Montezuma hizo su oracion, é amonestamiento, despojándose de su señorío, é las de aquellos con que les respondiéron aceptando lo que les mandaba, y exortaba, y á mi parecer su llanto queria decir, ó enseñar otra cosa de lo que él, y ellos dixéron ; porque las obediencias que se suelen dar á los Príncipes con riza, é con camaras ; é diversidad de Música, é leticia, enseñales de placer, se suele hacer ; é no con lucto ni lágrimas, é sollozos, ni estando preso quien obedece ; porque como dice Marco Varron : Lo que por fuerza se da no es servicio sino robo." Hist. de las Ind., MS, lib. 33. cap. 9.

The rumor of these strange proceedings was soon circulated through the capital and country. Men read in them the finger of Providence. The ancient tradition of Quetzalcoatl was familiar to all ; and where it had slept scarcely noticed in the memory, it was now revived with many exaggerated circumstances. It was said to be part of the tradition, that the royal line of the Aztecs was to end with Montezuma ; and his name, the literal signification of which is "sad " or "angry lord " was construed into an omen of his evil destiny.[5]

Having thus secured this great feudatory to the crown of Castile, Cortés suggested that it would be well for the Aztec chiefs to send his sovereign such a gratuity as would conciliate his goodwill by convincing him of the loyalty of his new vassals.[6] Montezuma consented that his collectors should visit the principal cities and province, attended by a number of Spaniards, to receive the customary tributes, in the name of the Castilian sovereign. In a few weeks most of them returned, bringing back large quantities of gold and silver plate, rich stuffs, and the various commodities in which the taxes were usually paid.

To this store Montezuma added, on his own account, the treasure of Axayacatl, previously noticed, some part of which had been already given to the Spaniards. It was the fruit of long and careful hoarding,—of extortion, it may be,—by a prince who little dreamed of its final destination. When brought into the quarters, the gold alone was sufficient to make three great heaps. It consisted partly of native grains ; part had been melted into bars; but the greatest portion was in utensils, and various kinds of ornaments and curious toys, together with imitations of birds, insects, or flowers, executed with uncommon truth and delicacy. There were, also, quantities of collars, bracelets, wands, fans, and other trinkets, in which the gold and feather-work were richly powdered with pearls and precious stones. Many of the articles were even more admirable for the workmanship than for the value of the materials ;[7] such indeed,—if we may take the report of Cortes to one who would himself have soon

---

[5] Gomara, Crónica, cap. 92.—Clavigero, Stor. del Messico, tom. II. p. 256.

[6] " Pareceria que ellos comenzaban á servir, y Vuestra Alteza tendria mas concepto de las voluntades, que é su servicio mostraban." Rel. Seg. de Cortés, ap. Lorenzana, p. 98.

[7] Peter Martyr, distrusting some extravagance in this statement of Cortés, found it fully confirmed by the testimony of others. " Referunt non credenda. Credenda tamen, quando vir talis ad Cæsarem et nostri collegii Indici senatores audeat exscribere. Addes insuper se multa prætermittere, ne tanta recensendo sit molestus. *Idem affirmant qui ad nos inde regrediuntur.*"
De Orbe Novo, dec. 5. cap. 3

an opportunity to judge of its veracity, and whom it would not be safe to trifle with,—as no monarch in Europe could boast in his dominions!

Magnificent as it was, Montezuma expressed his regret that the treasure was no larger. But he had diminished it, he said, by his former gifts to the white men. "Take it" he added, "Malinche, and let it be recorded in your annals, that Montezuma sent this present to your master."

The Spaniards gazed with greedy eyes on the display of riches,[10] now their own which far exceeded all hitherto seen in the New World and fell nothing short of the *El Dorado* which their glowing imaginations had depicted. It may be, that they felt somewhat rebuked by the contrast which their own avarice presented to the princely munificence of the barbarian chief. At least, they seemed to testify their sense of his superiority by the respectful homage which they rendered him, as they poured forth the fulness of their gratitude.[11] They were not so scrupulous, however, as to manifest any delicacy in appropriating to themselves the donative, a small part of which was to find its way into the royal coffers. They clamored loudly for an immediate division of the spoil, which the general would have postponed till the tributes from the remoter provinces had been gathered in. The goldsmiths of Azcapoxalco were sent for to take in pieces the larger and coarser ornaments, leaving untouched those of more delicate workmanship. Three days were consumed in this labor, when the heaps of gold were cast into ingots, and stamped with the royal arms.

Some difficulty occurred in the division of the treasure, from the want of weights, which, strange as it appears, considering their advancement in the arts, were, as already observed, unknown to the Aztecs. The deficiency was soon supplied by the Spaniards, however, with scales and weights of their own manufacture, probably not the most exact. With the aid of these they ascertained the value of the royal fifth to be thirty-

---

[8] " Las quales, demas de su valor, eran tales, y tan maravillosas, que consideradas por su novedad, y estrañeza, no tenian precio, ni es de creer, que alguno de todos los Príncipes del Mundo de quien se tiene noticia, las pudiesse tener tales, y de tal calidad.'' Rel. Seg. de Cortés, ap. Lorenzana, p. 99.—See, also, Oviedo, Hist. de las Ind., MS., lib. 33, cap. 9,—Bernal Diaz, Hist. de la Conquista, cap. 104.

[9] " Dezilde en vuestros aneles y cartas: Esto os embia vuestro buen vassallo Monteçuma.'' Bernal Diaz, ubi supra.

[10]   " Fluctibus auri
Expleri callor ille nequit.''
CLAUDIAN, In Ruf., lib. 1.

[11] " Y quãdo aquello le oyó Cortés, y todos nosotros, estuvímos espanta-

two thousand and four hundred *pesos de oro*.[12]   Diaz swells is to nearly four times that amount.[13]   But their desire of securing the emperor's favor makes it improbable that the Spaniards should have defrauded the exchequer of any part of its due ; while, as Cortés was responsible for the sum admitted in his letter, he would be still less likely to overstate it.   His estimate may be received as the true one.

The whole amounted, therefore, to one hundred and sixty- two thousand *pesos de oro*, independently of the fine ornaments and jewelry, the value of which Cortes computes at five hundred thousand ducats more.   There were, besides, five hundred marks of silver, chiefly in plate, drinking-cups, and other articles of luxury.   The inconsiderable quantity of the silver, as compared with the gold forms a singular contrast to the relative proportions of the two metals since the occupation of the country by the Europeans.[14]   The whole amount of the treasure, reduced to our own currency, and making allowance for the change in the value of gold since the beginning of the sixteenth century, was about six million three hundred thousand dollars, or one million four hundred and seventeen thousand pounds sterling; a sum large enough to show the incorrectness of the popular notion, that little or no wealth was found in Mexico.[15]   It was, indeed, small in com.

dos de la gran bondad, y liberalidad del gran Monteçuma, y con mucho acato le quitámos todos las gorras de armas, y le diximos, que se lo teniamos en merced, y con palabras de mucho amor." etc.   Bernal Diaz, ubi supra.

[12] Rel. Seg. de Cortés, ap. Lorenzana, p. 99.

This estimate of the royal fifth is confirmed (with the exception of the four hundred ounces) by the affidavits of a number of witnesses cited on behalf of Cortés, to show the amount of the treasure.   Among these witnesses we find some of the most respectable names in the army, as Olid, Ordaz, Avila, the priests Oimedo and Diaz,—the last, it may be added, not too friendly to the general.   The instrument, which is without date, is in the collection of Vargas Ponçe.   Probanza fecha á pedimento de Juan de Lexalde, MS.

[13] " Eran tres montones *de oro*, y pesado huvo en ellos sobre *seiscientos mil pesos*, como adelante diré, sin la plata, é otras muchas riquezas."   Hist. de la Conquista, cap. 104.

[14] The quantity of silver taken from the American mines has exceeded that of gold in the ratio of forty-six to one.   (Humboldt, Essai Politique, tom. III. p. 401.)   The value of the latter metal, says Clemencin, which, on the discovery of the New World was only eleven times greater than that of the former, has now come to be sixteen times.   (Memorias de la Real Acad. de Hist., tom., VI. Ilust. 20.)   This does not vary materially from Smith's estimate made after the middle of the last century.   (Wealth of Nations, book 1. chap. 11.)   The difference would have been much more considerable but for the greater demand for silver for objects of ornament and use.

[15] Dr. Robertson, preferring the authority, it seems, of Diaz, speaks of the value of the treasure as 600,000 *pesos*.   (History of America, vol. II. pp. 296, 298.)   The value of the *peso* is an ounce of silver, or dollar, which, making allowance for the depreciation of silver, represented, in the t me of

parison with that obtained by the conquerors of Peru. But few
European monarchs of that day could boast a larger treasure in
their coffers.[16]

The division of the spoil was a work of some difficulty. A
perfectly equal division of it among the Conquerors would have
given more than three thousand pounds sterling, apiece ; a magnificent booty ! But one fifth was to be deducted for the Crown.
An equal portion was reserved for the general, pursuant to the
tenor of his commission. A large sum was then allowed to
indemnify him and the governor of Cuba, for the charges of
the expedition and the loss of the fleet. The garrison of Vera
Cruz was also to be provided for. Ample compensation was
made to the principal cavaliers. The cavalry, arquebusiers and
crossbow-men, each received double pay. So that, when the turn
of the common soldiers came, there remained not more than a
hundred *pesos de oro* for each ; a sum so insignificant, in comparison with their expectations, that several refused to accept it.[17]

Loud murmurs now rose among the men. "Was it for this,"
they said, "that we left our homes and families, perilled our lives,
submitted to fatigue and famine, and all for so contemptible a
pittance ! Better to have stayed in Cuba, and contented ourselves
with the gains of a safe and easy traffic. When we gave up our
share of the gold at Vera Cruz, it was on the assurance that we
should be amply requited in Mexico. We have, indeed, found
the riches we expected ; but no sooner seen then they are snatched
from us by the very men who pledged us their faith ! " The
malcontents even went so far as to accuse their leaders of
appropriating to themselves several of the richest ornaments,
before the partition had been made ; an accusation that receives
some countenance from a dispute which arose between Mexia,

Cortés, nearly four times its value at the present day. But that of the *peso
de ora* was nearly three times that sum, or eleven dollars, sixty-seven cents.
(See Ante, Book II. chap. 6, note 18.) Robertson makes his own estimate,
so much reduced below that of his original, an argument for doubting the
existence, in any great quantity, of either gold or silver in the country. In
accounting for the scarcity of the former metal in this argument, he falls into
an error in stating that gold was not one of the standards by which the value
of other commodities in Mexico was estimated. Comp. Ante, Vol. I. p.
145.

[16] Many of them, indeed, could boast little or nothing in their coffers.
Maximilian of Germany, and the more prudent Ferdinand of Spain, left
scarcely enough to defray their funeral expenses. Even as late as the be
ginning of the next century, we find Henry IV. of France embracing his
minister, Sully, with rapture, when he informed him, that, by dint of great
economy, he had 36,000,000 livres, about 1,500,000 pounds sterling, in his
treasury. See Mémoires du Duc de Sully, tom. III. liv. 27.

[17] " Por sar tan poco, muchos soldados huuo que no lo quisiéron recebir."
Bernal Diaz, Hist. de la Conquista, cap. 105.

the treasurer for the Crown, and Velasquez de Leon, a relation of the governor, and a favorite of Cortés. The treasurer accused this cavalier of purloining certain of pieces of plate before they were submitted to the royal stamp. From words the parties came to blows. They were good swordsmen ; several wounds were given on both sides, and the affair might have ended fatally, but for the interference of Cortés, who placed both under arrest.

He then used all his authority and insinuating eloquence to calm the passions of his men. It was a delicate crisis. He was sorry, he said, to see them so unmindful of the duty of loyal soldiers, and cavaliers of the Cross, as to brawl like common banditti over their booty. The division, he assured them, had been made on perfectly fair and equitable principles. As to his own share, it was no more than was warranted by his commission. Yet, if they thought it too much, he was willing to forego his just claims, and divide with the poorest soldier. Gold, however welcome, was not the chief object of his ambition. If it were theirs, they should still reflect, that the present treasure was little in comparison with what awaited them hereafter ; for had they not the whole country and its mines at their disposal ? It was only necessary that they should not give an opening to the enemy, by their discord, to circumvent and to crush them. With these honeyed words, of which he had good store for all fitting occasions, says an old soldier,[18] for whose benefit, in part, they were intended, he succeeded in calming the storm for the present ; while in private he took more effectual means, by present judiciously administered, to mitigate the discontents of the importunate and refractory. And, although there were a few of more tenacious temper, who treasured this in their memories against a future day, the troops soon returned to their usual subordination. This was one of those critical conjunctures which taxed all the address and personal authority of Cortés. He never shrunk from them, but on such occasions was true to himself. At Vera Cruz he had persuaded his followers to give up what was but the earnest of future gains. Here he persuaded them to relinquish these gains themselves. It was snatching the prey from the very jaws of the lion. Why did he not turn and rend him ?

To many of the soldiers, indeed, it mattered little whether their share of the booty were more or less. Gaming is a deeprooted passion in the Spaniard, and the sudden acquisition of riches furnished both the means and the motive for its indulg-

---

[18] " **Palabras muy melifluas** ; . . . . . **razones** mui bien dichas, que las sabia bien proponer." Ibid., ubi supra.

ence.　Caras were easily made out of old parchment drum‑
heads, and in a few days most of the prize‑money, obtained
with so much toil and suffering, had changed hands, and many
of the improvident soldiers closed the campaign as poor as they
had commenced it.　Others, it is true, more prudent, followed
the example of their officers, who, with the aid of the royal jew‑
ellers, converted their gold into chains, services of plate, and
other portable articles of ornament or use.[19]

Cortés seemed now to have accomplished the great objects
of the expedition.　The Indian monarch had declared himself
the feudatory of the Spanish.　His authority, his revenues, were
at the disposal of the general.　The conquest of Mexico seemed
to be achieved, and that without a blow.　But it was far from
being achieved.　One important step yet remained to be taken,
towards which the Spaniards had hitherto made little progress,
—the conversion of the natives.　With all the exertions of
father Olmedo, backed by the polemic talents of the general,[20]
neither Montezuma nor his subjects showed any disposition to
abjure the faith of their fathers.[21]　The bloody exercises of their
religion, on the contrary, were celebrated with all the usual cir‑
cumstance and pomp of sacrifice before the eyes of the Span‑
iards.

Unable further to endure these abominations, Cortés, attended
by several of his cavaliers, waited on Montezuma.　He told the
emperor that the Christians could no longer consent to have the
services of their religion shut up within the narrow walls of the
garrison.　They wished to spread its light far abroad, and to
open to the people a full participation in the blessings of Chris‑
tianity.　For this purpose, they requested that the great *teocalli*

[19] Ibid., cap. 105, 106.—Gomara, Crónica, cap. 93.—Herrera, Hist. Gen‑
eral, dec. 2, lib. 8. cap. 5.
[20] "Ex jureconsulto Cortesius theologus effectus," says Martyr, in his
pithy manner.　De Orbe Novo, dec. 5, cap. 4.
[21] According to Ixtlilxochitl, Montezuma got as far on the road to conver‑
sion, as the *Credo* and the *Ave Maria*, both of which he could repeat; but
his baptism was postponed, and he died before receiving it.　That he ever
consented to receive it is highly improbable.　I quote the historian's words,
in which he further notices the general's unsuccessful labors among the
Indians.　"Cortés comenzó á dar órden de la conversion de los Naturales,
diciéndoles, que pues eran vasallos del Rey de España que se tornasen
Christianos como él lo era, y así se comenzáron á Bautizar algunos aunque
fuéron muy pocos, y Motecuhzoma aunque pidió el Bautismo, y sabia algunas
de las oraciones como eran el Ave María, y el Credo, se dilató por la Pasqua
siguiente, que era la de Resurreccion, y fué tan desdichado que nunca al‑
canzó tanto bien, y los Nuestros con la dilacion y aprieto en que se viéron,
se descuidáron, de que pesó á todos mucho muriese sin Bautismo."　Hist
Chich., MS., cap. 87.

should be delivered up, as a fit place where their worship might be conducted in the presence of the whole city.

Montezuma listened to the proposal with visible consternation. Amidst all his troubles he had leaned for support on his own faith, and, indeed, it was in obedience to it, that he had shown such deference to the Spaniards as the mysterious messengers predicted by the oracles. "Why," said he, "Malinche, why will you urge matters to an extremity, that must surely bring down the vengeance of our gods, and stir up an insurrection among my people, who will never endure this profanation of their temples?"[22]

Cortés, seeing how greatly he was moved, made a sign to his officers to withdraw, When left alone with the interpreters, he told the emperor that he would use his influence to moderate the zeal of his followers, and persuade them to be contented with one of the sanctuaries of the *teocalli*. If that were not granted, they should be obliged to take it by force, and to roll down the images of his false deities in the face of the city. "We fear not for our lives," he added, "for, though our numbers are few, the arm of the true God is over us." Montezuma, much agitated, told him that he would confer with the priests.

The result of the conference was favorable to the Spaniards, who were allowed to occupy one of the sanctuaries as a place of worship. The tidings spread great joy throughout the camp. They might now go forth in open day and publish their religion to the assembled capital. No time was lost in availing themselves of the permission. The sanctuary was cleansed of its disgusting impurities, An altar was raised, surmounted by a crucifix and the image of the Virgin. Instead of the gold and jewels which blazed on the neighboring Pagan shrine, its walls were decorated with fresh garlands of flowers; and an old soldier was stationed to watch over the chapel, and guard it from intrusion.

When these arrangements were completed, the whole army moved in solemn procession up the winding ascent of the pyramid. Entering the sanctuary, and clustering round its portals, they listened reverentially to the service of the mass, as it was performed by the fathers Olmedo and Diaz. And, as the beautiful *Te Deum* rose towards heaven, Cortés and his soldiers, kneeling on the ground, with tears streaming from their eyes,

---

[22] "O Malinche, y como nos quereis echar á perder á toda esta ciudad, porque estarán mui enojados nuestros Dioses contra nosotros, y aun vuestras vidas no sé en que pararan." Bernal Diaz, Hist. de la Conquista, cap. 107

poured forth their gratitude to the Almighty for this glorious triumph of the Cross.[22]

It was a striking spectacle,—that of these rude warriors lifting up their orisons on the summit of this mountain temple, in the very capital of Heathendom, on the spot especially dedicated to its unhallowed mysteries. Side by side, the Spaniard and the Aztec knelt down in prayer; and the Christian hymn mingled its sweet tones of love and mercy with the wild chant raised by the Indian priest in honor of the war-god of Anahuac! It was an unnatural union, and could not long abide.

A nation will endure any outrage sooner than that on its religion. This is an outrage both on its principles and its prejudices; on the ideas instilled into it from childhood, which have strengthened with its growth, until they become a part of its nature,—which have to do with its highest interests here, and with the dread hereafter. Any violence to the religious sentiment touches all alike, the old and the young, the rich and the poor, the noble and the plebeian. Above all, it touches the priests, whose personal consideration rests on that of their religion; and who, in a semi-civilized state of society, usually hold an unbounded authority. Thus it was with the Brahmins of India, the Magi of Persia, the Roman Catholic clergy in the Dark Ages, the priests of ancient Egypt and Mexico.

The people had borne with patience all the injuries and affronts hitherto put on them by the Spaniards. They had seen their sovereign dragged as a captive from his own palace; his ministers butchered before his eyes; his treasure seized and appropriated; himself in a manner deposed from his royal supremacy. All this they had seen without a struggle to prevent it. But the profanation of their temples touched a deeper feeling, of which the priesthood were not slow to take advantage.[24]

---

[23] This transaction is told with more discrepancy than usual by the different writers. Cortés assures the Emperor that he occupied the temple, and turned out the false gods by force, in spite of the menaces of the Mexicans. (Rel. Seg., ap. Lorenzana, p. 106.) The improbability of this Quixotic feat startles Oviedo, who nevertheless reports it. (Hist. de las Ind., MS., lib. 33, cap. 10.) It looks, indeed, very much as if the general was somewhat too eager to set off his militant zeal to advantage in the eyes of his master. The statements of Diaz, and of other chroniclers, conformably to that in the text, seem far the most probable. Comp. Diaz, Hist. de la Conquista, ubi supra.—Herrera, Hist. General, dec. 2, lib. 8, cap. 6.—Argensola, Anales, lib. 1, cap. 88.

[24] Para mí yo tengo por marabilla, é grande, la mucha paciencia de Montezuma, y de los Indios principales, que assí viréon tratar sus Templos, é Idolos: Mas su disimulacion adelante se mostró ser otra cosa viendo, que vna Gente Extrangera, é de tan poco número, les prendió su Señore é porque formas los hacia tributarios, é se castigaban é quemaban los principales.

The first intimation of this change of feeling was gathered from Montezuma himself. Instead of his usual cheerfulness, he appeared grave and abstracted, and instead of seeking, as he was wont, the society of the Spaniards, seemed rather to shun it. It was noticed, too, that conferences were more frequent between him and the nobles, and especially the priests. His little page, Orteguilla, who had now picked up a tolerable acquaintance with the Aztec, contrary to Montezuma's usual practice, was not allowed to attend him at these meetings. These circumstances could not fail to awaken most uncomfortable apprehensions in the Spaniards.

Not many days elapsed, however, before Cortéz received an invitation, or rather a summons, from the emperor, to attend him in his apartment. The general went with some feelings of anxiety and distrust, taking with him Olid, captain of the guard, and two or three other trusty cavaliers. Montezuma received them with cold civility, and, turning to the general, told him that all his predictions had come to pass. The gods of his country had been offended by the violation of their temples. They had threatened the priests, that they would forsake the city, if the sacrilegious strangers were not driven from it, or rather sacrificed on the altars, in expiation of their crimes.[25] The monarch assured the Christians, it was from regard to their safety, that he communicated this; and, "if you have any regard for it yourselves," he concluded, "you will leave the country without delay. I have only to raise my finger, and every Aztec in the land will rise in arms against you." There was no reason to doubt his sincerity. For Montezuma, whatever evils had been brought on him by the white men, held them in reverence as a race more highly gifted than his own, while for several, as we

---

é se aniquilaban y dissipaban sus tempios, é hasta en equellos y sus antecesores estaban. Recia cosa me parece soportarla con tanta quietud; pero adelante, como lo dirá la Historia, mostró el tiempo lo que en el pecho estaba oculto en todos los Indios generalmente." Hist, de las Ind., MS., lib. 33, cap. 10.

[26] According to Herrera, it was the Devil himself who communicated this to Montezuma, and he reports the substance of the dialogue between the parties. (Hist. General, dec. 2, lib. 9, cap. 6.) Indeed, the apparition of Satan in his own bodily presence, on this occasion, is stoutly maintained by most historians of the time. Oviedo, a man of enlarged ideas on most subjects, speaks with a little more qualification on this. " Porque la Misa y Evangelio, que predicaban y decian los christianos, le [al Diablo] daban gran tormento; y débese pensar, si verdad es, que esas gentes tienen tanta conversacion y comunicacion con nuestro adversario, *como se tiene por cierto en estas Indias*, que no le podia á nuestro enemigo placer con los misterios y sacramentos de la sagrada religion christiana." Hist. de las Ind., MS., lib. 33, cap. 47

have seen, he had conceived an attachment, flowing no doubt,
from their personal attentions and deference to himself.

Cortés was too much master of his feelings, to show how far
he was startled by this intelligence. He replied with admirable
coolness, that he should regret much to leave the capital so pre-
cipitately, when he had no vessels to take him from the country.
If it were not for this, there could be no obstacle to his leaving
it at once. He should also regret another step to which he
should be driven, if he quitted it under these circumstances,—
that of taking the emperor along with him.

Montezuma was evidently troubled by this last suggestion.
He inquired how long it would take to build the vessels, and
finally consented to send a sufficient number of workmen to the
coast, to act under the orders of the Spaniards ; meanwhile, he
would use his authority to restrain the impatience of the people,
under the assurance that the white men would leave the land
when the means for it were provided. He kept his word. A
large body of Aztec artisans left the capital with the most experienced Castilian ship-builders, and, descending to Vera Cruz,
began at once to fell the timber and build a sufficient number of
ships to transport the Spaniards back to their own country. The
work went forward with apparent alacrity. But those who had
the direction of it, it is said, received private instructions from
the general, to interpose as many delays as possible, in hopes
of receiving in the mean time such reinforcements from Europe,
as would enable him to maintain his ground.[26]

The whole aspect of things was now changed in the Castilian
quarters. Instead of the security and repose in which the troops
had of late indulged, they felt a gloomy apprehension of danger,
not the less oppressive to the spirits, that it was scarcely visible
to the eye ;—like the faint speck just descried above the horizon
by the voyager in the tropics, to the common gaze seeming only
a summer cloud, but which to the experienced mariner bodes
the coming of the hurricane. Every precaution that prudence

---

[26] " E Cortés proveió de maestros é personas que entendiesen en la labor
de los Navíos, é dixo despues á los Españoles desta manera : Señores y her-
manos, este Señor Montezuma quiere que nos vamos de la tierra, y conviene que
se hagan Navíos. Id con estos Indios é córtese la madera ; é entretanto Dios
nos proveherá de gente é socorro ; por tanto, poned tal dilacion que parezca
que haceis algo y se haga con ella lo que nos conviene ; é siempre me escrivid
é avisad que tales estáis en la Montaña, é que no sientan los Indios nuestra
disimulacion. E así se puso por obra." (Oviedo, Hist. de las Ind., MS.,
lib. 33, cap. 47.) So, also, Gomara. (Crónica, cap. 95.) Diaz denies any
such secret orders, alleging that Martin Lopez, the principal builder, assured
him they made all the expedition possible in getting three ships on the stocks.
Hist. de la Conquista, cap. 108.

could devise was taken to meet it. The soldier, as he threw himself on his mats for reposé, kept on his armor. He ate, drank, slept, with his weapons by his side. His horse stood ready caparisoned, day and night, with the bridle hanging at the saddle-bow. The guns were carefully planted so as to command the great avenues. The sentinels were doubled, and every man, of whatever rank, took his turn in mounting guard. The garrison was in a state of siege.[27] Such was the uncomfortable position of the army, when, in the beginning of May, 1520, six months after their arrival in the capital, tidings came from the coast, which gave greater alarm to Cortés, than even the menaced insurrection of the Aztecs.

[27] "I may say without vaunting," observes our stout hearted old chronicler Bernal Diaz, "that I was so accustomed to this way of life, that since the conquest of the country I have never been able to lie down undressed, or in a bed; yet I sleep as sound as if I were on the softest down. Even when I make the rounds of my *encomienda*, I never take a bed with me; unless indeed I go in the company of other cavaliers, who might impute this to parsimony. But even then I throw myself on it with my clothes on. Another thing I must add, that I cannot sleep long in the night without getting up to look at the heavens and the stars, and stay a while in the open air, and this without a bonnet or covering of any sort on my head. And, thanks to God, I have received no harm from it. I mention these things, that the world may understand of what stuff we, the true Conquerors were made, and how well drilled we were to arms and watching." Hist de la Conquista, cap. 108.

CHAPTER VI.

Fate of Cortes' Emissaries.—Proceedings in the Castilian Court.—Preparations of Velasquez.—Narvaez lands
in Mexico.—Politic conduct of Cortes.—He leaves the
Capital.

1520.

Before explaining the nature of the tidings alluded to in the
preceding chapter, it will be necessary to cast a glance over
some of the transactions of an earlier period. The vessel, which,
as the reader may remember, bore the envoys Puertocarrero and
Montejo with the despatches from Vera Cruz, after touching,
contrary to orders, at the northern coast of Cuba, and spreading
the news of the late discoveries, held on its way uninterrupted
towards Spain, and early in October, 1519, reached the little
port of San Lucar. Great was the sensation caused by her arrival and the tidings which she brought; a sensation scarcely
inferior to that created by the original discovery of Columbus.
For now, for the first time, all the magnificent anticipations
formed of the New World seemed destined to be realized.

Unfortunately, there was a person in Seville, at this time,
named Benito Martin, chaplain of Velasquez, the governor of
Cuba. No sooner did this man learn the arrival of the envoys,
and the particulars of their story, than he lodged a complaint
with the *Casa de Contratacion,*—the Royal India House,—charging those on board the vessel with mutiny and rebellion against
the authorities of Cuba, as well as with treason to the Crown.[1]
In consequence of his representations, the ship was taken possession of by the public officers, and those on board were prohibited from removing their own effects, or anything else from
her. The envoys were not even allowed the funds necessary
for the expenses of the voyage, nor a considerable sum remitted
by Cortés to his father, Don Martin. In this embarrassment
they had no alternative but to present themselves, as speedily as

---

[1] In the collection of MSS., made by Don Vargas Ponçe, former President of the Academy of History, is a Memorial of this same Benito Martin
to the Emperor, setting forth the services of Velasquez, and the ingratitude
and revolt of Cortés and his followers. The paper is without date; written
after the arrival of the envoys, probably at the close of 1519, or the beginning
of the following year.

possible, before the emperor, deliver the letters with which they had been charged by the colony, and seek redress for their own grievances. They first sought out Martin Cortés, residing at Medellin, and with him made the best of their way to court.

Charles the Fifth was then on his first visit to Spain after his accession. It was not a long one ; long enough, however, to disgust his subjects, and, in a great degree, to alienate their affections. He had lately received intelligence of his election to the imperial crown of Germany. From that hour, his eyes were turned to that quarter. His stay in the Peninsula was prolonged only that he might raise supplies for appearing with splendor on the great theatre of Europe. Every act showed too plainly that the diadem of his ancestors was held lightly in comparison with the imperial bauble in which neither his countrymen nor his own posterity could have the slightest interest. The interest was wholly personal.

Contrary to established usage, he had summoned the Castilian córtes to meet at Compostelia, a remote town in the North, which presented no other advantage than that of being near his place of embarkation.[2] On his way thither he stopped some time at Tordesillas, the residence of his unhappy mother, Joanna " the Mad." It was here that the envoys from Vera Cruz presented themselves before him, in March, 1520. At nearly the same time, the treasures brought over by them reached the court where they excited unbounded admiration.[3] Hitherto, the returns from the New World had been chiefly in vegetable products, which, if the surest, are, also, the slowest sources of wealth. Of gold they had as yet seen but little, and that in its natural state or wrought into the rudest trinkets. The courtiers gazed with astonishment on the large masses of the precious metal, and the delicate manufacture of the various articles, especially of the richly tinted feather work. And, as they listened to the accounts, written and oral, of the great Aztec empire, they felt assured that the Castilian ships had, at length, reached the golden Indies, which hitherto had seemed to recede before them.

In this favorable mood there is little doubt the monarch would have granted the petition of the envoys, and confirmed the

---

[2] Sandoval, indeed, gives a singular reason,—that of being near the coast, so as to enable Chièvres and the other Flemish blood suckers, to escape suddenly, if need were, with their ill-gotten treasures, from the country. Hist. de Cárlos Quinto, tom. I. p. 203, ed. Pamplona, 1634.

[3] See the letter of Peter Martyr to his noble friend and pupil, the Marquis de Mondejar, written two months after the arrival of the vessel from Vera Cruz. Opus Epist., ep. 650.

irregular proceedings of the Conquerors, but for the opposition of a person who held the highest office in the Indian department. This was Juan Rodriguez de Fonseca, formerly dean of Seville, now bishop of Burgos. He was a man of noble family, and had been intrusted with the direction of the colonial concerns, on the discovery of the New World. On the establishment of the Royal Council of the Indies by Ferdinand the Catholic, he had been made its president, and had occupied that post ever since. His long continuance in a position of great importance and difficulty is evidence of capacity for business. It was no uncommon thing in that age to find ecclesiastics in high civil, and even military employments. Fonseca appears to have been an active, efficient person, better suited to a secular than to a religious vocation. He had, indeed, little that was religious in his temper ; quick to take offence and slow to forgive. His resentments seem to have been nourished and perpetuated like a part of his own nature. Unfortunately his peculiar position enabled him to display them towards some of the most illustrious men of his time. From pique at some real or fancied slight from Columbus, he had constantly thwarted the plans of the great navigator. He had shown the same unfriendly feeling towards the Admiral's son, Diego, the heir of his honors ; and he now, and from this time forward, showed a similar spirit towards the Conqueror of Mexico. The immediate cause of this was his own personal relations with Velasquez, to whom a near relative was betrothed. [4]

Through this prelate's representations, Charles, instead of a favorable answer to the envoys postponed his decision till he should arrive at Coruña, the place of embarkation.[5] But here he was much pressed by the troubles which his impolitic conduct had raised, as well as by preparations for his voyage. The transaction of the colonial business, which, long postponed, had greatly accumulated on his hands, was reserved for the last week in Spain. But the affairs of the " young admiral " consumed so large a portion of this, that he had no time to give to those of Cortés ; except, indeed, to instruct the board at Seville to remit to the envoys so much of their funds as was required to defray the charges of the voyage. On the 16th of May, 1520, the impatient monarch bade adieu to his distracted kingdom, with-

[4] Zuñiga, Anales Eclesiásticos y Seculares de Sevilla, (Madrid, 1677,) fol. 414.—Herrera, Hist. General, dec. 2, lib. 5, cap. 14 ; lib. 9, cap. 17, et alibi.

[5] Velasquez, it appears, had sent home an account of the doings of Cortés and of the vessel which touched with the treasures at Cuba, as early as October, 1519. Carta de Velasquez al Lic. Figueroa, MS., Nov. 17, 1519.

out one attempt to settle the dispute between his belligerent vassals in the New World, and without an effort to promote the magnificent enterprise which was to secure to him the possession of an empire. What a contrast to the policy of his illustrious predecessors, Ferdinand and Isabella![6]

The governor of Cuba, meanwhile, without waiting for support from home, took measures for redress into his own hands. We have seen, in a preceding chapter, how deeply he was moved by the reports of the proceedings of Cortés, and of the treasures which his vessel was bearing to Spain. Rage, mortification, disappointed avarice, distracted his mind. He could not forgive himself for trusting the affair to such hands. On the very week in which Cortés had parted from him to take charge of the fleet, a *capitulation* had been signed by Charles the Fifth, conferring on Velasquez the title of *adelantado*, with great augmentation of his original powers.[7] The governor resolved, without loss of time, to send such a force to the Aztec coast, as should enable him to assert his new authority to its full extent, and to take vengeance on his rebellious officer. He began his preparations as early as October.[8] At first, he proposed to assume the command in person. But his unwieldy size, which disqualified him for the fatigues incident to such an expedition, or, according to his own account, tenderness for his Indian subjects, then wasted by an epidemic, induced him to devolve the command on another.[9]

The person whom he selected was a Castilian hidalgo, named Panfilo de Narvaez. He had assisted Velasquez in the reduction of Cuba, where his conduct cannot be wholly vindicated from the charge of inhumanity, which too often attaches to the early Spanish adventurers. From that time he continued to hold important posts under the government, and was a decided favorite with Velasquez. He was a man of some military capacity, though negligent and lax in his discipline. He possessed undoubted

---

[6] "Con gran música," says Sandoval, bitterly, "de todos los ministriles y clarines, recogiendo las áncoras, diéron vela al viento con gran regozijo, dexando á la triste España cargada de duelos, y desventuras." Hist. de Cárlos Quinto, tom. I. p. 219.

[7] The instrument was dated at Barcelona, Nov. 13, 1518. Cortés left St. Jago the 18th of the same month. Herrera, Hist. General, dec. 2, lib. 3, cap. 11,

[8] Gomara (Cronica, cap. 96) and Robertson (History of America, vol. II. pp. 304, 466) consider that the new dignity of *adelantado* stimulated the governor to this enterprise. By a letter of his own writing in the Muñoz collection, it appear he had begun operations some months previous to his receiving notice of his appointment. Carta de Velasquez al señor de Xèvres Isla Fernandina, MS., Octubre 12, 1519.

[9] Carta de Velasquez al Lic. Figueroa, MS. Nov. 17, 1519.

courage, but it was mingled with an arrogance, or rather overweening confidence in his own powers, which made him deaf to the suggestions of others more sagacious than himself. He was altogether deficient in that prudence and calculating foresight demanded in a leader who was to cope with an antagonist like Cortés.[10]

The governor and his lieutenant were unwearied in their efforts to assemble an army. They visited every considerable town in the island, fitting out vessels, laying in stores and ammunition, and encouraging volunteers to enlist by liberal promises. But the most effectual bounty was the assurance of the rich treasures that awaited them in the golden regions of Mexico. So confident were they in this expectation, that all classes and ages vied with one another in eagerness to embark in the expedition, until it seemed as if the whole white population would desert the island, and leave it to its primitive occupants.[11]

The report of these proceedings soon spread through the Islands, and drew the attention of the Royal Audience of St. Domingo. This body was intrusted, at that time, not only with the highest judicial authority in the colonies, but with a civil jurisdiction, which, as " the Admiral " complained, encroached on his own rights. The tribunal saw with alarm the proposed expedition of Velasquez, which, whatever might be its issue in regard to the parties, could not fail to compromise the interests of the Crown. They chose accordingly one of their number, the licentiate Ayllon, a man of prudence and resolution, and despatched him to Cuba, with instructions to interpose his authority, and stay, if possible, the proceedings of Velasquez.[12]

On his arrival, he found the governor in the western part of the island, busily occupied in getting the fleet ready for sea. The licentiate explained to him the purport of his mission, and the views entertained of the proposed enterprise by the Royal Audience. The conquest of a powerful country like Mexico required the whole force of the Spaniards, and, if one half were employed against the other, nothing but ruin could come of it. It was the governor's duty, as a good subject, to forego all private animosities, and to sustain those now engaged in the great work by

---

[10] The person of Narvaez is thus whimsically described by Diaz. "He was tall, stout limbed, with a large head and red beard, an agreeable presence, a voice deep and sonorous, as if it rose from a cavern. He was a good horseman and valiant." Hist. de la Conquista, cap. 205.

[11] The danger of such a result is particularly urged in a memorandum of the licentiate Ayllon. Carta al Emperador, Guaniguanico, Marzo 4, 1520, MS.

[12] Processo y Pesquiza hecha por la Real Audiencia de la Española Santo Domingo, Diciembre 24, 1519, MS.

sending them the necessary supplies. He might, indeed, proclaim his own powers, and demand obedience to them. But, if this were refused, he should leave the determination of his dispute to the authorized tribunals, and employ his resources in prosecuting discovery in another direction, instead of hazarding all by hostilites with his rival.

This admonition, however sensible and salutary, was not at all to the taste of the governor. He professed, indeed, to have no intention of coming to hostilities with Cortés. He designed only to assert his lawful jurisdiction over territories discovered under his own auspices. At the same time, he denied the right of Ayllon or of the Royal Audience to interfere in the matter. Narvaez was still more refractory; and, as the fleet was now ready, proclaimed his intention to sail in a few hours. In this state of things, the licentiate, baffled in his first purpose of stay-ing the expedition, determined to accompany it in person, that he might prevent, if possible, by his presence, an open rupture between the parties.[13]

The squadron consisted of eighteen vessels, large and small. It carried nine hundred men, eighty of whom were cavalry, eighty more arquebusiers, one hundred and fifty crossbow-men, with a number of heavy guns, and a large supply of ammunition and military stores. There were, besides, a thousand Indians, natives of the island, who went probably in a menial capacity.[14] So gallant an armada—with one exception[15]—never before rode in the Indian seas. None to compare with it had ever been fitted out in the Western World.

Leaving Cuba early in March, 1520, Narvaez held nearly the same course as Cortés, and running down what was then called the " island of Yucatan."[16] after a heavy tempest, in which some of his smaller vessels foundered, anchored, April 23, off San Juan de Ulua. It was the place where Cortés, also, had first landed; the sandy waste covered by the present city of Vera Cruz.

Here the commander met with a Spaniard, one of those sent by the general from Mexico, to ascertain the resources of the

[13] Parecer del Lic. Ayllon al adelantado Diego Velasquez, Isla Fernandina, 1520, MS.

[14] Relacion del Lic. Ayllon, Santo Domingo, 30 de Agosto, 1520, MS.— Processo y Pesquiza por la R. Audiencia, MS.

According to Diaz, the ordnance amounted to twenty cannon. Hist. de la Conquista, cap. 109.

[15] The great fleet under Ovando, 1501, in which Cortés had intended to embark for the New World. Herrera, Hist. General, dec. 1, lib. 4, cap. 11

[16] " De alli seguimos el viage por toda la costa de la Isla de Yucatan.' Relacion del Lic. Ayllon, MS.

country, especially, its mineral products. This man came on board the fleet, and from him the Spaniards gathered the particulars of all that had occurred since the departure of the envoys from Vera Cruz.—the march into the interior, the bloody battles with the Tlascalans, the occupation of Mexico, the rich treasures found in it, and the seizure of the monarch, by means of which, concluded the soldier, " Cortés rules over the land like its own sovereign, so that a Spaniard may travel unarmed from one end of the country to the other, without insult or injury." [17] His audience listened to this marvellous report with speechless amazement, and the loyal indignation of Narvaez waxed stronger and stronger, as he learned the value of the prize which had been snatched from his employer.

He now openly proclaimed his intention to march against Cortés, and punish him for his rebellion. He made this vaunt so loudly, that the natives, who had flocked in numbers to the camp, which was soon formed on shore, clearly comprehended that the new comers were not friends, but enemies, of the preceding. Narvaez determined, also,—though in opposition to the counsel of the Spaniards, who quoted the example of Cortés,—to establish a settlement on this unpromising spot ; and he made the necessary arrangements to organize a municipality. He was informed by the soldier of the existence of the neighboring colony at Villa Rica, commanded by Sandoval, and consisting of a few invalids, who, he was assured, would surrender on the first summons. Instead of marching against the place, however, he determined to send a peaceful embassy to display his powers, and demand the submission of the garrison.[18]

These successive steps gave serious displeasure to Ayllon, who saw they must lead to inevitable collision with Cortés But it was in vain he remonstrated, and threatened to lay the proceedings of Narvaez before the government. The latter, chafed by his continued opposition and sour rebuke, determined to rid himself of a companion who acted as a spy on his movements. He caused him to be seized and sent back to Cuba. The licentiate had the address to persuade the captain of the vessel to change her destination for St. Domingo ; and, when

---

[17] " La cual tierra sabe é ha visto este testigo, que el dicho Hernando Cortés tiene pacífica, é le sirven é obedecen todos los Indios ; é que cree este testigo que lo hacen por cabsa que el dicho Hernando Cortés tiene preso á un Cacique que dicen Montesuma, que es Señor de lo mas de la tierra, á lo que este testigo alcanza, al cual los Indios obedecen, é facen lo que les manda, é los Cristianos andan por toda esta tierra seguros, é un solo Cristiano la ha atravesado toda sin temor." Processo y Pesquiza por la R. Audiencia, MS.

[18] Relacion del Lic. Ayllon, MS.—Demanda de Zavallos en nombre de Narvaez, MS.

he arrived there, a formal report of his proceedings, exhibiting in strong colors the disloyal conduct of the governor and his lieutenant, was prepared, and despatched by the Royal Audience to Spain.[19]

Sandoval meanwhile had not been inattentive to the movements of Narvaez. From the time of his first appearance on the coast, that vigilant officer, distrusting the object of the armament, had kept his eye on him. No sooner was he apprised of the landing of the Spaniards, than the commander of Villa Rica sent off his few disabled soldiers to a place of safety in the neighborhood. He then put his works in the best posture of defence that he could, and prepared to maintain the place to the last extremity. His men promised to stand by him, and, the more effectually to fortify the resolution of any who might falter, he ordered a gallows to be set up in a conspicuous part of the town! The constancy of his men was not put to the trial.

The only invaders of the place were a priest, a notary, and four other Spaniards, selected for the mission, already noticed, by Narvaez. The ecclesiastic's name was Guevara. On coming before Sandoval, he made him a formal address, in which he pompously enumerated the services and claims of Velasquez, taxed Cortés and his adherents with rebellion, and demanded of Sandoval to tender his submission, as a loyal subject, to the newly constituted authority of Narvaez.

The commander of La Villa Rica was so much incensed at this unceremonious mention of his companions in arms, that he assured the reverend envoy, that nothing but respect for his cloth saved him from the chastisement he merited. Guevara now waxed wroth in his turn, and called on the notary to read the proclamation. But Sandoval interposed, promising that functionary, that, if he attempted to do so, without first producing a warrant of his authority from the Crown, he should be soundly flogged. Guevara lost all command of himself at this, and stamping on the ground repeated his orders in a more peremptory tone than before. Sandoval was not a man of many words. He simply remarked, that the instrument should be read to the general himself in Mexico. At the same time, he ordered his men to procure a number of sturdy *tamanes*, or Indian porters, on whose backs the unfortunate priest and his companions were bound like so many bales of goods. They

[19] This report is to be found among the MSS. of Vargas Ponçe, in the archives of the Royal Academy of History. It embraces a hundred and ten folio pages, and is entitled, " El Proceso y Pesquiza hecha por la Real Audiencia de la Española é tierra nuevamente descubierta. Para el Consejo de su Majestad."

were then placed under a guard of twenty Spaniards, and the whole caravan took its march for the capital. Day and night they travelled, stopping only to obtain fresh relays of carriers ; and as they passed through populous towns, forests, and culti-vated fields, vanishing as soon as seen, the Spaniards, bewildered by the strangeness of the scene, as well as of their novel mode of conveyance, hardly knew whether they were awake or in a dream. In this way, at the end of the fourth day, they reached the Tezcucan lake in view of the Aztec capital.[20]

Its inhabitants had already been made acquainted with the fresh arrival of white men on the coast. Indeed, directly on their landing, intelligence had been communicated to Mon-tezuma, who is said (it does not seem probable) to have con-cealed it some days from Cortés.[21] At length, inviting him to an interview, he told him there was no longer any obstacle to his leaving the country, as a fleet was ready for him. To the in-quiries of the astonished general, Montezuma replied by point-ing to a hieroglyphical map sent him from the coast, on which the ships, the Spaniards themselves, and their whole equipment, were minutely delineated. Cortés, suppressing all emotions but those of pleasure, exclaimed, " Blessed be the Redeemer for his mercies ! " On returning to his quarters, the tidings were re-ceived by the troops with loud shouts, the firing of cannon, and other demonstrations of joy. They hailed the new comers as a reinforcement from Spain. Not so their commander. From the first, he suspected them to be sent by his enemy, the governor of Cuba. He communicated his suspicions to his officers, through whom they gradually found their way among the men. The tide of joy was instantly checked. Alarming apprehensions succeeded, as they dwelt on the probability of this suggestion, and on the strength of the invaders. Yet their constancy did not desert them ; and they pledged themselves to remain true to their cause, and, come what might, to stand by their leader. It was one of those occasions that proved the entire influence which Cortés held over these wild adventurers. All doubts were soon dispelled by the arrival of the prisoners from Villa Rica.

One of the convoy, leaving the party in the suburbs, entered the city, and delivered a letter to the general from Sandoval,

[20] "E iban espantados de que veian tàtas ciudades y pueblos grandes, que les traian de comer, y vnos los dexavan, y otros los tomavan, y andar por su camino. Dizē que iban pensando si era encantamiento, ó sueño." Bernal Diaz, Hist. de la Conquista, cap. 111.—Demanda de Zavallos, MS.

[21] "Ya auia tres dias que lo sabia el Montecuma, y Cortes no sabia cosa ninguna. Bernal Diaz, Hist. de la Conquista, cap. 110.

acquainting him with all the particulars. Cortés instantly sent to the prisoners, ordered them to be released, and furnished them with horses to make their entrance into the capital,—a more creditable conveyance than the backs of *tamanes.* On their arrival, he received them with marked courtesy, apologized for the rude conduct of his officers, and seemed desirous by the most assiduous attentions to soothe the irritation of their minds. He showed his good-will still further by lavishing presents on Guevara and his associates, until he gradually wrought such a change in their dispositions, that, from enemies, he converted them into friends, and drew forth many important particulars respecting not merely the designs of their leader, but the feelings of his army. The soldiers, in general, they said, far from desiring a rupture with those of Cortés, would willingly coöperate with them, were it not for their commander. They had no feelings of resentment to gratify. Their object was gold. The personal influence of Narvaez was not great, and his arrogance and penurious temper had already gone far to alienate from him the affections of his followers. These hints were not lost on the general.

He addressed a letter to his rival in the most conciliatory terms. He besought him not to proclaim their animosity to the world, and, by kindling a spirit of insubordination in the natives, unsettle all that had been so far secured. A violent collision must be prejudicial even to the victor, and might be fatal to both. It was only in union that they could look for success. He was ready to greet Narvaez as a brother in arms, to share with him the fruits of conquest, and, if he could produce a royal commission, to submit to his authority.—Cortés well knew he had no such commission to show.[22]

Soon after the departure of Guevara and his comrades,[23] the general determined to send a special envoy of his own. The person selected for this delicate office was father Olmedo, who, through the campaign, had shown a practical good sense, and a talent for affairs, not always to be found in persons of his spiritual calling. He was intrusted with another epistle to Narvaez, of similar import with the preceding. Cortés wrote, also, to the licentiate Ayllon, with whose departure he was not acquainted, and to Andres de Duero, former secretary of Velasquez, and his

---

22 Oviedo, Hist. de las Ind., MS., lib. 33, cap. 47.—Rel. Seg. de Cortés, ap. Lorenzana, pp. 117-120.

23 "Our commander said so many kind things to them," says Diaz, "and anointed their fingers so plentifully with gold, that, though they come like roaring lions, they went home perfectly tame!" Hist de la Conquista, cap. 111.

own friend, who had come over in the present fleet. Olmeda was instructed to converse with these persons in private, as well as with the principal officers and soldiers, and, as far as possible to infuse into them a spirit of accommodation. To give greater weight to his arguments, he was furn'shed with a liberal supply of gold.

During this time, Narvaez had abandoned his original design of planting a colony on the sea-coast, and had crossed the country to Cempoalla, where he had taken up his quarters. He was here, when Guevara returned, and presented the letter of Cortés.

Narvaez glanced over it with a look of contempt, which was changed into one of stern displeasure, as his envoy enlarged on the resources and formidable character of his rival, counselling him, by all means, to accept his proffers of amity. A different effect was produced on the troops, who listened with greedy ears to the accounts given of Cortés, his frank and liberal man-ners, which they involuntarily contrasted with those of their own commander, the wealth in his camp, where the humblest private could stake his ingot and chain of gold at play, where all revel-led in plenty, and the life of the soldier seemed to be one long holiday. Guevara had been admitted only to the sunny side of the picture.

The impression made by these accounts was confirmed by the presence of Olmedo. The ecclesiastic delivered his missives, in like manner, to Narvaez, who ran through their contents with feelings of anger which found vent in the most opprobrious in-vectives against his rival; while one of his captains, named Salvatierra, openly avowed his intention to cut off the rebel's ears, and broil them for his breakfast ! [24] Such impotent sallies did not alarm the stout-hearted friar, who soon entered into communication with many of the officers and soldiers, whom he found better inclined to an accommodation. His insinuating elo-quence, backed by his liberal largesses, gradually opened a way into their hearts, and a party was formed, under the very eye of their chief, better affected to his rival's interests than to his own. The intrigue could not be conducted so secretly as wholly to elude the suspicions of Narvaez, who would have arrested Ol-medo and placed him under confinement, but for the interposi-tion of Duero. He put a stop to his further machinations by sending him back again to his master. But the poison was left to do its work.

Narvaez made the same vaunt, as at his landing, of his design to march against Cortés and apprehend him as a traitor. The

[24] Ibid., cap. 112.

Cempoallans learned with astonishment that their new guests, though the countrymen, were enemies of their former. Narvaez, also, proclaimed his intention to release Montezuma from captivity, and restore him to his throne. It is said, he received a rich present from the Aztec emperor, who entered into a correspondence with him.[20] That Montezuma should have treated him with his usual munificence, supposing him to be the friend of Cortés, is very probable. But that he should have entered into a secret communication, hostile to the general's interests, is too repugnant to the whole tenor of his conduct, to be lightly admitted.

These proceedings did not escape the watchful eye of Sandoval. He gathered the particulars partly from deserters, who fled to Villa Rica, and partly from his own agents, who in the disguise of natives mingled in the enemy's camp. He sent a full account of them to Cortés, acquainted him with the growing defection of the Indians, and urged him to take speedy measures for the defence of Villa Rica, if he would not see it fall into the enemy's hands. The general felt that it was time to act.

Yet the selection of the course to be pursued was embarrassing in the extreme. If he remained in Mexico and awaited there the attack of his rival, it would give the latter time to gather round him the whole forces of the empire, including those of the capital itself, all willing, no doubt, to serve under the banners of a chief who proposed the liberation of their master. The odds were too great to be hazarded.

If he marched against Narvaez, he must either abandon the city and the emperor, the fruit of all his toils and triumphs, or, by leaving a garrison to hold them in awe, must cripple his strength already far too weak to cope with that of his adversary. Yet on this latter course he decided. He trusted less, perhaps, to an open encounter of arms, than to the influence of his personal address and previous intrigues, to bring about an amicable arrangement. But he prepared himself for either result.

In the preceding chapter, it was mentioned that Velasquez de Leon was sent with a hundred and fifty men to plant a colony on one of the great rivers emptying into the Mexican Gulf. Cortés, on learning the arrival of Narvaez, had despatched a messenger to his officer, to acquaint him with the fact, and to arrest his

<hr/>

[20] Ibid., cap. 111. Oviedo says that Montezuma called a council of his nobles, in which it was decided to let the troops of Narvaez into the capital, and then to crush them at one blow, with those of Cortes1 (Hist. de las Ind., MS., lib. 33, cap. 47.) Considering the awe in which the latter alone were held by the Mexicans, a more improbable tale could not be devised but nothing is too improbable for history,—though, according to Boileau's maxim, it may be for fiction.

further progress.   But Velasquez had already received notice of it from Narvaez himself, who, in a letter written soon after his landing, had adjured him in the name of his kinsman, the governor of Cuba, to quit the banners of Cortés, and come over to him.   That officer, however, had long since buried the feelings of resentment which he had once nourished against his general, to whom he was now devotedly attached, and who had honored him throughout the campaign with particular regard. Cortés had early seen the importance of securing this cavalier to his interests.   Without waiting for orders, Velasquez abandoned his expedition, and commenced a countermarch on the capital, when he received the general's commands to wait him in Cholula.

Cortés had also sent to the distant province of Chinantla, situated far to the south-east of Cholula, for a reinforcement of two thousand natives.   They were a bold race, hostile to the Mexicans, and had offered their services to him since his residence in the metropolis.   They used a long spear. in battle, longer, indeed, than that borne by the Spanish or German infantry.   Cortés ordered three hundred of their double-headed lances to be made for him, and to be tipped with copper instead of *itztli.* With this formidable weapon he proposed to foil the cavalry of his enemy.

The command of the garrison, in his absence, he intrusted to Pedro de Alvarado,—the *Tonatiuh* of the Mexicans, —a man possessed of many commanding qualities, of an intrepid, though somewhat arrogant spirit, and his warm personal friend.   He inculcated on him moderation and forbearance.   He was to keep a close watch on Montezuma, for on the possession of the royal person rested all their authority in the land.   He was to show him the deference alike due to his high station, and demanded by policy.   He was to pay uniform respect to the usages and the prejudices of the people ; remembering that though his small force would be large enough to overawe them in times of quiet, yet, should they be once roused, it would be swept away like chaff before the whirlwind.

From Montezuma he exacted a promise to maintain the same friendly relations with his lieutenant which he had preserved towards himself.   This, said Cortés, would be most grateful to his own master, the Spanish sovereign.   Should the Aztec prince do otherwise, and lend himself to any hostile movement, he must be convinced that he would fall the first victim of it.

The emperor assured him of his continued good-will.   He was much perplexed, however, by the recent events.   Were the Spaniards at his court, or those just landed, the true representatives of their sovereign? Cortés, who had hitherto maintain-ed a reserve on the subject, now told him that the latter were indeed his countrymen, but traitors to his master. As such, it was his painful duty to march against them, and, when he had chastised their rebellion, he should return, before his departure from the land, in triumph to the capital. Montezuma offered to support him with five thousand Aztec warriors; but the general declined it, not choosing to encumber himself with a body of doubtful, perhaps disaffected, auxiliaries.

He left in garrison, under Alvarado, one hundred and forty men, two thirds of his whole force.[26] With these remained all the artillery, the greater part of the little body of horse, and most of the arquebusiers. He took with him only seventy soldiers, but they were men of the most mettle in the army and and his staunch adherents. They were lightly armed and en-cumbered with as little baggage as possible. Every thing de-pended on celerity of movement.

Montezuma, in his royal litter borne on the shoulders of his nobles, and escorted by the whole Spanish infantry, accompanied the general to the causeway. There, embracing him in the most cordial manner, they parted, with all the external marks of mu-tual regard.—It was about the middle of May, 1520, more than six months since the entrance of the Spaniards into Mexico. During this time they had lorded it over the land with absolute sway. They were now leaving the city in hostile array, not against an Indian foe, but their own countrymen. It was the beginning of a long career of calamity,—checkered, indeed, by occasional triumphs,—which was yet to be run before the Con-quest could be completed.[27]

[26] In the Mexican edition of the letters of Cortés it is called five hundred men. (Rel. Seg., ap. Lorenzana, p. 122.) But this was more than his whole Spanish force. In Ramusio's version of the same letter, printed as early as 1565, the number is stated as in the text. (Navigationi et Viaggi, fol. 244. In an instrument without date, containing the affidavits of certain witnesses as to the management of the royal fifth by Cortés, it is said, there were one hundred and fifty soldiers left in the capital under Alvarado. (Probanza fecha en la nueva España del mar océano á pedimento de Juan Ochoa de Lexalde, en nombre de Hernando Cortés, MS.) The account in the Mexican edition is unquestionably an error.

[27] Carta de Villa de Vera Cruz á el Emperador, MS. This letter without date was probably written in 1520.—See, also, for the preceding pages, Pro-banza fecha á pedimento de Juan Ochoa, MS. —Herrera, Hist. General, dec. 2, lib. 9, cap. 1, 21; lib. 10, cap. 1,—Rel. Seg. de Cortés, ap. Lorenzana, pp. 119, 120,—Bernal Diaz, Hist. de la Conquista, cap. 112-115—Oviedo, Hist. de las Ind., MS., lib. 33, cap. 47.